Statutory Nu
2nd editi

Statutory Nuisance
2nd edition

Robert McCracken QC
MA (Oxon), LARTPI
Sometime Chairman of the UK Environmental Law Association
Visiting Lecturer King's College London
Barrister of the Inner Temple and Lincoln's Inn
Francis Taylor Building, Temple, London

Gregory Jones
MA (Oxon), LLM (Lond), LARTPI, Fellow of the Institute of Quarrying
Visiting Lecturer King's College London
Barrister of Lincoln's Inn and King's Inns
Francis Taylor Building, Temple, London

James Pereira,
MA (Cantab), LLM (Lond), Fellow of the Royal Society of Arts
Barrister of the Middle Temple
Francis Taylor Building, Temple, London

Tottel Publishing, Maxwelton House, 41–43 Boltro Road, Haywards Heath, West Sussex, RH16 1BJ

© Tottel Publishing Ltd 2008

Reprinted 2010

The authors assert their moral right to be identified as authors of this work.

All rights reserved. No part of this publication may be reproduced in any material form (including photocopying or storing it in any medium by electronic means and whether or not transiently or incidentally to some other use of this publication) without the written permission of the copyright owner except in accordance with the provisions of the Copyright, Designs and Patents Act 1988 or under the terms of a licence issued by the Copyright Licensing Agency Ltd, Saffron House, 6–10 Kirby Street, London, England EC1N 8TS. Applications for the copyright owner's written permission to reproduce any part of this publication should be addressed to the publisher.

Warning: The doing of an unauthorised act in relation to a copyright work may result in both a civil claim for damages and criminal prosecution.

Crown copyright material is reproduced with the permission of the Controller of HMSO and the Queen's Printer for Scotland. Any European material in this work which has been reproduced from EUR-lex, the official European Communities legislation website, is European Communities copyright.

A CIP Catalogue record for this book is available from the British Library.

ISBN 978 1 84592 123 1

Typeset by Phoenix Photosetting, Chatham, Kent, UK
Printed in Great Britain by www.printondemand-worldwide.com

FOREWORD TO THE FIRST EDITION

Every law student used to spend a lot of time trying to understand the development of the law of nuisance and its relationship to other torts. It was not always easy and a more practical guide might have been very helpful. But nobody doubted its importance as part of the common law.

Parliament began to legislate in detail from the middle of the nineteenth century (see for example the Temporary Act of 1846 and the General Acts from the Nuisance Removal and Disease Prevention Act of 1848, through the Public Health Acts of 1875 and 1936 to the Environmental Protection Act of 1990). No doubt it was done with the intention of making the law not only effective in changing circumstances but also clear. However it has become very complex, and the precise ambit of the definition of statutory nuisances in contemporary society can lead to difficult questions. An example of the division of view is *Birmingham City Council v Oakley* where all the judges no doubt thought that the arrangements of the house by modern standards were unsatisfactory (a lavatory with no washbasin next to the kitchen) but divided on the question whether they fell within the class of prohibited acts, namely 'premises in such a state as to be prejudicial to health or a nuisance'.

This was a good illustration not of the literal versus the purposive interpretation but of asking the purposive question – what was Parliament trying to do? – the question which could lead to different answers.

But in addition to the detailed statutory provisions there are no less complex regulations dealing with different aspects of social policy which have to be considered and perhaps reconciled.

And so, as the authors say, 'Technical difficulties abound for environmental health officers, non-specialist lawyers and community groups.' They were courteous enough not to add judges to the list but they could have done so. There is no doubt that difficulties exist. The substantive provisions need careful analysis but the procedures are at least as important, particularly for local authorities given the powers and the responsibilities to abate nuisances which the private citizen either cannot or would find it practically difficult to tackle.

This book gives a useful analysis of what a statutory nuisance is and expounds in detail the procedures to be followed. It will provide a valuable guide to those who seek to serve an abatement notice, to those who say such a notice should never have been issued in the form in which it was issued and to those who have to defend themselves against prosecutions under sections 80 and 82 of the Act – in the latter case where proceedings are brought by a private individual. There is a careful analysis of the many other provisions of the 1990 Act and it is done with the practical as well as the policy aspects in mind. I consider that it would

Foreword to the first edition

be very useful as a guide and a checklist to those concerned with the application of the Act. The authors do not sit on the fence where there are debatable issues. They do not hesitate to say in effect 'we think' or 'we advise' or even 'you should'. They may prove right or they may prove wrong but their experience justifies them in giving a lead and that is what people really need.

Particular individuals will be concerned with particular types of nuisance. The courts in fairly recent years, as in the nineteenth century, have had to look at the question of noise, increasingly likely to be injurious to health as to reasonable living. The authors show the approach which has been adopted and which has to be worked out further. Indeed Parliament and the courts may have to be tougher and more comprehensive in their attitude.

But in addition to looking at the 1990 Act the authors have considered the provisions of other environmental legislation dealing with matters such as pollution in the Pollution Prevention and Control Act 1999 and the regulations made under it. The interaction of these various statutes and their influence on the interpretation of the 1990 Act may prove of increasing importance. In even less charted waters they consider the impact of the Human Rights Act 1998 on the procedures of the 1990 Act.

The style is clear and direct which in law of this kind is particularly important. It seems to me that this will be a very useful book to those who work in this area and to citizens who, or whose surroundings, need protection. It will need regular updating if this legislation and the case law proliferate. But the first edition was needed and is to be warmly welcomed.

Slynn of Hadley

The Rt Hon the Lord Slynn of Hadley, PC, Lord of Appeal in Ordinary and sometime Judge and Advocate General of the European Court of Justice

PREFACE

Statutory nuisance is an important, fast moving part of environmental law with a great potential for making a difference to people's lives. Our aim has been to produce a work useful to courts, companies, councils, community groups and their counsellors. The reports we have received from users of the 1st edition suggest that we have had a gratifying measure of success. The highest courts seem to have found the work useful.

We have not shied away from expressing our views on difficult points, though indicating the scope for differences of legal opinion. The inspiration for our approach is Blackstone's observation on nuisance to watercourses in his Commentaries: 'So closely does the law of England enforce that excellent rule of gospel morality of, "doing unto others, as we would that they should unto us"'. We have, however, found in our practices 200 years later that a fuller exposition of the law is necessary for the enforcement of the principle. The principle is not confined to Christianity; it is found in the Islamic Hadith 'None of you [truly] believes until he wishes for his brother what he wishes for himself'.

Francis Taylor Building,	Robert McCracken QC
Temple	Gregory Jones
	James Pereira
Ash Wednesday 2008	

ACKNOWLEDGEMENTS

We would like to thank Angus Walker, James Neill, Mark Westmoreland Smith, Cain Ormondroyd and Thomas Cross, barristers, for their assistance in the preparation of this work. Any errors are, of course, our own.

We express our grateful thanks to our new publishers Tottel and in particular to Andy Hill and Jane Bradford.

Our love and dedication of this edition of the book to our families.

Contents

Foreword to the First Edition	v
Preface	vii
Acknowledgements	viii
Table of Statutes	xv
Table of Statutory Instruments	xxiii
Table of Cases	xxv

Chapter 1   Nature and Scope of Statutory Nuisance

Introduction	1
First limb: prejudicial to health	2
Second limb: nuisance	3
Key considerations	6
Development plans	9
The categories of statutory nuisance	10
Some general points	25
The contaminated land exception	28

Chapter 2   Duties and Powers of Local Authorities

Introduction	33
The HRA 1998	33
The need to ensure proper delegation of powers	37
The duty to inspect the area	37
The duty to investigate complaints	40
The power to take criminal proceedings	56
The power to seek injunctions	56
A duty to consult?	61
Duties under the Regulation of Investigatory Powers Act 2000	62

Chapter 3   The Abatement Notice

Introduction	67
Authority to issue an abatement notice	67
Underlying principle of simplicity	68
Formalities	69
What should be required?	69
Should works or steps be required?	70
Formulation of abatement notice: practical guidance	73
Human Rights Act 1998	78
The 'best practicable means' defence	80
Letters before notice	81
Records of offers	81
The courts' power to quash or amend	82
Statutory authority	83
Recipient of the notice	84
Noise from the street	87
Unlawful shifting of the burden	88
How should an abatement notice be served?	88
Withdrawal of notices	89

Chapter 4   Challenging an Abatement Notice

Introduction	91
Challenges by recipients	91

Contents

Challenges by third parties	91
Appealing an abatement notice	92
The form of a complaint	93
The time period for appealing an abatement notice	94
Grounds of appeal	102
Amending the grounds of appeal	116
Pre-trial procedures	119
Rules of evidence	120
Order of evidence and speeches	123
The standard of proof	124
The burden of proof	124
The relevant date	125
Magistrates' powers on appeal	126
Powers of the magistrates to make orders against third parties	128
Appeals to the Crown Court and to the High Court	130

Chapter 5 Criminal Proceedings under EPA 1990, Section 80 for Breaches of the Requirements of an Abatement Notice

Introduction	139
Elements of the offence	139
The nature of the offence	140
Categories of offence	144
Drafting the information	145
Making prosecution evidence available to the defence	149
Disclosure of expert evidence	153
Application of PACE 1984	154
Course of a summary trial	158
Proving the offence	159
'Reasonable excuse'	160
Submission of no case to answer	162
Defence case	162
Statutory defences	163
Conviction and sentencing	167
Challenges to decisions by the magistrates' court	170
Challenges to decisions by the Crown Court	172

Chapter 6 Statutory Nuisance Proceedings Brought by an Individual

Introduction	175
Who can bring proceedings under section 82?	175
How are proceedings started?	176
Procedure at the hearing	189
Defences to proceedings for an order under section 82(2)	192
Penalties in proceedings under section 82(2): nuisance orders and fines	194
Orders against a local authority which is not a defendant to the proceedings	197
Costs in proceedings under section 82(2)	197
Failure to comply with a nuisance order made under section 82(2)	198

Chapter 7 Costs and Compensation

Introduction	201
Section 1 Civil Proceedings: costs on an appeal against an abatement notice	201
Section 2 Criminal Proceedings: costs on a prosecution for failure to comply with an abatement notice or nuisance order	208

Contents

Section 3 Costs on a private party's action for a nuisance order under section 82 of the EPA — 212
Section 4 Common questions — 215
Section 5 Costs of a civil appeal to the High Court and a criminal appeal to the Divisional Court or Criminal Court of Appeal — 218
Section 6 Application for costs: evidence and procedure in the magistrates' and crown court — 219
Section 7 Challenging a costs order — 222
Section 8 Compensation and damages — 222

Chapter 8   Noise and Smell
Noise: Introduction — 231
Quantification — 232
Background to technology — 236
Noise indices — 237
Qualitative factor adjustments — 238
Times and seasons — 238
Some important maximum levels — 239
BS 4142 industrial noises — 241
Smell — 242

Chapter 9   Other Powers Dealing with Problems Akin to Nuisance
Introduction — 245
Land adversely affecting the amenity of an area – Town and Country Planning Act 1990 section 215 — 245
Housing standards: Housing Act 2004 — 249
'Fly tipping' – Environmental Protection Act 1990 section 59 — 251
Powers concerned with litter, rubbish and refuse — 254
Demolition waste – Building Act 1984 section 79 — 260
Abandoned vehicles: Refuse Disposal (Amenity) Act 1978 sections 2 and 3 — 260
Miscellaneous public health powers — 261
Night-time noise in dwellings: Noise Act 1996 — 267
Control of noise from construction and engineering works: Control of Pollution Act 1974 sections 60 and 61 — 269
Noise abatement zones: Control of Pollution Act 1974 sections 63–66 — 272
Loudspeakers and street noise: Control of Pollution Act 1974 section 62 — 275
Audible intruder alarms — 276
Noise codes of practice: Control of Pollution Act 1974 section 71 — 276
Noise from vehicles — 276
Anti-social behaviour orders — 276

Chapter 10   Other Environmental Regimes
Introduction — 279
EPA 1990, Part I — 279
Pollution Prevention and Control Act 1999 — 281
Radioactive Substances Act 1993 — 282
Contaminated land regime under EPA 1990 Part IIA — 283
Water pollution controls: Water Resources Act 1991 Part III — 286
Waste management licensing under EPA 1990 Part II — 287
Clean Air Act 1993 — 288
Crown property — 290

Contents

Appendices – Contents	**293**
Appendix A Forms and Draft Notices	**295**
Draft abatement notices types: I, II, III and IV	296
Draft notice of proceedings under section 82	302
Court Forms (Magistrates' Courts (Forms) Rules 1981	303
Form 98 Complaint	303
Form1 Information	303
Pre-trial review standard questionnaire	304
Draft costs schedule	307
Appendix B Material Relating to Statutory Nuisance	**309**
Environmental Protection Act 1990, ss 78A, 79–82, 84, 157–160, Sch 3	309
Statutory Nuisance (Appeals) Regulations 1995, SI 1995/2644	330
Clean Air Act 1993, s 64	333
Control of Pollution Act 1974, ss 60, 61, 66, 67	335
Noise Act 1996	339
Statutory Nuisances (Insects) Regulations 2006, SI 2006/770	352
Statutory Nuisances (Artificial Lighting) (Designation of Relevant Sports) (England) Order 2006, SI 2006/781	354
Appendix C Material Relating to Magistrates' Court, Crown Court and High Court proceeding	**357**
Magistrates' Courts Act 1980, ss 40, 53, 64, 101, 108–111, 123, 127	357
Magistrates' Courts Rules 1981, SI 1981/552, rr 4, 14, 16, 34, 43, 99	360
Supreme Court Act 1981, s 48	362
Criminal Appeal Act 1968, s 50	363
Criminal Appeal Rules 1968, SI 1968/1262, r 10	364
Criminal Procedure Rules 2005, SI 2005/384, rr 1, 2, 3, 7.1–7.3, 21, 24, 37, 63.1–63.5, 63.9, 64	364
Practice Note (Magistrates: Clerk and Authorised Legal Adviser) [2000] 4 All ER 895	383
Practice Note (Justices' Clerks) [1954] 1 WLR 213	385
Appendix D Material Relating to Evidence	**387**
Civil Evidence Act 1995, ss 1–16, Sch 2	387
Magistrates' Courts (Hearsay Evidence in Civil Proceedings) Rules 1999, SI 1999/681	394
Police and Criminal Evidence Act 1984, ss 67, 76, 78	397
Appendix E Material Relating to Sentencing and Costs	**401**
Courts Act 1971, s 52	401
Prosecution of Offences Act 1985, ss 16–21	401
Supreme Court Act 1981, ss 28, 48, 51	410
Practice Direction (Costs in Criminal Proceedings) [2004] 2 All ER; [2004] 1 WLR 2657, Pts I–VI, VII.1, VII.3, VIII, IX	413
Criminal Procedure Rules 2005, SI 2005/384, rr 78.1–78.7	421
Powers of the Criminal Courts (Sentencing) Act 2000, ss 130, 131, 134	424
Appendix F Human Rights	**427**
Human Rights Act 1998, ss 1–13, 19, 21, 22, Sch 1, arts 2, 6, 7, 8, First Protocol, art 1	427
Appendix G Miscellaneous Statutory Material	**439**
Local Government Act 1972, s 222	439

Local Government (Miscellaneous Provisions) Act 1976, s 16   439
Environmental Information Regulations 2004, SI 2004/3391   440

Appendix H   Guidance Relating to Noise and Smell   **455**

PPG 24, Planning Policy Guidance: Planning and Noise, paras 1–27,
Glossary, Annexes 1, 2, 5   455
WHO Environmental Health Criteria 12 Noise (1980)   471
WHO Environmental Health Criteria Document on Community Noise   480
WHO Guidelines for Community Noise   491
Noise – DEFRA Guidance on sections 69 to 81 and section 86 of the
Clean Neighbourhoods and Environment Act 2005   494
Statutory Nuisance from Insects and Light – DEFRA Guidance on
sections 101 to 103 of the Clean Neighbourhoods and Environment
Act 2005   502
Nuisance Parking Offences and Abandoned Vehicles – DEFRA
Guidance   526
Environment Agency Technical Guidance Note IPPC H4 – Draft
Horizontal Guidance for Odour, Introduction, Apps 1, 2, 6, 7, 10   537

Index   **551**

Table of Statutes

	PARA
Agriculture Act 1947	
s 109	1.58
Alkali, &c, Works Regulations Act 1906:	5.96
Animal Boarding Establishments Act 1963	9.95
Anti-social Behaviour Act 2003	9.144
s 40, 41	9.144
Antisocial Behaviour etc (Scotland) Act 2004	
s 66, Sch 2, para 4(1), (4)	5.20
Breeding and Sale of Dogs (Welfare) Act 1999	9.95
Breeding of Dogs Act 1973	9.95
Breeding of Dogs Act 1991	9.95
Building Act 1984	
s 59(1)(a)–(d)	9.81
63	9.82
64, 65	9.77
66	9.76
76(1)	9.87, 9.88
(2), (3)	9.88
(4)(a)	9.89
(b)(i), (ii)	9.89
77	9.90, 9.91, 9.93
(1)(a), (b)	9.91
(2)	9.91
78	9.90, 9.92, 9.93
(1)–(3)	9.92
79(2)	9.66
83(3)	9.67
107–110	9.89
Civil Aviation Act 1982	
s 76	10.34
78(1)	10.34
81	10.34
Civil Evidence Act 1995	
s 12	4.93
Clean Air Act 1956	10.28
Clean Air Act 1968	1.80; 10.28, 10.32
Clean Air Act 1993	1.35, 1.43, 1.78; 10.28, 10.29
Pt I (ss 1–3)	10.30
s 1, 2	10.30
3(1), (3)	1.35
Pt III (ss 4–17)	10.31
s 20	10.31
42, 43	10.33
44	10.33
47	10.32
64	1.35

	PARA
Clean Neighbourhoods and Environment Act 2005	9.01, 9.99
s 3	9.71
(2)	9.71
4	9.71
(3)	9.71
18	9.47
27	9.45
64	9.98
(2)	9.98
Pt VII (ss 69–86)	9.140
s 86	2.41
101	1.58; 4.59
102	1.61
103	6.84
104	10.12
Control of Pollution Act 1974	1.47, 1.67; 2.45, 2.71; 4.108; 5.98; 9.125; 10.28
s 58	1.64; 8.09
(4)	5.84, 5.98
60	1.64; 2.45; 4.68; 8.01; 9.109, 9.111, 9.114, 9.115, 9.116, 9.119, 9.120, 9.121, 9.132
(1)	9.109, 9.110
(3)	9.111
(4)	9.114, 9.142
(5)	9.111
(6)	9.112
(7)	9.113
(8)	9.120
61	1.64; 2.45; 4.68; 5.97; 6.70; 8.01; 9.109, 9.121, 9.122
(4)–(8)	9.121
(9)	9.123
62	8.01; 9.136, 9.137
(1)	9.136, 9.138, 9.139
(1A), (1B)	9.136
(2), (3)	9.137
63	9.124
(1)	9.125
(3)	9.121
64	9.124, 9.126
(3)	9.127
(7)	9.126
65	2.45; 4.68; 5.97; 6.70; 9.124, 9.134, 9.135

Table of Statutes

	PARA
Control of Pollution Act 1974 – *contd*	
s 65(2)–(4)	9.129
(6), (7)	9.128
(8)	6.70; 9.135
66	2.45; 4.68; 5.97; 9.134, 9.135, 9.135
(1)–(3), (6)	9.131
(7), (8)	9.132
(9)	9.132, 9.142
67	2.45; 5.97; 9.124, 9.134
68	9.124
69	9.133
(1)	9.128
(3)(b)	9.128
71	9.141
73	9.131
74(1), (5)	9.128
Sch 1	9.125
Criminal Appeal Act 1968	
s 9, 50	7.88
Criminal Justice Act 1967	
s 9	5.72
10	5.04
Criminal Justice Act 1991	
s 18(2), (3)	5.111
Criminal Procedure and Investigations Act 1996	5.45, 5.48, 5.51
Pt I (ss 1–21)	5.49
s 1(1)	5.49
3	5.49, 5.50
(1)(a)	5.49
6, 6A	5.49
7A(2)	5.49, 5.50
(3)	5.50
(5)	5.49
8, 10	5.49
11	5.49
21(1)	5.51
Crown Proceedings Act 1947	
s 11	10.35
Dogs (Fouling of Land) Act 1996	9.98
Environment Act 1995	1.95
Pt II (ss 57–60)	10.12, 10.13
Sch 22	10.16
Environment Act 2005	
s 101(5)	4.59
102, 103	4.59
Environmental Protection Act 1990	1.35; 2.01, 2.05, 2.14, 2.15, 2.16, 2.26, 2.35, 2.37, 2.58, 2.83, 2.88; 3.02, 3.19, 3.20, 3.59, 3.76; 4.08, 4.17, 4.20, 4.68, 4.76, 4.86, 4.98, 4.108; 5.07, 5.31, 5.98; 6.02; 7.68; 9.32, 9.118; 10.29

	PARA
Environmental Protection Act 1990 – *contd*	
Pt I (ss 1–28)	1.35, 1.43, 1.45, 1.49, 1.63; 2.01, 2.81; 10.01, 10.02, 10.03, 10.04, 10.06, 10.07, 10.10
s 1(4)	1.98, 1.102
6	10.02
7(2), (4), (6)	10.02
10, 12–14	10.05
23(1)	10.05
Pt II (ss 29–78)	10.01, 10.07, 10.26, 10.27
s 29	9.42
33	9.33
(1)	9.31, 9.37
(a)	9.37
34, 42	10.26
45	3.75
59	9.31, 9.32, 9.36, 9.39, 9.40, 9.41 9.61
(3)	9.39
(4)	9.40
(5), (6)	9.41
(7)	9.42
71(2)	5.62
75	9.34
Pt IIA (ss 78A–78YC)	1.95, 1.98, 1.99, 1.102; 10.01, 10.12, 10.13; 10.14, 10.15, 10.16, 10.27
s 78A(2)	1.102
(4)	1.96, 1.98, 1.102
(5)	1.102
(9)	1.96, 1.97
78B, 78H	10.12
78L	10.12
78I(2)(b)	4.113
78M, 78N, 78P	10.12
Pt III (ss 79–84)	1.05, 1.64, 1.98, 1.102; 2.45, 2.51, 2.59; 4.118; 9.87, 9.88, 9.89, 9.101; 10.01, 10.06, 10.11, 10.12; 10.14, 10.15, 10.16, 10.22, 10.24, 10.27, 10.30, 10.32, 10.33, 10.34, 10.36
s 79	2.26; 4.13, 4.36, 4.38, 4.59; 10.16, 10.29, 10.37
(1)	1.02; 2.12, 2.13, 2.20, 2.41; 6.03, 6.30, 6.84; 9.08
(a)	5.13; 9.96; 10.13, 10.23
(b), (d)	10.06, 10.10
(e)	10.10, 10.13, 10.23
(fa), (fb)	4.59

Table of Statutes

	PARA
Environmental Protection Act 1990 – contd	
s 79(1)(g)	2.26, 2.89; 9.119, 9.122. 9.134; 10.10, 10.34
(ga)	6.08; 9.119, 9.122, 9.134, 9.143; 10.10
(1A)	1.79, 1.96, 1.99; 10.14, 10.16, 10.22
(1B)	1.96, 1.99; 10.16, 10.22
(2)	1.35; 4.59
(3)	10.30, 10.31
(i)–(iv)	1.35
(4)	1.36; 10.32
(5)	4.59
(5B)	1.62
(6)	10.34
(7)	1.04, 1.26, 1.34, 1.40, 1.55, 1.62, 1.64, 1.78, 1.79, 1.80; 3.63, 3.66; 10.13
(7A), (7B)	1.62
(7C)	4.59
(7C)(a)–(d)	4.59
(7D)	4.59
(8)	2.01
(9)	1.80, 1.82, 1.85; 2.21; 5.96
(9)(a)	2.21
(10)	1.45, 1.49, 1.63; 2.01, 2.81; 10.06
80	2.39, 2.41, 2.49, 2.81, 2.89; 4.13, 4.22, 4.35, 4.37, 4.61, 4.62, 4.72, 4.83; 5.14, 5.19, 5.21, 5.22, 5.23, 5.40; 6.13, 6.16, 6.80, 6.83; 7.07; 10.37
(1)	2.33, 2.34; 3.02, 3.09, 3.10; 4.66; 6.75; 7.07; 10.25
(a)	2.44; 3.18, 3.56; 6.74; 8.08; 9.119, 9.122, 9.134
(b)	2.66; 3.50, 3.56; 6.74; 9.119, 9.122, 9.134
(2)	4.66, 4.73, 4.74
(a)	3.63 ; 6.74
(b), (c)	3.64; 6.74
(2A)(b)	2.41, 2.89
(2C)(a), (b)	2.43
(2D)	2.43
(2E)	2.43
(3)	3.08; 4.03, 4.05, 4.11, 4.12, 4.15, 4.29, 4.65, 4.66, 4.89, 4.135; 5.01, 5.84

	PARA
Environmental Protection Act 1990 – contd	
s 80(4)	2.01, 2.68; 4.68; 5.01, 5.03, 5.05, 5.06, 5.09, 5.10, 5.12, 5.14, 5.17, 5.26, 5.30, 5.31, 5.44, 5.127; 9.119, 9.142
(5)	2.68
(5A)	1.58
(6)	5.19, 5.20, 5.31
(6A)	1.68
(7)	1.49, 1.57, 1.58, 1.60, 1.66, 1.67, 1.69, 1.70, 1.83, 1.94; 5.20, 5.84, 5.90, 5.94, 5.95
(7C), (7D)	1.58
(8)	1.70, 1.83; 5.95
(a)	1.49, 1.57, 1.60, 1.67; 5.20
(aa)	1.69
(aza)	1.63
(b)	1.35
(8B), (8C)	1.63
(9)	4.69; 5.90, 5.94, 5.97
(a)	5.97; 9.119, 9.134
(b), (c)	5.97; 9.134
(10)(aza)	1.63
(10A)	1.63
(11)	1.66, 1.79
80A(1), (2)	3.74
(3)	3.74; 4.37
(4)	3.74
81	4.74; 10.37
(1B)(a), (c)	3.74
(2)	2.79
(3), (4)	2.50
(5)	1.73; 2.10, 2.11, 2.71, 2.73, 2.75, 2.76, 2.77, 2.82; 4.68; 9.119
(6)	9.119
81A(9)	3.66
82	2.01, 2.44, 2.84; 4.04, 4.145; 5.05; 6.01, 6.02, 6.03, 6.04, 6.07, 6.12, 6.13, 6.15, 6.16, 6.17, 6.18, 6.23, 6.24, 6.27, 6.35, 6.39, 6.41, 6.42, 6.43, 6.44, 6.46, 6.49, 6.50, 6.51, 6.53, 6.54, 6.55, 6.57, 6.61, 6.62, 6.64, 6.68, 6.69, 6.70, 6.73, 6.74, 6.79, 6.80, 6.82; 7.47, 7.50, 7.54, 7.55, 7.57, 7.58, 7.74, 7.75, 7.90, 7.92, 7.93, 7.116; 9.53, 9.119, 9.123, 9.134, 90.135; 10.06, 10.10, 10.37

Table of Statutes

	PARA
Environmental Protection Act 1990 – *contd*	
s 82(1)	6.03, 6.14, 6.18, 6.38, 6.39, 6.46, 6.56, 6.57, 6.58; 7.54
(2)	6.11, 6.36, 6.52, 6.54, 6.56, 6.58, 6.66, 6.71, 6.75, 6.81, 6.83; 7.48, 7.49, 7.89; 10.15, 10.37
(a)	6.71
(3)	6.71
(4)	6.09, 6.11, 6.26; 7.51
(a), (b)	6.08
(c)	6.08, 6.67
(d)	6.08
(5)	6.09
(5A)	6.11
(5B)	6.10, 6.11
(6)	6.06, 6.11, 6.14, 6.18, 6.23, 6.24, 6.27, 6.29, 6.32, 6.33, 6.34, 6.36, 6.42, 6.43, 6.46, 6.67; 7.50, 7.93
(7)(a), (b)	6.20
(8)	6.83, 6.85; 9.142; 10.37
(9)	6.69, 6.84
(10), (10A)	6.84
(11)	6.09
(12)	6.55; 7.48, 7.50, 7.53, 7.55, 7.56
(13)	1.47; 6.35, 6.36, 6.79, 6.80; 7.56
Pt IV (ss 86–99)	9.44; 10.01
s 86	9.48
(11)	9.51
(13)	9.48
87	9.47, 9.48
(2)	9.48
(9)	1.83, 1.94
(10)	1.83
88(6A)	9.49
89(1), (3)	9.51
91	9.52
(12)	9.53
92	9.52
(9), (10)	9.52
92A	9.54
(3)	9.54
93	9.56
94	9.56
97(7)	1.36
98	9.45, 9.51
99(1)	9.59
152	9.100
157	5.113
159(2)–(4)	10.36
160	3.77; 6.34

	PARA
Environmental Protection Act 1990 – *contd*	
s 160(3)	3.79
(a), (b)	3.78
(4)	3.77
(a)	3.78
(5)	3.79
Sch 3	4.67, 4.73, 4.78
para 1	4.05
(3)	4.126
2	2.56, 2.60
(1)	2.59
(a)	2.19
(b)	2.66
(3)(a), (b)	2.61
(4)	2.58
(c)	2.51
(5)	2.62
(7)	2.60
2A	2.63
(1)	2.63
(2)–(4)	2.64
(5), (6)	2.65
3(1), (2)	2.62
4	4.119
6	3.08; 4.73, 4.119, 4.120, 4.121, 4.122
7	4.120
Sch 4	9.59
para 2(1), (2)	9.59
3(1)(a), (b)	9.59
(4), (5)	9.59
Firearms Act 1968	4.94, 4.96
Forestry Act 1967	
s 17(1)	4.28, 4.30
Freedom of Information Act 2000	2.26, 2.30
s 2(3)	2.26
39	2.26
Greater London Council (General Powers) Act 1968	
s 49(10)	4.95
Health and Safety at Work etc Act 1974	5.96
Highways Act 1980	
s 149(3)(a), (b)	9.63
151	9.63, 9.64, 9.65
(2), (3)	9.65
Housing Act 1957	2.35
Housing Act 2004	
Pt I (ss 1–54)	9.18, 9.19
s 2(1)	9.21
5, 6	9.19
11	9.20, 9.23
(2), (5), (8)	9.22
12	9.23
13(2)	9.23
(3), (4)	9.24
20, 40, 43	9.20

Table of Statutes

	PARA
Housing Act 2004 – *contd*	
Sch 1	
para 10	9.26
11, 12	9.25
14	9.27
Sch 3	
para 1–3	9.28
4	9.29
5	9.28
6	9.29
Human Rights Act 1998	2.01, 2.02, 2.04, 2.91; 3.07, 3.14, 3.53; 4.17, 4.20, 4.48, 4.127, 4.142; 5.02, 5.42, 5.46, 5.67, 5.84; 7.111, 7.112, 7.115, 7.116
s 1	4.06
2	2.05
3	2.03 ;4.22; 8.05
(1)	2.05; 5.51; 10.37
4	4.22
6	2.04; 3.38; 7.109; 8.05
(1)	2.03, 2.10
(3)(a)	2.10
7	2.03, 2.04
(1)	2.06
(b)	4.06, 4.40; 7.109
(7)	2.06
8	7.113
(1), (2)	7.109
(3)	7.113
(4)	7.114
9	4.06
22(4)	2.04; 3.07; 7.109
Sch 1	7.109; 8.05
Interpretation Act 1978	3.63
s 1	6.03
7	3.77
12	2.12
Sch 1	1.26, 1.79
5	6.03
Land Drainage Act 1991	
s 28	1.73
Limitation Act 1980	
s 2	4.22
Litter Act 1983	9.45
Local Government Act 1972	
s 222(1)	2.69, 2.73
Local Government Act 1974	
s 25	4.146
26	4.148
34(1)	4.146
Local Government (Miscellaneous Provisions) Act 1976	5.58
s 16	5.54, 5.60, 5.64
(2)	2.54; 5.60
Local Government (Scotland) Act 1975	
Pt II (ss 21–32)	4.146

	PARA
Magistrates' Courts Act 1980	4.09, 4.76, 4.78, 4.96, 4.113; 7.11
s 2, 3	6.46
52	4.10
(3)	7.18
53	4.109, 4.110; 7.20
(2)	7.11, 7.12, 7.19
64	7.03, 7.10, 7.11, 7.12, 7.14, 7.16, 7.19, 7.25
(1)	7.04, 7.05, 7.10, 7.11
(a)	7.04, 7.12
(b)	7.04
101	5.90
108	5.118
(1)	5.118
(3)	5.118
(b)	7.87
109	5.118; 7.41
(1)	7.27
110	5.118
111	4.126
(1)	5.122
112–114	4.126
123	4.79; 5.34; 6.41
127	6.42
142(1), (2)	5.113
Metropolitan Commons Acts 1866–1898	9.99
Mines and Quarries Act 1954	
s 151(1)	1.77
(2)(a)–(c)	1.77
Noise Act 1996	1.64; 2.52 ; 8.01; 9.101, 9.107
s 2(1), (2), (4)–(6)	9.102
3	2.98; 9.103, 9.105
(1)(a), (b)	9.103
(2), (4), (5)	9.103
4	9.104, 9.105
(2)	9.105
4A	9.105
5	9.102
6, 8	9.106
10(1)–(3)	9.107
(4)–(6)	9.108
(7)	2.50, 2.52, 2.67
(8)	9.108
Noise and Statutory Nuisance Act 1993	2.45
s 8	9.139
Sch 2	9.139
para 1	2.45; 4.68
Nuclear Installations Act 1965	10.01
Nuisance Removal Act 1846	1.03
Nuisance Removal Act 1855	1.03
Nuisance Removal and Diseases Prevention Act 1848	1.03
Parliamentary Commissioner Act 1967	4.149
Pet Animals Act 1951	9.95

Table of Statutes

	PARA
Planning and Compulsory Purchase Act 2004	1.21
s 17(3)	1.21
Planning (Listed Buildings and Conservation Areas) Act 1990	5.109
s 69, 71	2.12
Police and Criminal Evidence Act 1984	2.57; 5.55, 5.67
s 9	5.62
25	9.49
67(8), (9)	5.55
(11)	5.57, 5.59
76	5.56, 5.74
78	5.56, 5.62, 5.65, 5.66
Pollution Prevention and Control Act 1999	1.35, 1.63; 8.17; 10.01, 10.02, 10.07, 10.10, 10.27, 10.28
s 6	1.45, 1.49, 1.63; 10.02
Sch 2	
para 6	1.45, 1.49, 1.63; 10.02
Powers of Criminal Courts (Sentencing) Act 2000	
s 130(1)	7.89, 7.97
(3)	7.103
(4)	7.104
131	7.94, 7.104
133	7.108
134	7.96, 7.108
(2)	7.107
Prevention of Damage by Pests Act 1949	9.96
s 4	3.75
(1)	9.96
5	3.75; 9.97
22	9.97
Prosecution of Offences Act 1985	
s 16	7.30
(1)	7.31
(a)	7.58
(3)	7.42
(5)	7.75
(6)	7.31, 7.33, 7.42, 7.75
(7)–(9)	7.33
17	7.30
(1), (2)	7.75
(6)(c)	7.75
18	7.26, 7.30, 7.55
(1)	7.30, 7.38, 7.39
19	7.30
19A(3)	7.58
19B	7.56
20	7.30
21	7.30
(1)	7.43
Public Health Act 1875	1.03, 1.05, 1.42, 1.51, 1.64; 3.27

	PARA
Public Health Act 1936	1.03, 1.42, 1.64; 2.35; 4.66, 4.98, 4.137; 6.41; 9.76, 9.83, 9.94, 9.96
s 45	9.73
(2)	9.74
(3)	9.74, 9.75
48	9.73
50	9.79
(3)	9.80
51, 52	9.76
78	9.57
(2)	9.57
81, 82	9.83
83(1), (1A)	9.84
(2), (3)	9.85
84	9.85
90	9.73, 9.84
93	3.73
94	6.56
(1)	6.56
99	3.73
141	1.71
259	1.72
(1)(a)	1.72
(b)	1.72, 1.73
260, 261	9.94
268(2)(a), (b)	1.75
(3)	1.76
(5)(a)	1.76
280(3)	4.65
287	9.73
289	3.67
290(3)	4.65; 9.74, 9.80
(6)	9.75, 9.80
291	9.75, 9.80
Public Health Act 1961	
s 34	9.62
(2)	9.62
(b)	9.61, 9.62
(5)	9.61, 9.62
Public Health (Control of Disease) Act 1984	9.86
s 10, 29–32	9.86
Radioactive Substances Act 1993	10.01, 10.11
s 6, 8, 13, 14, 21, 22, 30	10.11
40	10.11
(1), (2)	1.71
Sch 3	1.71; 10.11
Refuse Disposal (Amenity) Act 1978	9.68
s 2(1)(a)	9.62, 9.69
(b)	9.62
3	9.70
(5)	9.70
4	9.70
6, 8	9.62
11	9.69

Table of Statutes

	PARA
Regulation of Investigatory Powers Act 2000	2.24, 2.93, 2.96
Pt II (ss 26–48)	2.93
s 26	2.95
(1)(c)	2.101
(2)	2.97
(3), (4)	2.100
(10)	2.97
29	2.101
48	2.94
(10)	2.97
Riding Establishments Act 1970	9.95
Road Traffic Act 1988	
s 5	5.63
172	5.63, 5.64
(2)(a)	5.63
Sanitation Act 1866	1.03
Supreme Court Act 1981	7.74
s 28	4.126; 5.127, 7.106
48	5.120; 7.23, 7.26, 7.29, 7.39
(2)	7.25
(4)	5.120
Taxes Management Act 1970	
s 103(1)	4.28
Town and Country Planning Act 1947	
s 33(1)	9.08, 9.09
Town and Country Planning Act 1971	
s 65	9.09
Town and Country Planning Act 1990	3.59; 7.113
s 12(3)	1.21
(4)(b)	1.21
36(2)	1.21
(3A)(b)	1.21
Pt III (ss 55–106)	9.05, 9.15, 9.16
s 77	2.15
Pt VII (ss 137–172)	9.13

	PARA
Town and Country Planning Act 1990 – *contd*	
s 172(2), (3)	5.06
173(3)	3.05
179(3)	5.81
181	9.13
186	3.44
187B	2.10, 2.75, 2.79
188	9.11
215	9.02, 9.03, 9.04, 9.07, 9.08, 9.09, 9.11, 9.13
(1)–(4)	9.02
216	9.03, 9.11
(2)–(4)	9.03
(5)(b)(i), (ii)	9.03
217	9.04
(1)(a)	9.05, 9.14
(b)	9.05, 9.14, 9.15, 9.16
(c), (d)	9.05
(3)	9.06
(4), (5)	9.04
218	9.06
219	9.07
284	4.134
285(3)	9.14
288(3)	4.24
289	4.84
Water Resources Act 1991	1.58; 9.94; 10.04, 10.21
s 18, 19	2.15
85	10.21, 10.22
88	10.21
104, 161	10.13
Sch 10	10.21, 10.24
Wildlife and Countryside Act 1981	10.17
Sch 5	1.58; 4.59
Zoo Licensing Act 1981	
s 4	9.95

Table of Statutory Instruments

	PARA
Air Navigation (General) Regulations 1993, SI 1993/1622	10.34
Civil Procedure Rules 1998, SI 1998/3122	
r 6.2.1	3.79
6.7	3.77
Pt 44	7.71
r 44.3(1), (2)	7.71
(3)	7.73
(4), (5)	7.72
Conservation (Natural Habitats, &c) Regulations 1994, SI 1994/2716	10.17
Contaminated Land (England) Regulations 2006, SI 2006/380	10.12
Control of Noise (Appeals) Regulations 1975, SI 1975/2116	9.114, 9.121, 9.127, 9.129, 9.132, 9.141
reg 5	9.114
(4)	9.114
10	9.132
(1)	9.116
(2)	9.117
Control of Noise (Code of Practice for Construction and Open Sites) (England) Order 2002, SI 2002/461	9.114
Control of Noise (Code of Practice for Construction and Open Sites) Order 1987, SI 1987/1730	9.114
Control of Noise (Code of Practice on Noise from Audible Intruder Alarms) Order 1981, SI 1981/1829	9.141
Control of Noise (Code of Practice on Noise from Ice Cream Van Chimes Etc) Order 1981, SI 1981/1828	9.141
Control of Noise (Code of Practice on Noise from Model Aircraft) Order 1981, SI 1981/1830	9.141
Control of Noise (Codes of Practice for Construction and Open Sites) Orders 1984, SI 1984/1992	9.115, 9.141
Control of Noise (Measurement and Register) Regulations 1976, SI 1976/37	9.126

	PARA
Controlled Waste Regulations 1992, SI 1992/588	9.43; 10.26
reg 7A	9.35
Costs in Criminal Cases (General) Regulations 1986, SI 1986/1335	7.30, 7.33
Criminal Procedure and Investigations Act 1996 (Defence Disclosure Time Limits) Regulations 1997, SI 1997/684	5.49
Criminal Procedure Rules 2005, SI 2005/384	5.02, 5.118, 5.128
r 1.1	5.02
(2)	5.02
1.2, 1.3	5.02
7.1(1), (2)	5.26
(3)	5.27
7.2	5.30
21.1	5.42, 5.44
24.1	5.54
(1)(a)(i), (ii)	5.52
24.2(1), (2)	5.53
37.1-37.5	5.68
63	5.118
63.2(2)-(5)	5.119
64.1-64.6	6.123
64.7(1)	5.128
(14)	5.128
78.2	7.44
Crop Residues (Restrictions on Burning) Regulations 1991, SI 1991/1399	9.100
Crop Residues (Restrictions on Burning) (No 2) Regulations 1991, SI 1991/1590	9.100
Crown Court Rules 1982, SI 1982/1109 r 26	4.126
Dog Control Order (Prescribed Offences and Penalties etc) Regulations 2006, SI 2006/1059	9.99
Environmental Information Regulations 1992, SI 1992/3240	2.26
Environmental Information Regulations 2004, SI 2004/3391	2.26, 2.29, 2.31, 2.32, 2.48; 6.63
reg 12	2.29
(1), (2), (11)	2.28
16	2.32
18	2.30

Table of Statutory Instruments

	PARA
Environmental Protection (Prescribed Processes and Substances) Regulations 1991, SI 1991/472	10.01, 10.03, 10.04
Housing, Health and Safety Rating System (England) Regulations 2005, SI 2005/3208	9.21
Justices' Clerk Rules 1970, SI 1970/231	6.45
Litter (Designated Educational Institutions) Order 1991, SI 1991/561	9.51
Litter (Relevant Land of Principal Litter Authorities and Relevant Crown Land) Order 1991, 1991/476	9.51
Litter (Statutory Undertakers) (Designation and Relevant Land) Order 1991, SI 1991/1043	9.51
Magistrates' Courts (Advance Information) Rules 1985, SI 1985/601	5.44
Magistrates' Courts (Forms) Rules 1981, SI 1981/553	4.08
Magistrates' Courts (Hearsay Evidence in Civil Proceedings) Rules 1999, SI 1999/681	4.93
Magistrates' Courts Rules 1981, SI 1981/552	4.100, 4.107
r 4	6.40
(1)	4.09
(2)	4.09; 5.26
(3)	5.30
14(1)	4.99
(2)	4.101
(3)	4.102
(5)	4.103
34	4.96, 4.109
76–81	4.126
98	6.44
100	6.50
Pollution Prevention and Control (England and Wales) Regulations 2000, SI 2000/1973	10.07, 10.08, 10.09, 10.10
reg 7, 8	10.07
Pt II (regs 9–22)	10.08
reg 9	10.07
Pt III (regs 23–26)	10.08
VII (regs 36–38)	10.08
Sch 1	10.07
10	10.10
Public Health (Infectious Diseases) Regulations 1988, SI 1988/1546	9.86
Radioactive Contaminated Land (Enabling Powers) (England) Regulations 2005, SI 2005/3467	10.12

	PARA
Road Vehicles (Construction and Use) Regulations 1986, SI 1986/1078	
reg 97	9.143
Rules of the Air Regulations 1996, SI 1996/1393	10.34
Statutory Nuisance (Appeals) (England) Regulations 2006, SI 2006/771	4.59
Statutory Nuisance (Appeals) Regulations 1995, SI 1995/2644	2.05; 3.08, 3.42, 3.43; 4.66, 4.72, 4.74, 4.78, 4.110; 5.101; 9.142
reg 2	4.105, 4.107
(2)	4.35, 4.38
(a)	4.35, 4.39, 4.59, 4.115
(b)	2.90, 4.06, 4.36, 4.39, 4.40
(c)	2.10; 4.41; 7.07
(d)	4.52
(e)	4.58
(i), (iv)	4.58
(g)	2.45, 4.68
(h)	2.45; 4.69
(i)	4.69
(3)	4.41
(4)	4.122
(5)	4.58, 4.78, 4.110, 4.117; 7.11, 7.19
(b)	4.112
(6)	4.118, 4.123
(7)	4.122, 4.123
3	3.56
(1)(a)	3.08, 3.36
(b)	3.08, 3.36
(i), (ii)	3.35
(2)(a)(i), (ii)	3.36
(b)	3.36
3(2)	4.141
(3)	3.36
4	4.34, 4.76
(2)	4.119
5(a), (b)	3.56
Statutory Nuisances (Artificial Lighting) (Designation of Relevant Sports) (England) Order 2006, SI 2006/781	1.63; 4.59
Statutory Nuisances (Insects) Regulations 2006, SI 2006/770	1.58
Waste Management Licensing Regulations 1994, SI 1994/1056	9.43, 9.36; 10.27
Sch 3	10.26
4	9.34, 9.35
Workplace (Health, Safety and Welfare) Regulations 1992, SI 1992/3004	
reg 3, 20, 21	9.74

Table of Cases

PARA

A

A v Hoare [2006] EWCA Civ 393 .... 4.22
AMEC Building Ltd and Squibb & Davies Ltd v Camden London Borough Council
 (1996) 55 Con LR 82, [1997] JPL B82, [1997] Env LR 330 .... 3.63, 5.07, 5.14
ARCO Chemie Nederland v M & V & EPON (Case C-418/97) [2003] Env LR 40,
 [2002] QB 646 .... 9.36; 10.26
Airey v Ireland (1979) 2 EHRR 305, ECtHR 6.62, 6.64
Albert and Le Compte v Belgium (1983) 5 EHRR 533 .... 3.41
Albion v Railtrack plc [1998] NPC 21, [1998] EHLR 83 .... 3.03
Anufrijeva v LB Southwark [2003] EWCA Civ 1406, [2004] QB 1124 .... 7.115
Ashingdane v United Kingdom (1985) 7 EHRR 528, ECtHR 3.40, 4.18, 4.30
Associated Provincial Picture Houses Ltd v Wednesbury Corpn [1948] 1 KB 223, [1947]
 2 All ER 680, 45 LGR 635, 112 JP 55, [1948] LJR 190, 92 Sol Jo 26, 177 LT 641, 63
 TLR 623, CA 3.75
Atkinson v DPP [2004] EWHC 1457, [2005] 1 WLR 96 .... 5.31
A-G of Gambia v N'Jie [1961] AC 617, [1961] 2 All ER 504, [1961] 2 WLR 845, 105
 Sol Jo 421, PC 6.03
Aviation and Shipping Co Ltd v Murray (Inspector of Taxes) [1961] 2 All ER 805,
 [1961] 1 WLR 974, [1961] 1 Lloyd's Rep 513, 39 TC 595, 40 ATC 143, [1961] TR
 133, 105 Sol Jo 441, CA 1.80
Aylesvury Vale District Council v Florent [2007] EWHC 724, [2008] JPL 70, QB 2.10

B

B v Secretary of State for the Home Department [2000] 2 CMLR 1086, [2000] Imm AR
 478, CA 2.09
Bamford v Turnley (1860) 3 B & S 62; on appeal (1862) 3 B & S 66, 31 LJQB 286, 9
 Jur NS 377, 10 WR 803, 122 ER 27, [1861-73] All ER Rep 706, 6 LT 721, Ex Ch .. 1.06
Barns (the) v Newcastle upon Tyne City Council [2005] EWCA Civ 1274 .... 2.39, 2.76,
 2.77, 4.61, 4.63
Barraclough v Secretary of State for the Environment and Leeds City Council [1990]
 JPL 911 .... 3.80
Battersea Borough Council v George (1906) 5 LGR 62, 71 JP 11, DC 5.11, 5.12
Baxter v Camden London Borough Council [1999] 4 All ER 449, 32 HLR 148, [1999]
 42 LS Gaz R 41, [1999] NLJR 1618, [1999] 45 EG 179, [1999] EGCS 122, 143 Sol
 Jo LB 249, 79 P & CR D13, [2000] Env LR 112, sub nom Baxter v Camden London
 Borough Council (No 2) [1999] 3 WLR 939, HL 1.31, 1.65, 8.03
Bellet v France (Series A no 333-B, 4 December 1995) 4.17
Berkeley v Secretary of State for the Environment [1999] 1 CMLR 945, [1998] Env LR
 741, [1998] PLCR 97, [1998] 3 PLR 39, [1998] NPC 18, CA; revsd [2000] 3 All ER
 897, [2000] 3 WLR 420, [2000] EGCS 86, HL 7.86
Birmingham City Council v Oakley (1998) 31 HLR 1070, [1999] Env LR D17; revsd
 [2000] 3 WLR 1936, [2000] NLJR 1824, HL 1.30, 1.31, 1.32
Birmingham District Council v Kelly (1985) 17 HLR 572, [1986] 2 EGLR 239 ...... 1.29, 6.77
Birmingham District Council v McMahon (1987) 86 LGR 63, 151 JP 709, 19 HLR
 452 .... 1.29, 1.79, 6.04, 6.57, 6.67
Bishop Auckland Local Board v Bishop Auckland Iron and Steel Co (1882) 10 QBD
 138, 47 JP 389, 52 LJMC 38, 31 WR 288, 48 LT 223, DC 1.09
Blackburn v ARC Ltd [1998] Env LR 469 .... 1.22

Table of Cases

	PARA
Bond v Chief Constable of Kent [1983] 1 All ER 456, [1983] 1 WLR 40, 76 Cr App Rep 56, 4 Cr App Rep (S) 324, 147 JP 107, [1983] Crim LR 166, 126 Sol Jo 707, [1983] LS Gaz R 29	7.92
Botross v London Borough of Hammersmith and Fulham (1994) 93 LGR 269, 16 Cr App Rep (S) 622, 27 HLR 179, [1994] NPC 134, [1995] COD 169, [1995] Env LR 217	6.39, 7.50, 7.89
Bowyer, Philpott and Payne Ltd v Mather [1919] 1 KB 419, 17 LGR 222, 83 JP 50, 88 LJKB 377, 120 LT 346, DC	2.72
Boynton v Helena Rubinstein Ltd (1960) 176 Estates Gazette 443	8.32
BPS Advertising Ltd v London Borough of Barnet [2006] EWHC 3335 (Admin)	7.64
Bradford Metropolitan District Council v Booth (2000) 164 JP 485	7.09, 7.12, 7.14, 7.20
Brighton and Hove Council v Ocean Coachworks (Brighton) Ltd (11 April 2000, unreported)	3.06, 3.56, 8.01, 8.10
Brind, ex p. See R v Secretary of State for the Home Department, ex p Brind	
Britt v Buckinghamshire County Council [1964] 1 QB 77, [1963] 2 All ER 175, [1963] 2 WLR 722, 61 LGR 223, 14 P & CR 318, 127 JP 389, 107 Sol Jo 153, [1963] RVR 215, CA	9.08, 9.09
Broad v Fernandez (10 July 1996, unreported)	6.51
Bryan v United Kingdom (1995) 21 EHRR 342, [1996] 1 PLR 47, [1996] 2 EGLR 123, [1996] 28 EG 137, [1996] JPL 386, ECtHR	3.38, 4.84
Budd v Colchester Borough Council [1997] COD 36, [1997] Env LR 128; affd (1999) 97 LGR 601, [1999] NPC 30, [1999] JPL 717, 143 Sol Jo LB 96, 143 Sol Jo LB 96, [1999] BLGR 601, [1999] EHLR 347, [1999] Env LR 739, CA	1.20, 1.52, 3.17, 3.24
Butland v Powys City Council [2007] EWHC 734	5.07
Butuyuyu v Hammersmith and Fulham London Borough Council (1996) 29 HLR 584, [1997] Env LR D13	4.15, 5.83

C

Cambridge Water Co v Eastern Counties Leather plc [1994] 2 AC 264, [1994] 1 All ER 53, CA; revsd [1994] 2 AC 264, [1994] 1 All ER 53, [1994] 2 WLR 53, [1994] 1 Lloyd's Rep 261, [1994] 11 LS Gaz R 36, [1994] NLJR 15, 138 Sol Jo LB 24, HL	1.06
Camden London Borough Council v Gunby [1999] 4 All ER 602, [2000] 1 WLR 465, 32 HLR 572, [1999] 29 LS Gaz R 30, [1999] NLJR 1146, [1999] 44 EG 147, [2000] Env LR D10	3.66
Camden London Borough Council v London Underground Ltd [2000] 01 LS Gaz R 25, ENDS Report 300, p 47, [2000] Env LR 369	3.31, 3.32, 3.56, 3.59, 3.60, 7.09
Carr v Hackney London Borough Council (1995) 93 LGR 606, 160 JP 402, 28 HLR 749	6.67
Cartwright v Post Office [1968] 2 QB 439, [1968] 2 All ER 646, [1968] 3 WLR 63, 112 Sol Jo 312; affd [1969] 2 QB 62, [1969] 1 All ER 421, [1969] 2 WLR 323, 112 Sol Jo 944, 208 Estates Gazette 1352, CA	9.08
Chief Constable of the North Wales Police v Evans [1982] 3 All ER 141, [1982] 1 WLR 1155, 147 JP 6, 126 Sol Jo 549, [1982] LS Gaz R 1257, HL	4.135
Cheshire County Council v Secretary of State for the Environment [1988] JPL 30	2.11
Chung Tak Lam v Brennan [1997] 3 PLR 22	7.115
City of Bradford MDC v Booth [2000] 164 JP 485, DC	7.05, 7.07, 7.10
Clarke v Garrett (1877) 28 UCCP 75	4.28
Cocks v Thanet District Council [1983] 2 AC 286, [1982] 3 All ER 1135, [1982] 3 WLR 1121, 81 LGR 81, 6 HLR 15, 126 Sol Jo 820, [1984] RVR 31, HL	4.22, 4.84
Cole v Wolkind (22 July 1980, unreported)	6.51
Cooke v Adatia (1988) 153 JP 129	5.13
Coventry City Council v Cartwright [1975] 2 All ER 99, [1975] 1 WLR 845, 73 LGR 218, 139 JP 409, 119 Sol Jo 235, DC	1.05, 1.48, 1.52
Coventry City Council v Doyle [1981] 2 All ER 184, [1981] 1 WLR 1325, 79 LGR 418, 125 Sol Jo 639, DC	5.18, 6.56, 6.67
Coventry City Council v Harris (1992) 4 Land Management and Env LR 168	1.65
Crowe v London Borough of Tower Hamlets noted in LAG May 1997	6.54
Cullen v Jardine [1985] Crim LR 668	5.27

Table of Cases

PARA

Cunningham v Birmingham City Council (1997) 96 LGR 231, 30 HLR 158, [1998] Env LR 1 .... 1.05
Crawley BC v Stuart Attenborough [2006] EWHC 1278 .... 7.07, 7.21

D

Danby v Beardsley (1880) 43 LT 603 .... 7.55
Davenport v Walsall Metropolitan Borough Council (1995) 28 HLR 754, [1996] COD 107, [1997] Env LR 24 .... 7.51, 7.53, 7.95, 7.96, 7.102
Davy v Spelthorne Borough Council [1984] AC 262, [1983] 3 All ER 278, [1983] 3 WLR 742, 82 LGR 193, 47 P & CR 310, 127 Sol Jo 733, [1984] JPL 269, HL 9.14
Debtor, A, Re, ex p Debtor (No 490 of 1935) [1936] Ch 237, 105 LJ Ch 129, [1934-1935] B & CR 329, 79 Sol Jo 839, 154 LT 44, 52 TLR 70, CA 1.81
Dee and Clwyd River Authority v Parry (1967) 65 LGR 488, DC 3.03
De Geouffre de la Pradelle v France (1992) A 253-B 4.17, 4.18, 4.19, 4.30
Dennis v Ministry of Defence [2003] EWHC 793, QB, [2003] EWHC LR 34 .... 1.18; 10.35
Dilieto (Alfonso) v Ealing London Borough Council [2000] QB 381, [1998] 2 All ER 885, [1998] 3 WLR 1403, [1998] PLCR 212 .... 4.84
DPP v Coleman [1998] 1 All ER 912, [1998] 1 WLR 1708, [1998] 2 Cr App Rep 7, [1997] 48 LS Gaz R 30 .... 5.128
DPP v Merriman [1973] AC 584, [1972] 3 All ER 42, [1972] 3 WLR 545, 56 Cr App Rep 766, 136 JP 659, 116 Sol Jo 745, HL 5.27
Disher v Disher [1965] P 31, [1963] 3 All ER 933, [1964] 2 WLR 21, 108 Sol Jo 37 .. 4.101
Dombo Beheer BV v Netherlands (1993) 18 EHRR 213, ECtHR 2.06, 3.38
Dover District Council v Farrar (1980) 2 HLR 32 .... 3.70, 6.67
Draper v Sperring (1861) 25 JP 566, 10 CBNS 113, 30 LJMC 225, 9 WR 656, 142 ER 392, 4 LT 365 .... 1.52
Dunsfold Park Ltd v Waverley Borough Council (12 January 2007) 4.107

E

Eagil Trust Co v Pigott-Brown [1985] 3 All ER 119 .... 7.21
East Dorset v Eaglebeam Ltd [2006] EWHC 2378, QB 2.11, 2.76, 2.77, 2.78, 2.79, 2.98
East Northamptonshire District Council v Fossett [1994] Env LR 388 .... 1.65, 5.13
East Riding of Yorkshire; C v Yorkshire Water Services [2001] Env LR 113 .... 1.26
East Staffordshire Borough Council v Fairless (1998) 31 HLR 677, [1998] 41 LS Gaz R 46, [1998] EGCS 140, [1999] EHLR 128, [1999] Env LR 525 .... 6.23, 6.24, 6.25, 6.26, 6.27, 6.29, 6.39, 6.67
Edwards v United Kingdom (1992) 15 EHRR 417, ECtHR 5.45
Ellerman's Wilson Line Ltd v Webster [1952] 1 Lloyd's Rep 179, DC 9.62, 9.69
Elliott v Brighton Borough Council (1980) 79 LGR 506, 258 Estates Gazette 441, [1981] JPL 504, CA 9.26
Ellis and Ruislip-Northwood UDC, Re [1920] 1 KB 343, 17 LGR 607, 83 JP 273, 88 LJKB 1258, 122 LT 98, 35 TLR 673, CA 9.08
Express Contract Drying Ltd v Blaenau Gwent CBC (20 November 2007) 4.88, 4.100

F

F (an infant) v Chief Constable of Kent [1982] Crim LR 682 .... 5.74
FFF Estates Ltd v Hackney London Borough Council [1981] QB 503, [1981] 1 All ER 32, [1980] 3 WLR 909, 79 LGR 38, 41 P & CR 54, 3 HLR 107, 124 Sol Jo 593, [1981] JPL 34, CA 9.08
Farley v Skinner [2001] UKHL 49, [2002] 2 AC 732 .... 10.34
Felix v DPP [1998] Crim LR 657 .... 9.48
Finbow v Air Ministry [1963] WLR 697 .... 3.31
Fischer v Austria (1995) 20 EHRR 349, ECtHR 3.38
Fose v Minister of Safety and Security (1997) 2 BHRC 434 .... 7.113
Funke v France [1993] 1 CMLR 897, 16 EHRR 297, ECtHR 5.61

Table of Cases

PARA

G

Galer v Morrissey [1955] 1 All ER 380, [1955] 1 WLR 110, 53 LGR 303, 119 JP 165, 99 Sol Jo 113, DC 1.52
Gillingham Borough Council v Medway (Chatham) Dock Co Ltd [1993] QB 343, [1992] 3 All ER 923, [1992] 3 WLR 449, 91 LGR 160, 63 P & CR 205, [1992] 1 PLR 113, [1992] JPL 458 .... 1.22; 3.59
Godfrey v Conwy County Borough Council [2001] Env LR 38 .... 5.102, 8.23
Golder v United Kingdom (1975) 1 EHRR 524, ECtHR 3.40
Goldman v Hargrave [1967] 1 AC 645, [1966] 2 All ER 989, [1966] 3 WLR 513, [1966] 2 Lloyd's Rep 65, 110 Sol Jo 527, [1967] ALR 113, PC 1.74
Gosnell v Aerated Bread Co Ltd (1894) 10 TLR 661 .... 1.15
Greater London Council v Tower Hamlets London Borough Council (1983) 15 HLR 54 .... 1.29, 3.71, 3.72, 6.67
Greenwich Borough Council v LCC (1912) 10 LGR 488, 76 JP 267, 23 Cox CC 32, 106 LT 887, DC 5.11
Griffin, Re, ex p Board of Trade (1890) 60 LJQB 235, 8 Morr 1, 39 WR 156, 7 TLR 146, CA 1.82
Griffiths v Pembrokeshire County Council [2000] 18 LS Gaz R 36, [2000] NLJR 512 .... 1.34, 7.66, 10.29
Guérin v France (29 July 1998) 4.18
Guerra v Italy (1998) 26 EHRR 357, ECtHR 2.07, 2.17, 2.25, 2.29, 2.48, 6.62, 7.116

H

Hall v Kingston upon Hull City Council [1999] 2 All ER 609, 96 LGR 184, 164 JP 9, sub nom Kingston upon Hull City Council v Hall 31 HLR 1078, sub nom R v Kingston upon Hull City Council, ex p Hall [1999] EGCS 4 .... 1.01, 3.01, 3.79, 6.02, 6.23, 6.67
Hall & Co Ltd v Shoreham-by-Sea UDC [1964] 1 All ER 1, [1964] 1 WLR 240, 62 LGR 206, 15 P & CR 119, 128 JP 120, 107 Sol Jo 1001, CA 3.75
Hammersmith London Borough Council v Magnum Automated Forecourts Ltd [1978] 1 All ER 401, [1978] 1 WLR 50, 76 LGR 159, 142 JP 130, 121 Sol Jo 529, CA 8.32
Hammertons Cars Ltd v London Borough of Redbridge [1974] 2 All ER 216, [1974] 1 WLR 484, 118 Sol Jo 240 .... 7.92
Hampstead and Suburban Properties Ltd v Diomedous [1969] 1 Ch 248, [1968] 3 All ER 545, [1968] 3 WLR 990, 19 P & CR 880, 112 Sol Jo 656 .... 1.18, 8.05
Handyside v United Kingdom 17 YB 228 (1974), EComHR 5.100
Handyside v United Kingdom (1976) 1 EHRR 737, ECtHR 3.16
Haringey London Borough Council v Jowett (1999) 32 HLR 308, [1999] EGCS 64, 78 P & CR D24, [1999] EHLR 410, [1999] BLGR 667, [1999] NPC 52 .... 1.31
Harris v Hickman [1904] 1 KB 13, 2 LGR 1, 68 JP 65, 73 LJKB 31, 48 Sol Jo 69, 89 LT 722, 20 TLR 18 .... 2.88
Hatton v United Kingdom (2002) 34 EHRR 1, (2003) 37 EHRR 28 .... 10.34
Hazlett v Sefton Metropolitan Borough Council [2000] 4 All ER 887, [1999] NLJR 1869, [2000] Env LR 416 .... 7.53, 7.77
Herbert v Lambeth London Borough Council (1991) 90 LGR 310, 13 Cr App Rep (S) 489, 156 JP 389, 24 HLR 299 .... 7.96
Hertsmere Borough Council v Alan Dunn Building Contractors Ltd (1985) 84 LGR 214 .... 5.31, 5.32
Hewlings v Mclean Homes East Anglia Ltd [2000] 39 LS Gaz R 41, [2000] EGCS 100, [2001] 2 All ER 281 .... 3.77, 3.78, 5.07, 6.27, 6.34, 6.67
Hilton v Hopwood (1899) 44 Sol Jo 90, DC 6.58
Horrix v Malam [1984] RTR 112, 148 JP 30 .... 5.27
Hounslow LBC v Thames Water Utilities Ltd [2003] EWHC 1197, [2004] QB 212 ... 1.26, 1.39
Hunter v Canary Wharf Ltd [1997] AC 655, [1997] 2 All ER 426, [1997] 2 WLR 684, [1997] 2 FLR 342, [1997] Fam Law 601, 30 HLR 409, [1997] 19 LS Gaz R 25, [1997] NLJR 634, 84 BLR 1, 141 Sol Jo LB 108, HL 1.09

Table of Cases

PARA

I

Iatridis v Greece (1999) 30 EHRR 97, ECtHR 7.116
Inter-Environnement Wallonie ASBL v Région Wallonie: C-129/96 [1998] All ER (EC)
  155, [1997] ECR I-7411, [1998] 1 CMLR 1057, [1998] Env LR 623, ECJ 9.35
Issa v Hackney London Borough Council [1997] 1 All ER 999, [1997] 1 WLR 956, 29
  HLR 640, [1997] Env LR 157, sub nom Hackney London Borough Council v Issa
  [1997] 1 LS Gaz R 24, 140 Sol Jo LB 262, CA 1.28

J

Jemmison v Priddle [1972] 1 QB 489, [1972] 1 All ER 539, [1972] 2 WLR 293, 56 Cr
  App Rep 229, 136 JP 230, 116 Sol Jo 99, DC 5.27
Johnson v Royal Society for the Prevention of Cruelty to Animals (2000) 164 JP 345,
  [2000] 20 LS Gaz R 42, DC 7.23, 7.26, 7.39, 7.46, 7.84, 7.87
Johnsons News of London v Ealing London Borough Council (1989) 154 JP 33, [1990]
  COD 135 .... 4.108
Johnston v Chief Constable of the Royal Ulster Constabulary: 222/84 [1987] QB 129,
  [1986] 3 All ER 135, [1986] 3 WLR 1038, [1986] ECR 1651, [1986] 3 CMLR 240,
  [1987] ICR 83, [1986] IRLR 263, 130 Sol Jo 953, [1987] LS Gaz R 188, ECJ 2.29
Jones v Williams (1843) 12 LJ Ex 249, 11 M & W 176, 152 ER 764 .... 4.133
Jordan v Norfolk County Council [1994] 4 All ER 218, [1994] 1 WLR 1353, 93 LGR
  50 .... 2.21
Joy v Federation Against Copyright Theft Ltd [1993] Crim LR 588 .... 5.55

K

Kane v New Forest DC [2002] 1 WLR 312 .... 7.115
Katte Klitsche de la Grange v Italy (1994) 19 EHRR 368, ECtHR 7.116
Kaur v Secretary of State for the Environment (1990) 61 P & CR 249, [1990] JPL 814: 3.34
Kavanagh v Chief Constable of Devon and Cornwall [1974] QB 624, [1974] 2 All ER
  697, [1974] 2 WLR 762, 138 JP 618, 118 Sol Jo 347, CA 4.94, 4.95, 4.96, 4.97, 4.98
Kellar v Stanley A Williams [2004] UKPC 30 .... 7.53
Kent County Council v Beaney [1991] 5 Env LR 89 .... 9.39
Kent County Council v Brockman [1994] Crim LR 296, [1996] 1 PLR 1 .... 5.81, 7.80
Kent County Council v Secretary of State for the Environment (1997) 75 P & CR 410,
  [1997] JPL 1115, [1997] COD 481, [1997] NPC 71, [1997] EGCS 64, CA 4.29
Khan (Sultan) v United Kingdom [2000] Crim LR 684 .... 2.93
Kirklees Metropolitan Borough Council v Field (1997) 96 LGR 151, 162 JP 88, 30 HLR
  869, [1997] 45 LS Gaz R 28, 141 Sol Jo LB 246, [1998] Env LR 337 .... 3.11, 3.12, 6.75
Kitson v Ashe [1899] 1 QB 425, 63 JP 325, 68 LJQB 286, 19 Cox CC 257, 80 LT 323,
  15 TLR 172, DC 1.77
Kokkinakis v Greece (1993) 17 EHRR 397, ECtHR 3.16, 5.100

L

Lambert (A) Flat Management Ltd v Lomas [1981] 2 All ER 280, [1981] 1 WLR 898,
  125 Sol Jo 218 .... 5.14, 5.84, 5.98, 5.99
Lambie v Thanet [2001] Env LR 21 .... 2.66, 3.02
Leeds v Islington London Borough Council (1998) 31 HLR 545, [1998] COD 293,
  [1998] 07 LS Gaz R 33, [1998] Env LR 655 .... 3.77, 3.79, 6.67
Leeds City Council v Spencer [1999] EGCS 69, [1999] EHLR 394, 11 Admin LR 773,
  [1999] NPC 55, CA 3.75
Leeman v Montagu [1936] 2 All ER 1677, 80 Sol Jo 691 .... 1.17, 8.03
Lewisham v Fenner [1995] 248 ENDS Report 44 .... 1.05
Lewisham v Yvonne Hall [2002] EWHC 960, [2003] Env LR 4 .... 5.13, 5.86
Lewisham London Borough Council v Marylebone Magistrates Court [2003] EWHC
  1184 (Admin) 5.49
Lithgow v United Kingdom (1986) 8 EHRR 329, ECtHR 4.18
Liverpool City Council v Worthington (1998) Times, 16 June 7.87
Lloyds Bank v Guardian Assurance plc (1986) Lexis, Enggen Library, Cases File 2.79

xxix

Table of Cases

	PARA
London Borough of Hackney v Moshe Rottenburg [2007] Env LR 24	5.13
Lonsdale (Earl) v Nelson (1823) 2 B & C 302, 2 LJOS 28, 3 Dow & Ry KB 556, 107 ER 396, [1814-23] All ER Rep 737	4.133
Lopez Ostra v Spain (1994) 20 EHRR 277, ECtHR	1.102, 2.13, 2.17, 2.48, 6.62, 7.116

M

McGillivray v Stephenson [1950] 1 All ER 942, 48 LGR 409, 114 JP 262, DC .. 3.24, 3.31, 3.56
McKay v First Secretary of State [2005] EWCA Civ 774, [2006] 1 PLR 19 .... 3.31, 3.57
McLean v Pinkerton (1882) 7 OAR 490 .... 4.24, 4.31
McQueen v Jackson [1903] 2 KB 163, 1 LGR 601, 67 JP 353, 72 LJKB 606, 20 Cox CC 499, 88 LT 871 .... 6.22
Mallie v Manchester City Council [1998] COD 19 .... 4.126
Malton Board of Health v Malton Manure Co (1879) 4 Ex D 302, 44 JP 155, 49 LJMC 90, 27 WR 802, 40 LT 755 .... 1.04, 1.42
Manchester Corpn v Farnworth [1930] AC 171, 94 JP 62, 99 LJKB 83, [1929] All ER Rep 90, 73 Sol Jo 818, 46 TLR 85, sub nom Farnworth v Manchester Corpn 27 LGR 709, 142 LT 145, HL 1.69, 1.85; 3.59
Maneli v Switzerland (1983) 5 EHRR 554 .... 7.31
Manley and Manley v New Forest District Council [1999] PLR 36, [2000] EHLR 113: 1.84, 8.03
Manorlike Ltd v Le Vitas Travel Agency and Consultancy Services Ltd [1986] 1 All ER 573, [1986] 1 EGLR 79, 278 Estates Gazette 412, CA 4.28
MArcic v Thames Water Utilities [2003] UKHL 60, [2004] 2 AC 42 .... 3.59
Marleasing SA v La Comercial Internacional de Alimentaci|fon SA: C-106/89 [1990] ECR I-4135, [1992] 1 CMLR 305, [1993] BCC 421, 135 Sol Jo 15, ECJ 2.05, 5.51
Maurice v LCC [1964] 2 QB 362, [1964] 1 All ER 779, [1964] 2 WLR 715, 62 LGR 241, 128 JP 311, 108 Sol Jo 175, [1964] RVR 341, CA 6.03
Mayer Parry Recycling Ltd v Environment Agency [1999] 1 CMLR 963, [1999] Env LR 489 .... 9.35
Mayers v Mayers [1971] 2 All ER 397, [1971] 1 WLR 679, 135 JP 487, 115 Sol Jo 111: 4.99
Meade v London Borough of Haringey [1979] 2 All ER 1016, [1979] 1 WLR 637, 77 LGR 577, [1979] ICR 494, 123 Sol Jo 216, CA 2.12
Metropolitan Asylum District Managers v Hill (1881) 6 App Cas 193, 45 JP 664, 50 LJQB 353, 29 WR 617, 44 LT 653, HL 1.28
Michael v Gowland [1977] 2 All ER 328, [1977] 1 WLR 296, 7 Fam Law 109, 141 JP 343, 120 Sol Jo 857 .... 5.122
Miles v Secretary of State for the Environment, Transport and Regions (4 June 1999, unreported); on appeal (11 August 2000, unreported), CA 9.09
Millard v Wastall [1898] 1 QB 342, 62 JP 135, 67 LJQB 277, 18 Cox CC 695, 46 WR 258, 42 Sol Jo 215, 77 LT 692, 14 TLR 172, DC 3.24
Miller v Minister of Pensions [1947] 2 All ER 372, [1948] LJR 203, 91 Sol Jo 484, 177 LT 536, 63 TLR 474 .... 4.104
Miller-Mead v Minister of Housing and Local Government [1963] 2 QB 196, [1963] 1 All ER 459, [1963] 2 WLR 225, 61 LGR 152, 14 P & CR 266, 127 JP 122, 106 Sol Jo 1052, [1963] RVR 181, CA 3.05, 3.57
Millington v Secretary of State for the Environment, Transport and the Regions and Shrewsbury and Atcham Borough Council [2000] JPL 297 .... 4.73
Monen v SSTLGR [2002] EWHC 81 .... 9.09
Mooney v Cardiff Justices (1999) 164 JP 220, [1999] 42 LS Gaz R 40, DC 7.31
Morton v Hampson [1962] VR 364 .... 4.24, 4.29
Muller v Switzerland (1988) 13 EHRR 212, ECtHR 3.16
Mullingar RDC v Lord Greville (1906) 41 ILTR 144 .... 7.53
Murdoch v Glacier Metal Co Ltd [1998] 07 LS Gaz R 31, [1998] Env LR 732, [1998] EHLR 198, CA 1.04, 8.23

N

National Coal Board v Neath Borough Council [1976] 2 All ER 478, 140 JP 436, sub nom National Coal Board v Thorne [1976] 1 WLR 543, 74 LGR 429, 120 Sol Jo 234, 239 Estates Gazette 121, DC 1.08, 1.09

Table of Cases

	PARA
Neath RDC v Williams [1951] 1 KB 115, [1950] 2 All ER 625, 49 LGR 177, 114 JP 464, 94 Sol Jo 568, 66 (pt 2) TLR 539	1.74
Network Housing Association v Westminster City Council (1994) 93 LGR 280, 27 HLR 189, [1995] Env LR 176	1.64, 3.25, 3.28
Neville v Gardner Merchant Ltd (1983) 82 LGR 577, 5 Cr App Rep (S) 349, 148 JP 238	7.59
Nichols, Albion and Lainson v Powergen Renewables Ltd & Wind 23 Prospect Ltd (20 January 2004)	6.09, 6.41, 6.42, 6.69
Northern Ireland Trailers Ltd v Preston County Borough (or Preston Corpn) [1972] 1 All ER 260, [1972] 1 WLR 203, 136 JP 149, 116 Sol Jo 100	6.41, 6.54
Nottingham Corpn v Newton [1974] 2 All ER 760, sub nom Nottingham City District Council v Newton [1974] 1 WLR 923, 72 LGR 535, 118 Sol Jo 462	2.35, 2.45, 6.76, 6.77
Nottingham No 1 Area Hospital Management Committee v Owen [1958] 1 QB 50, [1957] 3 All ER 358, [1957] 3 WLR 707, 55 LGR 550, 122 JP 5, 101 Sol Jo 852	10.36

O

O'Brien v Hertsmere Borough Council (1998) 76 P & CR 441	5.90
O'Nuallain v Dublin Corpn [1999] 4 IR 137	2.11
O'Toole v Knowsley Metropolitan Borough COuncil [1999] Env LR D28, [1999] 22 LS Gaz R 36	1.05, 5.13

P

P, Re [2007] EWCA Civ 2, [2007] HRLR 14	7.115
Palacegate Properties Ltd v LB Camden (2001) ACD 137	5.07, 5.76
Parramatta City Council, Re, ex p Tooth & Co Ltd (1955) 55 SRNSW 282	9.08
Pasmore v Oswaldtwistle UDC [1898] AC 387, 62 JP 628, 67 LJQB 635, [1895-9] All ER Rep 191, 78 LT 569, 14 TLR 368, HL	2.14
Patel and Patel v Blakey [1988] RTR 65, 151 JP 532, [1987] Crim LR 683	7.31
Pearshouse v Birmingham City Council (1998) 96 LGR 169, 31 HLR 756, [1999] COD 132, [1999] JPL 725, [1999] EHLR 140, [1999] BLGR 169, [1999] Env LR 536	1.01, 6.26, 6.27, 6.28, 6.29, 6.30
Pepper (Inspector of Taxes) v Hart [1993] AC 593, [1993] 1 All ER 42, [1992] 3 WLR 1032, [1992] STC 898, 65 TC 421, [1993] ICR 291, [1993] IRLR 33, [1993] NLJR 17, [1993] RVR 127, HL	1.103
Philis v Greece (Applications 12750/87, 13780/88 and 14003/88) (1991) 13 EHRR 741, ECtHR	4.18
Pike v Sefton Metropolitan Borough Council (29 February 2000, unreported)	1.29, 3.70, 6.67
Pine Valley Developments Ltd v Ireland (1991) 14 EHRR 319, ECtHR	7.116
Pollway Nominees Ltd v Havering London Borough Council (1989) 88 LGR 192, 21 HLR 462	1.29, 1.31
Polychronakis v Richards and Jerrom Ltd [1998] JPL 588, [1998] Env LR 347	5.03, 5.75, 5.78
Postermobile plc v Brent London Borough Council (The Times, 8 December 1997)	5.25
Powell v The Chief Executive of the City and County of Swansea [2003] EWHC 2185 (Admin) [2006] EWHC 1374	7.07
Practice Direction (costs: criminal proceedings) [2004] 2 All ER 1070, [2004] 1 WLR 2657	7.62
Practice Note [1962] 1 All ER 448, sub nom Practice Direction [1962] 1 WLR 227, 106 Sol Jo 133, DC	5.85
Pressos Compania Naviera SA v Belgium (1995) 21 EHRR 301, ECtHR	3.44
Price v Humphries [1958] 2 QB 353, [1958] 2 All ER 725, [1958] 3 WLR 304, 122 JP 423, 102 Sol Jo 583, DC	4.102

Q

Quigley v Liverpool Housing Trust [1999] EGCS 94, [2000] Env LR D9	1.27, 1.29; 6.67

R

R v A (No 2) [2001] UKHL 25, [2002] 1 AC 45	1.102

Table of Cases

	PARA
R v Associated Octel Co Ltd (costs) [1997] 1 Cr App Rep (S) 435, [1997] Crim LR 144, CA	7.59, 7.60, 7.83
R v Atath Construction Ltd [1991] 1 PLR 25	5.114
R v Barking and Dagenham Justices, ex p DPP (1994) 159 JP 373, [1995] Crim LR 953	5.85
R v Birmingham City Council, ex p Ferrero Ltd [1993] 1 All ER 530, 89 LGR 977, 155 JP 721, [1991] 26 LS Gaz R 32, CA	4.138
R v Blandford Justices, ex p G (infant) [1967] 1 QB 82, [1966] 1 All ER 1021, [1966] 2 WLR 1232, 130 JP 260, 110 Sol Jo 465, DC	5.118
R v Bow Street Metropolitan Stipendiary Magistrate, ex p Screen Multimedia Ltd (1998) Times, 28 January, DC	7.87
R v Brentford Justices, ex p Catlin [1975] QB 455, [1975] 2 All ER 201, [1975] 2 WLR 506, 139 JP 516, 119 Sol Jo 221	4.10, 6.44
R v Brentford Justices, ex p Wong [1981] QB 445, [1981] 1 All ER 884, [1981] 2 WLR 203, [1981] RTR 206, 73 Cr App Rep 67, [1981] Crim LR 336, 884, 125 Sol Jo 135	5.36, 5.37
R v Brightman [1990] 1 WLR 1255, 88 LGR 756, 60 P & CR 533, 154 JP 911, [1991] 1 PLR 25, 134 Sol Jo 1009, [1991] 1 EGLR 285, CA	5.114
R v Bristol City Council, ex p Everett [1998] 3 All ER 603, [1999] 1 WLR 92, 96 LGR 531, 77 P & CR 216, 31 HLR 292, [1998] NPC 86, [1998] 3 EGLR 25, [1998] 23 LS Gaz R 26, [1998] NLJR 836, [1998] 42 EG 166, 142 Sol Jo LB 173, [1999] EHLR 59, [1999] Env LR 256; affd [1999] 2 All ER 193, [1999] 1 WLR 1170, 31 HLR 1102, [1999] 3 PLR 14, [1999] NPC 28, [1999] 13 LS Gaz R 31, [1999] NLJR 370, [1999] EGCS 33, 143 Sol Jo LB 104, [1999] BLGR 513, [1999] Env LR 587, [1999] EHLR 265, CA	1.05, 2.83, 3.81, 4.13, 7.19
R v Browne (1943) 29 Cr App Rep 106, CCA	4.102
R v Browning (Derek) [1996] 1 PLR 61, [1995] NPC 191, CA	5.111
R v Cannock Justices, ex p Astbury (1972) 70 LGR 609, 224 Estates Gazette 1037	7.19
R v Carr-Briant [1943] KB 607, [1943] 2 All ER 156, 41 LGR 183, 29 Cr App Rep 76, 107 JP 167, 112 LJKB 581, 169 LT 175, 59 TLR 300, CCA	5.90
R v Carrick District Council, ex p Shelley (1996) 95 LGR 620, [1996] JPL 857, [1996] Env LR 273	1.47, 2.15, 2.34, 2.35, 2.36, 2.39, 4.49, 4.61, 4.62, 4.63, 4.109, 4.145, 10.23, 10.24
R v Central Criminal Court, ex p Bright (2000) Times, 26 July	5.62
R v Cheb Miller [2007] EWCA Crim 1891	5.67
R v Chief Constable of the Kent County Constabulary, ex p L (a minor) [1993] 1 All ER 756, 93 Cr App Rep 416, 155 JP 760, [1991] Crim LR 841	2.49
R v City of Liverpool Stipendiary Magistrate, ex p Ellison [1990] RTR 220n, 153 JP 433, [1989] Crim LR 369	4.79
R v Comr for Local Administration, ex p S [1999] ELR 102	4.150
R v Cooper (1982) 4 Cr App Rep (S) 55, [1982] Crim LR 308	7.101
R v Coventry Magistrates Court, ex p Crown Prosecution Service (1996) 160 JP 741, [1996] Crim LR 723	7.03
R v Crown Court at Liverpool, ex p Cooke [1996] 4 All ER 589, [1997] 1 WLR 700, [1997] 1 Cr App Rep (S) 7, 29 HLR 249	6.42, 6.43, 6.54, 6.56, 6.67, 7.54, 7.93, 7.97
R v Crown Court at Oxford, ex p Smith (1989) 154 LGR 458, 154 JP 422, [1990] COD 211, [1990] 2 Admin LR 389	9.08, 9.14
R v Crown Court at Preston, ex p Jolly (7 April 2000, unreported)	9.09
R v Dartford Justices, ex p Dhesi [1983] 1 AC 328, [1982] 3 WLR 331, [1982] RTR 449, 126 Sol Jo 526, sub nom Hill v Anderton [1982] 2 All ER 963, 75 Cr App Rep 346, 146 JP 348, [1982] Crim LR 775, HL	4.10
R v Day [1940] 1 All ER 402, 38 LGR 155, 27 Cr App Rep 168, 104 JP 181, 31 Cox CC 391, 162 LT 407, CCA	4.102
R v Derby (1990) 12 Cr App Rep (S) 502, CA	7.91
R v DPP, ex p Kebelene [2000] 2 AC 326, [1999] 4 All ER 801, [1999] 3 WLR 972, [2000] 1 Cr App Rep 275, [2000] Crim LR 486, [1999] 43 LS Gaz R 32, HL	2.08, 4.20, 5.23, 5.93
R v DPP, ex p Manning [2001] QB 330, DC	2.48

Table of Cases

	PARA
R v Duckworth (1995) 16 Cr App Rep (S) 529, CA	5.109

R v Dudley Magistrates' Court, ex p Hollis [1998] 1 All ER 759, [1999] 1 WLR 642, 30 HLR 902, [1998] 2 EGLR 19, [1998] 18 EG 133, [1998] JPL 652, [1998] Env LR 354 .... 6.54, 6.56, 6.67, 7.50, 7.51, 7.54

R v Durham County Council, ex p Huddleston [2000] 1 WLR 1484, [2000] 2 CMLR 313, 144 Sol Jo LB 149, [2000] 13 LS Gaz R 43, [2000] 1 PLR 22, [2000]EGCS 39, CA 2.05, 5.51, 10.37

R v Durham Quarter Sessions, ex p Virgo [1952] 2 QB 1, [1952] 1 All ER 466, 116 JP 157, [1952] 1 TLR 516, DC 5.118

R v East Sussex County Council, ex p Tandy [1998] AC 714, [1998] 2 All ER 769, [1998] 2 WLR 884, 96 LGR 497, [1998] 2 FCR 221, [1998] ELR 251, [1998] 24 LS Gaz R 33, [1998] NLJR 781, 142 Sol Jo LB 179, HL 2.18

R v Edmonton Justices, ex p Hughes [1983] 1 AC 328, [1982] 3 WLR 331, [1982] RTR 449, 126 Sol Jo 526, sub nom Hill v Anderton [1982] 2 All ER 963, 75 Cr App Rep 346, 146 JP 348, [1982] Crim LR 755, HL 4.10

R v Elmbridge Borough Council, ex p Activeoffice Ltd [1998] 01 LS Gaz R 23, 10 Amin LR 561, [1998] JPL B43, (The Times, 29 December 1997) 2.49, 5.23

R v Epping (Waltham Abbey) Justices, ex p Burlinson [1948] 1 KB 79, [1947] 2 All ER 537, 46 LGR 6, 112 JP 3, [1948] LJR 298, 92 Sol Jo 27, 63 TLR 628 .... 1.26; 2.80

R v Falmouth and Truro Port Health Authority, ex p South West Water Services (1999) 163 JP 589, [1999] EGCS 62, [1999] Env LR 833; affd [2000] 3 All ER 306, [2000] 3 WLR 1464, [2000] EGCS 50, CA 1.01, 1.72, 2.01, 2.08, 2.91, 3.11, 3.13, 3.25, 3.32, 3.33, 3.53, 3.60, 3.62, 4.22, 4.38, 4.39, 4.48, 4.84, 4.87, 4.136, 4.137, 4.139, 4.141, 6.75

R v Fenny Stratford Justices, ex p Watney Mann (Midlands) Ltd [1976] 2 All ER 888, [1976] 1 WLR 1101, 75 LGR 72, 140 JP 474, 120 Sol Jo 201, 238 Estates Gazette 417, DC 3.05, 6.76, 8.06, 8.07

R v Finch (1992) 14 Cr App Rep (S) 226, CA 5.115

R v Folkestone Magistrates' Court, ex p Kibble [1993] Crim LR 704, [1993] COD 401, Times, 1 March 10.15

R v Gateshead Justices, ex p Tesco Stores Ltd [1981] QB 470, [1981] 1 All ER 1027, [1981] 2 WLR 419, 73 Cr App Rep 87, 145 JP 200, [1981] Crim LR 495, 125 Sol Jo 204, 145 JP Jo 237 .... 4.10

R v Gloucestershire County Council, ex p Barry [1997] AC 584, [1997] 2 All ER 1, [1997] 2 WLR 459, 36 BMLR 69, [1997] NLJR 453, 141 Sol Jo LB 91, 1 CCL Rep 40, HL 2.18

R v Harris [1927] 2 KB 587, 20 Cr App Rep 86, 91 JP 152, 96 LJKB 1069, 28 Cox CC 432, [1927] All ER Rep 473, 137 LT 535, 43 TLR 774, CCA 4.102

R v Hertfordshire County Council, ex p Green Environmental Industries Ltd [2000] 2 AC 412, [2000] 1 All ER 773, [2000] 2 WLR 373, [2000] 09 LS Gaz R 42, [2000] NLJR 277, [2000] EGCS 27, HL 5.62, 5.64

R v Highbury Corner Magistrates' Court, ex p Edwards [1995] Crim LR 65, 26 HLR 682, [1994] Env LR 215 .... 6.03, 6.45, 6.49

R v Hill [1997] Crim LR 459, CA 5.115

R v Hillingdon London Borough Council, ex p Royco Homes Ltd [1974] QB 720, [1974] 2 All ER 643, [1974] 2 WLR 805, 72 LGR 516, 28 P & CR 251, 138 JP 505, 118 Sol Jo 389 .... 2.14

R v Horsham Justices, ex p Richards [1985] 2 All ER 1114, [1985] 1 WLR 986, 82 Cr App Rep 254, 7 Cr App Rep (S) 158, 149 JP 567, 129 Sol Jo 467, [1985] LS Gaz R 2499 .... 7.104

R v Hughes (1879) 4 QBD 614, 43 JP 556, 48 LJMC 151, 14 Cox CC 284, 40 LT 685, [1874-80] All ER Rep Ext 1535, CCR 6.41

R v Huntingdon Crown Court, ex p Jordan [1981] QB 857 .... 5.118

R v IRC, ex p Knight [1973] 3 All ER 721, [1973] STC 564, sub nom R v Havering Income Tax General Comrs, ex p Knight 49 TC 161, 52 ATC 282, [1973] TR 235, CA 4.28

R v JO Sims Ltd (1993) 96 Cr App Rep 125, 14 Cr App Rep (S) 213, [1993] Env LR 323, CA 5.110

R v Jan (Richard) [2006] EWCA Crim 2314 .... 2.98

xxxiii

Table of Cases

	PARA
R v Jenner [1983] 2 All ER 46, [1983] 1 WLR 873, 46 P & CR 411, 147 JP 239, 127 Sol Jo 324, [1983] JPL 547, CA	4.84
R v Kennet District Council, ex p Somerfield Property Co Ltd [1999] JPL 361, [1999] Env LR D13	1.22, 8.14
R v Kingston-upon-Hull Justices, ex p McCann (1991) 155 JP 569	5.42
R v Knightsbridge Crown Court, ex p Cataldi [1999] Env LR 62	4.108
R v Komsta and Murphy (1990) 12 Cr App Rep (S) 63, 154 JP 440, [1990] Crim LR 434, CA	5.104
R v Lambert [2001] UKHL 37, [2002] 2 AC 545	1.102
R v Leicester City Council, ex p Safeway Stores plc [1999] JPL 691	2.15
R v Leyland Justices, ex p Hawthorn [1979] QB 283, [1979] 1 All ER 209, [1979] 2 WLR 28, 68 Cr App Rep 269, 143 JP 181, 122 Sol Jo 627	5.51, 5.88
R v Liddle (1928) 21 Cr App Rep 3, CCA	4.102
R v Liverpool Crown Court, ex p Cooke [1996] 1 WLR 700	7.93
R v Liverpool Crown Court, ex p Roberts [1986] Crim LR 622	5.51, 5.73
R v Liverpool Juvenile Court, ex p R [1988] QB 1, [1987] 2 All ER 668, [1987] 3 WLR 224, 86 Cr App Rep 1, 151 JP 516, [1987] Crim LR 572, 131 Sol Jo 972, [1987] LS Gaz R 2045	5.74
R v Liverpool Magistrates' Court, ex p Abiaka (1999) 163 JP 497, [1999] 14 LS Gaz R 32, 143 Sol Jo LB 135, DC	7.82
R v Local Comr for Administration, for the South, the West, the West Midlands, Leicestershire, Lincolnshire and Cambridgeshire, ex p Eastleigh Borough Council [1988] QB 855, [1988] 3 WLR 113, 86 LGR 491, 132 Sol Jo 564, sub nom R v Comr for Local Administration, ex p Eastleigh Borough Council [1988] 3 All ER 151, CA:	4.149
R v McMahon (1933) 24 Cr App Rep 95, CCA	4.102
R v Manchester Stipendiary Magistrate, ex p Hill [1983] 1 AC 328, [1982]3 WLR 331, [1982] RTR 449, 126 Sol Jo 526, sub nom Hill v Anderton [1982] 2 All ER 963, 75 Cr App Rep 346, 146 JP 348, [1982] Crim LR 755, HL	4.09, 4.10, 4.32, 5.33, 6.41
R v Metropolitan Stipendiary Magistrate, ex p London Waste Regulation Authority [1993] 3 All ER 113	1.47, 9.38
R v Miller [1976] Crim LR 694, CA	7.98
R v Network Sites Ltd, ex p Havering London Borough (1997) 161 JP 513, [1997] Crim LR 595	5.34
R v Newton (1982) 77 Cr App Rep 13, 4 Cr App Rep (S) 388, [1983] Crim LR 198, CA	5.106, 5.108, 5.115
R v Northallerton Magistrates' Court, ex p Dove [2000] 1 Cr App Rep (S) 136, 163 JP 657, [1999] Crim LR 760, DC	7.63, 7.64, 7.65, 7.66, 7.67, 7.76, 7.83, 7.85, 7.87
R v North West Suffolk (Mildenhall) Magistrates' Court, ex p Forest Heath District Council [1998] Env LR 9	4.126
R v Nottingham Justices, ex p Brown [1960] 3 All ER 625, [1960] 1 WLR 1315, 125 JP 49, 104 Sol Jo 1036, DC	6.41
R v Olliver and Olliver (1989) 11 Cr App Rep (S) 10, 153 JP 369, [1989] Crim LR 387, CA	7.80
R v Oxford City Justices, ex p Smith [1982] RTR 201, 75 Cr App Rep 200, DC	5.36
R v Palmer (1989) 11 Cr App Rep (S) 407, CA	5.110
R v Panayioutou (1989) 11 Cr App Rep (S) 535, [1990] Crim LR 349, CA	5.104
R v Parlby (1889) 22 QBD 520, 53 JP 327, 58 LJMC 49, 37 WR 335, 60 LT 422, 5 TLR 257, DC	1.05, 1.26, 1.28
R v Parliamentary Comr for Administration, ex p Balchin [1996] NPC 147, [1997] COD 146, [1996] EGCS 166, [1997] JPL 917	4.149, 4.150
R v Parliamentary Comr for Administration, ex p Morris and Balchin (No 2) (1999) 79 P & CR 157, [1999] EGCS 78	4.149
R v Quinn [1990] Crim LR 581, CA	5.66
R v Rehman [2006] EWCA Crim 1900	5.67
R v Rimmington [2005] UKHL 63, [2006] 1 AC 459	1.09, 5.05
R v Robinson (1969) 53 Cr App Rep 314, [1969] Crim LR 314, 113 Sol Jo 143, CA	5.115
R v St Edmundsbury Borough Council, ex p Walton [1999] 3 PLR 51, [1999] NPC 44, [1999] EGCS 53, [1999] JPL 805, 143 Sol Jo LB 175, 11 Admin LR 648, [1999] Env LR 879	2.11, 3.03
R v Sandhu [1997] Crim LR 288, [1996] NPC 179, [1997] JPL 853, CA	5.67, 5.75, 5.109

Table of Cases

	PARA
R v Scunthorpe Justices, ex p McPhee and Gallagher (1998) 162 JP 635	5.34, 5.35
R v Secretary of State for the Environment, ex p Hillingdon London Borough Council [1986] 1 All ER 810, [1986] 1 WLR 192, 84 LGR 628, 52 P & CR 409, 130 Sol Jo 89, [1986] LS Gaz R 525, [1986] NLJ Rep 16, [1987] RVR 6, [1986] JPL 363; affd [1986] 2 All ER 273n, [1986] 1 WLR 807n, 84 LGR 628, 55 P & CR 241n, 130 Sol Jo 481, [1986] LS Gaz R 2331, [1987] RVR 6, [1987] JPL 717, CA	2.72
R v Secretary of State for the Environment, ex p Kent [1990] COD 78, [1990] JPL 124, CA	4.14
R v Secretary of State for the Environment, ex p Ostler [1977] QB 122, [1976] 3 All ER 90, [1976] 3 WLR 288, 75 LGR 45, 32 P & CR 166, 120 Sol Jo 332, 238 Estates Gazette 971, [1976] JPL 301, CA; affd sub nom Ostler v Secretary of State for the Environment [1977] 1 WLR 258, HL	4.14
R v Secretary of State for the Home Department, ex p Brind [1991] 1 AC 696, [1990] 1 All ER 469, [1990] 2 WLR 787, [1989] NLJR 1751, CA; affd [1991] 1 AC 696, [1991] 2 WLR 588, 135 Sol Jo 250, sub nom Brind v Secretary of State for the Home Department [1991] 1 All ER 720, HL	1.102, 3.07
R v Secretary of State for Transport, ex p Richmond-upon-Thames London Borough Council [1994] 1 All ER 577, [1994] 1 WLR 74	10.34
R v Sevenoaks District Council, ex p Palley [1995] JPL 915	5.23
R v Somerset County Council and ARC Southern Ltd, ex p Dixon (1997) 75 P & CR 175, [1997] NPC 61, [1997] COD 323, [1997] JPL 1030	6.04
R v Stafford Crown Court, ex p Wilf Gilbert (Staffs) Ltd [1999] 2 All ER 955	7.21
R v Stratford Justices, ex p Imbert [1999] 2 Cr App Rep 276, 163 JP 693	5.42, 5.43, 5.45, 5.46
R v Thames Magistrates' Court, ex p Stevens (2000) 164 JP 233, [2000] COD 211	5.34
R v Thomson Holidays Ltd [1974] QB 592, [1974] 1 All ER 823, [1974] 2 WLR 371, 58 Cr App Rep 429, [1974] Crim LR 198, 118 Sol Jo 96, CA	7.91
R v Tottenham Justices, ex p Joshi [1982] 2 All ER 507, [1982] 1 WLR 631, 75 Cr App Rep 72, 146 JP 268, [1982] Crim LR 307, 126 Sol Jo 209	7.87
R v Tower Hamlets London Borough Council, ex p Chetnik Developments Ltd [1988] AC 858, [1988] 2 WLR 654, 86 LGR 321, [1988] RA 45, 132 Sol Jo 462, [1988] 2 EGLR 195, [1988] 16 LS Gaz R 44, [1988] NLJR 89, [1988] 28 EG 69, sub nom Tower Hamlets London Borough Council v ChetnikDevelopments Ltd [1988] 1 All ER 961, HL	3.19, 4.135
R v Vaughan (1990) 12 Cr App Rep (S) 46, [1990] Crim LR 443, CA	7.92
R v Walden-Jones, ex p Coton [1963] Crim LR 839	1.54
R v Wealan (1881) 14 Cox CC 595	4.102
R v West London Justices, ex p Klahn [1979] 2 All ER 221, 143 JP 390, sub nom R v West London Metropolitan Stipendiary Magistrate, ex p Klahn [1979] 1 WLR 933, 123 Sol Jo 251, DC	6.45, 6.48
R v West London Magistrates' Court, ex p Kyprianou [1992-1003] Env LR D21	7.76, 7.85
R v Wheatley, ex p Cowburn (1885) 16 QBD 34, 50 JP 424, 55 LJMC 11, 34 WR 257, 54 LT 680, 2 TLR 137, DC	3.27
R v Whitter [1999] Env LR D21, CA	7.85
R v Wigg (1705) 2 Ld Raym 1163, 2 Salk 460	1.52
R v Wilson (1979) 69 Cr App Rep 83, CA	5.27
R v Yorkshire Water Services [2001] EWCA Crim 2635, [2002] 2 Cr App R 13	5.107
R (Alconbury Developments) v Secretary of State for Environment, Transport and the Regions [2001] UKHL 23, [2003] 2 AC 295	3.41, 4.22
R (Cambridge City Council) v Alex Nesting Ltd [2006] EWHC 1374	7.07
R (G) v London Borough of Ealing [2002] EWHC 250, [2002] ACD 298	4.22
R (Kurdistan Workers Party) v Secretary of State for the Home Department [2002] EWHC 644 (Admin), [2002] ACD 560	4.22
R (London Borough of Islington) v Inner London Crown Court [2003] EWHC 2500, [2004] Env LR 20	5.107
R (Maiden Outdooe Advertising Ltd) v Lambeth Borough Council [2003] EWHC 1224	4.22
R (on the application of Cowl) v Plymouth City Council [2001] EWCA Civ 1935, [2002] 1 WLR 803	2.15
R (on the application of OSS Group Ltd) v Environment Agency [2007] EWCA Civ 611	9.36; 10.26

Table of Cases

	PARA
R(SB) v Denbeigh High School [2007] 1 AC 100 (HL)	7.109
R (on the application of Sivasbramaniam) v Wandsworth County Court [2002] EWCA Civ 1738	2.14
R (Terrafirma) v Manchester City Council [2002] EWHC 702	2.11
R (Utllesford DC) v English Heritage [2007] EWHC 816	7.07
RSPCA v Eager (1995) Crim LR 59, DC	5.55
Robb v Dundee [2002] SC 301	1.05, 1.08, 1.09
Robinson v Torridge DC [2006] EWHC 877	1.72
Robinson v Waddington (1849) 13 QB 753, 18 LJQB 250, 13 Jur 537, 13 LTOS 281	4.24
Rockall v Department for Environment, Food and Rural Affairs [2007] EWHC 614, [2007] Env LR D16	4.28, 4.29, 4.30, 4.31, 5.33, 6.22
Rolls v Miller (1884) 27 Ch D 71, 53 LJ Ch 682, 32 WR 806, [1881-5] All ER Rep 915, 50 LT 597, CA	1.81
Roper v Tussauds Theme Parks Ltd [2007] EWHC 624, [2007] Env LR 31	6.71, 6.76, 6.77, 8.15
Rutili v Minister for the Interior: 36/75 [1975] ECR 1219, [1976] 1 CMLR 140, ECJ	2.29
Rye (Dennis) Pension Fund Trustees v Sheffield City Council [1997] 4 All ER 747, [1998] 1 WLR 840, 30 HLR 645, CA	4.136
Rylands v Fletcher (1868) LR 3 HL 330, 33 JP 70, 37 LJ Ex 161, 14 WR 799, [1861-73] All ER Rep 1, 19 LT 220	1.74

S

SFI Group plc (formerly Surrey Free Inns) v Gosport Borough Council [1999] EGCS 51, [1999] Env LR 750, [1999] BLGR 610, CA	4.57, 4.108, 4.112, 4.126
Saddleworth UDC v Aggregate and Sand Ltd (1970) 69 LGR 103, 114 Sol Jo 931, DC:	5.81, 5.96
Saidi v France (Application 14647/89) (1993) 17 EHRR 251, E Ct HR	5.45
St Helen's Smelting Co v Tipping (1865) 29 JP 579, 11 HL Cas 642, 35 LJQB 66, 11 Jur NS 785, 13 WR 1083, 11 ER 1483, 12 LT 776, [1861-73] All ER Rep Ext 1389	8.02
Salabiaku v France (1988) 13 EHRR 379, ECtHR	5.92
Salford City Council v McNally [1976] AC 379, [1975] 2 All ER 860, [1975] 3 WLR 87, 73 LGR 408, 139 JP 694, 119 Sol Jo 475, 236 Estates Gazette 555, HL	1.04, 1.05, 1.09, 1.29, 3.05, 6.71
Sandwell Metropolitan Borough Council v Bujok [1990] 3 All ER 385, [1990] 1 WLR 1350, 89 LGR 77, 155 JP 293, 23 HLR 48, 134 Sol Jo 1300, [1990] 42 LS Gaz R 34, HL	6.04, 6.18
Saunders v United Kingdom (1996) 23 EHRR 313, [1998] 1 BCLC 363, [1997] BCC 872, ECtHR	5.61, 5.63
Schofield v Schunck (1855) 19 JP 84, 24 LTOS 253	5.96
Scott (Procurator Fiscal, Dunfermline) v Brown (2000) UKHRR 239	5.63
Sedleigh-Denfield v O'Callaghan [1940] AC 880, [1940] 3 All ER 349, 84 Sol Jo 657, 164 LT 72, 56 TLR 887, sub nom Sedleigh-Denfield v St Joseph's Society for Foreign Missions 109 LJKB 893, HL	1.74, 3.65
Sevenoaks v Brands Hatch Leisure Group (CO/3076/99) (May 2000, unreported)	3.17, 3.35, 3.56, 3.57, 8.08
Sheffield City Council v ADH Demolition Ltd (1983) 82 LGR 177, [1983] LS Gaz R 1919, [1984] JPL 658	1.80
Shelfer v City of London Electric Lighting Co [1895] 1 Ch 287	1.18
Shelley, ex p. See R v Carrick District Council, ex p Shelley	
Skinner v Jack Breach Ltd [1927] 2 KB 220, 25 LGR 287, 91 JP 109, 96 LJKB 834, 28 Cox CC 353, 136 LT 726, 43 TLR 484	1.80
Soltau v De Held (1851) 2 Sim NS 133, 21 LJ Ch 153, 16 Jur 326, 61 ER 291	1.14, 8.04
South Buckinghamshire v Porter [2003] UKHL 26, [2003] 2 WLR 1547	2.10, 2.75
South Cambridgeshire District Council v Persons Unknown [2004] EWCA Civ 1280	2.79
Southwark London Borough Council v Ince and Williams (1989) 153 JP 597, 21 HLR 504	1.29, 1.31
Southwark London Borough Council v Simpson (1998) 31 HLR 725, [1999] Env LR 553, DC	1.05
Sovereign Rubber Ltd v Stockport Metropolitan Borough Council [2000] Env LR 194	3.57, 4.22, 4.37, 4.89, 4.113, 4.115, 4.143

Table of Cases

	PARA
Sporrong and Lünnroth v Sweden (1982) 5 EHRR 35, ECtHR	2.09, 4.21, 7.116
Springett v Harold [1954] 1 All ER 568, [1954] 1 WLR 521, 52 LGR 181, 118 JP 211, 98 Sol Jo 197	1.29
Stagecoach Ltd v McPhail 1988 SCCR 289	5.98
Stanley v London Borough of Ealing [2000] Env LR D18, DC	3.05, 3.28, 3.34, 3.56
Steele Ford & Newton v Crown Prosecution Service (No 2) [1994] 1 AC 22, [1993] 2 All ER 769, [1993] 2 WLR 934, [1993] 27 LS Gaz R 34, [1993] NLJR 847, 137 Sol Jo LB 152, HL	7.74
Steers v Manton (1893) 57 JP 584	1.52
Stepney Borough Council v Joffe [1949] 1 KB 599, [1949] 1 All ER 256, 47 LGR 189, 113 JP 124, [1949] LJR 561, 93 Sol Jo 119, 65 TLR 176	4.106
Sterling Homes (Midlands) Ltd v Birmingham City Council [1996] Env LR 121	3.01, 3.10, 3.25, 3.26, 3.56, 3.57, 4.85, 5.10, 5.17, 5.99, 5.100, 5.101
Stoke-on-Trent City Council v B & Q (Retail) Ltd [1984] AC 754, [1984] 2 All ER 332, [1984] 2 WLR 929, 82 LGR 473, 128 Sol Jo 364, 4 Tr L 9, HL	2.74, 2.75
Stovin v Wise (Norfolk County Council, third party) [1996] AC 923, [1996] 3 All ER 801, [1996] 3 WLR 388, 95 LGR 260, [1996] RTR 354, [1996] 35 LS Gaz R 33, [1996] NLJR 1185, 140 Sol Jo LB 201, HL	7.115
Strathclyde Regional Council v Tudhope [1983] JPL 536	8.09
Sturges v Bridgman (1879) 11 Ch D 852, 43 JP 716, 48 LJ Ch 785, 28 WR 200, 41 LT 219, CA	1.13
Sunday Times v United Kingdom (1979) 2 EHRR 245, ECtHR	3.16
Surrey Free Inns plc v Gosport Borough Council (1998) 96 LGR 369, [1998] Crim LR 578, [1998] 06 LS Gaz R 25, 142 Sol Jo LB 84, [1998] JPL B86, [1999] Env LR 1; affd [1999] LGR 610, sub nom SFI Group plc (formerly Surrey Free Inns) v Gosport Borough Council [1999] EGCS 51, [1999] Env LR 750, [1999] BLGR 610, CA	4.108, 4.115
Swansea City Council v Jenkins (1994) 158 JP 952	9.81

T

Tauiria v France (1995) 83 A 113, EComHR	2.06
Taylor v Walsall and District Property and Investment Co Ltd (1998) 30 HLR 1062, [1998] 06 LS Gaz R 24, 142 Sol Jo LB 75, [1998] Env LR 600	7.81, 7.83
Thompson v Stimpson [1961] 1 QB 195, [1960] 3 All ER 500, [1960] 3 WLR 818, 104 Sol Jo 912, 176 Estates Gazette 1179	6.22
Tombesi (criminal proceedings against): C-304, 330, 342/94, C-224/95 [1997] All ER (EC) 639, [1997] ECR I-3561, [1997] 3 CMLR 673, ECJ	9.35
Tower Hamlets London Borough Council v Manzoni and Walder (1983) 148 JP 123, [1984] JPL 436	1.64
Tsfayo v United Kingdom (application no 60860/00) (The Times, 23 November 2006):	4.22
Turner v Secretary of State for the Environment (1973) 72 LGR 380, 28 P & CR 123, 288 Estates Gazette 335	6.03, 6.04

V

Vale of White Horse District Council v Allen & Partners [1997] Env LR 212	2.73
Van de Walle v Texaco Belgium (Case C-1/03) [2005] All ER (EC) 1139	9.36; 10.26
Vaughan v Biggs [1960] 2 All ER 473, [1960] 1 WLR 622, 58 LGR 218, 124 JP 341, 104 Sol Jo 508, DC	9.45, 9.47
Vella v Lambeth [2005] EWHC 2473 (Admin), [2006] Env LR 33	1.32

W

Waddington v Miah [1974] 2 All ER 377, [1974] 1 WLR 683, 59 Cr App Rep 149, 138 JP 497, 118 Sol Jo 365, HL	5.100
Walter v Selfe (1851) 4 De G & Sm 315, 20 LJ Ch 433, 15 Jur 416, 64 ER 849, 17 LTOS 103; affd (1852) 19 LTOS 308	8.04

Table of Cases

	PARA
Wandsworth London Borough Council v Winder [1985] AC 461, [1984] 3 All ER 83, [1984] 3 WLR 563, 82 LGR 509, 15 HLR 1, 128 Sol Jo 384, [1984] LS Gaz R 1684, CA; affd [1985] AC 461, [1984] 3 All ER 976, [1984] 3 WLR 1254, 83 LGR 143, 17 HLR 196, 128 Sol Jo 838, [1985] LS Gaz R 201, [1985] NLJ Rep 381, HL	9.26
Warner v Lambeth London Borough Council (1984) 15 HLR 42	1.29, 3.73, 6.13, 6.67
Warwick RDC v Miller-Mead [1962] Ch 441, [1962] 1 All ER 212, [1962] 2 WLR 284, 60 LGR 29, 126 JP 143, 105 Sol Jo 1124, CA	2.72
Wealden District Council v Hollings [1992] 4 LMELR 126	1.16
Wellingborough District Council v Gordon (1990) 155 JP 494, [1991] COD 154, [1991] JPL 874, [1993] Env LR 218, (1990) Times, 9 November	5.13, 5.79, 5.80, 5.84, 10.15
West Bowers Farm Products v Essex County Council (1985) 50 P & CR 368, [1985] 1 EGLR 271, [1985] RVR 176, [1985] JPL 857, CA	1.101
West Mersea UDC v Fraser [1950] 2 KB 119, [1950] 1 All ER 990, 48 LGR 418, 114 JP 282, 94 Sol Jo 271, 66 (pt 1) TLR 891	1.26
Westminster Bank Ltd v Minister of Housing and Local Government [1971] AC 508, [1970] 1 All ER 734, [1970] 2 WLR 645, 69 LGR 61, 21 P & CR 379, 134 JP 403, 114 Sol Jo 190, 214 Estates Gazette 129, HL	3.75
Westminster City Council v Cinquemani [2002] EWHC 179	5.55, 5.67
Westminster City Council v McDonald [003] EWHC 2698, [2005] Env LR 1	5.13, 5.86
Westminster City Council v Zestfair Ltd (1989) 88 LGR 288, 153 JP 613, 133 Sol Jo 1262	4.95, 4.97, 4.98
Westminster Renslade Ltd v Secretary of State for the Environment (1983) 48 P & CR 255, 127 Sol Jo 444, [1983] JPL 454	3.75
Wheeler v JJ Saunders Ltd [1996] Ch 19, [1995] 2 All ER 697, [1995] 3 WLR 466, [1995] NPC 4, [1995] JPL 619, [1995] Env LR 286, CA	1.21; 3.59
Wilkinson, Re [1922] 1 KB 584, 66 Sol Jo 269, 126 LT 673, sub nom Re Wilkinson, Re Randall 91 LJKB 326	1.81
Wilks v Hungerford Market Co (1835) 2 Bing NC	2.98
Williams v Burgess (1840) 12 Ad & El 635, 9 Dowl 544, 10 LJQB 10, Arn & H 65, 5 Jur 71, 4 Per & Dav 443	4.24
Wilson's Music and General Printing Co v Finsbury Borough Council [1908] 1 KB 563, 6 LGR 349, 72 JP 37, 77 LJKB 471, 98 LT 574	2.88
Wincanton RDC v Parsons [1905] 2 KB 34, 3 LGR 771, 69 JP 242, 74 LJKB 533, 93 LT 13	9.78
Winterwerp v Netherlands (1979) 2 EHRR 387, ECtHR	3.07
Wivenhoe Port Ltd v Colchester Borough Council [1985] JPL 175; affd [1985] JPL 396, CA	1.10, 1.34, 5.96
Wycombe District Council v Jeffways and Pilot Coaches (HW) Ltd (1983) 81 LGR 662, CA	7.11, 7.12
Wyre Forest District Council v Bostock [1992] 4 LMELR 50, [1993] Env LR 235	2.73

X

X (minors) v Bedfordshire County Council [1995] 2 AC 633, [1995] 3 All ER 353, [1995] 3 WLR 152, 160 LG Rev 103, [1995] 3 FCR 337, [1995] 2 FLR 276, [1995] Fam Law 537, [1995] ELR 404, 26 BMLR 15, [1995] NLJR 993, HL	7.115

Y

Young v Information Commissioner and the Department of the Environment for Northern Ireland EA/2007/0048 (12 December 2007)	2.31

Z

Zimmermann and Steiner v Switzerland (1983) 6 EHRR 17, ECtHR	4.130, 4.131

Chapter 1

Nature and Scope of Statutory Nuisance

INTRODUCTION

1.01 Statutory nuisance legislation is designed to provide a summary procedure for the remedy of a disparate collection of unacceptable states of affairs, most of which put at risk human health or harm the amenity of neighbours. Summary remedies are provided by local authorities and magistrates' courts. They are intended to be speedy, cheap and readily accessible to ordinary people. As Rose LJ, VP,[1] has said of the private citizen's procedure:

> '... the system should be operable by people who may be neither very sophisticated nor very articulate and who may not in some cases have the benefit of legal advice ... the hallmarks of the statutory remedy can be summarised in two words "simple" and "speedy"'.[2]

Unfortunately, the law has become complex. Technical difficulties abound for environmental health officers, non-specialist lawyers and community groups. Legal expenses have become prohibitive; they are a serious deterrent to the performance of duties by local authorities and the exercise of rights by citizens. This book is intended to give the general lawyer, environmental health officer and intelligent layman an awareness of the possibilities that is otherwise only available at great expense from specialist practitioners. It is intended to facilitate the operation of the legislation in accordance with the spirit and intendment of Parliament and the salutary words of Pill LJ:

> 'I see no reason why the procedure laid down by Parliament should not be made an effective procedure. It is the duty of the Courts to ensure that it is'.[3]

---

1 Lord Justice of Appeal; Vice President of the Court of Appeal, Criminal Division
2 *Hall v Kingston upon Hull City Council* [1999] 2 All ER 609 at 618. He quoted at 617 of *Hall* the then Lord Chief Justice, Lord Bingham, who emphasised, in *Pearshouse v Birmingham City Council* [1999] Env LR 536, that it was important that the system should be operable by people 'who may be neither very sophisticated nor very articulate and who may not ... have the benefit of specialised and high quality advice.'
3 *R v Falmouth and Truro Health Authority, ex p South West Water Services* [2000] 3 WLR 1464 at 1494H.

1.02 Section 79(1) of the Environmental Protection Act 1990, as amended, ('EPA 1990') establishes nine categories of statutory nuisance.[1] They relate to:

(a) the state of premises
(b) smoke emissions
(c) fumes or gases from dwellings
(d) effluvia from industrial, trade or business premises
(e) accumulations or deposits
(f) animals
(fa) insects
(fb) light

1

1.02 *Nature and scope of statutory nuisance*

(g) noise from premises
(ga) noise from vehicles or equipment in a street
(h) other matters declared by other Acts to be statutory nuisances.

All of them (apart from the round up category which cross-refers to other legislative provisions) have a common feature. Their definitions have two limbs. They require the existence either of *'prejudice to health'* or *'a nuisance'*. The choice of phrasing is intentionally disjunctive; the requirement is for one or the other.

1   Discussed in more detail later in this chapter at paras **1.26–1.77**.

FIRST LIMB: PREJUDICIAL TO HEALTH

1.03   The history of the statutory scheme and its predecessor legislation is worth noting as recourse is often made by the courts to the presumption that Parliament intends, unless the contrary intention appears, that re-enacted words should have the same meaning as they originally had. Predecessor legislation included the temporary Nuisances Removal Act 1846, passed as an emergency measure, in an unusually hot summer when rumours of cholera and typhoid were rife, for the 'speedy removal of certain nuisances'. This Act was renewed by the Nuisance Removal and Diseases Prevention Act 1848, and consolidated with amendments in the Nuisances Removal Act 1855, and amended by the Sanitation Act 1866. This legislation was replaced by the great Public Health Acts of 1875 and 1936.

1.04   **Prejudicial to health** is a relatively straightforward term. It is defined by section 79(7) of the EPA 1990 as *'injurious or likely to cause injury to health.'*[1] Plainly, opinions will differ about what is likely to cause injury to health. Judges have suggested that it is broad enough to apply to that which interferes with the 'vigour and vitality' of the well.[2] The term applies to making sick people worse. Guidance from bodies such as the World Health Organisation,[3] the experience of relevant professionals and common sense will all contribute to what is ultimately a judgment. The making of such a judgment is an art. Quantitative standards and scientific measurements of factors such as damp are useful servants; the masters must be human judgment.

1   Evidently, this test is different from 'fitness for habitation' as Lord Wilberforce observed in *Salford City Council v McNally* [1976] AC 379 at 389.
2   *Malton Board of Health v Malton Manure Co* (1879) 4 Ex D 302.
3   The Court of Appeal in *Murdoch v Glacier Metal Co Ltd* [1998] Env LR 732 held such material to be relevant but not necessarily determinative.

1.05   Five points should in particular be noted.

- *First*: injury to the *health* of a person must be likely; the contemporary view is that the likelihood of *personal injury* is not sufficient.[1] Thus the then Lord Chief Justice said in *Coventry City Council v Cartwright*:[2]

  'The words are obviously very wide ... But I think the underlying conception ... is ... a threat to health in the sense of a threat of disease, vermin or the like'.

  In that case risk of injury from broken glass was held not to be prejudicial to health. Likewise a steep and dangerous staircase, liable to cause accidents, has been held not to be prejudicial to health by the Court of Appeal.[3] Buxton LJ said:

'It cries out form the page that the target of the legislation was disease not physical injury'.[4]

Interference with comfort is not sufficient to amount to prejudice to health although it may amount to nuisance.[5]

- *Second*: the term has a broad meaning. The effects on health may be indirect. Thus, sleeplessness has been held to be injurious to health.[6]
- *Third*: the test is an objective one. It depends not on the particular personal circumstances of the individual affected but on the potential effects on health generally.[7]
- *Fourth*: this type of statutory nuisance protects the health of anyone put at risk by the relevant state of affairs. Thus, it protects the occupants of a house against the conditions of the house; the state of a house can be prejudicial to the health of its occupants.[8] In this respect it is, in England and Wales,[9] different from the second limb, mere nuisance, which only protects neighbours or the nearby community but not those on the land from which the nuisance originates.
- *Fifth*: Courts are not entitled to form a view without expert evidence or in rejection of unanimous expert evidence but the relevant professional experience is not confined to the medical profession. The expertise of others such as building inspectors and environmental health officers is recognised by the courts.[10] Courts will disregard the opinions about this of those with no relevant expertise;[11] such people may, of course, give factual evidence of their observations.

1 There are suggestions in some nineteenth century cases that the equivalent provision of the 1875 Act would apply to premises 'so dilapidated as to be a source of danger to life or limb' see *R v Parlby* (1889) 22 QBD 520. Such premises may well today be regarded as a second limb statutory nuisance if they are hazardous to passersby.
2 [1975] 1 WLR 845, DC, per Lord Widgery at 849B–C.
3 *R v Bristol City Council, ex p Everett* [1999] 2 All ER 193, CA.
4 He remarked of the Public Health Act 1875 which he regarded as a pointer to the scope of the EPA 1990, Pt III.
5 *Salford City Council v McNally* [1976] AC 379, HL, see Lord Wilberforce at 389E and Lord Edmund Davies at 353G.
6 *Lewisham v Fenner* [1995] 248 ENDS Report 44.
7 *Cunningham v Birmingham City Council* [1998] Env LR 1. A kitchen was harmful to an autistic child. It was otherwise acceptable. The relevant test was not met.*Robb v Dundee* [2002] SC 301 It is not necessary, however, that actual injury has been caused to someone's health
8 *Salford City Council v McNally* [1976] AC 379, HL, see Lord Wilberforce at 389A.
9 As to Scotland, see para **1.08**.
10 *O'Toole v Knowsley* [1999] Env LR D29; *Patel v Mehtab* (1980) 5 HLR 78. *Southwark London Borough Council v Simpson* [1999] Env LR 553
11 *Southwark London Borough Council v Simpson* [1999] Env LR 553 where the then Lord Chief Justice, Lord Bingham, made clear that relevant experience included that of building surveyors and inspectors.

SECOND LIMB: NUISANCE

1.06 **Nuisance** is unacceptable interference with the personal comfort or amenity of neighbours or the nearby community. What is unacceptable is that which ordinary, decent people would consider unreasonable. Baron Bramwell said that there was a rule:

'[in the] use and occupation of land and houses ... [of] give and take, live and let live'.[1]

Lord Millett has recently formulated the underlying principle:

1.06 *Nature and scope of statutory nuisance*

'The governing principle is that of good neighbourliness, and this involves reciprocity. A landowner[2] must show the same consideration for his neighbour as he would expect his neighbour to show for him'.[3]

1   *Bamford v Turnley* (1860) 3 B & S 62 at 83–84.
2   Or anyone else using land (see Baron Bramwell in *Bamford v Turnley* above and Lord Goff of Chieveley in *Cambridge Water Co v Eastern Counties Leather plc* [1994] 2 AC 264 at 299 'the principle of give and take between neighbouring occupiers of land'.
3   *Baxter v London Borough of Camden* [2000] Env LR 112 at 126.

1.07 Blackstone's[1] observation on nuisance to watercourses in his Commentaries perhaps expresses the common law's aspiration in this area of law: 'So closely does the law of England enforce that excellent rule of Gospel morality, of "doing unto others, as we would they should do unto us". It is sadly the case that 200 years later a fuller exposition of the law is necessary for the practical application and enforcement of the principle, which our experience here and in other parts of the Commonwealth has shown not to be exclusive to Christianity.

1   Early, but practical, academic writer, Professor of Law at Oxford, author of the influential 'Commentaries on the Laws of England'.

1.08 It is important to note the fundamental principle, traditionally said to apply to the second limb, but not applicable to the first limb, expressed thus by Watkins J with whom the then Lord Chief Justice agreed:

'a nuisance cannot arise if what has taken place affects only the person or persons occupying the premises where the nuisance is said to have taken place'.[1]

The principle has, however, been doubted[2], at least for Scotland, by an Extra Division of the Court of Session. Lady Paton observed[3] that:

'The statute is not concerned with *culpa*[4], but uses the definition "nuisance" to denote a set of physical circumstances recognised by the law as something *plus quam tolerabile*[5] ... it may be unavoidable that the application of this UK statute will produce different results, depending on whether the premises in question are north or south of the border ...'

Lord Johnston opined[6] that:

'It therefore seems to me to be incongruous, if not meaningless in the context of the legislation, to deny a remedy to the persons occupying the premises where the features said to create a nuisance exist, *involving no actual and likely damage to health* ... [there must be] a factual basis for a claim in nuisance if liability was being sought to be established at common law in that respect against a third party. That does not mean that a third party has to be involved on any notion of neighbourhood'[our emphasis].

The decision would however have been the same even if the Court had not been of this view as a majority was satisfied both that conditions were prejudicial to health[7] and that it was the resident's fault as she was not using sufficiently the provided heating facilities[8].

1   *National Coal Board v Neath Borough Council* [1976] 2 All ER 478 at 482.
2   *Robb v Dundee City Council* [2002] SC 301.
3   At p 321–322 [6]–[8].
4   Blameworthiness, wrongfulness in the eyes of the law.
5   Beyond what the law considers can reasonably be tolerated.
6   At p 318 [19] and [20].

Second limb: nuisance **1.09**

7   Lord Cameron of Lochbroom at p 308–9 [14], and Lady Paton at p 321 [4].
8   Lord Cameron of Lochbroom at p 309 [15] Lord Johnston at p 319–320 [27]–[33].

1.09 There are two important differences between common law[1] and statutory nuisance.

- *First* the Divisional Court[2] have held that the term has, in one sense, a narrower meaning in the statutory context than it does at common law[3] (which provides the traditionally more difficult and expensive procedures in the civil courts for damages[4] and injunctions[5]). The existence of circumstances capable of amounting to a common law nuisance is, in one respect, a necessary but not a sufficient condition for the existence of this first limb of statutory nuisance.[6] The development of statutory nuisance in public health legislation[7] and judicial observations suggest that statutory nuisance, unlike common law nuisance, does not deal with harm to property unless that causes harm to people's comfort or amenity.[8] The great Victorian judge Stephen J put it thus:

'I think the legislature intended to strike at … anything which diminished the comfort of life though not injurious to health [and at anything which would in fact injure health]'.[9]

- *Second*, however, in another important sense, the test is wider. There is no need for the victim to have property rights of the kind required (in the majority's opinion[10] in *Hunter v Canary Wharf Ltd*[11]) before the common law provides a remedy in private nuisance. Private nuisance at common law protects private property rights;[12] statutory nuisance protects people not property.

1   Common law nuisance may be public or private. There is an interesting discussion of their relationship to each other and statutory nuisance in the Opinion of Lord Bingham of Cornhill *R v Rimmington* [2005] UKHL 63, [2006] 1 AC 459 [5]–[31]. Public nuisances cause common injury to members of the public by interference with rights enjoyed in common by them. They are crimes punishable on indictment. Statutory nuisance is intended to provide a speedy remedy for some of them.
2   References to the Divisional Court (DC) in this book are references to the Divisional Court of the Queen's Bench Division. It usually consists of the Lord Chief Justice or one Lord Justice of Appeal and one High Court Judge of the Queen's Bench Division. It can have more members. Nowadays three only sit where a question known to be difficult needs resolution. The decisions of a divisional court bind single High Court judges and lower courts such as the Magistrates' and Crown Court. It is not bound by, but follows as highly persuasive, its own previous decisions unless it believes they were wrong.
3   The traditional law of England and Wales which has evolved through its exposition by judges on a case by case basis.
4   Monetary awards as compensation for harm.
5   Court orders to do or desist from doing something, disobedience to which is punishable by fine or imprisonment.
6   *National Coal Board v Thorne* [1976] 1 WLR 543, DC.
7   Nuisance Removals Act 1855 and Public Health Acts 1875–1936.
8   *National Coal Board v Thorne* [1976] 1 WLR 543, DC.see also *Robb v Dundee* [2002] SC 301 lord cameron of Lochbroom
9   *Bishop Auckland Local Board v Bishop Auckland Iron and Steel Co* (1880) 10 QB 138 at 141 endorsed by Lord Wilberforce in the House of Lords in *Salford City Council v McNally* [1976] AC 379 at 389E.
10 Notwithstanding the powerful dissenting speech of a former President of the New Zealand Court of Appeal, Lord Cooke of Thornden.
11 [1997] AC 655.
12 The common law does not confine the protection of public nuisance to private property interests in buildings and land. Such nuisances must, however, generally affect a whole neighbourhood.

1.10 Nature and scope of statutory nuisance

1.10 The distinction between harm to property not protected by statutory nuisance and harm to people which is protected is not always easy to draw. Caution should be adopted in approaching the judgment (which he acknowledged was made hesitantly and in a sea of uncertainty) of Judge Butler QC in *Wivenhoe Port Ltd v Colchester Borough Council*.[1] He correctly expressed the principle in the following passage but, it is respectfully submitted, created the potential for confusion in its application by his treatment of the examples he discussed:

> 'To be within the spirit of the Act a nuisance to be a statutory nuisance had to be one interfering materially with the personal comfort of the residents, in the sense that it materially affected their wellbeing although it might not be prejudicial to their health. Thus, dust falling on motor cars might cause inconvenience to their owners; it might even diminish the value of their motor car; but this would not be a statutory nuisance. In the same way, dust falling on gardens or trees, or on stock held in shop would not be a statutory nuisance. But dust in eyes or hair, even if not shown to be prejudicial to health, would be so as an interference with personal comfort'.

He properly does not exclude dust on clothes, worn on the person or hung out to dry, as a statutory nuisance. His words might seem totally to exclude dust in a shop or a garden. It is difficult to think that the legislature intended to exclude something so damaging to personal comfort as the assault on domestic or workplace amenity occasioned by substantial dust deposits on domestic gardens or in the interior of shops. Occasional or small deposits of dust might not in fact, of course, amount to a nuisance. It seems unlikely that dust in gardens or shops should be ruled out in principle. The sound point underlying the learned judge's remarks was that the effect on, and diminution in value of, the garden or shop stock was *in itself* irrelevant.

1   [1985] JPL 175; affd [1985] JPL 396, CA.

1.11 Ordinary, decent people used to be equated with *the man on the Clapham Omnibus*. Nowadays it would be more realistic to think of the people who spend Saturday afternoon watching the match and Sunday morning washing their cars. They are not (yet) those, for the moment the leaders in progressive thought and life, who bicycle to farmers' markets to buy organic vegetables, have backyard recycling centres and heat their houses on methane gas produced from the night soil of their privies. Growing public concern, recognised both in government policy and emerging legislation, about climate change is however likely to create a more sympathetic attitude towards activities, such as wind turbines, which are perceived as making a contribution towards reducing our dependence on greenhouse gas producing technologies.

KEY CONSIDERATIONS

1.12 Relevant considerations to which the test of ordinary decent people will be applied include the following:

- location
- time
- duration
- frequency
- convention

- importance and value to the community of activity
- difficulty in avoiding external effects of activity.

Location

1.13 A noisy refrigeration unit or mechanical air extraction unit may be expected and unexceptional on an industrial estate. Most people would agree that they are out of place and unacceptable on a quiet suburban estate. The crowing of cocks is a traditional part of the countryside; it might be regarded differently in an urban area. The call of a muezzin to prayer might be acceptable in an area with a large Muslim population; it would be otherwise elsewhere. The principle was well expressed in the pithy language apt to nineteenth century conditions:

> 'What would be a nuisance in Belgrave Square would not necessarily be so in Bermondsey'.[1]

Mixed areas present difficulties. The Government and local authorities are keen to bring back life into town centres at night and the weekends. Two conflicting strands present particular difficulties. On the one hand they wish to encourage people to live in town centres (above shops, for example); on the other hand they are keen for town centres to be places of entertainment. They sometimes speak of the '24 hour city'. Statutory development plans may be able to offer useful guidance to courts (see paras **1.21–1.25** below).

1 *Sturges v Bridgman* (1879) 11 Ch D 852 per Thesiger LJ at 856.

Time

1.14 Mowing the lawn or ringing church bells may well be acceptable in the quietest and most peaceful of villages on a Sunday morning; they would not be, if done in the middle of the night.[1] A noisy party on a Saturday evening will be viewed quite differently from the same party on a Monday night. Grinding knives at a mobile machine outside a school at examination time would be viewed differently from the same activity during school holidays. The definition in development plans[2] of acceptable times for carrying out noisy activities might be a useful way particularly for residential areas both of increasing the predictability of intrusions into tranquillity and minimising the overall periods of time subject to them.

1 *Soltau v de Held* (1851) 2 Sim NS 133.
2 See below.

Duration

1.15 An hour's practice at a piano audible through a poorly insulated wall or ceiling in an adjoining dwelling is likely to be judged differently from a piano marathon. Likewise a quarter of an hour's smoke from a coffee roaster in a mixed area will not be judged in the same way as continuous smoke of the same kind from the same premises. Dogs may bark at visiting postmen and cats with impunity for their owners; but a dog barking the whole day would be viewed differently. Temporary construction works may be very noisy for a period; this may have to be accepted.[1]

1 *Gosnell v Aerated Bread Co Ltd* (1894) 10 TLR 661.

1.16 *Nature and scope of statutory nuisance*

Frequency

1.16 Noisy parties held every Saturday night will be viewed differently from an occasional one held on special occasions. Knife grinding at a mobile machine outside an office every morning would be viewed differently from the same noise made once a month at the same place. Unpleasant smells occasionally emitted from great manufacturing works might well be acceptable where regular emissions would not. The open air brass band contests held from teatime to midnight in the villages of Saddleworth on Whit Friday are a valued local tradition; such events on a weekly basis would be received quite differently. Courts may limit the frequency of activities. A farm was restricted to muck spreading on 15 days a year.[1]

1 *Wealden District Council* v *Hollings* [1992] 4 LMELR 126.

Convention

1.17 The existence of a widespread practice or common usage in an area is influential.[1] Many people find contemporary lawn mowers intensely irritating. One stops; another starts. They are used at the very time and in the very conditions that most people wish to enjoy 'a bit of peace and quiet' in their gardens. But their use at such times is an accepted widespread practice in England and Wales. So it is unlikely that a local authority or court would at present find them to be a nuisance. Likewise the practice of open air burning of meat at barbecues is now part of a Middle England summer. But in those areas where Monday is still washing day it would be considered unacceptable to burn leaves on that day.

1 See for example *Leeman v Montagu* [1936] 2 All ER 1677.

Importance and value to the community of activity

1.18 This must be viewed from the perspective of the community. Few would doubt that more latitude should be given to a great engineering works producing ploughshares for a continent and providing employment for a town than to a motocross course where the apprentices relax noisily. The hum of the works' extractor fans may be unavoidable; better that the terraces should house workers in some noise than that they house the unemployed in silence. But many would think that the peace of the company pensioners in their homes[1] should be valued more highly than the opportunity for a few to enjoy themselves in a manner inimical to the amenity of many. There comes a point however where the effect of even the most socially useful activity becomes unacceptable and a nuisance. The motive of the enterprise and the public value of its activities then provide no defence[2].

1 See for example *Hampstead and Suburban Properties Ltd v Diomedous* [1968] 3 All ER 545.
2 *Shelfer v City of London Electric Lighting Co* [1895] 1 Ch 287 at p 316 *Dennis v Ministry of Defence* [2003] EWHC 793 (QB).

Difficulty in avoiding external effects of activity

1.19 It is easy for a bar to stop playing loud amplified music; so little sympathy is likely for any suggestions that their interest in so doing should be preferred to the interests of affected neighbours. It might be much more difficult for a brewery to avoid regular smells; more weight would be given to their interest in so doing for that reason. It is difficult to stop schoolchildren from making a noise in play (and unnatural to make them play inside) so there would be no point in protesting about their noise during playtime. The ploughshare works might be able to install noise baffles around their extractor fans; if so there might be little sympathy for the continuation of the noise.

Ultimately a Matter of Judgement

1.20 Ultimately, however, as Schiemann LJ put it:

'in nuisance cases there is always an element of judgment in a continuum between a mildly irritating activity to something which is intolerable and positively criminal if it affects a large enough number of people'.[1]

1   *Budd v Colchester Borough Council* [1997] Env LR 128 at 134.

DEVELOPMENT PLANS

1.21 It may be that the statutory development plan which local authorities have to prepare under the Town and Country Planning legislation could provide greater guidance to environmental health officers and courts as to the reconciliation of the many potentially conflicting interests which must be addressed. Such plans are adopted by the democratically elected representatives of the local community after extensive consultation and independent scrutiny by professional inspectors at planning inquiries. National Government, however, tended to take a narrow view of the scope of development plans. In the authors' views, nevertheless, policies for the 'development *and use* of land'[1] could usefully address such conflicts.'Development of land' includes changes of use. The addition of the words highlighted indicates that such policies should extend beyond the mere control of changes of use and other forms of development. Sections 12(4)(b) and 36(3A)(b) of the Town and Country Planning Act 1990 used to require plans to include policies for '*the improvement of the physical environment*'. The replacement provision in the Planning and Compulsory Purchase Act 2004, however, no longer does. This does not, of course, prevent them either from so doing or seeking to preserve the physical environment.

1   That for which local planning authorities must set out their policies. The duty was formerly found in TCPA 1990, ss 12(3) and 36(2) but is now in the Planning and Compulsory Purchase Act 2004, s 17(3).

1.22 The Court of Appeal acknowledged in *Wheeler v JJ Saunders Ltd*[1] that planning decisions could alter the character of an area in a way which affected the acceptability of various types of activity and hence a judgment as to whether they were nuisances. The designation of areas as suitable or unsuitable for particular uses is one obvious way in which such plans can make an important contribution to the operation of the statutory nuisance regime. There are other such areas.

1   [1996] Ch 19 effectively disapproving of the broader approach taken in a lower court in *Gillingham Borough Council v Medway (Chatham) Dock Co Ltd* [1993] QB 343 where the puisne judge wrongly came close to treating the grant of planning permission as equivalent to statutory authority for the nuisance. See also *Blackburn v ARC Ltd* [1998] Env LR 469 and *R v Kennet District Council, ex p Somerfield Property Co Ltd* [1999] JPL 361. There is a discussion of the significance of statutory authority in Chapter 3 at paras **3.59–3.62**.

1.23 *Nature and scope of statutory nuisance*

1.23 Traditionally, local planning authorities have not drafted their plans with a view to giving guidance to courts on the exercise of their powers to control anti social uses of land. They are, however, well equipped to give such guidance. Such a role need not conflict with the supremacy which the magistracy and courts must have in resolving disputes which, if not handled with sufficient firmness, lead to violence and breaches of the peace.

1.24 It would, in the authors' view, be open to planning authorities to include policies setting out the local community's judgment on uses of land which did not amount to development. Thus, they might formulate policies reflecting the local community's judgment of the limits of acceptability of bonfires, burglar alarms, barbecues and other potential occasions of neighbour dispute. Unfortunately the prospects for a widespread extension of the role of development plans are not good; local planning authorities are likely to be reluctant to add to the number of controversial issues with which they have to deal.

1.25 Until, however, development plans are formulated with the intention of providing guidance to environmental health officers, community groups and courts on nuisance they must be approached with caution. They are at present prepared on the basis (albeit perhaps mistakenly) that they ought not to address such issues. They assume that an entirely independent regime will deal with issues other than the development of land.

THE CATEGORIES OF STATUTORY NUISANCE[1]

The state of premises

(a) any premises in such a state as to be prejudicial to health or a nuisance

1.26 The term 'premises' is defined in section 79(7) of the EPA 1990 so as to include land[2] and generally vessels, such as house boats.[3] The Interpretation Act 1978, Sch 1 defines the word 'land', if used in legislation, as including 'land covered with water' unless the statutory context requires otherwise. The courts have not decided whether the context does so require in statutory nuisance legislation. Tents, vans, sheds and similar structures used for human habitation are deemed to be houses[4]. This category does not apply to public sewerage systems and sewage treatment works[5].

1   EPA 1990, s 79(1).
2   The contaminated land exception, discussed in a later section, will be increasingly important in relation to land.
3   Extending the approach of the Divisional Court in *West Mersea UDC v Fraser* [1950] 2 KB 119.
4   Public Health Act 1936, s 268(1).
5   *R v Parlby* (1889) 22 QBD 520; *R v Epping (Waltham Abbey); JJ ex p Burlinson* [1948] 1 KB 79 per Lord Goddard CJ at p 8; *East Riding of Yorkshire; C v Yorkshire Water Services* [2001] Env LR 113; *Hounslow LBC v Thames Water Utilities Ltd* (DC) [2003] EWHC 1197 (Admin), [2004] QB 212 per Scott Baker LJ at [62].

1.27 Its most obvious use is to describe the whole or part of a building such as a dwelling-house. Lord Justice Sedley has observed[1]

'These are statutory provisions which have stood the test of time, and which serve as a very valuable protection against both bad housing management and for the protection of public health among, in general, the very poorest people in this country. They need all the help they can get .... It is important that for both sides that this legislation should be used intelligently and responsibly for the remedying of real need, not capriciously or factitiously ...'

1   *Quigley v Liverpool Housing Trust* DC [2000] Env LR D9.

1.28   The essence of this category is the unacceptability of a state of affairs on land or within a building. It is the unacceptability of the *state* or *condition* of the premises, not the *use* or *purpose* to which they are put which is important. Wills J put this point well:[1]

'... it is confined to cases in which the premises themselves are decayed, dilapidated, dirty, or out of order, as for instance, where houses have been inhabited by tenants whose habits and ways of life have rendered them filthy, or impregnated with disease, or where foul matter has been allowed to soak into walls or floors ...'

Thus a building which was a nuisance only by reason being *used* as a hospital for infectious diseases was not within the meaning of the same words in earlier legislation.[2] A house inadequately protected from the elements becomes damp; such premises are prejudicial to the health of its occupants.[3] A building infested with rodents would be prejudicial to the health of its occupants and the area. A building used as a laboratory in which there was stored for analysis much pestilential material would not thereby be in a *state* prejudicial to the health of the area. If the pestilential material impregnated the walls, floors and ceilings then the building would be in a state prejudicial to health.

1   *R v Parlby* (1889) 22 QBD 520.
2   *Metropolitan Asylum District Managers v Hill* (1881) 6 App Cas 193.
3   Eg *Issa v London Borough of Hackney* [1997] 1 All ER 999; [1997] Env LR 157, CA where houses with condensation and mould were held to be statutory nuisances.

1.29   There are many physical states of residential premises – commonly associated with poor maintenance or poor design – which are capable of supporting a finding that premises are prejudicial to health within the meaning of the statute. For example, evidence of excessive dampness in the living areas of a flat,[1] rising damp in the wall of a bedroom,[2] excessive condensation and associated mould growth,[3] severe dry rot[4] and poor sanitary conditions[5] may support such a finding. The cumulative effect of the defects in the premises should be examined as well as their individual effect. Want of decoration is not enough.[6] Proof that a landlord is in breach of his covenants as landlord is not, of course, necessary; it has been treated as persuasive.[7] A tenant cannot invoke the act if she refuses to move out temporarily to allow the landlord to carry out necessary works of repair.[8]

1   *GLC v London Borough of Tower Hamlets* (1983) 15 HLR 54.
2   *Pollway Nominees Ltd v London Borough of Havering* (1989) 21 HLR 462.
3   *Birmingham District Council v McMahon* (1987) 19 HLR 452; *Southwark London Borough Council v Simpson* (1998) 31 HLR 725; *Pike v Sefton Metropolitan Borough Council* DC [2000] Env LR D31.
4   *Warner v London Borough of Lambeth* (1984) 15 HLR 42.
5   *Salford City Council v McNally* [1976] AC 379.

1.29 *Nature and scope of statutory nuisance*

6 *Springett v Harold* [1954] 1 All ER 568.
7 *Birmingham District Council v Kelly* (1985) 17 HLR 572.
8 *Quigley v Liverpool Housing Trust* DC 24 June 1999 [2000] Env LR D9.

1.30 The design or layout of premises cannot in themselves render their state prejudicial to health. In *Birmingham City Council v Oakley*[1] the bathroom, lavatory and kitchen of the property were all located on the ground floor of the premises. There was no hand basin in the lavatory and no space to install one. The lavatory and bathroom were themselves located opposite sides of the kitchen. As a result, the only place for washing hands after using the lavatory was the bathroom or the kitchen sink. The magistrates found that this was unacceptable because of the risks of cross-infection of the kitchen area. It was found as a matter of fact that it was used by children which in large measure created the risk to health. The Divisional Court rejected as wrong in principle the argument advanced on behalf of the council that the case fell outside section 79 altogether because it was concerned with the use of the premises rather than their state.[2] As Simon Brown LJ put the matter:

> '... [where] ... the way the premises are used is the direct result of their layout and ... that is predictably so unhygienic as to create a health risk, then it is the state of the premises which is injurious to health ...'

Accordingly, the Court of Appeal held that the justices had been entitled to find that a statutory nuisance existed by reason of the absence of a washbasin with the lavatory and the layout of the premises, which made the house so unhygienic that it was or was likely to be injurious to health. The House of Lords,[3] by a majority of 3:2, reversed the decision of the Court of Appeal. As Lord Slynn of Hadley put it:

> 'There must be a factor which in itself is prejudicial to health. I do not think that the arrangement of the rooms otherwise not in themselves insanitary so as to be prejudicial to health falls within section 79(1)(a) ... The prejudice to health results from the failure to wash hands or the use of the sink or the basin after access through the kitchen'.

1 (1998) 31 HLR 1070.
2 (1998) 31 HLR 1070 at 1076.
3 [2000] 3 WLR 1936.

1.31 There has been some uncertainty about the extent to which a building may fall within the category if the problems experienced within it come from external sources such as road noise. The Divisional Court has held that premises could be prejudicial to health even though the cause was a defective wall outside them which the landlord did not control.[1] The penetration of noise into inadequately insulated premises has been treated as covered by this category.[2] This treatment should, however, be viewed with some caution in view of *Haringey London Borough Council v Jowett*[3] and doubts about it expressed by Lord Hoffmann and Lord Millet in *Birmingham v Oakley*. The Divisional Court held in *Jowett*, on questionable reasoning (perhaps not being directed to the authorities illustrating the difference between the nature of the nuisance under (ga) and (a)), that if the origin of noise was traffic then because of section 79(6A)[4] (which in fact only applies to (ga)), there could be no nuisance even under (a) where a dwelling-house was inadequately insulated against external noise.

1 *Polloway Nominees Ltd v London Borough of Havering* (1989) 21 HLR 462.

The categories of statutory nuisance **1.34**

2 *Southwark London Borough Council v Ince and Williams* (1989) 21 HLR 504. It is interesting that neither this case nor EPA 1990 Pt III were apparently drawn to the attention of the House of Lords in *Baxter v London Borough of Camden* [2000] Env LR 112 which proceeded on the assumption that there was no statutory duty (119 notional D-E) on a landlord to soundproof a dwelling even if the noise penetrating it was excessive (116 notional C).
3 (1999) 32 HLR 308, DC.
4 See (ga) at para **1.68** below.

1.32 The uncertainty appears to have been resolved by the Divisional Court in *Vella v Lambeth*[1]. It held that premises with inadequate sound insulation which failed to prevent the penetration of external noise did not fall within this category. The approach was a pragmatic one. The court was reluctant to oblige social housing providers to a potentially hugely expensive obligation to retro fit sound insulation. Lord Justice Keene emphasised[2] Lord Hoffmann's observation in *Oakley*[3] that:

'... it is [n]either sensible [n]or in accordance with modern notions of democracy to hold that when Parliament re-enacted language going back to the 19th century, it authorised the courts to impose upon local authorities and others a huge burden of capital expenditure to which the statutory language had never been held to apply.'

The court relied upon the proposition[4] that mere failure to prevent external activities from causing a risk to health cannot fall within (a). This reasoning needs further amplification, as it is well established that externally sourced damp penetration can fall within (a). In the authors' view perhaps the most satisfactory rationale for the distinction between penetration of noise, which is not covered by (a), and penetration of damp, which is covered by (a), is that in the former case there is no intermediate stage before the effect on health during which it may be said that the *state of the premises* has been affected by the intrusion. By contrast in the latter case there is an intermediate stage between the intrusion and the effect on health, during which it may be said that the state of the premises has deteriorated because of the intrusion. The key is to be found in the words of Lord Slynn of Hadley in *Oakley*[5]:

'The *state* of the house must *in itself* have been prejudicial to health' [our emphasis].

1 [2005] EWHC 2473 (Admin) [2006] Env LR 33 p 873.
2 At [72] and [80].
3 [2001] 1 AC 617, [2001] Env LR 37 at 632 D–F.
4 At [79].
5 At 627C.

1.33 The category does not apply to industrial, trade or business premises where the *'best practicable means'* have been used to prevent or counteract the nuisance.[1]

1 See para **1.83** below.

Smoke emissions

(b) smoke emitted from premises so as to be prejudicial to health or a nuisance

1.34 Smoke is the visible airborne product of combustion. It includes soot, ash, grit and gritty particles emitted in smoke.[1] This category covers antisocial

13

1.34 *Nature and scope of statutory nuisance*

garden fires such as those of wet leaves on washing days in areas where such days, traditionally Mondays, are still observed as ones when washing is hung out to dry². The burning of tyres on domestic land would be covered; such an activity at commercial vehicle premises would be excluded. Most urban dwellings are within smoke control areas and excluded from this category. Rural dwellings, however, are generally not excluded. The use of unconventional fuel such as plastic waste briquettes (producing foul, noxious smoke) in the domestic hearth would be covered. The inconsiderate practice of burning slack at low temperatures for long periods could be covered. The smoke of regular barbecues,³ from a public house garden (or from a domestic garden if of unacceptable frequency) could be covered. Smoke includes the smell of smoke.⁴

1   EPA 1990, s 79(7).
2   This practice has an important contribution to make in avoiding unnecessary energy use in indoor drying. Note in this context, however, in the general discussion above on the second limb 'nuisance' the note at para **1.10** on *Wivenhoe Port Ltd v Colchester Borough Council* and the potential problems caused by the treatment of examples discussed. The statutory nuisance consists not in any damage to the clothes but to the personal discomfort occasioned by the unacceptable options of dirty, damp or darkened clothes.
3   The smell of such barbecues would also be covered by categories (c) (para **1.36**) and (d) (para **1.39**) respectively.
4   *Griffiths v Pembrokeshire County Council* DC [2000] Env LR 622, per Kennedy LJ, VP.

1.35 The many exceptions to, and limitations on, this apparently simple provision of the EPA 1990 reflect the desire of Parliament to avoid duplication of other control regimes:¹

- smoke from the chimneys of private dwellings within smoke control areas (s 79(3)(i))
- dark smoke² from industrial or trade premises or from chimneys³ associated with buildings or fixed plant (s 79(3)(iv) and (ii))
- where the smoke comes from a chimney and the *'best practicable means'*⁴ have been used (s 80(8)(b))
- crown defence service property (s 79(2))
- smoke from railway steam engines (s 79(3)(iii)).

Proceedings may not be initiated by local authorities without the consent of the Government in respect of premises subject to Integrated Pollution Control or Local Authority Air Pollution Control if proceedings could be taken under Part I of the EPA 1990 or under the replacement regime of the Pollution Prevention and Control Act 1999⁵ The definition provisions of the Clean Air Act 1993⁶ apply.

1   Such as those under the Clean Air Acts, EPA 1990, Pt 1 requiring prior authorisation of potentially polluting activities through Integrated Pollution Control by the Environment Agency or Local Authority Air Pollution Control or the Pollution Prevention and Control Act 1999.
2   Section 79(7) gives '*Dark smoke*', and other terms used in s 79, the same meaning as in the Clean Air Act 1993. Section 3(1) of that Act defines it as as dark or darker than 2 on the Ringelmann chart. Section 3(3) empowers the relevant Secretary of State to specify other means of proving that smoke is dark.
3   See Clean Air Act 1993, s 64 reproduced in Appendix H.
4   See para **1.83**.
5   Pollution Prevention and Control Act 1999.
6   EPA 1990, s 79(7); see Clean Air Act 1993, s 64.

Fumes or gases from dwellings

(c) fumes or gases emitted from premises so as to be prejudicial to health or a nuisance

1.36 This only applies to private dwellings.[1] *'Fumes'* means any airborne solid[2] matter smaller than dust.[3] *'Gas'*[4] includes vapour and moisture precipitated from vapour. Vapour includes particles of liquid suspended in air.

An obvious problem which this can address is that caused by the flue emitting exhaust gases from a central heating boiler into a neighbour's bedroom window. Likewise the liquid droplets of spray paint used by a bad neighbour for his hobbies could be controlled.

1   EPA 1990, s 79(4).
2   Solids resist change in shape and volume. Liquids resist change in volume but not shape. Gases do not resist changes in shape or size,
3   Dust is often taken to be solids suspended in air as a result of the disintegration of matter consisting of particles between 1 and 76 micrometres in diameter (A Porteous 1: *Dictionary of Environmental Science and Technology* (2nd Edn) John Wiley, Chichester).
4   EPA 1990, s 97(7) and see note above.

1.37 Smells, such as the offensive exudations of home soap or candle making, or the pungent odours of some sorts of cooking are caused by small particles whether solid, liquid or gas. They are, in our view, within this category. Smells are not, however, expressly included. They are expressly included in the next category (which does not apply to residential premises). The principle of construction that where a list expressly includes a point in one instance but not in another the point cannot apply in the one wherein it is not expressly mentioned[1] might superficially suggest that smells are not covered by this category. If that were so it would never be possible to deal by this procedure with some repeated, intolerable smells from bad residential neighbours[2]. That would be inconsistent with the overall scheme of the Act. Smells from residential premises are also covered by the summary procedures of the Act if they are caused by the *state of* premises (Category (a), paras **1.26–1.33**). Those emanating from *accumulations or deposits* (Category (e), paras **1.46–1.50**) and those associated with *smoke* (Category (b), paras **1.34–1.35**) are also covered by the Act.

1   Succinctly expressed in the Latin 'expressio unius, exclusio alterius'.
2   In the authors' view the reason why smells are expressly included in the next category (d), which relates to industrial, trade and business premises, is that fumes and gases are excluded from that category. Parliament intended that in non-residential premises they are, in general, to be covered by other controls such as the prior authorisation regime of Integrated Pollution Control. However, Parliament recognised that such other regimes cannot be expected adequately to deal with smells. Smells, therefore, had to be expressly mentioned in respect of non-residential premises; whereas in residential premises they were included within 'fumes or gases'.

1.38 The defence of 'best practicable means' does not apply.

1.39 *Nature and scope of statutory nuisance*

Effluvia from industrial, trade or business premises

(d)   any dust, steam, smell or other effluvia arising on industrial, trade or business premises and being prejudicial to health or a nuisance

1.39   This category of nuisance cannot be used against residential property. It is not confined to *emissions* from premises. It is, therefore, capable of applying where the health[1] of workers on the originating premises is put at risk. This category, unlike (a), applies to sewage treatment works[2].

1   As to the second limb 'nuisance' see para **1.06** above. A nuisance can only be occasioned to neighbours or the nearby community.
2   *Hounslow LBC v Thames Water Utilities Ltd* (DC) [2003] EWHC 1197 (Admin), [2004] QB 212 per Scott Baker LJ at [70] and Pitchford J at [54].

1.40   **Dust** would apply to the break up of concrete or unloading of rubble by a builder or demolition contractor at their yard. It would apply to the delivery of coal at a merchant's yard. It could apply to the handling of bulk foodstuffs at a transhipment depot. It is defined so as to exclude dust emitted from a chimney as an ingredient of smoke.[1]

1   EPA 1990, s 79(7).

1.41   **Steam** is less of a problem today than when it was one of the principal sources of power for machinery. An ill directed jet, or drifting cloud, of steam from leaking pipe, or ill placed stack, of a great manufacturing works or small laundry could be disagreeable or damaging to the lungs of those working or living nearby.

1.42   **Smell** was not expressly included within the categories of the Public Health Act 1936.[1] The smells of cooking from fish and chip shops or curry houses, paint spraying from vehicle repair shops or cleaning fluids at dry cleaners illustrate some of the everyday problems associated with small businesses which may be remedied by this category. Great chemical works, oil refineries, paper mills or other large enterprises may also cause problems on a larger scale to whole towns. Local authorities are often apprehensive of fulfilling their duties as a result of the great resources which such businesses can deploy in avoiding changes to their practices. These resources include politically sensitive suggestions that vigorous enforcement of the requirement for best practicable measures will lead to relocation elsewhere in the United Kingdom or abroad (perhaps with the aid of Government or European Community grants).

1   Smells were included within the term '*effluvia*' which was covered by that Act and its predecessor the 1875 Act (see *Malton Board of Health v Malton Manure Co* (1879) 4 Ex D 302 where smells from processes including dissolving bones and coprolite in sulphuric acid caused people to close windows and some to experience nausea and vomiting).

1.43   **Effluvia** suggest something 'given off' into the air that is offensive to the senses. In other contexts, and probably in the predecessor legislation, it would be capable of referring to something harmful to health though not necessarily noticeable by the senses. In this context Parliament is unlikely to have intended that it should have that meaning. This category (unlike (c)) does not include 'fumes or gases'. They would be covered if 'effluvia' had that broad scope; they seem to have been deliberately omitted. The preceding instances in the list are all disagreeable to the senses. This round-up instance is therefore probably only intended to cover those things that have that characteristic.[1] Fumes and gases which are unpleasant to the senses would probably be encompassed within the concept of smells and other effluvia as used in this section. The category seems to exclude harmful fumes or gases which are not offensive to the senses. Parliament seems to have intended, and envisaged, that such emissions from non-residential premises should, and would, be adequately governed by other control regimes such as the prior authorisation regime of Part I of the EPA 1990. It is noteworthy that the Clean Air Act 1993 empowers the relevant Secretary of State[2] to apply to fumes and gases the provisions of that Act relating to grit dust and smoke on non-residential premises.

1 Succinctly expressed by the Latin phrase 'ejusdem generis' – a pithy shorthand for this principle of statutory interpretation.

1.44 The defence of *'best practicable means'* applies.[1] The terms *'industrial, trade or business premises'* are discussed below at paras **1.80–1.82**.

1 Discussed at paras **1.83–1.94**.

1.45 Proceedings may not be initiated[1] by local authorities without the consent of the Government in respect of premises subject to Integrated Pollution Control or Local Authority Air Pollution Control under Part I of the EPA 1990, if proceedings might be taken under that legislation or under the replacement regime of the Pollution Prevention and Control Act 1999.[2]

1 EPA 1990, s 79(10).
2 Pollution Prevention and Control Act 1999, s 6, Sch 2, para 6.

Accumulations or deposits

(e) any accumulation or deposit which is prejudicial to health or a nuisance

1.46 An *accumulation* is the result of a series of deposits whether by man, beast, nature or machine. A *deposit* is the result of a single instance. This category applies regardless of where the offending material is located. It might be in a street, a rag and bone merchant's yard or a hospital laundry. It protects the health of those who live or work on any premises where it is found as well as neighbours and the nearby community.

1.47 It covers piles of refuse, ordure or waste material whether on the street, on a farm, within premises or on the beach.[1] It does not need to be permanent.[2] It could be invoked by a resident of a block of flats or mixed use premises against another occupier of the same building. It could be invoked against someone who placed his rubbish in the street well in advance of its likely collection. It could be invoked in respect of a single dump of excrement by a street person. He would be unlikely to be served with an abatement notice; as will be seen, below however, landowners and local authorities[3] can be forced to take action in respect of statutory nuisances of which they have not been the first cause.

1 *R v Carrick District Council, ex p Shelley* [1996] Env LR 273.
2 This was so even under waste control under Control of Pollution Act 1973; *R v Metropolitan Stipendiary Magistrate, ex p London Waste Regulation Authority* [1993] 3 All ER 113, DC.
3 See EPA 1990, s 82(13) discussed in Chapter 6, paras **6.79–6.80**.

1.48 *Nature and scope of statutory nuisance*

1.48 In the absence of a nuisance, a pile of material which included dangerous but inert things such as knives or broken glass would not be prejudicial to health (see para **1.05** and *Coventry City Council v Cartwright*.[1] A used syringe potentially infected with HIV virus or hepatitis (now all too often encountered in city centres) would be included because of the risk of disease. A sealed sterile unused needle would present a risk of injury but not disease; it could not therefore be caught under the first limb.

1   [1975] 1 WLR 845.

1.49 The defence of 'best practicable means' applies on industrial or trade premises[1]. Proceedings may not be initiated[2] by local authorities without the consent of the Government in respect of premises subject to Integrated Pollution Control or Local Authority Air Pollution Control under Part I of the EPA 1990, if proceedings might be taken under that legislation or under the replacement regime of the Pollution Prevention and Control Act 1999.[3]

1   EPA 1990, s 80(7), (8)(a).
2   EPA 1990, s 79(10).
3   Pollution Prevention and Control Act 1999, s 6, Sch 2, para 6.

1.50 It will in the future be particularly important in respect of this category to consider the extent to which the contaminated land exception applies.[1]

1   See paras **1.95–1.104**.

Animals

(f) any animal kept in such a place or manner as to be prejudicial to health or a nuisance

1.51 This is less important today than it was in 1875 when the Public Health Act of that year made it a statutory nuisance. It is most likely to be useful in an urban area. It could be invoked by a resident in respect of a fellow occupier of a building who kept a smelly animal.

1.52 Keeping may be for a relatively short time; thus keeping pigs from morning until evening without feeding them amounted to keeping them.[1] Traditionally the keeping of pigs within a city was regarded as nuisance in itself.[2] It can apply where the animals are kept in a public place. Sheep droppings in a market have been held to be a nuisance.[3] It might well apply to demonstrations by farmers adopting French tactics. There seems to be no reason why it should not apply to noise from animals as Lord Widgery CJ was inclined to accept;[4] such noise was however held not to be a nuisance under this head by a predecessor of his Lord Godddard CJ.[5] It is sensible therefore to use category (g) as well in respect of animal noise.[6]

1   *Steers v Manton* (1893) 57 JP 584.
2   *R v Wigg* (1705) 2 Salk 460.
3   *Draper v Sperring* (1861) 25 JP 566.
4   *Coventry City Council v Cartwright* [1975] 1 WLR at 850G.
5   *Galer v Morrissey* [1955] 1 WLR 110.
6   In *Budd v Colchester Borough Council* [1999] Env LR 739 the Court of Appeal assumed that the barking of greyhounds could be a nuisance. It is not clear whether (g) or (f) was the basis.

1.53 An important question is the extent to which it applies to the actions of animals while they are temporarily away from the immediate control of their regular keeper.

1.54 A serious problem in urban areas is caused by those who keep dogs[1] but do not ensure that they defecate in their own gardens, in the gutter or other appropriate places such as those areas set apart for canine relief in parks. In the authors' view if it can be shown that an animal is regularly defecating in inappropriate public places (such as footways, play grounds or sitting areas in parks) then it is being kept in such a manner as both to be prejudicial to health and a nuisance.

1   See *R v Walden-Jones, ex p Coton* [1963] Crim LR 839.

1.55 A fox, by contrast, whose hole was within a garden would not be regarded as being kept (unless tamed); its depredations on neighbourhood refuse sacks would not be caught by this category. It might well be, however, that as premises include land[1], the garden in which the fox hole had not been dug out would be caught by category (a).

1   EPA 1990, 79(7).

1.56 Peacocks, although visually beautiful, produce raucous noise. This may be away from the premises of their owner, so category (g) may not be appropriate. Bees may swarm away from their keeper's land. So in urban areas where such occurrences are probably unacceptable it is likely that Parliament intended the category to apply to animals even where the harm that they cause is occasioned while temporarily away from their keeper's immediate control.

1.57 The defence of best practicable means is available in respect of industrial, trade or business premises.[1]

1   EPA 1990, s 80(7), (8)(a).

(fa) any insects emanating from relevant industrial, trade or business premises and being prejudicial to health or a nuisance[1]

1.58 Infestations of insects may be caused not only by deposits of rotting organic matter which would be covered by category (e) but also by the operation of food processing plants and poultry houses. Exceptions include not only pasture land, woodland, and market gardens but also land (in this context probably excluding buildings thereon) if part of agricultural units[2] which have been exempted by the Secretary of State or Welsh Assembly[3]. Insects which may be protected or associated with sites protected under nature conservation legislation are usually excepted[4]. The category does not apply to rivers, watercourses, lakes or ponds or land flooded by them. It does apply to sewers and drains[5].

1   This category was added by the Clean Neighbourhoods and Environment Act 2005, s 101; see the DEFRA Guidance Note 'Statutory Nuisance from Insects and Artificial Light', reproduced in Appendix H. It does not yet apply to Scotland but the Public Health Etc (Scotland) Bill may introduce this category to Scotland.
2   Land occupied as a unit for purposes defined as agricultural under section 109 of the Agriculture Act 1947; EPA 1990 s 79(7D).
3   EPA 1990 s 79(7), (7C) and see for England the Statutory Nuisances (Insects) Regulations 2006 (SI 2006/770) (reproduced in Appendix B) which exempt various categories of agricultural units regarded as having particular environmental value.
4   EPA 1990 s 79(5A) (insects included in the Wildlife and Countryside Act 1981, Sch 5 unless included only under s 9(5) of that Act) and 79(7C)(e) (sites of special scientific interest).
5   EPA s 79(7C); 'Drain' is defined in the Water Resources Act 1991.

1.59 *Nature and scope of statutory nuisance*

1.59 It is arguable[1] that the specific provision now made under this category effectively excludes from category (e) deposits or accumulations causing, and from category (a) premises whose state causes, emanations of insects. If so the effect of the insertion of this new category would have been to restrict the availability of statutory nuisance remedies for insects. As the category only relates to insects which leave industrial, trade or business premises its existence cannot prevent the operation of categories (a) and (e) to protect the occupants of such premises which are infested by insects nor can it prevent the operation of such categories in respect of emanations of insects from other premises such as houses. The oddity of the scheme which would result from attributing to Parliament the intention to restrict the operation of categories (a) and (e) suggests that the amendment introducing the new category is not intended to impose such a restriction.

1   It is a general principle of statutory interpretation that if Parliament makes specific provisions subject to exceptions then more general provisions not subject to such provisions do not apply.

1.60   The defence of best practicable means is available.[1]

1   EPA 1990, s 80(7),(8)(a).

Light Pollution

(fb)   artificial light emitted from premises so as to be prejudicial to health or a nuisance[1]

1.61   Light pollution, whether obliterating views of the night sky, or irritating neighbours is an increasing, and increasingly recognised, problem. It seems unlikely, however, that society is yet ready to treat views of the Milky Way or moonlight views of St Paul's as worthy of protection by these means[2]. Security and other lights, such as coloured or flashing advertising lights, may nevertheless be extremely powerful and problematic at a local level and are no doubt the intended objects of this section. Sunlight reflected from photovoltaic cells, wind turbines and glasshouses is not covered as it is not artificial.

1   This category was added by the Clean Neighbourhoods and Environment Act 2005, s 102; see the DEFRA Guidance Note 'Statutory Nuisance from Insects and Artificial Light', reproduced in Appendix H. It does not yet apply to Scotland but the Public Health Etc (Scotland) Bill may introduce this category to Scotland.
2   It is worth noting, however, that illumination of the Taj Mahal does not take place at the time of the full moon. It may be that pressure to reduce energy wastage will alter attitudes to street lighting.

1.62   The exceptions[1] are extensive. They are[2]:

- airports
- harbour premises
- railway premises[3]
- tramway premises
- bus stations and associated facilities
- public service vehicle operating centres
- goods vehicle operating centres
- lighthouses
- prisons.[4]

1   EPA 1990, s 79(5B).
2   The definitions of the terms are set out in EPA 1990, s 79(7).
3   Unless they are (1) within (a) a museum or other place of cultural, scientific or historic interest or (b) a funfair or other premises used for entertainment, recreation or amusement (EPA 1990,

s 79(5B), (7A)) and (2) not associated with other railway premises (as defined in EPA 1990, s 79(7B)).
4   Including young offenders institutions EPA 1990, s 79(7).

1.63 The defence of 'best practicable means' applies to light from both[1] industrial, trade or business premises and from outdoor non domestic[2] sports facilities designated[3] by the Secretary of State or Welsh Assembly. Proceedings may not be initiated by local authorities without the consent of the Government in respect of premises subject to Integrated Pollution Control or Local Authority Air Pollution Control under Part 1 of EPA 1990 or the replacement regime of the Pollution Prevention and Control Act 1999[4], if proceedings might be taken under those Acts[5].

1   EPA 1990, ss 80(8)(aza), 82(10)(aza).
2   EPA 1990, ss 80(8C), 82(10A). Domestic premises are those used wholly or mainly as a private dwelling and include for these purposes land enjoyed with a private dwelling.
3   EPA 1990, ss 80(8B), 82(10A) designation may be by inclusion in a list prepared by a specified body (such as Sport England) and see the Statutory Nuisances (Artificial Lighting) (Designation of Relevant Sports) (England) Order 2006 (reproduced in Appendix B) for the wide range of activities so designated in England.
4   PPCA 1990, s 6 and Sch 2 para 6.
5   EPA 1990, s 79(10).

Noise from premises

(g)   noise emitted from premises so as to be prejudicial to health or a nuisance

1.64 Noise from premises was not a statutory nuisance in the 1875 or 1936 Public Health Acts. Today it is one of the most important categories. It includes vibration.[1] Premises means a separate unit of occupation; thus loud music emanating from a neighbouring flat or bar in the same building would be caught by the subsection. By contrast tenants could not use this subsection for noise from a malfunctioning water supply system within their own flat. It can be invoked in respect of noise originating in the open provided that it is possible to define distinct areas from which it is *emitted* and into which it penetrates.[2] Such noise might be from sound amplification systems used in public or private gardens. The courts have held that noise is emitted from premises even if it merely passes through them and is not produced therein.[3] The provisions of the Noise Act 1996 and sections 60 to 61 of the Control of Pollution Act 1974 should be noted in relation to night time noise from dwellings and licensed premises, and construction activities[4].

1   EPA 1990, s 79(7).
2   *Tower Hamlets London Borough Council v Manzoni and Walder* [1984] JPL 436 decided that noise from the street was not covered by Control of Pollution Act 1974, s 58. The term 'premises' is defined in EPA 1990, Pt III to include 'land'. There is thus no good reason why it should not apply to noise originating on a field used for noisy activities such as motorcross or commercial war games penetrating neighbouring houses, gardens or cloisters.
3   *Network Housing Association v Westminster City Council* [1995] Env LR 176.
4   See paras **9.101–9.108** and **9.109–9.123** respectively.

1.65 Duration is especially important here. For example, in *Coventry City Council v Harris*[1] the Crown Court allowed an appeal against an abatement notice upheld by the magistrates forbidding a brass player from practising in his semi-detached house; it substituted a limit of one hour a day. A single instance of intense prolonged noise may (unusually) suffice (for example, an all night rave).[2] The noise from the ordinary use of a dwelling-house cannot amount to a

1.65 *Nature and scope of statutory nuisance*

statutory nuisance even though inadequate sound insulation may create problems for neighbours.[3]

1   (1992) 4 Land Management and Env LR 168.
2   *East Nothamptonshire District Council v Fossett* [1994] Env LR 388.
3   *Baxter v London Borough of Camden* [2000] Env LR 112, HL.

1.66 Premises are defined in section 80(7) of the EPA 1990 to include vessels. The territorial sea is included within the area of local authorities.[1] Thus, music from a party boat moored at or plying down a river or offshore is caught.

1   EPA 1990, s 80(11).

1.67 The defence of best practicable means applies to industrial trade and business premises.[1] It is a defence to show that the noise was consistent with the requirements of consent or other notice issued under the Control of Pollution Act 1974.

1   EPA 1990, s 80(7), (8)(a).

Noise from vehicles or equipment in a street

(ga)   noise that is prejudicial to health or a nuisance and is emitted from or caused by a vehicle, machinery or equipment in a street or, in Scotland, road

1.68 This useful provision does not apply to traffic noise (the cumulative noise of vehicles moving or waiting to move along the highway), defence forces or political demonstrations.[1] It applies to individual vehicles. Examples that spring to mind, especially where operated during the night or at other antisocial times, include:

- refrigerated lorries waiting to deliver goods
- compressors used to dig up the street or pump water to flower pots
- vehicles using reversing bleepers
- street cleaning industrial vacuum cleaners
- car alarms
- hedge cutters
- grass strimmers
- generators used by film companies on location
- coaches, buses or other diesel vehicles parked with engines running.

1   EPA 1990, s 80(6A).

1.69 The defence of best practicable means applies to industrial, trade and business activities.[1] 'Statutory undertakers' who supply water, gas, and electricity have powers granted by Parliament to carry out certain works. They are not guilty of nuisance in exercising those powers provided that they cause no more collateral harm to the community than is reasonably necessary;[2] they sometimes think that this protection is greater than in fact it is. Clearly, however, the community must from time to time put up with emergency repairs during the quiet times of the night or weekend.

Special provisions as to service of notices apply.[3]

1   EPA 1990, s 80(7), (8)(aa).

The categories of statutory nuisance **1.73**

2   *Manchester City Council v Farnworth* [1930] AC 171, HL, see especially Viscount Dunedin at 183.
3   EPA 1990, s 80A.

Other matters declared by other Acts to be statutory nuisances

(h) any other matter declared by any enactment to be a statutory nuisance

1.70 Much of what was incorporated by this round up category in the 1936 legislation is now embodied in the earlier categories. The defence of best practicable means does not apply[1] to this category. The main examples are set out in the following paragraphs.

1   EPA 1990, s 80(7) and (8).

Domestic water supply[1]

1.71 This covers any well, tank, cistern or water-butt used for domestic water supply which is so placed, constructed or kept as to render the water liable to contamination or otherwise prejudicial to health. This is particularly important in blocks of flats where communal water storage tanks may be inaccessible and contamination (by animals or otherwise) may be easily overlooked. It does not apply to radioactive contamination.[2]

1   Public Health Act 1936, s 141.
2   Radioactive Substances Act 1993, s 40(1), (2), Sch 3.

Water courses, ditches and ponds[1]

1.72 This covers two types of problem. The first is where areas of water are, in themselves, *so foul or in such a state*[2] as to be prejudicial to health or a nuisance. Cattle slurry ponds or industrial waste ponds evidently have such potential. The second is where watercourses[3] are so *choked or silted up as to obstruct or impede the proper flow of water*[4] and thereby to cause a nuisance or give rise to conditions prejudicial to health. There is some authority for the proposition that the mere presence of a bridge which caused intermittent flooding at times of high river flow can constitute 'choking' of a watercourse[5].

1   Public Health Act 1936, s 259.
2   Public Health Act 1936, s 259(1)(a).
3   Excluding watercourses ordinarily navigated by vessels employed in the carriage of goods by water (Public Health Act 1936, s 259(1)(b)). The term has been held not to apply to wide expanses of water such as estuaries *R v Falmouth and Truro Port Health Authority, ex p South West Water Services* [2000] 3 All ER 306, [2000] 3 WLR 1464.
4   Public Health Act 1936, s 259(1)(b).
5   Per Hodge J in *R (Robinson) v Torridge DC* [2006] EWHC 877 (Admin) [2006] Env LR 40 at 1036. Oddly, in this judicial review application, all of his observations on the substantive dispute which led to the litigation were *obiter dicta* (judicial asides, not part of the decisive reasoning) as he considered that the question before him was hypothetical and therefore not suitable for a declaration; nevertheless he dealt at length with the substantive dispute and gave guidance because he thought it would be useful in ongoing magistrates court litigation.

1.73 The range of potential recipients of abatement notices and defendants to proceedings for the second type is subject to an important limitation. No liability may be imposed on someone who has not, by act or default, caused the

1.73 *Nature and scope of statutory nuisance*

nuisance to arise or allowed it to continue.[1] 'Default' has been held to require more than merely doing nothing unless there is a common law or statutory duty[2] to do something.[3]

1 Public Health Act 1936, s 259(1)(b).
2 Such as perhaps the duty which may arise under the Land Drainage Act 1991, s 28 when the Agricultural Land Tribunal orders ditches to be cleansed (provided that such a ditch can be regarded as a 'watercourse' for the purposes of the Public Health Act 1936, s 259 (1)(b).
3 *Neath RDC v Williams* [1951] 1 KB 115.

1.74 In general, a landowner or occupier has no duty to clear obstructions which occur naturally in a natural watercourse.[1] Thus, where a natural watercourse became silted up by natural causes and caused a nuisance by flooding the landowner was held not to be liable under this provision.[2] By contrast if a watercourse is created or substantially altered by humankind then the landowner or occupier is responsible for its design, construction and maintenance and may be in 'default' in respect of their inadequacies.[3]

1 Traditionally landowners are not liable for the consequences of what happens to their land if it is used naturally *Rylands v Fletcher* (1868) LR 3 HL 330. More recently however the courts seem to be prepared to hold that if a landowner has substantial means and a small expenditure of effort or resources can avert serious consequences then he is under a duty to avert those consequences *Goldman v Hargrave* [1967] 1 AC 645 and *Leakey v National Trust* [1978] QB 849.
2 *Neath RDC v Williams* [1951] 1 KB 115.
3 *Sedleigh-Denfield v O'Callaghan* [1940] AC 880 especially at 892. Lord Goddard CJ in *Neath* was careful to distinguish this situation: [1951] 1 KB 115 at 120, 121.

Tents, vans and sheds

1.75 Tents, vans and sheds, and similar structures used for human habitation, are statutory nuisances in two situations:

- if they are in such a state or so overcrowded as to be prejudicial to the health of the inmates[1]
- if their use causes, on or off the site, a nuisance or conditions prejudicial to health because of the absence of proper sanitary facilities or other reasons.[2]

1 Public Health Act 1936, s 268(2)(a).
2 Public Health Act 1936, s 268(2)(b).

1.76 Any person for the time being in charge of such habitation is an 'occupier'. An abatement notice may also be served on the occupier of the land on which the habitation is located. He has a defence that he did not authorise the location of the habitation.[1] A court dealing with statutory nuisances of this type has power to make an order prohibiting such human habitations at specified places or areas.[2]

1 Public Health Act 1936, s 268(3).
2 Public Health Act 1936, s 268(5)(a).

Quarries and disused mines

1.77 This applies to:

- quarries[1] (whether or not they are being worked) if–
  (i) they do not have an efficient and properly maintained barrier designed to prevent people from accidentally falling into them and

(ii) they are a danger to the public because of their proximity to the highway[2] or places of public resort[3]
- shafts or outlets of mines, either abandoned or disused for 12 months, which do not have efficiently maintained plugs or other devices for preventing people from accidentally entering them.[4]

1 Mines and Quarries Act 1954, s 151(2)(c).
2 A public right of way on foot, horseback or by bicycle is a highway.
3 Whether or not they have a right to resort to them *Kitson v Ashe* [1899] 1 QB 425. Thus, open land in mineral extraction areas to which the public go in large numbers despite the absence of rights so to do would be covered.
4 Mines and Quarries Act 1954, s 151(1), (2)(a)(b). The provision only applies to mines for minerals other than coal, stratified ironstone, shale or fireclay, which were abandoned after 9 August 1872 if they are a danger to the public because of their accessibility from a highway or place of public resort (s 151(2)(b)). See previous notes about 'highway' and 'public resort'.

SOME GENERAL POINTS

1.78 *Definitions*: terms used in section 79 of the EPA 1990[1] have the same meaning as in the Clean Air Act 1993. The definition section of the 1993 Act is reproduced in the Appendices.

1 EPA 1990, s 79(7).

Premises

1.79 Premises is defined in Section of the EPA 1990, s 79(7) to include land and any vessel. Houseboats or rubbish barges may thus be covered. The territorial sea is included within the area of local authorities.[1] The Interpretation Act 1978 Schedule 1 defines the word 'land' if used in legislation, unless the context otherwise requires, as including land covered with water. It is important to bear in mind the contaminated land exception to the statutory nuisance regime created by section 79(1A) of the EPA 1990 but which only came into force in April 2000. Premises can be the whole of a building or the parts of it if there are separate units of occupation.[2]

1 EPA 1990, s 80(11).
2 See *Birmingham District Council v McMahon* (1987) 19 HLR 452.

Meaning of 'industrial, trade or business premises'

1.80 The meaning of industrial, trade or business premises is important both because some categories of statutory nuisance only arise in respect of such premises (for example (d) effluvia) and because the defence of 'best practicable means'[1] often applies to such premises.

Such premises mean those used for, or where matter is burnt in connection with, any such purpose.[2] *Industrial* uses are not confined to manufacturing but extend to treatment or processes.[3] *Trade* has a wide meaning:

'A trade is an organised seeking after profits as a rule with the aid of physical assets'.[4]

'No doubt in many contexts the word "trade" indicates a process of buying and selling but that is by no means an exhaustive definition of its meaning. It may also mean a calling or industry or class of skilled labour'.[5]

1.80 *Nature and scope of statutory nuisance*

A demolition site without productive activity has been held to fall within the definition of 'industrial or trade premises' for the Clean Air Act 1968.[6]

1 Discussed at paras **1.83–1.94**.
2 EPA 1990, s 79(7).
3 EPA 1990, s 79(9).
4 *Aviation and Shipping Co Ltd v Murray* [1961] 1 WLR 974.
5 *Skinner v Jack Breach Ltd* [1927] 2 KB 220.
6 *Sheffield City Council v ADH Demolition Ltd* (1983) 82 LGR 177.

1.81 *Business* has a wider definition.[1] It includes the work of the brain. It can apply to professional activities.[2] It covers:

> 'almost anything which is an occupation, as distinguished from a pleasure–anything which is an occupation or duty which requires attention is a business'.[3]

Agriculture, horticulture and forestry seem to be included. In the authors' view the term is wide enough in this context to apply to public services provided on an organised basis by public authorities. Thus a hospital or non-privatised statutory undertaker would be within it. Residential premises used for small scale ancillary business or professional activities would not, in the authors' view, be within the category.

1 *Re A Debtor, ex p Debtor (No 490 of 1935)* [1936] Ch 237.
2 *Re Wilkinson* [1922] 1 KB 584 at 587.
3 *Rolls v Miller* (1884) 27 Ch D 71 at 88.

1.82 It is not clear that within the context of legislation with this purpose that a single, isolated instance of an activity would be excluded as it would be in other contexts.[1] It is not clear, for example, that a single event should be *necessarily* excluded from the control of category (d) because the land is not otherwise used for industrial trade or business purposes. On the other hand, there is perhaps good reason for thinking that Parliament did not intend that a single, isolated event should have the benefit of the defence of 'best practicable means'. That defence is intended to protect livelihoods from summary justice. Such an intention can hardly be held about a one-off, one night rave held in a disused[2] warehouse by an anarchist group.

1 *Re Griffin, ex p Board of Trade* (1890) 60 LJ QB 235 at 237 is not necessarily a good guide in this context.
2 Such premises would not otherwise fall within the definition. The past use clearly would. The premises would not otherwise actually *be* used for industrial, trade or business purposes which is the definition in EPA 1990, s 79(9) of industrial, trade or business premises.

The defence of 'best practicable means'

1.83 The defence of 'best practicable means' (which must be established by the person relying on it) is often available as a defence against a local authority abatement notice[1] or a citizen's action.[2] The local authority and magistrates provide speedy, cheap accessible remedies. Parliament considered it wrong to apply them where the fuller, slower more expensive conventional court procedures ought to be available to protect important interests and activities such as those of industry, trade and business. They affect people's livelihoods and the provision of material necessities to society. The defence is not available to common law actions in civil courts for nuisance or applications by local authorities to the High Court[3] for injunctions in respect of statutory nuisance under section 81(5) of the EPA 1990. Injunctions are only issued as a matter of

Some general points **1.91**

discretion. The court can however take into account the extent to which best practicable means have been achieved.

1 EPA 1990, s 80(7), (8).
2 EPA 1990, s 87(9), (10).
3 This is discussed in Chapter 4, para **4.68** n 1.

1.84 The decision on whether best practicable means have been adopted will often depend on the definition of the activity. Thus a discotheque must have loud amplified music; best practicable means must relate to that. A restaurant need not have any music at all; thus best practicable means might be the avoidance of amplified music. Not surprisingly the Divisional Court have held that the test is applied to the location at which the activity is located; satisfaction of the duty cannot require relocation to other premises.[1]

1 This principle was held in relation to the aptly named 'Howling Dog Kennels' *Manley and Manley v New Forest District Council* [2000] EHLR 113.

1.85 The term is to be interpreted by the courts in accordance with the provisions of section 79(9) of the EPA 1990.[1] These are:

1 The similarity between this statutory definition and the judicially evolved doctrine of reasonable necessity as a defence for statutory undertakers to common law nuisance is noteworthy (see Viscount Dunedin in *Manchester City Council v Farnworth* [1930] AC 171 at 183). This is discussed later in Chapter 3 at paras **3.59–3.62**.

1.86 *(a) 'practicable' means reasonably practicable having regard among other things to local conditions and circumstances, to the current state of technical knowledge and to the financial implications*

1.87 Much is left to the judgment of the court. The adjective 'reasonably' gives much discretion to the court deciding what is practicable. The phrase 'among other things' indicates that the list of factors that follows is not exhaustive. Other related considerations may also be material. The listed considerations themselves give much discretion to the court. The cost of a means of avoiding the harm is relevant though not decisive. The standard of harm prevention may vary from place to place; thus a poor, run-down area with a workforce of low skills and enterprises with little capital might be allowed not to install expensive, difficult to operate harm reduction measures which would be required elsewhere.

1.88 *(b) the means to be employed include the design, installation, maintenance and manner and periods of operation of plant and machinery and the design construction and maintenance of buildings and structures'*

1.89 Thus, the phrase has a much wider meaning than the ordinary use of language would suggest. It applies to the type of buildings and equipment, how they have been maintained, how and when they are used. It is not enough to say: 'This is the latest, quietest refrigeration unit.' It is necessary to show that it is being looked after properly and being used for no longer than necessary.

1.90 *(c) the test is to apply only in so far as compatible with any duty imposed by law*

1.91 No one may assert that the best practicable means test effectively permits or requires the non-performance of a legal duty. Thus, if the law requires audible reversing alarm for certain vehicle manoeuvres it is not open to

1.91 *Nature and scope of statutory nuisance*

a complainant to suggest that the alarm should be silenced; it would however be open to her to suggest that reversing manoeuvres should only take place outside the hours of quietness. (See also the comments on (d) at paras **1.92–1.94**).

1.92 *(d) the test is to apply only so far as compatible with safety and safe working conditions, and with the exigencies of any emergency or unforeseeable circumstances*

1.93 Naturally the avoidance of prejudice to health or nuisance should not lead to risk to the physical safety of workers or others or failure to respond to emergencies and other dangers.

1.94 The somewhat infelicitous drafting of (c) and (d) does give rise to a difficulty of interpretation. Sections 80(7) and 87(9) of the EPA 1990 impose on a defendant the burden of proving that the best practicable means have been adopted. It might be thought, therefore, that insofar as the test does not apply that is a problem only for defendants. Our view is, however, that the intention of Parliament is clearly that a defendant should not lose the benefit of the defence merely because of non-compliance with what would otherwise be best practice during an emergency. Nor can he be required to endanger employees or others to avoid a nuisance. It may well be, however, that he must adopt other means, such as different hours of working, to avoid both the risk to safety and the prejudice to health or nuisance.

THE CONTAMINATED LAND EXCEPTION

1.95 The Environment Act 1995 introduced Part IIA into the EPA 1990 establishing a new regime to deal with contaminated land. The government, therefore, decided that the statutory nuisance regime of Part III should cease to be available for that which would be covered by the new special regime. There remains much uncertainty about the scope of this exception even though the contaminated land regime came into force in April 2000.

1.96 Section 79(1A) provides that:

> No matter shall constitute a statutory nuisance *to the extent that* it consists of, or is caused by, any land being in a contaminated state [our emphasis].

This exception applies if, and only if land is in such a condition by reason of *substances in, on or under it* that the land causes:[1]

- *either* the possibility of *harm to the health of living organisms, or other interference with the ecological systems of which they form part, and in the case of man includes harm to his property*[2]
- *or* the likelihood of *the entry into controlled waters of any poisonous noxious or polluting matter or any solid waste matter.*[3]

If either of the above conditions is satisfied the land is said to be in a *contaminated state.*[4]

1 EPA 1990, s 79(1B) (our emphasis).
2 EPA 1990, ss 79(1B) and 78A(4). It is then said to be in a *contaminated state* for the purposes of the exception.
3 EPA 1990, ss 79(1B) and 78A(9). It is then said to be in a *contaminated state* for the purposes of the exception.
4 EPA 1990, s 79(1B).

The contaminated land exception **1.100**

1.97 *Substances* are defined in section 78A(9) of the EPA 1990 to mean 'any natural or artificial substance, whether in solid or liquid form, or in the form of a gas or vapour'.

1.98 Part III of the EPA 1990, as already noted, in general excludes from statutory nuisance control those activities that are controlled by other regimes. Many activities are controlled under Part 1 of the Act. Part I has a wide definition of harm to the environment; it includes offence caused to any of man's '*senses*'.[1] Part IIA of the Act has a narrower definition of harm which *excludes* offences to the senses.[2] The scheme of the Act is thus to leave within Part III statutory nuisance control that which offends the senses but to exclude from its control risk from land contaminated by substances dangerous to ecosystems, the health of living creature and man's property. The latter should in the future be controlled, if at all, only by the contaminated land regime of Part IIA of the Act.

1   EPA 1990, s 1(4).
2   EPA 1990, s 78A(4).

1.99 The exception is potentially extremely wide. Its scope has not yet been clarified by the courts. It would be easy for a superficial examination of the language without an appreciation of the scheme of the legislation to lead to a much greater width than was intended.

The following observations are therefore suggested as a guide.

- The exception does not apply where offence to the senses is caused or amenity is harmed without harm to health, ecosystems or man's property. Thus a pile of smelly but otherwise harmless material would not be caught by the exception. A mound of odourless but lethal heavy metal waste would be caught.
- The exception applies only if the *state/condition* of the land is such that it causes Part IIA harm.[1] It does not apply if the *use* of the land causes such harm. Thus, if a garden is impregnated with heavy metals contaminating a stream the exception is likely to apply. If, however, someone carries out home soldering and thereby emits toxic fumes into the neighbourhood without spilling any thing onto the ground the exception would not apply.
- The exception only applies where 'substances' cause harm. That term's meaning must be determined in the context of contaminated land. It seems to refer to that which *by its nature* has properties which cause the risks against which Part IIA provides protection.
- The wording both of section 79(1A) and 79(1B), emphasised above, indicate that Parliament intended a narrow construction of the exception. The exception is applied only '*to the extent that* a matter consists of or is caused by any land being in a contaminated state.' In the authors' view this wording is intended to leave subject to the Part III statutory nuisance control matters which are offensive to man's senses or harmful to amenity *even if they are also harmful to ecosystems, health or property.*

1   EPA 1990, Pt IIA harm is harm of the type defined in s 79(1B).

1.100 A substance may have properties which are harmful in the latter respect and also have properties which are offensive to the senses. Land is,

1.100 *Nature and scope of statutory nuisance*

however, contaminated only to the extent that it is in a condition which causes harm or possibility of harm to ecosystems, health or property. The properties which cause offence to the senses and damage to amenity do not constitute such a condition. In respect of those properties a state of contamination does not exist. The exception only applies therefore to the extent that the substances in, on or under land cause harm, or a risk of harm to ecosystems, health or property. Only to that extent does a state of contamination exist. To the extent that the substances cause offence to the senses the exception does not apply.

1.101 There is precedent for the principle that one physical process or situation can have juridically a dual nature in the context of land use regimes. The Court of Appeal accepted in *West Bowers Farm Products v Essex County Council*[1] that a single process can have a dual nature for the development control purposes of the Town and Country Planning Acts. Thus the operation of removing earth and minerals to form a reservoir on a farm both constituted agricultural operations which were permitted by the then General Development Order and a change of use which required planning permission.

1   (1985) 50 P & CR 368, [1985] JPL 857.

1.102 The other construction that a piece of land can only be controlled either by Part IIA or Part III of the EPA 1990 but not by both has the obvious superficial attraction of simplicity. It is, however, not merely inconsistent with the wording but leads to the following absurdity. A substance might cause slight harm to property of a type which would not warrant action under Part IIA. It might also cause gross offence to the sense of smell. Unless the exception subsection is interpreted in the way suggested no action could be taken under Part III; however, no action could rationally or lawfully[1] be taken under Part IIA. Offence to the senses does not constitute harm for the purposes of Part IIA.[2] Such a result, if it involved serious harm to someone's home, would hardly be consistent with the European Convention on Human Rights (ECHR).[3] The European Court of Human Rights (ECtHR) have held in *Lopez Ostra v Spain*[4] that:

> 'severe environmental pollution may affect individuals' well being and prevent them from enjoying their homes in such a way as to affect their private and family life adversely without seriously endangering their health.'

1   The circumstances where action can be taken under EPA 1990, Pt IIA are, to some extent, more limited, both as a matter of law and as a result of legally binding government guidance, than those where the exception to the statutory nuisance regime applies. The definition of land in a 'contaminated state' for the purposes of the exception to Pt III (statutory nuisance) is wider than the definition (s 78A(2)) of 'contaminated land' for the purposes of Pt IIA (contaminated land regime). The exception applies whenever there is *possibility of harm* or *likelihood of pollution*. However, it is only if (s 78A(2)) the regulatory authority thinks that there is a *significant* risk of *significant* harm that land is 'contaminated land' for Pt IIA purposes. Only then does the Pt IIA regime bite. Decisions as to the existence of *significant* risk of *significant* harm *must* be made in accordance with Government guidance (s 78A(5)). That guidance could not, as a matter of law, treat something which was merely offensive to the senses as being harmful within the meaning of that term in Pt IIA (s 78A(4)). (In fact government guidance issued in April 2000 (Annex 3, Pt 3, para 23) has adopted a very narrow test for *significant* harm. Thus for Pt IIA purposes human skin ailments are not covered unless they are extensive. Harm to ecological systems is not covered unless they are found within internationally or nationally important sites. Harm to property in the form of buildings is not covered by Pt IIA unless structural failure is caused or substantial damage, such as to make it uninhabitable, occurs.)

The contaminated land exception **1.104**

2   EPA 1990, s 78A(4) (in marked contrast to the definition of harm for Pt 1 which expressly includes offence to any of man's senses (EPA 1990, s 1(4)).
3   Courts in England and Wales have always sought to construe legislation so as to be consistent with the Convention (see Lord Diplock's opinion in *R v Home Secretary, ex p Brind* [1991] 1 AC 696). Section 3 of the Human Rights Act 1998 now imposes a strong obligation on the Courts to construe domestic legislation, whenever passed, in a way which is compatible with the codified Convention rights. The correct approach is that so far as is possible, the relevant statute should be construed as compatible, even if that reading may not be the most obvious way to read the relevant section and words have to be implied into the statute see *R v Lambert* [2001] UKHL 37 [2002] 2 AC 545, at 42, 78 and 79 and *R v A* (No 2) [2001] UKHL 25 [2002] 1 AC 45, Lord Steyn at 44
4   (1994) 20 EHRR 277 where the ECHR held that states must protect people's homes from smells even if they did not cause disease.

1.103 The wide construction of the scope of the contaminated land exception would leave a substantial gap between the area controlled by the statutory nuisance regime and that controlled by the contaminated land regime. This was not the intention of the legislation according to the government ministers' statements to Parliament. Their explanation of how it was intended to work is an important guide to how the Act should be interpreted.[1] Viscount Ullswater said:

> '... we do not believe that land should be considered contaminated on the basis of smells and odours which are not themselves harmful to health or the wider environment. The statutory nuisance powers will still potentially be available to deal *as necessary* with those other problems[2] ... we have revised the formulation in order to ensure that *so far as possible* there is neither an overlap between the two regimes *nor a lacuna*[3] *between them*'[4] [our emphasis].

1   *Pepper v Hart* [1993] AC 593, HL.
2   260 HL Official Report (5th Series) col 1440, 31 January 1995.
3   Latin for gap.
4   565 HL Official Report (5th series) col 1493, 11 July 1995.

1.104 The wide construction of the exception would make the statutory nuisance regime unavailable in some circumstances where it was necessary to deal with smells. It would create a lacuna where a narrower construction of the exception would have made it possible to avoid that lacuna. The narrower construction of the scope of the exception is therefore, despite its difficulties, to be preferred.

Chapter 2

Duties and Powers of Local Authorities

INTRODUCTION

2.01 The Environmental Protection Act 1990 (EPA 1990) entrusts local authorities with primary, but not exclusive, responsibility for the operation of the statutory nuisance regime.[1] It requires local authorities to carry out certain duties, for example to survey their area and investigate an individual complaint. It also gives them powers. With the coming into force of the Human Rights Act 1998 (HRA 1998) on 2 October 2000, local authorities are also obliged to ensure that they exercise those powers and duties in a manner which is consistent with rights given by the European Convention on Human Rights (ECHR).

1 The ability to enforce the statutory nuisance regime is not restricted to local authorities only. Private citizens may bring proceedings under EPA 1990, s 82 in respect of statutory nuisance (see Chapter 6). They may also take private criminal proceedings for a breach of an abatement notice issued by a local authority under s 80(4) although it is more usual for the local authority to do so. A port authority has statutory nuisance powers and duties in respect of statutory nuisance by virtue of EPA 1990, s 79(8) (see for example *R v Falmouth and Truro Port Health Authority, ex p South West Water Services* [2000] 3 All ER 306, [2000] 3 WLR 1464, CA). It is also necessary for a local authority to obtain the consent of the Secretary of State before instituting summary proceedings in respect of certain proceedings which may also be covered by Pt 1 of EPA 1990; see EPA 1990, s 79(10).

2.02 The detailed points we make elsewhere in the book on the possible impact of HRA 1998 upon the law and practice of statutory nuisance require some general knowledge of the 1998 Act. We recognise that the HRA 1998 may remain unfamiliar to some readers, particularly to those who are not lawyers. Accordingly, we have included an introduction to the general principles and operation of the HRA 1998 along with a description of those Convention rights most likely to affect the law of statutory nuisance.

THE HRA 1998

Obligations imposed by the HRA 1998 on 'a public authority'

2.03 Section 6(1) of the HRA 1998 makes it unlawful for public authorities to act or to fail to act in a way that would be incompatible with a Convention right. 'Public authority' is widely defined and includes[1] any body the functions of which include functions of a public nature. There can be no doubt that a local authority charged with the exercise of powers and duties in respect of statutory nuisance is a 'public authority' for the purposes of the HRA 1998.[2] Section 7 of the HRA 1998 provides that:

(1) A person who claims that a public authority has acted (or proposes to act) in a way which is made unlawful by section 6(1) may

2.03 *Duties and powers of local authorities*

(a) bring proceedings against the authority under this Act in the appropriate court or tribunal; or
(b) rely on the Convention rights or rights concerned in any legal proceedings,

but only if he is (or would be) a victim of the unlawful act.

1   With the exception of Parliament itself.
2   The government expressly included local government as an example of the type of person or organisations whose acts or omissions might be challenged under HRA 1998, s 3 in the White Paper: *Rights Brought Home: the Human Rights Bill* (Cm 3782), para 2.2.

2.04 By sections 6 and 7 the HRA 1998 provides, that in addition to the ability to rely upon Convention rights in any legal proceedings, a specific right of action against a public authority for acting in breach of Convention rights or failing to act in accordance with them. There is a general time limit of one year. Any shorter time limit imposed by the rules of court continues to apply.[1] Remedies can include damages or other relief that is 'just and appropriate.' Significantly, reliance can be placed on Convention rights, whether the act in question took place before or after the commencement of the HRA 1998 if proceedings are brought *by or at the instigation* of a public authority.[2] Where proceedings relate to an act occurring before 2 October 2000, a person is not entitled to rely upon a Convention right under the HRA 1998 if he is *bringing* the proceedings. In other words, in respect of acts occurring before the coming into force of the HRA 1998 a person may use the 1998 Act as a shield but not a sword.

1   So, for example, the three month rule for judicial review is not affected, see further the Hon Sir Stephen Richards 'The Impact of Article 6 of the ECHR on Judicial Review' [1999] JR 106.
2   HRA 1998, s 22(4).

Duty to interpret legislation in accordance with the HRA 1998

2.05 By section 3(1) legislation of any kind, whether passed before or after the coming into force of the HRA 1998 and including delegated legislation must 'so far as it is possible to do so' be construed and given effect in a way which is compatible with Convention rights.[1] This means that the provisions of the EPA 1990 and the regulations made thereunder (such as the Statutory Nuisances (Appeals) Regulations 1995[2]) must be construed in accordance with the HRA 1998 'so far as possible.' The courts of England and Wales are not *bound* to follow the decisions of the European Court of Human Rights (ECtHR). Section 2 of the HRA 1998 requires courts and tribunals, when construing Convention rights, to take account of decisions of the ECtHR and to have regard to the opinions of the Commission.

1   In practice the approach is similar to that required in EC law pursuant to article 10 of the EC Treaty. (See *Marleasing SA v La Comercial Internacional de Alimentacifon* [1990] ECR 1-4135). The process of 'convergent construction', sometimes inaccurately known as 'indirect effect', is helpfully explained by Sedley LJ in *R v Durham County Council, ex p Huddleston* [2000] 1 WLR 1484, [2000] 1 PLR 122, CA. For a lucid examination of the recent case law concerning s 3 HRA 1998 see Jan van Zyl Smit *The New Purposive Interpretation of Statutes: HRA Section 3 after* Ghaidan v Godin-Mendoza (2007) 70(2) MLR 294-317.
2   SI 1995/2644. Reproduced in full at Appendix B.

Victim

2.06 Reliance can be placed upon Convention rights where the person is a 'victim' of the challenged action or failure to act.[1] A victim is a person who is 'actually and directly affected by the act or omission, the subject of the complaint,' albeit that immediate threat or risk may suffice. In the context of statutory nuisance, a person who is served with an abatement notice would be capable of being a 'victim' as would a third party who could show that there was some evidence that the statutory nuisance had a material effect on their lives or health or their property.[2] Non-human companies may also have Convention rights.[3]

1 HRA 1998, s 7(1) and (7) limits recourse to those who would be victims within article 34 of the ECHR. Article 34 provides 'The Court may receive applications from any person, non-governmental organisation or group of individuals claiming to be victims of a violation.'
2 *Tauiria v France* (1995) 83 A 113 (a decision of the now defunct European Commission on Human Rights).
3 *Dombo Beheer BV v Netherlands* (1993) 18 EHRR 213.

Convention rights

2.07 The following Convention rights are those which are likely to be most relevant to statutory nuisance:[1]

- Article 6: The right to a fair hearing by an independent tribunal.
- Article 8: The right to respect for home (private and family life).
- Article 2: the right to life.[2]
- First Protocol, Article 1: the right to protection of property.

1 See Appendix F for the full text of these provisions.
2 In *Guerra v Italy* (1998) 26 EHRR 357 a claim was made concerning liability for illegal toxic emissions from a factory which resulted in 150 people being admitted to hospital with acute arsenic poisoning. Since some of the workers had died from cancer, the applicants argued that the state's failure to provide information about the risks was a violation of article 2. The ECtHR found it unnecessary to consider the case under article 2 since it had found that the absence of information about living near the factory breached the applicant's rights to respect for their private and family life under article 8 of the Convention.

The principles of deference and proportionality

2.08 Before the ECtHR itself, contracting states are entitled to rely in some instances on the so-called doctrine of the 'margin of appreciation' which allows the contracting state some latitude in taking measures necessary in a democratic society for the well-ordering of the state. It has been said that the margin of appreciation does not apply when the English and Welsh courts consider the HRA 1998.[1] However, in practice an analogous doctrine of deference will apply. As Lord Hope stated in *R v DPP, ex p Kebelene*:[2]

> 'In this area difficult choices may have to be made by the executive or the legislature between the rights of the individual and the needs of society. In some circumstances it will be appropriate for the courts to recognise that there is an area of judgment within which the judiciary will defer, on democratic grounds, to the considered opinion of the elected body or person whose act or decision is said to be incompatible with the Convention. This point is well made at p 74, para 3.21 of *Human Rights Law and Practice* (Butterworths, 1999), of which Lord Lester of Herne Hill QC and Mr David Pannick QC are the General Editors, where the area in which these choices

may arise is conveniently and appropriately described as the "discretionary area of judgment".[1]

This principle of deference is relevant when considering aspects of the statutory nuisance regime whose purpose is to protect the health and amenity of the public.[3]

1 See for example, the Rt. Hon Sir John Laws 'The Limitations of Human Rights' (1998) 63 PL 254 at 258.
2 [1999] 3 WLR 972.
3 See, for example, the emphasis given by the Court of Appeal in *R v Falmouth and Truro Port Health Authority, ex p South West Water Services* [2000] 3 All ER 306, [2000] 3 WLR 1464 to the purpose of EPA 1990 in prohibiting nuisances prejudicial to health.

2.09 The court will be expected to apply the principle of proportionality in assessing whether the measures employed by the state are justified. In *Sporrong and Lünnroth v Sweden*[1] the ECtHR described the principle in respect of the ECHR in these terms:

'... the Court must determine whether a fair balance has been struck between the demands of the general interests of the community and the requirements of the protection of the individual's fundamental rights.'[2]

1 (1982) 5 EHRR 35.
2 In *B v Secretary of State for the Home Department* [2000] 2 CMLR 1086 Sedley LJ described the principle as follows: '... in essence it amounts to this: a measure that interferes with a [European] Community or human right must not only be authorised but must correspond to the pressing social need and go no further than is strictly necessary in a pluralistic society to achieve its permitted purpose; or more shortly, must be appropriate and necessary to its legitimate aim.'

2.10 The impact of the proportionality in the context of Convention rights is likely to be particularly relevant to two aspects of statutory nuisance. Firstly, it is already in essence to be found in the ground of appeal against an abatement notice that the 'authority has refused unreasonably to accept compliance with alternative requirements, or, the requirements of the abatement notice are otherwise unreasonable in character or extent, or are unnecessary' (see reg 2(2)(c) of the Statutory Nuisances (Appeals) Regulations 1995[1]). Second, the principle of proportionality will be relevant to the exercise of the court's discretion whether to grant an injunctive remedy pursuant to section 81(5) of the EPA 1990 in respect of a statutory nuisance. Some guidance in this respect can be gleaned from *South Buckinghamshire v Porter* [2003] UKHL 26, [2003] 2 WLR 1547 in which the House of Lords considered the correct approach to the exercise of the court's discretion to grant an injunction under section 187B of the Town and Country Planning Act 1990 (as amended) (TCPA 1990) to restrain a breach of planning control where the defendant's Convention rights were engaged, in that case the right to respect for home and family life under article 8 of ECHR for gypsies who had stationed their caravans on sites in breach of planning control. Lord Bingham stated at paragraph 37:

'As a public authority, the English court is prohibited by section 6(1) and (3)(a) of the Human Rights Act 1998 from acting incompatibly with any Convention right as defined in the Act, including Article 8. It follows, in my opinion, that when asked to grant injunctive relief under section 187B the court must consider whether, on the facts of the case, such relief is proportionate in the Convention sense, and grant relief only if it judges it to be so.'

The duty to inspect the area **2.12**

This passage applies equally to a court considering an application for an injunction to restrain a statutory nuisance that would interfere with rights protected under the ECHR. In practice, however, the nature of the rights and the balancing exercise is likely to be different in the case of an injunction to restrain a statutory nuisance than for an injunction removing gypsies from a site and possibly, in the process, making them homeless. Indeed, a person creating a nuisance is himself quite likely to be adversely affecting the Convention rights of local residents disturbed by the nuisance. A useful analogy is to be found in *Aylesbury Vale District Council v Florent* [2007] EWHC 724, QB, [2008] JPL 70 in which the court in considering whether to grant an injunction under section 187B of the TCPA 1990 had to balance the rights under article 1 to the first protocol to the ECHR of the owners of a clay pigeon shoot against the article 8 rights of local residents disturbed by the noise levels occurring in breach of planning conditions imposed upon the clay pigeon shoot.

1   SI 1995/2644. Reproduced in full at Appendix B.

THE NEED TO ENSURE PROPER DELEGATION OF POWERS

2.11 It is important for local authorities to ensure that a proper system of delegation is in place if decisions are to be made by officers. Decisions made by officers that have not been given the requisite delegated powers are liable to be quashed – see, for example, *R v St Edmundsbury Borough Council, ex p Walton*.[1] As a matter of good practice, we recommend that there should be an annual review by the local authority of its schemes of delegation in order to ensure that:

- the scheme is up to date to take into account any statutory amendments or case law; and
- the scheme remains one that is authorised by the relevant committee of the council. It is not unknown for schemes of delegation to be passed for the duration only of a year.

1   [1999] Env LR 879. This decision has been cited with approval and applied in the Irish High Court: *O'Nuallain v Dublin Corpn* [1999] 4 IR 137 per Smyth J at 149. For general guidance on the court's approach to delegation of powers in respect of enforcement decisions, see also *Cheshire County Council v Secretary of State for the Environment* [1988] JPL 30 and for a consideration of possible conflicting authorities on whether a delegated officer can discharge his duties through junior officers not named in the particular scheme of delegation, see *R (Terrafirma) v Manchester City Council* [2002] EWHC 702 (Admin). For a decision which addresses the level of evidence that a local authority must produce in order to demonstrate that the duly delegated officer had properly considered that criminal porceedings for breach of an abatement notice would be inadequate pursuant to EPA 1990, s 81(5), see *East Dorset v Eaglebeam Ltd* [2006] EWHC 2378, QB.

THE DUTY TO INSPECT THE AREA

2.12 Section 79(1) of the EPA 1990 requires a local authority to:

'... cause its area to be inspected from time to time to detect any statutory nuisances which ought to be dealt with under section 80.'

The use of the words 'from time to time' introduces a degree of uncertainty.[1] There is no fixed period to indicate when a local authority should conduct its inspection. Total inaction over a sufficiently long period of time would probably

2.12 *Duties and powers of local authorities*

be regarded as in breach of this duty.[2] A one-off inspection is unlikely to be sufficient.[3] The duty requires that the whole of the authority's area must be inspected at some time and inspected again as necessary.

1   The phrase 'from time to time' also appears in other statutory schemes: see the duty imposed upon local planning authorities to determine 'from time to time' what parts of their area are to be designated as a conservation area (Planning (Listed Buildings and Conservation Areas) Act 1990 (P(LBCA)A 1990), s 69) and the duty on local planning authorities 'from time to time' to formulate and publish proposals for the preservation and enhancement of any conservation areas (P(LBCA)A 1990, s 71).
2   *Meade v London Borough of Haringey* [1979] 1 WLR 637.
3   Interpretation Act 1978, s 12.

2.13 The appropriate course of action is for the local authority to have a programme of inspection covering the entire authority area. Simply reacting to complaints made by members of the public would not, in our view, comply with the statutory duty. After all, there is already a separate express duty under section 79 (1) of the EPA 1990 for a local authority to investigate complaints made by persons living in its area.[1] The wording of the section expressly provides for local authority inspections in addition to the investigation of complaints. Many local authority representatives (not just environmental health officers) will have an opportunity to observe that which may or may not become a statutory nuisance in their day-to-day work. It is important that local authorities put in place a system to record and ensure that their officers' observations are used efficiently. It is sensible for local authorities to monitor the efficiency of the programme particularly by examining the extent to which nuisances are being investigated only where complaints are made. This duty must also now be viewed in the context of the local authority's obligations under article 8 of the ECHR. For example, in *Lopez Ostra v Spain*,[2] the ECtHR found that the applicants' homes had not been respected where a waste treatment plant had been built close to her homes in a town with a heavy concentration of leather manufacturing. The treatment plant operated without a licence releasing fumes and vapours that caused health problems to residents. The state had failed in its duty of respect for the applicants' private and family life by failing to exercise the powers it had to prevent the nuisance and by failing to take the measures necessary to protect the applicants' homes. A failure by a local authority to maintain a proper system of inspection of its area for statutory nuisances (and a failure to investigate complaints, as to which see below) may therefore result in a breach of article 8. It is worth noting that in *Lopez Ostra v Spain*, the ECtHR expressly held that an infringement of article 8 could occur even in the absence of evidence of damage to health.

1   Paragraph 15 of the National Assembly of Wales Circular NAfW 18/2007 *Night Noise from Licensed Premises and Dwellings Guidance on the Noise Act 1996 as amended by the Antisocial Behaviour Act 2003 and the Clean Neighbourhoods and Environment Act 2005* acknowledges that the duty under EPA 1990, s 79 to inspect is an 'additional' duty to the duty to investigate complaints.
2   (1994) 20 EHRR 277. See also *Guerra v Italy* (1998) 26 EHRR 357 concerning the failure of the state to protect the home environment from pollution.

Remedies for non-compliance with the local authority's duty to inspect its area

2.14 Some commentators[1] have suggested that the only remedy for failure to discharge the duty of inspection is that provided for in the EPA 1990, namely for the Secretary of State to make an order compelling the authority to do so under paragraph 4 of Schedule 3 to the Act, and if the authority still fails to do so, either seeking a court order to compel it, or taking over the function himself. This view is based on the principle 'that where a remedy is given by a statute, it thereby deprives the person who insists upon a remedy of any other form'[2] in particular, an action by way of judicial review.[3]

1 See for example *Encyclopaedia of Environmental Health Law and Practice*, p 2913/164.
2 *Pasmore v Oswaldtwistle UDC* [1898] AC 387 at 394 per Earl of Halsbury LC.
3 A statutory right of appeal will not necessarily prevent an aggrieved person proceeding by way of judicial review. It is a factor to be taken into account by the court when considering whether to exercise its discretionary supervision by way of judicial review. In *R v London Borough of Hillingdon, ex p Royco Homes Ltd* [1974] QB 720, it was held that judicial review was available to quash a planning permission granted subject to conditions which were on their face clearly made without jurisdiction or in error of law, even though there is a statutory process to appeal against conditions attached to a planning permission. However, this was an exceptional case: where there is a right of appeal which the claimant has failed to pursue or where permission to appeal has been refused, judicial review will not normally be entertained (see *R (on the application of Sivasubramaniam) v Wandsworth County Court* [2002] EWCA Civ 1738).

2.15 In our view, it is unlikely that the remedy of reference to the Secretary of State is exclusionary (ie the only way of enforcing a breach of the duty). Where the Secretary of State has a *duty* to make an enforcement order in respect of some breach, an individual might have greater difficulty in seeking to enforce the same breach by means of judicial review.[1] Under the EPA 1990, the Secretary of State's power to force a local authority to act is discretionary. It is not so clear whether a discretionary power of the Secretary of State prevents challenges by means of judicial review.[2] In any event, in our view it is rather artificial to look upon a power or duty entrusted to the Secretary of State to take action as an alternative remedy for a person aggrieved by the failure of a local authority to take action to inspect its area for nuisances, since there is no express power to apply to the Secretary of State to take action.

1 Water Resources Act 1991, s 18 provides that if the Secretary of State is satisfied that a water company is failing any of its duties under that Act, he must issue an enforcement notice (subject to some exceptions in s 19). Some commentators think that as a result of the power given to the Secretary of State it would not be possible for an individual to challenge the water company's breach by judicial review. If, however, the Secretary of State unlawfully failed to act, then that failure could be challenged by way of judicial review (see by analogy *R v Carrick District Council, ex parte Shelley* [1996] Env LR 273).
2 For example, a person opposed to a grant of planning permission could seek to persuade the Secretary of State to call in the application for his own determination, as he has a power to do so provided by the Town and Country Planning Act 1990, s 77. However, it is well established that such a person can nevertheless challenge the grant of planning permission directly by means of judicial review. In the case of *R v Leicester City Council, ex p Safeway Stores plc* [1999] JPL 691, in the context of challenging an approval of reserved matters as part of a planning permission the applicant had sought to persuade the Secretary of State to call in the application on three occasions. Dyson J held that there might be circumstances in which attempts to persuade the Secretary of State to determine an application were a good reason for refraining from embarking on judicial review proceedings, but that that case was not one of them, particularly after two refusals stating that the Secretary of State only called in reserved matters applications in very exceptional circumstances. On the general approach to pursuit of alternative remedies as a reason for delaying in bringing proceedings for judicial review see *R (on the application of Cowl) v Plymouth City Council* [2001] EWCA Civ 1935, [2002] 1 WLR 803, where the Court of Appeal emphasised that litigation was a last resort, and proper attention had to be given to alternative dispute resolution, including any complaints mechanism.

2.16 An aggrieved person risks losing if he elects the wrong course. Until the courts resolve the matter, the best course for an applicant would be one of 'twin-

2.16 *Duties and powers of local authorities*

tracking': that is, challenging the authority's refusal to act by means of judicial review, while simultaneously seeking to persuade the Secretary of State to exercise his powers under the EPA 1990. There are thus two remedies: judicial review and action by the Secretary of State. In our view, judicial review is not ousted by the existence of the Secretary of State's power. The Secretary of State in practice does not exercise this power; indeed, we are unaware of him ever having exercised it. The real remedy lies, therefore, with judicial review.

2.17 It may seem that situations will be rare where a person will be aggrieved by a local authority's failure to inspect its area rather than its failure to investigate his particular complaint of a statutory nuisance. Evidence of the absence of a scheme of inspection is likely to provide *prima facie* support not only for a breach of the local authority's duty to inspect, but also for a complaint of a failure to investigate a particular complaint. Local authorities are likely to be obliged to supply information on their compliance with these duties.[1]

1   ECHR, article 8; see *Lopez Ostra v Spain* (1994) 20 EHRR 277 and *Guerra v Italy* (1998) 26 EHRR 357.

2.18 In our view, it is unlikely that a local authority would be able to plead successfully lack of resources for failing to discharge the duty properly to establish and operate a system of inspection. However, a local authority could take into account the question of finances in deciding what method of inspection it should employ.[1] However, if the result of taking financial consequences into account is that the method employed is so feeble that it is not effective then, in our view, the local authority would be in breach of its duty. The scheme of inspection must be effective. Community groups and concerned individuals should not hesitate in seeking details of the scheme of monitoring that their authority employs. Most of the information should be available publicly.

1   In *R v Gloucestershire County Council, ex p Barry* [1997] AC 584, a case about a local authority's duty to provide social services to disabled people, the House of Lords were unanimous in holding that financial constraints cannot relieve a local authority of its duties, although the House of Lords held by a majority of three to two that financial constraints *were* relevant in deciding whether it was necessary to meet needs of disabled people. The approach in *Ex p Barry* was confirmed in *R v East Sussex County Council, ex p Tandy* [1998] AC 714 in the context of special educational needs. The House of Lords held that a local authority could not lawfully take into account financial resources when determining what was suitable education within the meaning of Education Act 1998, s 298 for a particular child. However, a local authority was entitled, when there is more than one way of providing such suitable education, to have regard to its resources in deciding between different ways of providing such education. See further the commentary on this case by Philip Petchey and Oliver Hyams at [1998] Ed CR 217.

2.19 An authorised person may enter premises in pursuance of this duty.[1]

1   EPA 1990, Sch 3, para 2(1)(a).

THE DUTY TO INVESTIGATE COMPLAINTS

2.20 Section 79(1) of the EPA 1990 further requires local authorities 'where a complaint of a statutory nuisance is made to it by a person living within its area, to take such steps as are reasonably practicable to investigate the complaint.'

2.21 The words 'reasonably practicable' do not qualify the duty but rather qualify the nature of the steps to be employed pursuant to that duty.[1] It was held in *Jordan v Norfolk County Council*,² in the context of complying with the terms of an injunction, that financial considerations were relevant to the test of reasonable practicability. In that case the estimated cost of reinstating some land in which the council had erroneously installed a sewage pipe and which it was obliged to reinstate 'as far as is reasonably practicable' was out of all proportion to the value of the land. The phrase 'reasonably practicable' is not defined in the EPA 1990 as such. However, s 79(9) of the EPA 1990 may be thought to provide some assistance. In addressing the manner in which 'best practicable means' is to be interpreted, it provides that reference should be made to a number of provisions including s 79(9)(a) which states:

> '"practicable" means reasonably practicable having regard amongst other things to local conditions and circumstances, to the current state of technical knowledge and to the financial implications.'

1 In practice, this is likely to give rise only to minor problems. There may be an instance where someone unknown has deposited a pile of stinking waste on some land. The local authority might not be able to discover the person responsible without excessive and costly investigation. Instead, it simply arranges for the removal of the material.
2 [1994] 4 All ER 218.

2.22 Many local authorities operate 'noise patrols' that respond to telephone complaints of nuisance. However, one problem that frequently arises is where the alleged nuisance takes place at times when the noise patrol does not operate. Funding is usually the issue.¹ The Local Government Ombudsman's guidance entitled *Neighbour nuisance and anti-social behaviour* suggests the steps which the ombudsman considers a local authority should take, even in circumstances where resources are at issue. It states that:

> 'if councils do not have the resources to visit anything other than the most urgent complaints out of working hours, they should make this clear to complainants. It is good practice for councils to have a written policy setting out how any out-of-hours service works and when it will be used. In general, this information should be passed on to the complainant, if needs be in the form of a leaflet. However, records kept by complainants of nuisance out of hours can be used to identify a pattern, which may then lead to planned visits to witness the behaviour at the most likely time. If a council has a limited out-of-hours service, or none at all, this does not mean it does not have to investigate a complaint about nuisance which occurs at night or over a weekend. If such a complaint is recurring, the council must take steps to address the complaint. This may involve making special arrangements or liaising with another agency, for example, the police.'²

1 See also para **2.18,** n 1.
2 Section G, paras 15–16.

2.23 The Local Government Ombudsman's mention of the police is interesting. The attitude of most police forces in the country towards complaints of nuisance is usually uncooperative. They now tend to regard issues of nuisance as a matter for local authorities.¹

1 Indeed, anecdotal evidence of EHOs suggests a reluctance of the police even to accompany EHOs to scenes where the EHOs fear physical intimidation. Views may differ upon whether the activities of people who subject their neighbours to excessive noise decibel levels and react aggressively to polite requests to lower the noise have no bearing on whether the neighbourhood feels a safer place in which to live. However, the stance adopted by the police – no doubt in part resource driven – does represent, in our view, a regrettable withdrawal from

2.23 *Duties and powers of local authorities*

an aspect of community relations which can escalate to physical or verbal abuse of a criminal nature requiring yet more intensive use of police and public resources, which, if treated early could often be solved without recourse to the criminal justice system.

2.24 Although there is no case law on the meaning of 'reasonably practicable' in the context of statutory nuisance, there have been decisions of the Local Government Ombudsman on the subject. The following actions were held to fall short of investigating a complaint as far as reasonably practicable:

- waiting five months before evaluating a complaint[1]
- dropping a complaint because a complainant had not followed it up[2]
- failing to keep records of correspondence and telephone calls in connection with a complaint[3]
- failing to investigate a complaint because it concerned noise on a Sunday[4]
- only conducting two monitoring exercises in two years when there had been a considerable number of complaints backed up by evidence.[5]

The possible impact of the Regulatory of Investigatory Powers Act 2000 (RIPA) and the ECHR in connection with surveillance is considered further at paras **2.93–2.101**.

1 Complaint 88/A/1864 against the London Borough of Barnet.
2 Complaint 88/A/1864.
3 Complaint 88/A/1864.
4 Complaint 88/C/1571 against the Metropolitan Borough of Rotherham.
5 Complaint 88/C/1571.

The duty to make environmental information available

2.25 There is a general requirement to make certain information available pursuant to the state's environmental obligations under articles 2 and 8[1] of the ECHR. These have been considered in *Guerra v Italy*[2] in which ECtHR held that the local authority's failure to give the local people:

> '... essential information that would have entitled them to assess the risks they and their families might run if they continued to live at Manfredonia, a town particularly exposed in the event of an accident at the factory [amounted to a breach of article 8]'.

1 The rights to life and the right to respect of the home respectively.
2 (1998) 26 EHRR 357.

2.26 More specifically, the Environmental Information Regulations 2004, SI 2004/3391 (EIR 2004) provide a powerful tool for requiring the disclosure of environmental information. The regulations came into force on 1 January 2005, a product both of the international obligations of the Aarhus Convention to which the United Kingdom is a signatory state, and EC Directive 2003/4/EC.[1] These Regulations impose a duty on 'public authorities' (defined in regulation 2(2)) to make publicly available environmental information which it 'holds' (for the meaning of which see regulations 4(1) and 5(1)). A local authority charged with statutory nuisance responsibilities under the EPA 1990 is within the definition of public authority under the EIR 2004. The meaning of 'environmental information' is addressed at regulation 2. It is wide. It encompasses:

'any information in written, visual, aural, electronic or any other material form on–
  (a) the state of the elements of the environment, such as air and atmosphere, water, soil, land, landscape and natural sites including wetlands, coastal and marine areas, biological diversity and its components, including genetically modified organisms, and the interaction among these elements;
  (b) factors, such as substances, energy, noise, radiation or waste, including radioactive waste, emissions, discharges and other releases into the environment, affecting or likely to affect the elements of the environment referred to in (a);
  (c) measures (including administrative measures), such as policies, legislation, plans, programmes, environmental agreements, and activities affecting or likely to affect the elements and factors referred to in (a) and (b) as well as measures or activities designed to protect those elements;
  (d) reports on the implementation of environmental legislation;
  (e) cost-benefit and other economic analyses and assumptions used within the framework of the measures and activities referred to in (c); and
  (f) the state of human health and safety, including the contamination of the food chain, where relevant, conditions of human life, cultural sites and built structures inasmuch as they are or may be affected by the state of the elements of the environment referred to in (a) or, through those elements, by any of the matters referred to in (b) and (c).'

Requests may therefore be made for information held by the public authority concerning matters which may constitute a statutory nuisance within the meaning of section 79 of the EPA 1990. For example, noise emissions under category (b) might qualify as a statutory nuisance under section 79(1)(g) or indeed a request may be made for any reason the local authority may have for not taking enforcement action for a breach of an abatement notice. The Freedom of Information Act 2000 (FOIA 2000) is unlikely, in practice, to have much application in respect of statutory nuisance, given the wide definition of 'environmental information' under the EIR 2004 since, where information comes within the definition of 'environmental information', it is in practice to be dealt with under the EIR 2004 (see section 39 of the FOIA 2000, although the subordination is not absolute: see section 2(3) of the FOIA 2000; the practical consequence is that the EIR 2004 effectively 'trumps' the FOIA 2000 in respect of 'environmental information' – this is important because where the two differ it is where the EIR 2004 favours greater disclosure).

1   The EIR 2004 represent an enhanced replacement of the Environmental Information Regulations 1992, SI 1992/3240 which sought to implement EC Directive 90/313/EEC on freedom of access to information on the environment.

2.27 Environmental information must be disclosed on request unless one of a series of exceptions applies and 'in all the circumstances of the case the public interest in maintaining the exception outweighs the public interesting in disclosing the information'. Under regulation 12, there are two categories of exceptions:
  • standalone exceptions[1] and
  • 'adverse effect' exceptions[2].

2.27 *Duties and powers of local authorities*

The latter category of exception is particularly narrow since, in order to come within it, there must be evidence to show that the provider of the information would be adversely affected if that information were disclosed to the public. Moreover, in accordance with article 4 of the Directive, all exceptions must be interpreted in a restrictive way.

1 Information falling into the following categories:
 (a) the public authority does not hold that information when an applicant's request is received
 (b) the request for information is manifestly unreasonable
 (c) the request for information is formulated in too general a manner and the public authority has complied with its duty to assist the applicant to reformulate the request (see reg 9)
 (d) the request relates to material which is still in the course of completion, to unfinished documents or to incomplete data or
 (e) the request involves the disclosure of internal communications.
2 Information falling into the following categories:
 (a) international relations, defence, national security or public safety
 (b) the course of justice, the ability of a person to receive a fair trial or the ability of a public authority to conduct an inquiry of a criminal or disciplinary nature
 (c) intellectual property rights
 (d) *the confidentiality of the proceedings of that or any other public authority where such confidentiality is provided by law
 (e) *the confidentiality of commercial or industrial information where such confidentiality is provided by law to protect a legitimate economic interest
 (f) *the interests of the person who provided the information where that person–
  (i) was not under, and could not have been put under, any legal obligation to supply it to that or any other public authority
  (ii) did not supply it in circumstances such that that or any other public authority is entitled apart from these Regulations to disclose it and
  (iii) has not consented to its disclosure
 (g) *the protection of the environment to which the information relates.
The exceptions marked with an asterisk are ones where public authorities are not entitled to rely on them to refuse to disclose environmental information on emissions.

2.28 Even if an exception applies, the public authority must nonetheless disclose the information if the public interest in maintaining the exception does not outweigh the public interest in disclosing the exception.[1] There is a statutory presumption in favour of disclosure.[2] Furthermore, even where information within a document qualifies as an exception, there remains an obligation on the public authority to redact the document as far as possible so as to disclose material in the document not covered by the exception.[3]

1 EIR 2004, reg 12(1).
2 EIR 2004, reg 12(2).
3 EIR 2004, reg 12(11).

2.29 It is most unlikely that the EIR 2004, which implements an EC directive, could lawfully be applied in such a way which would be contrary to the ECHR.[1] Indeed, the residual 'public interest test' provides an opportunity to apply the ECHR, for it is difficult to see how it could be in the 'public interest' to refuse to disclose something which would result in the infringement of a person's Convention rights. For example, in order for the exceptions contained at regulation 12 of the EIR 2004 to stand in circumstances where a violation of article 8.1 had been demonstrated, it would need to justify the particular exception under article 8.2 as a measure necessary in a democratic society. Each exception would need to be assessed in the context of the particular case. However, where there is a threat to life under article 2, there is no such method of justification in the context of a failure to provide environmental information. In *Guerra v Italy*,[2] whilst the majority of the ECtHR did not consider article 2, two concurring members of the Court thought there would have been a violation of article 2. Judge Jambrek stated:

> 'If the information is withheld by a government about circumstances which forseeably and on substantial grounds present a real risk of danger to health and physical integrity, then such a situation may also be protected by Article 2 of the Convention.'

1 Such conflicts are likely to be rare because the European Court of Justice (ECJ) has recognised that the general principles contained in the ECHR are a source of EC law; see eg 36/75: *Rutili v Minister for the Interior* [1975] ECR 1219, [1976] 1 CMLR 140, para 32. See also, the joint statement by the European Parliament, the Council and the Commission on fundamental rights: OJ 1988 C 103/1. The case law of the ECJ acknowledges the 'special significance' of the Convention (222/84: *Johnston v Chief Constable of the RUC* [1986] ECR 1651, para 18). There remains the question, however, whether or not the final arbiter of any conflict would be the ECJ or the domestic courts with final recourse to the ECtHR. The opinion of the ECJ was sought pursuant to EC art 300(6) on whether accession to the ECHR by the EC itself would be compatible with the EC Treaty. The ECJ held that it would not be compatible (Opinion 2/94 [1996] ECR I-1759).
2 (1998) 26 EHRR 357.

2.30 The enforcement and appeal procedures of the FOIA 2000 have been incorporated into the EIR 2004[1] so that, following the internal review, the dissatisfied applicant can apply to the Information Commissioner and then, if further dissatisfied, to the Information Tribunal on the same basis as the FOIA 2000.

1 EIR 2004, reg 18.

2.31 An area where the EIR 2004 may have a particular role is in the identification of complaints. Sometimes, for obvious reasons, complainants may wish to remain anonymous. The difficulty is that determining whether a nuisance has been caused will often depend upon identifying the location which is said to have suffered the nuisance. Some assistance may be derived from the decision of the Information Commissioner concerning an application for disclosure of details of complaints and the complainant's identity to Bridgenorth District Council[1] and the decision of the Information Tribunal in *Young v Information Commissioner and the Department of the Environment for Northern Ireland*[2], both concerning planning enforcement actions and from which it appears that, generally and subject to the particular circumstances of the case, the balance is likely to be struck in allowing disclosure of the nature of the complaints but not the identity or addresses of the complainants.

1 FS50062329, 12 July 2005.
2 EA/2007/0048, 12 December 2007.

2.32 A detailed analysis of the scope of the EIR 2004 is plainly outside the scope of this text. The Information Commissioner and the Information Tribunal maintain websites from which their decisions can be downloaded.[1] Although not binding decisions, these are helpful resources. For example, the decision of the Information Tribunal concerning the level of charges which it may be reasonable for a public authority to make in respect of providing copies of environmental information requested under the EIR 2004 should be required reading for anyone wishing to make an EIR 2004 request. Useful further guidance can be gleaned from the following sources:

- published by the UN's European Economic Commission, *The Aarhus Convention: An Implementation Guide* (www.unece.org/env/pp/acig.pdf)

2.32 *Duties and powers of local authorities*

- published pursuant to EIR 2004, regulation 16[2] by the Secretary of State in February 2005, the *Code of Practice on the discharge of the obligations of public authorities under the Environmental Information Regulations 2004* (www.defra.gov.uk/corporate/opengov/eir/pdf/cop-eir.pdf)
- since 21 September 2005 DEFR also publishes *A guide to the environmental information regulations* which is updated (www.defra.gov.uk/corporate/opengov/eir/guidance/index.htm)
- guidance on the EIR 2004 from the Information Commissioner (www.ico.gov.uk/tools_and_resources/document_library/environmental_information_regulation.aspx).

1 Decision notices of the Information Commissioner can be found at www.ico.gov.uk/tools_and_resources/decision_notices.aspx and for the Information Tribunal at www.informationtribunal.gov.uk/Decisions/eir.htm.
2 EIR 2004, reg 16 provides for the Secretary of State to publish '... a Code of Practice providing guidance to public authorities as to the practices which it would, in the Secretary of State's opinion, be desirable for them to follow in connection with the discharge of their functions under the [EIR 2004]'.

The duty to issue an abatement notice

2.33 Section 80(1) of the EPA 1990 provides that:

'[W]here a local authority is satisfied that a statutory nuisance exists, or is likely to occur or recur, in the area of the authority, the local authority shall serve ... an abatement notice.'

2.34 This was interpreted as a duty (in other words 'shall' means 'must' in this context) by Carnwath J in *R v Carrick District Council, ex p Shelley*.[1] In that case, two sewage discharges permitted by consents from the National Rivers Authority (the precursor to the Environment Agency) were perceived nevertheless to be a statutory nuisance by the local authority. Since the consents were being appealed by the water authority, the local authority decided to 'monitor the situation', ie do nothing for the time being. This was held to be in breach of its obligations under section 80(1) of the EPA 1990.

1 [1996] Env LR 273.

2.35 An earlier case, *Nottingham Corpn v Newton*[1] held that in a case where another route was available to the local authority the 'shall' did not impose a duty to take the EPA 1990 route. The Divisional Court held that *the authority in question* could have acted under the Public Health Act 1936 (a predecessor of the 1990 Act) or the Housing Act 1957 to deal with a house that was in a state prejudicial to health. Once it had chosen which route to take, there was a duty to go down that route. In both *Ex p Shelley* and *Nottingham*, two schemes of enforcement existed that could be employed in order to address the nuisance. However, the situations were distinguishable because in *Ex p Shelley* only one scheme of enforcement, that of statutory nuisances under the EPA 1990, was open to the local authority; the other scheme was a matter for the Environment Agency over which the local authority would have no control.

1 [1974] 1 WLR 923 at 927A–C. This case was not cited in the *Ex p Shelley* judgment.

2.36 The *Ex p Shelley* approach is consistent with that adopted by the Local Government Ombudsman. Following a complaint that the condition of a flat

The duty to investigate complaints 2.39

was prejudicial to health following wood treatment work, the local authority referred the complaint to the Health and Safety Executive rather than itself deciding whether there was a statutory nuisance. This was held to be maladministration.[1]

1   Complaint 90/A/3123 against London Borough of Kensington & Chelsea.

2.37   The EPA 1990 is concerned with the prevention as well as the existence of statutory nuisances. If a local authority is satisfied that a statutory nuisance is likely to occur, it must issue a notice. If criminal proceedings are initiated in such a case, it will only be necessary to show that the local authority was satisfied as to the likelihood of a nuisance occurring rather than the existence of a statutory nuisance.

2.38   The existence of a duty to issue an abatement notice gives rise to an interesting question in the light of the existence of various statutory defences and grounds of appeal, in particular in respect of 'best practicable means'.[1] It might appear that a local authority must go ahead with issuing an abatement notice even if it is likely that the recipient of the notice will be able to appeal successfully that it is taking best practicable means to prevent the nuisance, or on other grounds. It cannot, however, be the case that a local authority is obliged to issue a notice even when it knows that the recipient will have a cast iron ground of appeal to have the notice quashed on the grounds of best practicable means. If that were so, taken to its logical (albeit extreme) conclusion, if the appeal were successful the local authority would nonetheless continue to be obliged to issue a notice if satisfied that a statutory nuisance still existed.

1   See further the discussion on this point in Chapter 4 at paras **4.61–4.68**.

2.39   There are a number of possible answers to this problem:

- *Ex p Shelley* is wrong in holding that 'shall' means 'must' for the purposes of section 80 of the EPA 1990
- the Secretary of State acted contrary to the intention of Parliament by allowing a ground of appeal based upon the best practicable means
- *Ex p Shelley* is correct, but where the local authority was satisfied that the recipient would be able to appeal successfully on the grounds that he had employed the best practicable means, the local authority should issue a notice restricting rather than abating the nuisance by requiring the employment of best practicable means (see further paras **2.44–2.45** on the power to restrict a statutory nuisance);
- *Ex p Shelley* is correct, but where the local authority was satisfied that the recipient would be able to appeal successfully on the grounds that he had employed the best practicable means, it is not under a duty to issue a notice.

The suggestion that the local authority might simply seek to restrict the nuisance appears attractive since it would require the maker of the nuisance to ensure that he maintain and keep up to date with the best practicable means or else risk an immediate prosecution. However, it would in our view seem curious that a notice representing formal enforcement action could be issued in circumstances which Parliament and the Secretary of State appear to contemplate are acceptable. Accordingly, in our view, the last view probably represents the correct approach although the matter cannot be said to be entirely free from doubt.[1] Indeed, it appears that the Secretary of State is of the view that a local authority must issue

2.39 *Duties and powers of local authorities*

an abatement notice regardless of whether it is of the view that a recipient may be employing best practicable means. Paragraph 36 of the DEFRA *Guidance on Sections 69 to 81 and Section 86 of the Clean Neighbourhoods and Environment Act 2005* (section 86 of which introduces a power to defer the service of an abatement notice in respect of noise nuisance only: see further paras **2.41–2.43**) states that the provision was introduced because:

> 'There is no provision for the exercise of discretion as to whether or not to take this action, even if the local authority suspects that "best practicable means" may be in place (only the courts can rule on whether "best practicable means" are in place).'

We respectfully disagree. Carnwath J's analysis in *Ex p Shelley* reflects the statutory scheme seen as a whole.[2] This purpose would be frustrated if local authorities were not in general obliged to issue an abatement notice although satisfied that a statutory nuisance existed and equally frustrated if they were forced to court to fight a case where they are in agreement with the appellant. If the Secretary of State holds this view it is somewhat odd that the provision for deferral of an abatement notice was restricted only to noise abatement notices.[3]

1 See further the discussion of this matter in Chapters 3 and 5.
2 It is perhaps significant to note that despite the widespread litigation in this field no-one appears to have sought to challenge the validity of Carnwath J's approach either in the Divisional Court or the Court of Appeal. However, it is also true that the problem that we have identified in respect of this ground of appeal does not appear to have been raised before Carnwath J in *Ex p Shelley*, or, indeed, before any other court in subsequent litigation. In *The Barns v Newcastle Upon Tyne City Council* [2005] EWCA Civ 1274, the Court of Appeal accepted the correctness of *Ex p Shelley*, which was not challenged by the City Council.
3 It is the authors' experience that prior to the decision in *Ex p Shelley*, many local authorities tended to seek to negotiate the best compromise possible with nuisance-makers rather than move to issue an abatement notice.

2.40 In summary therefore, we are of the view that the correct position is probably as follows. Where the local authority cannot say that an appeal based on best practicable means can be made out, it should issue a notice. Where it is of the view that a best practicable means ground of appeal is likely to succeed in quashing the notice, the duty does not arise.

2.41 As stated at para **2.39**, section 86 of the Clean Neighbourhoods and Environment Act 2005 has subsequently inserted new provisions into section 80 of the EPA 1990. The new provisions deal only with statutory nuisance falling within paragraph (g) of s 79(1) of the EPA (that is '*noise* emitted from premises so as to be prejudicial to health or a nuisance'). The amended section 80 now provides in respect of this particular type of nuisance that, where it is satisfied that a statutory nuisance exists or is likely to occur or recur in its area, a local authority may, as an *alternative* to its duty to serve an abatement notice, 'take such other steps as it thinks appropriate for the purpose of persuading the appropriate person to abate the nuisance or prohibit or restrict its occurrence or recurrence' (subsection (2A)(b)). Where it does so, the Secretary of State advises that a record for its reason for so doing must be kept.[1]

1 Paragraph 34 of the DEFRA Guidance on Sections 69 to 81 and Section 86 of the Clean Neighbourhoods and Environment Act 2005

2.42 This provision is intended to encompass discussion and negotiations between the local authority and the nuisance-maker with the aim of avoiding the service of an abatement notice. The Secretary of State considers that:

The duty to investigate complaints **2.43**

'In some circumstances an informal approach will engender greater co-operation and a faster resolution of a noise nuisance. Sometimes it can be counterproductive and/or unnecessary to issue an abatement notice – for example, the notice may provoke one party to withdraw from negotiations, actually aggravate a situation, or enable the person responsible to avoid having to abate the problem by, for example, holding a one-off noisy party). The option to defer serving an abatement notice for up to seven days in order to pursue specific steps may support resolution without recourse to a formal abatement notice.'[1]

A local authority would clearly have to exercise caution before pursuing this 'alternative route' in instances where the 'noise emitted from premises' is prejudicial to health, as opposed to noise which is merely a nuisance. Where the noise nuisance is prejudicial to health, a decision to defer the service of the notice pending discussions or negotiations clearly risks extending the time during which the health of an affected person is prejudiced.

1   Paragraph 36 of the DEFRA *Guidance on Sections 69 to 81 and Section 86 of the Clean Neighbourhoods and Environment Act 2005*.

2.43 If the authority should choose to adopt the alternative course, there is then provision for a 'relevant period' for deferral (stated in subsection (2D) to be 'seven days starting with the day on which the authority was first satisfied that the nuisance existed, or was likely to occur or recur'). The Secretary of State advises local authorities that:

'it will usually be appropriate to advise the person responsible for the nuisance in writing that a noise nuisance exists or is likely to occur or recur, and of the decision to defer service of an abatement notice provided the nuisance is dealt with within seven days. The local authority may also inform the noisemaker that if the nuisance continues after seven days of the notification of deferral, an abatement notice will be served. Outlining the consequences of an abatement notice in this initial letter advising of the decision to defer is recommended.'[1]

After the expiry of the seven day period, the authority shall then serve the notice on the 'appropriate person' (defined in subsection (2E) as 'the person on whom the authority would otherwise serve the notice had it chosen to serve straight away') if either of two conditions are satisfied:

- 'the authority is satisfied at any time before the end of the relevant period that the steps taken will not be successful in persuading the appropriate person to abate the nuisance or prohibit or restrict its occurrence or recurrence' (subsection (2C)(a)) or
- 'the authority is satisfied at the end of the relevant period that the nuisance continues to exist, or continues to be likely to occur or recur, in the area of the authority'(subsection (2C)(b)).

This appears to mean, although it is not entirely clear, that unless the authority is satisfied that the discussions and/or negotiations are successful at the end of the seven-day period so that the original nuisance has been abated and/or is unlikely to recur, it must then issue the abatement notice; it does not need to do so otherwise. This view appears to be supported by the guidance given by DEFRA.[2] However, it is not necessarily true that the nuisance actually has to be abated by the conclusion of the seven-day period. The provision appears to mean that the local authority needs only be satisfied that

2.43 *Duties and powers of local authorities*

the nuisance will (at some point) be abated in order for the service of a notice to be avoided.

1 Paragraph 37 of the DEFRA *Guidance on Sections 69 to 81 and Section 86 of the Clean Neighbourhoods and Environment Act 2005*.
2 Paragraphs 38–39 of the DEFRA *Guidance on Sections 69 to 81 and Section 86 of the Clean Neighbourhoods and Environment Act 2005*.

Power merely to restrict a nuisance

2.44 This is a power that, in the authors' experience, is rarely exercised by local authorities. Perhaps this is because it may not be entirely clear what Parliament intended by this provision. Curiously, there is no similar power to restrict a nuisance *expressly* provided in section 82 of the EPA 1990 in respect of abatement orders issued by magistrates' courts. We have discussed above the possibility that this power might be exercised where a statutory nuisance exists but where best practicable means is being employed by the relevant 'industrial, trade or business premises'. There may of course be other circumstances where the local authority may consider that best practicable means which otherwise might be available is not being employed at the date the notice is served. It may also be satisfied that the employment of best practicable means would not fully abate the nuisance. Arguably it could then, in our view, exercise its power under section 80(1)(a) of the EPA 1990 to issue a notice restricting the nuisance to a level that corresponds to the best practice rather than its complete elimination.[1] However, the consequence of so doing would effectively reverse the burden of proof for any alleged breach of the notice. Ordinarily, best practicable means being a statutory defence, the burden is on the defendant to show to the civil standard of proof that it was being employed at the relevant date. If best practicable means is included as a requirement of the abatement notice, then, in order to prove a breach of the notice, the prosecution must prove beyond reasonable doubt that best practicable means was not being employed. That would seem to undermine the structure of the statutory nuisance scheme. We consider that a notice may be issued so as simply to restrict in time a nuisance where the activity causing it is going to be relocated. The notice is effectively required to deal only with the intervening period prior to re-location.

1 In our view, the use of the alternative power to restrict rather than abate the nuisance provided in EPA 1990, s 80(1)(a) is to be exercised narrowly in accordance with the overall purposes of the statutory scheme.

2.45 It could be said that the power to restrict (rather than prohibit) a nuisance might also be exercised where the local authority is satisfied that the nuisance in question is already covered by a consent either under the Control of Pollution Act 1974 or the Noise and Statutory Nuisance Act 1993. The requirements of the abatement notice would be restricted to the terms of the consent.[1] However, since the local authority is responsible for the issue of consents under both schemes then pursuant to the *Nottingham*[2] case, there would be no duty upon the local authority to chose to go down the statutory nuisance route under Part III of the EPA 1990 rather than to enforce under another statutory regime.

1 Statutory Nuisance (Appeals) Regulations 1995, SI 1995/2664, reg 2(2)(g): in the case of noise emitted from premises in categories (g) or (ga), the requirements of the notice are more onerous than the existing controls in relation to the noise under the Control of Pollution Act 1974, ss 60, 61, 65, 66, or 67 as appropriate; or reg 2(2)(h): in the case of noise in the street, the requirements of the notice are more onerous than the requirements of any condition of a

consent given under the Noise and Statutory Nuisance Act 1993, Sch 2, para 1 in respect of the same noise for loudspeakers on the street (Statutory Nuisance (Appeals) Regulations 1995, reg 2(2)(g)).
2   *Nottingham Corpn v Newton* [1974] 1 WLR 923.

Decisions by the Local Government Ombudsman on local authorities' duty to issue abatement notices

2.46   Decisions by Local Government Ombudsman are not legal precedents for deciding cases. They do, however, provide useful guidance to local authorities upon what they should do in order to fulfil their statutory responsibilities. They may also be illustrative of bad practice. Two decisions of the Local Government Ombudsman are noteworthy. First, it was not acceptable to refrain from issuing an abatement notice because the nuisance was due to an activity which had been encouraged by another department of the local authority, nor not to have served an abatement notice 20 months after deciding a nuisance existed.[1] Secondly, a local authority which refrained from issuing an abatement notice for a considerable period of time because it was assessing its prospects of success on appeal was held to have been guilty of maladministration.[2] We would support what is the main thrust of the Ombudsman's decision. It would be entirely inappropriate for a local authority to allow its consideration of whether best practical means was being employed to cause any *substantial* delay the issue of the abatement notice.

1   Complaint 88/C/1373 against Sheffield City Council.
2   Complaint 88/C/1571 against Metropolitan Borough of Rotherham.

What happens when an abatement notice is breached?

2.47   If there has been a breach of an abatement notice there are four options that a local authority can consider:

- do nothing
- attempt to abate the nuisance itself
- institute criminal proceedings in the magistrates' court or
- institute civil proceedings in the High Court.

These are the subject of this and the following three sections.

2.48   If the local authority chooses to do nothing, there is at present no express general requirement to give reasons (for example to a person who made a complaint of a nuisance). In the case of *R v DPP, ex p Manning*[1] it was held that the Crown Prosecution Service was only under a duty to give reasons not to prosecute in an extreme case, such as an alleged murder. The Local Government Ombudsman, however, made a finding of maladministration when a local authority had properly decided to do nothing after investigating a complaint, but had not told the complainant.[2] Moreover, it might well be difficult for a local authority to fail to act without providing very clear and cogent reasons where the nuisance affected someone's home and thereby involved a person's right to respect for his home under article 8 of the ECHR. Indeed, in certain circumstances a failure of the local authority to act regardless of whether it gives its reasons may be capable of amounting to a breach of article 8.[3] Where a local authority decided not to take enforcement action, its decision and any reasons for it presumably will be noted and would be subject to a request for disclosure under the EIR 2004 (see paras **2.25–2.32**).

2.48 *Duties and powers of local authorities*

1 [2001] QB 330.
2 Complaint 92/B/3695 against Bromsgrove District Council.
3 See *Lopez Ostra v Spain* (1994) 20 EHRR 277 and *Guerra v Italy* (1998) 26 EHRR 357.

2.49 In another case relating to the powers of the Crown Prosecution Service, it was held that its discretion to institute criminal proceedings could be the subject of judicial review only where it was regardless of, or contrary to, the Director of Public Prosecution's settled policy.[1] Many local authorities will have their own enforcement policies which apply to statutory nuisance and a failure without good reason to follow such policy may give rise to legal challenge. Moreover, according to a written answer given by the Deputy Prime Minister on 22 July 2002 in the House of Commons, as of that date, 96 per cent of all central and local government enforcement organisations had adopted the Enforcement Concordat. This is likely to include most local authorities responsible for enforcing the statutory nuisance regime. Under the heading 'Principles of Good Enforcement: Procedures' is included the following provision in respect of the procedure to be followed when action is taken:

'Before formal enforcement action is taken, officers will provide an opportunity to discuss the circumstances of the case and, if possible, resolve points of difference, unless immediate action is required (for example, in the interests of health and safety or environmental protection or to prevent evidence being destroyed).

Where immediate action is considered necessary, an explanation of why such action was required will be given at the time and confirmed in writing in most cases within five working days and, in all cases, within 10 working days.'

However, in reality the courts are reluctant to quash by judicial review a decision to prosecute, preferring instead such matter to be dealt with by way of an abuse of process argument before the court hearing the prosecution.[2]

1 *R v Chief Constable of Kent County Constabulary, ex p L* (1991) 93 Cr App Rep 416. For an attempt to seek judicial review of a decision to prosecute in a planning enforcement case see *R v Elmbridge Borough Council, ex parte Activeoffcie Ltd* (1997) Times, 29 December, DC where the court held that the underlying test was whether the decision was reasonable.
2 By way of an example in the context of statutory nuisance, in *Islington LBC v Match EC1* (4 September 2006, unreported) following a two-day hearing at Marylebone Magistrates' Court District Judge Roscoe in a reserved judgment rejected an abuse of process argument against a prosecution by the London Borough of Islington. Match EC1 Ltd, a café bar, had argued that a prosecution for breach of a noise nuisance abatement notice under s 80 of EPA 1990 was an abuse of process because it alleged that the council had granted planning permission and building regulation approval for the sub standard work. It also argued that it had been led to believe that it would not be prosecuted until the council had taken planning enforcement action against the freeholders. Both arguments were rejected by the court holding that first, even if planning permission had been given the two were separate regimes and secondly, on the facts of the case, the council had later made clear in sufficient time its intention to prosecute.

Power of abatement by the local authority

2.50 A local authority has the power to abate the nuisance itself if an abatement notice has not been complied with.[1] The local authority need not take the person responsible for the nuisance to court. The local authority can recover expenses reasonably incurred in abating the nuisance from the person responsible under section 81(4) of the EPA 1990.

1 1990 Act, s 81(3).

The duty to investigate complaints **2.58**

2.51 Section 10(7) of the Noise Act 1996 further provides that in order to abate a statutory nuisance of category (g), namely noise emanating from premises, persons authorised by a local authority may seize and remove equipment which is being or has been used in the emission of the noise in question. It is difficult to see how this adds much to the general power of entry which is provided by the EPA 1990, which includes the power to 'take away such ... articles as he considers necessary for [the discharge of any of the local authority's functions under Part III]',[1] other than to make it more explicit.

1   EPA 1990, Sch 3, para 2(4)(c).

2.52 The Schedule to the Noise Act 1996 sets out what must be done with equipment seized under section 10(7), whereas the EPA 1990 makes no such provision. In this sense the Noise Act 1996 is more restrictive.

The power to suspend a notice and the duty to consult

2.53 This power is considered in detail in Chapter 3 at paras **3.35–3.37**.

The power to require information

2.54 A local authority has a power to require certain information under section 16 of the Local Government (Miscellaneous Provisions) Act 1976. It is an offence under section 16(2) not to comply with such a request. Pursuant to this power, a local authority may, for example, require someone to admit whether or not they are the owner or occupier of the premises to which an abatement notice relates. It is immediately apparent why such a power can be important for local authorities dealing with alleged breaches of abatement notices.

2.55 The use of information obtained by coercion in criminal proceedings for a failure to comply with an abatement notice may be incompatible with article 6 of the ECHR. The implication of article 6 and the right against self-incrimination are discussed in further detail in Chapter 5 at paras **5.60–5.64**.

The power to enter premises or open vehicles

2.56 The power to enter premises may be invoked in pursuance of any of a local authority's duties or powers relating to statutory nuisance and its extent is set out in paragraph 2 of Schedule 3 to the EPA 1990.

2.57 The Police and Criminal Evidence Act 1984 (PACE) provides Codes of Practice for police officers and other persons 'charged with the duty of investigating offences or charging offenders' and Code B relates to entry and search powers. However paragraph B:1.3B states:

> '... this code does not apply to the exercise of a statutory power to enter premises or to inspect goods, equipment or procedures if the exercise of that power is not dependent on the existence of grounds for suspecting that an offence may have been committed and the person exercising the power has no reasonable grounds for such suspicion.'

2.58 The power to enter and search premises under the EPA 1990 is a general one and is not dependent upon the existence of grounds for suspecting that an

2.58 *Duties and powers of local authorities*

offence may have been committed. The only alleged offence that may be investigated by means of this power is that of failure to comply with an abatement notice. Such an offence cannot be committed until after an abatement notice has been issued and the deadline for compliance has expired. Any exercise of powers of entry and search before that time, therefore, cannot be because of suspicion that an offence *has been* committed.[1] An authorised person may take equipment and other persons with them as necessary, carry out inspections, measurements and tests, and take away samples and articles.[2]

1   Some might argue that even if evidence gathered from such a search is later used in court as part of a prosecution and the evidence was gathered with that possibility in mind, Code B should not apply because the suspicion is that an offence is *going to be* committed. For more details about the procedures for prosecution for a failure to comply with an abatement notice see Chapter 5.
2   EPA 1990, Sch 3, para 2(4).

2.59 By virtue of Schedule 3, paragraph 2(1) of the EPA 1990, any person authorised by a local authority may, on production of (if so required) his authority, enter any premises at any reasonable time:

- for the purpose of ascertaining whether or not a statutory nuisance exists or
- for the purpose of taking any action, or executing any work authorised by Part III of the EPA 1990.

2.60 However, in the case of a property used wholly or mainly for residential purposes, admission is conditional upon having first given 24 hours' notice of intended entry to the occupier. In the case of an emergency, prior notice is not required.'Emergency' is specifically defined for the purposes of Schedule 3, paragraph 2 of the EPA 1990[1] as:

'... a case where the person requiring entry has a reasonable cause to believe that circumstances exist which are likely to endanger life or health and that immediate entry is necessary to verify the existence of those circumstances or to ascertain their cause and to effect a remedy.'

Accordingly, an authorised person does *not* have a right to enter a residential property without giving 24 hours' notice where the nuisance relates simply to a nuisance that is not likely to endanger life or health. In our view, the restrictions placed upon this right satisfy the balance of interests to be struck under the ECHR.

1   EPA 1990, Sch 3, para 2(7).

2.61 A right to enter a premises does not give the authorised person a right to force an entry, even where the premises is unoccupied. An authorised person may be entitled to enter a premises by force where the justice of the peace has issued a warrant for that purpose. A sworn information must be placed before the justice of the peace. The justice must be satisfied that:[1]

- admission to any premises has been refused
- refusal is apprehended
- the premises are unoccupied
- the occupier is temporarily absent, or that the case is one of emergency or
- an application for admission would defeat the object of the entry

and:

- that there is a reasonable ground for entry into the premises for the purpose required.

1   EPA 1990, Sch 3, para 2(3)(a) and (b).

2.62 Obstruction of entry is an offence under the EPA 1990.[1] Persons conducting a search can also be guilty of an offence if they disclose a trade secret encountered during the exercise of this power.[2] Premises must be left in the same state of security against trespassers as when they were found.[3]

1   EPA 1990, Sch 3, para 3(1).
2   EPA 1990, Sch 3, para 3(2).
3   EPA 1990, Sch 3, para 2(5).

2.63 Powers of entry to and opening of vehicles, machinery and equipment in a street are provided by paragraph 2A of Schedule 3 to the EPA 1990. Any person authorised by a local authority may enter or open a vehicle, machinery or equipment in the case of noise in the street emitted from or caused by the vehicle, machinery or equipment (statutory nuisance category (ga)).[1]

1   EPA 1990 Sch 3, para 2A(1).

2.64 A vehicle, machinery or equipment must be left in the same state of security against theft as when it was found[1] and no more damage should be done to it than necessary.[2] If securing it is not possible, it must be immobilised or removed to a safe place.[3]

1   EPA 1990, Sch 3, para 2A(2).
2   EPA 1990, Sch 3, para 2A(4).
3   EPA 1990, Sch 3, para 2A(3).

2.65 Before the entry or opening of vehicles, machinery or equipment in the street is carried out, the police must be notified and if the object in question is removed, the police must be told of its whereabouts.[1]

1   EPA 1990, Sch 3, para 2A(5) and (6).

2.66 It should also be noted that the Divisional Court has recently held that a local authority can draft an abatement notice which requires as a 'step' actions to be taken by its own officers entering on to the premises causing the nuisance. In *Lambie v Thanet District Council*,[1] the local authority had served an abatement notice on a public house alleging nuisance caused by the use of amplified music and a public address system. One of the requirements of the notice was to 'install and have set by officers from the Environmental Service department sound-restricting device which shall be operational any time music is played'. Langley J held that the wording of section 80(1)(b) and Schedule 3, paragraph 2(1)(b) of the EPA 1990 was sufficiently wide to permit authorised officers to enter premises to set a sound-restricting device.

1   [2001] Env LR21.

Powers of seizure

2.67 Authorised persons may enter premises for the purposes relating to statutory nuisance. They have the power to seize and remove equipment causing noise nuisances.[1]

1   Noise Act 1996, s 10(7).

2.68 *Duties and powers of local authorities*

THE POWER TO TAKE CRIMINAL PROCEEDINGS

2.68 Section 80(4) of the EPA 1990 provides that it is an offence not to comply with an abatement notice. The penalty, if the offence is committed on industrial, trade or business premises, is a fine of up to £20,000 and otherwise is up to level 5 (currently £5,000) plus a tenth of the fine for each day the offence continues after conviction.[1]

1 EPA 1990, s 80(5).

2.69 By section 222(1) of the Local Government Act 1972, a local authority may prosecute in any legal proceedings where it considers it expedient for the promotion or protection of the interests of the inhabitants of its area.

2.70 Thus a local authority has a power rather than a duty to take criminal proceedings in respect of non-compliance with an abatement notice, and only if it considers it is in the interests of the inhabitants of its area.[1] However, article 8 of the ECHR may make it difficult for a local authority not to take criminal proceedings or injunctive proceedings where the statutory nuisance adversely affects the home of a person.

1 Chapter 5 deals in detail with the conduct of criminal prosecution.

THE POWER TO SEEK INJUNCTIONS

2.71 This power is provided by section 81(5) of the EPA 1990. If the abatement by other means is considered by the local authority to be inadequate, the authority may take proceedings in the High Court (ie seek an injunction). A failure to comply with the terms of a court injunction is a contempt of court for which the offender may be fined and imprisoned. The defendant is provided with an additional defence, namely that he has a notice or consent under the Control of Pollution Act 1974. We also consider it likely that the employment of best practicable means by the defendant would often be accepted by the High Court as a reason for not granting an injunction.

2.72 The authority must be of the opinion that criminal proceedings are inadequate. However, if the power to reach such an opinion has been properly delegated, it can be reached by a committee, sub-committee or officer of the council. Note that the decision cannot be made by a single member.[1] The decision ordinarily should be taken before a claim is issued but it has been held to be acceptable to take it a few days afterwards.[2] Any delegation to a committee or officer cannot however be made retrospectively.[3]

1 *R v Secretary of State for the Environment, ex p London Borough of Hillingdon* [1986] 1 WLR 192.
2 *Warwick RDC v Miller-Mead* [1962] 1 All ER 212.
3 *Bowyer, Philpott and Payne Ltd v Mather* [1919] 1 KB 419.

2.73 In the case of *Vale of White Horse District Council v Allen & Partners*[1] it was held that it must be the case that criminal proceedings are considered inadequate, not just that High Court proceedings would be more convenient.[2]

1 [1997] Env LR 212.
2 It was further held in that case that a local authority's power to seek injunctions generally under Local Government Act 1972, s 222(1) was not free-standing in relation to statutory nuisance. This was despite Court of Appeal observations that the powers were concurrent: see *Wyre*

The power to seek injunctions **2.76**

Forest District Council v Bostock [1993] Env LR 235. Bell J held in *Vale of White Horse* that s 222(1) was an enabling power to allow an authority to sue under EPA s 81(5) in its own name.

2.74 The power to seek an injunction should not be exercised lightly, as Lord Templeman stated in *Stoke-on-Trent City Council v B & Q (Retail) Ltd*:[1]

'[T]he right to invoke the assistance of the civil court in aid of the criminal law is a comparatively modern development. Where Parliament imposes a penalty for an offence, Parliament must consider the penalty is adequate and Parliament can increase the penalty if it proves to be inadequate. It follows that a local authority should be reluctant to seek and the court should be reluctant to grant an injunction which if disobeyed may involve the infringer in sanctions far more onerous than the penalty imposed for the offence.'

1   [1984] AC 754.

2.75 However, the situation under section 81(5) of the EPA 1990 is somewhat different in that Parliament has specifically provided resort to an injunction if the local authority considers the criminal procedure inadequate. Examples include emergencies or highly profitable nuisance. The *B & Q* case[1] is an example of the latter: the local authority considered that the company would not be deterred by the maximum criminal penalty as it was making considerably more money in profits by breaking the law than it would pay in penalty (in that case, by opening on a Sunday before the Sunday trading laws were liberalised). The ECHR will also influence the exercise of the court's discretion as to whether and in what terms to grant an injunctive remedy. Guidance in this respect can be gleaned from *South Buckinghamshire v Porter*[2] in which the House of Lords considered the correct approach to the exercise of the court's discretion to grant an injunction under section 187B of the TCPA 1990 to restrain a breach of planning control where the defendant's Convention rights were engaged (see para **2.10** for a fuller discussion on the impact of the HRA 1998).

1   *Stoke-on-Trent City Council v B&Q (Retail) Ltd* [1984] AC 754.
2   [2003] UKHL 26, [2003] 2 WLR 1547.

2.76 It is not possible for a local authority to seek an injunctive remedy under section 81(5) unless it has first served an abatement notice under section 80(1). In *The Barns v Newcastle Upon Tyne City Council*,[1] it was held that the provisions in the Act were intended to be *consecutive* steps when dealing with a statutory nuisance. First, the authority should serve the abatement notice; where there was no compliance, there should be either prosecution in the magistrates' court or self-help by the local authority requiring the wrongdoer to compensate the local authority for its expenses; as a last resort, there was action in the High Court for an injunction under s 81(5). It was reasoned that if Parliament had intended to empower a local authority to apply to the High Court without first serving an abatement notice, then clear provisions to that effect would have been expected. Read literally, some of the strictly speaking *obiter* reasoning in *The Barns v Newcastle Upon Tyne City Council* would appear to create a number of quite cumbersome obstacles for local authorities seeking effective enforcement of the statutory nuisance regime. *East Dorset District Council v Eaglebeam Ltd*[2] puts these matters into context and is therefore an important decision for local authorities.

1   [2005] EWCA Civ 1274.
2   [2006] EWHC 2378, QB (26 July 2006).

2.77 *Duties and powers of local authorities*

2.77 In *East Dorset District Council v Eaglebeam Ltd*[1], the court held that where an abatement notice had been served on a company of which an individual was the owner and director, a local authority was entitled to issue proceedings for injunctive relief pursuant to section 81(5) against the individual, notwithstanding that the individual had not been served with an abatement notice in his personal capacity. The rationale being that the underlying principle in *The Barnes v Newcastle Tyne City Council* was that a person should first be served with an abatement notice in order that he be given an opportunity to abate the nuisance. Where, as in the case of a director, the individual has been afforded this opportunity, by virtue of the service of the abatement notice on the company, it was not unfair for the local authority to seek injunctive relief against the individual in circumstances where the service of an abatement notice on the company had failed satisfactorily to abate the nuisance.

The court also rejected the submission that the injunction proceedings were an abuse of process when there was an on-going appeal in the magistrates' court against the abatement notice issued by the local authority. Similarly, the court did not consider that *The Barns v Newcastle Upon Tyne City Council* meant that in addition to serving a notice it was necessary for a local authority actually to have prosecuted or attempted self-help before it could seek an injunction. Rather it had to demonstrate that such options were not adequate to deal with the problem.

1   [2006] EWHC 2378, QB (26 July 2006).

2.78 Injunctions are also useful to local authorities in situations where the person served with an abatement notice has complied, or purported to comply, with the requirements of the notice. In the *East Dorset* case, Sir John Blofeld granted an injunction restraining motocross activities by respondents who, in spite of taking some steps to reduce the noise following the abatement order, had been aware that motocross was sufficiently noisy to be both a statutory and a public nuisance. In light of the fact that the respondent had deliberately continued with the motocross in those circumstances, the injunction was granted.

Interim injunctions

2.79 It should be noted that when seeking to enforce the law by means of an interim injunction, a local authority does not have to give an undertaking in damages.[1] In other words, the local authority does not need to undertake to the court to pay damages to the defendant if it later transpires that the injunction should not have been granted (an undertaking which applicants for injunctions usually have to give). An interim injunction would be appropriate where a local authority wished to stop an activity at short notice if, for example, an activity was likely to be noisy. In that case, it can apply for an injunction without giving notice to the other party, who could later claim that the injunction had been wrongly granted. In hearing an interim application, the High Court would need to be satisfied as to the location of the activity and generally the identities of those responsible for it[2] or the landowner, that an injunction was the appropriate remedy and that the activity would cause a nuisance if it went ahead.

An injunction can be different from, and more extensive than, the terms of the original abatement notice.[3] Often the question of costs will be reserved until the substantive hearing but it is to be noted that in the *East Dorset* case where there had been extensive argument on various legal matters as well as live evidence over several days, the court ordered that the defendant pay the local authority's costs for the hearing of the interim injunction.

1   *Kirklees Metropolitan Borough Council v Wickes Building Supplies Ltd* [1993] AC 227.
2   The High Court is sometimes willing to grant injunctions against those whose names are not known (see in the context of TCPA 1990, s 187B, *South Cambridgeshire District Council v Persons Unknown* [2004] EWCA Civ 1280, (2004) Times, 11 November).
3   *Lloyds Bank v Guardian Assurance plc* (1986) Lexis, Enggen library, cases file.

The power to deal with statutory nuisances arising outside the local authority area

2.80 Section 81(2) of the EPA 1990 provides that where the act, default or sufferance which resulted in the statutory nuisance took place outside the area of the local authority where its effects were experienced, the duties and powers of the authority are as if that act, default or sufferance had taken place within its area. In *R v Epping (Waltham Abbey) Justices, ex p Burlinson*[1] it was held that this section may be invoked by one local authority against another.

1   [1948] 1 KB 79.

The requirement to seek permission from the Secretary of State

2.81 Under section 79(10) of the EPA 1990, before summary proceedings can be instituted for statutory nuisances of smoke from premises, dust, steam, smell or other effluvia from industrial, trade or business premises, or any accumulation or deposit (categories (b), (d) and (e)) which could have been prosecuted under Part I of the Act, the permission of the Secretary of State must be obtained. Part I of the Act[1] is concerned with pollution by the emission of prescribed substances that are not the subject of a consent. It should be noted that 'summary proceedings' means the laying of an information in the magistrates' court, not the issue of an abatement notice, despite the heading of section 80 of the 1990 Act.

1   For the enforcement of which the Environment Agency rather than the local authority is responsible.

2.82 The requirement to seek permission is only in the case of instituting summary proceedings – the duty to issue an abatement notice is intact. Furthermore, if the local authority is of the opinion that criminal proceedings would be inadequate, then it could leapfrog this requirement by seeking an injunction in the High Court under section 81(5) of the EPA 1990 without the permission of the Secretary of State.

The power to withdraw or vary an abatement notice

2.83 It is not clear from the EPA 1990 whether once served, an abatement notice can be withdrawn or varied. The issue came before the courts in the case of *R v Bristol City Council, ex p Everett*.[1] In that case, the local authority had originally issued an abatement notice in regard to a steep staircase because in its opinion it was likely to cause someone to fall and injure themselves, but following legal advice it withdrew the notice. Richards J in the High Court held

2.83 *Duties and powers of local authorities*

that, indeed, personal injury was outside the scope of the statutory nuisance regime and that, furthermore, there was an implied power for a local authority to withdraw an abatement notice. He stated:

> 'In the absence of an implied power to withdraw an abatement notice, the enforcement provisions would in my view be unduly rigid. It seems senseless that an authority should be unable to withdraw an abatement notice which, for whatever reason, it no longer considers to be appropriate. It is particularly unsatisfactory that the recipient of the notice should remain subject to it and, by reason of a failure to comply with its requirements, should remain in breach of the criminal law in circumstances where the local authority does not consider the notice to be appropriate and has no intention of bringing a prosecution for breach of it. A power of withdrawal is therefore consistent with, and serves to promote rather than to undermine, the legislative scheme. I see no difficulty in implying such a power.'

1   [1999] 1 WLR 92; [1999] 2 All ER 193.

2.84 The Court of Appeal adopted Richards J's judgment with little further comment. However, whilst the court's decision may be pragmatic the rationale is not entirely convincing. Once the notice has been issued in the absence of an express power of withdrawal, the local authority might be thought to *functus officio* rather like a local planning authority which has issued a planning permission. The commentator to the High Court judgment in the *Environmental Law Reports* stated that an aggrieved person who disagrees with the local authority's decision to withdraw a notice can take action under section 82 of the EPA 1990 (summary proceedings by persons aggrieved). However, once an abatement notice has been breached in the absence of a defence a criminal offence has been committed. Persons *other than* the local authority may prosecute the alleged offender, and in this sense the offence is in the public domain and it is arguable that the local authority is therefore not entitled to withdraw the notice that gave rise to it. It is no answer to say that such persons could commence section 82 proceedings. They would then have to prove beyond reasonable doubt the existence or threat or a statutory nuisance. They could not prosecute simply on the basis that the defendant had failed to comply with one of the specified works or steps required by the notice.[1]

1   Accordingly, third parties may have standing to challenge by judicial review a decision by a local authority to withdraw an abatement notice: see para **2.92**.

2.85 It is possible to envisage situations where withdrawal might seem the sensible course. For example, if a notice was served on a discotheque requiring the premises to be vacated between the hours of midnight and 8 am, and the premises are later converted to an old people's home, the owners of the home would be at risk of prosecution for operating their premises during the forbidden hours. However, withdrawal of the notice would not be necessary in order to ensure a sensible result. In the event of a prosecution, the owners could plead that they had a reasonable excuse for failing to comply with the notice.

'Minded to act' notices

2.86 Some authorities notify persons they consider might be causing a statutory nuisance before issuing an abatement notice. This is done informally or by means of a semi-formal 'minded to act' or 'intimation' notice. Such notices have no statutory basis or force. We do not recommend the practice of issuing 'minded to act' notices. It may sometimes be appropriate for a local authority to write to a potential recipient informing him of its investigation and provisional views. However, it is in our view unhelpful to elevate a letter into the status of a 'notice'.

2.87 In any event, care should be taken with the timing and phrasing of any such letter, notice or pre-action correspondence. Such a letter should not state or suggest that the local authority is already satisfied that a statutory nuisance exists, because in that case it would generally be under a duty to issue an abatement notice. Any 'minded to act' letter would have to be issued before the local authority were satisfied as to the existence of the statutory nuisance, and probably before it had finished its investigations. Similarly, the wording should not imply that the local authority had reached a decision about the existence of a statutory nuisance (or the likelihood of its occurrence). Unless a local authority has genuinely not yet decided whether a statutory nuisance exists (or is likely to occur), it should issue an abatement notice as there is no requirement to warn the recipient of such a notice in advance (and see paras **2.90–2.92**).

2.88 Furthermore, if a person acts upon a 'minded to act' notice and incurs expense, and could have recovered the expense from another person under the EPA 1990 following the issue of an actual abatement notice, then it appears that he will be unable to recover anything in these circumstances,[1] unless that other person is the local authority itself and the person doing the work states that he is doing it under protest.[2] To avoid any legal dispute, then, it would be better for a local authority not to issue 'minded to act' notices.[3]

1 *Harris v Hickman* [1904] 1 KB 13.
2 *Wilson's Music and General Printing Co v London Borough of Finsbury* [1908] 1 KB 563.
3 But see paras **3.43–3.44**.

2.89 As noted above at para **2.44**, there is now a provision under the amended section 80 of the EPA 1990 empowering a local authority to choose whether to issue an abatement notice forthwith or to 'take such other steps as it thinks appropriate for the purpose of persuading the appropriate person to abate the nuisance or prohibit or restrict its occurrence or recurrence' (subsection (2A)(b)). This power may address concerns that the issue of 'minded to act' notices is *ultra vires* where the authority is satisfied that a statutory nuisance exists (since in such a circumstance it is under a *duty* to issue a notice). It appears that under the amended section 80, the issue of 'minded to act' notices could fall within subsection (2A)(b). It should be noted however, that the amended provisions only apply to statutory nuisances falling under the definition of section 79(1)(g) of the EPA (namely those relating to noise), see further para **2.44**.

A DUTY TO CONSULT?

2.90 In contrast with the advice not to issue a warning to a person it considers is causing a statutory nuisance, the question remains as to whether there is a duty to consult with such a person before issuing an abatement notice. The answer would appear to be that there is generally no such duty. A legitimate expectation may arise if the local authority has adopted an enforcement protocol or policy guidance as to how it will approach the task of issuing abatement notices. Many local authorities are also signatories to the Enforcement

2.90 *Duties and powers of local authorities*

Concordat, which presumes that, unless there are good reasons before taking immediate formal enforcement action, an authority will discuss the matter first. Where immediate action is required – and the Concordat expressly envisages this in the case of environmental protection – the Concordat provides that an explanation should be given and furnished to the person against whom action is taken (see para **2.49**). It may also be that failure to follow correctly the local authority's own guidance or the Enforcement Concordat may amount to '[an] informality defect, or error in, or in connection with , the abatement notice' and give grounds for an appeal under regulation 2(2)(b) of the Statutory Nuisance (Appeals) Regulations 1995 (see further para **4.37**). Furthermore, it is possible that article 6.1 of the ECHR may in certain circumstances give rise to a duty of consultation.

2.91 The general position prior to the coming into force of the HRA 1998 was considered in *R v Falmouth and Truro Port Health Authority, ex p South West Water Services*[1] where it was held that there is no general duty of consultation. The water authority, which was the recipient of an abatement notice, claimed that it had a legitimate expectation to be consulted following earlier letters. The Court of Appeal rejected this argument. It held that where consultation was not provided for by statute, only the clearest of assurances would give rise to a legitimate expectation.

1 [2000] 3 All ER 306, [2000] 3 WLR 1464.

2.92 However, in certain circumstances a duty to consult may arise under article 6 of the ECHR. For example, in the context of the issue of an unsuspended abatement notice, the recipient's property rights may potentially be affected. They are protected by article 1 of the first protocol to the ECHR. Article 6 provides that civil rights and obligations should not be determined without a public hearing by an independent tribunal. It may be difficult save in some cases of urgency for a local authority to show that it has adequately balanced the interests of the recipient of the notice before serving an unsuspended notice if there has been no consultation. Equally, it might also be difficult for a local authority to justify withdrawing an abatement notice in respect of a nuisance affecting people's homes without first consulting with those persons affected. A further discussion of these points is to be found in Chapter 3.

DUTIES UNDER THE REGULATION OF INVESTIGATORY POWERS ACT 2000

2.93 The Regulation of Investigatory Powers Act 2000 (RIPA) seeks to ensure that surveillance carried out by the organs of the state does not infringe an individual's Convention rights under the ECHR, in particular, article 8. RIPA 2000 was enacted in response to the European Court of Human Rights case of *Khan (Sultan) v United Kingdom* [2000] Crim LR 684.

2.94 Local authority enforcement is covered by Part II of the RIPA. Section 48 of the RIPA defines 'surveillance' as including 'monitoring, observing or listening to persons, their movements, their conversations or their other activities or communications'. It includes 'recording anything monitored, observed or listened to in the course of surveillance'. It is for this reason that

Duties under the Regulation of Investigatory Powers Act 2000 2.98

some local authorities have adopted policy requirement to apply the RIPA to any complaints of statutory nuisance involving noise including loud swearing or abusive conversation.

2.95 It is commonplace for investigations of a noise statutory nuisance to involve monitoring and obtaining recordings of noise levels. An important question is whether such activities amount to surveillance. Section 26 of the RIPA 2000 applies to:

- directed surveillance
- intrusive surveillance and
- the conduct and use of covert human intelligence sources.

2.96 Although the matter is not free from doubt, it is our view that the majority of ordinary investigations and evidence gathering associated with statutory nuisance are likely to fall outside these categories and therefore would not be subject to RIPA 2000. However it is important that careful consideration is given as to whether the evidence is governed by the RIPA 2000 and if so has been collected in accordance with its provisions.

2.97 Directed surveillance is defined as something that is covert but not intrusive when undertaken as a specific investigation or operation and carried out in such a way as to make it likely that private information is obtained about a person.[1] 'Private information' is defined to include any information relating to a person's private or family life.[2] 'Surveillance' includes 'monitoring, observing or listening to persons and any recordings made as a result of such activities.'[3] Noise nuisance investigations when carried out covertly involving residents might appear to come within this definition. It is not free from doubt whether the evidence gleaned from such investigations would amount to 'private information'. However, in our view, given that nuisance arises when activities impact adversely upon other outside the private domain, it is difficult to see that, for example, evidence from neighbours or an EHO of excessive noise from music played loudly in someone's flat causing a nuisance in another's flat really is information relating to a person's *private* life. Nor do we consider that a person should be able successfully to assert that it is part of his 'family life' to make excessive noise which may annoy his neighbours.

1   RIPA 2000, s 26(2).
2   RIPA 2000, s 26(10).
3   RIPA 2000, s 48(10).

2.98 Local authorities may only authorise directed surveillance when it is 'for the purpose of preventing or detecting crime or of preventing disorder'.[1] An investigation prior to the issue of an abatement notice – as opposed to a potential breach of an abatement notice – is not on its face for the purpose of preventing or detecting a criminal offence. In a report to one local authority concerning the analogous position of an investigation prior to issue of a planning enforcement notice, the Surveillance Commissioner's office stated:

> 'There is some doubt whether investigation of a planning breach prior to the service of an enforcement notice (following which continued breach may amount to a "crime") can be authorised. The limitation of the grounds of necessity available to local government may inhibit it. But it seems to me reasonable to hope that the courts will adopt a broad view of the concept "prevention of crime".'

2.98 *Duties and powers of local authorities*

In the event, in some instances the statutory nuisance may also amount to a public nuisance[2] which is capable of amounting to a common law criminal offence[3] and might therefore be thought to come within the purpose for which directed surveillance may be permitted. Furthermore if a person is served with a warning notice under section 3 of the Noise Act 1996, the person responsible for the noise may be committing an offence if the noise nuisance continues.

1 SI 2003/3771.
2 For a recent example of concurrent public and statutory nuisance see *East Dorset District Council v Eaglebeam Ltd* [2006] EWHC 2378, QB.(26 July 2006).
3 *Wilks v Hungerford Market* Co 2 Bing NC.281 1835. This offence has been referred to in the Magistrates' Courts Act 1980, Sch 1 and in *R v Jan (Richard)* [2006] EWCA Crim 2314.

2.99 Directed surveillance must be authorised in each case by a designated person. A designated person must be an assistant chief officer or an officer responsible for management of an investigation.[1] This has been extended to a 'service manager or equivalent'[2]. However, the authorising officer should not normally be directly involved in the surveillance.[3] A local authority should ensure that the relevant office has been properly delegated with the relevant powers or his authority may be challenged in court (see para **2.11**). Although we have expressed our doubts as to whether ordinary investigations of statutory nuisance would come within the definition of 'directed surveillance', if it were not so, the burden placed upon local authorities could be considerable. Where the council provides a night noise patrol service investigating many complaints during the night, each would require separate authorisation if directed surveillance were held to be involved.

1 SI 2000/2417.
2 SI 2003/3771.
3 Code of Guidance, para 4.14.

2.100 Section 26(3) of the RIPA 2000 defines intrusive surveillance as covert surveillance that is carried out on any residential premises, or in any private vehicle, which involves the presence of an individual on those premises, or in that vehicle, or is carried out by means of a surveillance device. Local authorities are not authorised by RIPA 2000 to carry out intrusive surveillance. However, it is important to note that covert surveillance undertaken by a person off the premises of the person causing the nuisance, would be either not be covered by the RIPA at all, or would be directed not intrusive surveillance, unless it involved the use of a surveillance device. For the use of a surveillance device to be intrusive, it would have to be placed covertly in the premises of the person causing the nuisance for which there is no power under the EPA 1990. Alternatively, to be intrusive, the device would have to be one that 'consistently provides information of the same quality and detail as might be expected to be obtained from a device actually present on the premises'.[1] For it to apply in a statutory nuisance case it would have to be established that a noise monitoring device is a surveillance device for purposes of the RIPA 2000. Whether the measurement and recording of noise levels is capable of amounting to surveillance seems in our view to be doubtful since the point of measurement is to assess the level of noise at the noise sensitive premises, not the level of noise at source.

1 RIPA 2000, s 26(4).

2.101 If one assumes, contrary to our view, that noise evidence from neighbours about a nuisance experienced at their home premises can amount to

Duties under the Regulation of Investigatory Powers Act 2000   **2.101**

'private information' about the maker of the nuisance, it may well be that if the neighbour of a person causing a statutory nuisance is asked by an EHO to collect evidence covertly, he might be acting as a covert human intelligence source.[1] Authorisation for the use of covert human intelligence sources is provided by section 29 of the RIPA and the process is similar to that applying in respect of directed surveillance.

1   RIPA 2000, s 26(1)(c).

Chapter 3

The Abatement Notice

INTRODUCTION

3.01 Abatement notices are a drafting challenge. Their wording is often the subject of close scrutiny at court. A notice may, if it is seriously defective, be quashed, rather than amended, on appeal, at the magistrates', Crown or Divisional courts. It may be incapable of founding a conviction in criminal proceedings.[1] As Kennedy LJ,[2] has said:

'... local authorities, who are entitled to serve abatement notices have access to legal and technical advice. It is understandable that greater particularity [than in a s 82 notice] should be required in such a notice served by a public body with penal consequences if it is not complied with or appealed against'.[3]

1   *Sterling Homes (Midlands) Ltd v Birmingham City Council* [1996] Env LR 121.
2   Formerly Vice-President, QBD.
3   *East Staffordshire Borough Council v Fairless* (1998) 31 HLR 677 quoted in *Hall v Kingston upon Hull City Council* [1999] 2 All ER 609 at 617.

3.02 No particular form for an abatement notice has been stipulated in the Environmental Protection Act 1990 (EPA 1990) or in regulations made under it. Some bases from which to draft abatement notices are set out in Appendix A. Section 80(1) of the 1990 Act simply requires local authorities to serve notices which impose:

'all or any of the following requirements
(a) requiring the abatement of the nuisance or prohibiting or restricting its occurrence or recurrence;
(b) requiring the execution of such works and the taking of such other steps, as may be necessary for any of those purposes
[specifying] the time or times within which the requirements of the notice are to be complied with'.

These provisions have been given a broad meaning. Langley J held in *Lambie v Thanet*[1] that they extended to a requirement to permit a local authority environmental health officer to enter premises to set a sound limiter.

1   [2001] Env LR 21 p 397.

AUTHORITY TO ISSUE AN ABATEMENT NOTICE

3.03 An abatement notice may only be served by a local authority. It is important to ensure that those who purport to issue them have authority under the scheme of delegation to do so. The Divisional Court tends nowadays to be unsympathetic to technical arguments based on alleged defects in the internal procedures of local authorities.[1] Recipients of abatement notices are, however, often both enthusiastic for such points and persuasive in the magistrates' court.

3.03 *The abatement notice*

1   See eg *Albion v Railtrack plc* [1998] EHLR 83 but contrast with *R v St Edmundsbury Borough Council, ex p Walton* [1999] Env LR 878 where a planning permission was quashed because the officers, who decided not to require formal environmental assessment pursuant to Directive 85/337/EEC, did not have authority to make that decision and *Dee and Clwyd River Authority v Parry* (1967) 65 LGR 488 where a water pollution prosecution failed because the prosecutor could not prove his authority to prosecute.

UNDERLYING PRINCIPLE OF SIMPLICITY

3.04   *The key question* to be asked is:

Would someone in the position of the recipient know what he had to do or abstain from doing to avoid prosecution?

3.05   The underlying principle which should govern the drafting of such notices is to ensure that they let the recipient know what is wrong and tell him in simple, straightforward terms what, if any, particular measures he is required to take to put it right.[1] It is neatly encapsulated in the remark of the then Vice President of the Queen's Bench Division Kennedy LJ about the notice in *Stanley v Ealing*[2] that it was 'sufficiently precise to enable the respondent to know what was wrong and what he had to do about it.' Lord Wilberforce suggested in 1975 that the keynote is the need to use discretion and common sense.[3] The then Lord Chief Justice, Lord Widgery observed in 1974 that it is necessary to look at the whole circumstances of the case and to try to make an order which is in its terms sensible and just having regard to the entire prevailing situation.[4] The Divisional Court has recently reiterated this approach by observing[5] that:

> '... it beholds those who seek to attack the validity of an Abatement Notice to approach the matter with practical common sense'.

1   The classic formulation in the related area of planning control is that of Upjohn LJ in *Miller-Mead v Minister of Housing Local Government* [1963] 2 QB 196 at 232: '... in my judgment the test must be: does the notice tell him fairly what he has done wrong and what he must do to remedy it?' Town and Country Planning Act 1990, s 173(3) requires the local planning authority to tell the wrongdoer what he must do to remedy the breach of planning control. In statutory nuisance under EPA 1990, Pt II, by contrast, the authority can generally leave to the wrongdoer the choice of means and methods for abating and preventing the recurrence of the nuisance (see below).
2   [2000] Env LR D18.
3   *Salford City Council v McNally* [1976] AC 379 at 390A.
4   *Nottingham City District Council v Newton* [1974] 1 WLR 923 at 930A endorsed by the Divisional Court in *R v Fenny Stratford Justices, ex p Watney Mann (Midlands) Ltd* [1976] 1 WLR 1101.
5   *Stanley v London Borough of Ealing* [2000] Env LR D18.

3.06   As the then Lord Chief Justice, Lord Bingham of Cornhill observed[1] that there was 'no necessary complexity in this topic'. He suggested some simple questions to which the notice should provide the answer, such as:

> 'What was the statutory nuisance the subject of the notice? What did the Notice require the recipient to do? Were any works to be carried out?'

He agreed with Astill J that the notice must be clear to the recipient. The test is whether those who receive it and have to work to it can understand its requirements.

1   *Brighton and Hove Council v Open Coachworks (Brighton) Ltd* DC [2001] Env LR 4 p 77.

3.07 The above approach should in the authors' view minimise the difficulties associated with challenges based upon articles 6,[1] 7(1),[2] the First Protocol[3] of, and the principle of certainty[4] inherent in, the European Convention on Human Rights (ECHR). The position has always been as Lord Bridge of Harwich explained in *R v Home Office, ex p Brind*[5] that:

> '... the courts will presume that Parliament intended to legislate in conformity with the Convention, not in conflict with it ...'

Decisions of national courts ought therefore generally always to have been consistent with the Convention. Challenges based on the Convention are still likely to be small, now that the Human Rights Act 1998 (HRA 1998) is, and has been since October 2000[6], in force.

1 This includes at article 6, para 3(a) of the Convention the right to be informed in detail of the nature and cause of a criminal charge (see Appendices).
2 Ie the prohibition on retrospective criminalisation (see Appendix F).
3 Ie the protection of property rights (see para **2.92** on unsuspended notices).
4 *Winterwerp v Netherlands* (1979) 2 EHRR 387.
5 [1991] 1 AC 696 at 747H and 748A.
6 The Act to some extent operates retrospectively on action taken by public authorities before that date (s 22(4)).

FORMALITIES

3.08 There is no prescribed form. Schedule 3 (6) of the EPA 1990 requires that the notice inform the recipient of any right of appeal to the magistrates and the time limit for such appeals. The time limit for such an appeal is 21 days from the date of service.[1] Appeals are currently governed by the Statutory Nuisance (Appeals) Regulations 1995.[2] If the notice requires works to be undertaken or relates to noise necessarily caused in the performance of a legal duty then if the notice is not to be suspended pending any appeal a statement to that effect must be made[3]. Magistrates sometimes decline to hear prosecutions pending the determination of appeals even where the notice has not been suspended[4].

1 EPA 1990, s 80(3).
2 SI 1995/2644.
3 See Statutory Nuisance (Appeal) Regulations 1995, SI 1995/2644, reg 3(1)(a) and (b) discussed below at para **3.35**.
4 The lawfulness of this does not appear to have been tested by an application for a mandatory order (formerly a mandamus – a court order requiring a public body to perform its duty).

WHAT SHOULD BE REQUIRED?

3.09 The introductory words[1] *'all or any'* of section 80(1) of the EPA 1990 indicate that it is unnecessary to impose as requirements on the recipient all the possible elements of a notice. The wording does not, however, make clear whether the local authority must include all the elements which they consider applicable.

1 See para **3.02**.

3.10 *The abatement notice*

SHOULD WORKS OR STEPS BE REQUIRED?

Background to current position

3.10 The decisions of the Divisional Court on section 80(1) of the EPA 1990 have demonstrated some judicial ambivalence. In some cases such as *Sterling Homes (Midlands) Ltd v Birmingham City Council*[1] (which arose out of noises from 'Big Bertha' disturbing nearby residents) it has held that local authorities can choose simply to require the abatement of the nuisance; the obligation to specify the 'works' and the 'steps' only arises if they choose to include in their notices a requirement for works to be done or steps to be taken.[2]

1   [1996] Env LR 121.
2   See McCullough J in *Sterling Homes (Midlands) Ltd v Birmingham City Council* [1996] Env LR 121 at 133, 134. He observed that even if the notice specified works, they might not succeed in abating the nuisance and further action would be taken. He considered that 'it may clearly be helpful if local authorities feel able to specify what works should be done or what steps should be taken, but I see little advantage in obliging them to do so'.

3.11 In other cases the emphasis has been different. For example, in *Kirklees Metropolitan Borough Council v Field*[1] it held that if works or action are required as a matter of fact they should be specified if there might be any doubt about them.[2] In the latter case the Divisional Court sat as a three judge court with the express intention of resolving the uncertainty that two judge court decisions had left. Its formulation was as follows:

> '... an abatement notice must inform the landowner of what is wrong so that he knows what is wrong ... but as it must also ensure that the landowner knows what he is to do to abate the nuisance it may be necessary to specify the works required'.[3]

Brooke LJ emphasised[4] that Parliament cannot have intended that citizens might be exposed to criminal penalties for failure to execute works which were 'positively needed' to abate a nuisance. He also expressed the somewhat optimistic hope that Owen J's judgment would make the position completely clear in the future.

1   [1998] Env LR 337 now overruled by *R v Falmouth and Truro Port Health Authority, ex p South West Water Services* [2000] 3 All ER 306, [2000] 3 WLR 1464, CA and para **3.13**.
2   [1998] Env LR 337 at 342 per Owen J with whom Brooke LJ and Gage J agreed.
3   [1998] Env LR 337 at 342.
4   [1998] Env LR 337 at 343.

3.12 What is clear, unfortunately, is that *Kirklees*[1] did not end disputes about the adequacy of abatement notices. The facts of the *Kirklees* case were somewhat unusual. A rock face and wall was in imminent danger of collapse. Some positive action had to be taken. Inaction or abstention from action would not resolve the problem. It was therefore plainly necessary to undertake *works*. The local authority left it to the recipients to decide what those should be. The Divisional Court held that to be wrong. (The facts were, therefore, very different from those involving nuisances subject to the 'best practicable means' defence which could be abated either by abstention from an activity or by the continuation of activities after the execution of works or the carrying out of steps.)

1   *Kirklees Metropolitan Borough Council v Field* [1998] Env LR 337.

Should works or steps be required? **3.16**

Current position after *Falmouth*

3.13 The Court of Appeal[1] held in *R v Falmouth and Truro Port Health Authority, ex p South West Water Services* that an abatement need not require any steps or works even if the authority think that, or if, as a matter of fact, they are necessary. Simon Brown LJ put it thus:

> 'It is therefore necessary to decide whether ... an abatement notice must specify the works or steps in every case (like the present) where the nuisance can only be abated by the execution of works or the taking of steps ... I would therefore overrule *Kirklees* and hold that in *all* cases the local authority can if it wishes leave the choice of means of abatement to the perpetrator of the nuisance.'[2]

This is not necessarily the final word. Two qualifications need to be made.

1 The Court of Appeal is superior in the hierarchy of the courts to the Divisional Court so it can overrule the Divisional Court.
2 *R v Falmouth and Truro Port Health Authority, ex p South West Water Services* [2000] 3 All ER 306; [2000] 3 WLR 1464, CA.

3.14 First the House of Lords may take a different view.[1] The Court of Appeal might itself take a different view now that the ECHR has been incorporated into English law.[2] An argument might be advanced that failure to require particular works known to be necessary would leave the wrongdoer exposed to criminal prosecution for failure to do something which he had not been told that he was required to do. It might be urged that this would be inconsistent with articles 6(3)(a)[3] and 7[4] of the ECHR and the principle of certainty.[5]

1 In a future case. The House of Lords Appeals Committee refused leave to appeal on the papers in this case.
2 By the HRA 1998.
3 Ie the right to be informed in detail of the nature and cause of a criminal charge (see Appendix F).
4 Ie the prohibition on retrospective criminalisation (see Appendices).
5 See also paras **3.38–3.44**.

3.15 In the authors' view such arguments should be examined critically and viewed with great caution. In most cases the wrongdoer can avoid prosecution by abstaining from the activity that causes the nuisance. This is so even if the defence of best practicable means applies. The only situation where this would not be so would be where there was a legal duty to do that which, in the absence of particular measures, would cause a nuisance. There the only way that some exposure to legal sanction could be avoided would be by taking those measures.

3.16 Even in those cases, however, courts should, in the authors' view, be cautious about accepting arguments based on articles 6(3)(a) and 7. Those who undertake activities are generally much better placed than local authorities in terms of expertise and resources to devise measures to avoid carrying them out in a way that causes nuisance. An element of judgment must inevitably be exercised by criminal courts about the factual situations that they examine. For example courts must judge whether a particular piece of driving falls below the standard of care which society requires drivers to take. Subjects of the law are entitled to know what tests the court will apply; they cannot know in advance how the tests will apply to particular factual situations. The European Court of Human Rights (ECtHR) has acknowledged in *Sunday Times v United Kingdom*[1]

3.16 *The abatement notice*

that '... many laws are inevitably couched in terms which to a greater or lesser extent are vague ...' In *Handyside v United Kingdom*[2] it held that although article 7 '... includes the requirement that the offence should be clearly described by law' that test was satisfied if the legislation in question provided a general description which was then interpreted and applied by the courts.

1   (1979) 2 EHRR 245; also in *Muller v Switzerland* (1988) 13 EHRR 212.
2   (1976) 1 EHRR 737, (1974) 17 YB 228. See also *Kokkinakis v Greece* (1993) 17 EHRR 397.

3.17 *Second* Simon Brown LJ himself acknowledged that the Court of Appeal have considered[1] that it may be irrational for an authority not to specify works or steps. Laws LJ considered in *Sevenoaks v Brands Hatch*[2] that 'there may well be some utility in recognising a class of case where it may be irrational for a local authority not to specify works.' There is a general principle of law that a public authority must not act in a way which the courts regard as irrational or otherwise 'unreasonable in the Wednesbury sense'.[3] Such circumstances will, in the authors' view, be rare. Arguments by wrongdoers that the circumstances exist will, of course, be less rare.

1   *Budd v Colchester Borough Council* [1999] Env LR 739, CA.
2   [2001] Env LR 5 p 86. Laws LJ's observation was not part of his decisive reasoning (*ratio decidendi*). It was a judicial aside (*obiter dictum*) and therefore is not binding on later court decisions.
3   Wade & Forsyth *Administrative Law* (8th edn, 2000), Chapter 12 (abuse of discretion, principle of reasonableness).

Mere restriction rather than abatement?

3.18   Section 80(1)(a) of the EPA 1990 gives local authorities a discretion to require the *restriction* rather than the abatement or prohibition of its occurrence or recurrence. On one interpretation, this means that, and no more than that, they may restrict that of which unreasonable quantities amount to a nuisance to a level at which it is no longer a nuisance. Thus open air opera performances in an otherwise quiet village might be restricted to a short season or a limited number of nights. The difficulty with this view is that in general this would amount to abating rather than restricting the *nuisance*.[1] So the word would be unnecessary; statutes are so far as possible interpreted on the basis that Parliament does not use words unnecessarily.[2]

1   See discussion of significance of frequency and level of activity in Chapter 1 (nature and scope of statutory nuisance), paras **1.12**–**1.20**.
2   See Bennion *Statutory Interpretation* (3rd edn, 1997) pp 898–900.

3.19   The better interpretation, however, in the authors' view, is that this provision empowers local authorities to serve a notice which falls short of eliminating the nuisance. The circumstances in which it would be reasonable for an authority to adopt such an approach are limited. Generally, they will not be staying within the limits of the discretion given to them under the EPA 1990 unless they require the elimination of statutory nuisances (which are by their nature either prejudicial to health or otherwise unacceptable). It is a general principle of law that where Parliament gives public authorities a power as to the exercise of which they have a discretion that discretion is not unlimited. The limits of their discretion are to be found by an examination of the purpose and objects for which Parliament gave the power.[1] The purpose and object of this legislation is the speedy elimination of that which puts health at risk or is otherwise unacceptable in the areas to which it applies.

1   The classic exposition of this general principle is to be found in Lord Bridge of Harwich's speech in the House of Lords in *R v Tower Hamlets London Borough Council, ex p Chetnik Developments Ltd* [1988] AC 858 at 872–873.

3.20 The range of circumstances in which local authorities can legitimately, within the limits of their discretion, under-enforce is limited. Some circumstances may, however, justify under-enforcement. The scheme of the EPA 1990 is that in situations to which is applied the defence of 'best practicable means' the elimination of nuisances should not be enforced by the statutory nuisance regime. Where, therefore, it is clear to an authority that a potential recipient of a notice would be entitled to the 'best practicable means' defence in respect of a certain level of activity it would be consistent with the scheme of the Act for them to require the restriction of the nuisance to a level which corresponds to best practice rather than its complete elimination.

3.21 Another example might be where the recipient of the notice was proposing to relocate his activities, and elimination of the nuisance would involve expenditure whose benefits could not be transferred. In those circumstances it might well be reasonable in the interim before relocation to tolerate for a limited period a restriction of, rather than the elimination of, the nuisance.

The more specific: the easier to enforce

3.22 An advantage to a local authority of specifying works or steps is that proof of non-compliance with such requirements may be much easier than proof of the continuation of a nuisance; there is less scope for differences of judgment between the local authority and the courts. So, even though they may not be required to specify any measures, they should think carefully about how much more difficult it may be for them to bring a successful prosecution for non-compliance if they do not. Fewer staff resources are required to enforce a requirement to install triple glazing than to prove that a noise nuisance has recurred.

FORMULATION OF ABATEMENT NOTICE: PRACTICAL GUIDANCE

3.23 The following propositions of guidance in the formulation of abatement notices may be made:

1   Where abstention from or ordinary care in undertaking an activity will resolve the problem then the notice need only, and generally should only, describe the nuisance, require its abatement and prohibit its recurrence

3.24 Thus in *Budd v Colchester Borough Council*[1] the Divisional Court considered that the nuisance of greyhounds barking could be resolved by getting rid of the greyhounds or by treating them in a different way, or by insulating their premises. The notice did not need to specify which. The Court of Appeal[2] upheld its decision. In 1950, it was held that there was no need in relation to foul smells from the improper keeping of pigs to do more than require the abatement of the nuisance.[3] In 1894, it was held that no works had

3.24 *The abatement notice*

to be executed to avoid the recurrence of the nuisance of black smoke belching forth from a factory chimney.[4] As the Borough of Ramsgate's inspector of nuisances submitted to the court *'all that is required is care in the stoking'*.

1   [1997] Env LR 128, see esp 133.
2   [1999] Env LR 739.
3   *McGillivray v Stephenson* [1950] 1 All ER 942.
4   *Millard v Wastall* [1898] 1 QB 342, 'This is one of those nuisances ... like ... keeping an animal so as to be a nuisance ... do not necessarily require the execution of any works in order to abate them' (per Lawrance J at 344).

2   Where the terms of the notice require steps to be taken or works undertaken to abate the nuisance, the notice must specify them clearly

3.25   Failure to take steps or do works required by an abatement notice will be in itself a criminal offence. There will be no need to prove that a nuisance has continued or recurred. So the recipient of such a notice must know what he has to do to avoid criminal liability. The Court of Appeal confirmed in *R v Falmouth and Truro Port Health Authority, ex p South West Water Services* that if the local authority do require steps to be taken or works undertaken then they must be clearly specified.[1] Simon Brown LJ expressly stated that two decisions asserting this rule were still good law.

'*Network*[2] and *Sterling*[3] remain good law'.

1   [2000] 3 WLR 1464, CA at 1486E–1487E.
2   *Network Housing Association v Westminster City Council* [1995] Env LR 176.
3   *Sterling Homes (Midlands) Ltd v Birmingham City Council* [1996] Env LR 121.

3.26   In *Sterling*[1] the Divisional Court found invalid on grounds of uncertainty a notice in these terms:

'Do hereby require you to abate the said nuisance within fifty six days ... and for that same purpose require you to carry out *such works as may be necessary* to ensure that the noise and vibration does not cause prejudice to health or a nuisance, take any steps as may be necessary for that purpose' [our emphasis].

1   *Sterling Homes (Midlands) Ltd v Birmingham City Council* [1996] Env LR 121.

3.27   The classic case is *R v Wheatley*.[1] Drains were untrapped. The premises would remain a nuisance until appropriate physical apparatus had been installed. The order of the justices (the equivalent under the Public Health Act 1875 of an abatement notice) merely required the owner of the premises to:

'execute such works and do such things as may be necessary ... so that the same shall no longer be a nuisance or injurious to health'.

This was too vague and general. The court was emphatic that if any works and things were required they should be specified in the order.[2]

1   (1885) 16 QBD 34.
2   'If after he had incurred expense in doing what he thought was necessary, the nuisance was not abated, he might be required by the justices to incur further expense by executing further works, and I cannot think that such a state of things was intended by the legislature' per Mathew J (1885) 16 QBD 34 at 38. This approach is common sense; but it must be remembered that if the works required do not in fact remedy the problem the person responsible still has the general obligation to abate it. He may therefore have to undertake further work.

Formulation of abatement notice: practical guidance 3.31

3.28 A more recent strong example involved deficient sound insulation between flats of a housing association in Westminster. The notice required works which would achieve a level of sound attenuation but did not specify what those works should be to achieve that result. The Divisional Court regarded as notoriously difficult the question of sound levels and nuisance. The council therefore:

> 'should have made up their own minds as to the work required and stated it in the notice'.[1]

Giving the recipient an option as to the works to be undertaken was described by Simon Brown LJ as a poisoned chalice.[2] The notice need not, however, be as detailed as a builder's specification.[3] Whether works have been sufficiently described in an abatement notice is something which magistrates have to decide 'applying practical common sense'.[4]

1 *Network Housing Association v Westminster City Council* [1995] Env LR 176 at 183 per Buckley J. Simon Brown LJ in *Falmouth City Council* said expressly that this remained good law.
2 Buckley J was disturbed at the contemplation within the notice of the possible need to undertake a succession of works: 'That will not do' ([1995] Env LR 176 at 184).
3 *Network Housing Association v Westminster City Council* [1995] Env LR 176 per Buckley J.
4 *Stanley v London Borough of Ealing* [2000] Env LR D18 per Kennedy LJ.

3.29 An example of *steps* which had positively to be taken would be those involved in the removal of an accumulation of putrescible waste constituting a nuisance. It might, however, in such a case be obvious from a mere description of the nuisance what steps needed to be taken. If there were within a builder's yard piles of inert waste (not prejudicial to health or a nuisance) and piles of foul smelling ordure and rotting bones attracting vermin (which were both a nuisance and prejudicial to health) it would be necessary to make it clear which piles had to be removed.

3.30 One of the most important categories of works which may need to be undertaken are those necessary to prevent a dwelling house from being prejudicial to the health of its occupants. Premises inadequately protected from damp might well need works to be undertaken, for example the installation of a damp proof course. It makes sense for the local authority to specify such works rather than to leave it to the owner. If so the specification must be by reference to what must be done not by reference to the result sought.

3 Where the notice or accompanying documentation imply that works or steps will be required, the works or steps must be specified

3.31 The Divisional Court has on occasion been prepared to treat words apparently requiring works or steps as mere surplusage and uphold a notice on the basis that in reality all that it was requiring was the abatement of a nuisance which could be done by abstention from or ordinary care in undertaking an activity.[1] It would be a potentially expensive mistake for a local authority to rely on this approach. The London Borough of Camden did so in dealing with noisy lift machinery at Russell Square Station that was causing a nuisance to a nearby flat. London Underground's own report said that:

> 'No attempt has been made to control the vibration or noise in the lift machine room. Therefore the conclusions from the local authority are

3.31 *The abatement notice*

justified and it is clear that the best practical means has not been applied in this situation ...'

It might seem a difficult case for a local authority to lose. Unfortunately, however, the notice and an accompanying letter referred to works without specifying them.[2] Rose LJ[3] observed:

'... it seems to us sensible, particularly if there is ambiguity in the notice, to look at any accompanying letter in order to determine objectively how the notice would be understood by its recipient ...'

These are perhaps examples of the application of the general principle that in interpreting documents courts look to objectively assessed substantive intention rather than literal meaning of superficially examined words. It is traditionally expressed in the Latin phrases '*Falsa demonstratio non nocet*' and '*ut res magis valeat quam pereat*'[4]. Thus the Court of Appeal in *McKay v First Secretary of State*[5] was willing to treat an appeal clearly expressed to be against one enforcement notice as relating to a different enforcement notice as the context made it clear that that was the intention.

1   Eg *McGillivray v Stephenson* [1950] All ER 942.
2   London Underground has a statutory duty to provide passenger transport services. So abatement of the nuisance by complete cessation of activity at Russell Square would not have been lawful.
3   *London Borough of Camden v London Underground Ltd* [2000] Env LR 369, DC.
4   'A[n obviously] mistaken description does not count' and '[we will interpret it if possible] so that the thing should be valid rather than fail [in its purpose]'.
5   [2005] EWCA Civ 774 [2006] 1 PLR 19 at p 363 applying the approach of McNair J in *Finbow v Air Ministry* [1963] WLR 697.

3.32 Neither the notice nor the letter had specified the works to be undertaken. Camden compounded their errors by not ensuring that the preliminary hearing which the stipendiary magistrate held (into other matters discussed below) dealt with the validity of the notice. The hearing lasted six days. London Underground claimed £91,097 costs; they were awarded £37,540.[1]

1   It is possible that the case would have been decided differently after *Falmouth* [2000] 3 All ER 306, [2000] 3 WLR 1464, CA. It would be rash, however, to assume that future similar cases would be decided differently. The DC treated the totality of material surrounding the abatement notice as effectively requiring works to be undertaken; *Falmouth* does not remove the duty to specify any such works. Laws LJ discussed both *Falmouth* and *Camden v London Underground* in *Sevenoaks v Brands Hatch* [2001] Env LR 5 p 86 without suggesting that *Camden* would have been differently decided after *Falmouth*. Silber J attached importance to the requirement in *Camden* 'special attention to be paid to the low frequency element of a noise' which, he evidently thought, created uncertainty without giving freedom of choice of means to the recipient.

4   If in doubt leave works and steps out; simply require the abatement and prohibit the recurrence of the nuisance

3.33 The Court of Appeal decision in *R v Falmouth and Truro Port Health Authority, ex p South West Water Services*[1] discussed above suggests a safe course if there is any doubt about whether works or steps should be required, and if so, how they should be described to satisfy the courts' standards for clear specification. The safe course will be to leave it to the wrongdoer to choose for himself the means and methods for compliance.

1   [2000] 3 All ER 306, [2000] 3 WLR 1464.

5 Can the notice say 'Do what y requires you to do' or 'Do x to the satisfaction of y?'

3.34 A Divisional Court decision suggests that these are lawful terms for a notice. Thus a requirement to provide suitable refuse storage for the property:

'to comply with the requirements of the environmental health officer'.[1]

was not regarded as necessarily bad. However, Kennedy LJ emphasised that there was simply no finding of fact in the Case Stated that the recipient did not know what the requirements of the environmental health officer were. By contrast, Sir Frank Layfield QC held a planning enforcement notice which required works *to be agreed with the local planning authority* to be bad for uncertainty.[2] Such formulations are always likely to have, at best, a precarious validity. The authors' view is that they should be avoided.

1 *Stanley v London Borough of Ealing* [2000] Env LR D18, DC
2 *Kaur v Secretary of State* [1990] JPL 814.

6 Decide whether the notice will or should be suspended

3.35 Abatement notices are not suspended pending appeal to the magistrates unless:[1]

- compliance would involve any person in expenditure on the carrying out of works before the hearing of the appeal or
- they are based on categories (g) or (ga) and relate to noise necessarily caused in the performance of some duty imposed by law.

1 Statutory Nuisance (Appeals) Regulations 1995, SI 1995/2664, reg 3(1)(b)(i)(ii).

3.36 In such cases abatement notices are generally suspended. The local authority can only prevent them from being suspended if:[1]

- the nuisance is injurious to health[2] or
- the nuisance is likely to be of limited duration so that suspension would render it of no practical effect[3] or
- the expenditure on works would not be disproportionate to the public benefit to be expected in the period before the appeal is determined.[4]

The notice must then state[5] (or the notice will be suspended):

- that paragraph 2 of regulation 3 of the Statutory Nuisance (Appeals) Regulations 1995 applies
- that it will have effect notwithstanding any appeal to the magistrates
- which of the grounds applies.

1 Statutory Nuisance (Appeals) Regulations 1995, SI 1995/2644, reg 3(2)(a)(b).
2 Reg 3(2)(a)(i).
3 Reg 3(2)(a)(ii).
4 Reg 3(2)(b).
5 Reg 3(3).

3.37 An aggrieved recipient of such a notice may raise in his defence to a prosecution brought before any appeal has been heard facts or matters which suggests that the conditions for effectiveness before appeal have not been met.

3.38 *The abatement notice*

HUMAN RIGHTS ACT 1998

3.38 The ECHR[1] was incorporated into national law in October 2000.[2] Section 6 of the HRA 1998 makes it unlawful for public authorities to act in a way which is incompatible with a Convention right. Recipients may be tempted to argue that an *unsuspended* abatement notice, which takes effect before any appeal is heard by the magistrates, is inconsistent with article 6(1) of the ECHR which entitles everyone:

> 'in the determination of his civil rights and obligations ... [to] a fair and public hearing'.

The ECtHR has held that article 6(1) applies to rights such as those which are restricted by environmental control regimes.[3] Non human companies may also rely on this 'human' right.[4]

1 The term generally used to refer to the 'Convention for the Protection of Human Rights and Fundamental Freedoms' of the Council of Europe (Rome 1950).
2 HRA 1998, s 22(4) applies it retrospectively where people rely on it against actions taken by public authorities before October 2000.
3 *Fischer v Austria* (1995) 20 EHRR 349; *Bryan v United Kingdom* (1995) 21 EHRR 342. *Alconbury Investments REF*
4 *Dombo Beheer BV v Netherlands* (1993) 18 EHRR 213.

3.39 In the authors' view however, such attacks on unsuspended notices need not generally be successful. Courts have tended to be reluctant to accept arguments that public bodies have acted inconsistently with the Convention. Article 1 of the first protocol permits states to interfere with or deprive people of property 'in the public interest.' It also provides that the protection of property:

> 'shall not impede the right of a state to enforce such laws as it deems necessary to control the use of property in accordance with the public interest'.

3.40 Article 6 rights are not absolute. Access to courts may be limited where a legitimate aim is pursued by proportionate means.[1] In the period before a magistrates' court hearing takes place the interests of *either* the subject of the nuisance (whose rights are infringed by its continuance) or the recipient of the notice are bound to be adversely affected by the suspension or immediate effect of the notice. Interim protection of one of those interests is, in our view, a legitimate aim. The immediacy of effect of abatement notices was one of the most important recent improvements in statutory nuisance procedure.

1 *Golder v United Kingdom* (1975) 1 EHRR 524; *Ashingdane v United Kingdom* (1985) 7 EHRR 528.

3.41 Administrative decisions which do not themselves comply with article 6 may, nonetheless, not involve conflict with the Convention if there is a right of recourse to a court which complies with article 6.[1] Such is the situation where a notice is not suspended.

1 *Albert and Le Compte v Belgium* (1983) 5 EHRR 533; *Kaplan v United Kingdom* (1980) 4 EHRR 64; *R (Alconbury developments) v Secretary of State for Environment, Transport and the Regions* [2001] UKHL 23, [2003] 2 AC 295.

3.42 Some amendments to the Statutory Nuisance (Appeals) Regulations 1995[1] nonetheless appear to us to be desirable. However, it is important that authorities should not in the meantime be deterred from offering immediate

Human Rights Act 1998 **3.44**

protection to their communities from some statutory nuisances such as those which involve risk to health or nuisances to homes.[2] The following procedure should reduce risk of problems.

1 SI 1995/2644.
2 Protected especially by article 8 of the Convention.

Practical advice

3.43

- Authorities should consider whether the interests of the subjects of the nuisance or the recipient of the notice should prevail in the period before any appeal is heard by magistrates. They should attach particular importance to factors such as risk to health or the effect of nuisances on people's homes. Respect for homes is a specific right under article 8 of the Convention.
- If (a) provisionally they think that a notice should not be suspended, (b) it is a complex matter and (c) it is reasonable and practical to do so, it may be worth consulting in writing the proposed recipient of the notice and inviting any representations he wishes to make in writing by a specified date on the notice. This may not, however, be practical and reasonable. The situation may call for urgent action. The time for response may justifiably be short. The authority may well not be able to engage in any, or any extensive, discussion with the recipient.
- They should record their decision and the reasons for it in writing.
- If they decide to suspend the notice pending appeal they should specify a time for compliance which runs from the date of the magistrates' decision if an appeal is made.[1]
- If they decide that the notice should be immediately effective then they should state briefly on the notice why they have so decided (eg because of risk to health or effect on people's homes).
- They should also make any statements on the notice which are required by the Statutory Nuisance (Appeals) Regulations 1995.[2]

1 See Appendices.
2 SI 1995/2644. See discussion at para **3.36**.

3.44 An interesting argument for recipients in that situation would be that the legislation should have provided for compensation to be paid if an appeal against an unsuspended notice was subsequently successful.[1] The ECtHR has observed:

'Compensation terms under the relevant legislation are material to the assessment whether the contested measure respects the requisite fair balance and, notably, whether it imposes a disproportionate burden on the [subject][2]'.

Compensation is relevant. It is by no means clear however that a disproportionate burden is placed on the subject merely because a magistrates' court takes a different view from the local authority. If negligence or other fault has been involved (which should involve only a small minority of cases where appeals are successful) then the law may have changed. The old strict restrictions on liability even in those circumstances may no longer be justified.[3]

1 As is the case in respect of planning enforcement notices that become effective before appeal ('stop notices'). Compensation is payable if it transpires on appeal that there was no breach of planning control (Town and Country Planning Act 1990, s 186).

3.44 *The abatement notice*

2 *Pressos Compania Naviera SA v Belgium* (1995) 21 EHRR 301.
3 See Chapter 7, paras **7.115–7.116**.

THE 'BEST PRACTICABLE MEANS' DEFENCE

3.45 A difficulty arises where the notice relates to one of the categories of statutory nuisance to which the defences of *best practicable means* applies. It may well be that the nuisance could be abated simply by ceasing the activity. But the recipient has a defence to a prosecution, even if a nuisance is found to exist, if he is adopting the best practicable means to prevent or counteract the effects of the nuisance.

3.46 One view is that there would be no point in serving a notice if the defence could successfully be made out. Parliament cannot have intended that there should be a duty to serve a notice in that situation. That is our hesitant view of the law.[1] It is also our more strongly held view of the appropriate guide to prudent local authorities unwilling to expose themselves to unnecessary costs orders in the magistrates' courts.

1 See also the discussion of this issue in Chapter 2 at paras **2.44–2.46**.

3.47 Another view is that Parliament intended that the notice should be served. A prosecution for non-compliance can, however, only be brought if the best practicable means defence were not being used. Best practicable means often involves practices which involve changes in manner of operation from day to day or hour to hour. It is appropriate that those who rely on that defence as a justification for the perpetuation of a nuisance should be at risk of immediate prosecution if they fail to maintain at all times the use of best practicable means.

3.48 But if the local authority consider that the best practicable means are not being adopted, must, or should, the notice specify what the best practicable means would be? 'Works and steps' are wide enough terms to cover much of what is encompassed within the concept of best practicable means. If they do so specify, the recipient knows where he is and the local authority can in due course prosecute for non-compliance with the specific, clear requirements of the notice.

3.49 On the other hand the issues relating to best practicable means may be highly technical. They may be matters in respect of which it would be difficult to expect a local authority to have sufficient expertise to form a view. The wise course may be to leave it to the recipient to choose what they are.

3.50 It is arguable that there is no power to require works or steps if cessation of or abstention from an activity would abate the nuisance. Section 80(1)(b) of the EPA 1990 provides that an abatement notice may require only the execution of works or the taking of steps insofar as they are necessary to abate or prevent the occurrence or recurrence of a nuisance. They cannot, it might be argued, be necessary if cessation of or abstention from an activity would abate it or avoid its recurrence. This is an area which must be approached with common sense. If the reality is that the recipient is probably not going to choose to abstain from an activity which causes a nuisance then the authority are entitled, if they choose to do so, to require works or steps. What is necessary must be judged on the balance of probabilities. For example, if the probability is that the club will continue to play amplified music below a bedroom window then triple glazing may well, on the balance of probabilities, be necessary.

3.51 The local authority is free to leave it to the recipient to decide whether to cease or abstain from an activity rather than to undertake works or take steps. He is free to appeal on the grounds that he has adopted the best practicable means. In his appeal he will have to specify the means that he is asserting are the best practicable ones.

3.52 The magistrates have to decide whether the recipient has made out his defence. If he does not make out his defence it is useful for the magistrates to explain fully their findings as to the respects in which he has failed to adopt best practicable means. That will be helpful both to the local authority in deciding whether to initiate, and the recipient in avoiding the risk of, a prosecution.

LETTERS BEFORE NOTICE

3.53 Where the best practicable means defence might apply it is prudent[1] for the local authority to write to the potential recipients of the notice explaining that they have a duty to serve a notice unless the recipient can demonstrate that he is adopting the best practicable means. They should invite him to comment and provide material by way of technical literature and examples of best practice elsewhere which show that they are adopting best practicable means. The local authority should seek to visit the premises and talk to the operators as well as the 'front men.' They should be conscious of the possibility of the need to equip themselves to present convincing evidence in court in due course.

1   The High Court suggested in *R v Falmouth and Truro Port Health Authority, ex p v South West Water Services* [1999] Env LR 833 that it would usually be unreasonable not to consult before serving a notice and that failure to do so could constitute failure to meet a legitimate expectation and therefore make the decision invalid. This suggestion was not sound and was rejected by the Court of Appeal (*R v Falmouth and Truro Port Health Authority, ex p South West Water Services* [2000] 3 WLR 1464. The statutory appeal procedure defines and meets any legitimate expectation. As Pill LJ observed at 1493H 'The perpetrator of a nuisance however well informed cannot be permitted to dictate the time for compliance. It has been a theme underlying the water undertaker's case that the health authority were obliged to bargain with them as the body with expertise in sewage. Realism must of course govern the activities of public bodies but the health authority cannot properly put itself into the hands of the alleged perpetrator of a public nuisance.' Some degree of consultation may also, as discussed in an earlier section, be appropriate in relation to unsuspended notices as a result of the HRA 1998.

RECORDS OF OFFERS

3.54 It is not uncommon for potential recipients to suggest improvements which might overcome the problems. These should be carefully noted. A reminder in writing should be sent to the recipients setting them out what they have offered to do. But an authority is only absolved from the duty to serve an abatement notice if the nuisance has been abated and is unlikely to recur. If, therefore, the offer from the potential recipient is to do something (for example, install different or additional equipment) which will not immediately, but only at some time in the future, abate or prevent the recurrence of, the nuisance the duty to serve a notice remains.

3.55 *The abatement notice*

3.55 The prudent course, fair to all affected parties, where complicated or expensive steps or works are needed is to write to the prospective respondent setting out the steps or works, assessed on a precautionary basis, that the local authority is considering specifying in the notice and giving it an opportunity to say what, if any, other steps it considers more appropriate and the reasons for so considering. Such an approach should be well received by the courts; this is especially important in relation to costs if at trial the respondent persuades the court that other steps (which it did not suggest to the local authority beforehand) are more appropriate.[1]

1   See also Chapter 2, at paras **2.86–2.89**.

THE COURTS' POWER TO QUASH OR AMEND

3.56 Magistrates have power to quash abatement notices and to vary them in favour of the recipient.[1] Some Divisional Court judges have suggested, without deciding the point, that they may have the power to quash an abatement notice in part, striking out the bad parts, but upholding the valid parts which are severed.[2] Courts must disregard informalities, defects or errors which are not material.[3] Courts are sometimes willing to disregard potentially troublesome parts of notices as 'mere surplusage'[4] or as being 'superfluous'.[5] Astill J, with whom the then Lord Chief Justice agreed, was prepared to ignore as meaningless in context a requirement for the 'carrying out of works.'[6] Had those words not been ignored the notice would have fallen foul of the requirement that any works required by a notice must be specified. The courts look to the substance of requirements. Thus they do not regard as insufficiently specified works and steps (section 80(1)(b) of the EPA 1990) descriptions of what will be regarded as abatement of the nuisance (section 80(1)(a)) even if they are preceded by inappropriate labels such as 'works' or 'steps'.[7]

1   Statutory Nuisance (Appeals) Regulations 1995, SI 1995/2664, reg 5(a), (b). This subject is discussed more fully in Chapter 3 'Challenges to abatement notices'.
2   Eg Jowitt J in *Stanley v London Borough of Ealing* [2000] Env LR D 18 and McCullough J in *Sterling Homes (Midlands) Ltd v Birmingham City Council* [1996] Env LR 121. Partial quashing may not be different from varying. Insofar as it was such an analysis would the advantage for community that a partial quashing would not need to be 'in favour of the appellant' as does a variation.
3   Statutory Nuisance (Appeals) Regulations 1995, SI 1995/2664, reg 3.
4   *McGillivray v Stephenson* [1950] 1 All ER 942 at 944 per Humphreys J. In *London Borough of Camden v London Underground Ltd* [2000] Env LR 369 Rose LJ at 378, para 24 decided that he did not need to consider this possibility as the notice was incurably defective for lack of particulars.
5   *Brighton and Hove Council v Ocean Coachworks (Brighton) Ltd* DC [2001] Env LR 4 at p 77.
6   *Brighton and Hove Council v Ocean Coachworks (Brighton) Ltd* (above).
7   See eg *Sevenoaks v Brands Hatch* DC [2001] Env LR 5 p 86 per Laws LJ at paras 20, 25 and 26.

3.57 Critics of notices often devote much energy to the proper juridical analysis of the nature of the alleged defects and their effects on the status of the notice. They commonly assert that the defects make the notice a nullity[1] or irremediably voidable. Lively and enjoyable though this debate about the juridical status of defective notices can be, it is in the authors' view sterile. The courts tend to deprecate it.[2] The key question is 'Is the notice adequate to found a prosecution for non compliance?'[3] If not, the notice must either be quashed, as a whole or in part, or varied.

1   It often used to be said that fundamental defects apparent on the face of a document render them a nullity (see Upjohn LJ in *Miller-Mead v Minister of Housing and Local Government* [1963] 2 QB 196 at 226). It led Mr Nigel Macleod QC sitting as a Deputy Judge to make a decision *McKay v Secretary of State for the Environment* [1994] JPL 806 of which Sedley LJ dryly observed in *Sovereign Rubber Ltd v Stockport Metropolitan Borough Council* [2000] Env LR 194 'it would take a great deal to persuade me to follow it'. Sedley LJ at 203 acknowledged that, in extreme cases, a notice may be the subject of judicial review for bad faith, serious non compliance with the requisite procedures or such deficiency that the notice cannot be described as an abatement notice at all. Where, however, the magistrates quash, they quash a defective abatement notice not a nullity.
2   Laws LJ observed in *Sevenoaks v Brands Hatch* DC [2001] Env LR 5 at p 86: 'the metaphysical language of "nullity" or "voidness" is not apt in this context. The question always and only is whether a lawful notice has been given.'
3   See Kennedy LJ's remarks in *Sterling Homes (Midlands) Ltd v Birmingham City Council* [1996] Env LR 121 at 135 notional A and 136 notional D–E.

3.58 If the respondent can show that the nuisance could be abated by less onerous steps or works than those specified in the notice, it can be amended by the substitution of those less onerous steps or works. Local authorities need to bear in mind that a notice that is defective in a way that cannot be remedied by a variation in favour of the recipient, cannot be amended.

STATUTORY AUTHORITY

3.59 Where Parliament requires or authorises an activity,[1] it usually expressly or impliedly authorises what would otherwise be a common law nuisance if it is reasonably necessary to the activity authorised. The Divisional Court in *London Borough of Camden v London Underground Ltd*[2] opined that second limb statutory nuisances (but not first limb 'prejudicial to health' ones) enjoyed such an immunity. That opinion was not necessary for their decision and is not therefore binding. The House of Lords in *Manchester Corporation v Farnworth*[3] defined the test of reasonable necessity is such a way that it is difficult in practice to distinguish it from the test of best practicable means:

'When Parliament has authorised a certain thing to be made or done in a certain place, there can be no action for nuisance caused by the making or doing of that thing if the nuisance is the inevitable result of the making or doing so authorised. The onus of proving that the result is inevitable is on those who wish to escape liability for nuisance, but the criterion of inevitability is not what is theoretically possible but what is possible according to the state of scientific knowledge at the time, having also in view a certain common sense appreciation, which cannot be rigidly defined, of practical feasibility in view of situation and expense ...'

So it may not often matter whether the immunity does or does not exist. The immunity has been enlarged by the House of Lords in *Marcic v Thames Water Utilities*[4] in respect of statutory undertakers subject to a specialist control regime. The extent of the enlarged immunity is not clear. It may now be the case that where a potential nuisance could only be avoided by the expenditure of money controlled by a specialist regulator who has environmental responsibilities and enforcement powers, nuisances can no longer exist merely for failure to incur expenditure on works.

1   There may well be an alternative specialist statutory control regime. An interesting example of the approach of the courts to the relationship of nuisance to statutory control regimes other than the EPA 1990 is *Marcic v Thames Water* [2003] UKHL 60, [2004] 2 AC 42. At first instance in *Gillingham Borough Council v Medway (Chatham) Dock Co Ltd* [1993] QB 247 there was

3.59 *The abatement notice*

a suggestion that a permission granted by a planning authority under the Town and Country Planning Act 1990 constituted statutory authority for nuisances. This view was rejected by the Court of Appeal in *Wheeler v Saunders* [1995] 2 ALL ER 697 (see also discussion of this in Chapter 1).
2   [2000] Env LR 369.
3   [1930] AC 171 per Viscount Dunedin at 183.
4   [2003] UKHL 60, [2004] 2 AC 42.

3.60 However, the existence of a statutory duty is important in the context of drafting abatement notices. An organisation under a statutory duty cannot abate a nuisance simply by ceasing the activity which he is obliged to undertake. Therefore, the abatement of a nuisance requires the taking of steps or undertaking of works. The courts are, therefore, more likely in such circumstances to be receptive to the argument that it would be unreasonable for a local authority not to specify the works or steps required and that by failing so to specify they had stepped outside the lawful limits of their discretion under the EPA 1990.[1]

1   This seems to have been the underlying assumption of the Divisional Court in *London Borough of Camden v London Underground Ltd* [2000] Env LR 369; Rose LJ set out the statutory duty under London Regional Transport Act 1984, s 2, at the outset of the court's judgment. The later Court of Appeal decision *R v Falmouth and Truro Port Health Authority, ex p South West Water Services* [2000] 3 All ER 306, [2000] 3 WLR 1464, CA, might however lead to a different approach in the future.

3.61 Ironically, however, it may be in just such cases that local authorities would lack the technical expertise and resources to tell the statutory undertaker how best to carry out his duties. In these circumstances, it would be prudent for the local authority to write to the potential recipients and give them an opportunity to suggest what would amount to best practice. It would also be sensible to contact other similar undertakers and local authorities to find out what are the general practices.

3.62 Where there is a statutory power (as opposed to a duty) it would be possible simply to cease the activity which is authorised, but not required. It may well be however that recipients will, nonetheless, argue[1] that, as cessation of the authorised activity cannot be required, then if the taking of ordinary care is not enough, it would be irrational for the authority not to specify steps or works.

1   Claiming (often wrongly in our view) that they fall within the sort of circumstances envisaged by Simon Brown LJ in *R v Falmouth and Truro Port Health Authority, ex p South West Water Services* [2000] 3 All ER 306, [2000] 3 WLR 1464, CA, as making it irrational not to specify works or steps.

RECIPIENT OF THE NOTICE

3.63 *The person responsible for the nuisance:* this is the person on whom the notice should generally be served.[1] Such a person may be a natural person such as man or a legal person such as a limited company. He is defined in general as *the person to whose act, default or sufferance the nuisance is attributable.*[2] The Interpretation Act 1978 provides that the singular includes the plural. There may well be more than one person responsible. Thus a householder may invite a disc jockey to provide music for a party; both are responsible. A notice served on the wrong person is a nullity.[3]

1   EPA 1990, s 80(2)(a).

2   EPA 1990, s 79(7).
3   *Amec v Camden* [1996] Env LR 330.

3.64   There are three general exceptions:[1]
- where the person responsible cannot be found
- where the nuisance has not yet occurred
- where the nuisance arises from any defect of a structural character.

In the first two exceptions the notice should be served on the owner of the premises.[2] In the third exception the notice should be served on either the owner or the occupier.[3]

1   Special considerations apply to noise from the street; see para **3.74** below.
2   EPA 1990, s 80(2)(b).
3   EPA 1990, s 80(2)(c).

3.65   *Acts* are relatively straightforward. If a fish and chip shop proprietor regularly dumps a pile of foul smelling fish skins in someone else's yard he is plainly responsible for the nuisance. *Default* and *sufferance* are more problematic.

Default arises where a duty is not performed. It can be difficult to determine which of the several people who have interests in land and premises have the relevant duty.

Sufferance encompasses a positive grant of permission to do something or acquiescence in the doing of it. It also encompasses failure to do anything about a nuisance caused on one's land by a trespasser or otherwise without permission where the nuisance ought to have been noticed and dealt with.[1]

1   The House of Lords held in *Sedleigh-Denfield v O'Callaghan* [1940] AC 880 that an occupier is responsible for a nuisance if with knowledge or presumed knowledge of its existence he fails to take reasonable means to bring it to an end when he has adequate time to do so.

3.66   The term *owner* is not defined.[1] Ownership is a protean concept;[2] it has many possible meanings. It must, therefore, be interpreted in the context of the purpose and scheme of this Part of the EPA 1990. The sense of the Act seems to be that the owner is someone with an interest in the property which carries with it responsibility for the upkeep of the structure. This includes those entitled to receive the rent of the property such as managing agents.[3]

1   It is defined *solely for the purposes of the charging provisions* of EPA 1990, s 81A(9). This suggests that the definition provided there was not intended to apply generally or it would have been included in the general definition provisions of s 79(7).
2   Ownership of movable things such as bag of potatoes can be exclusive and absolute. Immovable things such as buildings and land cannot traditionally be owned absolutely. People may simultaneously have interests and estates in them. There is usually a hierarchy. Eg the Duke of Indolence has a large freehold estate in Mudshire; Mr Gradgrind has a lease for 25 years, part of it on which he has built a factory; Mr Industrious has a yearly sublease of a shed at the edge of the factory site.
3   The Divisional Court so held recently in *London Borough of Camden v Gunby* CO/4777/98 [1999] 4 All ER 602. This decision has resolved some of the doubts caused by the application to EPA 1990, s 81A alone of the express definition in s 81A(9) of 'owner' as including 'a person ... who, whether in his own right or as a trustee for any other person, is entitled to receive the rack rent of the premises ...'

3.67   The EPA 1990 cannot have intended that obligations which could not legally be performed should be imposed, therefore notice should not require the doing of that which the local authority knows the recipient cannot do. Section

3.67 *The abatement notice*

289 of the Public Health Act 1936 permits a landlord to enter the land of his tenant to comply with a notice.

3.68 '*Any defect of a structural character*' refers to defects in or relating to a structure as opposed to fittings. The term is not confined to fundamental defects which put at risk the very structure itself.

3.69 There is often dispute between landlord and tenant as to who is responsible for conditions within premises. The landlord may suggest that the lifestyle of the complainant is to blame for the state of the premises complained of.

3.70 For example, in *Dover District Council v Farrar*,[1] there was evidence of excessive condensation which had resulted in mould growth in the bedrooms and bathroom of the council run house. The justices found that the heating provision in the house would have been adequate to combat the condensation had it been properly used, but it had not been used by the tenant because of the cost of doing so. In these circumstances, the Court upheld the justices' decision that the council was not responsible for the statutory nuisance, stating that:

> '... putting it in its simplest terms, the cause of this so called statutory nuisance was the unwillingness of the tenants themselves to spend the amount of money that was required to provide themselves with adequate heating with the system provided in the first place by the ... Council ... So we are dealing here with a case in which the cause of the condensation and hence the dampness, hence the mould and hence the prejudice to health is the unwillingness, possibly inability, of the complainants themselves to afford the costs of the heating ...'[2]

1 [1980] 2 HLR 32.
2 See also *Henry Pike v Sefton Metropolitan Borough Council* DC [2000] Env LR D31.

3.71 The defence will fail where the facilities provided by the landlord even if used properly are not adequate to maintain the premises in a state that does not cause a statutory nuisance. In *Greater London Council v London Borough of Tower Hamlets*[1] the heating and ventilation system provided by the local authority landlord were woefully inadequate for the purposes of combating excessive condensation which had lead to mould growth in the flat. The tenant had the heating on constantly or nearly constantly, but to no avail. Accordingly, the local authority were found liable as the 'person responsible' for the statutory nuisance. As Griffiths LJ stated:[2]

> 'A landlord is required to apply his mind to the necessity of ventilation and, if need be, to insulation and heating. The landlord must provide a combination of these factors to make a house habitable for the tenant.'

1 (1983) 15 HLR 54.
2 (1983) 15 HLR 54 at 61.

3.72 Tenants sometimes refuse to accept solutions put forward by the landlord to remedy the state of affairs. For example, where the heating and ventilation installed is inadequate, the landlord may suggest alternative means – such as the provision of additional electric heaters – to combat the conditions in the house. Provided that the alternative means put forward by the landlord are both reasonable and adequate, he will not be responsible for a statutory nuisance which results from the tenant's refusal to accept those alternative means.[1] Alternative means would be unreasonable where they require the tenant to use abnormal quantities of fuel.[2]

1 See *Greater London Council v London Borough of Tower Hamlets* [1983] 15 HLR 54 at 61 per Griffiths LJ: 'If it is shown ... that the landlord has done everything reasonable and the cause of the continuing condensation is that the tenant is unwilling to use the appliances or any reasonable alternative means of heating the flat, then the landlord cannot be held responsible for the ensuing state of the premises.'
2 *GLC v Tower Hamlets* (1983) 15 HLR 54.

3.73 A defence may also be open to a landlord where the tenant has refused the offer of alternative accommodation. In *Warner v London Borough of Lambeth*,[1] substantial dry rot was found in the tenant's local authority flat, which was found as a matter of fact to render the premises prejudicial to health. Work commenced to rectify the situation while the tenant's family were still in occupation, but the tenant found this intolerable and subsequently refused entry to the workmen. Before proceedings were started by the tenant, the Council made offers to re-house the family in three alternative homes. These offers were refused on various grounds, including that the alternatives were either too small or too close to a railway line. On the facts, these grounds were found to be unreasonable.

The magistrates found that although the local authority were responsible for the nuisance arising, they were not the person by responsible for the nuisance continuing. Accordingly, the local authority was not responsible. On appeal by the tenant, the Divisional Court held that the requirement under section 93 of the Public Health Act 1936 that a local authority abatement notice be served on a person whose 'act, default or sufferance the nuisance arises or continues ...' applied equally to the service of a nuisance order under section 99[2] of that Act which dealt with proceedings by a private party. Accordingly, the magistrates' finding that the local authority was responsible for the nuisance arising but that the tenant was responsible for it continuing justified the magistrates in dismissing the tenant's complaint.

1 (1984) 15 HLR 42.
2 Proceedings by private individual, now covered by EPA 1990, s 82.

NOISE FROM THE STREET

3.74 Special provisions apply here. If the noise has not yet occurred or comes from an unattended vehicle, machinery or equipment the local authority can decide whether to serve it on any[1] of the persons responsible (if such a person can be found) or to fix it to the vehicle, machinery or equipment.[2] If the local authority choose not to serve the notice on someone who can be found, then if someone[3] responsible can be found within an hour of the fixing of the notice onto the noise source, then at least one such person[4] too must be served with a copy of the notice.[5] Where the authority choose not to serve the notice on a person who can be found then the time for compliance must be extended by an additional period specified in the notice if such a person is found within the hour.[6]

1 EPA 1990, s 81(1B)(a).
2 EPA 1990, s 80A(1) and (2).
3 EPA 1990, s 81(1B)(c).

3.74 *The abatement notice*

4   EPA 1990, s 81(1B)(c).
5   EPA 1990, s 80A(3).
6   EPA 1990, s 80A(4).

UNLAWFUL SHIFTING OF THE BURDEN

3.75 The courts will prevent local authorities from using their statutory powers for ulterior purposes such as to escape their own responsibilities. Thus, the Court of Appeal held in *Leeds City Council v Spencer*[1] that a council was not entitled to serve a notice under section 4 of the Prevention of Damage by Pests Act 1949 requiring the removal of a putrefying collection of household waste which they had a public duty to remove under section 45 of the EPA 1990. They failed therefore to recover under section 5 of the 1949 Act the costs of doing the work themselves. Their actions were held to be unreasonable in a 'Wednesbury'[2] sense and beyond their powers. This approach would also be applied to the use of abatement notices to avoid their responsibilities.[3] Some caution should be exercised in applying this principle. The House of Lords have held that where the local authority has a choice of means of achieving a public objective it may choose a means which does not involve it in paying compensation.[4]

1   [1999] EHLR 394, CA.
2   Lawyers tend to describe actions by public bodies which are so unreasonable that they go outside the limits of their discretion and are, therefore, unlawful as being 'Wednesbury unreasonable.' This phrase derives from a classic statement of the relevant legal principles by the then Master of the Rolls, Lord Greene, in *Associated Provincial Picture Houses Ltd v Wednesbury Corpn* [1948] 1 KB 223.
3   Another example is the use of the planning system to create public rights over land without compensation *Hall & Co Ltd v Shoreham-by-Sea UDC* [1964] 1 WLR 240. There has been much litigation in the planning field on this subject (see cases such as *Westminster Renslade Ltd v Secretary of State for the Environment* [1984] JPL 454).
4   *Westminster Bank Ltd v Minister of Housing and Local Government* [1971] AC 508.

HOW SHOULD AN ABATEMENT NOTICE BE SERVED?

3.76 The EPA 1990 does not prescribe how service should be effected. Section 160 facilitates service by setting out procedures compliance with which will achieve effective service.

> 'Any ... notice required or authorised to be served on or given to a person ... may be served or given by delivering it to him, or leaving it at his proper address, or by sending it by post to him at that address'.

3.77 These provisions are introduced by the auxiliary 'may'. The Divisional Court has recently held that they are permissive.[1] They are sufficient but not necessary conditions for effective service. Other means of service may be effective. It would, nonetheless, be sensible for local authorities to follow the procedures of section 160 of the EPA 1990 unless there is a good reason for adopting a different course of action. Three methods of serving abatement notices will therefore benefit from the statutory approval:

- delivery to the recipient
- leaving it at the recipient's *'proper address'*
- posting[2] it to the recipient's *'proper address'*.

The *'proper address'* of a person is his last known address.[3]

1   *Hewlings v McLean Homes East Anglia Ltd* [2001] Env LR 17, DC where the then Vice President of the Criminal Division of the Court of Appeal, Rose LJ and Rafferty J declined to follow the unnecessary asides ('obiter dicta') of Schiemann LJ in *Leeds v London Borough of Islington* [1998] Env LR 657 to opposite effect.
2   Unless the contrary is proved letters are assumed to have arrived on the day when they would be received in the ordinary course of post (Interpretation Act 1978, s 7). The Civil Procedure Rules (CPR) 6.7 suggests second working day for first class post.
3   EPA 1990, s 160(4) the definition of proper address is introduced by the auxiliary 'shall [be]'. Thus the specified addresses will be the only addresses that will do for the purposes of the section.

3.78 Bodies corporate such as companies may be served through their official secretaries or clerks.[1] Their registered or principal UK office will both be proper addresses.[2] It is wise, however, to serve through the company secretary at the registered office; there is then little scope for argument about the adequacy of service. Any partner or the person having control and management of a partnership business may be served.[3] The proper address is the principal office of the business.[4]

1   EPA 1990, s 160(3)(a).
2   EPA 1990, s 160(4)(a) as interpreted in *Hewlings v McLean Homes East Anglia Ltd* [2001] Env LR 17, DC.
3   EPA 1990, s 160(3)(b).
4   EPA 1990, s 160(4). See para **3.77**, n 3.

3.79 Potential recipients may prefer to be served at other addresses. If they specify an address for this purpose it will also[1] be a proper address for the purpose of the section.[2]

1   EPA 1990, s 160(5).
2   Addresses specified for the purpose of other legislation such as the Landlord and Tenant Acts will not become proper addresses under this subsection: *Leeds v London Borough of Islington* [1998] Env LR 665. The person who specifies the alternative address on behalf of the recipient need not be one of the office holders identified in EPA 1990, s 160(3); *Hall v Hull* [1999] 2 All ER 609.

3.80 Reliance should not be placed on faxes unless consent and acknowledgement of service are obtained.[1] Other forms of electronic mail should not be used.

1   Notwithstanding *Barraclough v Secretary of State for the Environment* [1990] JPL 911. Note Civil Procedure Rules 6.2.1; Practice Direction Service (CPR 6 PD 3.1.1) requires consent in writing for fax. Service is deemed on the day following if the transmission is after 4 pm.

WITHDRAWAL OF NOTICES

3.81 There is no express power to permit the withdrawal of a notice. Mummery LJ[1] in the Court of Appeal and Richards J[2] in the Queen's Bench Division have both expressed the view that such power must be implied. This view is discussed in Chapter 2.[3]

1   *R v Bristol City Council ex p Everett* [1999] Env LR 587, CA at 600.
2   *R v Bristol City Council ex p Everett* [1999] Env LR 256, DC at 270–272.
3   See paras **2.83–2.85**.

Chapter 4

Challenging an Abatement Notice

INTRODUCTION

4.01 The recipient has a clear interest in being able to challenge an abatement notice. The notice is intended to affect the way he orders his affairs. If he fails to comply with its terms he may face a criminal conviction. The terms of an abatement notice may be of great interest to others also. Very often the decision by the local authority to issue the notice will have been made in response to complaints from third parties, for example, neighbours complaining about excessive noise. Third parties may well be dissatisfied with the terms of the notice. They may, for example, feel that the steps required are not adequate or that the time given to comply with the terms of the notice is too long.

4.02 Both recipients and third parties may challenge abatement notices but in different ways. The scope for challenge by third parties is very limited.

CHALLENGES BY RECIPIENTS

4.03 An abatement notice may be open to challenge by the recipient of the notice in the following ways:

- An appeal by way of complaint to the magistrates' court pursuant to section 80(3) of the Environmental Protection Act, as amended (EPA 1990). This is the principal method of challenge.
- In some (unusual) circumstances by way of judicial review by the recipient.
- Sometimes as a collateral defence to criminal proceedings brought in respect of an alleged breach of the requirements of the notice.[1]
- By complaint to the Local Government Ombudsman where the recipient considers that the notice has been issued as the result of maladministration. This is likely to provide a limited form of redress and may be rejected if the Ombudsman is of the view that the recipient should have pursued another remedy before the court.

1   See further, Chapter 5 at paras **5.98–5.102**.

CHALLENGES BY THIRD PARTIES

4.04 Third parties have *no* right of appeal to the magistrates' court under the EPA 1990, but:

- In certain circumstances third parties may be able to seek judicial review of the decision by the local authority to issue the notice.
- Third parties may complain to the Local Government Ombudsman if they believe the local authority has been guilty of maladministration.
- It is open to an aggrieved third party to take his own proceedings under section 82 of the EPA 1990 in order to persuade the court to issue a statutory nuisance order in different terms. This would not involve a

4.04 *Challenging an abatement notice*

formal challenge to the abatement notice issued by the local authority. However, in reality, it would inevitably involve direct criticism of the notice issued by the local authority in order for the third party to establish the need for the court to issue an order pursuant to section 82 of the EPA 1990 in addition to the notice issued by the local authority.[1] In practice, this is the most important avenue of redress afforded to third parties dissatisfied by the action or inaction of the local authority.

1 A third party might seek to bring civil nuisance proceedings against the recipient of an abatement notice. However, because of the differences between the statutory nuisance procedure and civil law nuisance such as the absence of an express defence of best practicable means and the availability of damages in cases of civil nuisance, an action for civil law nuisance may not necessarily indicate any dissatisfaction with the abatement notice served by the local authority. Indeed, the fact that the local authority has issued an abatement notice may be the evidential basis for bringing the civil law nuisance action. For it may be difficult in practice for the recipient of an abatement notice to challenge a civil law action for nuisance on the basis that he had not caused a nuisance where an abatement notice has been issued and has not been quashed.

APPEALING AN ABATEMENT NOTICE

4.05 A recipient of an abatement notice may appeal against the notice within the period of 21 days beginning with the date on which he was served with the notice.[1] Schedule 3 paragraph 1 of the EPA 1990 states that the appeal is made by way of a 'complaint' to the magistrates' court. When reference is made to an 'appeal' or 'complaint' to the justices it is effectively referring to the same thing.

1 EPA 1990, s 80(3).

4.06 In determining an appeal, the justices are obliged to act in accordance with the provisions of the Human Rights Act 1998 (HRA 1998).[1] Section 7(1)(b) of that Act provides that a person is entitled to rely on a right under the European Convention of Human Rights (ECHR)[2] where he claims that a public authority, has acted in *a way* that contravenes a Convention right. This is a wide provision. It is therefore capable of having an impact upon appeals against abatement notices, in particular, because recipients of notices are entitled to appeal against the abatement notice on the ground that there has been some informality, defect, or error, in or in connection with, the abatement notice.[3] It is the authors' view that a breach of a recipient's Convention right is capable of amounting to such a defect, error or informality.[4]

1 HRA 1998, s 9. For a general introduction to those aspects of the HRA 1998 and the provisions of the European Convention on Human Rights most relevant to statutory nuisance see Chapter 2 'Local authority powers and duties'.
2 'Convention rights' are defined in HRA 1998, s 1; see further Chapter 2 para **2.07**.
3 Statutory Nuisance (Appeals) Regulations 1995, SI 1995/2664, reg 2(2)(b), reproduced in full at Appendix B. See further paras **4.37–4.41** for a more detailed discussion on this ground of appeal.
4 The fact that a Convention right has been breached does not mean that the notice will necessarily be quashed. What happens will depend upon the nature of the breach. Where appropriate the justices have a power to vary the notice in order to overcome any mischief that may have been caused by the breach of the Convention right. As to the exercise of this power see further at paras **4.110–4.117**.

What is a complaint?

4.07 The making of a complaint is the first stage of procedure in civil proceedings before the magistrates' court. This means that:

- an appeal against an abatement notice is a 'complaint'
- the recipient of an abatement notice who appeals to the magistrates' court is the 'complainant' and
- the local authority that issued the notice is the 'defendant'.

THE FORM OF A COMPLAINT

Written complaint

4.08 In most cases the complaint will be made in writing to the court. The form of a written complaint is prescribed.[1] It stipulates that the complaint should set out the name and address of the complainant and defendant along with short particulars of the matters or complaint stated and the relevant statute.[2]

1 Magistrates' Courts (Forms) Rules 1981, SI 1981/553.
2 In this case the relevant statute will be the EPA 1990.

Oral complaint

4.09 A complaint need not be made in writing or on oath.[1] It may be made by the complainant in person or by his counsel or solicitor, or other person authorised on his behalf.[2] Accordingly, it is possible for a recipient of an abatement notice to attend the court and make a complaint orally thereby initiating his appeal against the abatement notice.[3]

The complainant will be expected to provide orally the same details that are required for a written complaint. In practice, it is highly unusual for someone to proceed in this way.

1 See Magistrates' Courts Rules 1981, SI 1981/552, r 4(2) which provides that subject to any provision in the Magristrates' Courts Act 1980 or other enactment a complaint need not be in writing. There is no requirement under the EPA 1990.
2 Magistrates' Courts Rules 1981, SI 1981/552, r 4(1).
3 See *R v Manchester Stipendiary Magistrate, ex p Hill* [1983] 1 AC 328, HL, at 342E-F per Lord Roskill.

Issuing the summons

4.10 After a complaint is made, a justice or justices' clerk must apply his mind to the complaint. He must go through the judicial exercise of deciding whether or not to issue a summons.[1] In particular, he must consider whether:

- the court has *prima facie* power to make the order sought
- the court will have the territorial jurisdiction to act; and
- the matter has been brought within the period of any limitation period.

1 Magistrates' Courts Act 1980, s 52. See also *R v Brentford Justices, ex p Catlin* [1975] QB 455, [1975] 2 All ER 201; *R v Gateshead Justices, ex p Tesco Stores Ltd* [1981] QB 470, [1981] 1 All ER 1027; *R v Manchester Stipendiary Magistrate, ex p Hill, R v Dartford Justices, ex p Dhesi*, and *R v Edmonton Justices, ex p Hughes* [1983] 1 AC 328, sub nom *Hill v Anderton* [1982] 2 All ER 963, HL.

4.11 In the authors' experience the most common instance where the justices (or their clerk) have refused to issue a summons for a complaint against an abatement notice is when the complainant has failed to lodge the complaint

4.11 *Challenging an abatement notice*

within the 21-day limit provided by section 80(3) of the EPA 1990 (discussed at paragraph **4.12** below).

THE TIME PERIOD FOR APPEALING AN ABATEMENT NOTICE

4.12 The magistrates' court grants a power to hear appeals by way of complaint against abatement notices. The time period for making an appeal is set down in the statute. Section 80(3) of the EPA 1990 provides that:

> '[A person served with an abatement notice] may appeal against the notice to a magistrates' court ... within the period of twenty-one days beginning with the date on which he was served with the notice'.

Does the magistrates' court have discretion to allow an extension of the time to appeal by way of complaint?

4.13 No express statutory provision is made for applications to the court for an extension of time for an appeal to be made. The power to appeal would therefore appear[1] be limited to those appeals made within the requisite 21-day period.

1   It cannot be said that the mere absence of an express statutory provision has always prevented the court from taking the view that implied power may exist. Such an example can be found in respect of the court's approach to whether a local authority has an implied power to withdraw an abatement notice. No express power exists either in ss 79 or 80 of the EPA 1990. Notwithstanding the absence of such an express power in *R v Bristol City Council, ex p Everett* [1999] Env LR 256 at 270–272 Richards J held that a power could be implied. In the Court of Appeal ([1999] Env LR 587 at 600) the appeal was dismissed for other reasons; Mummery LJ simply stated that Richards J had been correct to hold that '... the Council clearly had an implied power to withdraw the notice ...'. For a discussion and criticism of this view see Chapter 2 at paras **2.83–2.85**.

4.14 Where a time limit is prescribed by statute rather than by the rules of court and the statute provides no power to allow an extension of time, the court does not have power to exercise its discretion to extend time.[1]

1   See *R v Secretary of State for the Environment, ex p Ostler* [1977] QB 122 and *R v Secretary of State for the Environment, ex p Kent* [1990] JPL 124.

4.15 The use of the word 'may' in section 80(3) of the EPA 1990 does *not* imply that the appeal may be made to the justices outside that period. It indicates that the right of appeal is an opportunity not a duty. The right of appeal to the magistrates' court against an abatement notice is a right given by statute and must therefore be limited by the terms of that statutory right. The court has no general supervisory powers over local authorities in respect of abatement notice to supplement those powers granted by statute.

Accordingly, a failure to appeal within the prescribed time period deprives the justices of jurisdiction.[1] It does not matter that the failure to appeal in time is not the fault of the complainant.

1   In *Hope Butuyuyu v London Borough of Hammersmith* [1997] Env LR D13 counsel for both parties accepted before the Divisional Court that the time period of 21 days was absolute for appeals against abatement notices. The matter was therefore not the subject of argument. In our view, for the reasons set out above, counsel were right to agree that the period is absolute.

4.16 Providing that proper service has been effected time will start to run even though the recipient may be actually unaware of the existence of the notice. Such a situation is not wholly unimaginable. For example, it may be the custom for the owner of an Italian restaurant to close each year for a month's holiday in the summer during which time he and his wife holiday with their relatives in Italy. The notice arrives on the same day of his departure but after he has left for the airport. When he returns from his holiday he finds that the period for appeal has just expired. He is unable to appeal the notice.[1]

1   As to whether it would be open to seek to persuade the justices on any prosecution that his absence and hence failure to challenge the terms of the notice amounted to a 'reasonable excuse', see Chapter 5, paras **5.78–5.84**.

Compatibility of non-extendable 21 days' limit with the HRA 1998

4.17 The 21-day period is relatively short. It is also absolute. The consequences of a failure to appeal within time may be severe for the recipient; but the EPA 1990 imposes no express obligation upon a local authority to give prior warning to the recipient.[1] Non extendable time limits for statutory appeals and challenges have been recognised to present a possible infringement of article 6 of the ECHR.[2] For the right of access to a court to be effective, an individual must have a clear, practical opportunity to challenge an act which is an interference with his or her rights (see *De Geouffre de la Pradelle v France*, judgment of 16 December 1992, Series A no 253-B, para 43, para 34, and *Bellet v France*, judgment of 4 December 1995, Series A no 333-B, p 42).

1   As to the circumstances where a local authority may be obliged to consult before issuing a notice, see Chapter 3 on the drafting of unsuspended abatement notices and more generally see also Chapter 2, paras **2.90–2.92**.
2   The Hon Sir Stephen Richards (as he then was), writing extra-judicially, 'The Impact of Art. 6 of the ECHR on Judicial Review' [1999] JR 106 at 109.

4.18 The European Court on Human Rights (ECtHR) has repeatedly held that:

> '... the right to a court enshrined in Article 6 is not an absolute one. It may be subject to limitations but these must not restrict or reduce the access left to the individual in such a way or to such an extent that the very essence of the right is impaired'.[1]

In *Ashingdane v United Kingdom*[2] the ECtHR held that:

> '[Such] a limitation will not be compatible with Article 6 para 1 (art 6-1) if it does not pursue a legitimate aim and if there is not a reasonable relationship of proportionality between the means employed and the aim sought to be achieved'.[3]

1   See eg *De la Pradelle v France* (1992) A 253-B, para 28; and *Philis v Greece* (1991) 13 EHRR 741, para 20.
2   (1985) 7 EHRR 528. See also *Guérin v. France*, judgment of 29 July 1998, *Reports* 1998-V, p. 1867, para 37.
3   *Ashingdane v United Kingdom* (1985) 7 EHRR 528, para 54. See also *Lithgow v United Kingdom* (1986) 8 EHRR 329, para 194(c).

4.19 There would seem to be little doubt that the aim of the 21-day time limit, that of seeking a degree of legal certainty and ensuring that the harm created by the statutory nuisance is addressed promptly, would be regarded as

4.19 *Challenging an abatement notice*

legitimate.¹ However, it remains to be seen whether the *non-extendable* time limit of 21 days could be successfully attacked on the grounds that it is disproportionate to the aims to which it seeks to achieve. Whilst the filing of grounds of appeal could be said to be a relatively simple exercise, most recipients would wish to seek legal advice before appealing. 21 days presents a very tight schedule for taking and acting on legal advice especially if the recipient is away for the first part of the 21-day period. Indeed, as discussed at paras **4.30–4.33** depending upon what day of the week the notice is served the time for appealing may actually be as little as 19 days. Clearly, a judgment would have to be made by the court as to whether 21 days amounts to an appropriate balance between the potential harm of the nuisance problem and the consequent need for speedy action to abate it and the practical difficulties for the recipient in meeting the tight schedule.²

1 See the concurring opinion of Judge Martens in *De la Pradelle v France* (1992) 253A-B at para 7.
2 Indeed, the short time limit presents a neat illustration of some of the tensions that exist between competing 'human rights'. The need to abate the nuisance may involve the protection of someone's right to home guaranteed under article 8: the short non-extendable time limit for appealing, however, risks offending another's property rights under article 1 to the First Protocol and article 6 of the Convention guaranteeing the right to a fair hearing.

4.20 If there were a power under the EPA 1990 for the court to extend the period for appeal on demonstration of good reason for the delay, it is very unlikely that the 21-day period would be in breach of article 6 of the European Convention or article 1 to the First Protocol to the Convention. In this respect, it should be noted that article 1 to the First Protocol of the Convention gives contracting states a wide margin of appreciation allowing them to interfere with ECHR rights. This applies in respect of the first part of article 1, involving the 'peaceful' (the word 'peaceful' is used in its legal rather than its lay sense¹) enjoyment of possessions, and an even greater margin of appreciation in respect of the second part of the article, relating to the *regulation* of the use of property. It is not entirely clear into which part of article 1 a restriction upon the use of property following the imposition of an abatement notice would fall. It has been said that the doctrine of margin of appreciation does not apply when a national court is considering the HRA 1998. But in practice an analogous doctrine will apply. As Lord Hope stated in *R v DPP, ex p Kebelene*:²

> 'In this area difficult choices may have to be made by the executive or the legislature between the rights of the individual and the needs of society. In some circumstances it will be appropriate for the courts to recognise that there is an area of judgment within which the judiciary will defer, on democratic grounds, to the considered opinion of the elected body or person whose act or decision is said to be incompatible with the Convention.'

1 In this context, it is *not* used to mean 'not noisy'!
2 [1999] 3 WLR 972.

4.21 The European Court on Human Rights has held in *Sporrong and Lünnroth v Sweden*,¹ that whilst prohibitions on construction works imposed by Swedish authorities amounted to the interference with the 'peaceful enjoyment of possession' (ie the first part of article 1), this interference could be justified if it could be shown that:

> 'a fair balance was struck between the demands of the general interests of the community and the requirements of the protection of the individual's fundamental rights'.

The court held that in such an area there was a room for the margin of appreciation because:

> '[it] was natural that, in an area as complex and difficult as that of the development of large cities, the Contracting States should enjoy a wide margin of appreciation in order to implement their town planning policy.'

One can reasonably suppose that the court might take a similar view of the complex process involved in the law of statutory nuisance of ensuring an appropriate environment for people to live. The court, nonetheless, went on to hold that in view of the inflexibility of the particular law concerned, there had been a failure to strike the appropriate balance and, accordingly, decided that there had been a breach of the Convention. This reinforces our view that the main problem with the 21-day time limit for appeals is not the brevity of the period allowed but the absence of flexibility to extend the period, regardless of the circumstances of the particular case.

1   (1982) 5 EHRR 35.

4.22 If circumstances were such that the court considered that the time period in question was too short the issue arises as to what could be done. It would be open to a recipient of a notice to seek a declaration of incaptibility under section 4 of the HRA 1998.[1]

Given that the time period of 21-days is enshrined in statute, the question arises as to whether the magistrates' court itself pursuant to the rule of interpretation under section 3 of the HRA 1998 could consider that section 80 of the EPA 1990 could be interpreted so as to afford itself a discretion to extend the period of time for appeal so as to avoid a possible breach of article 6 ECHR.[2]

There is no preclusive provision in the EPA 1990 restricting challenges to the validity of abatement notices being restricted only to challenges by way of appeal under section 80 EPA 1990[3]. Indeed, where a recipient alleges that the abatement notice is a nullity then judicial review rather than an appeal under s.80 EPA 1990 is the appropriate procedure by which to challenge the notice[4]. A challenge by way of judicial review may not be an adequate alternative if the recipient is not entitled to challenge the factual merits of the notice. However, were a court to consider that in circumstances of the particular case the time period afforded to the recipient to appeal the notice had been inadequate for the purposes of article 6 ECHR, the administrative court has the ability if it so wishes to be flexible in such matters[5] Similarly, the possibility of challenging the notice by way of a defence of 'reasonable excuse' to a prosecution for breach of an abatement notice is not likely to be viewed as an adequate substitute either by the European Court of Human Rights or the English courts[6] because it is not desirable that someone should have to await criminal prosecution before establishing the extent of his civil law rights and obligations. Accordingly, section 7(1)(b) of the HRA 1998 will entitle the defendant to rely upon an infringement of his human rights in the abatement notice proceedings as part of a defence of 'reasonable excuse.'

1   Such a declaration could not be granted by the magistrates' court, the recipient of the notice would have to take proceedings before a court empowered to make such an order, such as the High Court (see *R (Kurdistan Workers Party) v Secretary of State for the Home Department* [2002] EWHC 644 (Admin) [2002] ACD 560 at [86] but that would not quash the notice.
2   In *A v Hoare* [2006] EWCA Civ 393 the claimant argued that the court should apply section 3 HRA 1998 to interprete section 2 of the Limitation Act 1980 so as to allow an extension of

4.22 *Challenging an abatement notice*

time. However, the Court of Appeal held that the date of action had accrued prior to the coming into force of the HRA 1998 and therefore section 3 did not apply. The House of Lords allowed the claimant's appeal but without reliance upon section 3 of the HRA 1998 (*A v Hoare, C v Middlesbrough Council, X v London Borough of Wandsworth, H v Suffolk Council, Young v Catholic Care (Diocese of Leeds)* [2008] UKHL 6; Times, 31 January 2008).

3   For guidance on the factors that would ordinarily be applied see *R v Falmouth and Truro Port Health Authority, ex p South West Water Services* [2000] 3 ALL ER 306; [2000] 3 WLR 1464, CA.
4   *Sovereign Rubber Ltd v Stockport Metropolitan Borough Council* [2000] Env LR 194.
5   Cross-examination can be permitted at the discretion of the judge in proceedings for judicial review. Hitherto, the power has been rarely exercised (see eg *Cocks v Thanet District Council* [1983] 2 AC 286: at 294H per Lord Bridge). If the question as to existence or likely occurrence of a statutory nuisance is regarded as a precedent fact then it may be that the court will hear live evidence and cross examination in order to determine for itself whether that condition has been properly satisfied. (see *R (Maiden Outdoor Advertising Ltd) v Lambeth Borough Council* [2003] EWHC 1224 (Admin)). Indeed, following the coming into force of the HRA 1998 the courts have acknowledged that in some contexts nothing short of a full merits review will suffice even in judicial review (see *R (G) v London Borough of Ealing* [2002] EWHC 250 (Admin) [2002] ACD 298 at [15] and see the reasoning of the European Court of Human Rights in *Bryan v United Kingdom* [1996] JPL 386); cf *R (Alconbury Developments Ltd) v Secretary of State for the Environment, Transport and the Regions* [2003] 2 AC 295, [2001] UKHL 23 and *Tsfayo v United Kingdom* (Application No 60860/00) (ECtHR) The Times, 23 November 2006.
6   'The *principal object* of the statutory appeal against an abatement notice is plainly to relieve the person served of the need to await a prosecution and to risk a conviction before being able to contest the need for the contents of the notice.'[Emphasis added] *per* Sedley LJ in *Sovereign Rubber Ltd v Stockport Metropolitan Borough Council* [2000] Env LR 194 at 198.

When does time start to run?

4.23   Given that the period for appealing is absolute and that 21 days is relatively short, it is important that the calculation of the time for appeal is made correctly.

4.24   The time starts to run on the day upon which the recipient was 'served with the notice.' This is to be contrasted with other statutory provisions where time starts to run on the date that the particular notice, decision, order etc. was issued.[1]

The statute also expressly provides that the period of 21 days *begins* with the date on which he was served with the notice. Accordingly, 'day one' for the purposes of calculating the 21 days' appeal period is the day of service, and not, as would otherwise be the case in the absence of such an express statement, the day immediately after the service of the notice.[2]

1   See eg Town and Country Planning Act 1990 (as amended), s 288(3).
2   *Williams v Burgess* (1840) 10 LJQB 10; *Robinson v Waddington* (1849) 18 LJQB 250; *Radcliffe v Batholomew* [1892] 1 QB 161. The same is true in Australia: *Morton v Hampson* [1962] VR 364 at 365, *per cur* (written joint judgment of Herring CJ, Sholl and Little JJ) and, in Canada: *McLean v Pinkerton* (1882) 7 OAR 490.

When does the time end?

4.25   As a matter of good practice, recipients should, in any event, avoid lodging appeals on the last day. There is always a risk that there may have been a miscalculation in the time for appealing or that some problem arises with the physical filing of the appeal.

4.26   In most cases there really should be no need for the appeal to be made hard up against the time period. This is because the grounds of appeal can be shortly stated in fairly general terms. If the recipient or his advisors are in doubt as whether or not a particular ground should be included as part of the appeal,

The time period for appealing an abatement notice 4.29

it is usually best to include any ground that may be possibly relevant. It is always possible to withdraw grounds of appeal.

4.27 Once the appeal has been made it should be reviewed as soon as possible. If there are grounds that are to be abandoned they should usually be abandoned promptly by notification to the clerk of the court and to the local authority. Late abandonment of appeals may give rise to costs penalties where the local authority may have incurred additional costs in preparing to meet a ground of appeal that has been recently abandoned.[1]

1   As to whether there is a power to award costs in such a situation see Chapter 7.

4.28 The statute provides that an appeal may be made 'within' 21 days from the date of the notice having been served on the recipient.[1] Does 'within' 21 days mean before the twenty first day or does it include the twenty first day? In other words, does the appeal need to be filed by close of business on the twentieth day or close of business on the twenty first day? The court has considered the meaning of 'within' in the context of time limits elsewhere and come to the conclusion that it means that appeals made during the last day are still made 'within' the prescribed time period.[2]

1   See Chapter 3 para **3.03** for what constitues good service.
2   English authorities include: *R v IRC, ex p Knight* [1973] 3 All ER 721 where 'within three years' for the purposes of the Taxes Management Act 1970, s 103 (1) was held to mean 'not later than three years;' and *Manorlike Ltd v Le Vitas Travel Agency* [1986] 1 All ER 573 where it was held that a notice to quit requiring tenants to vacate premises 'within a period of three months' did not necessarily require them to vacate before the end of the period, and was therefore not inconsistent with a clause in the lease specifying 'not less than three months previous notice in writing.' In Canada, where a statute required an execution to be returnable 'within thirty days', a writ issued on April 24 was held to be in force on May 24 – the day of issue being excluded but the last day held to be within time (*Clarke v Garrett* (1877) 28 UCCP 75); see also Judge Widdfield *Words and Phrases Judicially Defined* (Toronto, 1914) More recently, in *Rockall v Department for Environment, Food and Rural Affairs* [2007] EWHC 614 (Admin); [2007] Env LR D16 the court proceeded on the basis that, for the purposes of section 17(1) of the Forestry Act 1967, a requirement for proceedings to be instituted within six months from the first discovery of the offence by the person taking the prosecution meant that where the first discovery had been on 12 August 2005 the six months expired on 12 February 2006. 12 February being a Sunday, the court was also of the view that proceedings had to be instituted by Friday 10 February 2006.

4.29 One must always remember that decisions relating to the same statutory wording in other statutory schemes may not be applied strictly to other statutes where the context and purpose of the provision may be very different.[1] However, we consider it unlikely that the court would take the view that a different interpretation is justified in respect of section 80(3) of the EPA 1990. The following lucid expression of the general approach to the meaning of 'within' has been given by the full court of the Supreme Court of the State of Victoria in Australia:

'The modern rule in relation to a period of time fixed by statute "within" which an act is to be done after a specified event is that ... *the time expires on the last day of the period*'[2] [Emphasis added]

In our view this statement also represents the law in England and Wales concerning the meaning of 'within' generally and in particular as contained in section 80(3) of the EPA 1990.

1   See *Rockall v Department for Environment, Food and Rural Affairs* [2007] EWHC 614 (Admin); [2007] Env LR D16 and *Kent County Council v Secretary of State for the*

4.29 *Challenging an abatement notice*

Environment [1997] JPL 1115, CA *per* Swinton Thomas LJ at 1119–1120 and Otton LJ at 1120–1121.
2   *Morton v Hampson* [1962] VR 364 at 365, *per cur* (written joint judgment of Herring CJ, Sholl and Little JJ).

Court closure on last day permitted for making an appeal

4.30   There are no days expressly excluded from the period of calculation. Accordingly, upon one view if the twenty-first day is a Sunday, Monday will be too late;[1] in such circumstances, our clear view is that a recipient should act on the basis that Monday would be too late. Yet it is difficult to see what real justification exists for taking this approach. Courts are closed on Sundays and it might seem unfair that the effective period during which a recipient can appeal should depend upon accidents of the calendar. In *Rockall v Department for Environment, Food and Rural Affairs* [2007] EWHC 614 (Admin); [2007] Env LR D16 the Divisional Court took the view that for the purposes of section 17(1) of the Forestry Act 1967 where the time period (in that case, six months) expired on 12 February 2006 and 12 February 2006 was a Sunday, proceedings had to be instituted by Friday, 10 February 2006. Monday 13 February 2006 would have been too late. Nonetheless, it is arguable that for the reasons set out below that lodging the complaint on the Monday in the case of statutory nuisance where the time period is 21-days rather than six months would be in time. It is hard to see a justification for why the 21-day period should be reduced to 19 days by the arbitrary factor of what particular day of the week the local authority served the notice.[2] Moreover, it is arguable that this arbitrary reduction of the time period to appeal is not proportionate and does not entail the necessary clarity required by article 6 of the European Convention on Human Rights for provisions restricting access to the court.[3]

1   See *Encyclopedia of Environmental Health Law and Practice*, Vol 1 paras 1-517 at 1277.
2   If the local authority served the notice on a Monday, day 21 would fall on a Sunday, giving the recipient effectively 19 days to lodge an appeal. If a local authority served the notice on a Sunday, day 21 would fall on a Saturday, also giving the recipient effectively 19 days to lodge an appeal. If a period for appeal coincided with the Easter Bank holiday and day 21 fell on Easter Monday, the last day of lodging the appeal would be Maunday Thursday, thus reducing the effective period for appeal to 17 days.
3   See for example *Ashingdane v United Kingdom* (1985) 7 EHRR 528, and the entirety of the concurring opinion of Judge Martens in *De la Pradelle v France* (1992) A 253-B.

4.31   In the authors' view the correct approach under the common law is to examine whether the act in question is to be done entirely by the person himself or requiring some assistance by the court. A Canadian judgment neatly encapsulates this approach:

> '... when Sunday is the last day for the party to do an act, and the time is fixed by statute, Sunday is part of the specified time, and a further day is not given to the party because he does not do the act or cannot do it upon the Sunday. But where the act is to be done by the Court and the Court is closed upon a Sunday or other holiday, the party has until the next following day on which the Court can act.'[1]

However, in *Rockall v Department for Environment, Food and Rural Affairs*,[2] the Divisional Court assumed that where the last day fell on a Sunday the prosecutor or complainant should ensure that the necessary documentation is available or retrievable by the justices or their clerk on the preceding Friday. In that case, the court held that such a requirement would be satisfied where a transmission by fax or electronic where it could properly be inferred that the information was retrievable, whether retrieved in fact or not.

1   *McLean v Pinkerton* (1882) 7 OAR 490.
2   [2007] EWHC 614 (Admin); [2007] Env LR D16.

4.32 What then is the position in respect of the lodging of a complaint? In *R v Manchester Stipendiary Magistrates, ex p Hill*,[1] Lord Roskill stated:

> '... *the making of a complaint is a matter for the complainant* ... *it is for* ... *the complainant to decide* ... *how the complaint shall be formulated* ... the making of a complaint to a justice of the peace or the clerk to the justices to my mind means, in reference to a written information or complaint, *procuring delivery of the document to a person authorised to receive it on behalf of the justices of the peace and the clerk to the justices'*. [our emphasis]

Accordingly, the duty is upon the recipient of the notice to make a complaint by 'procuring delivery of the document to a person authorised to receive it.' This would mean that simply posting the complaint through the letterbox of the courthouse would not be good enough since the receipt must be procured to a person. In our view, it is arguable that the making of a complaint does involve some element of court participation; there must be someone authorised by the justices or their clerk to receive the complaint. Upon that view, Monday would not be too late. However, we emphasise as a matter of prudence that recipients should act on the basis that Monday is too late and ensure that a complaint is made by the close of court business on the preceding Friday.

1   [1983] 1 AC 328.

4.33 A complaint will be regarded as having been made when it is received at the courthouse by an official working at the court. It does not matter that the clerk or the justices do not get around to issuing the summons immediately. It is that it is available or retrievable whether or not it was in fact retrieved by the clerks within the 21 days. Accordingly, the summons may be issued outside the 21-day period provided that the complaint has been made within the prescribed period.

Service of copies of 'notices of appeal' on third parties

4.34 Regulation 4 of the Statutory Nuisance (Appeals) Regulations 1995[1] provides for two categories of third persons upon which a notice of appeal (ie 'the complaint') can be served.

- The first part of regulation 4 provides that where the grounds for appeal include grounds (i) or (j) (ie that a notice should be served on someone else instead or in addition respectively), the third person(s) named in the ground of appeal, the appellant *'shall'* also serve the third party mentioned with a copy of the notice of appeal (ie the complaint, see further below).
- The second part of regulation 4 provides that copies of the appeal notice *may* be served on 'any other person having an estate or interest in the premises, vehicle, machinery or equipment in question.'

There would seem to be little doubt that the use of the word 'shall' in respect of the first category should be interpreted in a mandatory sense. Clearly, those

4.34 *Challenging an abatement notice*

grounds of appeal are likely to be of most interest to the third party, more so than even to the local authority. Service of the notice in the second category appears to be discretionary but may in our view be mandatory in the circumstances we address below. The consequences for third parties are considered further in this Chapter at paras **4.70–4.77**.

1   SI 1995/2664, as amended by SI 2006/771. Reproduced in full at Appendix B.

GROUNDS OF APPEAL

4.35 The grounds of appeal are set out at regulation 2(2) of the Statutory Nuisance (Appeals) Regulations 1995.[1]

1   SI 1995/2664, as amended by SI 2006/771. Reproduced in full at Appendix B.

Regulation 2(2)(a): that the abatement notice is not justified by section 80 of the EPA 1990

4.36 This ground of appeal goes to whether a statutory nuisance existed or is likely to occur or recur. The issue most likely to arise under this ground is whether the matters complained of be a statutory nuisance.[1]

Obviously, if the matters alleged to be a statutory nuisance are not within the definition at section 79 of the EPA 1990 then this ground of appeal will inevitably succeed. More usually, however, the issue under this ground will turn on whether an activity listed in section 79 is of such a character so as to be 'prejudicial to health or a nuisance'.

Where the notice alleges that the nuisance is likely to occur or recur an issue may arise under this ground that there is insufficient evidence to show that the nuisance is likely to occur or recur notwithstanding that it may have occurred in the past. Particular attention should be paid to the terms of the abatement notice.[2]

1   As to which see the discussion in Chapter 1, paras **1.06–1.11**.
2   Not all abatement notices, for example, will necessarily be drafted to prohibit the recurrence of the alleged nuisance but may simply require the abatement of the nuisance. See the further discussion in Chapter 5, paras **5.10–5.18** on the possible effect of this difference in drafting in the context of criminal proceedings.

Regulation 2(2)(b): that there has been some informality, defect, or error in, or in connection with, the abatement notice

4.37 This ground also applies to notices served under section 80A(3) of the EPA 1990 in respect of noisy machinery etc on the street. For the types of informality, defects, or errors in connection with an abatement notice see paras **3.24–3.30**. Where the defect is so fundamental so as to make the notice a nullity, it may be more appropriate to seek judicial review. In *Sovereign Rubber Ltd v Stockport Metropolitan Borough Council*[1] Sedley LJ stated:

'I do not doubt that an abatement notice may fall to be quashed as a nullity in an extreme case, for example where bad faith can be shown or serious non-compliance with requisite procedures or such deficiency that the document cannot be described as an abatement notice at all. But any quashing on such grounds must be way of judicial review. A recipient of an abatement notice who appeals to the Justices ... is *ex hypothesi* appealing against a notice which, though arguably deficient, is valid. If it so deficient that it cannot be cured by variation in favour of the appellant, the Justices have jurisdiction to quash it, but this is the quashing of an abatement notice, not of a nullity.'

The law on the distinction between errors of law which result in a nullity and those which affect only the validity of the notice is complex. What should a recipient do if faced with a ground of challenge which might amount to a nullity but is not sure? In such circumstances the safest course is probably to appeal under section 80 as well as lodging judicial review proceedings. Depending upon the circumstances one or other of the proceedings could be stayed pending the outcome of the other.

1   [2000] Env LR 194 at 203–204.

4.38 The wording of this ground also raises an interesting question as to whether a defect etc in the decision-making process leading to the issue of an abatement notice is 'in connection with' the notice. If it is, it could form a ground of appeal under this regulation. If it is not, then it cannot be appealed to the justices and can be raised only by way of judicial review. An example arose in *R v Falmouth and Truro Port Health Authority, ex p South-West Water Services*.[1] At first instance, Harrison J considered whether an allegation of a lack of consultation before the issue of an abatement notice could form the subject of an appeal to the justices. He said:

> 'I doubt very much whether the consultation issues could been raised under ground (a) of regulation 2(2) of the 1995 Regulations because the ground relates to the question whether the notice is justified by s 80, whereas the consultation issues were mainly directed at the investigation stage under s 79 of the Act. However, whether that is so or not, I take the view that the issues of consultation and legitimate expectation are issues which are particularly suitable for a decision by judicial review.'[2]

1   At first instance reported at [1999] Env LR 833.
2   [1999] Env LR 833 at 867.

4.39 The Court of Appeal[1] did not agree that questions of legitimate expectation and consultation were particularly suitable for judicial review per se but it is also apparent from the judgment of Pill LJ that he considered that these issues *could* have been raised by way of appeal to the justices. In our view Pill LJ was right. Harrison J appears to have addressed the wrong ground of appeal, namely regulation 2(2)(a). He should have addressed ground 2(2)(b). In the authors' view ground 2(2)(b) can include an allegation relating to the process leading up to the service of the notice. The following two reasons support this:

- the ordinary meaning of the words 'in connection with' suggest that the ground is not limited to defects etc only to be found on the face of the notice. There is nothing in the context of statutory scheme read as a whole that it should be given a more restricted meaning; and
- the inclusion of the additional words 'error' and 'informality' strongly suggest that the procedure by which the notice was issued may also be challenged under this ground. It is difficult to imagine what could meant by an 'informality' if this ground were to be restricted to defects on the face of the abatement notice.

4.39 *Challenging an abatement notice*

1   R v Falmouth and Truro Port Health Authority, ex p South-West Water Services [2000] 3 All ER 306, [2000] 3 WLR 1464.

4.40 As has already been stated at para **4.06**, section 7(1)(b) of the HRA 1998 provides that a person is entitled to rely on a Convention right[1] where he claims that a public authority has acted in *a way* that contravenes a Convention right. This is a wide provision. It is likely to have a real impact upon appeals against abatement notices in particular, because recipients of notices are entitled to appeal against the abatement notice on the ground that there has been some informality, defect, or error, in or in connection with, the abatement notice.[2] As discussed in Chapter 2, para **2.28**, we consider that this ground of appeal might also embrace a failure by a local authority to follow its adopted enforcement policy when issuing an abatement notice.

1   'Convention rights' are defined at HRA 1998, s 1.
2   Statutory Nuisance (Appeals) Regulations 1995 SI 1995/2664, reg 2(2)(b). Reproduced in full at Appendix B.

4.41 Appeals based on some informality, defect, or error will not succeed if the court is satisfied that the problem is not a material one.[1] Whether the problem is material will depend upon the nature the particular problem. Obvious typographical errors in the notice are not likely to be regarded as material.

1   Statutory Nuisance (Appeals) Regulations 1995, SI 1995/2664, reg 2(3). Reproduced in full at Appendix B.

Regulation 2(2)(c): (1) The authority has refused unreasonably to accept compliance with alternative requirements, or, (2) The requirements of the abatement notice are otherwise unreasonable in character or extent, or are unnecessary

4.42 This ground of appeal includes two separate limbs giving rise to *independent* grounds of appeal. Arguably, it could be further subdivided into three if the second limb is regarded as comprising two parts, (i) unreasonable in character or extent and (ii) unnecessary.

Alternative scheme

4.43 The first part deals with the situation where the recipient has already suggested an alternative scheme of measures that would ensure the abatement of the nuisance. This ground of appeal cannot arise unless the recipient has proposed the scheme *before* the notice has been served. This ground arises where the potential recipient has suggested requirements that will deal adequately with the nuisance but the local authority has served a notice requiring other steps to be carried out.

4.44 This ground of appeal does not go to the issue whether or not a nuisance has been created. It is predicated on the basis that a nuisance has been created. This ground of appeal is concerned with what steps can be required to abate the nuisance (as evidenced by the reference made to 'compliance with alternative requirements').

4.45 A potential recipient might propose a series of steps to be included in an abatement notice but reserve his right to appeal in the event that a notice is served, even if the notice incorporates the scheme proposed by the recipient. For example, the recipient may wish to appeal on the grounds that the matter complained of does not amount to a statutory nuisance.

4.46 The steps required by the local authority may be reasonable in themselves, but if the local authority has no good reason not to accept the steps previously suggested by the recipient this ground of appeal will succeed.

A local authority will be entitled to reject the suggested requirements where, for example, the requirements suggested by the recipient do not abate[1] the nuisance or else are not sufficiently clear or precise.

1   There may be circumstances where employment of best practicable means would not abate the nuisance. In such circumstances, the most that probably could be required would be a restriction of the nuisance to the level achieved by the employment of best practicable means. On this point see the discussion below on the best practicable means ground of appeal at paras **4.64–4.68**.

4.47 Where the justices uphold this ground of appeal they will vary the notice to include the steps suggested by the recipient of the notice. This does not mean that the justices are obliged simply to adopt the whole package of measures that have been proposed by the recipient of the notice. It is open to the justices to accept only some of those proposed by the recipient but retain some steps contained in the notice drafted by the local authority.

4.48 The existence of *this* ground of appeal does not mean that the local authority is generally obliged to enter into consultations with the potential recipient of a notice before a notice is issued.[1] There *may*, however, be circumstances unrelated to this ground of appeal where the local authority should consult the intended recipient before issuing an abatement notice.[2]

1   *R v Falmouth and Truro Port Authority, ex p South West Water Services* [2000] 3 WLR 1464, CA at 1475H–1476B per Simon Brown LJ and 1493H–1494A per Pill LJ.
2   In our view, a local authority, pursuant to its obligations under HRA 1998, may in *certain circumstances* be obliged to consult before serving an abatement notice which is not suspended, as to which see the discussion in Chapter 2 at paras **2.90–2.92**.

4.49 In reality in most cases potential recipients of abatement notices will have been given some indication that a local authority proposes to issue a notice whether by letter or a visit by the environmental health officer. Depending upon the circumstances of the case, it may be advantageous to the potential recipient to propose a series of steps to the local authority before a notice is served. Indeed, it may be equally advantageous to the potential recipient to enter into negotiations with the environmental health officer with a view to putting in place a voluntary package of measures and thereby avoid a notice being served. Whilst such a solution is of undoubted value to the potential recipient of the notice there are two important reservations to the foregoing. First, where a local authority is satisfied that a statutory nuisance exists it is *obliged* to serve an abatement notice[1] and in those circumstances it is not open to the local authority to agree to a voluntary package as an alternative to the service of an abatement notice. Second, the local authority should not allow discussions to cause undue delay to the service of an abatement notice.[2]

1   *R v Carrick District Council, ex p Shelley* [1996] Env LR 273.
2   Where a local authority did not serve an abatement notice until 20 months after it decided a nuisance existed the Local Government Ombudsman held that it had been guilty of maladministration: Complaint 88/C/1373 against Sheffield City Council.

4.50 *Challenging an abatement notice*

Requirements unreasonable in character or extent and/or unnecessary

4.50 The second part of this ground of appeal arises where the particular requirements set out in the notice go beyond that which is reasonably necessary to abate the nuisance, whether or not the alternatives have been canvassed previously with the local authority.

4.51 The recipient will not succeed on this ground merely because he can show that there is an alternative scheme of steps that will abate the nuisance. That ground is only open to a recipient who has proposed such an alternative scheme to the local authority prior to the issue of the abatement notice (see para **4.43** above in respect of the first limb). Under the ground of appeal contained in the second limb the recipient must go further and show that the steps required by the abatement notice are unreasonable in character or extent or are unnecessary.

4.52 What is unreasonable or unnecessary is a question for the justices. It will vary depending upon the circumstances of the cases; not least, the nature and extent of the nuisance. The principle of proportionality may provide a useful tool in determining what is reasonable in the circumstances. Examples may include the following:

- Where a notice requires that a certain noise level must not be exceeded throughout the day and night. That requirement *may* be unreasonable because at certain times of the day the background noise level is higher. Reasonableness may require that different permitted noise levels for the day and for the night be required, or that the noise level should be measured by reference to the existing background noise levels. An unchanging fixed noise level may be criticised by the recipient as iniquitous. Such a requirement will not always be unreasonable. It will depend upon the circumstances. For example, it may be reasonably necessary in order to ensure that the condition is effectively enforced. Furthermore, a noise may be extremely annoying because of its frequency notwithstanding that it registers below or only marginally above the background noise level in terms of DbA; and
- Where the steps required are extremely rigorous and expensive but ensure that there is not even a theoretical risk of a recurrence of the statutory nuisance, the justices may take the view that the additional steps required in order to ensure that complete absence of risk of recurrence go beyond that which could be reasonably required. The degree of acceptable risk would depend in large part upon the likelihood of it recurring without such measures and factors such as the risk to health and the harm caused by other types of nuisance if the nuisance were to recur.

Regulation 2(2)(d): That the time or times within which the requirements of the notice are to be complied with is or are not reasonably sufficient for the purpose

4.53 This ground is self-explanatory. It should be noted that the time for compliance with different requirements in the notice may vary for each

Grounds of appeal 4.58

individual requirement. For example, a notice may require complete abatement of the nuisance within six months but may require a limit to the hours of operation of the offending machinery to be put in place within two months, sound insulation to be installed within five months and the machine to be re-engineered with a new silencer by the end of the six months. The recipient is entitled to appeal against any or all of the time limits imposed by the notice.

The recipient will need to bring forward evidence to show why it is unreasonable to expect compliance within the times required. It may be, for example, that works required under the notice will take longer to install than permitted in the notice. Perhaps it will take more than six months to obtain the necessary equipment to fit the silencer to the machine. It may also be the case that the carrying out of steps required by the notice may require additional forms of regulatory consent such as planning permission or listed building consent.

4.54 Often a recipient will argue that extra time should be allowed in order for him to honour existing contracts. This is unlikely to be regarded as reasonable particularly if it means a significant extension in time for compliance or where the notice has been issued in order to prevent prejudice to health.

4.55 Ordinarily, where the notice has been suspended and the recipient is appealing on other grounds he is entitled to argue that no account should be taken of the additional time between the date of the issue of the notice and the determination of the appeal. Until the determination of the appeal the appellant is entitled to hope that his appeal will be successful.[1]

1   Where the notice has not been suspended the recipient is obliged in any event to comply with the notice within the time provided.

4.56 But what is the position where the only ground of appeal is that the notice does not provide a sufficient time within which to comply with its terms? It could be said that the justices should take account of the intervening period between receipt of the notice and the matter coming to appeal. This is because the recipient knew that at some date he was going to have to comply with the notice in any event. By the time the matters come to court he should have already progressed with taking steps to secure compliance. The better view, however, is that no account should be taken of any time intervening even where the recipient has appealed solely on the ground that the original period for compliance is too short. The notice is regarded as taking effect from the date of the determination of appeal and the court should consider the position as of that date as if the notice had just been issued.

4.57 The above approach is consistent with the view that the court looks at matters as of the date of the service of abatement notice.[1] Just as the recipient cannot pray in aid subsequent works to show that no nuisance currently exists at the time of the appeal in order to have the notice quashed nor should the local authority be entitled to rely on events subsequent to the issue of the notice. If the notice has been suspended it would be wrong as a matter of principle to prejudice the recipient by presuming that he should have been making efforts to comply with the notice during a time it was suspended.

1   *SFI Group plc v Gosport Borough Council* [1999] Env LR 750.

4.58 If a recipient has taken steps to comply with the notice notwithstanding that the notice is suspended it would be unreal for the court to ignore what has

4.58 *Challenging an abatement notice*

been carried out and extend the period for compliance for that which is no longer required. For example, if a notice gives three months for compliance and the recipient says that six months are necessary. The appeal comes before the court three months later. During the intervening period the recipient has carried out three months' worth of works. If the court accepts the recipient's case, he requires only three more months – the period allowed for by the notice. Accordingly, it would be *now* no longer necessary in practice to extend the time for compliance. Yet, it would be wrong for the justices to take the view that since there is now no need to extend the period for compliance the recipient has lost his appeal. This is because the ground of appeal uses the present tense and relates to the situation as at the time the notice was issued. At the time it was quite right to make the appeal. Moreover, it is also undesirable as a matter of policy to discourage a recipient of a notice to carry out any works before the determination of the appeal. The correct approach in such a situation is to view the notice at the date it was issued and uphold the appeal but to extend the period for compliance for as long as the court considers it is now necessary to complete the works as of the date of the hearing. Accordingly, it may be that, as in the example given above, an extension is no longer necessary. However, the notice should be varied to extend the period of time for compliance from the date on which the notice was issued. Regulation 2(5) of the Statutory Nuisance (Appeals) Regulations 1995[1] provides that a notice varied by the court 'shall have effect, as so varied, as if it had been so made by the local authority.' Nonetheless, it is common practice for the court to vary notices by inserting a period of compliance running from the date of the court order rather than the date when the notice was first issued by the local authority.

1   SI 1995/2664. Reproduced in full at Appendix B.

Regulation 2(2)(e): The best practicable means were used to prevent, or to counteract, the effects of the nuisance

4.59 This ground of appeal applies to nuisances contained in categories (a), (d), (e), (fa)[1], (fb)[2] and (g) of section 79 of the EPA 1990, and category (b) where the smoke emitted is from a chimney. It also arises in respect of noise emitted from vehicles etc in the street: (category ga). However, this ground of appeal will only apply to any of these nuisances if they arise on premises used for industrial, trade or business purposes or, in the case of category (ga), is caused by a vehicle etc used for those purposes. Amendments made to the Statutory Nuisance (Appeals) Regulations 1995 by the Statutory Nuisance (Appeals) (England) Regulations 2006[3], enable an appeal based on best practicable means against an abatement notice which cites either an insect or artificial light statutory nuisance. Section 79(1)(fa) (the insect nuisance) is added to the list of provisions at regulation 2(2)(e)(i) of the 1995 Regulations (*regulation 2(2)(a)*). Section 79(1)(fb) (the artificial light nuisance) is made the subject of a new regulation 2(2)(e)(iv) of the 1995 Regulations, providing that best practicable means are a ground of appeal against an abatement notice in respect of this nuisance where the artificial light is emitted either from industrial, trade or business premises, or by lights used for the purpose only of illuminating an outdoor relevant sports facility[4] (*regulation 2(2)(b)*).

1   The Clean Neighbourhood and Environment Act 2005, s 101 adds to the descriptions of statutory nuisances contained in EPA 1990, s 79(1): '(fa) any insects emanating from relevant industrial, trade or business premises and being prejudicial to health or a nuisance'. This provision does not apply to insects from domestic premises or insects listed in the Wildlife and

Grounds of appeal 4.61

Countryside Act 1981, Sch 5 unless they are included in that Schedule solely to prevent their trade or sale. The measure is intended to provide local authorities with a remedy to nuisances from insect infestations (whether naturally occurring or caused by human activities) on 'relevant' industrial,trade or business premises. However, it is not meant to be used against most naturally occurring concentrations of insects on open land or in ways that would adversely affect biodiversity. Accordingly, subsection (5) inserts two new subsections (7C) and (7D) into EPA 1990, s 79 which exclude from the definition of 'relevant' industrial, trade and business premises: (a) land used as arable, grazing, meadow or pasture land (but not structures placed on the land), (b) land used as osier land, reed beds, or woodland, (c) land used for market gardens, nursery grounds or orchards, (d) land forming part of an agricultural unit (but not covered by (a) to (c)) and which is of a description specified in regulations, and (e) land included in a Site of Special Scientific Interest,and land covered by, and the waters of, rivers, watercourses (except sewers and drains), lakes and ponds. Land which falls under (d) above is described by regulations. These regulations prescribe the descriptions of land under EPA 1990, s 79(7C)(d) (introduced by the Clean Neighbourhoods and Environment Act 2005, s 101(5)), that form part of an agricultural unit and which are (in addition to the types of land already listed at s 79(7C)(a)–c)) to be exempt from 'relevant industrial etc. premises' from which the new statutory nuisance from insects (EPA 1990, s 79(1)(fa)) is capable of emanating. Certain types of land are exempted from being capable of statutory nuisance from insects in order to safeguard endangered species,and protect biodiversity.

2 Section 102 adds to the descriptions of statutory nuisances listed in EPA 1990, s 79(1) '(fb) artificial light emitted from premises so as to be prejudicial to health or a nuisance'.However, this does not include artificial light emitted from the following premises. These are premises used for transport purposes and other premises where high levels of light are required for safety and security reasons:
- airports
- harbours
- railway premises
- bus stations and associated facilities
- public service vehicle operating centres
- goods vehicle operating centres
- lighthouses
- prisons
- premises occupied for defence purposes

These premises are listed in a new subsection (5B) to EPA 1990, s 79 and are defined in subsection (7) and in new subsections (7A) and (7B) of that Act (inserted by the Clean Neighbourhoods and Environment Act 2005, s 102 (4)–(6)). The exemption for defence premises is made by section 102(3) of the 2005 Act, amending EPA 1990, s 79(2). Section 103 extends the defence of 'best practicable means' to these new statutory nuisances where either is emitted from industrial, trade or business premises or, in the case of light, also from relevant outdoor sports facilities which are not industrial etc premises. Most artificially illuminated sports facilities will be regarded as businesses and so will benefit thereby from the 'best practicable means' defence. However, there may be some that are not; such as local authority grounds or facilities run by amateur clubs.

3 SI 2006/771.

4 The Statutory Nuisances (Artificial Lighting) (Designation of Relevant Sports) (England) Order 2006 designates the 'relevant sports', the facilities for which will be able to use the defence of 'best practicable means' in appealing against, or as a defence against prosecution for breaching or failing to comply with, an abatement notice for statutory nuisance from artificial light under EPA 1990, s 79(1)(fb).

4.60 This ground of appeal is only open to a recipient who was employing best practicable means *on the date the notice was issued.*

4.61 What constitutes 'industrial, trade or business premises' and 'best practicable means' is discussed in detail in Chapters 3 and 5. However, the very fact that the Secretary of State has included best practicable means as a ground of appeal is itself worthy of comment. In particular, a question arises as to how the mandatory obligation requiring a local authority to serve an abatement notice when satisfied of the existence of a statutory nuisance[1] can be reconciled with the ability of the recipient to appeal that notice and have it quashed on the

4.61 *Challenging an abatement notice*

ground that notwithstanding the existence of the statutory nuisance he has employed best practicable means. It cannot be the case that a local authority is obliged to issue a notice even when it knows that the recipient will have a cast iron ground of appeal to have the notice quashed on the grounds of best practicable means. If that were so, taken to its logical (albeit extreme) conclusion, if the appeal were successful the local authority would nonetheless continue to be obliged to issue a notice if satisfied that a statutory nuisance still existed.

1   In *R v Carrick District Council, ex p Shelley* [1996] Env LR 273, Carnwath J examined the wording of EPA 1990, s 80 and commented at 277–278 that: 'So far as the decision to serve an abatement notice is concerned, if the authority are satisfied on the balance of probabilities that there is a statutory nuisance, they have a duty to serve the notice.' This was followed in *The Barnes v Newcastle Upon Tyne City Council* [2005] EWCA Civ 1274 in which the proposition was not challenged by the local authority.

4.62   As we stated at Chapter 2, para **2.39**, there are a number of possible answers to this problem:

- *Ex p Shelley*[1] is wrong in holding that 'shall' means 'must' for the purposes of section 80 of the EPA 1990
- the Secretary of State acted contrary to the intention of Parliament by allowing a ground of appeal based upon the best practicable means
- *Ex p Shelley* is correct, but where the local authority was satisfied that the recipient would be able to appeal successfully on the grounds that he had employed the best practicable means, the local authority should issue a notice restricting, rather than abating, the nuisance by requiring the employment of best practicable means (see further paras **2.44–2.45** on the power to restrict a statutory nuisance)
- *Ex p Shelley* is correct, but where the local authority was satisfied that the recipient would be able to appeal successfully on the grounds that he had employed the best practicable means, it is not under a duty to issue a notice.

1   *R v Carrick District Council, ex p Shelley* [1996] Env LR 273.

4.63   The suggestion that the local authority might simply seek to restrict the nuisance appears attractive since it would require the maker of the nuisance to ensure that he maintains and keeps up to date with the best practicable means or else risks an immediate prosecution. However, it would, in our view, seem curious that a notice representing formal enforcement action could be issued in circumstances which Parliament and the Secretary of State appear to contemplate are acceptable. Accordingly, in our view, the last view probably represents the correct approach though the matter cannot be said to be entirely free from doubt.[1] However, it appears that the Secretary of State is of the view that a local authority must issue an abatement notice regardless of whether it is of the view that a recipient may be employing best practicable means. Paragraph 36 of the DEFRA *Guidance on Sections 69 to 81 and Section 86 of the Clean Neighbourhoods and Environment Act 2005*, section 86 of which introduces a power to defer the service of an abatement notice in respect of noise nuisance only (see further paras **2.41–2.43**), states that the provision was introduced because 'There is no provision for the exercise of discretion as to whether or not to take this action, even if the local authority suspects that "best practicable means" may be in place (only the courts can rule on whether "best practicable means" are in place).' We respectfully disagree. Carnwath J's analysis in *Ex p*

Shelley[2] reflects the statutory scheme seen as a whole.[3] This purpose would be frustrated if local authorities were not in general obliged to issue an abatement notice although satisfied that a statutory nuisance existed, and equally frustrated if they were forced to court to fight a case where they are in agreement with the appellant. If the Secretary of State holds this view, it is somewhat odd that the provision for deferral of an abatement notice was restricted only to noise abatement notices.[4]

1   See further the discussion of this matter at paras **2.39** and **3.45–3.52**.
2   *R v Carrick District Council, ex p Shelley* [1996] Env LR 273 at 277–278.
3   It is perhaps significant to note that despite the widespread litigation in this field no-one appears to have sought to challenge the validity of Carnwath J's approach either in the Divisional Court or the Court of Appeal. However, it is also true that the problem that we have identified in respect of this ground of appeal does not appear to have been raised before Carnwath J in *Ex p Shelley* or, indeed, before any other court in subsequent litigation. In *The Barns v Newcastle Upon Tyne City Council* [2005] EWCA Civ 1274, the Court of Appeal accepted the correctness of *Ex p Shelley* which was not challenged by the City Council.
4   It is the authors' experience that prior to the decision in *Ex p Shelley* many local authorities tended to seek to negotiate the best compromise possible with nuisance makers rather than move to issue an abatement notice.

4.64   The above matters are not free from doubt. Indeed, it can be argued that Secretary of State acted *ultra vires* in prescribing a ground of appeal based upon the employment of best practicable means.

4.65   Section 80(3) of the EPA 1990 makes provision for the rights of appeal. Appeals to the magistrates' court are set out at paragraph 1 to Schedule 3:

'(4) The Secretary of State may make regulations as to appeals to which this paragraph applies and the regulations *may in particular* –
  (a)   include provisions comparable to those in section 290 of the Public Health Act 1936 (appeals against notices requiring the execution of works);' [our emphasis].

The best practicable means ground of appeal, regulation 2(e), along with those contained in regulation 2(f), (g), (i) and (j), did not appear in section 290(3) of the Public Health Act 1936.[1]

1   Public Health Act 1936, s 280(3) provided that:
    A person served with such a notice as aforesaid may appeal to a court of summary jurisdiction on any of the following grounds which are appropriate in the circumstances of the particular case:
    (a) that the notice or requirement is not justified by the terms of the section under which it purports to have been given or made;
    (b) that there has been some informality, defect or error in, or in connection with, the notice;
    (c) that the authority have refused unreasonably to approve the execution of alternative works, or that the works required by the notice to be executed are otherwise unreasonable in character or extent, or are unnecessary;
    (d) that the time within which the works are to be executed is not reasonably sufficient for the purpose;
    (e) that the notice might lawfully have been served on the occupier of the premises in question instead of on the owner, or on the owner instead of the occupier, and that it would have been equitable for it to have been so served;
    (f) where work is work for the common benefit of the premises in question and other premises, that some other person, being the owner or occupier of premises to be benefited, ought to contribute towards the expenses of executing any works required.

4.66   The other grounds of appeal contained in the Statutory Nuisance (Appeals) Regulations 1995[1] reproduce those previously found in the Public Health Act 1936 and relate to some matter the local authority has to satisfy itself

4.66 *Challenging an abatement notice*

about before issuing the abatement notice (see section 80(1), (2) of the EPA 1990).[2] It is reasonable to suppose that the power of the Secretary of State to make provision for grounds of appeal was intended to be restricted to matters which related to the decision making process and conclusions reached by the local authority in sections 80(1) and (2).

1   SI 1995/2644.
2   As previously stated, EPA 1990, s 80(3) provides for the power of appeal; the remainder of s 80 (ie sub-ss (4)–(10)) deals with criminal proceedings relating to a breach of an abatement notice.

4.67 It is, of course, correct to note that Schedule 3 of the EPA 1990 does not purport to provide an exhaustive list of the circumstances within which the Secretary of State can make regulations. However, it is right to suppose that the Secretary of State cannot act to undermine the basis of the statutory scheme.[1] On this basis no ground of appeal based upon best practicable means could validity exist. A local authority would therefore be obliged to issue an abatement notice despite accepting that the recipient would have a statutory defence of best practicable means to any prosecution. A purpose would nonetheless be served because the recipient of the notice will be obliged to ensure that he is always employing best practicable means in order to avoid successful prosecution.

1   To take a more extreme hypothetical example in order to illustrate this point, suppose that the Secretary of State purported to include a ground of appeal that allowed a recipient to appeal a notice 'if the nuisance had been caused in connection with a trade or business.' Such a ground of appeal would create a massive exception, allowing all trades and businesses to avoid the statutory nuisance regime. It would clearly be outside the scope of the Secretary of State's powers since it did not accord with the implied intention of the statutory scheme, notwithstanding the absence of an exhaustive list of possible categories of grounds of appeal. Similarly, it is submitted that the inclusion of a ground of appeal on the basis of best practicable means may well be ultra vires the scope of power when properly understood against the context of the legislative scheme. The classic formulation of the general principle relating to the exercise of statutory discretion is to be found in the speech of Lord Bridge of Harwich in *R v London Borough of Tower Hamlets, ex p Chetnik Developments Ltd* [1988] AC 858 at 872–873.

4.68 In the light of the above arguments what course should be followed by local authorities? The scheme of the act is that abatement notices are enforced by prosecution for non-compliance.[1] The EPA 1990 provides a defence where the defendant can show best practicable means were being employed at the date of the alleged breach of the abatement order. It would therefore appear, in our view, to be inconsistent with the scheme of the Act for a local authority to issue a notice where it is satisfied that best practicable means were already being adopted.[2] Although the contrary is clearly arguable, the prudent course for authorities is not to serve abatement notices where they are satisfied that best practicable means would apply because they would expose themselves to what might be substantial costs on the magistrates' courts if the best practicable means ground of appeal is validly included in the regulations. It will always be open to aggrieved members of the public to seek a court order against the local authority that adopts the position recommended by us. It will also to be open to a local authority to take a contrary view of the validity of the best practicable means ground of appeal. In the authors' view this question of law would be much better addressed by such judicial review in advance of the service of the notice.

1   Abatement notices are not the only form of remedy under the statutory scheme. EPA 1990, s 80(4) allows a local authority to seek an injunction where it considers that proceedings for an offence would be an inadequate remedy. It must satisfy the condition specified in s 81(5) are

met (see further paras **2.71–2.78**). In the first edition of this text published in 2000, we suggested that it is not a condition that an abatement notice has already been issued. Accordingly, we suggested that the fact that the defendant may be employing the best practicable means may not necessarily preclude the imposition of an injunction to restrain the nuisance. Just as in the case of a civil action for nuisance, the court retains its discretion as to whether or not to grant injunctive relief. The court would be able to take into account the interest of businesses employing best practicable means when considering how best to exercise its discretion in the circumstances of the particular case. Indeed, it could very well be an intended consequence of the regime under the EPA 1990 that someone who has employed best practicable means to abate the nuisance should only be further restricted in his activities by way of injunction issued by the County or High court rather than by the local justices. Rosalind Malcolm has stressed the local nature of the jurisdiction exercised by the justices of the peace in the context of statutory nuisance (Malcolm 'Statutory Nuisance: The Validity of Abatement Notices' [2000] JPL 894 at 895–896): 'For the local magistracy, employment and social matters will carry weight. To close a local factory would be a result which they would barely contemplate. This characteristic of the enforcement of the law relating to statutory nuisance is not accidental. It originates from nineteenth century public health legislation where the local Justices were a potent force in the local community and where the control of such issues increasingly became a matter for local government.' [our emphasis] However, following *The Barns v Newcastle Upon Tyne City Council* [2005] EWCA Civ 1274 it is not possible to seek an injunction pursuant to EPA 1990, s 81(5) in the absence of an abatement notice having been issued.

2   Although it appears that the Secretary of State may take a different view, see paragraph 36 of the DEFRA *Guidance on Sections 69 to 81 and Section 86 of the Clean Neighbourhoods and Environment Act 2005*, and Chapter 2 at para **2.39**.

Regulation 2(2)(g): Noise emitted from premises and noise in the street
In the case of noise emitted from premises in categories (g) or (ga) that the requirements of the notice are more onerous than the existing controls in relation to the noise under the Control of Pollution Act 1974, sections 60, 61, 65, 66, or 67 as appropriate, or, in the case of noise in the street, the requirements of the notice are more onerous than the requirements of any condition of a consent given under the Noise and Statutory Nuisance Act 1993, Schedule 2, paragraph 1 in respect of the same noise for loudspeakers on the street

4.69   These two grounds of appeal (noise emitted from premises and noise in the street) can be dealt with together. They relate only to the noise nuisances. Presumably the reasoning behind these two grounds of appeal is that it would be unreasonable for the local authority to issue an abatement notice where under some other provision it has effectively given consent by deeming it acceptable for any particular level of noise and the person concerned is not exceeding that level. Certainly, this *rationale* would justify the statutory defence provided at section 80(9) of the EPA 1990.[1]

1   The existence of these two grounds of appeal raises a similar issue experienced in relation to the ground of appeal based upon the employment of best practicable means and the duty to issue a notice when satisfied of the existence of a statutory nuisance which are discussed at paras **4.61–4.68** in respect of the best practicable means ground of appeal contained in reg 2(2)(e).

4.70 *Challenging an abatement notice*

Regulation 2(2)(h): Service on an appropriate person
The abatement notice should have been served on some person instead of the appellant, being:
(i) the person responsible for the nuisance; or
(ii) the person responsible for the vehicle, machinery, or equipment; or
(iii) in the case of a structural defect, the owner of the premises; or
(iv) in the case where the person responsible for the nuisance cannot be found or the nuisance has not yet occurred, the owner or occupier of the premises.

Regulation 2(2)(i): Service on person instead of appellant
The abatement notice might have been lawfully served on some person instead of the appellant being:
(i) in the case where the appellant is the owner of the premises, the occupier of the premises; or
(ii) in the case where the appellant is the occupier of the premises, the owner of the premises;
and that it would have been equitable for him to have been served.

Regulation 2(2)(j): Service on person in addition to appellant
The abatement notice might have been lawfully served on some person in addition to the appellant, being:
(i) a person also responsible for the nuisance;
(ii) a person who is also owner of the premises;
(iii) a person who is also the occupier of the premises;
(iv) a person who is also responsible for the vehicle, machinery, or equipment
and it would have been equitable for him to have been so served.

4.70 Ground (h) concerns the question as to whether the recipient of the notice is an appropriate person on whom to serve a notice. This is discussed in Chapter 3 paras **3.63–3.73**. Under ground (h) the recipient needs to show that he is not the person upon whom a notice should lawfully have been served but that someone else should have been served instead. Put in simple terms, this ground of appeal is that the recipient of the notice is not the person legally responsible for the alleged nuisance.

4.71 Both grounds (h) and (i) allege that the notice should have been served on someone else 'instead'. However in respect of ground (i) the recipient is not arguing that he is legally not responsible for the nuisance but rather that someone else is also responsible and that it would be equitable for that person to be served instead. Ground (j) alleges that the notice should have been served upon someone else 'in addition' to the recipient.

4.72 Grounds (i) and (j) deal with the situation where there may be more than one person legally responsible but where the court considers that equity requires that because another person also responsible should have been served, either 'instead' (ground (i)) or in 'addition' (ground (j)). Grounds (i) and (j) introduce the concept of equity to the process, something not apparent in section 80 of the EPA 1990 itself. Thus, a recipient may be responsible for the nuisance but nonetheless succeed in having the notice quashed under ground (i) on the basis that it was not fair for him to have been served with an abatement notice when there is another *also* responsible upon whom the notice should rather have been served. Neither the EPA 1990 nor the 1995 Appeal Regulations give any guidance as to how the court should exercise this judgment. Clearly the circumstances will depend upon the particular facts of the case.

4.73 Grounds (i) and (j) create some problems for practitioners. Some assume that the local authority has a discretion as to who can be served. It is arguable that section 80(2) of the EPA 1990 does *not* afford local authorities such a discretion. Section 80(2) provides that subject to certain exceptions the local authority 'shall' serve a notice upon the person 'responsible' for the nuisance. If 'shall' in section 80(2) has the same mandatory meaning as 'shall' in section 80 (1) then a local authority would be obliged to serve a notice upon everyone who is legally responsible for the nuisance regardless of whether the local authority considers it equitable to do so.[1] Yet it should also be noted that Schedule 3 paragraph 4(d) provides that the Secretary of State could 'prescribe the cases in which the appellant may claim that an abatement notice should have been served on some other person and prescribe the procedure to be followed in those cases.' Whether grounds (h), (i) and (j) prescribe the type of cases envisaged by the EPA 1990 is debatable. In particular, it is questionable whether Schedule 3 paragraph 4(d) permits the Secretary of State to prescribe grounds (h) and (i) which allow a recipient of a notice who is legally responsible for the nuisance to escape receipt of an abatement notice altogether on the basis that an abatement notice should have been served on someone else.

1   '[I]t is impermissible to interpret a definition section in an Act in the light of a definition contained in a statutory instrument made under that Act': *Millington v Secretary of State for the Environment, Transport and the Regions and Shrewsbury and Atcham Borough Council* [2000] JPL 297 at 303 per Schiemann LJ. Accordingly, it would also be wrong to interpret the meaning of EPA 1990, s 80 (2) in the light of the grounds of appeal contained made by the Secretary of State under EPA 1990 s 81 and Sch 3.

4.74 As matters currently stand, a tension arises from the fact that the grounds of appeal prescribed by the Statutory Nuisance (Appeals) Regulations 1995[1] appear to include considerations for the court to take into account on appeal not open to the local authority when considering whether and upon whom a notice should be served.[2] On balance, however, it is our view that the purpose of the EPA 1990 is to secure by simple means the speedy and effective abatement of nuisance and there is therefore no need to serve more than one notice where it is fair to do so. This would suggest that the local authority does have a discretion under section 80(2) of the EPA 1990 as to whether to serve a notice upon all, some or even only one of the persons responsible for the nuisance, provided that exercise of discretion is exercised lawfully and equitably.

1   SI 1995/2644.
2   On the other hand, the advice provided by the Secretary of State at paragraph 36 of the DEFRA *Guidance on Sections 69 to 81 and Section 86 of the Clean Neighbourhoods and Environment*

4.74 *Challenging an abatement notice*

Act 2005 is that whether a person is employing best practicable means can only be determined by the courts. This means that the local authority, once satisfied of the existence of a statutory nuisance must issue an abatement notice and leave to the court the determination of whether or not best practicable means was being applied. If this view were correct – and the authors respectfully disagree (see Chapter 2 para **2.39**), then it would not be anomalous for the court to be able to consider matters such as whether it was 'equitable' for the receipient to have been served with the notice even if that were a factor which the local authority itself had no discretion to consider when issuing the notice.

4.75 The result of a successful appeal under either grounds (h) or (i) would result in the quashing of the notice served against the recipient. However, a successful appeal under ground (j) would not result in a quashing or variation of the notice since this ground of appeal does not assert that the notice should not have been served on the recipient but merely that an abatement notice should have been served on someone else as well. See paras **4.118–4.123**.

4.76 The outcome of appeals made under grounds (i) and (j) are plainly relevant to third parties. Regulation 4 of the Statutory Nuisance (Appeals) Regulations 1995[1] requires the person appealing under either of these grounds to serve a copy of 'the notice of his appeal' on any person referred to. The reference to 'notice of appeal' is rather unhelpful. It can only refer to the complaint.[2]

1 SI 1995/2664. Reproduced in full at Appendix B.
2 This unhelpful duplicity of terms is a consequence of the confusion to which we have already made reference arising out of the fact that the EPA 1990 is an appeal but provides that an appeal is to be made by way of a 'complaint' to the magistrates' court governed by the Magistrates' Court Act 1980.

4.77 There is no time period prescribed for service of copies of the complaint on third parties mentioned in the appeal. However, notice would have to be given far enough in advance for the third party to be able to prepare properly and attend court. The prudent course is to serve a copy of the complaint on the third party at the same time the complaint is lodged with the magistrates' court.

AMENDING THE GROUNDS OF APPEAL

4.78 The Statutory Nuisance (Appeals) Regulations 1995[1] are silent about the possibility of amendment to the grounds of appeal. An appeal against an abatement notice must be made within 21 days. Does this mean that a failure to appeal upon a particular ground within the 21-day period prevents the appellant amending his grounds of appeal to include it at a later date?

Regulation 2(5) of the 1995 Regulations provides that on hearing the appeal the court may amongst other things 'vary the abatement notice in favour of the appellant in such a manner as it thinks fit.' This appears to give the court a wide power regardless of the specifics of the grounds of appeal. Further, Schedule 3 of the EPA 1990 at paragraph 2 provides that the Magistrates' Courts Act 1980 (MCA 1980) shall apply to the procedure governing the complaint. Section 123 of the MCA 1980 provides that no objection can be taken to any defect in the substance or form of a complaint.

1 SI 1995/2664. Reproduced in full at Appendix B.

4.79 From an examination of the approach adopted by the court in respect of amendments of charges by prosecutors in criminal proceedings under section

123 of the MCA 1980 the following may be deduced in respect of amendments to the grounds of appeal (or complaint) to an abatement notice:

An appellant may abandon a ground of appeal and substitute a fresh appeal save where the local authority can show that it would be inappropriate to do so, for example where:

- there is bad faith on the part of the appellant, or
- where unfairness or prejudice would result from the amendment, or
- the court is satisfied that the amendment does not amount to an abuse of procedure.[1]

1   See *R v City of Liverpool Stipendiary Magistrate, ex p Ellison* [1989] Crim LR 369 and *Stone's Justices' Manual* (2007) Vol I, 1-440.

4.80   The authorities from which the above principles are derived are concerned principally with amendments to criminal charges. In our view, they also represent sound guidance for complaints against abatement notices. If anything, it is probably correct to suppose that the court is likely to be more willing to allow a complainant in a civil appeal to amend his grounds of appeal since the local authority is not in the position of a defendant facing newly constituted criminal charges.

4.81   There may, however, be circumstances where the court refuses to allow an amendment to a complaint against an abatement notice. An instance could arise where the appellant deliberately waits until the last moment to amend his grounds of appeal either to catch the local authority unprepared or else to force the local authority into applying for an adjournment in order to deal with the new ground of appeal. An adjournment may be to the advantage of a cynical appellant since in most cases the provisions of the notice will have been suspended upon the outcome of the appeal. If the court takes the view that the appellant has sought to abuse the process it may refuse to allow the amendment. In any event, in deciding whether to allow an amendment the court should always seek an explanation from the appellant as to why any new ground was not originally included and why the amendment has not been made at an earlier stage.

4.82   Where an amendment is made late so as to incur an adjournment the appellant may also be penalised in respect of the award of costs made at the final judgment.[1]

1   On the power to award costs of adjournments in abatement notice appeals, see Chapter 7, paras **7.16–7.17** and **7.28**.

Challenging a non-suspended notice

4.83   In some cases a notice will be suspended pending determination of an appeal. A recipient of a non-suspended notice is entitled to appeal under section 80 of the EPA 1990 to the justices in the same way as where the notice is not suspended. But what can the recipient of a notice do if the terms of the notice are not suspended pending his appeal? The only civil law avenue open to the recipient is to challenge the decision not to suspend the notice by way of judicial review.

4.84   The court has noted on a number of occasions that the judicial review is not usually appropriate for issues involving disputes of fact.[1] Moreover, the conventional view is that even if a challenge by way of judicial review were to

4.84 *Challenging an abatement notice*

be permitted, '[The applicant] would of course be limited to arguing administrative law grounds for such a challenge and would not be able to argue the merits.'[2]. This view *may* now have to be reassessed in the light of the incorporation of the ECHR.[3]

1 See for example, cases concerning planning law: *R v Jenner* [1983] 2 All ER 46 at 49C per Watkins LJ (a case concerning a defence to a failure to comply with a stop notice) and the comments by Sullivan J in *Alfonso Dilieto v London Borough of Ealing* [1998] PLCR 212 at 223A-D. The latter case was concerned with whether a defendant, charged with a failure to comply with a breach of condition notice to which there was no appeal, could challenge the factual basis upon which the notice was issued as a defence to a prosecution for failure to comply with the terms of the breach of condition notice. The argument advanced by the prosecution that such challenges should brought by way of judicial review and not as part of a defence to a prosecution for failing to comply with the breach of condition notice was rejected.
2 See Woolley, Pugh-Smith, Langham and Upton *Environmental Law* (2000, OUP), para 19.39 at 842.
3 Article 6 of the ECHR provides that everyone is entitled to a fair hearing in the determination of their civil law rights and obligations. Article 1 to the First Protocol to the European Convention also guarantees the right to quiet enjoyment of property subject to a margin of appreciation. The issuing of an abatement notice has a clear and direct effect upon the recipient's property rights. Yet insofar as the notice is suspended he is denied a right of appeal and the extent of his remedy by way of judicial review is unclear and limited particularly in the light of the Court of Appeal's decision in *R v Falmouth and Truro Port Health Authority, ex p South West Water Services* [2000] 3 All ER 306, [2000] 3 WLR 1464, CA. In *Bryan v United Kingdom* (1995) 21 EHRR 342; [1996] 1 PLR 47 the European Court of Human Rights had to consider whether the limited grounds of statutory appeal afforded under Town and Country Planning Act 1990, s 289 complied with article 6(1). That section provided a limited ground of appeal akin to judicial review of decisions by the Secretary of State. The court held that was compatible because the appellant had been afforded an opportunity to argue matters of fact before the Secretary of State by way of a public inquiry if he so chose. In the case of a challenge to a decision not to suspend the issue of an abatement notice, recipients may seek to argue that a failure to afford a right of appeal on the facts at issue would infringe article 6(1) of the ECHR. The merits of such a challenge are discussed in further detail in Chapter 3. It is possible for the court to accommodate such a review by way of judicial review. Cross-examination is currently permitted in judicial review albeit in rare circumstances at the discretion of the court (see for example *Cocks v Thanet District Council* [1983] 2 AC 286 at 294H per Lord Bridge).

4.85 In the event of a prosecution for the failure to comply with the terms of a notice that had not been suspended pending an appeal the defendant would be allowed to raise as part of his defence any argument that the notice was invalid of the notice.[1] Clearly, the particular aspect of invalidity would have to have some relevance to the nature of the breach he is alleged to have committed. As to the possible defences to a prosecution for non-compliance with a non-suspended notice, see Chapter 5, paras **5.90–5.102**.

1 See for example *Sterling Homes (Midlands) Ltd v Birmingham City Council* [1996] Env LR 121.

4.86 It is undesirable that the recipient of a notice should have to await prosecution in order to test whether it was right to issue the notice. This is particularly so because the EPA 1990 provides no right to compensation where a notice is not suspended and the recipient has to comply with the requirements of the notice pending appeal. Indeed, it may be that the requirements are such that the appeal has become of academic importance, where for example the recipient is required to install sound insulation. Once that has been done and the expense incurred there is hardly likely going to be much point in removing it in the event of a successful appeal.

4.87 In the light of the views expressed by the Court of Appeal in *R v Falmouth and Truro Port Authority, ex p South West Water Services*,[1] the opportunity for challenging an abatement notice, even one that is not suspended, by way of judicial review is limited (as to general scope to seek judicial review of abatement notices generally see further paras **4.135–4.145**). The normal course must be for a recipient of a non-suspended notice to make an immediate appeal to the justices seeking an immediate hearing of the matter. Following *Ex p South West Water*, unless the recipient can show that he cannot obtain a sufficiently speedy hearing of his appeal before the justices it is unlikely, in our view, that an application by way of judicial review will be entertained by the court.[2]

1   [2000] 3 All ER 306, [2000] 3 WLR 1464, CA.
2   As we have stated earlier, it is arguable that the justices have the power to hear the question of whether the notice should be suspended immediately whilst adjourning the substantive grounds of appeal against the notice to be heard at a later date. Until a final decision is made the justices will be entitled to revisit the question of whether the notice should have been suspended at the adjourned hearing. Justices will be familiar with the notion of 'split hearing' since they are a common feature of the family law proceedings that come before the magistrates' courts.

PRE-TRIAL PROCEDURES

4.88   There are no express provisions in the rules for the magistrates' court to order, for example, disclosure by the parties or for the compulsory exchange of evidence before the hearing date. However, it is common and good practice for the court to hold a pre-trial review in more complicated cases in order to address matters in the same way as a directions hearing. Indeed, it is the practice of some District Judges to issue directions without even the attendance of the parties.[1] Some cases are sufficiently straightforward that they will be unlikely to warrant a pre-trial hearing.

1   An example is the direction issued on 15 November 2007 requiring the complainant to furnish further particulars of its grounds of appeal issued by District Judge Richard Williams (the Law Courts, Bridgend) in *Express Contract Drying Limited v Blaenau Gwent CBC*.

4.89   Some have contended that nonetheless the court retains an inherent power to make such orders.[1] However, the better view, as matters presently stand, is that there are no formal powers directly open to the court to make such orders. This means that a party could theoretically spring surprise evidence and even witnesses on an opposing party on the very day of the hearing. This approach, however, is not to be recommended as a general course of action. In practice, the court will rightly expect some degree of co-operation between the parties. Sedley LJ has recently put the matter thus:[2]

> 'The principal object of the statutory appeal against an abatement notice is plainly to relieve the person served of the need to await a prosecution and to risk a conviction before being able to contest the need for the contents of the notice. Precisely because an appeal under section 80(3) is therefore not a criminal proceeding *it is reasonable to expect some sensible co-operation between the persons served and the local authority in producing an intelligible and workable notice, unless it really is arguable that no statutory nuisance exists.*' [Emphasis added]

Magistrates and their clerks will not appreciate surprise production of technical evidence. The bench is likely to find the case complicated enough without the manoeuvring of uncooperative parties. The introduction of surprise evidence may also lead to a justified application for an adjournment. It should also be remembered that many courts have their own practice guidance that may

4.89 *Challenging an abatement notice*

provide, for example, for a pre-trial hearing or for legal authorities to be sent to the clerk and the other side some days before the hearing date.

1   See eg Delwyn Jones, 'Statutory nuisance appeals with special reference to smells' [1995] JPL 797 at 800.
2   *Sovereign Rubber Ltd v Stockport Metropolitan Borough Council* [2000] Env LR 194 at 198.

4.90 Set out in Appendix A is a suggested checklist that we recommend for the parties and the courts. We would hope that this form or a type similar to it would be sent out by the court when the summons is issued. However, we would suggest in the absence of such a form the parties might do well to propose it to the other side and the court as a convenient way of progressing the management of the case.

The suggested form sets out the questions that will need to be addressed. It is entirely consistent with the notion of 'case management' hearings now found elsewhere in civil proceedings. It will assist in determining whether there is a need for a pre-trial hearing.

4.91 Very often the grounds of appeal will reveal little about the exact nature of the complaint. The appellant is not obliged to particularise the exact nature of the appeal but it is clearly helpful for the local authority to know the nature of the complaint that it has to meet. This is especially so if a ground of appeal is that the appellant was employing the best practicable means. There may be cases where it would save court time if the matter were placed before a District Judge. If the case is heard by a District Judge, there is less difficulty in listing a part-heard case if it runs over time since it is necessary only to ensure that the District Judge is free rather than three lay persons. An agreement that the matter should go before a District Judge does not oblige the court to list it before a District Judge. Indeed, the court may be reluctant to do so if it would involve an undue delay whilst the necessary arrangements were put in place. It is helpful for the court to know whether the parties consider that a site visit is necessary. Once again this is a matter entirely at the discretion of the court. It is probably prudent for the bench not to visit the site unaccompanied or at least it should not do so unless it has previously informed the parties. This is to avoid any challenges to the court's decision based upon breaches of natural justice for the tribunal to take into account information not before the parties. There are of course obvious dangers with site visits. The site may have in fact changed since the date of the notice. However, an accompanied visit to the site may help the court picture the actual layout and relationship of the site particularly in cases of noise nuisance.

4.92 Where the parties are going to call expert evidence it is helpful if the expert reports are exchanged with allowance for the possibility of an exchange of rebuttal reports. Sometimes it may be possible for the parties to work together in producing a schedule of matters agreed and not agreed so that court time is saved by focusing upon those matters that are actually disputed by the parties.

RULES OF EVIDENCE

4.93 There is some debate about the extent to which the rules of evidence apply to appeals against abatement notices. Hearsay evidence may be permitted in civil cases before the magistrates' court. The rules relating to the admission

Rules of evidence **4.95**

of hearsay evidence have been set down in the Magistrates' Court (Hearsay Evidence in Civil Proceedings) Rules 1999.[1] The rules are reproduced in full at Appendix D. They greatly relax the restrictions previously applying to hearsay evidence in civil cases.

1   SI 1999/681 (made pursuant to Civil Evidence Act 1995, s 12).

4.94   However, it has been argued that, if one accepts that the magistrates are sitting in a regulatory capacity, then the court would not be bound by any rules of evidence.[1] Support for this view can be gained from the Court of Appeal's decision in *Kavanagh v Chief Constable of Devon and Cornwall*.[2] The case concerned an appeal against the refusal by the Chief Constable to issue a firearms certificate Mr Kavanagh appealed to the Crown Court which was of the view that it was entitled to hear all of the matters that had influenced the Chief Constable in reaching his decision with regard to the appellant. Lord Denning MR examined the jurisdiction of the magistrates' court. He drew a distinction between its capacity as a criminal court where the rules of evidence for criminal cases applied and where the court was exercising 'administrative jurisdiction'.

> 'When so doing, the justices never held themselves bound by the strict rules of evidence. They acted on material that appeared to be useful in coming to a decision, including their own knowledge. No doubt they admitted hearsay, though there is nothing to be found in the books about it. To bring the procedure up to modern requirements, I think they should act on the same lines as any administrative body which is charged with an inquiry. They may receive material which is logically probative even though it is not evidence in a court of law. Hearsay evidence can be permitted where it can fairly be regarded as reliable.'

In the same case Roskill LJ stated;

> '... when one looks at the relevant sections of the Firearms Act 1968, one finds references to the need for the officers concerned to be 'satisfied' of certain matters. This seems to me the key to the present case. In reaching a decision whether or not he is 'satisfied', he is entitled and indeed obliged to take account all relevant matters, whether or not any reports and information given to him would be strictly admissible in a court of law ... It would be strange indeed if the appeal which formerly lay to the quarter sessions and now lies to the Crown Court had to be dealt with on a wholly different evidential basis from that on which senior police officers concerned had to deal with the original applications.'

1   Tom Graham 'Statutory nuisance: what are the rules governing appeal?' [1996] JPL 194.
2   [1974] 2 All ER 697.

4.95   The Court of Appeal's decision in *Kavanagh v Chief Constable of Devon and Cornwall* was considered and applied by the Divisional Court in *Westminster City Council v Zestfair Ltd*.[1] That case concerned an appeal to the magistrates' court under section 49(10) of the Greater London Council (General Powers) Act 1968 by way of complaint against the refusal by the local authority to re-register their premises as a night café.

> 'The practical question, as appears from counsel's submissions, was whether an officer or officers of the council could give evidence to the court of complaints made to them as to nuisances alleged to have been caused by reason of the conduct of the premises. It is common ground that the licensing

4.95 *Challenging an abatement notice*

sub-committee, provided they act fairly, are entitled to have regard to material which would not ordinarily be admissible in a civil proceeding in a court of law.

The stipendiary magistrate ruled that hearsay evidence should not be admitted. Having heard the oral evidence he made an order setting aside the refusal to register the premises as a night café and granted registration subject to the council's standard conditions.

The question for the opinion of the High Court is whether the stipendiary magistrate is correct in law in holding that the hearing of an appeal under s 49(10) of the Greater London Council (General Powers) Act 1968 (which by virtue of r 34 of the Magistrates' Court Rules 1981 is by way of complaint) is governed by the rules of evidence applicable to civil proceedings or, in hearing such an appeal, whether the court is entitled and required to admit all the evidence, including hearsay evidence, which was originally before the local authority licensing sub-committee whose decision is the subject of the appeal.'

1   (1989) 153 JP 613.

4.96 The Divisional Court rejected the argument that the word 'evidence' in the MCA 1980 (section 53 and rule 34 of the Magistrates' Courts Rules 1981) means evidence properly admissible in civil proceedings which does not include hearsay. The Divisional Court considered itself bound by the principle articulated in *Kavanagh* and rejected the notion that the case was distinguishable on the grounds that it was decided under the Firearms Act 1968 and that different considerations applied. The Divisional Court considered that the public interest was concerned in both cases.

4.97 In giving the judgment of the Divisional Court, Pill J underlined the caution given by Cusack J in *Kavanagh*:

'... that if some of the matters before the court 'are hearsay and are not supported by the evidence of witnesses in ... court ... it will be for the court to consider carefully what weight is to be attached to the evidence which is put before it in that fashion.'[1]

1   (1989) 153 JP 613.

4.98 In our view there is no relevant distinction in respect of the hearing of complaint against abatement notices under the EPA 1990 that would justify taking a different approach to that of *Kavanagh*[1] and *Westminster City Council v Zestfair Ltd*.[2] This means that at a hearing of a complaint against an abatement notice environmental health officers will be able to give evidence of complaint about nuisances that they have received from third parties in the absence of the third parties themselves. It should be remembered that the original jurisdiction to issue abatement notices was different to that of today in so far as it related to proceedings taken under the Public Health Act 1936. Prior to the reforms of the EPA 1990 it was necessary for the local authority to apply to the justices for a nuisance order to be issued. In the light of the quite proper caution given in *Kavanagh* and *Westminster City Council v Zestfair* as to the weight to be given to evidence which would not be admissible in ordinary civil proceedings, it is clearly advantageous to ensure where possible that evidence adduced complies with the civil rules of evidence in order to increase the weight which can be

Order of evidence and speeches **4.102**

given it by the court. As has already been stated the rules relating to the admission of hearsay evidence in civil proceedings have been greatly relaxed and so it is less likely that material considered by the local authority would not be admissible even under the rules of civil evidence. One real distinction is that under the rules there is a requirement to give notice to the court and the other side. The best practice would be to follow the rules for notice where possible when relying upon hearsay evidence.

1 *Kavanagh v Chief Constable of Devon and Cornwall* [1974] 2 All ER 697.
2 (1989) 153 JP 613.

ORDER OF EVIDENCE AND SPEECHES

4.99 The rules are clear in the way in which the complaint is supposed to proceed. Under the rules the appellant proceeds first to present his case. He is permitted an opening address before calling his evidence.[1] The court may dismiss the appellant's case at its conclusion either of its own motion or following a submission of no case to answer by the local authority. In either event the appellant must be offered the opportunity to address the court before such a dismissal.[2]

1 Magistrates' Court Rules 1981, r 14(1).
2 *Mayers v Mayers* [1971] 2 All ER 397.

4.100 In the authors' experience some appellants have successfully persuaded magistrates' courts that the local authority should proceed to present its case first before the appellant. They have argued that since for the most part the burden of proving that the notice is a good one rests with the local authority the local authority must go first. In the authors' view this arguments is wrong.[1] The appellant should go first and he bears the burden of proof. The tactical advantage to the appellant in arranging that the local authority go first is obvious. The appellant's advocate can snipe at the notice before having to show his own hand in any detail. But this order does not accord with the order of speeches and evidence set down in the Magistrates' Court Rules 1981.[2] It is also unlikely to be an expeditious way to hear the matter, for the local authority is likely to be calling its evidence without knowing the details of the appellant's complaint. The result is that it is more likely that the local authority may need to call rebuttal evidence following the presentation of the appellant's case.

1 In *Express Contract Drying Limited v Blaenau Gwent CBC* the local authority had agreed to present evidence first. District Judge Richard Williams with the agreement of the parties considered that he could rule on a submission on a no case to answer by the appellant in relation to whether the local authority's evidence demonstrated that the appellant had caused the alleged nuisance, in this case, an alleged odour (Judgment 20 November 2007).
2 See *Stone's Justices' Manual* (2007) Vol I 1-5943.

4.101 At the conclusion of the appellant's evidence the local authority may address the court whether or not it afterwards calls evidence.[1] The local authority retains this right even if it has previously made an unsuccessful submission of no case to answer.[2]

1 Magistrates' Court Rules 1981, r 14(2).
2 *Disher v Disher* [1965] P 31, [1963] 3 All ER 933.

4.102 At the conclusion of the evidence, if any, from the local authority, the appellant may call evidence to rebut that evidence.[1] In civil cases the right to call 'rebutting evidence' corresponds to the similar right in criminal trials. This

123

4.102 *Challenging an abatement notice*

means that rebutting evidence must be confined to a matter that arose unexpectedly in the course of the defence.[2] In criminal cases it has been held that it is only proper for the prosecution to call rebuttal evidence if during the defendant's case some matter has arisen which no human ingenuity could foresee.[3] However, the test in civil proceedings for statutory nuisance may be less severe. One needs to bear in mind that the appellant is not a prosecuting authority. The purpose of the appellant calling further evidence would not be to show that the local authority was guilty of some criminal offence but to support its contention that the abatement notice appeal should be allowed.

1 Magistrates' Courts Rules 1981, r 14(3).
2 *R v Wealan* (1881) 14 Cox CC 595.
3 *R v Harris* [1927] 2 KB 587, 91 JP 152; *R v Liddle* (1928) 21 Cr App Rep 3; *R v McMahon* (1933) 24 Cr App Rep 95; *R v Day* [1940] 1 All ER 402, 104 JP 181; *R v Browne* (1943) 29 Cr App Rep 106; *Price v Humphries* [1958] 2 QB 353, [1958] 2 All ER 725.

4.103 Closing speeches are not automatically available to either party. However, both the appellant and the local authority may address the court for a second time with the permission of the court. In the authors' experience it is the normal practice for closing speeches to be made other than in the most straightforward cases. Should the court refuse a request by a party for a closing speech it is likely that the hearing will not be regarded as fair as a matter of common law natural justice or for the purposes of article 6 of the ECHR. Indeed, the terms of rule 14(5) are such that the appellant may be allowed a closing speech even if the local authority does not wish to have one itself. Where the court grants permission to one party it cannot refuse permission to the other.[1] Where the local authority obtains permission to address the court a second time its second address must be made before the second address, if any, of the appellant.[2] This is because the appellant bears the burden of proof (see para **4.105** below) and therefore gets the last word.

1 Magistrates' Courts Rules 1981, r 14(5).
2 Magistrates' Courts Rules 1981, r 14(5).

THE STANDARD OF PROOF

4.104 The standard of proof is the ordinary civil law standard.

In *Miller v Minister of Pensions*[1] Denning J (as he then was) described as well-settled the degree of cogency required to discharge the legal burden in a civil case. He stated:

> 'It must carry a reasonable degree of probability, but not so high as is required in a criminal case. If the evidence is such that a tribunal can say: "we think it more probable than not", the burden is discharged, but if the probabilities are equal it is not.'

1 [1947] 2 All ER 372.

THE BURDEN OF PROOF

4.105 The regulations do not specifically provide that the appellant must prove any of the grounds set out in regulation 2 of the Statutory Nuisance (Appeals) Regulations 1995.[1]

1 SI 1995/2664. Reproduced in full at Appendix B.

4.106 In *Stepney Borough Council v Joffe*[1] concerning an appeal over the refusal by a local authority to grant a street trading licence, Lord Goddard CJ confirmed that the appeal before the justices was a *de novo*[2] hearing but noted that this did not mean that the court:

'... ought not to pay great attention to the fact that the duly constituted and elected local authority have come to an opinion on the matter and ought not lightly to reverse their opinion.'

Applying the ordinary principle that he who asserts must prove, it is generally accepted that it was for the appellant to prove his case on the civil standard if the appeal was to succeed.[3] However, in our experience it is not infrequently submitted by advocates for appellants that the local authority bears the burden of demonstrating that the notice is a good one.

1 [1949] 1 KB 599, [1949] 1 All ER 256.
2 A completely new hearing.
3 See eg Delwyn Jones 'Statutory nuisance appeals with special reference to smells' [1995] JPL 797 at 800.

4.107 In our view the better view is that the appellant bears the burden of making out his appeal. Once the appellant has established a *prima facie* case in support of his grounds of appeal then the local authority will have to meet the case.[1] This view accords with the procedure for complaints set out in the Magistrates' Courts Rules 1981[2] which provides that the court may dismiss the appeal and the end of the appellant's case either of its own motion or following an application of no case to answer by the local authority. It is also sensible to proceed in this way because there are some grounds of appeal that the appellant will be particularly well placed to deal with, for example, whether the appellant has employed the best practicable means or that the local authority has unreasonably refused alternative solutions to abate the nuisance. Indeed the way in which the grounds of appeal are drafted in regulation 2 of the 1995 Appeal Regulations indicate that it is expected that the appellant will have to make out his case. It would be absurd to suggest that the local authority was under a burden to show that it had *not* unreasonably refused to accepted alternative solutions.

1 This passage as it appeared in the first edition of this text was approved by District Judge English sitting at the South West Surrey Magistates' Court in *Dunsfold Park Limited v Waverley Borough Council* (12 January 2007).
2 SI 1981/552.

THE RELEVANT DATE

4.108 In considering the appeal the court must consider the facts at the date the notice was served.[1] Previously a view had persisted that the court should examine the situation as of the date of the hearing.

1 See *Surrey Free Inns plc v Gosport Borough Council* [1999] Env LR 1, DC, followed in *R v Knightsbridge Crown Court, ex p Cataldi* [1999] Env LR 62. Both cases were heard together and upheld by the Court of Appeal sub nom *SFI Group plc (formerly Surrey Free Inns plc) v Gosport Borough Council* [1999] Env LR 750. These decisions effectively overruled *Johnson News of London v London Borough of Ealing* (1989) 154 JP 33, decided under the Control of Pollution Act 1974 but followed in subsequent cases under the EPA 1990.

4.109 Under the old view a recipient of a notice might be able to cure the nuisance by the time of the hearing and thus defeat a notice that had been

4.109 *Challenging an abatement notice*

properly served. There was something inherently unattractive to this scenario, the more so because a local authority is under a statutory duty to serve an abatement notice when it forms a view that the nuisance exists.[1] If the appeal is upheld the local authority is deprived of its costs. In the *Surrey Free Inns* case, Stuart-Smith LJ rightly considered that it would be 'remarkable' if that had been the intention of Parliament. The distinction is particularly important for cases which turn on whether the best practical means have been employed. As the law now stands where improvements post-date the notice they cannot be used to defeat the notice. Such evidence might become admissible where for example an appellant argues that such and such works would be impossible to carry out but there is evidence that he has in fact subsequently carried them out.[2]

1   *R v Carrick District Council, ex p Shelley* [1996] Env LR 273.
2   The footnote which appears in *Stone's Justices' Manual* (2007) Vol I 1-5963 to the Magistrates' Courts Rules 1981 r 34 that '... as the appeal [under section 53 of the MCA 1980] is by way of a rehearing the court is entitled to consider all the relevant evidence including that arising between the original decision appealed against and the appeal (*Rushmoor Borough Council v Richards* (1996) 160 LG Rev 460, DC)' must be read with caution in respect of appeals against abatement notices. Only evidence that goes to the issue whether the notice should have been issued on the date it was served is relevant.

MAGISTRATES' POWERS ON APPEAL

4.110 Section 53 of the MCA 1980 provides that upon hearing a complaint the magistrates 'shall make the order for which the complaint is made or dismiss the complaint'. A 'complaint' against an abatement notice will very often include a series of complaints based upon the various grounds of possible appeal set out the Statutory Nuisance (Appeals) Regulations 1995.[1] The complaint will be made out in part if one ground of appeal succeeds.[2] More particularly, the 1995 Regulations provide that the magistrates may quash the notice, vary the notice in favour of the appellant, or dismiss the appeal.[3] The first and last options are self-explanatory. The second warrants further thought. Any variation that relaxes the vigour of the requirements of the notice would be permitted because it is plainly in the appellant's favour. Conversely, an amendment making the terms of the notice obviously stricter would not be permitted.

1   SI 1995/2644.
2   There may of course be costs implications where a complainant fails on other grounds of appeal (as to which see Chapter 7, paras **7.10–7.15**).
3   SI 1995/2644, reg 2(5).

4.111 More problematic is an amendment that clarifies a notice so as to make it plainly enforceable. On one view that is in the appellant's favour because he knows more clearly what he should do. By contrast, it could be argued that it is outside the scope of the magistrates' powers because it makes a potentially unenforceable notice enforceable against the appellant – something that cannot be said to be to his advantage.

4.112 The issue arose in part before Mance J in the hearing before the divisional court in the *Surrey Free Inns* case.[1] In that case the appellant operated a bar where live and recorded music was played. The council issued an abatement notice that required amongst other things the recipient 'to cease the playing of amplified music at levels which cause nuisance at neighbouring premises'. Mance J held that this was not a requirement of works or steps but simply a repetition of the requirement to abate the nuisance and prohibit its recurrence. Nonetheless he went on to consider the question of the power of the court to vary the notice. He noted that the Crown Court in that case had expressed the view that if this limb of the notice had been read as containing an impermissibly unspecific requirement to do works or take steps, then it would have been open to the court to delete the limb, leaving the first limb (the simple requirement to abate and prohibit the recurrence of the nuisance caused by the playing of amplified music) standing validly by itself. The appellant argued that that would have involved a variation of the notice and, as such, would not be permissible, because it would not be 'in favour of the appellant' as required by regulation 2(5)(b) of the 1990 Regulations (reproduced in the 1995 Appeal Regulations). Mance J stated:

> 'It seems to me open to argument whether deletion of an insufficiently specific requirement which the council was not obliged to introduce in the first place, thus leaving the person responsible to abate in any way he chose, constitutes a variation at all, as opposed to a partial quashing of the notice. Assuming that it does, it would seem to me, as at present advised, to be in that person's favour. It is unnecessary to pursue this point further.'

Accordingly, there is some *obiter* support for the proposition that the magistrates' court may at least delete a provision that is otherwise unspecific or unclear. Mance J did not address the question whether the justices are entitled to amend an unspecific requirement otherwise than by way of simple deletion. The answer is not clear.

1   *Surrey Free Inns plc v Gosport Borough Council* [1999] Env LR 1, DC, at 10. The point was not addressed by the Court of Appeal.

4.113 It is to be noted that the Secretary of State was given a power under Schedule 3, paragraph (4)(c) of the EPA 1990 to prescribe circumstances where the justices may make a decision less favourable than that that is appealed. He has not exercised this power.[1] However, the reason why notices are required to be specific is because the recipient must know what he must do in order to comply with the notice and avoid the risk of a criminal conviction. Accordingly, in our view the justices are permitted to make drafting amendments to a requirement in order to ensure that the requirement contained in that notice is made clear to the recipient. There is a requirement that the parties should co-operate to make a workable notice.[2]

1   The contaminated land regime was based upon the structure of statutory nuisance. By contrast, the Secetary of State has exercised his power under EPA 1990, s 78L(2)(b), under regulation 11 of the Contaminated Land (England) Regulations, to allow the Secretary of State on appeal to vary a remediation notice contrary to the interets of the appellant. Regulation 8 also provides the Secretary of State with the power to prevent an appellant from withdrawing an appeal.
2   *Sovereign Rubber Ltd v Stockport Metropolitan Borough Council* [2000] Env LR 194 at 206 per Sedley LJ.

4.114 We acknowledge that the matter is not free from doubt. Moreover, if we are correct, the power to make such amendments must be exercised with extreme caution lest the process of amendment could lead to the imposition of a requirement more onerous that that expressed unclearly in the original form. We acknowledge too, the force of the argument that if the notice is not specific so as to be clear it is rather difficult for the justices to be sure that by amending the terms of the notice they are not in fact making it more onerous that was originally intended.

4.115 *Challenging an abatement notice*

4.115 In the course of argument before the Court of Appeal in *SFI Group plc v Gosport Borough Council*[1] the question also arose as to what the magistrates' court had to decide when an appeal is brought under regulation 2(2)(a) of the Statutory Nuisance (Appeals) Regulations 1995.[2] Is the court confined to deciding whether the local authority was *bona fide* satisfied that a statutory nuisance existed? Or is the court concerned to see whether the underlying facts that constitute the nuisance or its likely occurrence or recurrence existed at the date of the notice? Stuart-Smith LJ had 'no doubt it is the latter' holding that:

> 'The notice is not justified if no statutory nuisance existed or was likely to occur or recur at the date of its service; that is a question of fact to be determined by the magistrate's court if it is in dispute. The court is not bound to accept the subjective view of the [environmental health officer] in the absence of bad faith or Wednesbury grounds.'[3]

Whether a statutory nuisance exists is a matter for the magistrates. They are not obliged to follow the views of one witness even where the other party has called no 'evidence' to contest or controvert it. This is because the question of whether a statutory nuisance exists is a matter for the justices and is not a matter of expert opinion.[4]

1 [1999] Env LR 750.
2 SI 1995/2664. Reproduced in full at Appendix B.
3 [1999] Env LR 750 at 763, para 29.
4 *Sovereign Rubber Ltd v Stockport Metropolitan Borough Council* [2000] Env LR 194 at 206 per Sedley LJ.

4.116 In our view the power to vary the abatement notice in favour of the appellant does not extend to varying the notice so as to replace the name of the original recipient with the name of a third party cited in the recipient's ground (h), (i) or (j) grounds of appeal. It would seem odd if the magistrates were prohibited from varying the notice to the disadvantage of the appellant but could vary the notice to the manifest disadvantage of a third party – someone who is given no right of appeal against the notice since he has never been served with a notice.

4.117 Regulation 2(5) of the 1995 Regulations provides that where an abatement notice is varied by the court it 'shall be final and shall otherwise have effect, as so varied, as if it had been so made by the local authority.' This provision must be read in the context of the statutory scheme as a whole. It refers to the power of the court. At first instance that court will be the magistrates' court. There is a power of appeal to the Crown Court to both parties. The mention of the court's decision being 'final' is not intended to oust the right of appeal.

POWERS OF THE MAGISTRATES TO MAKE ORDERS AGAINST THIRD PARTIES

4.118 Regulation 2(6) of the Statutory Nuisance (Appeals) Regulations 1995[1] provides that:

> '... on hearing of an appeal the court may make such order as it thinks fit
> (a) with respect to the person by whom any work is to be executed and the contribution to be made by any person towards the cost of the work, or

Powers of the magistrates to make orders against third parties 4.122

(b) as to the proportions in which any expenses which may become recoverable by the authority under Part III of the 1990 Act are to be borne by the appellant and by any other person.'

1   SI 1995/2664. Reproduced in full at Appendix B.

4.119 This would appear to be an order *outside* the terms of the abatement notice. Its scope is unclear. An order under Schedule 3, paragraph 6 of the EPA 1990 is subject to the requirements of paragraph 7 that includes a requirement that service under paragraph 4 should have taken place. Accordingly, in practice the power provided under paragraph 6 for the magistrates to make to order in respect of 'any person' is limited to the recipient of the notice or those persons mentioned in paragraph 4 who have been duly notified. The intention therefore is to deal with the position of third parties who may have been cited in successful ground (h) (i) or (j) appeals and possibly also those mentioned in regulation 4(2) of the 1995 Regulations with an estate or interest in the premises, vehicle machinery etc.

4.120 Schedule 3, paragraph 6 of the EPA 1990 gives the magistrates an apparently wide discretion to make orders as they think fit against third parties as to financial contributions (which may presumably amount to the total cost) to the costs of works to be carried out (paragraph 6(a)) and in respect of a contribution to the costs of works carried out directly by the local authority (paragraph 6(b)). Paragraph 6 is subject to paragraph 7 which provides for account to be taken between owners and occupiers of the terms of any tenancy arrangements and the nature of the works required (paragraph 7(b)). Before an order is made under paragraph 6 the magistrates must be satisfied that a person has been served with a notice in pursuance of paragraph 4 above.

4.121 Under Schedule 3, paragraph 6(a) of the EPA 1990 the magistrates can make an order as they think fit 'with respect to the person by whom work is to be executed.' It is not happily drafted but would appear to mean that the magistrates can order a third party to carry out works. It is to be noted that paragraph 6 gives the magistrates powers only in respect of work to be done *not* steps.

4.122 Schedule 3, paragraph 6 of the EPA 1990 is thoroughly unsatisfactory. It introduces a power, at the very least, for the magistrates to order third parties to make contributions towards works to be carried out and at the most perhaps a power to order third parties to carry out works. Where it turns out that someone else is really responsible or more or equally responsible as the recipient for the nuisance there is nothing wrong in principle in seeking to decide the appropriate appointment in one hearing. The problem lies in the fact that the Statutory Nuisance (Appeals) Regulations 1995[1] fail to set out the position of the third party. Whilst it is true there is a notice requirement (see regulation 2(4) and (7) of the 1995 Regulations) the regulations fail:

- to give the third party an express right to appear at the hearing (although natural justice and article 6 of the ECHR would mean that any refusal to do so would be insupportable),
- to set out any mechanism for the third party to challenge the terms of the abatement notice,
- to make an express provision for the costs of third parties.

1   SI 1995/2664. Reproduced in full at Appendix B.

4.123 *Challenging an abatement notice*

4.123 Regulation 2(7) of the 1995 Regulations impliedly recognises the demands of natural justice that require a third party at least to have been notified of the possibility that they might be exposed to sanction. It is surprising that there is no express requirement for a third party to be served also with a copy of the abatement notice itself. In our view if there is to be any question of third parties being exposed to any form of liability under an order made pursuant to regulation 2(6), natural justice and article 6 of the ECHR require that they be afforded the same rights of appeal before the justices as the recipient of the notice. In other words, a third party should be entitled not only to a copy of the abatement notice but also appear before the magistrates at the hearing to attack all aspects of the notice.

APPEALS TO THE CROWN COURT AND TO THE HIGH COURT

4.124 Following the determination by the magistrates' court each party to the proceedings may appeal to the Crown Court.[1] The appeal should be lodged within 21-days of the order of the magistrates' court.

1   See *Stone's Justices' Manual* (2007) Vol I 1-821.

4.125 Any party to the proceedings (including a local authority) may appeal, without leave, to the Crown Court.[1] The relevant procedure is found in the Crown Court Rules 1982, which apply in respect of civil (though not criminal) appeals.[2] The appellant to the Crown Court must give notice of appeal, in writing, to the magistrates' court and all other parties, not later than 21 days after the day on which the decision appealed against is given.[3] The time for giving notice of appeal may be extended, either before or after it expires, by a written application specifying the grounds for an extension, sent to the Crown Court.[4] An appellant to the Crown Court may abandon an appeal by giving notice in writing to the magistrates, and sending a copy to the Crown Court, not later than the third day before the day fixed for hearing the appeal.[5] The Crown Court will usually comprise a judge sitting with two magistrates, and the appeal is a *de novo* hearing.[6] However, since the matter is a civil appeal there would appear to be no reason why evidence such as that given under cross-examination by witnesses at the previous hearing could not be put before the Crown Court. Accordingly, it may be helpful to ensure that there is someone (for example an instructing solicitor or pupil barrister) to make a clear contemporaneous note of the oral evidence given at the hearing before the justices. There may be concession that could usefully be put to the witness at the hearing before the Crown Court especially if it appears that the witness is attempting to resile from that which he said previously. The Crown Court has wide powers on appeal. It may confirm, reverse or vary any part of the decision appealed against from the magistrates' court, remit the matter with its opinion thereon to the magistrates, or make such other order as it thinks just, and by such order exercise any power which the magistrates had (for example under the Statutory Nuisance (Appeals) Regulations 1995, regulation 2(5)).[7] However, should the Court fail to give proper, adequate and intelligible reasons for its decision, this will constitute a ground for judicial review.[8]

1   EPA 1990, Sch 3, para 1(3).
2   See rule 6(1) of the Crown Court Rules 1982, which has been revoked in respect of criminal proceedings. For criminal appeal procedure see the Criminal Procedure Rules 2005.
3   Rule 7(1)–(3). For method of service see rule 28 and the presumption of due delivery in s 7 of the Interpretation Act 1978.

4   Rule 7(5) and (6). Where the Crown Court refuses to allow an application for an extension of time, it should give a brief statement why (*Re Worth (application for judicial review)* (1979) 1 FLR 159).
5   Rule 11. If an appellant fails to comply with the requirements of this Rule, the judge still has a discretion to allow the abandonment of the appeal (*R v Crown Court at Manchester, ex p Welby* (1981) 73 Cr App Rep 248).
6   Supreme Court Act 1981, s 79(3); *Sirros v Moore* [1975] QB 118.
7   Supreme Court Act 1981, s 48(2).
8   *R v Crown Court at Canterbury, ex parte Howson-Ball* [2001] Env LR 36.

4.126 It should be noted that where the challenge to the decision of the justices involves no issue of fact but simply a question of law it is possible to challenge the decision by way of case stated.¹ In *R v North West Suffolk (Mildenhall) Magistrates' Court, ex p Forest Heath District Council* [1998] Env LR 9 the Divisional Court made clear that an appeal by way of case, the High Court would not able to interfere with a finding of fact by the Magistrates' Court unless it was perverse. It held that '... it is not be perverse, even if it may be mistaken, to prefer the evidence of A to that of B where they are conflict.' In such a case appeal should be made by way of re-hearing on the merits to the Crown Court.

The decision of the Crown Court may be challenged by case stated² or judicial review³ also depending upon the nature of the challenge.

1   Appeals from a magistrates' court by case stated are regulated mainly by MCA 1980, ss 111–114, 144 and 148 and Magistrates' Courts Rules, SI 1981/552, rr 76–81. A downside of proceeding immediately to the High Court on appeal by way of case stated is that s 28(A) of the Supreme Court Act 1981 provides that save as otherwise provided by the Administration of Justice Act 1960 the decision by the High Court on civil appeals by way of case stated from the magistrates' court is final. By virtue of s 18(c) of the Supreme Court Act 1981 it has the effect of precluding all appeals from the High Court of civil case stated appeals from the magistrates' court (*Mallie v Manchester City Council* [1998] COD 19).
2   Appeals from the Crown Court by way of case stated are governed by Supreme Court Act 1981, s 28 and Crown Court Rules 1982, SI 1982/1109, r 26. Unlike in the case of civil case stated appeals from the magistrates' court there is no prohibition on seeking to appeal from the High Court's decision to the Court of Appeal (*SFI Group plc v Gosport Borough Council* [1999] Env LR 739 is an example of such a case which proceeded in this way).
3   Judicial review will usually only be appropriate where the decision is not one form which an appeal by way of case stated can be made, for example a procedural decision on the admissibility of evidence.

Impact of the HRA 1998 upon listing of complaints against abatement notices

4.127 The HRA 1998 is likely also to impact upon the listing arrangements for certain complaints against abatement notices made to the magistrates' court. This is most likely to occur where a non-suspended abatement notice has been served. A failure to secure a speedy (and in the case of a non-suspended, notice that may mean almost immediate) hearing date for the complaint may amount to the denial of a fair hearing, guaranteed under article 6 of the ECHR. Unless a speedy date is achieved it is likely that the recipient will have already been obliged to comply with the terms of a non-suspended notice even though that notice may subsequently be shown to have been unjustified. However, it should not be thought that the need for a speedy hearing is restricted only to the Convention rights of the recipient of the notice. Those whose health or well-being are intended to be protected by the abatement notice may also have human rights, in particular, the right to home is guaranteed under article 8 of the Convention. Where a notice has not been suspended and the hearing does not take place within a reasonable time their Convention rights may also be violated:

4.127 *Challenging an abatement notice*

'The principle that legal proceedings should be concluded within a reasonable time is a key element of Article 6(1).'[1]

1 AH Robertson and JG Merrills *Human Rights in Europe: A Study of the European Convention on Human Rights* (3rd edn, 1993) at p 100.

4.128 What constitutes a 'reasonable time' depends upon the circumstances of the litigation. However, the following principal factors have emerged from the ECtHR's case law,[1] namely:

- the complexity of the case,
- the way in which the administrative and judicial authorities have dealt with it,
- the conduct of the applicant,
- what is at 'stake for the applicant'.

1 AH Robertson and JG Merrills *Human Rights in Europe: A Study of the European Convention on Human Rights* (3rd edn, 1993), p 101.

4.129 The interplay between the Convention rights of third parties is also likely to be relevant. The need to hear an appeal against a non-suspended abatement notice requiring immediate compliance will usually be pressing. The recipient's conduct is relevant. Accordingly, the recipient of the notice should not delay in lodging a complaint and seeking an immediate listing from the magistrates' court for the hearing.

4.130 But what if the magistrates' court is simply too busy with other cases to afford an immediate listing? In *Zimmerman and Steiner v Switzerland*[1] the ECtHR rejected the argument that a delay of three and a half years in dealing with an action for nuisance could be excused by the national courts' excessive workload. The Court was prepared to accept that:

'... a temporary backlog of business does not involve liability on the part of the Contracting State provided that they take, with the *requisite* promptness, remedial action to deal with any exceptional situation.' [Emphasis added]

1 (1983) 6 EHRR 17.

4.131 In the case of an urgent listing for a non-suspended abatement notice the period of time in question will be counted in days and weeks rather than years. However, in our view, what period of delay is acceptable must be viewed against the circumstances of the case. As the ECtHR stated in *Zimmerman and Steiner v Switzerland*[1] the system must deal with 'exceptional' situations with 'requisite' promptness.

1 (1983) 6 EHRR 17.

4.132 The situation becomes more problematic if the delay is caused by the complexity of the issues raised in the case rather than because of a court backlog. Indeed, it is said that:

'... the best chance of proving that there has been no violation [of article 6] will often be to show that the length of the proceedings was attributable to the complexity of the case'... [1]

However, in the case of statutory nuisance, the instances where the complexity of the case could amount to a valid reason for delaying the hearing of an appeal against an abatement notice should be infrequent. It is to be remembered that the statutory nuisance regime is meant to be a summary and speedy procedure.[2] With the possible exception of a ground of appeal based upon best practical means, the local authority should already be well versed in the general issues of the case, having considered them prior to the issue of the notice. The recipient of the notice is unlikely to wish to delay the hearing of the appeal although he may feel that he has been forced into a hearing before he is fully prepared.[3]

1 AH Robertson and JG Merrills *Human Rights in Europe: A Study of the European Convention on Human Rights* (3rd edn, 1993), p 102. See, eg, *Buchholz v Germany* (1981) 3 EHRR 597.
2 See para **1.01**.
3 It is arguable that the magistrates' may have the power to hear immediately an appeal into the question as to whether the notice should be suspended and to adjourn to a later date to hear any arguments about the substance of the notice if the complainant so wishes.

4.133 There is no reason why in principle decisions by magistrates' courts on listing matters should not be amenable to judicial review. Ordinarily the High Court will be reluctant to interfere to decisions made by the clerk to the magistrates' court on listing matters save where it could not be should that there was a breach of a fundamental right, such as the right to a fair hearing.[1]

1 Like many aspects of the ECHR, this aspect of article 6 could be said to be another statement of a principle already found in the common law, namely, *justice delayed is justice denied*. It is relevant to note that the abatement of a dangerous nuisance without notice in the exercise of common law powers was held to be a circumstance where the obligation to give notice and opportunity to be heard would obstruct the taking of prompt action. (See *Lonsdale (Earl) v Nelson* (1823) 2 B & C 302, 311-312; *Jones v Williams* (1843) 11 M & W 176, 181-182 (dicta); more generally, see De Smith, Woolf and Jowell *Judicial Review of Administrative Action* (6th edn, 2007) para 7-059). Whilst it may be presumed that codification of these principles by the HRA 1998 will encourage the court to be more confident in intervening than previously was the case under the common law, the court will nonetheless frequently be faced with a balancing exercise between the human rights of the recipient of the notice and the human rights of those suffering by the nuisance.

Absence of preclusive provision

4.134 A preclusive provision is a clause in a statute which provides that a matter may *only* be challenged by way of a particular procedure.[1] There is no 'preclusive provision' in respect of challenges to abatement notices. This means that in certain circumstances an abatement notice may be, for example, challenged by way of judicial review.

1 For an example of such a provision see Town and Country Planning Act 1990 (as amended), s 284.

When an abatement notice may be challenged by way of judicial review

Challenge by a recipient

4.135 Judicial review is a limited form of challenge.[1] By contrast to the justices deciding an appeal under section 80(3) of the EPA 1990, the role of the High Court is not to supplant its own decision on the merits for those of the local authority. Its purpose is to examine whether the decision has been made (1) within the limits of administrative discretion[2] and (2) whether a lawful procedure has been followed.[3]

1 For an authoritative text on the principles of judicial review see de Smith, Woolf and Jowell, *Judicial Review of Administrative Action* (6th edn, 2007).

4.135 *Challenging an abatement notice*

2 As to point (1) see *R v London Borough of Tower Hamlets, ex p Chetnik Developments Ltd* [1988] AC 858. Lord Bridge affirmed the principle that there is no such thing as an unfettered discretion. At 872F-G he cited with approval a passage from William Wade QC in *Administrative Law* (5th edn, 1982) with approval to the effect that:

'Unfettered discretion is wholly inappropriate to a public authority, which processes solely in order that it may use them for public good ... Unreviewable administrative action is just as much a contradiction in terms as unfettered discretion, at any rate in the case of statutory powers. The question which has to be asked is what is the scope of judicial review. But that there are legal limits to every power is axiomatic.' Lord Bridge himself continued to say: 'Some statutory discretions may be so wide that they can for practical purposes be challenged if shown to have been exercised irrationally or in bad faith. But if the purpose which the discretion is intended to serve is clear, the discretion can only be validly exercised for reasons relevant to the achievement of that purpose.'

3 As to point (2) Lord Hailsham LC put the matter thus in *Chief Constable of North Wales Police v Evans* [1982] 1 WLR 1155 at 1161: 'The purpose of judicial review is to ensure that the individual receives fair treatment, and not to ensure that the authority, after according fair treatment, reaches on a matter which it is authorised by law to decide for itself a conclusion which is correct in the eyes of the court.'

4.136 The circumstances where it may be appropriate for a recipient of an abatement notice to proceed by way of judicial review rather than or in addition to an appeal under the regulations were considered by Simon Brown and Pill LJJ in the Court of Appeal in *R v Falmouth and Truro Port Health Authority, ex p South West Water Services*[1] and by Harrison J in the same case at first instance.[2]

1 [2000] 3 All ER 306, [2000] 3 WLR 1464, CA. Neither the Court of Appeal, nor Harrison J at first instance referred to the then recent judgment of the Court of Appeal: *Dennis Rye Pension Fund Trustees v Sheffield City Council* [1998] 1 WLR 840 in which Lord Woolf MR stated that in considering whether proceedings should have been brought by way of judicial review or ordinary action, the court should look at the practical consequences of the choice rather than just the technical questions of the distinction between public and private law.

2 *R v Falmouth and Truro Port Health Authority, ex p South West Water Services* [1999] Env LR 833.

4.137 In *R v Falmouth and Truro Port Health Authority, ex p v South West Water Services*,[1] the applicant, a sewage undertaker, had sought judicial review of an abatement notice issued by the port authority. The basis of the application was that the port authority had acted in breach of the applicant's legitimate expectation to be consulted before the issue of the notice, that the notice was defective and that the Carrick Road were not a 'watercourse' within the meaning of the Public Health Act 1936 and so whatever their state were not capable of constituting a public nuisance. An appeal had also been made to the magistrates' court but the notice had not been suspended pending the determination of an appeal. However, the applicant had succeeded in obtaining a stay in those proceedings pending the outcome of the judicial review from Collins J when he granted permission to bring proceedings for judicial review.

1 [2000] 3 WLR 1464, CA.

4.138 The respondent port authority argued that all the issues raised in the applicant's case could have been dealt with on appeal to the magistrates and that being so the applicant had an alternative remedy. It was accepted by the port authority that a discretion existed to allow judicial review despite the existence of an alternative remedy. However, it contended that pursuant to the principles laid down in *R v Birmingham City Council, ex p Ferrero Ltd*[1] this was not an appropriate where the discretion could be so exercised. Simon Brown LJ pointed out that:[2]

'... in cases like ... the present appeal, *the need to safeguard the public, even sometimes at the expense of the other party, is likely to be the paramount consideration. In deciding whether, exceptionally, to allow an application for judicial review, the judge should never lose sight of this.* Questions of convenience, expedition and effectiveness should be assessed accordingly. If for example, in this case ... the enforcing authority had defeated all grounds of challenge, then the decision to allow a judicial review would have delayed abatement, quite possibly with damaging public health consequences. This should be recognised.' [our emphasis]

1   [1993] 1 All ER 530.
2   [2000] 3 WLR 1464, CA at 1490B.

4.139   Applying those principles to the facts of *Falmouth* where the notice had been issued but not suspended, Simon Brown LJ found:

'Given (a) that the water undertaker's appeal did not operate to suspend the notice, (b) that it might not be heard before (and at best would be heard only shortly before) the three month period for compliance expired (bearing in mind that the appeal would be heard on all issues and involve extensive oral evidence), (c) that to avoid the risk of committing an offence the water undertaker would have to start work on an alternative sewage scheme before its appeal could be heard, (d) that it would not be compensated for its work even if its appeal succeeded, and (e) that if its appeal failed, it would almost certainly wish to appeal by case stated to the Divisional Court, I think that a *limited judicial review* [on the meaning of "watercourse"]could properly have been permitted.' [our emphasis][1]

1   [2000] 3 WLR 1464, CA at 1490F–G.

4.140   The five reasons ((a)–(e)) as to why, in this particular case, it was appropriate to go by way of judicial review are, sound. However, those considerations would remain equally powerful in the event that the issue was one involving a complicated factual dispute (for example an appeal based upon best practicable means or a dispute as to the existence of the nuisance). It would seem just as unfair that the water undertaker would be faced in the position of having to carry out the works that may prove unnecessary without the prospect of compensation. Simon Brown LJ also suggested (and indeed more significantly) that:

'... non consultation might well have been thought an inappropriate basis upon which to quash an abatement notice in a public health case.'[1]

1   [2000] 3 WLR 1464, CA at 1490D–E, and see also 1479D–E.

4.141   Simon Brown LJ took the view that it would not be appropriate to quash a decision for of lack of consultation because of the legislative purpose behind the statutory nuisance regime. However, it is not clear whether Simon Brown LJ's comment is confined to cases where the notice has been issued where it is prejudicial to health or whether he would consider it to extend to cases where a notice has been issued to abate a nuisance but one which is not prejudicial to health. It is also interesting to note the approach adopted in the judgment of Pill LJ. Whilst Pill LJ expressly stated that he agreed with the *conclusions* of Simon Brown LJ on each of the issues addressed it is apparent that Pill LJ's approach is stricter on the circumstances where challenges by way of judicial review may be permitted. Pill LJ held

4.141 *Challenging an abatement notice*

'In the present context, the need to safeguard the public is, as Simon Brown LJ has stated, likely to be the paramount consideration. An indication of statutory intention to that effect emerges in the power of the health authority under Regulation 3(2), exercised in this case, to require, where here the alleged nuisance is injurious to health, that the notice shall have effect notwithstanding any appeal to a magistrates' court which has not been decided by the court.

Given the public health context and the provision of a statutory remedy, I question whether matters of convenience and expedition should be allowed to permit proceedings by way of judicial review the effect of which is to circumvent or ... subvert a detailed statutory procedure. If the statutory intention to provide that any appeal to the magistrates' court, the aim must be to make that remedy effective rather than to surmise that it is so ineffective that judicial review is permitted. *I do not accept for a moment the water undertaker's submission that Magistrates' Court proceedings could not have been brought on within the three month period.*' [our emphasis][1]

1   [2000] 3 WLR 1464, CA at 1494 E–H.

4.142 The need for proceeding by way of judicial review would be thus obviated if the matter could be brought speedily before the justices. Accordingly, in the authors' view the appropriate course of action to pursue where a notice has been issued but not suspended is for the appeal to be brought by expedition before the justices. If the magistrates' court cannot produce such an expedited hearing then it would seem that the only route would be by way of judicial review. As to the possible impact of the HRA 1998 upon listing in magistrates' courts see paras **4.127–4.133**.

4.143 Where the notice is not suspended the scope for judicial review remains limited. Where the recipient considers that the abatement notice and/or the decision to issue the notice is so fundamentally flawed that it amounts to a nullity, he should challenge it by way of judicial review. It is true that in recent times the courts have generally deprecated the practice of applicants for judicial review seeking to argue that something of consequence flows from the distinction between whether a flaw in the decision results in a nullity or invalidity. However, Sedley LJ has expressed the view that an allegation that an abatement notice is a nullity should proceed by way of judicial review rather than by appeal to the magistrates' court. As a result careful consideration should be given to seeking judicial review where the recipient seeks to argue that the notice is a nullity.[1]

1   *Sovereign Rubber Ltd v Stockport Metropolitan Borough Council* [2000] Env LR 194 at 204.

Application for judicial review by third parties

4.144 The right of appeal to the magistrates' court is confined to the recipient of the notice. It may be asked why anyone else who is not bound by its provisions should wish to challenge an abatement notice. Such a person may be a complaint who feels that the requirements of the notice do not go far enough. As has already been stated the scope for judicial review is usually limited to errors of law.

4.145 It could also be argued that third parties have an alternative remedy under the section 82 of the EPA 1990 grievance procedure. However, it is to be

Appeals to the Crown Court and to the High Court **4.148**

noted that third parties were able to seek judicial review proceeding against a failure by a local authority to issue an abatement notice in *Ex p Shelley*.[1] In practice it will be rarely be advantageous to a third to seek judicial review of a decision to issue an abatement notice. Furthermore there are serious costs implications to consider before embarking upon high court litigation. An unsuccessful applicant for judicial review may face having to pay both the costs of the local authority and those of the recipient of the notice who will no doubt argue that he had a separate interest in defending the decision.

1 *R v Carrick District Council, ex p Shelley* [1996] Env LR 273. Moreover, it could be said, if the local authority has issued a notice requiring certain steps it is difficult to see that a third party would have much prospect of persuading the justices to issue another notice with different requirements. Indeed, it could be rather unsatisfactory for a particular recipient to be a recipient of two abatement notices with different and possibly conflicting requirements. It should also be recalled that the local authority need only defend the issue of the notice and its requirements to the standard of the balance of probabilities. A third party acting under EPA 1990, s 82 must satisfy the justices beyond reasonable doubt.

Complaints to the Local Government Ombudsman

4.146 The Local Government Act 1974 established two commissioners for Local Administration, one for England and one for Wales.[1] The work is performed by local commissioners appointed by the Crown. The local commissioners are entitled to investigate complaints against any local authority[2] and this includes committees, members and officers.[3] The commissioner for local government administration is more commonly known as the Local Government Ombudsman. Complaints to the Ombudsman by third parties aggrieved at the local authority's failure to deal properly with a statutory nuisance have met with success on a number of occasions. Commonly, the complaint will be that the local authority has delayed unduly before taking any action.

3.5% of complaints handled by the Local Government Ombudsman in 2005/06 – amounting to 658 – related to environmental health and most of them were in respect of nuisance complaints.[4] 'Advice and Guidance from the Local Government Ombudsman' can be found in the special report 'Neighbour Nuisance and Anti-social Behaviour' at http://www.lgo.org.uk/pdf/neighbour-nuisance-asb.pdf.

1 Scotland has its own system (Local Government (Scotland) Act 1975, Pt. II).
2 Except a parish council.
3 Local Government Act 1974, ss 25, 34(1).
4 Helen Reay, Investigator for the Local Government Ombudsman, '*Stop the Nuisance*'. 5 January 2007.

4.147 This route is less likely to be so attractive for the recipient of the notice. The Local Government Ombudsman has no power to overturn or amend the notice. In most cases he is likely to be of the view that the recipient has an alternative remedy before the court and will therefore unwilling to interfere.

4.148 The complainant must allege that injustice has been suffered as a consequence of maladministration.[1] Accordingly, in order to succeed a complainant must satisfy the Ombudsman that (1) there has been maladministration and (2) he has suffered injustice as a result.

1 Local Government Act 1974, s 26.

4.149 *Challenging an abatement notice*

Maladministration

4.149 The meaning of maladministration has been considered by the courts on a number of occasions. In *R v Parliamentary Comr for Administration, ex p Morris and Balchin*,[1] Sedley J (as he then was) examined the previous case law and textbook authority on public law. He noted that all had drawn on the so-called 'Crossman catalogue' offered to Parliament during the passage of the Parliamentary Commissioner Act 1967. Sedley J concluded that:

> 'It is accordingly accepted that maladministration includes bias, neglect, inattention, delay, incompetence, inaptitude,[2] perversity, turpitude and arbitrariness in reaching a decision or exercising a discretion, but that it has nothing to do with the intrinsic merits of the decision itself: see *R v Local Comr for Administration, ex p Eastleigh Borough Council* [1988] QB 855 at 863.'

1   [1997] JPL 917.
2   Sedley J noted that commentators have repeatedly substituted the word 'ineptitude'.

Injustice

4.150 The meaning of 'injustice' had not been subject to any judicial scrutiny until fairly recently. In *ex p Balchin*[1] Sedley J cited with approval the following passage from *Judicial Review of Administrative Action*:[2]

> '"Injustice" has been widely interpreted so as to cover not merely injury redressible in a court of law, but also "the sense of outrage aroused by the unfair or incompetent administration, even where the complainant has suffered no actual loss" (citing Mr RHS Crossman, speaking as leader of the House of Commons)'

Sedley J himself continued by stating:

> 'It follows that the defence familiar in legal proceedings, that because the outcome would have been the same in any event there has been no redressible wrong, does not run in an investigation by the Commissioner.'[3]

1   [1997] JPL 917.
2   De Smith, Woolf and Jowell *Judicial Review of Administrative Action* (5th edn, 1995), para 1-102.
3   This approach was accepted by Dyson J in *R v Parliamentary Comr for Administration, ex p Balchin (No 2)* (1999) 79 P & CR 157, [2000] JPL 267. However, in *R v Comr for Local Administration, ex p S* [1999] ELR 102 Collins J took the view that although the council had been guilty of maladministration in its handling of a child's special educational needs the child had suffered no injustice because the outcome would have been the same in any event. The judgment does not address Sedley J's earlier decision in *Ex p Balchin*. The judgment of Collins J in *Ex p S* is not referred to in the later *Ex p Balchin (No 2)*. There now exists an apparent conflict of High Court authority as to the meaning of 'injustice'. In our view the approach adopted by Sedley J and Dyson J is to be preferred.

4.151 Where the Ombudsman is satisfied that maladministration and injustice have occurred he may recommend that the local authority take action, this may also include a recommendation to pay compensation to the complainant. Local authorities are not obliged to follow the recommendations of the Ombudsman but if they refuse to adhere to his recommendation they are obliged to publish the results of his decision and their reasons for not following his recommendation in the local newspaper.[1]

1   See further Jones and Grekos, *Great Expectations? The Ombudsman and the meaning of 'Injustice'* [2001] JR 20.

Chapter 5

Criminal Proceedings under EPA 1990, Section 80 for Breaches of the Requirements of an Abatement Notice

INTRODUCTION

5.01 Proceedings under section 80(4) of the Environmental Protection Act 1990 (EPA 1990) for a breach of an abatement notice are criminal in nature.[1] The recipient faces the prospect of possible conviction and the imposition of a fine. The prosecution bears the heavy burden of proving beyond reasonable doubt that the defendant committed the offence. It must be particularly careful to prove each element of the offence. The rules of criminal evidence weigh in favour of the defendant. Material that may have been admissible before the justices in a hearing in an appeal by the recipient of an abatement notice under section 80(3) of the EPA 1990 may not be admissible in criminal proceedings under section 80(4). The scope for hearsay evidence in criminal proceedings is much more restricted than in civil proceedings. Relevant evidence may be excluded on the basis that it has been improperly obtained.

1 This chapter addresses formal proceedings in the criminal court. Note, however, that an authorised officer of a London Borough Council may enforce a breach of an abatement notice by a fixed penalty notice, in which case the recipient of the fixed penalty notice may discharge any liability to conviction for the offence by payment of a fixed penalty: see London Local Authorities Act 2004, ss 15-18 and Schedules 2 and 3. The fixed penalties introduced in March 2007 are £100 and £400, the latter being for industrial trade and business premises.

5.02 Additionally, the introduction of the Human Rights Act 1998 (HRA 1998) means that the court must ensure, in particular, that the proceedings do not breach the defendant's right to a fair hearing under article 6 of the European Convention on Human Rights (ECHR), including the right against self incrimination, and the prohibition under article 7(1) against the imposition of retrospective offences. Cases must be prepared and conducted in accordance with the overriding objective under the Criminal Procedure Rules 2005[1] to deal with cases justly.[2]

1 SI 2005/384 as amended.
2 See r 1.1–1.3 and the list of factors included within the notion of dealing with cases justly (r 1.1(2)).

ELEMENTS OF THE OFFENCE

5.03 Section 80(4) of the EPA 1990 provides that:

'If a person on whom an abatement notice is served, without reasonable excuse contravenes or fails to comply with any requirement or prohibition imposed by the notice, he shall be guilty of an offence.'

Accordingly, the prosecution must lead evidence to establish that:

- the defendant was served with the abatement notice in question

5.03 *Criminal proceedings under EPA 1990, section 80*

- the defendant failed to comply with a requirement or prohibition contained in the notice and
- no reasonable excuse exists for the breach (where the defendant has raised a prima facie evidence of a 'reasonable excuse'[1]).

1   *Polychronakis v Richards and Jerrom Ltd* [1998] Env LR 347.

5.04 The prosecution should seek to obtain a schedule of admissions on matters admitted by the defendant pursuant to section 10 of the Criminal Justice Act 1967. Where the defendant refuses to admit anything or only very limited matters, the prosecution will at least be alerted as to exactly what it will be required to prove.

THE NATURE OF THE OFFENCE

5.05 Section 80(4) of the EPA 1990 does *not* create an offence of either causing a nuisance or a statutory nuisance.[1] Indeed, such an offence exists only in section 82 concerning complaints by persons aggrieved. The section 80 offence relates solely to a failure to comply with the requirements imposed by an abatement notice. The requirements included within the notice therefore set the bounds of the offence.

1   If the nuisance were of a nature sufficient to amount to a public nuisance its creation would be an offence at common law, see *R v Rimmington* [2006] AC 459.

Requirement to have been served with an abatement notice

5.06 A person can only be guilty of this offence if he is a person, 'on whom the abatement notice [has been] served.' This is an important provision. The mechanism for the service of notices under the EPA 1990 is set out at section 160. If a person has not properly been served with an abatement notice he cannot be guilty of the offence under section 80(4).[1]

1   This is to be contrasted to the operation of planning enforcement notices served under Town and Country Planning Act 1990 (as amended), s 172. Subject to a statutory defence, an owner of the land to which an enforcement notice applies is guilty of an offence if the terms of the enforcement notice have not been satisfied (s 172(2) and (3)). This may be so, notwithstanding the fact that he purchased the land following the service of the enforcement notice upon the previous owner and that he himself had not been served with the enforcement notice.

5.07 The service of the abatement notice[1] is an element of the offence, which the prosecution must prove. If the prosecution fails to lead evidence on this point the defence will be able to make an application of no case to answer. In *AMEC Building Ltd v London Borough of Camden*[2] the local authority had served notices upon a sister company of the defendant company which had a registered office at the same address. It was apparent from the evidence, however, that the correct company had in fact received the notices and had written back stating that it intended to comply with the notices. The company was subsequently prosecuted for having failed to comply with the terms of the notice. The Divisional Court held that the notices were not directed at the defendant but at the sister company and, therefore, had not been properly served. The EPA 1990 did not recognise the service of the wrong person whether or not the correct person subsequently received the notice; therefore, the defendant was not bound by the requirements of the notice. Proof of receipt of the notice was held to be inadequate.

1   Although it is not normally put in issue by the defendant, the prosecution ought to be in a position to prove that the abatement notice is formally valid in the sense that it was duly authorised and has not been set aside on appeal or by way of judicial review, see, by analogy, the position with planning enforcement notices explained in *Palacegate Properties Ltd v LB Camden* (2001) ACD 137, transcript paragraphs 28 (Laws LJ) and 38 (Longmore J).

The nature of the offence **5.11**

2 [1997] Env LR 330, see also *Butland v Powys City Council* [2007] EWHC 734 (Admin) (address specified for 'correspondence' was not the correct address for service of an abatement notice). The court has shown itself prepared to take a flexible approach to what amounts to proper service in proceedings brought by an individual under s 82, see *Hewlings v McLean Homes* [2001] Env LR 17 and Chapter 3, paras **3.76–3.80**.

5.08 The requirement of service means that a failure to effect proper service may prevent a successful prosecution. Local authorities, therefore, should take precautions when serving an abatement notice to ensure that service is recorded and can be proved in any future criminal proceedings.

5.09 The service requirement also creates difficulties where the premises may have passed to another person. For example, an abatement notice may specify that the operating hours of a car breaker's yard be restricted to prohibit car breaking activities during weekends and between specified hours during the week. That notice is served on the then current owners of the site. Later, the original owners, having complied with the notice, sell the business to another person. The new owner may have been well aware of the terms of the abatement notice but if he proceeds to operate the yard outside the requirements of the abatement notice he will not be guilty of an offence under section 80(4) of the EPA 1990. The original owner *may* still be prosecuted for the breach of the abatement notice. For example, if he has simply sold on the business without having taken steps to ensure compliance with the notice he may be regarded as having caused the breach of the abatement notice. If he has secured compliance with the notice and then sells the property on to another making that person fully aware of the terms of the notice then, depending on the circumstances, he might be regarded either as not having breached the terms of the notice or else having a 'reasonable excuse.'

The terms of the abatement notice

5.10 As previously stated, the offence created by section 80(4) of the EPA 1990 is that of failing without reasonable excuse to comply with a requirement imposed by an abatement notice served on the accused.[1] Accordingly, the range of the possible breach(es) will be determined by the way in which the notice has been drafted. If the notice simply states that the recipient is expected to abate the nuisance the question for the court would then be whether the defendant failed to comply with the requirement to abatement the nuisance.

1 See *Sterling Homes (Midlands) Ltd v Birmingham City Council* [1996] Env LR 121 per McCullough J.

5.11 Sometimes the notice is drafted so as simply to require the abatement of the nuisance and does not also include the prohibition of its recurrence. This is a form of drafting that we do not generally recommend. For example, once a deposit or accumulation has been removed it might seem that the nuisance has been abated once and for all. Any further accumulation or deposit might be seen as a different nuisance. A defendant may be able to argue that, where there has been a nuisance which has ceased for a considerable period of time (for example, black smoke), the further appearance of black smoke represents a new nuisance albeit one of the same type. Accordingly, a defendant might argue that, if the notice does not seek to prohibit recurrence he has not breached the terms of the notice. It is important to distinguish between temporary cessation of an intermittent activity and abatement followed by recurrence. An example of the former is where a person plays loud music on alternate nights the occurrence of which constitutes a nuisance.[1]

5.11 *Criminal proceedings under EPA 1990, section 80*

1   *Battersea Borough Council v George* (1906) 71 JP 11 is an example of the latter. A nuisance was abated immediately after the receipt of the notice. It occurred two years later. The court found that the magistrate had been entitled to hold that the nuisance was a distinct nuisance and not a failure to give effect to the notice. In *Greenwich Borough Council v London County Council* (1912) 106 LT 887 six months had passed between the abatement of a smoke nuisance and its recurrence. It was held that there was sufficient evidence to justify the magistrate in finding that the later nuisance was a separate and independent occurrence and not a recurrence of the first nuisance, and that therefore there had not been a failure to comply with the notice to abate the earlier nuisance.

5.12   The notice may not simply require merely the abatement of the nuisance but it may also specify certain steps that the recipient must carry out for the purpose of abating the nuisance. A failure to comply with any required steps specified in the notice constitutes a separate breach of the notice. Thus, where the notice requires the abatement of the nuisance and also requires certain specified works to be carried out for that purpose, a failure to abate the nuisance and a failure to carry out any of the specified steps may each constitute a separate breach of section 80(4) of the EPA 1990.[1]

1   *Battersea Borough Council v George* (1906) 71 JP 11.

5.13   In order for there to be a breach of the requirement to abate the nuisance it is *not* necessary for the prosecution to adduce evidence from a neighbouring occupier that he had actually suffered interference with the quiet enjoyment his property.[1] Whether or not a nuisance is being caused is a matter of fact for the magistrates, and in principle the prosecution is entitled to rely upon the expert judgment of environmental health officers without recourse to technical evidence or scientific measurements.[2] The court is not bound to accept the expert judgment of environmental health officers that a statutory nuisance is being caused; it can reach its own subjective judgment on that matter.[3]

1   *Wellingborough Borough Council v Gordon* [1993] Env LR 218; [1991] JPL 874, followed in *East Northamptonshire District Council v Brian Fossett* [1994] Env LR 388; *Westminster City Council v McDonald* [2003] EWHC 2698 (Admin), [2005] Env LR 1. See also *Cook v Adatia* (1989) 153 JP 129 where the only evidence as to the noise came from an expert who measured it. See also *O'Toole v Knowsley Metropolitan Borough Council* [1999] 22 LS Gaz R 36 on evidence required to show prima facie case that premises were prejudicial to health pursuant to EPA 1990, s 79(1)(a).
2   *Westminster City Council v McDonald* [2003] EWHC 2698 (Admin), [2005] Env LR 1; *LB Lewisham v Yvonne Hall* [2002] EWHC 960 (Admin), [2003] Env LR 4.
3   *London Borough of Hackney v Moshe Rottenburg* [2007] Env LR 24.

5.14   Where the recipient has failed to carry out works required by the notice it is not necessary for the prosecution to show that the nuisance has not been abated. It need prove only that the works were not carried out. In *AMEC Building Ltd v London Borough of Camden*[1] Ebsworth J put the matter thus:

> '[The council] relies upon the structure and purpose of the relevant provision of the Acts . . . Section 80 placed a duty on a local authority to serve a notice where it is dissatisfied that a statutory nuisance exists or is likely to occur or recur. There is no need for a nuisance to exist or to have existed in the past. The notices require abatement of an existing nuisance and/or requiring the [execution] of works and the taking of clearly identified steps to abate, prevent the occurrence or recurrence. Those steps are set out in the schedule accompanying the notice.
>
> If the alleged contravention in the summons is a failure to abate, then [The council] accepts that there is a need for the prosecution to prove the occurrence or recurrence of the nuisance.

The nature of the offence **5.17**

If the summons is for a failure to execute specified works or take steps required there is no such need. The reason for that [the council] says, is that the failure to execute works may be a serious matter, for example where the local authority has identified a potential nuisance and seek to prevent its occurrence. [The council] relies upon section 80(7) as consistent with that. The use of the words 'statutory nuisance' is consistent with that distinction. There would be no need for those words to appear if the section did not contemplate the existence of offences under section 80(4), which did not involve the existence of offences under section 80(4), which did not involve the existence of a statutory nuisance. That interpretation is in my opinion correct.'[2]

Ebsworth J found that in *Lambert Flat Management Ltd v Lomas*,[3] which considered the position under section 58 of the Control of Pollution Act 1974, supported the view that she had adopted.

1 [1997] Env LR 330.
2 [1997] Env LR 330 at 337–338.
3 [1981] 1 WLR 898.

5.15 There may, however, be circumstances where the failure to carry out either at all, or only partially, the required works, in the absence of an existing nuisance or where the likelihood of the nuisance occurring or recurring is remote, could amount to 'a reasonable excuse'. An example might be where an abatement notice was served in respect of noise coming from a nightclub, which required the installation of soundproofing. The premises might have been subsequently converted into use as an old age people's home. There being little or no prospect of all night discos, there might be said to be a 'reasonable excuse' for not installing the sound-proofing required in the abatement notice.

5.16 If the defendant has not been charged with the failure to comply with the requirement to abate the nuisance, evidence relating to the existence of a nuisance might well be inadmissible since it is unlikely to go to an issue before the court, save where it was relevant in showing that the particular step had not in fact been carried out, or where the defendant seeks to argue that he had a reasonable excuse due to the fact that the nuisance had abated in any event.

5.17 What happens where the recipient has carried out all the works (or steps required by the notice) but the nuisance remains unabated? Notices that require works or steps to be carried out do so for the express purpose of abating the nuisance. A failure to abate the nuisance would seem to be contrary to section 80(4) of the EPA 1990 notwithstanding that the person may have carried out all the works or other steps expressly required of him.[1] Recipients of a notice specifying certain works or steps are well advised to take all measures to ensure the abatement of the nuisance and not merely assume that carrying out the works or steps specified in the notice is good enough.

1 However, obiter dicta in *Sterling Homes (Midlands) Ltd v Birmingham City Council* [1996] Env LR 121 would seem to suggest that the appropriate course is for the local authority to issue a further abatement notice in such circumstances. It might be that a recipient of a notice who has carried out the works or steps required of him in the notice to abate the nuisance has a 'reasonable excuse' if the notice remains unabated. The issue was not directly canvassed in *Sterling Homes* and there is no direct case authority on the point. The authors consider that where a notice has required the abatement of nuisance as well, the occurrence of a nuisance will amount to an offence even if the steps or works required have in fact been completed.

5.18 *Criminal proceedings under EPA 1990, section 80*

5.18 Where premises are in such a state as to be prejudicial to health or a nuisance it has been suggested in *Coventry City Council v Doyle*[1] that simply removing the occupants does not constitute abatement of the nuisance. However it the same case it was held that different considerations might apply if the premises had effectively been rendered incapable of being occupied.

1   [1981] 1 WLR 1325.

CATEGORIES OF OFFENCE

5.19 Section 80 of the EPA 1990 provides:

'(5) Except in a case falling within subsection (6) below, a person who commits an offence under subsection (4) [ie failure without reasonable excuse to comply with abatement notice] shall be liable on summary conviction to a fine of an amount not exceeding level 5 on the standard scale together with a further fine of an amount equal to one-tenth of that level for each day on which the offence continues after the conviction.

(6) A person who commits an offence under subsection (4) above on industrial, trade or business premises shall be liable on summary conviction to a fine not exceeding £20,000.'[1]

A distinction is drawn between those who commit an offence on an industrial, trade or business premises and others. It should be noted that the distinction relates to the type of premises upon where the offence was committed and not to the occupation of the defendant or the activity itself. The EPA 1990 does not define what industrial, trade or business premises mean.[2]

1   In Scotland the maximum level is £40,000: see the Anti Social etc (Scotland) Act 2004, s 66, Sch 2, Pt 1, para 4(1), (4).
2   As to the case law on their meaning at paras **1.80–1.82**.

5.20 The definition is relevant for a number of reasons. Those falling within it will be exposed to a potentially greater fine.[1] On the other hand, there is no provision providing for a continuing offence in respect of an offence committed on industrial, trade or business premises.[2] Furthermore, the defence of best practicable means is also available to a much greater range of statutory nuisances where the offence is committed on an industrial, trade or business premises than where it is committed elsewhere.[3]

1   EPA 1990, s 80(6). The maximum fine is £20,000 except in Scotland where it is £40,000: see para 5.19, n 1.
2   EPA 1990, s 80(6).
3   See EPA 1990, s 80(7) and (8)(a).

5.21 Accordingly, in deciding what type of offence has been committed under section 80 of the EPA 1990, the following matters need to be considered:

- Is this a first offence?
- Is this the same offence for which a conviction has been obtained already?
- Is it an offence that could be said to have continued each day following a previous conviction? This could depend upon the nature of the breach alleged.
- Is this an offence committed on 'industrial, trade or business premises'?

Identifying the appropriate defendant(s)

5.22 It is only a 'person on whom an abatement notice is served' who can commit an offence under section 80 of the EPA 1990 for breach of an abatement notice.

Deciding whether to prosecute

5.23 Where a local authority is satisfied that an offence under section 80 of the EPA 1990 has occurred it has discretion whether, or not, to prosecute rather than a duty. The High Court is generally reluctant to allow challenges to the exercise of discretion to prosecute by public bodies. Nonetheless, such a decision is amenable to judicial review and there is no reason to suppose that it cannot be quashed if taken unlawfully.[1] Where there has been no error of law and the decision is not unreasonable (in the *Wednesbury* sense) the court will not interfere.[2]

1 See by way of analogy where the court quashed a decision by a local planning authority not to take non-criminal planning enforcement proceedings: *R v Sevenoaks District Council, ex p Palley* [1995] JPL 915.
2 See *R v Elmbridge Borough Council, ex p Active Office* [1998] JPL B43; (1997) Times, 29 December. See also the more recent decision of the House of Lords in *R v DPP, ex p Kebilene* [2000] 2 AC 326.

5.24 But a prosecution may be an abuse of process, as illustrated in the following example. The defendants have acted upon an assurance given by the local authority that certain works satisfied the requirements laid down in the notice. They have then been prosecuted subsequently without notice by the local authority for a failure to carry out the specified works. Such a prosecution is likely to be an abuse of process.

5.25 The council officers should ensure that they have authority to prosecute. Anyone can prosecute for the breach of an abatement notice so an absence of authority may not be fatal to the prosecution. But if the council officers do not have authority to prosecute, the prosecution is a private prosecution brought by the individual laying the information and not the local authority.[1]

1 See by way of analogy, the situation in *Postermobile plc v London Borough of Brent* (1997) Times, 8 December. For cases on delegated authority see Chapter 2, para **2.11**.

DRAFTING THE INFORMATION

5.26 Criminal proceedings in the magistrates' court are commenced by the prosecutor[1] or his counsel or solicitor or other person authorised in that behalf laying an information.[2] An information may be put in writing, signed and delivered to the magistrates' court or a prosecutor can go before the magistrates or a clerk to the justices and make his allegation orally relying upon the clerk or magistrates to write it down accurately.[3] The magistrates' court's rules of procedure give guidance on the drafting of informations issued or made by the magistrates' court.[4] It is rare for an information alleging a breach of an abatement notice to be made orally. The information is important because it provides both the mechanism for commencing proceedings and the basis for the charges.

1 As stated above, any person can prosecute an offence under s 80(4) by laying an information, though normally it is the local authority that is the prosecutor.
2 Criminal Procedure Rules 2005, (SI 2005/384, as amended), r 7.1(2).
3 Criminal Procedure Rules 2005, rr 7.2, 7.3, 12.
4 Criminal Procedure Rules 2005, r 7.1(1).

5.27 Not more than one offence can be charged in a single information,[1] although two or more separate criminal acts may be alleged in the same

5.27 *Criminal proceedings under EPA 1990, section 80*

information if the accused's conduct comprised one single act.[2] So in the case of a breach of an abatement notice the same information could contain allegations that a person breached a notice by exceeding the permitted noise level and also by operating outside permitted hours. In *DPP v Merriman*[3] the House of Lords held:

> 'When two or more acts of a similar nature committed by one or more defendants are connected with one another in the time and place of their commission, or by their common purpose, in such a way that they can be fairly regarded as forming part of the same transaction or criminal enterprise, they can be charged as one offence in a single indictment.'[4]

1   Criminal Procedure Rules, r 7(3). Rule 7.3(3) allows an information bad for duplicity to be rescued even after the trial has commenced, subject to the right of the defendant to have the proceedings adjourned where he has been unfairly prejudiced, see r 7.3(5).
2   *Jemmison v Priddle* [1972] 1 QB 489 and *Horrix v Malam* [1984] RTR 112.
3   [1973] AC 584, HL at 607.
4   See *Cullen v Jardine* [1985] Crim LR 668 and see *R v Wilson* (1979) 69 Cr App Rep 83.

5.28 However, where the defendant has operated his nightclub in breach of the terms of the abatement notice on different nights it is more likely that each day's breach would properly be regarded as a separate offence since there is more likely to have been a clear break in the acts committed on the different days.

5.29 Accordingly, if officers of the local authority have visited the premises more than once and found nuisances occuring on a number of occasions, they should consider charging in respect of each day the nuisance has occurred. If the local authority charges only in respect of one day, the potential fine will be smaller. Moreover, the prosecution may not be able to refer to incidents occurring on the other days since they would be irrelevant to proving the offence charged and prejudicial to the defendant.

5.30 Using as far as possible non-technical language the information must give reasonable particulars of the nature of the charge. It need not state every element of the offence. Nor is it required to specify that the accused does not fall within the ambit of a statutory defence, for example, the employment of best practicable means. Where, as in the case of a breach of an abatement notice, the offence is created by statute, the information must refer to the statute and relevant section concerned (in this case, section 80(4) of the EPA 1990 (as amended)).[1]

1   See Criminal Procedure Rules 2005, r 7.2.

Time for laying the information

5.31 Contravention for a failure to comply with an abatement notice is a 'summary only' offence.[1] There is no express provision in the EPA 1990 extending the ordinary period for laying the information. Accordingly, the magistrates' court has no jurisdiction to hear the case if the information is laid outside six months of the date of the alleged offence.[2] It is necessary, therefore, to establish:

- the date on which the offence was committed and
- the date when the information was laid.

Drafting the information **5.34**

The six months' period runs from the date upon which the offence is alleged to have occurred, *not* the date when the local authority first learned of the offence.[3] Accordingly, where the breach alleged is a failure to abate the nuisance as required by the notice, the prosecution has six months from the date of the breach of the notice to lay the information in respect of their particular breach. If, on evidence before the court of whatever nature, the magistrates doubt the date of the information so that it could have been laid out of time, the burden lies on the prosecution to show, to the criminal standard of proof that the information was laid within time.[4]

1   EPA 1990, s 80(4) and (6).
2   Magistrates' Courts Act 1980, s 127. A 'summary only' offence is one that is tried only before a magistrate's court with a right of appeal to the Crown Court before a judge and two justices.
3   *Hertsmere Borough Council v Alan Dunn Building Contractors* (1985) 84 LGR 214.
4   *Atkinson v DPP* [2004] EWHC 1457 (Admin), [2005] 1 WLR 96 (DC) at [18].

5.32 The abatement notice may very often require works to be completed within a period of time. If the recipient has failed to carry out the works, in the absence of a reasonable excuse, prima facie an offence will have been committed. It is necessary to consider whether the step required in the notice constituted a 'to do' requirement within a fixed or otherwise ascertainable period of time. In such cases, time will start to run from the day when the recipient of the notice was required to have carried out the works.[1] For example, where an abatement notice issued on 1 January 2000 contains a requirement to 'install double glazing within six months of the issue of abatement notice' a breach of that requirement of the notice occurs at the beginning of July 2000. An information in respect of that particular breach, therefore, must be laid *by* the beginning of December 2000.

1   *Hertsmere Borough Council v Alan Dunn Building Contractors* (1985) 84 LGR 214.

5.33 The information is considered as having been laid when the prosecutor 'procures delivery of the document to a person authorised to receive it on behalf of the justices of the peace and the clerk to the justices'[1] or the day on which he attends the justices or their clerk to make an oral information. Accordingly, where an information is sent by fax to the court office and it can be established by inference or otherwise that it was transmitted to the court's fax machine within time that is sufficient to constitute the laying of the information in time.[2]

1   *R v Manchester Stipendiary Magistrates, ex p Hill* [1983] 1 AC 328.
2   *Rockall v Department for Environment, Food and Rural Affairs* [2007] EWHC 614 (Admin). The general principle is that time limits should only bite in relation to steps over which the complainant has control (ibid).

Amending the information

5.34 Section 123 of the Magistrates' Court Act 1980 provides a wide power to amend an information. In most cases, any prejudice to the defendant caused by the amendment can usually be satisfied by granting an adjournment. Where an information has been laid within the six-month period it may be possible to amend it after the expiry of that period. It can be amended even to allege a different offence or different offences, provided that:

- the different offence or different offences allege the 'same misdoing' as the original offence and
- the amendment can be made in the interests of justice.[1]

5.34 *Criminal proceedings under EPA 1990, section 80*

1   *R v Scunthorpe Justices, ex p McPhee and Gallagher* (1999) 162 JP 635 at 639F. See also *R v Thames Magistrates' Court, ex p Stevens* [2000] COD 211 and *R v Network Sites Ltd, ex p Havering London Borough* (1997) 161 JP 513.

5.35   The phrase 'same misdoing':

'should not be construed too narrowly . . . [it means] that the new offences should arise out of the same(or substantially the same) facts as give rise to the original offence.'[1]

What does this mean in the case of statutory nuisance? It probably means that the prosecution may be able to amend the information to allege more or different breaches of the steps or works required by an abatement notice committed. These are likely to have arisen out of substantially the same facts that gave rise to the original judgment. However, is the prosecutor entitled to amend the information so as to allege further breaches committed on other days? In our view, the prosecutor is *probably* not entitled to include breaches committed more than six months before the date on which the amendment is sought. The court would be anxious not to allow a prosecutor to abuse the process of amendment made by including breaches that occurred on different days but are now immune for action because more than six months have expired.

1   *R v Scunthorpe Justices, ex p McPhee and Gallagher* (1999) 162 JP 635 at 639F.

Discretion to decline to try an information

5.36   In rare circumstances the magistrates can refuse to try an information which has been laid within time. The purpose of the six month provision for the laying of informations is to ensure that the trials take place speedily. Parliament's intention would be frustrated if the prosecutor laid the information just within the six-month period but then delayed unduly in serving the summons on the defendant. The court has recognised that magistrates do have discretion to acquit without hearing the evidence if either:

- the prosecution has abused correct court procedure by deliberate delay[1] or
- their inefficiency has led to extreme delay which might prejudice the accused of the trial were to go ahead.[2]

1   See eg *R v Brentford Justices, ex p Wong* [1981] QB 445.
2   *R v Oxford City Justices, ex p Smith* (1982) 75 Cr App Rep 200.

5.37   For example, where a local authority laid an information at the end of the six month period for a breach of an abatement notice but waited four more months before serving the summons because it wished to find out more information about the nature of any possible best practicable means defence before finally deciding to prosecute, the court is likely to consider that to be an abuse and acquit the defendant.[1]

1   See eg *R v Brentford Justices, ex p Wong* [1981] QB 445.

Relevant date for deciding when a breach has occurred

5.38   The relevant date for deciding whether the nuisance has been abated or the notice otherwise breached is the date of the offence alleged on the information. It is not the date on which the case is heard. In other words, a defendant cannot claim that there has been no breach of the abatement notice because by the time of the hearing before the magistrates' court, the notice has been complied with. Indeed, if the defendant has failed to carry out the necessary works within the time required by the notice it is no defence that he has complied with the notice before the information was laid but after the time required in the notice, although this could form the basis of mitigation.

MAKING PROSECUTION EVIDENCE AVAILABLE TO THE DEFENCE

5.39 A central feature of the criminal trial system in England and Wales is the duty of the prosecution to disclose evidence that it has at its disposal to the defence. It is interesting to note at the outset the reason for this. It is summarised by Sprack in *Emmins on Criminal Procedure*[1] as follows:

> 'The rationale for this duty is the disparity of resources between the Crown on the one hand (with its access to the investigative facilities of the police and the specialists services such as those of forensic scientist), and the individual accused of an offence on the other hand. In an effort to ensure a fair trial for the accused, and to achieve "equality of arms" as far as possible between the Crown and the accused, there developed a common law duty owned by the prosecution to the defence.'

1   8th edn (2000) at p 121.

5.40 Although anyone can bring criminal proceedings against another for a breach of an abatement notice, it is most usually the local authority that prosecutes. Although a local authority may not have the resources of the Criminal Prosecution Services (CPS), the comments made in the passage quoted above remain generally good. A local authority will have the benefit of enforcement officers and environmental health officers who are experts. The need for 'equality of arms' remains. When considering the extent to which the common law and express statutory provisions provide for advance disclosure it is important to note that the concept of 'equality of arms' is something which the European Court on Human Rights (ECtHR) has expressly recognised as a part of the rights guaranteed under article 6 of the ECHR. The Human Rights Act 1998 is therefore an important consideration in this context. As the Attorney General's 'Guidelines on Disclosure'[1] advise:

> 'Every accused has the right to a fair trial, a right long embodied in our law and guaranteed under art 6 of the European Convention on Human Rights (ECHR). A fair trial is the proper object and expectation of all participants in the trial process. Fair disclosure to an accused is an inseparable part of a fair trial.'

Although the Guidelines have been drafted with their focus on Crown Court proceedings, they provide that 'the spirit of the Guidelines must be followed where they apply to proceedings in the magistrates' court.'[2] They are therefore relevant to summary only proceedings for a breach of an abatement notice under section 80 of the EPA 1990.

1   April 2005, Introduction
2   See para 7.

5.41 The duty to make evidence available to the defence can be divided into two components:

5.41 *Criminal proceedings under EPA 1990, section 80*

- advance information of material upon which the prosecution intends to rely (advance information)
- material of relevance to the case on which the prosecution does not intend to rely (initial or primary disclosure).

Advance information

5.42 Notwithstanding the apparent[1] absence of an express statutory right to disclosure of advanced information in summary only proceedings, the defence should seek, nonetheless, advance disclosure from the prosecuting local authority. In our view, the best practice for prosecutors is generally to comply with any defence request to supply the statement of witnesses whom the prosecution intends to call. Indeed, in our view, it would be imprudent for the prosecution not to make that information available prior to the hearing even in the absence of such a request from the defence, particularly, where the defendant is not legally represented. In *R v Kingston-upon-Hull Justices, ex p McCann*[2] Bingham LJ[3] made clear that:

> 'Ordinarily I have no doubt that Crown Prosecutors are well advised to adopt a policy of disclosing to the defence the material upon which they intend to rely ... In some circumstances it may even be that disclosure is necessary in the interests of fairness. On the other hand, circumstances may arise in which the Crown Prosecution Service may properly seek to limit the extent of the disclosure. The primary example of such circumstances is where the prosecution witnesses may be at risk.
>
> Furthermore a failure to disclose in advance may lead to applications to adjourn and that is not conductive to the efficient disposal of criminal cases.'

1 Rule 21.1 of the Criminal Procedure Rules expressly provides that the rules of disclosure of advanced information apply only to offences triable either way, and therefore do not apply to summary only offences such as the offence of failing to comply with an abatement notice. However, the qualification in the text has been made in the light of our view that the HRA 1998 may have introduced such an implied statutory right by virtue of its incorporation of article 6 of the ECHR.
2 (1991) 155 JP 569.
3 (1991) 155 JP 569 at 573E-574B. Endorsed in *R v Stratford Justices, ex p Imbert* [1999] 2 Cr App Rep 276, DC.

5.43 Collins J stated in *R v Stratford Justices, ex p Imbert*[1] that:

> '... disclosure ought to be given if requested (and perhaps on payment of a reasonable fee for copying)[2] unless there are good reasons, such a protection of a witness, not to, at least where the offences charged could possibly lead to imprisonment. In this case, all witnesses were police officers. I can see no good reason not to have disclosed and the failure had led to unnecessary expense and delay. Furthermore, a failure to disclose in advance may lead to applications to adjourn that it is not conducive to the efficient disposal of criminal cases.'

1 [1999] 2 Cr App Rep 276.
2 Local authorities should be very cautious in insisting upon payment of photocopying fees for the production of these documents, particularly where the defendant may claim that he does not have the resources to pay for the documents. Any right to disclosure cannot depend upon one's financial means.

Making prosecution evidence available to the defence 5.46

5.44 The statutory rules relating to advance information do *not* apply to 'summary only' offences such as a breach of an abatement notice under section 80(4) of the EPA 1990.[1]

1   Criminal Procedure Rules 2005, r 21.1.

5.45 The non-application of the advance information rules to summary proceedings has been held by the Divisional Court in *Ex p Imbert* not to be inconsistent either with the Criminal Procedure and Investigations Act 1996 (CPIA 1996) (as to which, see paras **5.48–5.51**) and article 6(3)(a) of the ECHR.[1] Article 6(3)(a) provides that a defendant is 'to be informed promptly ... and in detail, of the nature of the accusation against him ...' The Divisional Court[2] in *Ex p Imbert* relied upon a number of decisions of the ECtHR in order to emphasise that article 6 related to the fairness of the proceedings as a whole. In particular the court relied upon a passage from the judgment in *Saidi v France*[3] that:

'... the taking of evidence is governed primarily by the rules of domestic law and it is in principle for the national courts to assess the evidence before them. The Court's task ... is to ascertain whether the proceedings in their entirety, including the way in which evidence was taken, were fair.'

But, as the passage states, that judgment concerned the *taking* of evidence rather than the disclosure of the prosecution case to the defendant. In *Edwards v United Kingdom*[4] relevant material had been withheld from the defence in a criminal trial. The ECtHR held:

'The Court considers that it is a requirement of fairness under article 6(1) which is recognised under English law, that the prosecution authorities disclose to the defence all material evidence for or against the accused and the failure to do so in the present case gave rise to a defect in the proceedings.'

1   [1999] 2 Cr App Rep 276, DC. The Divisional Court itself recognised that it comments were obiter because following the grant of leave the CPS had agreed to make the statements available to the defence without conceding that they were required to do so. However, the Divisional Court gave two reasoned judgments upon the issues raised.
2   Applications for judicial review of decisions relating to criminal matters go before the Divisional Court.
3   (1993) 17 EHRR 251.
4   (1992) 15 EHRR 417.

5.46 The ECtHR concluded, however, that the defects in the original hearing were remedied by the opportunities afforded to the defendant in his appeal to the Court of Appeal. In our view the comments made by the Divisional Court in *Ex p Imbert* may have to be revisited following the implementation of the HRA 1998. It seems to us that where the prosecution does not provide advance information and there is a failure by the justices to grant an adjournment that may in many cases lead to a breach of article 6. Moreover, the absence of advance information may in certain circumstances be a violation of article 6(3)(b), which lays down the right 'to have adequate time and facilities for [the] defence' as well as a violation of article 6(3)(a). In this respect we endorse the view expressed by Sprack in *Emmins on Criminal Procedure*:[1]

'In order that the trial should be fair, it is necessary that the defence should be able to consider the prosecution evidence, and prepare upon the basis of

5.46 *Criminal proceedings under EPA 1990, section 80*

knowledge rather than guesswork. Sometimes the nature of that evidence will be predicable, and the defence advocate will be able to respond with the necessary agility of thought. But, in other instances, the defence may be ambushed by an unexpected line of evidence.'

It is not difficult to imagine circumstances in the context of a statutory nuisance prosecution where the failure to supply material in advance of material even of a relatively non-technical nature may create difficulties for the defence.

1   11th edn (2006) at p 128–129.

5.47 It is, however, conceivable that there may be circumstances in the context of a statutory nuisance prosecution, where it may be necessary for the prosecution not to give advance warning of the existence or identity of a particular witness. One could imagine the situation where an individual or individuals who have a history of violence and intimidation have caused the breach of an abatement notice. The prosecution may fear that witnesses would be intimidated from giving evidence if the defendant knew of their intention beforehand.

Initial or primary disclosure

5.48 Initial or primary disclosure relates to the disclosure of material in the possession of the prosecution upon which it does not intend to rely. In the case of a statutory nuisance prosecution it could include statements by neighbours stating that they were not disturbed by the defendant's activity on the day in question or noise readings made by an environmental health officer showing low noise readings. This duty was evolved by judges at common law, it has now been made the subject of statutory regime set out in the CPIA 1996,[1] supplemented by a Code of Practice issued under that Act.

1   As amended by the Criminal Justice Act 2003.

5.49 Part I of the CPIA 1996 contains certain rules relating to prosecution (and defence) disclosure. It applies to 'summary only' proceedings where the accused pleads not guilty and the court proceeds to summary trial.[1] In these circumstances, the obligations of primary or initial disclosure under section 3 of the 1996 Act requires the prosecutor to disclose any previously undisclosed material to the accused, if it 'might reasonably be considered capable of undermining the case for the prosecution against the accused or of assisting the case for the accused'.[2] The test for primary disclosure is therefore an objective one. Once the prosecutor has complied or purported to comply with this duty, the defence *may* give the prosecutor and the court a defence statement within the prescribed time.[3] A defence statement is a written statement setting out the nature of the defence (including any particular defences on which he intends to rely), indicating the matters of fact on which the accused takes issue with the prosecution and why, and indicating any point of law (including points on the adminissibility of evidence or involving abuse of process arguments) which he wishes to take and any authority he intends to refer to for that purpose.[4] Serving a defence statement can provide a focus to trigger further prosecution disclosure which is subject to certain time limits.[5] It also enables the defendant to apply for a disclosure order in certain circumstances.[6] However, faults in disclosure by the defendant may enable to court to draw adverse inferences against the defendant, though no defendant may be convicted solely on the basis of such an inference.[7]

1   11th edn (2006) at 143.
2   CPIA 1996, s 3(1)(a).
3   CPIA 1996, s 6; CPIA 1996 (Defence Disclosure Time Limits) Regulations 1997, SI 1997/684.
4   CPIA 1996, s 6A
5   CPIA 1996, ss 7A(2), 7A(5) and 10. Late disclosure by the prosecution may render proceedings an abuse of process: see for example *Lewisham London Borough Council v Marylebone Magistrates Court* [2003] EWHC 1184 (Admin).
6   CPIA 1996, s 8.
7   CPIA 1996, s 11.

5.50   The prosecution duty of initial or primary disclosure under section 3 of the 1996 Act is an on-going one. There is a duty to keep the question under review the question of whether there is further material meeting the section 3 test, in particular after the giving of a defence statement.[1] If at any time after complying or purporting to comply with the section 3 duty, but before the acquittal or conviction of the accused or the withdrawal of the proceedings, there is material that meets the section 3 test that has not been disclosed, the prosecution must disclose it as soon as reasonably practicable or within certain time limits where a defence statement has been given.[2]

1   CPIA 1996, s 7A(2).
2   CPIA 1996, s 7A(3).

5.51   The common law imposed a duty of primary disclosure upon the prosecution. The basis for this duty was the requirement of natural justice.[1] The CPIA 1996 purports to disapply 'the rules of the common law which relate to the disclosure of material by the prosecutor.'[2] Does this mean that the defendant who decides not provide a statement is now no longer entitled under the principles of natural justice to further (or secondary) disclosure of prosecution material? It has been argued that the right is retained by the defendant notwithstanding the words of the CPIA 1996.[3] Indeed, this provision of the CPIA 1996 would be incompatible with article 6 of the ECHR if disclosure were no longer applicable. There is a duty of 'convergent construction' under section 3(1) of the HRA 1998.[4] Therefore, the CPIA 1996 will probably be construed so as to be convergent. In our view, the best practice is for the prosecution to disclose both primary and secondary material in summary abatement notice proceedings.

1   See eg *R v Leyland Justices, ex p Hawthorne* [1979] QB 283 (failure to reveal potential witness); *R v Liverpool Crown Court, ex p Roberts* [1986] Crim LR 622 (failure to disclose a previous inconsistent statement by a prosecution witness).
2   CPIA 1996, s 21(1).
3   Leng and Taylor *Blackstone's Guide to the Criminal Procedure and Investigations Act 1999*.
4   Section 3(1) of the HRA 1998 provides that legislation of any kind, whether passed before or after the coming into force of the HRA 1998 must 'so far as it is possible to do so' be construed and given effect in a way which is compatible with Convention rights. The approach is similar to the 'duty of interpretation' or 'convergent construction' imposed upon domestic courts when interpreting domestic law in compliance with the provisions of EC law pursuant to article 10 of the EC Treaty (see *Marleasing v CIA* [1990] ECR 1-4135). The process of convergent construction has been explained by Sedley J in *R v Durham County Council, ex p Huddleston* [2000] 1 WLR 1484, [2000] 1 PLR 122, CA.

DISCLOSURE OF EXPERT EVIDENCE

5.52   Where the defendant pleads not guilty and the case is to proceed to trial, if any party proposes to adduce expert evidence (whether of fact or opinion) in the proceedings (otherwise than in relation to sentence) that party shall as soon

5.52 *Criminal proceedings under EPA 1990, section 80*

as practicable furnish the other party or parties with a statement in writing of any finding or opinion which he proposes to adduce by way of such evidence.[1] Where a request in writing is made to him on that behalf by another party, he must provide that party with a copy of (or where more practicable, a reasonable opportunity to examine) the record of any observation, test, calculation or other procedure on which such finding or opinion is based and any document or other thing or substance in respect of which any such procedure has been carried out.[2] The rules of disclosure apply to prosecution and defence alike.

1   Criminal Procedure Rules 2005, r 24.1(1)(a) and (i).
2   Criminal Procedure Rules 2005, r 24.1(ii).

5.53 A party is not obliged to comply with the duty to disclose expert evidence where he has reasonable grounds for believing that to do so might lead to the intimidation or attempted intimidation of any person on whose evidence he intends to rely or otherwise to the course of justice being interfered with.[1] Notice that the evidence is being withheld and the grounds for doing so must be given to the other party.[2]

1   Criminal Procedure Rules 2005, r 24.2(1).
2   Criminal Procedure Rules 2005, r 24.2(2).

5.54 A party who seeks to adduce expert evidence in any proceedings and who fails to comply with r 24.1 of the Criminal Procedure Rules (see para **5.52** above) shall not adduce that evidence in those proceedings without the leave of the court.

APPLICATION OF PACE 1984

5.55 Where environmental health or other council officers have visited the site on a number of occasions it is likely that they will have spoken with the defendant or his employees. The substance of the Police and Criminal Evidence Act 1984 (PACE 1984) and the Codes of Practice also apply to persons 'other than police officers who are charged with the duty of investigating offences or charging offences'.[1] In *Joy v Federation Against Copyright Theft Ltd*[2] it was held that the duty referred to in section 67(9) of PACE 1984 was any type of legal duty, whether imposed by statute, common law or by contract. Accordingly, an investigator employed by the respondent was held to be subject to such a duty. The court has held that an inspector employed with the RSPCA may be such a person.[3] Accordingly, there can be little doubt that local authority officers investigating a possible breach of an abatement notice come within the section.

1   PACE 1984, s 67(9).
2   [1993] Crim LR 588.
3   *RSPCA v Eager* (1995) Crim LR 59, DC.

5.56 The provisions of PACE 1984 are important because evidence obtained in breach of the Code[1] can be excluded (under section 76 and 76A (confessions)[2], section 78 (unfair evidence) or under general common law). The Codes are admissible in evidence in all criminal and civil proceedings 'if relevant to any question arising in the proceedings' and shall be 'taken into account in determining that question'.[3]

1   The Codes of Practice that are likely to be most relevant to cases of breaches of abatement notices are:

Code A (in so far as it relates to the search of any vehicle)
Code C (relating to the questioning of persons and/or tape recording of interviews).
Code B (relating to entry and search of premises) (as to which see Chapter 2)
It should be remembered that the Codes are primarily intended to give the procedure to be adopted in police investigations. The court will apply a degree of common sense in applying them to the particular circumstances of a local authority summary prosecution for the breach of an abatement notice.
2 The impact of the ECHR and the right to silence is addressed at paras **5.60–5.64**.
3 PACE 1984, s 67(11).

5.57 If an officer has 'reasonable grounds for suspicion' that the person to whom he is speaking has committed an offence, he should caution that person. The caution shall be in the following terms:

> 'You do not have to say anything. But it may harm your defence if you do not mention when questioned something which you later rely on in court. Anything you do say may be given in evidence.'

Minor deviations do not constitute a breach of this requirement provided that the sense of the caution is preserved.

5.58 As a matter of good practice an investigating officer with the local authority should:

- inform that person suspected of having committed an offence of their legal rights including the right to have a lawyer present
- make a written note of any interview (if possible even of one held on site) and if possible get that person to read it through and sign the note as an approved record of interview.

Even if the officer is not sure an offence has been committed, the best policy is, when in doubt, caution.

5.59 The threshold for 'reasonable grounds for suspicion' under section 67(11) of PACE is relatively low. The caution should be administered when, objectively, there are grounds for suspicion, falling short of prima facie evidence of guilt, that the person questioned has committed an offence.[1]

1 *Westminster City Council v Cinquemani* [2002] EWHC 179 Admin.

The right against self incrimination

5.60 A local authority has a power to require certain information under section 16 of the Local Government (Miscellaneous Provisions) Act 1976. It is an offence under section 16(2) not to comply with such a request. Pursuant to this power a local authority may, for example, require someone to admit whether or not they are the owner or occupier of the premises to which an abatement notice relates. It is immediately apparent why such a power can be important for local authorities dealing with alleged breaches of abatement notices.

5.61 The use of information obtained by coercion in criminal proceedings for a failure to comply with an abatement notice might be incompatible with article 6 of the ECHR. The right to a fair trial in a criminal case includes, 'the right of anyone charged with a criminal offence ... to remain silent and not to contribute to incriminating himself'.[1] In *Saunders v United Kingdom*[2] the ECtHR held that the admission in evidence at the applicant's trial of transcripts

5.61 *Criminal proceedings under EPA 1990, section 80*

of interviews with DTI inspectors violated article 6.1 since at the time of the interrogation the applicant was under a duty to answer questions which was enforceable by criminal proceedings for contempt.

1   *Funke v France* (1993) 16 EHRR 297.
2   (1996) 23 EHRR 313.

5.62   In *R v Hertfordshire County Council, ex p Green Environmental Industries*[1] the House of Lords distinguished *Saunders*. In the *Ex p Green* case the local authority in its capacity was a waste regulation authority had served a notice under section 71(2) of the EPA 1990 requiring certain information to be provided. Lord Hoffman held that a requirement to provide information backed up a threat of conviction, if it was not complied, with could be justified in the public interest as in the present case where the question of public health could be an issue. However, in the *Ex p Green* case the recipient of the notice had refused to provide the information. Accordingly, the House of Lords did not consider whether the material obtained from a person by use of coercive powers could be used to prove criminal proceedings against him. In *R v Central Criminal Court, ex p Bright*,[2] the Divisional Court declined to re-examine the case law of the ECtHR, considering itself bound by the consideration of that case law by the House of Lords in *Ex p Green*. The case concerned the power under section 9 of PACE 1984 that allows a Crown Court to make production orders even where they might infringe a person's right against self-incrimination. The Divisional Court held[3] that safeguards were provided by the existence of statutory requirements and by judicial discretion (for example, that under section 78 of PACE 1984), which required the implications of self-incrimination to be considered. They held that such orders could be made.

1   [2000] 2 AC 412, [2000] 1 All ER 773.
2   [2001] 1 WLR 662.
3   There was some judicial disagreement within the court on certain aspects.

5.63   In *Stott (Procurator Fiscal, Dunfermline) v Brown*[1] the Privy Council held that it was not a breach of a defendant's right to a fair trial under article 6 of the ECHR on a charge of driving with excess alcohol in her blood contrary to section 5 of the Road Traffic Act 1988 for a prosecutor to rely at the trial on the defendant's admission, obtained compulsorily under section 172(2)(a) of that Act, that she had been the driver of the car. Lord Bingham noted that the ECtHR had recognised the need for a fair balance between the general interest of the community and the personal rights of the individual, the search for which balance had been described as inherent in the whole of the Convention. Lord Bingham noted the serious problem caused by the high incidence of death and injury caused by the misuse of motor vehicles. The question was therefore whether section 172 represented a disproportionate response, or one that undermined a defendant's right to fair trial, if an admission of being the driver was relied on at trial. Lord Bingham noted that section 172 provided for the putting of a single, simple question. The answer could not of itself incriminate a suspect, since it was not without more an offence to drive a car. Lord Bingham noted that an admission of driving might, of course, as in the present case provide proof of a fact necessary to convict, but the section did not sanction prolonged questioning about the facts alleged to give rise to criminal offences, such as was understandably held objectionable in *Saunders v United Kingdom*,[2] and the penalty was moderate and non-custodial.

1   (2000) UKHRR 239.
2   (1996) 23 EHRR 313.

5.64 In the authors' view Lord Bingham's analysis can be applied to the use of the power under section 16 of the Local Government (Miscellaneous Provisions) Act 1976 for a local authority to require the owner or occupier of a premises to reveal his interest in the land and for that material to be admitted before the court in a prosecution against that person under section 80 of the EPA 1990. It is to be noted that just like section 172 of the Road Traffic Act 1988, section 16 provides a power only for a limited number of questions and a small fine if the recipient refuses to provide a response. Whilst the approaches of the House of Lords in *Ex p Green*[1] and the Privy Council in *Stott*[2] have yet to be considered by the ECtHR, in our view they represent a correct application of article 6.

1 [2000] AC 412, [2000] 1 All ER 773.
2 (2000) UKHRR 239.

Contravention of PACE 1984 or the Codes (or other illegal or unfair conduct)

5.65 A Contravention of PACE 1984 or the Codes (or other illegal or unfair conduct) may result in the evidence, which was thereby obtained being ruled inadmissible. This is the effect of section 78 of PACE 1984, which provides that the court may exclude evidence on which the prosecution proposes to rely if:

'... having regard to all the circumstances, including the circumstances in which the evidence was obtained, the admission of the evidence would have such an adverse effect on the fairness of the proceedings that the court ought not to admit it.'

5.66 Section 78 of PACE 1984, therefore, gives the court a discretion to exclude any illegally or unfairly obtained evidence whatever its nature or source, including evidence gathered in breach of a Code of Practice. The wide range of this discretion was confirmed by the Court of Appeal in *R v Quin*[1] by Lord Lane CJ:

'The function of the judge is ... to protect the fairness of the proceedings, ... proceedings may become unfair if, for example, one side is allowed to adduce relevant evidence which, for one reason or another, the other side cannot properly challenge or meet, or where there has been an abuse of process, eg because evidence has been obtained in deliberate breach of procedures laid down in an official code of practice.'

Evidence which has been properly obtained but which is not relevant to an issue before the court but acts simply to prejudice the court against the accused can also be excluded under section 78 of PACE 1984.[2]

1 [1990] Crim LR 581.
2 *R v Sandhu* [1997] Crim LR 288, [1997] JPL 853.

5.67 If a contravention of PACE 1984 or the Codes (or, in our view the HRA 1998) leads to the accused making a confession, the contravention, *may*, depending up on its precise nature, either be sufficient of itself to make the confession inadmissible[1] or be a contributory factor which taken together with other circumstances render the evidence inadmissible.[2] The test in any particular case is whether the admission of the evidence obtained in breach of the Code would render the trial unfair.[3] The task of the court is not merely to consider whether there would be an adverse effect on the fairness of the

5.67 *Criminal proceedings under EPA 1990, section 80*

proceedings, but whether the effect is so adverse that justice requires the evidence to be excluded.[4]

1 See *Westminster City Council v Cinquemani* [2002] EWHC 179 Admin for an example of one such case.
2 Since the passing of PACE 1984 the courts have shown a greater readiness to exercise the discretion in favour of the defence than in the days of the Judge's Rules, the old common law approach to excluding unfair material. (On this point see further *Emmins on Criminal Procedure* (11th edn (2006)).
3 *R v Cheb Miller* [2007] EWCA Crim 1891 at [9]
4 *R v Rehman* [2006] EWCA Crim 1900 at [16]

COURSE OF A SUMMARY TRIAL[1]

5.68 The clerk begins by putting the information to the accused. The accused must either plead guilty or not guilty.

1 See Criminal Procedure Rules 2005, r 37.1–37.5.

Prosecution case

5.69 If the accused pleads not guilty, the prosecution has the right to an opening speech. Unless the case is complicated this will usually be short. However, magistrates are likely to be less familiar with statutory nuisance cases than, for example, road traffic offences and so a short opening dealing with the statutory scheme as well as the facts will often be appropriate even in a fairly uncomplicated statutory nuisance case.

5.70 After the opening prosecution witnesses are called. The witness give their evidence-in-chief and are then open to cross-examination by the defence and finally if necessary re-examined by the advocate for the prosecution. They may also be asked questions by the bench.

5.71 Generally speaking, witnesses as to fact will remain outside the court until called to give evidence although the procedure may vary depending upon the circumstances of the case.

5.72 The prosecution may also make use of section 9 of the Criminal Justice Act 1967 under which written statements may be read as evidence in criminal proceedings provided:

- the statement contains a declaration that it is true to the best of the maker's knowledge and belief and he realises the risk of prosecution for willful misstatements and
- a copy has been served on the defence and there has been no objection within seven days of service to the statement being read.

5.73 If a prosecution witness departs significantly in his evidence from earlier statements of which the prosecution is aware the defence should be informed so that they can use the consistency as a basis for cross examination.[1]

1 *R v Liverpool Crown Court, ex p Roberts* [1986] Crim LR 622.

5.74 A difficult question is how the magistrates deal with issues relating to the admissibility of evidence. In deciding whether a piece of evidence is it be admitted they will inevitably learn of its substance. There is also a problem as to when they should rule on the admissibility of evidence. The general principle is that they have an unfettered discretion as to how they deal with objections to evidence. They can rule on it as a preliminary point or they can deal with it immediately before the evidence would otherwise be given in the normal course of evidence or they can receive it provisionally and then decide to ignore it once all the evidence in the case has been received.[1] The position has been to some extent changed by section 76 of PACE 1984. If the defence represents that a confession was obtained by oppression or in circumstances likely to render it unreliable, the general principle will not apply and the magistrates are obliged forthwith to hold a 'trial within a trial' at which the confessions admissibility.[2]

1   *F (an infant) v Chief Constable of Kent* [1982] Crim LR 682.
2   See *R v Liverpool Juvenile Court, ex p R* [1988] QB 1. The position is complicated because it has also been held that where the court is being asked to exclude a confession as a matter of discretion, ie because there has been a breach of the Code, the usual rule, that it is left up to the magistrates how they deal with it, will apply.

PROVING THE OFFENCE

5.75   The prosecution must call evidence to show:

- the existence of the abatement notice
- that the notice was served on the defendant
- that the defendant has contravened or failed to comply with requirement in the notice. The evidence required will of course vary depending upon the nature of the alleged contravention. For example, if the allegation is simply a failure to comply with a requirement contained in the notice to carry out certain works by a particular date it is not necessary to call evidence that a nuisance is occurring. Indeed, in such circumstances (ie where no allegation of an offence is being made in respect of the continuation of a nuisance) such evidence may be thought to be irrelevant and inadmissible.[1] It would nonetheless be relevant to sentencing and *might* amount to a defence of 'reasonable excuse'. In many instances of course a defendant will face charges that he has failed to abate the nuisance and has also failed to carry out steps required by the notice and
- where the defendant discharges the evidential burden of showing a possible defence of 'reasonable excuse' the prosecution must prove beyond reasonable doubt that no reasonable excuse existed.[2]

1   *R v Sandhu* [1997] Crim LR 288, [1997] JPL 853.
2   *Polychronakis v Richards and Jeromm Ltd* [1998] Env LR 347.

5.76   Although it is not normally put in issue by the defendant, the prosecution ought to be in a position to prove that the abatement notice is formally valid in the sense that it was duly authorised and has not been set aside on appeal or by way of judicial review.[1]

1   By analogy with the position with planning enforcement notices as explained in *Palacegate Properties Ltd v LB Camden* (2001) ACD 137, transcript paragraphs 28 (Laws LJ) and 38 (Longmore J).

5.77   A failure to call evidence in respect of the above points may lead to a successful application by the defence of 'no case to answer'. In order to secure a conviction the court will need to be satisfied that these matters are proved to the criminal standard of proof.

5.78 *Criminal proceedings under EPA 1990, section 80*

'REASONABLE EXCUSE'

5.78 In *Polychronakis v Richards and Jeromm Ltd*,[1] the Divisional Court (curiously in our view) held that once a defendant had raised the issue of a reasonable excuse and had laid the evidential basis for that contention, it was for the prosecution to satisfy the court to the criminal standard of proof that the excuse was not a reasonable one.

1 [1998] Env LR 347.

5.79 What may amount to a reasonable excuse is not defined. However, in *Wellingborough Borough Council v Gordon*[1] Taylor LJ accepted the submission that,

> '... the defence of reasonable excuse is not available to a defendant who contravenes the notice deliberately and intentionally in circumstances wholly under his control. It would have been available, however, if the contravention occurred in an emergency or in circumstances beyond his control. If for example, a man devoted to DIY had made a habit of hammering through the night and notice was served prohibiting noise nuisance of that kind, he could plead reasonable excuse if a window had broken during the night in a storm and, to exclude the elements, he hammered some boarding into position.'

In the particular case, Taylor LJ had to decide a noise abatement notice had been served prohibiting the playing of loud music. The defendant organised a party three years later to celebrate his birthday. He held it on the day after his birthday so as to minimise disturbance. The defendant invited all his neighbours, most of whom attended. None of the neighbours who were not at the party complained. During the night two police officers hearing loud noise requested the defendant to reduce the noise level which he did. Taylor LJ held that whilst the prosecution might be regarded as a sledgehammer to crack a nut it did not amount to a reasonable excuse.

1 [1993] Env LR 218.

5.80 It would also appear that the fact that loud music forms part of one's culture does not amount to a 'reasonable excuse'.[1] It has also been suggested that the fact that a noise nuisance arises in the course of religious worship on premises lawfully used for such purposes may not amount to a reasonable excuse although such circumstances would be relevant considerations for the purposes of deciding whether a reasonable excuse existed.[2]

1 *Wellingborough Borough Council v Gordon* [1993] Env LR 218 at 223 per Moorland J.
2 See *London Borough of Hackney v Moshe Rottenburg* [2007] Env LR 24 at [23]. The comments are not part of the essential reasoning in the case and therefore are not binding on other courts.

5.81 A claim by a defendant that he did not possess either the physical or economic abilities to carry out the steps required in a notice might possibly constitute a 'reasonable excuse'.[1] For example, because the defendant had become bankrupt following the expiry of the period of appeal against the abatement notice. This particular type of excuse would generally be limited, in any event, to a contravention relating to the defendant's failure to undertake the works or steps required by the notice. An analogy can be found in the approach of the Divisional Court in *Kent County Council v Brockman*[2] to the statutory defence, under section 179(3) of the Town and Country Planning Act 1990, 'that [the defendant] did everything he could be expected to secure compliance with [a planning enforcement notice].' In that case the court held that 'personal circumstances of a defendant' could be taken into account. Buckley J held[3] that 'To hold someone guilty of a criminal offence for not doing something which they are genuinely incapable of doing, would be quite contrary to any tenets of criminal law known to me at least.' Simon Brown LJ noted, however, that:

> 'All will turn on the circumstances of a particular case, but I would expect the court to be fairly rigorous in the proof which it expects or demands of a defendant, and not allow itself to be hoodwinked by protestations of impecuniosity on behalf of any individual.'

1 See eg, the approach of the court in *Saddleworth UDC v Aggregates and Sand Ltd* (1970) 114 Sol Jo 931 in respect of best practicable means.
2 [1996] 1 PLR 1.
3 [1996] 1 PLR 1 at 3E.

5.82 Contravention of the notice caused by events beyond control of defendant, for example, a power supply failure may amount to a 'reasonable excuse'.

5.83 In *Hope Butuyuyu v London Borough of Hammersmith and Fulham Council*[1] the Divisional Court considered the question of personal hardship as constituting a 'reasonable excuse' by way of defence to a charge of contravening the requirements of an abatement notice. In this case, the appellant had been convicted of contravening a notice relating to noise. She had been diagnosed as HIV positive and her son suffered from cancer at the time the notice was served. Her son later died. The council had written expressing sympathy and telling her to abate the noise but had failed to explain the appeal procedure. On a later prosecution for non-compliance, it was argued that the failure to appeal the original notice had been due to her illness, and that of her son, and that her failure to appeal within 21 days against the notice should not prevent her from raising the question of the lack of justification for serving the notice in the prosecution proceedings as a 'reasonable excuse.' She was convicted and appealed. The Divisional Court held that it was not possible to provide a comprehensive definition of what matters were or were not capable of amounting to a reasonable excuse in the context of a failure to appeal an abatement notice within the time stipulated. Such circumstances would vary considerably from case to case. In this case the magistrates had put out of account any consideration of the personal circumstances of the appellant at the time of service of the notice. The magistrates' view had been that these reasons must amount, in effect to non-receipt of the notice, however, in the court's view, this involved too narrow a view of the defence put forward. The conviction was quashed.

1 [1997] Env LR D13.

5.84 Other case law suggests that 'reasonable excuse' does not include matters that should have been raised upon appeal under section 80(3) of the EPA 1990 challenging the validity of the notice, unless there has been some special reason for not entering the appeal.[1] Ackner LJ said in respect of the equivalent provisions contained in the Control of Pollution Act 1974 that:

> 'Section 58(4) was not designed, in my judgment, to give the recipient of the notice a choice of forum in which to mount his attack on the notice. It is

5.84 *Criminal proceedings under EPA 1990, section 80*

designed to provide a defence to a criminal charge where he had some reasonable excuse, such as special difficulty in relation to compliance with the notice.'[2]

Taylor LJ in the *Wellingborough* case[3] cited this passage with approval.'Reasonable excuse' would almost certainly not include matters covered by statutory defences set out at section 80(7) of the EPA 1990.[4] A breach of the defendant's Convention rights under HRA 1998 can be raised as a defence.[5] If relevant, it is capable to amounting to a 'reasonable excuse'. For example, it may be that where a recipient of a notice has been unable to appeal within the prescribed 21 days he may, nonetheless, be entitled to challenge the basis of the abatement notice on the grounds that the 21 days time limit was too short to afford him a proper hearing in accordance with article 6 of the ECHR in order to challenge the notice.

1   *A Lambert Flat Management Ltd v Lomas* [1981] 1 WLR 898.
2   [1981] 1 WLR 898 at 907.
3   *Wellingborough Borough Council v Gordon* [1993] Env LR 218.
4   This is important because the burden of proof differs depending whether the defendant relies on a statutory defence or 'reasonable excuse'. See paras **5.78** and **5.90**.
5   Note that to some extent the HRA 1998 is retrospective in its effect (s 22(4)).

SUBMISSION OF NO CASE TO ANSWER

5.85 At the conclusion of the prosecution evidence, the defence may make a submission of no case to answer. The submission should be upheld if either:

- there is no evidence to prove an essential element of the offence charged or
- the prosecution evidence has been so discredited as a result of cross-examination or is so manifestly unreliable that no reasonable tribunal could safely convict on it.[1]

If the justices are provisionally minded to uphold the submission of no case to answer, they should call on the prosecution to address them, to avoid the possibility of injustice.[2]

1   See *Practice Direction (submissions of no case)* [1962] 1 WLR 227.
2   *R v Barking and Dagenham Justices, ex p DPP* (1994) 159 JP 373.

5.86 Where the offence involves proving that a noise nuisance had not been abated, there is no requirement that the prosecution adduce technical noise measurements or evidence from occupiers of a particular building. The prosecution is entitled to rely upon the judgment and expertise of its environmental health officers without the need for technical noise evidence.[1]

1   *Westminster City Council v MacDonald* [2003] EWHC 2698 (Admin), *Lewisham v Yvonne Hall* [2002] EWHC 960 (Admin).

DEFENCE CASE

5.87 The accused himself is competent but not compellable as a witness in his own defence.

5.88 If the prosecution know of a witness who can give material evidence and they do not themselves propose to call him, they are under a duty to make him available to the defence.¹ If the defendant himself is to be called he should give evidence before any other witnesses to be called by the defence unless those other witnesses just be character witnesses. Once they have given evidence-in-chief they may be cross-examined by the prosecution and re-examined by the accused's advocate. The bench may also ask questions of them.

1   *R v Leyland Justices, ex p Hawthorn* [1979] QB 283.

5.89 The defence has the right to either an opening or a closing speech, and will usually opt for the latter so as to have the advantage of the last word. Either party can apply to the magistrates to grant them a second speech. This is a matter solely within the court's discretion, but if one party obtains a second speech, the other must be given one as well. A second prosecution speech will be made before the defence closing speech. In our view should a defendant request a closing speech in a complicated abatement notice case any refusal by the magistrates to grant such a request might amount to a breach of article 6 of the ECHR. The prosecution will be entitled to respond on any matter of law.

STATUTORY DEFENCES

5.90 Where a defendant relies upon a statutory defence the burden of proof rests with the defendant.¹ The standard of proof is the civil one: on the balance of probabilities.² The statutory defences to a contravention of the terms of an abatement notice are contained at section 80(7) and (9) of the EPA 1990.

1   See eg *O'Brien v Hertsmere Borough Council* (1998) 76 P & CR 441 and MCA 1980, s 101.
2   *R v Carr-Briant* [1943] KB 607.

5.91 Article 6.2 of the ECHR provides that:

'Everyone charged with a criminal offence shall be presumed innocent until proven guilty.'

5.92 Article 6.2 may be used to call into question provisions that place part of the burden of proof or disproof on the defence. Each provision must be examined in its context. The issue of presumptions has been addressed by the ECtHR in *Salabiaku v France*:¹

'Presumptions of fact and law operate in every legal system. Clearly the Convention does not prohibit such presumptions in principle. It does however require the Contracting States to remain within certain limits in this respect as regards criminal law ... Article 6(2) does not therefore regard presumptions of fact or law provided for in the criminal law with indifference. It requires States to confine them within reasonable limits 'which take into account the importance of what is at stake and maintain the rights of the defence.'

1   (1988) 13 EHRR 379 at para [28].

5.93 In *R v DPP, ex p Kebiline*,¹ Lord Hope analysed the caselaw of the ECtHR and concluded:

'The cases show, although article 6(2) is in absolute terms, it is not regarded as imposing an absolute prohibition on reverse onus clauses, whether they be

5.93 *Criminal proceedings under EPA 1990, section 80*

evidential (presumption of fact) or persuasive (presumption of law). In each case the question will be whether the presumption is within reasonable limits'[2]

1   [1999] 3 WLR 972.
2   [1997] 3 WLR 972 at 997.

5.94 In our view article 6 ECHR is not infringed by the imposition on the defence of the burden of proof to balance of probabilities test in respect of the statutory defences contained at section 80(7) and (9). It seems reasonable, for example, where a defendant has been found to be responsible for creating something which society finds unacceptable that he be required to show that he has employed the best practicable means. Similarly it is reasonable to expect a defendant who is creating a nuisance to be able to show that that he in possession of a relevant consent issued under CoPA 1974.

Best practicable means

5.95 Section 80(7) of the EPA 1990, subject to section 80(8) requires the defence to prove that 'best practicable means [bpm] were used to prevent, or to counteract the effects of, the nuisance.' The defence is not available in respect of:[1]

- nuisances comprised of fumes or gases emitted from premises
- smoke nuisance unless the smoke is emitted from a chimney
- nuisances comprising premises, dust, steam, smell or effluvia, accumulations and deposits, animals, insects or noise except where the nuisance arises on industrial, trade or business premises
- nuisance comprising artificial light emitted from premises unless it is either (a) emitted from industrial, trade or business premises or (b) by lights used for the purposes of illuminating an outdoor 'relevant sports facility'[2]
- other matters declared by other Acts to be statutory nuisances.

1   See s 80(8) of the EPA 1990, which must be read together with the list of statutory nuisances under s 79(1) of the EPA 1990. Does the bpm defence apply to a breach of a requirement contained in a notice to carry out works? The wording of EPA 1990, s 80(7) makes bpm available where 'best practicable means were used to prevent, or to counteract the effects of the nuisance.' It does not say, for example, that 'best practicable means were used in order to comply with the requirements of the abatement notice.' However, in our view, on the wording of the section this defence is also probably not available where the offence charged relates simply to a failure to carry out works required in an abatement nuisance.
2   For the meaning of 'relevant sports facility', see ss 80(8A)–(8C) of the EPA 1990.

5.96 What constitutes 'best practicable means' (bpm)? Judicial authority is limited. Old authorities[1] must be treated with caution in the light of the full definition employed in section 79(9) of the EPA 1990, but may be encountered. For a fuller consideration on the meaning of bpm see paras **1.83–1.94** and **4.59–4.68**. The following old authorities must be read against the statutory definition now contained in the EPA 1990:

- Those means that are best available to secure the end in view, not merely those ordinarily accepted in the trade in question (*Scholefield v Schunck*[2]).
- But, in *National Smokeless Fuels v Perriman*,[3] an industrial tribunal case, on a similar wording under the Alkali, &c, Works Regulations Act 1906 and the Health and Safety at Work etc Act 1974, it was indicated that not only technical factors should be taken into account in deciding whether bpm had been used, but also social and economic factors such as working agreements made with trades unions, and the costs, excessive or otherwise, of introducing abatement technology.

- In *Saddleworth UDC v Aggregates and Sand Ltd*[4] it was held that mere lack of finance on the part of the party served would not appear to be relevant to bpm. It has also been held that the increased expenditure or the resulting unprofitability of an activity would not amount to bpm (*Wivenhoe Port Ltd v Colchester Borough Council*[5]). It should be noted that *Wivenhoe Port Ltd v Colchester Borough Council* being simply a direction to a jury at a Crown Court is not a binding precedent. Both decisions in any event must be read with caution. It is probably right that mere lack of funds on the part of the defendant cannot establish bpm. If the works required could be achieved but only by using technology of a disproportionate cost it may be considered that it is not something that could be regarded as a 'practicable' means of complying with the notice.

1   See also *Manley v New Forest DC* [2007] EWHC 3188 (Admin) (DC) at [23], where reference to *Saddleworth UDC v Aggregates and Sand Ltd* (1970) 114 Sol Jo 931 was said to be 'of no avail' because it was decided under earlier, different legislation.
2   (1855) 19 JP 84.
3   (1987) 1 Environmental Law No 2.
4   (1970) 114 Sol Jo 931, but see fn 1.
5   [1985] JPL 175. This case is often misrecorded as a decision of the High Court upheld on appeal by the Court of Appeal at [1985] JPL 396. The case to which we refer was a decision of the Crown Court. The report at [1985] JPL 396 records a decision of the Court of Appeal involving the same parties but a different case!

Other statutory defences

5.97 Other statutory defences are provided at section 80(9) of the EPA 1990 in respect of certain noise nuisance committed when various notices or consents covered the premises issued pursuant to the Control of Pollution Act 1974 (CoPA 1974). It shall be a defence to proof:

(1) that the alleged offence was covered by a notice served under section 60 or a consent given under sections 61 or 65 of the CoPA 1974. These notices relate to construction sites etc (section 80(9)(a) of the EPA 1990) or

(2) where the alleged offence was committed at a time when the premises were subject to a notice under section 66 of the CoPA 1974 (a so-called 'noise reduction notice'), that the level of noise emitted form the premises at the time was not in contravention of the noise reduction notice (section 80(9)(b) of the EPA 1990) or

(3) where the alleged offence was committed at a time when the premises were not subject to a notice under section 66 of the CoPA 1974 and when a level fixed under section 67 of that Act (new buildings liable to abatement order) applied to the premises, that the level of noise emitted from the premises did not exceed that level (section 80 9(c) of the EPA 1990).

The defences set out at (2) and (3) above apply whether or not the notice in question is subject to an appeal at the date the offence was alleged to have been committed.

Challenging the validity of an abatement notice

5.98 Although there is a right of appeal against the issue of an abatement notice, there is no preclusive provision in the EPA 1990 restricting the forum in which challenges may be made. Superficially it might appear, therefore, that a defendant could challenge the validity of a notice or a particular requirement as part of a defence to a prosecution for contravention of that notice. In fact, the court have held the scope of such challenges to be quite limited. In Scotland, in *Stagecoach Ltd v McPhail*,[1] a noise nuisance case under the CoPA 1974, the

5.98 *Criminal proceedings under EPA 1990, section 80*

High Court of Justiciary held that failure to appeal against the notice deprived the accused of the right to challenge its terms at any subsequent trial. In *A Lambert Flat Management Ltd v Lomas*[2] Ackner LJ stated that:

'... can the respondent urge, as a reasonable excuse for failing to comply with the notice, that the same was invalid for one or more of the reasons provided by the regulations as permissible grounds of appeal? I am assuming ... that there was no special reason such as illness, non-receipt of the notice or other potential excuse for not entering an appeal.

The answer to my mind is clearly in the negative ... section 58(4) [of the 1974 Act] was not designed ... to give the recipient of the notice the choice of forum in which to mount his attack on the notice. It was designed to provide a defence to a criminal charge where he had some reasonable excuse, such as some special difficulty in relation to compliance with the notice. It does not provide an opportunity and justification of the notice where the defendant has not availed himself of his statutory opportunity to do this by way of appeal.'

1   1988 SCCR 289.
2   [1981] 1 WLR 898.

5.99 *Lambert* represents the general position. However, in *Sterling Homes (Midlands) Ltd v Birmingham City Council*[1] the court recognised that a notice could be challenged in criminal proceedings where its terms were imprecise that it was incapable of founding the basis for a criminal charge. Having cited the above passage (para **5.98**) from *Lambert Flat Management Ltd v Lomas*[2] McCullough J stated that he did not think that Ackner LJ's remarks could have been addressed to the situation present in *Sterling Homes*. He said:

'The point we have to consider is more fundamental. An allegation in an abatement notice that the person served is responsible for a nuisance and a requirement in that notice that he remedy the nuisance by carrying out *specified* works or by taking other *specified* steps are effective until successfully appealed against. A requirement to carry out *unspecified* works or to take other *unspecified* steps imposes on the recipient of the notice no obligation. On the point presently under consideration, the question (unlike that in *A Lambert Flat Management Ltd v Lomas*) is not whether Sterling had reasonable excuse for not complying with the 'requirements'; it is whether there were any 'requirements'; ...' [emphasis in the original]

1   [1996] Env LR 121.
2   [1981] 1 WLR 898.

5.100 In our view the approach adopted by *Sterling Homes* accords with the obligation under article 7(1) of the ECHR. Article 7(1) prohibits the retrospective application of criminal offences so as to penalise conduct that was not criminal at the time the relevant act or omission occurred.[1] Article 7 requires the criminal law to be sufficiently accessible and precise to enable an individual to know in advance whether his conduct is criminal.[2]

1   The principle is also found in the common law against retrospective criminal sanction (see eg *Waddington v Miah* [1974] 1 WLR 683 at 694 per Lord Reid).
2   See eg *Handyside v United Kingdom* (1974) 17 YB 228 at 290 and *Kokkinakis v Greece* (1993) 17 EHRR 397 at para 52.

5.101 Accordingly, properly understood the *Sterling Homes* case[1] is authority for the proposition that a defendant may question the validity of the notice as a defence to criminal proceedings on the basis that it is insufficiently precise to form the basis of a criminal conviction. *Sterling Homes* does not support the view that the defendant may simply argue any of the possible grounds of appeal provided under the Statutory Nuisance (Appeals) Regulations 1995.[2]

1   *Sterling Homes (Midlands) Ltd v Birmingham City Council* [1996] Env LR 121.
2   SI 1995/2644.

5.102 A notice that does not specify or expressly require steps to be carried out but merely requires the abatement of the nuisance will usually comply with article 7 ECHR since the test for whether a nuisance exists or not is sufficiently clear.[1]

1   *Godfrey v Conwy County Borough Council* [2001] Env LR 38 674.

CONVICTION AND SENTENCING

5.103 The current maximum penalty for breaches of nuisance abatement notices on non-industrial, trade or business premises is £5,000, plus £500 for each day the offence continues after conviction. For nuisances arising on industrial, trade or business premises, the maximum penalty is £20,000[1] but there is no provision for further daily fines.

1   £40,000 in Scotland: see para **5.20**, n 1.

5.104 Where the defendant has pleaded not guilty the court will have heard the relevant facts relating to the offence. Where the defendant has pleaded guilty, on the other hand, it is the duty of the advocate acting for the prosecution to summarise the facts of the offence. This includes the nature and gravity of the offence. The reaction of the defendant is also relevant. If he was cooperative, the prosecution should say so. At the sentencing stage the prosecution should adopt a neutral attitude towards the case. They should not suggest a particular sentence, nor advocate a severe sentence. However, the prosecution should:

- where appropriate apply for compensation, confiscation or forfeiture, backing up the application with evidence and argument if necessary
- the prosecution should also draw attention to any guideline cases[1] (as to examples of which see further below). It should assist the court by drawing attention to any limits on the court's sentencing powers, so that no unlawful sentence is passed. This duty applies also to defence counsel.[2] This will be especially important for the court in statutory nuisance cases where they will not be so readily familiar with the appropriate sentencing principles.

1   *R v Panayiotou* (1989) 11 Cr App Rep (S) 535.
2   *R v Komsta* (1990) 12 Cr App Rep (S) 63.

5.105 Evidence that may not be admissible in proving conviction may be relevant for sentencing. It is important that the defendant's representative establishes with the prosecution exactly what the prosecution intend to say. It may be that there is a 'substantial conflict between the two sides' involving a 'sharp divergence on questions of fact'. Where that is so, the court must hear submissions on the point and decide either

- to accept the defence account 'as far as that is possible' or
- give both parties the opportunity to call evidence about the disputed matters and then decide what happened.

5.106 *Criminal proceedings under EPA 1990, section 80*

5.106 Where dispute exists, the court cannot come down in favour of the prosecution version of events without having heard evidence. Where evidence is heard a so-called *Newton* hearing takes place.[1] The procedure is discussed below.[2]

1   *R v Newton* (1982) 77 Cr App Rep 13.
2   See para **5.115**.

5.107 There is no direct guidance on the levels of fines to be imposed. However a number of principles of sentencing can be gleaned from guidance given by the courts in cases involving regulatory offences. In the statutory nuisance case of *R (London Borough of Islington) v Inner London Crown Court* [1] the Divisional Court cited a number of factors that were relevant to sentencing, including

> '... the degree of culpability involved in the commission of the offence, the damage which was done, whether there was any previous record, the need to strike a balance between a fitting expression of censure and the counterproductive effect of imposing too great a financial penalty, the defendants' attitude and performance after the events, including [any] plea of guilty, and, in an appropriate case, the duty of a court to determine what the penalty for one incident should be rather than to tot up the various manifestations of the incident.'

1   [2003] EWHC 2500 (Admin), [2004] Env LR 20 at [21], following the guidance given by the Criminal Court of Appeal in *R v Yorkshire Water Services* [2001] EWCA Crim 2635, [2002] 2 Cr App R 13 (a water pollution case). These factors should not be taken as an exhaustive list but merely guidance of the kind of factors that can be relevant in any given case.

5.108 The court will have to take a view on the nature and degree of the breach. If the defendant has simply been prosecuted for failing to comply with a requirement as to the steps or works of the notice it may be relevant whether or not a nuisance occurred. If there has not already been a finding relating to the existence or recurrence of the nuisance then in the absence of an agreement between the parties it may be necessary to carry out a so-called *Newton* hearing[1] (as to which see paragraph **5.115** below).

1   *R v Newton* (1982) 77 Cr App Rep 13.

5.109 As referred to above, the defendant's state of mind will be relevant to sentencing. So that where he '... was warned and advised of the dangers, chose to ignore that advice, chosen incompetent builder and was generally happy to ride roughshod over the regulations. Those are all matters relevant to sentence'.[1] Culpability will be an important factor. In other words was the offence committed through lack of care, or with disregard for the need to comply with the requirements of the notice. To that end it appears that the court will also take notice of the status and occupation of the defendant. In *R v Duckworth*[2] a case involving unlawful demolition of part of a listed building case, the defendant was a chartered surveyor with relevant experience. That was regarded as an aggravating factor.

1   *R v Sandhu* [1997] JPL 853 in respect of an offence committed under the Planning (Listed Buildings and Conservation Areas) Act 1990 but in our view equally applicable to statutory nuisance.
2   (1995) 16 Cr App Rep (S) 529.

5.110 The degree of any financial gain that the defendant has attempted to achieve will also be relevant. It is a general principle of sentencing that a person should not profit from crime. If someone has decided to save money and not pay for the relevant works to comply with the notice the cost of those works are relevant to the level of fine to be imposed.[1] Similarly, if someone has made a profit, for example, by operating a late nightclub in breach of the terms of the nuisance or operated outside of the hours restricted by the terms of a notice in order to meet a contract deadline. The financial gain made by the defendant should be taken into account when sentencing.[2]

1   See by way of analogy *R v Palmer* (1989) 11 Cr App Rep (S) 407, a case where the accused had unlawfully felled a tree protected by a Tree Preservation Order in order to avoid having to install a root barrier between the tree and his house. The court took as its starting point the cost of the works that were no longer necessary following the unlawful felling. Of course, in the case of statutory nuisance the works are likely to be remain required in order to abate the nuisance even following a conviction, so that it may not bee appropriate to take into account the full amount.
2   See eg *R v Jo Sims Ltd* [1993] Env LR 323, 14 Cr App Rep (S) 213.

5.111 The financial means of the defendant are also relevant to sentencing,[1] as are any relevant previous convictions. As to the latter it is often very difficulty for local authorities to find evidence of previous convictions. Regulatory planning and environmental offences which are likely to be relevant to sentencing for breach of statutory nuisance abatement notice are usually prosecuted by local authorities or other agencies such as the Environmental Agency. Accordingly, they do not appear on the Crown Prosecution's central database.[2] Also relevant will be whether the defendant has pleaded guilty and at what stage in the proceedings the plea was entered.

1   There is a statutory obligation under Criminal Justice Act 1991, s 18(2), (3) for the court to have regard to the financial circumstances of the defendant. See also *R v Browing* [1996] 1 PLR 61, CA.
2   Up to date information on recent fines imposed for breaches of abatement notices appears from time to time in the ENDS reports.

5.112 Accordingly, whilst it is helpful to look at fines imposed by magistrates' courts for this offence it is evident that caution must be applied and that they should not been seen as binding precedent. The level of the fine will depend on a number of factors not simply the particular breach that may have been committed and the ability of the defendant to pay.

5.113 It should be noted that, if after convicting an accused, the magistrates have second thoughts about the correctness of their decision, they may direct that different justices rehear the case.[1] They may themselves reconsider a sentence where it is in the interest of justice for them so to do.[2] The power is not available if the Crown Court or High Court has determined an appeal.

1   MCA 1980, s 142(2).
2   MCA 1980, s 142(1).

Offences by companies

5.114 Many offences will be committed by companies. Under section 157 of the EPA 1990 it is possible to prosecute not only the company concerned but also any officer of the company who consented to or connived in the commission of the offence, or whose neglect contributed to it. This may help to ensure non-recurrence, see, for example, *R v Atath Construction Ltd; R v Brightman*[1] in which a development company was fined £500 for an offence relating to the unauthorised felling of a tree in a conservation area, and Mr Brightman (the managing director of the company) was personally fined a further £500 – and each had to pay £1000 towards the costs of the prosecution. For a prosecution to succeed against an officer of the company, however, it will be necessary to show that the officer concerned was a decision-maker within the company with the power and responsibility to decide corporate policy and strategy.[2] The prosecution must also be careful to ensure that it can produce the relevant admissible documentation to show that the person in question is a director or officer of the company.

1 [1991] 1 PLR 25.
2 *Woodhouse v Walsall Metropolitan Borough Council* [1993] Env LR 30.

Procedure for *Newton* style hearings

5.115 Where a *Newton*[1] style hearing is required witnesses are called and cross-examined just as at full trial to establish the various matters relevant to sentencing, such a the defendant's state of knowledge, the degree of financial gain realised, the financial means of the defendant and the extent of the seriousness of the breach. The proper procedure to be followed in such cases has been considered in the note on *R v Hill*.[2] A similar procedure should be followed where a conviction follows a non-guilty plea and where there is still relevant evidence to be canvassed as to the mental state of the defendant, or some other similar issue.[3]

1 See *R v Newton* (1982) 77 Cr App Rep 13.
2 [1997] Crim LR 459.
3 See *R v Robinson* (1968) 53 Cr App Rep 314 and *R v Finch* (1992) 14 Cr App Rep (S) 226.

CHALLENGES TO DECISIONS BY THE MAGISTRATES' COURT

5.116 A decision by a magistrates' court can be challenged[1] in the following ways, depending on the circumstances:

- appeal to the Crown Court or
- appeal to the Divisional Court by way of case stated by the magistrates for the Divisional Court's opinion or
- application to the Divisional Court for judicial review of the magistrates' decision and the issue of an appropriate order.

1 Only an overview of the relevant procedure is given here. Readers are referred to one of the many specialist texts on criminal procedure for a more extensive treatment of the appeals procedure.

Crown Court

5.117 Appeal to the Crown Court is open only to a person convicted. The other two procedures are open to a person aggrieved by a magistrates' court decision, which includes both the accused and the prosecutor.

5.118 Appeals to the Crown Court from a magistrates' court are governed by the MCA 1980, sections 108 to 110 and rule 63 of the Criminal Procedure Rules 2005.[1] A person convicted by a magistrates' court following a guilty plea is *generally*[2] prohibited from appealing the conviction, and may only appeal against his sentence.[3] An appeal to the Crown Court against a sentence may be brought in respect of 'any order made on conviction by a magistrates' court'[4] other than ones to pay the costs of the prosecution.

Challenges to decisions by the magistrates' court 5.123

1 SI 2005/384.
2 There are circumstances where the plea may be regarded as not being a genuine admission of guilt, see eg, *R v Durham Quarter Sessions, ex p Virgo* [1952] 2 QB 1; *R v Blandford Justices, ex p G* [1967] 1 QB 82; or made under duress, see eg, *R v Huntingdon Crown Court, ex p Jordan* [1981] QB 857.
3 MCA 1980, s 108(1).
4 MCA 1980, s 108(3).

5.119 Notice of appeal must be given in writing to a court officer of the relevant magistrates' court and to any other party to the appeal not later that 21 days after the day on which the decision appealed against is given.[1] The Crown Court has the power to extend time for appealing either before or after the 21 day period expires.[2] The notice of appeal must state the grounds of appeal.[3]

1 Criminal Procedure Rules 2005, r 63.2(2) and (3).
2 Criminal Procedure Rules 2005, r 63.2(5).
3 Criminal Procedure Rules 2005, r 63.2(4).

5.120 The appeal is before a judge and two magistrates. The powers of the Crown Court are set out at section 48 of the Supreme Court Act 1981 (as amended). The Crown Court may confirm, reverse or vary any part of the decision appealed against. It may remit the matter to the magistrates with its opinion, or make such other order as it considers just. The Crown Court has a power to increase the sentence imposed by the magistrates' court but the sentence cannot exceed that which the magistrates could have passed.[1]

1 Supreme Court Act 1981, s 48(4).

5.121 In the case of appeals against convictions for breaches of abatement notices the procedure will normally take the form of rehearing. In other words the prosecution will have to prove its case again from scratch.

Appeal by way of case stated and application for judicial review

5.122 Appeals by way of case stated from the magistrates' court[1] are open to anyone who was a party to the proceedings in respect of a decision that is wrong in law or in excess of jurisdiction.[2] Such appeals are heard by the Divisional Court. An application for the magistrates to state a case must be made within 21 days of the acquittal or conviction, or if the magistrates convicted an accused and adjourned before sentencing him within 21 days of sentence.[3] The application must be in writing and set out the question of law or jurisdiction for determination of the Divisional Court.[4] The Divisional Court has the power not only to overturn the decision of the magistrates' court but remit the case to the magistrates with a direction, for example, a direction to convict.

1 See generally, Criminal Procedure Rules 2005, r 64.1–64.6.
2 MCA 1980, s 111(1).
3 MCA 1980, s 111(2). There is no power for the court to extend the 21-day period (*Michael v Gowland* [1977] 1 WLR 296). As to the possible impact of HRA 1998 on this restriction, see paras **4.17–4.22**.
4 Criminal Procedure Rules 2005, r 64.1

5.123 Judicial review is also concerned primarily with errors of law. Judicial review proceedings are heard by the High Court. An application for judicial review may be more appropriate where, for example, the issue relates to a breach of natural justice. The remedies available under judicial review are more

5.123 *Criminal proceedings under EPA 1990, section 80*

extensive than those available for case stated. The High Court may in judicial review order that the magistrates' decision be quashed, may require the magistrates' to do something, or prohibit them from doing something.

5.124 It is not necessary to be a *party* to the proceeding to have sufficient locus standi to challenge a decision by the magistrates' court. It is possible that a neighbour who has suffered as a result of an alleged breach of an abatement notice could seek judicial review of a decision by the magistrates' court acquitting a defendant where the decision has been made following an error of law. However, the authors are unaware of anyone having done this. Article 8 of the ECHR would mean that it would be difficult to refuse permission on the grounds of lack of standing to a third party who could show their home or life was potentially affected.

5.125 Where there is a choice between case stated and judicial review the case stated procedure is usually to be preferred because it allows the magistrates' court to state the case without the need for the chairman of the bench to swear a witness statement.

CHALLENGES TO DECISIONS BY THE CROWN COURT

5.126 A decision by the Crown Court, like that of the magistrates' court, may be challenged, depending on the circumstances, by:

- appeal to the Divisional Court by way of case stated by the Crown Court for the Divisional Court's opinion or
- application to the Divisional Court for judicial review of the Crown Court's decision and the issue of an appropriate order.

5.127 Appeal by way of case stated may be used to question the Crown Court's decisions in matters not relating to trial on indictment.[1] It is plain, therefore, that the allowing or dismissal of an appeal from a magistrates' court summary conviction under section 80(4) of the EPA 1990 is a decision totally unconnected with trial on indictment. Therefore the unsuccessful party in the Crown Court[2] may further appeal by case stated to the Divisional Court. Just as with appeals by way of case stated from the magistrates' court, a Crown Court decision may only be questioned on the ground that it was wrong in law or in excess of jurisdiction.

1 Supreme Court Act 1981, s 28.
2 Whether it be the prosecution who have had a summary conviction overturned or the defence who have had the same result before the Crown Court as they had in the magistrates' court.

5.128 An application to the Crown Court to state a case should be made to the appropriate officer of the court within 21 days of the decision challenged being made.[1] The Criminal Procedure Rules make provision for the extension of this and other time limits for appeals by way of case stated, before or after expiry of the relevant period.[2] In this respect, the position differs from appeals from the magistrates' court, where the time limit for making the initial application to the Magistrates' court is a statutory one, and cannot be extended (see para **5.122** n 3).

1 Criminal Procedure Rules 2005, r 64.7(1). The procedure for an application for extension of time is set out in *DPP v Coleman* [1998] 2 Cr App R 7.
2 Criminal Procedure Rules 2005, r 64.7(14).

5.129 The main difference between the procedure for magistrates stating a case and the procedure for the Crown Court doing so is that the appellant from the Crown Court has the responsibility for drawing up an initial draft case which is put before the judge who presided at the proceedings in which the disputed decision was made.[1]

1   Criminal Procedure Rules 2005, r 64.7(8).

5.130 Judicial review of decisions of the Crown Court is available in the same way as for decisions of the magistrates' court.[1] In general, the purpose of judicial review is to prevent magistrates' courts and the Crown Court exceeding their jurisdiction; to compel them to exercise the jurisdiction which is rightfully theirs, and to control the way they exercise that jurisdiction in the sense of correcting fundamental irregularities in their procedures. Errors of law made by magistrates' courts or the Crown Court when exercising their proper jurisdiction in the proper manner should be questioned by case stated, not by an application for judicial review.

1   Judicial review is not available to challenge a decision of the Crown Court when it is exercising its jurisdiction in matters relating to trial on indictment. This restriction does not apply to the statutory nuisance regime where the offences are summary only.

Chapter 6

Statutory Nuisance Proceedings Brought by an Individual

INTRODUCTION

6.01 Section 82 of the Environmental Protection Act 1990 (EPA 1990) gives to any person aggrieved by the existence of a statutory nuisance a right to make a complaint direct to the magistrates' court. The magistrates may make an order requiring abatement of the nuisance or prohibiting its recurrence; they may also impose a fine.

6.02 The procedure is a useful tool to the private person, particularly in cases where the local authority has failed to take action or where the authority itself is responsible for the nuisance. It is of particular significance to tenants suffering from poor housing conditions. As the Divisional Court observed:

> 'This aspect of the 1990 Act is intended to provide ordinary people, numbered amongst whom are those that are disadvantaged (whether by reason of their health or financial circumstances or otherwise), with a speedy and effective remedy for circumstances which will often have an adverse effect (or a potentially adverse effect) upon their health and/ or the health of their children.'[1]

This chapter examines the procedure in detail.

1   *Hall v Kingston upon Hull City Council* [1999] 2 All ER 609 at 624d–f per Mitchell J. See also Sedley LJ in *Quigley v Liverpool Housing Trust* [1999] EGCS 94), DC: 'These are statutory provisions which have stood the test of time, and which serve as a very valuable protection both against bad housing management and for the protection of public health among, in general, the very poorest people in this country.' By way of contrast, see the view of local housing authorities and housing associations, researched and documented in *The Use of section 82 of the Environmental Protection Act 1990 Against Local Authorities and Housing Associations* (HMSO, 1996), para 3 of which reads: 'Action under section 82 of the 1990 Act was seen as a drain on limited financial resources, interfering with planned repairs and improvement programmes and ... diverting staff from other duties ...'

WHO CAN BRING PROCEEDINGS UNDER SECTION 82?

6.03 Any person[1] who is 'aggrieved' by the existence of a statutory nuisance[2] can bring proceedings under section 82 of the EPA 1990 by complaining about the nuisance directly to the magistrates' court. The requirement that the person starting proceedings be a person aggrieved acts as a filter to prevent vexatious or wholly unmeritorious claims. Cases decided in other contexts give the term 'person aggrieved' a wide meaning, excluding mere busy bodies who have no particular concern with the matter complained of, but including anyone whose interests are prejudicially affected.[3] Being a person aggrieved does not require interference with a private law right held by that person.[4]

6.03 *Statutory nuisance proceedings brought by an individual*

1   'Person' includes a body of persons incorporate or unincorporate, unless contrary intention is shown: Interpretation Act 1978, s 1 and Sch 5. Arguably therefore, a duly formed company could be a 'person aggrieved' for the purposes of EPA 1990, s 82. In *R v Highbury Corner Magistrates' Court, ex parte Edwards* [1994] Env LR 215 Marjorie Edwards lived in council property. The magistrates' Chief Clerk refused to issue her a statutory nuisance summons against the council under the Environmental Protection Act 1990 s 82(1)) because of duplication with her civil proceedings against the council for breach of covenants. She applied for judicial review of the refusal. The court held that contrary to the Clerk's conclusion, the criminal proceedings were potentially wider in effect than the civil proceedings.
2   For the meaning of statutory nuisance, see EPA 1990, s 79(1) and Chapter 1.
3   *A-G of Gambia v N'Jie* [1961] AC 617 at 634.
4   Eg *Maurice v London County Council* [1964] 2 QB 362 at 377–378; *Turner v Secretary of State for the Environment* (1973) 28 P & CR 123 at 137–138.

6.04 A similar approach is taken in statutory nuisance cases. Hence a person whose health is prejudiced by the state of premises in which they are living would be a person aggrieved[1], as would someone whose reasonable enjoyment of their property is adversely affected.[2] But where a person complained of a nuisance affecting the block of flats in which he lived but not actually his own flat, he was held not to be a person aggrieved.[3] It may be otherwise where the proceedings are started by an incorporated residents' association (for example, the Heathfield House Residents' Association Ltd) amongst whose members are occupants of flats which are affected by the nuisance. In such a case, the residents' association would have a clear and legitimate concern about the condition of the flats in question, and a purposive approach to the EPA 1990 and section 82 in particular would suggest that a representative body with a legitimate concern in the matter should have standing to bring proceedings under section 82.[4] In each case, the question is simply whether, in the ordinary sense of the word, the person or group of persons are aggrieved by the existence of the alleged statutory nuisance.[5] It is important, therefore, for the person starting proceedings directly in the magistrates' court to show how and why he is adversely affected by the alleged the statutory nuisance.[6]

1   Whether or not the person had a lease or was present as a mere licensee.
2   *Sandwell Metropolitan Borough Council v Bujok* [1990] 3 All ER 385 at 1357F.
3   *Birmingham District Council v McMahon* (1987) 86 LGR 63, 151 JP 709.
4   See by way of analogy the approach taken in judicial review proceedings in *R v Somerset County Council and ARC Southern Ltd, ex p Dixon* [1997] JPL 1030.
5   See, by analogy, *Turner v Secretary of State for the Environment* (1973) 28 P & CR 123 at 139.
6   See paras **6.46–6.47** and **6.55–6.58**.

HOW ARE PROCEEDINGS STARTED?

6.05 There are two important procedural steps before the hearing takes place:

- giving notice of intention to start proceedings
- applying to the magistrates' court for a summons by 'laying an information'.

(i) Giving notice

6.06 Before starting proceedings at the magistrates' court, the person aggrieved must give the proposed defendant(s) notice in writing of his intention to bring the proceedings. This is a statutory requirement under section 82(6) of the EPA 1990. As proceedings may be invalid if proper notice has not been given to the appropriate person(s), it is important that the notice requirements are complied with.

To whom should notice be given?

6.07 *The general rule* The general rule is that notice must be given to the person or persons who are to be the defendant(s) to proceedings under section 82 of the EPA 1990.

6.08 Usually the proceedings are commenced against the 'person responsible' for the statutory nuisance.[1] There are three exceptions to this:

- where the nuisance arises from premises because of any defect of a structural character, the proceedings should be brought against the owner of the premises[2]
- where the person responsible for the nuisance cannot be found, the proceedings should be brought against the owner or occupier of the premises[3]
- where the nuisance alleged is caused by noise emitted from or caused by a vehicle, machinery or equipment in a street[4] and the vehicle, machinery or equipment is unattended, the proceedings should be brought against the person responsible for the vehicle, machinery or equipment.[5]

1 See EPA 1990, s 82(4)(a); for the meaning of 'person responsible' see paras **3.63–3.73**.
2 EPA 1990, s 82(4)(b).
3 EPA 1990, s 82(4)(c).
4 Ie, a nuisance as defined under EPA 1990, s 79(1)(ga).
5 EPA 1990, s 82(4)(d).

6.09 Where more than one person is responsible for the nuisance, the general rule is that the proceedings should be brought against each of those persons, whether or not what any one of them is responsible for would by itself amount to a nuisance.[1] In *Nichols, Albion and Lainson v Powergen Renewables Limited and Wind 23 Prospect Limited* (South Lakeland Magistrates' Court, October 2003) in a complaint against noise from a wind farm proceedings were brought not only against the two companies concerned with operating the turbines but also against the Council, on the basis that they were, together with the companies, 'the persons responsible for the continuance and recurrence of the said statutory nuisance, in that they have repeatedly failed and delayed to take any action against the first and second defendants in respect of the occurrence of the said statutory nuisance, and have thereby caused or materially contributed to its continuance.' However, at a pre-trial hearing District Judge Peter Wallis ruled that the Council was not competent as a defendant and that they should be struck out of the proceedings. In so doing, the judge noted that under section 82(11) the court was empowered to direct the local authority to enforce any nuisance order made, and that were the Council to be a defendant, it would be placed in an impossible position: as counsel for the Council put it, section 82(11) in terms makes the Council the policeman to ensure any order is adhered to, and it is difficult to see how Parliament could have intended that to be done by a guilty party.

1 EPA 1990, s 82(4), (5).

6.10 In the case of a nuisance caused by a vehicle, machinery or equipment in a street where the vehicle, machinery or equipment *is not* left unattended, the proceedings should be started against each of the persons responsible for the nuisance who can be found. Where the nuisance is caused by a vehicle, machinery or equipment in a street where the vehicle, machinery or equipment

6.10 *Statutory nuisance proceedings brought by an individual*

is left unattended, the proceedings should be brought against any person responsible for the vehicle, machinery or equipment.[1]

1   EPA 1990, s 82(5B).

6.11 *Does notice need to be given to every possible defendant under section 82?* Where proceedings could be brought against more than one person, it is not clear whether a failure to give notice to any one of those persons will render invalid proceedings against those to whom notice has been given. The wording of sections 82(4) to 82(5B) of the EPA 1990 suggests that where proceedings can be taken against more that one defendant, then they must be taken against each defendant.[1] On the other hand, the wording of section 82(6) which sets out the requirement to give notice of intention to start proceedings suggests that notice need only be given to the person or person(s) against whom the person aggrieved intends to start proceedings.[2]

1   EPA 1990, s 82(4) provides that proceedings for an order under s 82(2) 'shall be brought' against the person(s) specified. The relevant part of the wording carrying the mandatory auxillary is not qualified by sub-ss (5A) and (5B).
2   EPA 1990, s 82(6): 'Before instituting proceedings ... against any person, the person aggrieved ... shall give *to that person* ... notice ...' (our emphasis).

6.12   In the authors' view, the correct position is probably that notice need only be given to the person against whom it is intended to start proceedings, whether or not there are other persons against whom proceedings could also be started. A defendant who has been properly served with notice of intention to start proceedings cannot be prejudiced by the fact that another person, who is not a party to the proceedings, was not given notice. Furthermore, although it may in some cases be desirable that all of the persons responsible for a nuisance are before the court on the hearing of a complaint made under section 82 of the EPA 1990, there can be no prejudice if the defendants have been given notice. A conviction will result where a particular defendant, who was properly served with notice of the intended proceedings, is proven to be responsible for the nuisance which is shown to exist or be likely recur on the same premises or in the same road at the date of trial. The fact that others may also be responsible does not affect the criminal liability of the particular defendant in question. Finally, such an interpretation complies with the spirit behind section 82. It would be placing an undue and costly burden upon the lay person were he required to find and proceed against each and every person responsible for the nuisance, rather than simply starting proceedings against any one of those persons whom he had found.

6.13   Where the local authority is served with a notice in its capacity as landlord and it considers that there is a nuisance but that the tenant who intends to start proceedings under section 82 of the EPA 1990 is in fact responsible for it, the local authority may consider serving an abatement notice on the tenant under section 80.[1] Similarly, it is arguable that a private individual who is a landlord may be a 'person aggrieved' for the purposes of section 82 and may therefore serve a counter-notice under section 82 on his tenant if he considers that the tenant is in fact responsible for the nuisance. In either case, if the nuisance is not abated, the court can then hear both cases together and decide who is responsible.

1   See also *Warner v Lambeth London Borough Council* (1984) 15 HLR 42, DC, at 52 where Glidewell LJ suggests that a local authority landlord, served with a s 82 notice by a tenant who may himself be the person responsible for the state of the premises, could serve an abatement notice under EPA 1990, s 80 in response.

How are proceedings started? 6.18

6.14 *Need the nuisance exist at the date that the notice is given?* The wording of section 82(6) of the EPA 1990 does not on its face require that the nuisance should in fact exist at the time that the proposed defendant is given notice of intended proceedings. Section 82(6) refers to 'the person aggrieved by the nuisance' giving notice. It does not use the expression 'the person aggrieved *by the existence of* the nuisance'[1] as used under section 82(1).

1 Our emphasis.

6.15 On one view, the requirement of notice serves to allow potential nuisance-makers to re-arrange their affairs so that they have the opportunity to avoid incurring criminal liability from proceedings under section 82 of the EPA 1990. On this view, prospective notice may be given, warning that if the activity giving rise to the nuisance is allowed to exist then proceedings will be commenced against the person responsible.

6.16 Another view is that section 82 of the EPA 1990 only exists to allow a citizen to bring proceedings after the statutory nuisance has come into existence and after the person responsible has had an the opportunity to abate the nuisance given him by the service of notice. In this respect one can contrast the wording of section 82 with that of section 80 which expressly includes a statutory nuisance that is 'likely to occur'. On this view, notice can only properly be given once the statutory nuisance has come into existence. The aggrieved person has an alternative remedy in that he could seek a civil *quia timet* injunction (that is a pre-emptive injunction).

6.17 In the authors' view, the former interpretation of the scheme of the EPA 1990 is probably preferable. Take the case where the restaurant on the ground floor under Mr Smith's first floor residential premises is due to host a world Karioke festival over the course of a week. Mr Smith gives three days' notice that he will bring proceedings under section 82 of the EPA 1990 if the nuisance comes into existence. Interpreted in the context of the Act, it is strongly arguable that the phrase *'aggrieved by the nuisance'* is sufficiently broad to encompass a person aggrieved by the prospect of the nuisance as well as the existence of one.

6.18 Although the position is uncertain, in the authors' view there are a number of reasons why section 82(6) of the EPA 1990 ought to be construed so as to allow prospective notice to be effectively given. First, there is no express requirement under section 82(6) that the nuisance should exist or have existed at that time that notice is given. Secondly, the requirement that a statutory nuisance be shown to exist at the time the information is laid[1] with the magistrates[2] under section 82(1) will prevent any frivolous claims being made. Thirdly, the notice provisions were inserted into the EPA 1990 to avoid the position under the earlier legislation where proceedings could be commenced without the proposed defendant being given any notice. This was objectionable because it denied the proposed defendant any opportunity to abate the nuisance before criminal proceedings were commenced.[3] Allowing prospective notice under section 82(6) would not undermine the proposed defendant's opportunity to avoid criminal proceedings.

1 For the formalities of starting proceedings under EPA 1990, s 82, see paras **6.38–6.53**.
2 See below.
3 See *Sandwell Metropolitan Borough Council v Bujok* [1990] 3 All ER 385.

6.19 *Statutory nuisance proceedings brought by an individual*

6.19 In practice, this issue is unlikely to arise often. The person who will be aggrieved will usually not know about the circumstances giving rise to the nuisance until the nuisance in fact exists.

What period of notice must be given?

6.20 The person aggrieved must usually give not less than 21 days' notice of his intention to start proceedings.[1] The only exception is in respect of noise nuisances,[2] where not less than 3 days' notice must be given.[3]

1   EPA 1990, s 82(7)(b).
2   Ie noise emitted from premises and noise emitted from or caused by any vehicle, machinery or equipment in a street.
3   EPA 1990, s 82(7)(a).

6.21 Notice will become effective on the day upon which it is received or deemed to be received.

6.22 To reckon the period when the notice expires, the day upon which the notice is effective – that is, the day upon which the recipient receives or is deemed to receive the notice – and the day upon which it is intended to start proceedings should be excluded. In other words, 3 or 21 'clear days' notice should be given. So if notice were given on Monday 1st of a month, proceedings could not be started until Friday 5th (in the case of a three-day notice) or Tuesday 23rd (in the case of a 21-day notice).[1] Any calculation of the period should include days which are holidays or weekends.[2]

1   *Thompson v Stimpson* [1961] 1 QB 195 ('not less than four weeks' notice' under the Rent Act 1957 means four clear weeks); also *Re Railway Sleepers Co* (1885) 29 Ch D 204; *McQueen v Jackson* [1903] 2 KB 163.
2   There is no express requirement to leave out of account holidays or weekends. There is no justification to imply such a requirement, which would conflict with the intention of the EPA 1990 to provide a speedy summary procedure for the abatement of nuisances. Why should a person aggrieved by noise from his neighbour's new swimming pool heater installed and switched on on a Friday of a bank holiday weekend and who gives notice straight away still not be able to start proceedings until the following Friday at the earliest? Three days' notice should mean what it says in this context. In the event the approach to anology time limits for bringing proceedings the Divisional Court has assumed that no allowance be made for weekends (see *Rockall v Department for Environment, Food and Rural Affairs* [2007] EWHC 614 (Admin); [2007] 3 All ER 258: (2007) NPC 34: Times, May 11, 2007; [2007] Env LR D16).

The content of the notice

6.23 The EPA 1990 does not prescribe any particular format for a notice. Section 82(6) simply requires that the notice must be in writing and specify the matter complained of, and the courts have expressly avoided an overly formal or legalistic approach to the contents of the notice, mindful that the procedure under section 82 should be accessible to the lay person.[1] In practice, notice is usually given by way of a letter from the person aggrieved or his representative to the person who would be the defendant in any subsequent proceedings under section 82.

1   See in particular *Hall v Kingston upon Hull City Council* [1999] 2 All ER 609 at 624d-f per Mitchell J: 'This aspect of the 1990 Act is intended to provide ordinary people ... with a speedy and effective remedy ... Parliament's intention, in the absence of compelling statutory language, should not in our view be frustrated by introducing into this straight forward and swift statutory remedy any technical obstacle of which the ordinary citizen will almost certainly be unaware.'

How are proceedings started? 6.27

6.24 It is suggested that the notice, to be valid, should contain at least the following:

- the name and address of the person to whom the notice is being given
- the name and address of the person giving the notice[1]
- the address of the premises which are the subject of the complaint, or the location of the accumulation of deposit, animal, vehicle, machinery or equipment as the case may be and
- a straight forward description of the matter complained of.

As a matter of good practice,[2] two further matters should be included:

- a statement that the notice is formal notice under section 82 of the EPA 1990 of intention to start proceedings under that section and
- the date after which proceedings may be started against the person on whom the notice is served.[3]

1   If the notice is sent by that persons legal representative, then the representative's name and address should be given in addition to the name and address of the person making the complaint.
2   Failure to comply with which should not make the notice invalid.
3   Failure to do so should not make the notice defective, provided proceedings are not in fact started until after the relevant period has expired: see the terms of EPA 1990, s 82(6) itself; *East Stafford Borough Council v Fairless* [1999] Env LR 525; and *Pearshouse v Birmingham City Council* [1999] Env LR 536.

6.25 There is no requirement that the notice specify the steps that might be required to abate the nuisance.[1]

1   *East Stafford Borough Council v Fairless* [1999] Env LR 525.

6.26 Nor, it is suggested, need the notice specify the capacity in which the proposed defendant is to be proceeded against, for example, whether as owner or as the person responsible for the alleged nuisance.[1] In *East Staffordshire Borough Council v Fairless*[2] the Divisional Court considered that the capacity of the proposed defendant need not be specified. In the later case of *Pearshouse v Birmingham City Council*[3] a differently constituted Divisional Court considered itself to have adopted an approach 'wholly consistent' with the *East Staffordshire* case. However, Collins J, citing section 82(4) of the EPA 1990, stated[4] that:

> 'It is clearly necessary to specify ... the basis upon which the recipient of the notice is said to be obliged to abate the nuisance.'

1   For the classes of people who may be prosecuted, see above and EPA 1990, s 82(4).
2   [1999] Env LR 525.
3   [1999] Env LR 536.
4   [1999] Env LR 536 at 549.

6.27 Given the court's non-technical approach to the section, the absence of any express requirement in section 82(6) of the EPA 1990 to identify the capacity of the proposed defendant, and the fact that a defendant is likely to know the capacity in which proceedings are brought (and to suffer no prejudice if he is unsure) it is respectfully submitted that the approach in *East Staffordshire*[1] is to be preferred.[2] Collins J's comments in *Pearshouse*[3] appear to be obiter, in any event. However, prudent litigants may wish to specify the capacity of the proposed defendant out of an abundance of caution.

6.27 Statutory nuisance proceedings brought by an individual

1   [1999] Env LR 525.
2   The Divisional Court in *Hewlings v Mclean Homes East Anglia Ltd* [2000] EGCS 100, DC provides further support for a non-technical approach to the service of notice for the purposes of EPA 1990, s 82.
3   [1999] Env LR 536.

6.28 It is important that the notice sufficiently describes the matters at which the complainant is aggrieved. As a general rule, the notice must give such detail of what is complained of as is reasonable in all the circumstances.[1] The description need only be in very broad terms. So in a case where a tenant is giving notice to his landlord:

> 'What is necessary ... is for the tenant (or whoever) to indicate very broadly the nature of the complaint. For example, if the tenant is concerned about dampness in the premises, he need say no more than: 'The premises are damp and that is damaging my health.' Or if there is a leaking roof, reference can be made to that. Nor does it matter ... that the tenant is wrong in identifying particular defects which do not amount to a statutory nuisance and omits (because he is not aware of their significance) defects which in the end do turn out to amount to a statutory nuisance. It is not for him to prejudge the matter. It is for him to draw to the attention of the [proposed defendant] the matter which is really troubling him.'[2]

1   *Pearshouse v Birmingham City Council* [1999] Env LR 536 at 522 per Bingham CJ.
2   *Pearshouse v Birmingham City Council* [1999] Env LR 536 at 550, 551 per Collins J; and see Bingham CJ at 552.

6.29 In determining whether the matters complained of have been made sufficiently clear, the court will look at all the circumstance of the case and any relevant background material rather than confining itself to any one document, such as a letter, which purports to be the notice itself. So where a letter purporting to be a notice under section 82(6) of the EPA 1990 is accompanied by a surveyor's report, both the letter and the report can be examined to determine whether the matter of complaint has been made sufficiently clear.[1] Similarly, where there is ongoing correspondence between the parties before the service of the notice, very little by way of elaboration may be required in the notice.[2]

1   *East Staffordhire Borough Council v Fairless* [1999] Env LR 525 at 534.
2   *Pearshouse v Birmingham City Council* [1999] Env LR 536 at 552.

6.30 However, a notice which purports to describe the matters complained of simply by reference to the definition of a statutory nuisance in the relevant subsection of section 79(1) of the EPA 1990 without more is likely to be defective.[1] So while a notice which states that 'the premises are damp because of leaking windows and the dampness is prejudicial to the health of the occupant and a nuisance' is likely to be sufficient, a notice which alleges simply that 'the premises are in such a state as to be prejudicial to the health of the occupant and a nuisance' would not be.

1   *Pearshouse v Birmingham City Council* [1999] Env LR 536 at 549.

6.31 In the authors' view, the key issue is whether in all the circumstances of the case the notice was sufficient to draw to the recipient's attention the gist of the matter troubling the complainant.

How are proceedings started? **6.37**

6.32 An example of a written notice for the purposes of section 82(6) of the EPA 1990 is found in Appendix A.

How to give notice under section 82(6)

6.33 Section 160 of the EPA 1990 sets out provisions for serving or giving notices generally, including notices under section 82(6). Readers are referred to Chapter 3[1] for an analysis of these provisions.

1   See paras **3.76–3.80**.

6.34 It is important to realise that section 160 of the EPA 1990 is permissive in its terms rather than compulsory, and the Divisional Court has shown that in the context of proceedings under section 82, it is not prepared to take a strict approach to compliance with section 160 of the Act.[1] However, in the authors' view, the provisions of section 160 provide a mechanism for giving notice which should be followed wherever possible when giving notice under section 82(6).

1   See *Hewlings v Mclean Homes East Anglia Ltd* [2001] 2 All ER 281, [2000] EGCS 100, DC where the Divisional Court held that whilst EPA 1990, s 160 provided a means for service of notice which was sufficient to ensure adequate service under the Act, compliance with its requirements was optional and service would not necessarily be invalid were s 160 had not strictly been complied with. The Divisional Court clearly indicated that in the context of a citizen's action under s 82, a strict approach to the service of notice of intention to start proceedings would not be adopted by the court.

Position where the relevant defendant cannot be found

6.35 Section 82 of the EPA 1990 expressly contemplates proceedings where the relevant defendant cannot be found. In these circumstances, the complainant will have to seek an order from the court against the local authority for the area. Such an order may be made pursuant to the court's discretion under section 82(13) to make any order against the local authority which it could have made against the relevant defendant had that defendant been found.

6.36 There is no express statutory requirement to give the local authority notice of intention to start proceedings in these circumstances. In the authors' view, there are two reasons why such notice is not required by the EPA 1990. First, section 82(6) only requires notice to be given to the person against whom the proceedings under section 82(2) are to be started. Indeed, the express requirement in section 82(13) that the local authority be heard before an order is made against it contemplates that it may not in fact be a party to the proceedings from the outset. Secondly, where the defendant cannot be found the proceedings are for a discretionary order made pursuant to the court's powers under section 82(13). They are not proceedings for a mandatory order under section 82(2). As section 82(6) only requires notice to be given where the proceedings are instituted for an order under section 82(2), no notice need be given where the order sought would be made under section 82(13).

6.37 However, the authors advise that, for reasons of courtesy, fairness and prudence notice should be given to the local authority in these circumstances. Indeed, the magistrates' court may well refuse to make an order against the local authority where no notice of the proceedings has been given.

6.38 *Statutory nuisance proceedings brought by an individual*

Applying to the magistrates' court for a summons

Laying an information

6.38 The language used in section 82(1) of the EPA 1990 is confusing. That provision refers to the person aggrieved starting proceedings by making a complaint. The making of a complaint has a technical meaning in the context of magistrates' court procedure, because the lodging of a formal document called 'a complaint' is the first step in applying to the magistrates' court in *civil* proceedings.

6.39 In *criminal* proceedings, a summons is applied for by 'laying an information.' The confusion thus arises because proceedings under section 82 of the EPA 1990 are criminal in nature, and are, therefore, commenced by laying an information with the magistrates,[1] even though section 82(1) itself refers to the person aggrieved making 'a complaint.'[2] The information may be laid by the person aggrieved himself or by his legal representative.

1 See *Botross v London Borough of Hammersmith and Fulham* [1995] Env LR 217, (1994) 27 HLR 179; *East Staffordshire Borough Council v Fairless* [1999] Env LR 525 at 527. Starting proceedings by laying an information is dealt with in some detail in Chapter 5, paras **5.26–5.38**.
2 Reference to making 'a complaint' appears to be a legislative oversight induced by a late amendment to the Environment Bill: see 522 HL Official Report (5th series) cols. 1279–1280, which was considered by the court in the *Bottross* case ([1995] Env LR 217).

6.40 There is no requirement that an information be laid in writing or made on oath,[1] though it is usual practice for the information to be laid in written form.[2]

1 Magistrates' Court Rules 1981, SI 1981/552, r 4.
2 See further Chapter 5.

6.41 The question arises as to whether proceedings erroneously started by way of a formal complaint rather than by laying an information, can nevertheless proceed as though they had been properly commenced by way of a complaint. Although the written forms of the two documents are almost identical,[1] and in each case the receipt of the information or complaint is followed by the issuing of a summons by the magistrates' court clerk, it appears that commencing proceedings under section 82 of the EPA 1990 by way of a formal complaint rather than the laying of an information will render the proceedings defective from the outset.[2] Thus, where proceedings are commenced by way of a formal complaint rather than the laying of an information, this will provide a defence to the proceedings.[3]

In *Nichols, Albion and Lainson v Powergen Renewables Limited and Wind 23 Prospect Limited* South Lakeland Magistrates' Court, 20 January 2004) proceedings had been commenced by way of a document describing itself as a complaint, rather than an information. It was submitted by the companies (supported by the Council) that the proceedings should therefore have been commenced by laying an information, whereas the document sent to the court was clearly a complaint. It referred to 'the complaint' and 'the matter of complaint' and it described the parties as complainants and defendants, not informants and accused. It was submitted that consequence was that the magistrates' court had no jurisdiction to try the criminal proceedings, since an information had not been laid; this was a fundamental defect rendering subsequent proceedings a nullity.

At a preliminary hearing on 23 October 2003 the District Judge held that the essence of an information was that it provided the accused with sufficient information to know the nature of the alleged offence he had to meet. The document sent to the court by the residents in this case amply satisfied that requirement, and accordingly could properly be regarded as by nature an information, even though it described itself as a complaint. Since section 82 of the 1990 Act is intended to provide a speedy and accessible remedy to members of the public aggrieved by nuisances, technical issues (on which the legislation is unhelpfully and misleadingly drafted) ought not to be allowed to defeat the merits of the claim in circumstances where the defendants had not been prejudiced. As a decision of the magistrates' court, this ruling is not a binding authority. We are not persuaded that the approach of the learned District Judge is correct.

1   Cf Form 1 (information) and Form 98 (complaint): Magistrates' Courts (Forms) Rules 1981, SI 1981/553, Sch 2.
2   *R v Nottingham Justices, ex p Brown* [1960] 1 WLR 1315, DC; *R v Manchester Stipendiary Magistrate, ex p Hill* [1983] 1 AC 328 at 342B per Lord Roskill: 'In their criminal jurisdiction, ... what is required to give them that jurisdiction is that an information has been laid before them' and 344C, '... it is the laying of the information ... which is the foundation of the magistrates' court's jurisdiction to try an information summarily ...' See also *Northern Ireland Trailers Ltd v Preston Corpn* [1972] 1 All ER 260 where it was argued in the Divisional Court that proceedings for a nuisance order under Public Health Act 1936, s 94 (the equivalent, under the earlier legislation, of EPA 1990, s 82) begun by information, rather than complaint, were a nullity. The court dismissed this ground of appeal on the basis that an information was the correct means by which to commence proceedings, but in doing so implicitly accepted that had the wrong procedure been used the proceedings would indeed have been a nullity.
3   The point may be raised notwithstanding Magistrates' Court Act 1980, s 123 which provides: '(1) No objection shall be allowed to any information or complaint, or to any summons or warrant to procure the presence of the defendant, for any defect in it in substance or in form ...' See *R v Nottingham Justices, ex p Brown* [1960] 1 WLR 1315 at 1318 per Parker CJ, commenting on the identical provisions of MCA 1952, s 100. It makes no difference that the defendant has appeared and been convicted pursuant to the proceedings defectively commenced: [1960] 1 WLR 1315 at 1319, distinguishing *R v Hughes* (1879) 4 QBD 614.

The 'six-month rule' in proceedings under section 82

6.42   In relation to criminal proceedings in the magistrates' court, the general rule that an information must be laid within six months of the offence alleged[1] in it applies in principle to proceedings under section 82 of the EPA 1990 as to other proceedings.[2] However, because an offence under the section will be made out only where the alleged nuisance is shown to exist or be likely to recur at the dates the trial starts, the six-month rule is unlikely to give rise to the issue of whether the offence is 'out of time'.[3] There is no requirement that the information be laid within six months of the expiry of the statutory notice under section 82(6).[4]

1   See MCA 1980, s 127.
2   As to the six-month rule in criminal proceedings, see Chapter 5, paras **5.31–5.38**.
3   In *Nichols, Albion and Lainson v Powergen Renewables Limited and Wind 23 Prospect Limited* (South Lakeland Magistrates' Court, 20 January 2004) The District Judge accepted the submission that under section 127 of the Magistrates'Courts Act 1980, in respect of a proceedings brought pursuant to section 82 he was concerned only with instances of alleged nuisance occurring within the six months prior to the formal complaint. As a judgment of a magistrates' court this is not a binding authority.
4   *R v Crown Court at Liverpool, ex p Cooke* [1996] 4 All ER 589, especially at 599b obiter per Sir Iain Glidewell.

6.43   The relevance of the six-month rule arises in relation to compensation orders[1] which may be sought in criminal proceedings under the EPA 1990. This

6.43 *Statutory nuisance proceedings brought by an individual*

is because the rule places a limitation on how for back from the date of the hearing the court can look when taking into account the duration or effects of the nuisance for the purposes of assessing the amount of compensation to be paid. Where the period between the expiry of the section 82 notice and the date the information was laid is no more than six months, the magistrates may take into account the injury, loss or damage due to the continuation of the nuisance from the date specified in the information to the date of the hearing. However, where the period between the expiry of the section 82(6) notice and the laying of the information is greater than six months, the magistrates court may only take into account the injury, loss or damage caused by the continuation of the nuisance from six months before the laying of the information to the date of the hearing.[2]

1   See Chapter 7, para **7.93**.
2   *R v Crown Court at Liverpool, ex p Cooke* [1996] 4 All ER 589 at 595d. The notice is relevant only in so far as proceedings cannot be commenced before the expiry of the notice.

Material which should be submitted when laying the information

6.44   Once an information has been laid by a person aggrieved at the existence of the alleged statutory nuisance, the next step in the proceedings is usually the issuing of a summons by the magistrates' court clerk. The summons is addressed to and served on the defendant. It sets out the allegation made in the information, and requires the defendant to attend court at a particular day and time to answer the allegations made.[1] However, the magistrates' court has a discretion whether or not to issue a summons. Section 82 of the EPA 1990 does not impose a duty on the magistrates' court to issue a summons in every case where a complaint is made to it. It is therefore important that when the information is laid, sufficient material is put before the magistrate or the magistrates' clerk to satisfy him that it is proper for him to issue the summons.

1   For the form of a summons, see Magistrates' Court Rules 1981 (SI 1981/552 (as amended)), r 98. Provided the information was properly laid, a defect in the summons will not invalidate the proceedings: *R v Brentford Justices, ex p Catlin* [1975] QB 455. The principles applicable to amending a defective summons appear to be the same as those applicable to amending a defective information: *Broad v Fernandez* (10 July 1996, unreported), DC; and see paras **6.51–6.52**. It is usual for the magistrate or the magistrates' clerk to draft the summons.

6.45   In *R v West London Metropolitan Stipendiary Magistrate, ex p Klahn*[1] the Divisional Court set out the following guidance on the approach which a magistrate or magistrates' court clerk[2] should adopt when considering whether or not to issue a summons:

> '... he should at the very least ascertain (1) whether the allegation is of an offence known to the law and if so whether the essential elements of the offence are prima facie present; (2) that the offence alleged is 'not out of time'; (3) that the court has jurisdiction; (4) whether the informant has the necessary authority to prosecute. In addition ... it is clear that he may also and indeed should consider whether the allegation is vexatious ... The magistrate must be able to satisfy himself that it is a proper case to issue a summons ...'[3]

1   [1979] 1 WLR 933.
2   In *R v Highbury Corner Magistrates' Court, ex p Edwards* (1994) 26 HLR 682 the Divisional Court accepted that the principles set out in *Ex p Klahn* [1979] 1 WLR 933 applied equally to the approach to be taken by the magistrates' court clerk. The individual clerk's power to issue a summons is conferred by the Justices' Clerks Rules 1970, SI 1970/231.

How are proceedings started? 6.49

3   *R v Metropolitan Stipendiary Magistrates, ex p Klahn* [1979] 1 WLR 933 at 935H–936C per Lord Widgery CJ.

6.46 Thus in the context of proceedings under section 82 of the EPA 1990, the information should be accompanied by material upon which the magistrate or clerk, as the case may be, can satisfy himself that:

- there is an allegation of a statutory nuisance
- the proceedings are being started by a person aggrieved by the statutory nuisance alleged
- that the statutory nuisance still exists or is likely to recur[1]
- the requisite notice under section 82(6) has been given to the proposed defendant
- the particular court in question is the correct magistrates' court to hear the case[2]
- the person starting the proceedings has the necessary authority to do so[3]
- the proceedings have not been brought vexatiously.

1   See wording of EPA 1990, s 82(1). In the authors' view, a summons can properly be issued where the magistrate or clerk is of the view that the nuisance has been abated but the complainant alleges that it is likely to recur. The contrary is however arguable.
2   A magistrates' court has jurisdiction to try only those summary offences which were committed within its area: MCA 1980, ss 2, 3.
3   This will usually not present a problem. However, if the complaint is made by a company, the necessary authority to start proceedings should be obtained.

6.47 At the time that the summons is applied for, there is no obligation upon the person starting the proceedings formally to prove the above matters; it is sufficient that he provides information which on the face of it establishes them. The information, a copy of the notice of intended proceedings, and a covering letter which addresses the above points should be sufficient. If an expert report is available, this should be submitted as well, but it will not usually be necessary to do so.

6.48 If the magistrate does not have sufficient information before him upon which he can be satisfied of the above matters, the summons cannot be issued. However, it has been suggested that the magistrate or magistrates' clerk may have a residual discretion to hear the proposed defendant if he feels it necessary for the purposes of reaching his decision. Such a power should only be exercised in exceptional circumstances, and must not result in any preliminary hearing of the complaint itself.[1]

1   *R v West London Metropolitan Stipendiary Magistrate, ex p Klahn* [1979] 1 WLR 933 at 936B per Widgery CJ.

6.49 Where the above matters are made out, it does not follow that the summons must necessarily be issued, as the decision still lies at the discretion of the magistrate or magistrates' court clerk (as the case may be). However, it would require exceptional circumstances to justify a decision not to issue a summons in such a case.[1]

1   See *R v Highbury Corner Magistrates' Court, ex p Edwards* (1994) 26 HLR 682, where the Divisional Court quashed the decision of a magistrates' court clerk who had refused to issue a summons on the erroneous belief that the complainant had a co-extensive remedy in civil proceedings (which had already been commenced against the same defendant as the EPA 1990, s 82) and that therefore it was not an appropriate case to issue a summons.

6.50 *Statutory nuisance proceedings brought by an individual*

The form of the information itself

6.50 The information must describe the allegation against the defendant in ordinary language, as far as possible avoiding the use of technical terms. It must also contain a reference to section 82 of the EPA 1990 under which the offence is charged.[1]

1   Magistrates' Courts Rules 1981, SI 1981/552, r 100.

Defective information

6.51 Where the information is defective, two possibilities arise. First, in the case of an information which is defective because it fails altogether to disclose an offence, there will be unfairness to the defendant who does not know what he has to do by way of defence to the prosecution. In these cases, the complainant should apply to have the information amended. If the court allows the amendment, it is likely to grant an adjournment to allow the defence time to prepare its case in the light of the particulars given in the amended information. If it does not allow the amendment or the application to amend the information is not made, then the case will almost certainly be dismissed because of the defective information. Secondly, in the case of an information which does disclose an offence but is simply sparse in the amount of information which it conveys to the defendant, the deficiency may be made good either formally by amendment or informally by the complainant providing further particulars to the defendant either before the trial begins or in court.[1]

1   See *Cole v Wolkind* (22 July 1980, unreported), DC per Donaldson LJ at 4C of the transcript. In *Broad v Fernandez* (10 July 1996, unreported), DC – a case concerning proceedings under EPA 1990, s 82 – Smith LJ expressly adopted and purported to apply the same guidance, but appears to have considered that where the information discloses no offence, the court would have no jurisdiction and the case would have to be dismissed. In the authors' view, the views of Donaldson LJ are to be preferred, giving as they do greater flexibility to the magistrates to make a decision in accordance with the justice of the particular case.

6.52 In this context, people will need to be alert to defendants who raise arguments based upon articles 6 and 7[1] of the European Convention on Human Rights (ECHR). In the authors' view, to ensure that a fair trial is given in accordance with article 6, the court should always grant an adjournment, or at least offer the defendant the choice of an adjournment, whenever the information is amended to a material extent. As to an argument under article 7, in the authors' view, this is unlikely to succeed. The information is not concerned with the offence itself – which is set out under section 82(2) of the EPA 1990 – but with the allegations said to amount to an offence in the particular circumstances of the case. No argument based upon retrospective criminalisation should therefore arise.

1   Freedom from retroactive criminal legislation.

6.53 A standard form information for proceedings under section 82 of the EPA 1990 is found at Appendix A.

PROCEDURE AT THE HEARING

What must be proved

(i) The alleged nuisance exists at the date of the hearing or (if abated) is likely to recur

6.54 An offence will be committed under section 82 of the EPA 1990 if the nuisance alleged in the information is proved to exist at the date of the trial, or if the magistrates find that although the nuisance has been abated, it is likely to recur on the same premises or in the same street (as the case may be).[1] If the trial commences but is adjourned to another date, it must be shown that the nuisance existed at the date the trial commenced.[2] Where there is an appeal to the Crown Court against a conviction under section 82 by the magistrates' court, the person aggrieved must still show that the nuisance complained of existed on the day that the magistrates' court hearing started, rather than on the day that the appeal in the Crown Court commenced.[3]

1 See EPA 1990, s 82(2); *R v Liverpool Crown Court, ex p Cooke* [1997] 1 WLR 700 at 703D, 705H; *R v Dudley Magistrates' Court, ex p Hollis* [1999] 1 WLR 642.
2 *Crowe v London Borough of Tower Hamlets* noted in *LAG*, May 1997.
3 *Northern Ireland Trailers Ltd v Preston Corpn* [1972] 1 WLR 203, DC.

(ii) Is there an obligation on the person aggrieved to prove that the alleged nuisance existed at the time the information was laid and that he was in fact a person aggrieved by the existence of that nuisance at that time?

6.55 It is always prudent for the person aggrieved to prove that the nuisance existed at the time the information was laid, as section 82(12) of the EPA 1990 gives him a statutory right to his costs where he does so.[1]

1 For a discussion of the scope of EPA 1990. s 82(12), see Chapter 7, paras **7.47–7.58** below.

6.56 It is unclear whether section 82 of the EPA 1990 requires that the person aggrieved formally prove that the alleged nuisance existed at the time that the information was laid or that he was in fact a 'person aggrieved' by the existence of that statutory nuisance at that time. Judicial pronouncements on the nature of the offence under section 82(2) suggest that there is no requirement to formally prove that the statutory nuisance existed at the date the information was laid or that the person who started the proceedings was in fact a person aggrieved by the existence of the alleged statutory nuisance at that time.[1] On the other hand, section 82(1) provides that the magistrates may only act under section 82 in proceedings commenced by someone aggrieved at the existence of a statutory nuisance.

1 See *Ex p Cooke* and *Ex p Hollis* cited above. In *Coventry City Council v Doyle* [1981] 2 All ER 184 the Divisional Court (Donaldson LJ and Hodgson J) considered whether under Public Health Act 1936, s 94(1) the magistrates had to look to the date the information was laid or the date of the hearing before them when determining whether a statutory nuisance existed or was likely to recur for the purposes of deciding whether to convict a defendant in proceedings brought by a person aggrieved under s 99 of the 1936 Act. In concluding that the relevant date was date of the hearing and not the date the complaint was made, neither judge suggested that the state of affairs at the date on which the complaint was made bore any relevance to the issue before the justices.

6.57 In practice, the fact that the person starting the proceedings was not a person aggrieved by the existence of the alleged statutory nuisance for the purposes of section 82(1) of the EPA 1990 will provide a defence to proceedings under section 82.[1] Accordingly, evidence should be submitted to prove that when the information was laid, the person starting the proceedings was aggrieved by the alleged statutory nuisance which already existed at that time.

1   *Birmingham District Council v McMahon* (1987) 86 LGR 63.

6.58 This is unlikely to give rise to any practical difficulties. Provided that the statutory nuisance is proven to exist or be likely to recur at the date of the hearing before the justices (a certain pre-requisite to proving an offence under section 82(2) of the EPA 1990), usually very little will be needed to prove that the statutory nuisance also existed at the date that the information was laid. Of course, a sensible approach to this issue must be taken. In the authors' view, section 82(1) cannot sensibly require the person starting the proceedings to show that at the instant the information was laid the statutory nuisance existed. It will be enough to show that the state of affairs or regular practice giving rise to the statutory nuisance existed at that time. Usually the information will allege that the nuisance existed on a certain day, has not been abated, and continues. Proof that it did in fact exist on the day stated in the information and that there were no changes in circumstances before the information was laid will usually be sufficient.[1]

1   Some support for the proposition that the date of the hearing is not the only relevant date and that the complainant must show that he was in fact aggrieved by the existence of the statutory nuisance before that time may be gleaned from *Hilton v Hopwood* (1899) 44 Sol Jo 90.

Onus and burden of proof

6.59 These matters must be proved by the person starting the proceedings to the criminal standard of 'beyond reasonable doubt,' and not the civil standard of the balance of probabilities.

6.60 In the case of a nuisance which at the time of the hearing has been abated but which it is alleged is likely to recur, the person aggrieved need not show that the nuisance is certain to recur. It is enough that he can show a likelihood of its recurrence, the degree of likelihood being a matter of judgment for the magistrates on the facts of the case.

The conduct of the proceedings

6.61 The proceedings follow the same procedure as those for the criminal offence of failing to comply with an abatement notice.[1] However, there are a number of additional issues worth outlining given the general recognition of section 82 of the EPA 1990 as a important tool for the individual litigant who may often be unable to afford full representation. These are set out below.

1   See Chapter 5.

6.62 First, where the nuisance complained of by the person aggrieved is affecting his enjoyment of his home, issues may arise under article 8 of the ECHR, which gives a qualified right to respect for private and family life and the home.[1] The European Court of Human Rights (ECtHR) has held that article 8 may give rise to a *positive* obligation upon a public authority to take steps

Procedure at the hearing **6.64**

necessary to ensure effective protection of the right to respect for private and family life and the home.[2] In *Guerra v Italy*[3] the claimant lived in a town about a kilometre from a fertiliser factory. The factory had been releasing various toxic and flammable gasses which had led, in one instance, to 150 people being hospitalised due to arsenic poisoning. The Italian authorities had drawn up a safety report and adopted an emergency plan and measures required for informing the local population of the risks of pollution, under domestic law. The authorities had refused to disclose the information which the local population needed. The ECtHR found that the information was essential to enable the local residents to assess the risks which they and their families might run if they continued to live in the town which was particularly exposed to danger in the event of an accident at the factory. Accordingly, the state's failure to release the information to the public, in the circumstances of that case, amounted to an infringement of article 8. Thus, in cases of serious nuisances affecting article 8 rights, it may be open to the private individual to require disclosure of information held by the local authority where that information concerns the nuisance in respect of which the individual is seeking a nuisance order from the court under section 82 of the EPA 1990.

1 On the availability of damages under the HRA 1998 against a local authority for breaches of article 8 arising from the failure to take action against a statutory nuisance, see Chapter 7, paras **7.109–7.116**.
2 *Lopez Ostra v Spain* (1994) 20 EHRR 277; *Guerra v Italy* (1998) 26 EHRR 357; *Airey v Ireland* (1979) 2 EHRR 305.
3 (1998) 26 EHRR 357.

6.63 Under domestic law, regulations such as the Environmental Information Regulations 2004[1] create powers and impose duties on local authorities to disclose information relating to nuisances. Where the local authority choose not to disclose information in circumstances where they have a power to do so, there may be an infringement of article 8 rights.[2]

1 The Environmental Information Regulations 2004, SI 2004/3391 and Chapter 2, paras **2.26–2.32**.
2 See further, Chapter 2, para **2.25**.

6.64 Secondly, it is arguable that in some cases the state may be required to provide assistance to a private litigant who seeks to protect his article 8 rights by proceedings under section 82 of the EPA 1990. In *Airey v Ireland*[1] Mrs Airey sought judicial separation from her husband under Irish law. She lacked the means to pay for a lawyer and legal aid for civil proceedings was not available. The ECtHR held that that unavailability of legal aid was a breach of Mrs Airey's rights under articles 6 and 8 of the ECHR. The court held that there had to be effective access to the courts under article 6 and effective protection and respect for private and family life under article 8. The complexity of the issues of law and fact involved in Mrs Airey's case and the emotive nature of family disputes meant that effective protection could not be secured by compelling her to act in person. By way of analogy, proceedings under section 82 of the EPA 1990 will in many circumstances involve complex issues of law and fact, often requiring expert evidence. Although the proceedings are classified in domestic law as criminal proceedings, in substance the proceedings may be seen as civil for the purposes of article 6:[2] they have at their heart the purpose of regulating the use of land.[3] This will be more readily evident when article 8 rights are involved. Accordingly, in a complex case the state *may* be under an obligation to provide financial support to the private litigant to enable legal representation and the

6.64 *Statutory nuisance proceedings brought by an individual*

presentation of expert evidence, where this is essential to ensure a fair trial or protection of article 8 rights, and he would not otherwise be able to afford such assistance. However, in the authors' view the courts are likely to strive to adopt a restrictive approach to the application of these principles.

1 (1979) 2 EHRR 305.
2 The distinction between civil and criminal law is relevant under article 6 of ECHR because an obligation upon the state to provide assistance to a party who wishes to commence proceedings will only usually arise, if at all, in the context of civil, rather than criminal proceedings.
3 The requirement that a litigant in proceedings under EPA 1990, s 82 be a 'person aggrieved' will often (though by no means always) mean that the procedure overlaps with remedies available in civil law.

6.65 A third aspect of proceedings worth remembering is the obligation upon legal representatives not to mislead the court, which in practice encompasses an obligation to disclose legal authorities of which the advocate is aware and which support legal propositions which run contrary to his case. The obligation to disclose such authorities is generally considered to be enhanced where the opposite party in the litigation is not legally represented. Thus, a litigant in person facing a party who is represented should remind the other side's representatives of their duty to the court and request disclosure of any adverse authorities.

DEFENCES TO PROCEEDINGS FOR AN ORDER UNDER SECTION 82(2)

6.66 There are no *express* statutory defences to proceedings for an order under section 82(2) of the EPA 1990.

6.67 However, the wording of section 82 of the EPA 1990 allows for the following lines of defence to be taken:

- the notice given for the purposes of section 82(6) was not sufficiently detailed[1]
- the notice under section 82(6) was served on the wrong person[2]
- the complainant is not a 'person aggrieved' by the existence of a statutory nuisance[3]
- the defendant is not the person responsible for the nuisance, the owner or occupier of the relevant premises or the person responsible for the vehicle, machinery, or equipment (as the case may be)[4]
- (in the case of an owner of occupier who is prosecuted under section 82(4)(c)), the person responsible for the nuisance can be found, and
- the nuisance alleged in the complaint does not exist at the date of trial and is not likely to recur.[5]

1 *East Stafford Borough Council v Fairless* [1999] Env LR 525; *Pearshouse v Birmingham City Council* [1999] Env LR 536.
2 *Leeds v London Borough of Islington* [1998] Env LR 665; *Hall v Kingston upon Hull City Council* [1999] 2 All ER 609; *Hewlings v Mclean Homes East Anglia Ltd* [2001] 2 All ER 281, [2000] EGCS 100.
3 *Birmingham District Council v McMahon* (1987) 151 JP 709.
4 *Quigley v Liverpool Housing Trust Anglia Ltd* [1999] EGCS 94, *Warner v London Borough of Lambeth* (1984) 15 HLR 42; *Dover District Council v Farrar* (1980) 2 HLR 32; *GLC v London Borough of Tower Hamlets* (1983) 15 HLR 54; *Henry Pike v Sefton Metropolitan Borough Council* (29 February 2000, unreported), DC; *Carr v London Borough of Hackney* (1995) 28 HLR 749.
5 *Coventry City Council v Doyle* [1981] 2 All ER 184; *R v Liverpool Crown Court, ex p Cooke* [1997] 1 WLR 700; *R v Dudley Magistrates' Court, ex p Hollis* [1999] 1 WLR 642.

Defences to proceedings for an order under section 82(2) 6.70

6.68 The poor drafting of section 82 of the EPA 1990 leaves complete uncertainty as to whether or not a best practicable means defence can be run as a defence to the making of a nuisance order. On the one hand, it is odd that the defence is available on a prosecution for non-compliance with a nuisance order but is not available at the earlier stage in proceedings in which the nuisance order is itself made. This means for example that the following might be possible. A business is causing a statutory nuisance but at all times is employing best practicable means. A person aggrieved brings proceedings under section 82. The proceedings are successful. An abatement order is issued and the business fined. It continues to operate in exactly the same manner and thereby has a complete defence to a prosecution for breach of the abatement order. This seems odd. Why should the business to be exposed to criminal sanction when Parliament considers that continuation of the very same activity should be lawful?

6.69 In *Nichols, Albion and Lainson v Powergen Renewables Limited and Wind 23 Prospect Limited* (South Lakeland Magistrates' Court, 20 January 2004) counsel for the local residents argued that for the purpose of the proceedings the only question was the existence or likely recurrence of the nuisance, not whether best practicable means were being used. The District Judge however accepted submissions for the defendants that in practical terms BPM could not simply be ignored at the earlier stage. The judge held:

> '. . . it is clear to me that I must give consideration to the means employed by the defendants in order to attempt to obviate an alleged nuisance for the very simple and obvious reason that to disregard those means at the s 82(2) stage would have two most undesirable consequences as follows:–
>
> (a) if (for want of a better description) "best practicable means" are being employed the framing of an abatement order would be a well-nigh impossible task, and
>
> (b) the defendants would not be in a position to comply with any such order and accordingly would automatically be in breach of it.
>
> Obscure though the intentions of Parliament may have been, I beg leave to doubt whether the situation I have just described was either intended or contemplated by that august body.'

The *Nichols* judgment being that of a magistrates' court is not a binding authority and, indeed, there is some force in the literal argument that it is inconsistent with the scheme of the Act and section 82 in particular for the aggrieved person to be exposed to the risk of having to incur substantial costs where his action is defeated by a plea of best practicable means in proceedings for a nuisance order and it is for that reason that it does not appeal as a defence in section 82 proceedings save only at s 82(9) as a defence to a breach of an abatement order already made.

6.70 It is not a defence to proceedings under section 82 that the matter amounting to a statutory nuisance was authorised by a consent under sections 61 or 65 of the Control of Pollution Act 1974.[1]

1 See COPA 1974, ss 61(9) and 65(8).

6.71   *Statutory nuisance proceedings brought by an individual*

PENALTIES IN PROCEEDINGS UNDER SECTION 82(2): NUISANCE ORDERS AND FINES

The court's powers

6.71 Where an offence under section 82(2) of the EPA 1970 is proven by a complainant with standing to do so, the magistrates' court *must* make an order – often referred to as a 'nuisance order' – for either or both of the purposes set out under that section, namely:

(i) an order requiring the defendant to abate the nuisance within the time specified in the order, and to execute any works necessary for that purpose (section 82(2)(a))

(ii) an order prohibiting a recurrence of the nuisance, and requiring the defendant within a time specified in the order, to execute any works necessary to prevent the recurrence (section 82(2)(a)).

In either case, where the court is satisfied that the alleged nuisance exists and is such as to render any premises unfit for human habitation, it may also prohibit the use of those premises for human habitation until such time as the court is satisfied that the premises have been rendered fit for that purpose (section 82(3)).

The Divisional Court appeared to endorse the view that whilst obliged to make an order which would abate the statutory nuisance, was obliged to have regard to all relevant circumstances so that it did not, by an order which was penal in its nature, require of the persons subject to it more than was reasonably necessary or proportionate in order to achieve the statutory requirement of abating the nuisance.[1]

1   In *Roper v Tussauds Theme Parks Limited* [2007] EWHC 624; [2007] Env LR 31 at [14] and [15] citing as authority *Nottingham Corporation v Newton* [1974] 2 All ER and *Salford City Council v McNally* [1976] AC 379.

6.72 In addition, the court *may* impose a fine on the defendant not exceeding level 5 on the standard scale.[1]

1   At the time of writing, level 5 is £5,000.

The terms of the nuisance order

6.73 A nuisance order under section 82 of the EPA 1990 is issued by the court. As with a local authority abatement notice, failure to comply with the terms of the order is a criminal offence. It follows that the need for clarity and certainty which underlies the drafting of local authority abatement notices applies equally[1] to the drafting of nuisance orders under section 82: the recipient of such notices must know what the matter is that is complained of and what is required by the notice to put it right. Beyond that level of generality, the question arises as to what extent the case law applicable to the drafting of local authority abatement notices applies to the drafting of nuisance orders under section 82.

1   See the discussion of this topic in Chapter 3, paras **3.04–3.07**.

6.74 It is useful to compare the relevant statutory provisions in section 80 of the EPA 1990 and those in section 82. There are a number of significant differences between them:

- first, whereas section 80(1)(a) allows the local authority simply to *restrict* the occurrence or recurrence of the nuisance rather than requiring its abatement or prohibiting altogether its recurrence, an order under section 82(2) *must* either require the abatement of the nuisance (where it exists at the date of trial) or prohibit its recurrence (where the nuisance although abated, is likely to recur at the date of trial) or both. There is no power to restrict the occurrence of the nuisance
- secondly, while section 80(1)(b) expressly allows the abatement notice to require the taking of steps, section 82(2) expressly provides that a nuisance order can require works but does not refer to a requirement of steps
- thirdly, whereas section 80 allows the local authority abatement notice to impose 'all or any' of the statutory requirement set out in section 80(1)(a) and (b), the court acting under section 82 must make an order 'for either or both' of the statutory purposes under section 82(2)(a) and (b). This is significant because section 80(1)(a) refers to the abatement, prohibition or restriction of the nuisance but not the means by which this is to take place; whereas section 80(1)(b) refers to the means by which those purposes may be carried out: works and any such other steps as may be necessary. Under section 80(1) therefore, the local authority can 'pick and mix' the ends which the notice is to achieve (section 80(1)(a)) and the means by which it is to achieve those ends (section 80(1)(b)). By contrast, both section 82(1)(a) and 82(1)(b) refer to the requirement of works, the difference between the two sub-sections being whether the order requires abatement (section 82(1)(a)) or prohibits recurrence (section 82(1)(b)) of the statutory nuisance
- fourthly, in terms of the scheme of the two sections, it is of note that whereas there is a right of appeal against an abatement notice on grounds which address the terms of the notice itself, there is no similar right of appeal against a nuisance order.[1]

1 The person convicted under EPA 1990, s 82 may, of course, appeal the conviction or sentence to the Crown Court. An appeal against the terms of a nuisance order could be made by way of an appeal against sentence.

6.75 In the authors' view, the differences between section 80(1) and section 82(2) of the EPA 1990 may be material. It would be inappropriate to assume that the guidance given by the courts as to when works need to be specified in an abatement notice would apply equally to nuisance orders.[1] Until judicial guidance is given on the issue, it is suggested that the following principle be applied: a nuisance order may simply require the abatement of the nuisance or prohibit its recurrence without specifying works unless either (i) the notice on its face contains a requirement that works be carried out or (ii) as a matter of fact, the recipient of the notice will be compelled to carry out works if he is to comply with the notice.[2] In either (i) or (ii), the works required must be specified.

1 It is interesting to note that the classic cases on the need to specify works arose in the context of orders made by the magistrates' court under earlier legislation. The leading decisions on the content and validity of local authority abatement notices under EPA 1990, s 80(1) and the requirement to specify works have focused on the s 80 power rather than the s 82(2) power.
2 These are, in effect, the principles set out in *Kirklees Metropolitan Borough Council v Field* [1998] Env LR 337 (overruled so far as local authority abatement notices are concerned in *R v Falmouth and Truro Port Health Authority, ex p South West Water Services* [2000] 3 All ER 306, [2000] 3 WLR 1464, CA).

6.76 As to the actual requirements of a notice, the magistrates have a wide discretion as to what works (if any) the order should require and the time within which work should be done, provided always that the requirements of the notice are directed towards the abatement of the nuisance and/or the prohibition of its recurrence, as the case may be. As the Divisional Court has said:[1]

> 'In deciding within the wide ambit of detailed discretion just what the terms of the nuisance order should be, I have no doubt it is the duty of the justices, as common sense dictates, to look at the whole circumstances of the case and to try and make an order which is in its terms sensible and just having regard to the entire prevailing situation.'

1   *Nottingham City District Council v Newton* [1974] 1 WLR 923, DC, at 930A, followed in *R v Fenny Stratford Justices, ex p Watney Mann (Midlands) Ltd* [1976] 2 All ER 888. Lord Wilberforce in *Salford v McNally* referred to the *Nottingham* case and emphasised that the 'keynote' of the magistrates approach should be to 'use discretion and common sense.' See also *Roper v Tussauds Theme Parks Limited* [2007] EWHC 624 (Admin); [2007] Env LR 31 at [14]–[15] which appears to suggest that commercial considerations can be taken into account. In the event the HRA 1998 would mean that the concept of proportionaity should also come into play in the making of the order.

6.77 In deciding what terms to impose, the magistrates should apply their own minds to the evidence before them to assess what is reasonably necessary to abate the nuisance in question and are not bound by the suggestions put forward by the parties, whether or not such suggestions are agreed.[1] In principle, a nuisance order can require not merely repairs but also improvements to premises, and the order may properly require works to be carried out which impose upon the landlord obligations which go beyond the obligations placed upon him as landlord.[2] However, where the landlord is a local authority, the courts have emphasised the need for the magistrates to bear in mind the heavy housing responsibilities which the authority bear and the need to avoid making an order which would require money being spent abortively on abating the nuisance.[3]

1   *Birmingham District Council v Kelly* (1985) 17 HLR 572 at 583. Ironically, had it not been for the fact that the works contained in the order made by the magistrate in that case were suggested and agreed by the parties, the nuisance order would have been quashed and remitted back to the magistrate for reconsideration: see at 581 and 583. For an exmple of where the parties did not agree the terms of an order and where the court adopted the order suggested by one party suibject to one modification see *Roper v Tussauds Theme Parks Limited* [2007] EWHC 624 (Admin); [2007] Env LR 31.
2   *Birmingham District Council v Kelly* (1985) 17 HLR 572 at 581.
3   *Birmingham District Council v Kelly* (1985) 17 HLR 572 at 581; *Nottingham City District Council v Newton* [1974] 1 WLR 923, DC, at 930B.

The power to fine

6.78 In contrast with the duty to make a nuisance order, the court has a choice as to whether or not it fines the defendant. Experience suggests that a fine will be unlikely, unless there a particular aggravating factors such as unacceptable conduct on the part of the defendant.[1]

1   *The Use of Section 82 of the Environmental Protection Act 1990 Against Local Authorities and Housing Associations* (HMSO, 1996), para 2.99-2.100.

ORDERS AGAINST A LOCAL AUTHORITY WHICH IS NOT A DEFENDANT TO THE PROCEEDINGS

6.79 Where the relevant defendant cannot be found, the court has a *discretion* under section 82(13) of the EPA 1990 to make any order against the local authority which it could have made against the relevant defendant to the proceedings had he been found. Section 82 therefore contemplates proceedings in circumstances where no person responsible for the nuisance, no owner or occupier of the premises, or no person responsible for the vehicle, machinery or equipment (as the case may be) can be found and therefore there is no defendant to the proceedings. For example, where a pile of stinking ordure has been dumped on land overnight and needs to be removed, and no one can find the person who dumped it nor is the owner or occupier of the land known, it will fall to the local authority to have the pile removed. If it fails to issue a notice itself (because the relevant parties cannot be found) and decides to take no action, then a person aggrieved may seek to use proceedings under section 82 to obtain an order against the local authority under section 82(13).

6.80 The factors which the magistrates' court will consider when deciding whether or not to make an order against the local authority under section 82(13) of the EPA 1990 are wide. They include, but are not limited to, the following:

- the nature, seriousness, effects and likely duration of the statutory nuisance in question
- whether the local authority were themselves aware of the situation giving rise to the statutory nuisance
- whether the local authority had themselves considered whether the situation complained of amounted to a statutory nuisance, and their reasons for deciding that it did not or did
- the reasons (if any) why the local authority did not themselves issue a notice under section 80
- whether the person aggrieved had given the local authority any notice of his intention to start proceedings under section 82
- other steps which have or are being taken or which are planned for the abatement of the statutory nuisance
- the consequences to both parties and to the public at large if the order is made as compared to the consequences if the order is not made.

COSTS IN PROCEEDINGS UNDER SECTION 82(2)

6.81 A person aggrieved who proves that the alleged nuisance existed at the time the information was laid has a right to recover from the defendant to the proceedings such amount of costs as the court considers would reasonably compensate the person aggrieved for any expenses properly incurred in the proceedings. The right exists whether or not the person bringing the proceedings proves that the nuisance existed or was likely to recur at the date of the hearing.

6.82 Details of the costs regime in proceedings under section 82 of the EPA 1990 are to be found in Chapter 7, paras **7.47–7.58**.

6.83 *Statutory nuisance proceedings brought by an individual*

FAILURE TO COMPLY WITH A NUISANCE ORDER MADE UNDER SECTION 82(2)

6.83 A person who, without reasonable excuse,[1] contravenes any requirement or prohibition imposed by an order under section 82(2) of the EPA 1990 commits an offence (see section 82(8)). In the authors' view, anyone may prosecute for contravention of the nuisance order, though it would be unusual for anyone but the local authority or person aggrieved to want to do so. One situation which could well arise is where a tenant obtained an order against the local authority under section 82(2), but then moves out of his flat which is the subject of the nuisance order. In these circumstances, the new tenant would be able to bring a prosecution in the magistrates' court for the local authority landlord's failure to comply with the nuisance order which his predecessor had obtained.

1   Reasonable excuse for non-compliance with an abatement notice under EPA 1990, s 80 is discussed in Chapter 5, paras **5.78–5.84**. The same considerations apply under EPA 1990, s 82(4).

6.84 It is a defence to prove that 'best practicable means'[1] were used to prevent, or to counteract the effects of, the nuisance.[2] The defence of best practicable means is not available in the case of:

(i) a nuisance falling within paragraph (a), (d), (e), (f), (fa), (fb)[3] or (g) of section 79(1) of the EPA 1990, except where the nuisance arises on industrial, trade or business premises[4]

(ii) a nuisance falling within paragraph (ga) of section 79(1) of the EPA 1990, except where the noise is emitted from or caused by a vehicle, machinery or equipment being used to industrial, trade or business purposes

(iii) a nuisance falling within paragraph (b) of section 79(1) of the EPA 1990, except where the smoke is emitted from a chimney

(iv) a nuisance falling within paragraph (a) or (h) of section 79(1) of the EPA 1990, and

(v) a nuisance which is such as to render premises unfit for human habitation.

1   For the defence of best practicable means, see Chapter 5, paras **5.95–5.96**.
2   EPA 1990, s 82(9).
3   The Clean Neighbourhoods and Environment Act 2005, s 103 amended EPA 1990, s 82 as follows:
   '(4) In section 82(10) (summary proceedings by aggrieved person: defence of best practicable means not available in certain cases)–
   (a)   in paragraph (a) after "paragraph (a), (d), (e), (f)" insert ", (fa)", and
   (b)   after paragraph (a) insert–
       "(aza) in the case of a nuisance falling within paragraph (fb) of section 79(1) above except where–
       (i)   the artificial light is emitted from industrial, trade or business premises, or
       (ii) the artificial light (not being (i) to which sub-paragraph (i) applies) is emitted by lights used for the purpose only of illuminating an outdoor relevant sports facility;".
   (5) After section 82(10) insert–
       "(10A) For the purposes of subsection (10)(aza) "relevant sports facility" has the same meaning as it has for the purposes of section 80(8)(aza)."'
4   It is of note that an offence under the equivalent provision of EPA 1990, s 80 carries a £20,000 fine.

6.85 A person convicted of an offence under section 82(8) of the EPA 1990 may be fined an amount up to level 5 on the standard scale,[1] together with a

Failure to comply with a nuisance order made under s 82(2) **6.85**

further fine of an amount equal to one-tenth of that level for each day on which the offence continues after the conviction.[2]

1 At the time of writing, this is £5,000.
2 Ie £500 a day.

Chapter 7

Costs and Compensation

INTRODUCTION

7.01 'At the end of a hearing the judge's mind is turning towards his next case. Counsel is busy indorsing and tying up his brief. Emotions are high – someone has won and someone has lost and dealing with the costs is a sordid anticlimax. Nevertheless, the fruits of victory can be soured if the proper orders are not made for costs.'[1]

1   *Cook on Costs 2008* (Rev edn, 2007) at p 221.

7.02 This chapter gives an outline of the general principles applicable to the courts' powers to award costs to parties to proceedings, with emphasis on the particular issues of practical relevance to those involved in statutory nuisance cases.

SECTION 1 CIVIL PROCEEDINGS: COSTS ON AN APPEAL AGAINST AN ABATEMENT NOTICE

Appeal in the magistrates' court

7.03 The magistrates' court has no general discretion to award costs as it sees fit. It can only award costs in accordance with its powers under statute.[1] In proceedings on an appeal against an abatement notice, the statutory power to award costs is found in section 64 of the Magistrates' Court Act 1980 (MCA 1980), which provides:

'(1) On the hearing of a complaint a magistrates' court shall have power in its discretion to make such order as to costs,
   (a) on making the order for which the complaint is made, to be paid by the defendant to the complainant;
   (b) on dismissing the complaint to be paid by the complainant to the defendant as it thinks just and reasonable . . .'

1   *R v Coventry Magistrates' Court, ex p Crown Prosecution Service* (1996) 160 JP 741 at 743G.

The scope of MCA 1980, section 64

7.04 The opening words of section 64(1) MCA make it clear that the Magistrates' Court has a discretion whether or not to make an order for costs. Thus, in an abatement notice appeal no party has an absolute right to recover its costs, whether or not it is successful. Where a costs order is made, the order shall be that which the court considers 'just and reasonable' in accordance with section 64. Moreover, although the opening works of sub-paragraphs (a) and (b) might be read as meaning that the magistrates may only award the complainant its costs where it makes 'an order for which the complaint is made',[1] and may only award the defendant its costs 'on dismissing the complaint', cases that have considered section 64 have made it clear that this is not the case.[2]

201

7.04 *Costs and compensation*

1 MCA 1980, s 64(1)(a).
2 MCA 1980, s 64(1)(b).

General Guidance on section 64

7.05 In *City of Bradford MDC v Booth*[1] the court gave the following general guidance on the approach that the magistrates' court should take to MCA 1980, s 64. It held that the proper approach to section 64 could be summarised conveniently in three propositions:[2]

> '1 Section 64(1) confers a discretion upon a magistrates' court to make such order as to costs as it thinks just and reasonable. That provision applies both to the quantum of the costs (if any) to be paid, but also as to the party (if any) which should pay them.
> 2 What the court will think just and reasonable will depend on all the relevant facts and circumstances of the case before the court. The court may think it just and reasonable that costs should follow the event, but need not think so in all cases covered by the subsection.
> 3 Where a complainant has successfully challenged before justices an administrative decision made by a ... regulatory authority acting honestly, reasonably, properly and on grounds that reasonably appeared sound, in the exercise of its public duty, the court should consider, in addition to any other relevant fact or circumstances, both (i) the financial prejudice to the particular complainant in the particular circumstances if an order for costs in not made in its favour; and (ii) the need to encourage public authorities to make and stand by honest, reasonable and apparently sound administrative decisions made in the public interest without fear of exposure to undue financial prejudice if the decision is successfully challenged.'

1 [2000] 164 JP 485 DC.
2 At [23]–[26].

7.06 The guidance is largely self-explanatory, but the following observations can be made. First, 'all the relevant facts and circumstances of the case before the court' fall to be taken into account when the discretion is exercised. This would include factors such as the extent to which each party has won or lost, the time and expense involved in dealing with particular issues, and the conduct of the parties, not just during the trial itself but also at pre-trial stages. For example, the extent to which a party has co-operated in reaching agreement with the other side on non-controversial matters would be relevant.

7.07 Secondly, although the third proposition is potentially wide in its effect, its significance and effect on the discretion to award costs will vary in different cases and in different contexts. *Bradford v Booth* was a licensing case, and the guidance has subsequently been applied in other licensing fields.[1] In the authors' view, the principles underlying the guidance quoted above should also be applicable to appeals against abatement notices under section 80 of the Environmental Protection Act 1990 (EPA 1990). An abatement notice is served pursuant to the local authority's duty as regulatory authority under section 80(1) of the EPA 1990. The decision to issue and serve the notice is an administrative decision. On any appeal, the authority will be bound to appear to defend the notice and its decision to issue it. Although the appeal may involve issues of 'unreasonableness'[2], many of the issues raised will involve matters of judgment

Section 1 Civil proceedings: costs on an appeal 7.11

upon which the local authority may well have acted honestly, properly and on grounds that reasonably appeared to be sound albeit the appeal may succeed. Accordingly, the broader considerations set out in the *Bradford* case should be applicable.

1 *Powell v The Chief Executive of the City and County of Swansea* [2003] EWHC 2185 (Admin); *R (Cambridge City Council) v Alex Nesting Ltd* [2006] EWHC 1374 (Admin); *Crawley BC v Stuart Attenborough* [2006] EWHC 1278 (Admin); *R (Utllesford DC) v English Heritage* [2007] EWHC 816 (Admin).
2 For example, an appeal under Statutory Nuisance (Appeals) Regulations 1995, reg 2(2)(c).

7.08 With those general observations in mind, consideration is given below to the way in which the court would usually exercise its discretion in particular circumstances and to some of the issues that sometimes arise when costs are being considered.

Outright success and outright failure

7.09 Where the appellant succeeds on all grounds of appeal, it will usually be just and reasonable for the court to award him his costs, or a reasonable amount thereof.[1] Where all the grounds of appeal are dismissed, the court will usually award the local authority its costs, or a reasonable amount thereof. A deduction from the costs awarded may of course be made where the successful party has behaved unreasonably. Thus, if such a party has unreasonably caused an otherwise unnecessary adjournment not only may the successful party not recover his costs of the adjournment but a reduction may be made sufficient to compensate the ultimately unsuccessful party for his own costs of the adjournment.

1 Where the amount of costs incurred are reasonable for the amount of work carried out on the case, a successful appellant may nevertheless have his costs award reduced where he is to some extent to blame for the proceedings: see for example *Camden London Borough Council v London Underground Ltd* [2000] Env LR 369.

Partial success and partial failure

7.10 In practice the approach of magistrates to section 64(1) of the MCA 1980 in cases where the appellant has succeeded on some but not all grounds differs from court to court. In cases of partial success where the appellant has failed to have the abatement notice quashed but only succeeds in having it varied, it appears to be common place for magistrates' clerks to advise the bench that no order for costs should be made under section 64, or that the local authority cannot recover any of its costs because the complaint is being upheld. Such advice is wrong. The parties should refer the court to the *Bradford* case to ensure that the court properly exercises its discretion looking at all the circumstances of the case. In cases of partial success, it is often appropriate to make partial awards of costs in favour of (and therefore also against) each party. These awards can then be offset, resulting in a single liability of one party to the other.

7.11 Because of the wording of the MCA 1980, s 64, in cases of partial success arguments can sometimes arise about whether the court is 'making an order for which the complaint is made' or dismissing it.[1] Under the MCA 1980, the magistrates on hearing a complaint must either make an order for which the complaint is made or dismiss the complaint.[2] In practice, this means that the

7.11 *Costs and compensation*

court must either quash the abatement notice, vary the notice in favour of the appellant, or dismiss the appeal.[3] In the authors' view, 'the complaint' can properly be seen as a combination of what the appellant is seeking and the grounds upon which he is seeking it. Thus, in substance there may be situations where the complaint will be both upheld and dismissed.[4]

1   See wording of MCA 1980, s 64(1).
2   MCA 1980, s 53(2).
3   Statutory Nuisance (Appeals) Regulations 1995, SI 1995/2664, reg 2(5). Whilst there is no requirement that the complaint specify the order which the court will be asked to make (see Magistrates' Court Forms, Form 98 (complaint) and *Wycombe District Council v Jeffways and Pilot Coaches (HW) Ltd* (1983) 81 LGR 662, CA, discussed in this chapter) clearly some grounds of appeal, if successful, will naturally lead the court to quash the notice while others may lead to the notice being varied.
4   Notwithstanding the terms of MCA 1980, s 53(2).

7.12 In *Wycombe District Council v Jeffways and Pilot Coaches (HW) Ltd*[1] one of the issues before the Court of Appeal was whether the magistrates were making an order for which the complaint was made in circumstances where the magistrates had varied the abatement notice but the appellant had stated in the details of his complaint that he was seeking to have the notice quashed (rather than varied). The court held that such an order was an order for which the complaint was made,[2] or was at least *substantially* such an order and, accordingly, the magistrates were entitled in principle to award the appellant its costs under section 64(1)(a) of the MCA 1980.[3] It is, therefore, strongly arguable that any appeal which is partially successful, whether it leads to the notice being quashed or simply varied, will result in the magistrates 'making an order for which the complaint is made' for the purposes of section 64(1)(a) of the MCA 1980.[4] It follows from this that the complaint is not being dismissed.[5]

1   (1988) 81 LGR 662, CA.
2   (1983) 81 LGR 662, CA, at 676 per O'Connor LJ.
3   (1983) 81 LGR 662, CA, at 675 per Stephenson LJ. His lordship observed that as there is no obligation on the appellant to specify the particular order(s) which he seeks, the complaint made is simply for 'an order on appeal against the notice'. The complaint may thus be properly seen as a complaint either for an order quashing the notice or an order varying it, as the case may be, even if the appellant is only seeking to have the notice quashed: see 675. Sir George Baker agreed with the reasoning of both Lord Justices. If it is concluded that the order is not at least substantially an order for which the complaint was made, then the magistrates would be acting outside their powers: see MCA 1980, s 53(2).
4   It is of note that the variation made to the notice in the *Wycombe* case was a relatively minor variation in operating hours. It therefore appears that the test of 'substantial' success adopted by Stephenson LJ has a low threshold.
5   It could be argued that there may be a category of cases in which the complaint is being substantially dismissed, albeit the notice is varied in some way. In the authors' view, such an approach to MCA 1980, s 64 is not sensible, nor does a broad discretion under s 64 need to rest upon such an approach: see *Bradford Metropolitan District Council v Booth* (2000) 164 JP 485, DC. See discussion at para **7.14**.

7.13 If in a case of 'partial success' the magistrates' court is in substance making an order for which the complaint is made, can it nevertheless make a costs award in favour of the local authority? Consider the case where an abatement notice is served on a factory requiring various steps to be carried out to abate noise from the plant, with a compliance period of four weeks. The factory owner in his appeal argues that the notice is unlawful because the requirements are unclear and there was no statutory nuisance at the time the notice was served. He also argues that he should be allowed six weeks to comply. Supposing the magistrates' court grants him the extension of time but dismisses his appeal on all other grounds. In such a case the local authority may justifiably consider themselves the victors and will often apply for some or all of their costs. However, it is often argued by appellants that because the notice is being varied, the complaint is being upheld and not dismissed, and therefore there is no discretion to award costs in favour of the local authority.

7.14 Our view is that in cases of partial success, the proper approach is for the court to view the complaint as having been in part upheld and in part dismissed. Accordingly, costs may be ordered in favour of the substantial victor. This approach to section 64 of the MCA 1980 is consistent with the philosophy which underlines recent decisions of the Divisional Court, such as *Bradford Metropolitan District Council v Booth*, referred to above.

7.15 Given the inherent uncertainties as to the outcome of the court's exercise of its discretion on costs, local authorities facing an appeal against an abatement notice are advised to be flexible towards what are often minor issues arising from the notice such as the time for compliance. This is particularly so given that magistrates who are finding against an appellant on several grounds of appeal may be inclined to give the appellant some cause for comfort by extending the time for compliance. For appellants, it is clearly worth seeking relatively minor or uncontroversial amendments to the notice if only to reduce the risk of an adverse costs order at the end of the trial.

Interim hearings and adjournments

7.16 It is doubtful that the magistrates' court has any power to award the costs of an interim hearing at the conclusion of that hearing itself, unless the at the conclusion of the hearing the complaint is dismissed.[1] If the complaint is not dismissed there and then, the costs of the interim hearing should be dealt with at the conclusion of the case as a whole.

1   See wording of MCA 1980, s 64.

7.17 Similarly, where a hearing of the complaint is adjourned to another date, the complaint is neither dismissed nor upheld and, therefore, there is no power to make an order for the costs of the adjourned hearing at the time of the adjournment. The costs of the adjournment should be dealt with at the conclusion of the case as a whole.

Abandonment of the appeal to the magistrates' court

7.18 Where an appeal is started by the making of a complaint to the magistrates' court but the case is abandoned by the appellant, the magistrates' court may make such order as to costs to be paid by the appellant to the other party to the appeal as it thinks just and reasonable.[1] Usually this will involve the appellant paying or making some contribution towards the other party's costs incurred as a result of the (abandoned) appeal.

1   Courts Act 1971, s 52(3).

Withdrawal of the abatement notice before the conclusion of the appeal

7.19 A difficulty arises where an appeal is made against the abatement notice, but the notice is subsequently withdrawn[1] by the local authority at any time

7.19 *Costs and compensation*

before the magistrates' make their decision on appeal. In such a case, although the complaint is still before the magistrates' court, it would appear[2] that there is no longer a notice which is the subject of appeal. It might be unjust if in such a case the appellant was denied all opportunity to claim his costs. The difficulty in these cases arises because section 64 of the MCA 1980 contemplates that the magistrates should only make an order as to costs on dismissing the complaint or making an order for which the complaint was made. Furthermore, section 53(2) of the MCA 1980 provides that on the hearing of a complaint, the magistrates shall make an order for which the complaint is made or dismiss the complaint. In the context of a statutory nuisance appeal, this means varying or quashing the notice or dismissing the appeal.[3] These does not appear to be any statutory power to make any other form of order.[4]

1 For the power of withdrawal, see Chapter 2, paras **2.83–2.85**.
2 *R v Bristol City Council, ex p Everett* [1999] 1 WLR 92 (Richards J); judgment upheld at [1999] 1 WLR 1170, CA, in which an implied power of a local authority to withdraw an abatement notice was held to exist, did not discuss the consequences of withdrawal of the abatement notice, save to suggest that from the time of withdrawal the notice ceased to be of any effect. The position may be different once an appeal has been made against the notice: *R v Cannock Justices, ex p Astbury* (1972) 70 LGR 609.
3 Statutory Nuisance (Appeals) Regulations 1995, SI 1995/2644, reg 2(5), and see further the discussion of MCA 1980, s 64 in this chapter.
4 Such as some form of declaration that the notice was unlawful or that the complaint was well-founded.

7.20 In the authors' view, once the abatement notice is withdrawn the magistrates probably cannot make an order for which the complaint is made; that is, they cannot vary or quash the notice,[1] because there is no longer a notice to quash or vary.[2] Assuming that the proper order is for the complaint to be dismissed, the question then arises as to the scope of the court's power in these circumstances. There are two alternative views. Either the magistrates' court does not have power to award the complainant his costs, since the court is not making an order for which the complaint was made, or, consistently with *Bradford v Booth*, the court has a discretion as to whether and how much costs to award whom. In the authors' view, the approach in *Bradford v Booth* would tend to support the position that the court may still exercise its discretion and award costs to either party as it considers just and reasonable.[3]

1 It would follow on the wording of MCA 1980, s 53 that the appeal should be dismissed.
2 It would also be somewhat artificial for a court to purport to quash a notice which has been withdrawn by the local authority. However, were it to do so then it could plainly award the appellant his costs, having made an order for which the complaint was made.
3 While the uncertainty surrounding the withdrawal of notices persists, prudent appellants may consider asking for an order for costs *as part of the complaint*. In this way, the court could arguably make an order for costs in favour of the appellant rather than dismiss the complaint where the abatement notice is withdrawn where it considered it just to do so.

Reasons for Costs Orders

7.21 It has been held that the magistrates need not go in detail into the reasons for their decision, but they ought to give sufficient reasons to make it clear that they appreciated the principles under which they were exercising their discretion. Part of the rationale behind not requiring detailed reasons appears to be to discourage satellite litigation on the question of costs.[1]

1 *Crawley BC v Stuart Attenborough* [2006] EWHC 1278 (Admin) at [10]–[11], where Scott-Baker LJ cast doubt on the correctness of decisions to the effect that there was no general duty to give reasons for costs decisions (see *R v Stafford Crown Court ex parte Wilf Gilbert (Staffs)*

Section 1 Civil proceedings: costs on an appeal 7.27

Ltd [1999] 2 All ER 955 and *Eagil Trust co v Pigott-Brown* [1985] 3 All ER 119). The judge considered it doubtful that such decisions survived the Criminal Procedure Rules which loosened the opportunity to appeal against costs decisions.

Appeal to the Crown Court

7.22 On an appeal to the Crown Court, a distinction must be drawn between the power to award costs of proceedings in the Crown Court, and the power to make a fresh order relating to the costs of the proceedings which have already taken place in the magistrates' court.

Costs of the proceedings in the Crown Court

7.23 As to costs of the Crown Court proceedings, the Court may make such order as it thinks just.'[1] This is obviously a wide discretion. The usual costs order will be that the outright or substantial winner gets his costs. However, the court may make partial awards of costs or award both parties a proportion of their costs. This may be appropriate where each has succeeded to some extent or where the conduct of the outright or substantial winner has led to costs being incurred unnecessarily.

1 Supreme Court Act 1981, s 48, applying *Johnson v RSPCA* (2000) 164 JP 345.

Costs of the proceedings in the magistrates' court

7.24 The way in which the Crown Court exercises its power to award costs of proceedings in the magistrates' court will depend on whether or not the appeal to the Crown Court succeeds.

7.25 Where the appeal is successful, the Crown Court may make any order as to costs as it thinks just, and by such order may exercise any power which the magistrates' court could have exercised. In other words, the Crown Court can exercise the costs power of the magistrates' court under section 64 MCA 1980.[1]

1 Supreme Court Act 1981 s 48(2).

7.26 Where the appeal is dismissed, by analogy with the position in criminal appeals it appears that the Crown Court may nonetheless interfere with the costs award made by the magistrates' court. However, the Crown Court should hesitate before doing so.[1] Where it chooses to interfere with the previous costs order, it may make such order as to costs as it thinks just.[2]

1 *Johnson v RSPCA* (2000) 164 JP 345, DC, in the context of criminal appeals (see paras **7.39–7.40**). The divisional court held that both Prosecution of Offences Act 1985 (POA 1985), s 18 and Supreme Court Act 1981 (SCA 1981), s 48 independently of each other conferred a sufficiently wide power upon the Crown Court for it to interfere with the magistrates' costs order on an unsuccessful appeal against conviction: see 351D. Although POA 1985, s 18 would not be available to the Crown Court on a civil appeal, SCA 1981, s 48 is applicable to civil appeals.
2 SCA 1981, s 48.

Abandonment of the appeal to the Crown Court

7.27 Where notice to abandon an appeal has been duly given by an appellant and the other party to the appeal wishes to apply for its costs, it must do so to the magistrates' court from whose decision the appeal was made. The

7.27 *Costs and compensation*

magistrates' court may order the appellant to pay such costs as appear to them to be just and reasonable in respect of expenses properly incurred by the other party in connection with the appeal. Only costs incurred before the notice of abandonment was given to that party may be recovered.[1]

1 MCA 1980, s 109(1).

Interim hearings and adjournments

7.28 The costs occasioned by any interim hearing or adjournment lie at the discretion of the court. Such costs are usually left to the conclusion of the proceedings as a whole.

Withdrawal of the abatement notice after an appeal to the Crown Court is made but before that appeal is determined

7.29 Where the abatement notice is withdrawn while the appeal to the Crown Court is pending or before a final decision on such an appeal is made, the Crown Court may make such order as to costs as it considers just.[1]

1 In other words, it may exercise its general discretion as to costs under SCA 1981, s 48. Because of this general discretion in the Crown Court, it matters not for the purposes of the costs of the Crown Court proceedings whether the appeal is formally dismissed or upheld following withdrawal of the abatement notice.

SECTION 2 CRIMINAL PROCEEDINGS: COSTS ON A PROSECUTION FOR FAILURE TO COMPLY WITH AN ABATEMENT NOTICE OR NUISANCE ORDER[1]

Prosecution in the magistrates' court

Prosecution an outright success

7.30 Where a defendant is convicted in the magistrates' court, the court may make such order as to costs to be paid by the accused to the local authority as it considers 'just and reasonable'.[2] The magistrates' court does not have a power to make an order for the local authority's costs to come out of central (public) funds.[3]

1 See generally the POA 1985, ss 16–21, Costs in Criminal Cases (General) Regulations 1986, SI 1986/1335, *Practice Direction (Costs: criminal proceedings)* [2004] 2 All ER 1070.
2 POA 1985, s 18(1).
3 *Practice Direction (Costs: criminal proceedings)* [2004] 2 All ER 1070, para III.1.1 and para VI.1.1; [2004] 1 WLR 2657.

Defendant wholly successful/abandonment of prosecution

7.31 Where an information is laid in the magistrates' court and not proceeded with, or the magistrates' court find in favour of the defendant at the end of the trial, the court may order the payment of the defendant's costs out of public funds. The court may award him such amount as it considers 'reasonably sufficient to compensate him for any expenses properly incurred by him in the proceedings'.[1] The court should usually award the defendant the whole of that amount unless there are positive reasons for not doing so.[2]

Section 2 Criminal proceedings: costs on a prosecution 7.37

1 POA 1985, s16(1), (6). The magistrates' court can award costs under this section even where the court has no jurisdiction to proceed with the trial because the information was laid out of time: *Patel and Patel v Blakey* (1987) 151 JP 532. There is no power to award interest on costs awarded out of central funds in a criminal cause or matter: see *Archbold: Criminal Pleading, Evidence and Practice* (2008 edn) para 6.22.
2 *Practice Direction (Costs: criminal proceedings)* [2004] 2 All ER 1070, para II.1.1; [2004] 1 WLR 2657. As to 'positive reasons' see para II.2.1-2.2 of the *Practice Direction* and also *Mooney v Cardiff Justices* (2000) 164 JP 220; *R v South West Surrey Justices, ex p James* [2000] Crim LR 690, DC; *R (J Sainsbury plc) v Plymouth Magistrates' Court* [2006] All ER (D) 137. Reasons which involve a suspicion that an acquitted defendant is in fact guilty have been held to infringe the right to a fair trial under article 6(2) of the ECHR: *Manelli v Switzerland* (1983) 5 EHHR 554, *Hussain v UK* (2006) The Times, 5 April 2006.

7.32 The court should be careful to ensure that it has before it sufficient evidence justifying a finding that such positive reasons exist before denying the defendant his costs. In the case of discontinued proceedings, there is no obligation upon the court to hear oral evidence as to the facts of the case which has been abandoned and the court may proceed to consider costs on the basis of a summary of the facts given by the prosecutor.[1]

1 *Mooney v Cardiff Justices* (2000) 164 JP 220.

7.33 Usually the court will assess the amount that the defendant should receive. However, where the defendant does not agree with the amount assessed by the court the matter will fall to be determined by formal taxation.[1]

1 See generally, POA 1985, s 16(6)–(9). The relevant regulations are the Costs in Criminal Cases (General) Regulations 1986, SI 1986/1335. For a commentary on the legislative scheme, see *Archbold: Criminal Pleading, Evidence and Practice* (2008 edn) paras 6-16 to 6-19.

7.34 Where the court makes an order for costs out of central funds, costs not properly incurred will be disallowed. Costs not properly incurred include costs in respect of work unreasonably done, for example, where the case has been conducted unreasonably so as to incur unjustified expense, or costs have been wasted by failure to conduct proceedings with reasonable competence or expedition.[1]

1 For a description of the relevant rules and procedure, see *Practice Direction (Costs: criminal proceedings)* [2004] 2 All ER 1070, part V; [2004] 1 WLR 2657.

Partial success

7.35 Where the defendant is acquitted on some but not all of the charges which are before the court, the court may exercise its discretion to make a costs order in favour of the defendant for the costs to come out of public funds, but may order that only part of the costs actually incurred be paid. The court should make whatever order seems just having regard to the relative importance of the charges and the conduct of the parties generally. Where the court considers that it would be inappropriate that the defendant should recover all of the costs properly incurred, the amount must be specified in the order.[1]

1 *Practice Direction (Costs: criminal proceedings)* [2004] 2 All ER 1070, para II.1.1 and II.2.2; [2004] 1 WLR 2657.

7.36 Correspondingly, the court has the power to award the prosecution its costs applying the principles set out above (see para **7.30**).

Appeal against conviction or sentence in the Crown Court

7.37 The powers of the Crown Court are the similar to those of the magistrates' court. However, as with civil proceedings in the Crown Court, it is

7.37 *Costs and compensation*

important to keep in mind the distinction between the costs of the proceedings in the Crown Court and the costs of the proceedings which have already taken place in the magistrates' court.

All grounds of appeal dismissed: costs of the proceedings in the Crown Court

7.38 Where the Crown Court dismisses in full an appeal against conviction or the sentence imposed on that conviction, it may make such order as to the costs to be paid by the accused to the local authority as it considers just and reasonable.[1] The court does not have a power to make an order for the local authority's costs to come out of public funds.[2]

1   POA 1985, s 18(1).
2   *Practice Direction (Costs: criminal proceedings)* [2004] 2 All ER 1070, para III.1.1 and VI.1.1; [2004] 1 WLR 2657.

All grounds of appeal dismissed: costs of the proceedings in the magistrates' court

7.39 Where the Crown Court dismisses an appeal against conviction or the sentence imposed on that conviction, the Crown Court may exceptionally interfere with the award of costs made in the magistrates' court, even though there is no right of appeal on costs alone[1]. In *Johnson v RSPCA*,[2] the Divisional Court held that there was no express or implied restriction on the Crown Court's statutory powers[3] which prevented the Crown Court from interfering with the costs order of the magistrates' court. Nor was there any policy reason why it should not have the power to do so. The Crown Court may lawfully reduce or increase the award of costs which the magistrates made even if the appeal is dismissed. However, the court stressed that a cautious approach should be taken to varying the costs order of the magistrates' court and that the prosecutor would be expected to inform the appellant in advance and with detailed reasons of his intention to ask the Crown Court to interfere with the costs order of the lower court. Schiemann LJ set out the following useful guidance:[4]

> '1   In the usual case where the issue is whether the magistrates order in respect of costs should be modified after an unsuccessful appeal the Crown Court should hesitate to do so. In the usual case the magistrates will be far better placed than the Crown Court judge to decide how much of the costs of legal proceedings before them the prosecution should recover. They know, especially in a long case, who wasted time, called unnecessary witnesses and so on.
>
> 2   If a prosecutor respondent proposes to ask the Crown Court to vary in his favour a costs order made in the court below he should set that out in detail and in writing to the appellant well before the case is listed to be heard so that the appellant's mind is directed to the possible consequences of any decision by him to pursue an appeal. If that step is omitted we would, bearing in mind that the prosecutor has no free-standing right to appeal in relation to costs, generally expect the Crown Court not to interfere with the costs order made in the court below.'

1   The prosecution have no right of appeal to the Crown Court, and the defence cannot appeal a costs order alone by virtue of MCA 1980, s 108(3)(b).
2   (2000) 164 JP 345.
3   Namely, POA 1985, s 18(1) and SCA 1981, s 48.
4   (2000) 164 JP 345 at 353F–354A.

Section 2 Criminal proceedings: costs on a prosecution 7.46

7.40 In general, modification of the magistrates' costs order following an unsuccessful appeal to the Crown Court will be the exception rather than the rule. Note that the prosecutor may ask the Crown Court to vary the magistrates' cost order even though the appeal is made by the defendant.

Abandonment of appeal

7.41 Where an appeal to the Crown Court is abandoned by the appellant before any hearing of the appeal takes place, the other party to the appeal may apply for its costs to the court whose decision was being appealed. That court may award such costs as appear to it to be just and reasonable in respect of expenses that are referable to the appeal before the notice of appeal was received.[1] Where the appeal is abandoned at the appeal hearing itself, the Crown Court may exercise its own powers to award costs.[2]

1   MCA 1980, s 109.
2   Supreme Court Act 1981, s 48(2).

Wholly successful appeal: costs of proceedings in the Crown Court

7.42 Where the Crown Court allows an appeal against conviction or sentence, it may award the defendant such amount as it considers 'reasonably sufficient to compensate him for any expenses properly incurred by him in the proceedings.'[1] The principles applicable to the making of an order for costs in these circumstances are the same as those applicable where a defendant is successful in the magistrates' court.[2]

1   POA 1985, s 16(3), (6), *Practice Direction (Costs: criminal proceedings)* [2004] 2 All ER 1070, para I.1.3; [2004] 1 WLR 2657.
2   See paras **7.31–7.34**.

Wholly successful appeal: costs of proceedings in the magistrates' court

7.43 Unless the Court expressly orders otherwise, an order by the Crown Court for costs in favour of the defendant who has succeeded in full on appeal will include the costs of those proceedings in the magistrates' court.[1]

1   POA 1985, s 21(1) (definition of 'proceedings' includes proceedings in the court below), *Practice Direction (Costs: criminal proceedings)* [2004] 2 All ER 1070, para I.1.3; [2004] 1 WLR 2657.

7.44 Where the Crown Court decides to make an express order addressing costs in the magistrates' court, it may make any order as to the costs of those proceedings which the magistrates' court itself could have made.[1]

1   Criminal Procedure Rules 2005, r 78.2. As to order which the magistrates' court could have made, see paras **7.30–7.36**.

Partial success: costs of proceedings in the Crown Court

7.45 Where the appellant has succeeded on some but not all grounds of appeal, the principles described in paras **7.38** and **7.42** will apply to the extent that each party has been successful.

Partial success: costs of the proceedings in the magistrates' court

7.46 Where some aspects of the appeal succeed but others are dismissed, the Crown Court can be expected to vary the costs award made in the magistrates'

7.46 *Costs and compensation*

court to reflect the partial success that the appellant has had. In principle, the Crown Court may also revisit the whole of the costs order made in the magistrates' court though it will hesitate before doing so.[1]

1   See *Johnson v RSPCA* (2000) 164 JP 345.

SECTION 3 COSTS ON A PRIVATE PARTY'S ACTION FOR A NUISANCE ORDER UNDER SECTION 82 OF THE EPA[1]

7.47   On proceedings under section 82 of the EPA 1990 the person aggrieved may be able to claim his costs of bringing the proceedings either against the defendant(s) to the complaint or against the local authority who is not a defendant to the complaint, depending on the circumstances of the case.

1   The procedure under EPA 1990, s 82 is discussed in Chapter 6.

Section 82(12): a statutory right to costs against the defendant to the complaint

7.48   Section 82(12) of the EPA 1990 provides that:

'Where on the hearing of proceedings for an order under subsection (2) above it is proved that the alleged nuisance existed at the date of the making of the complaint or summary application, then, whether or not at the date of the hearing it still exists or is likely to recur, the court ... shall order the defendant[s] ... in such proportions as appears reasonable to pay to the person bringing the proceedings such amount as the court considers reasonably sufficient to compensate him for any expenses properly incurred by him in the proceedings.'

These provisions are examined below.

'On the hearing of proceedings for an order under subsection(2)'

7.49   Section 82(2) of the EPA 1990 gives the magistrates' court the power to power to order the defendant(s) to abate the nuisance, prevent its recurrence, or execute any works necessary to achieve those ends. The hearing for the order will be held after the person aggrieved has made his complaint. The statutory right to costs can only arise where the application for costs is made at this hearing.

'It is proved that the alleged nuisance existed at the date of the making of the complaint ... whether or not at the date of the hearing it still exists or is likely to recur'

7.50   It must be proven – to the criminal standard of 'beyond reasonable doubt'[1] – that the alleged nuisance existed at the date the complaint was made under section 82 of the EPA 1990. It is not enough that the nuisance was likely to recur at that date, or that the nuisance has recurred since or still exists. Similarly, it is not enough to prove that a nuisance other than the one alleged in the complaint existed. The complainant will not be entitled to costs under section 82(12) of the EPA 1990 if the defendant has abated the nuisance by the day the complaint is made. However, provided the relevant notice requirements under section 82(6) have been complied with, the right to costs may exist even

Section 3 Costs on a private party's action for a nuisance order 7.54

if the nuisance has been abated by the time of the hearing and even if the defendant has not been given a reasonable time to abate the nuisance before the complaint was made.[2]

1 *Bottross v London Borough of Hammersmith and Fulham* (1994) 27 HLR 179. It follows that the person aggrieved must also prove the identity of the defendant beyond reasonable doubt.
2 See generally *R v Dudley Magistrates' Court, ex p Hollis* [1999] 1 WLR 642.

'The court shall order the defendant[s]'

7.51 The court is under a duty to make the order provided the statutory criteria are met.[1] The defendant(s) to the proceedings may be the person responsible for the nuisance, the owner, or occupier of relevant premises.[2] A local authority may fall into this category, for example as a landlord in council run housing.

1 And see *R v Dudley Magistrates' Court, ex p Hollis* [1998] Env LR 354 and *Davenport v Walsall Metropolitan Borough Council* [1997] Env LR 24.
2 See EPA 1990, s 82(4).

'In such proportions as appears fair and reasonable'

7.52 The court has a wide discretion to apportion liability to pay the costs awarded. Relevant factors in exercising the discretion will include the extent of responsibility for the nuisance, the steps each party took in trying to abate the nuisance before the complaint was made, the provisions of any legal agreement between the defendants such as a lease, the degree to which each party has co-operated with the court, and the ability of each party to pay costs.

'Such amount as the court considers reasonably sufficient to compensate him for any expenses properly incurred by him in the proceedings'

7.53 There is no right to recover all expenses properly incurred, but only the amount that the court considers will provide reasonably sufficient compensation.[1] Expenses may be properly incurred[2] in the proceedings even though those proceedings or part of them were not successful. However, in so far as part of the case was 'doomed from the outset,' the court is likely to find that expenses in relation to that part were improperly incurred.[3]

1 However, the court does not have a discretion to award a lesser sum that this: see *Mullingar RDC v Greville* (1906) 41 ILTR 144.
2 For the relevance of fee agreements between client and solicitor, see *Hazlett v Sefton Metropolitan Borough Council* [2000] 4 All ER 887; *Kellar v Stanley A Williams* [2004] UKPC 30.
3 See *Davenport v Walsall Metropolitan Borough Council* [1997] Env LR 24 at 41. The test for 'improper' conduct under EPA 1990, s 82(12) is not as high as the test which the court would apply on an application for a wasted costs order: *Davenport* at 39.

Discretion to award costs to the person aggrieved outside of section 82

7.54 Although section 82(1) of the EPA 1990 refers to the court acting 'on a complaint', proceedings under section 82 are properly commenced by the laying of an information because the proceedings are criminal in nature.[1] An offence is committed where the nuisance exists or is likely to recur at the date of the hearing.[2]

7.54 *Costs and compensation*

1 See Chapter 6 for the procedure under EPA 1990, s 82.
2 *R v Liverpool Crown Court, ex p Cooke* [1997] 1 WLR 700 at 703D, 705H; *R v Dudley Magistrates' Court, ex p Hollis* [1998] Env LR 354 at 360. See para **6.54**.

7.55 There is some uncertainty as to whether section 82 requires the defendant to formally prove that the statutory nuisance also existed on the date that the complaint was made which is discussed at paras **6.55–6.58**.[1] If an offence may be proven without showing that the nuisance existed at the time the complaint was made, it follows that the defendant may be convicted in circumstances where the right to costs under section 82(12) does not arise. In such a case, would the court nevertheless have power to award costs to the person aggrieved? In the authors' view it would. Section 18 of the POA 1985 provides that where any person is convicted of an offence before a magistrates' court, the court may make such order as to costs to be paid by the accused to the prosecutor as it considers just and reasonable. The Act gives no definition of 'prosecutor' for the purposes of section 18. However, because the person aggrieved lays the information before the magistrates' court and is responsible for proving the matters alleged in it, he would appear to fall within the definition of a 'prosecutor' at common law.[2] Accordingly, he should have the benefit of the courts power to award costs under section 18 of the POA 1985.[3]

1 In the authors' view, the party bringing proceedings under EPA 1990, s 82 is advised to adduce evidence to prove that he was aggrieved by the existence of the statutory nuisance at the time that the information was laid.
2 Defined as the party 'actively instrumental in putting the law into force': *Danby v Beardsley* (1880) 43 LT 603 at 604. See generally vol 45(2) *Halsbury's Laws* (4th edn reissue) para 460.
3 See para **7.30**. In simple terms, POA 1985, s 18 allows the court to award the prosecutor his costs to be paid by the accused.

Costs against the local authority who is not the defendant to the complaint

7.56 Where it appears to the magistrates that the relevant defendant[1] to the proceedings cannot be found, the magistrates may direct the local authority to do anything which they would have directed the defendant to do. The magistrates' powers therefore extend to ordering the local authority to pay the person aggrieved such amount of compensation for expenses incurred as the court could have awarded under section 82(12) of the EPA 1990. The local authority must be given an opportunity of being heard before such a direction is given.[2] Note however that the court's power to award costs in these circumstances arises under section 82(13) and is discretionary: there is no right to recover such costs from the local authority.

1 See para **7.51**.
2 See EPA 1990, s 82(13). Note also that s19B POA 1985 gives a discretion to the Magistrates' Court, Crown Court and Court of Appeal to make a costs order against third parties who are not parties to the proceedings, where there has been "serious misconduct" by that third party: see *Practice Direction (Costs: criminal proceedings)* [2004] 2 All ER 1070 para VII.3.1; [2004] 1 WLR 2657.

Costs of the defendant(s) to proceedings under section 82

7.57 A successful defendant to proceedings under section 82 of the EPA 1990 may be awarded his costs by the court out of central (public) funds. The power to award costs in these circumstances is the same as that which arises when the defendant is acquitted in criminal proceedings.[1]

1 For the (exceptional) power to award costs against a prosecutor for unnecessary or improper conduct, see Costs in Criminal Cases (General) Regulations 1986 (as amended) and *DPP v Denning* [1991] 2 QB 532 at 541C-D on the meaning of 'improper conduct.' See para **7.31**.

Is a private party in proceedings under section 82 at risk in costs?

7.58 There is no general power to award costs against the prosecutor personally.[1] Where the private party fails in his prosecution for a nuisance order under section 82 of the EPA 1990, he will not usually be liable for the defendant's costs because the defendant will usually recover his costs out of central (public) funds. This is the usual order even if the information, once laid, is not proceeded with.[2]

1 A court may exceptionally order a party's legal or other representative to personally pay some or all of the costs of the other side to the extent that the representative has acted unreasonably, negligently or improperly and costs have been incurred thereby: POA 1985, s 19A (known as a 'wasted costs' order). However, this provision applies to *representatives* of a party (see POA 1985, s 19(A)(3)), and is therefore not apt to encompass a litigant acting in person.
2 POA 1985, s 16(1)(a).

SECTION 4 COMMON QUESTIONS

Can the investigative costs of salaried officers be claimed?

7.59 As with many areas of environmental law, a large proportion of the costs of proceedings will be attributable to the preparation of expert evidence and investigations with a view to commencing proceedings. The leading case on the recovery of such costs is *R v Associated Octel Co Ltd*.[1] The case concerned a prosecution under environmental health legislation arising from the escape of ethyl chloride from the defendant's plant which resulted in a serious fire. The defendant pleaded guilty, but appealed against the inclusion in the costs award of the costs of investigations carried out by the Health and Safety Laboratory and the building of a model of the plant (costing some £9,300). The Court of Appeal dismissed the appeal. The following principles can be derived from its judgment:

(i) prosecution costs of investigations and preparation of evidence prior to charging the defendant are in principle recoverable
(ii) it will usually be just and reasonable to award the full amount of investigative costs which arose out of that for which the defendant was responsible, provided those costs are not manifestly excessive, and
(iii) recoverable costs include the costs of salaried officers who are paid out of public funds to investigate such matters, provided the investigations were due to the offences committed[2] and were not part of a routine inspection.[3]

1 [1997] 1 Cr App Rep (S) 435, CA.
2 Or the nuisance caused, in the case of civil proceedings.
3 See also *Neville v Gardner Merchant Ltd* (1983) 148 JP 238 at 242; The court in *R v Associated Octel Co Ltd* [1997] 1 Cr App Rep (S) 435, CA, approved the approach taken in *Neville*.

Can the costs of gathering evidence which is not used at trial be claimed?

7.60 The costs of investigation leading to evidence which was not or would not have been used at trial, may be recovered where it can be shown that the investigations were a necessary result of the incident in question or that the evidence had some beneficial use in the proceedings overall.[1]

1 *R v Associated Octel Co Ltd* [1997] 1 Cr App Rep (S) 435, CA.

7.61 *Costs and compensation*

7.61 Relevant questions when considering whether the costs of gathering evidence which was not or would not have been used at trial are:

(i) how serious is the nuisance or the breach of the abatement notice? The court will often be sympathetic to the argument that serious matters need to be investigated thoroughly and with care. This is particularly so where the case involves tangible environmental harm or a delicate balancing of competing land use interests

(ii) has the other party contributed in some way to the need to carry out the investigations? For example, was misleading information supplied by the defendant, or have the prosecution unreasonably refused to rely upon data supplied by the defendant's expert?

(iii) has the evidence been used in other ways which have contributed to the court process? For example, was it used to assess the other side's evidence, or to decide on the plea entered?

(iv) has the evidence contributed to a shortening of the court time that was or would have been taken up by the trial? For example, has the evidence assisted experts in reaching agreement over certain matters, or led to a narrowing of issues between the parties?

What is the position regarding the costs of witnesses generally?

7.62 The costs of attendance of a witness required by the accused, a private prosecutor (which would include a local authority) or the court are allowed out of central funds unless the court orders otherwise. A witness includes any person properly attending to give evidence whether or not he gives evidence or is called, but does not include a character witness unless the court has certified that the interests of justice require his attendance.[1]

1 *Practice Direction (Costs: criminal proceedings)* [2004] 2 All ER 1070, para IV.1; [2004] 1 WLR 2657.

What is the relationship between the amount of costs awarded and the level of fine imposed?

7.63 An award of costs may be unlawful where it is grossly disproportionate to the level of fine which the court has imposed. This aspect of the power to award costs is of particular importance in environmental prosecutions where the costs of bringing the proceedings may greatly exceed the amount of any fine which the court has power to impose.

7.64 In *R v Northallerton Magistrates' Court, ex p Dove*[1] the Divisional Court set out a number of propositions relevant to this issue, which can be summarised as follows:

(i) an order to pay costs to the prosecutor should never exceed the sum which, having regard to the defendant's means and any other financial order imposed upon him, the defendant was able to pay and which it was reasonable to order the defendant to pay

(ii) the costs order should never exceed the sum which the prosecutor had actually and reasonably incurred

(iii) the purpose of the costs order was to compensate the prosecutor and not to punish the defendant;

(iv) while there was no requirement that any sum ordered by justices to be paid to a prosecutor by way of costs should stand in any arithmetical relationship to any fine imposed, the costs order to be paid should not in the ordinary way be 'grossly disproportionate' to any fine and

(v) if the total of the costs sought and the proposed fine exceeded the sum which in all the circumstances the defendant could reasonably be expected to pay, it is preferable to achieve an acceptable total by reducing the sum of costs awarded rather than reducing the fine imposed[2].

1 (1999) 163 JP 657, [2000] 1 Cr App Rep (S) 136, DC. See also *BPS Advertising Ltd v London Borough of Barnet* [2006] EWHC 3335 (Admin).
2 The practical effect of this could operate as a disincentive for local authorities that are considering prosecuting defendants of limited means.

7.65 In *Ex p Dove*[1] itself, an award of costs which was about 4.5 times the level of the fine imposed was quashed as being grossly disproportionate. However, it would be wrong to draw any general rule from the facts of that case. The court stressed that there is no requirement that amount of costs should have a particular arithmetical relationship with the level of fine imposed. The means of the defendant are likely to be of equal if not greater importance, and each case is likely to turn on its own facts.

1 *R v Northallerton Magistrates' Court, ex p Dove* (1999) 163 JP 657, [2000] 1 Cr App Rep (S) 136, DC.

7.66 Where there is an unsuccessful appeal to the Crown Court against conviction in the magistrates' court, the prosecutor may well have incurred on appeal a similar level of costs as he incurred in the court below. How is the Crown Court to approach the issue of proportionality where the prosecutor's costs for both sets of proceedings may have doubled but the fine imposed by the Court has remained the same? The issue was recently raised in *Richard Griffiths v Pembrokeshire County Council*[1] where Kennedy LJ, having considered *Ex p Dove*,[2] said:

'It can, in my judgment, be cogently argued that when a defendant appeals against conviction and his appeal fails, he has put the prosecutor (and thus in a case such as this, council taxpayers) to avoidable expense, and subject to his means, he should bear the whole of the prosecutor's reasonable costs of resisting the appeal. I see no reason for making any link between the penalty imposed in the lower court and the costs ordered to be paid on appeal. That said, if the costs claimed on appeal are far in excess of those awarded in the lower court an independent bystander might well conclude that the unsuccessful applicant was being punished for having chosen to exercise his statutory right to appeal, so a balance has to be struck.'

1 [2000] Env LR 622
2 *R v Northallerton Magistrates' Court, ex p Dove* [1999] 163 JP 657; [2000] 1 Cr App Rep (S) 136, DC.

7.67 Thus the proportionality principle in *Ex p Dove*[1] only applies to the relationship between the costs of the summary trial and the fine imposed. Where the costs of an unsuccessful appeal are in issue, the relationship between the costs imposed by the magistrates' court and the costs imposed by the Crown Court is the relevant consideration, and a link should not usually be made between the penalty imposed in the lower court and the costs ordered to be paid on appeal.

1 (1999) 163 JP 657, [2000] 1 Cr App Rep (S) 136, DC.

7.67 *Costs and compensation*

Are the costs incurred in connection with the service of the abatement notice recoverable by the local authority following an unsuccessful appeal by the recipient of the notice?

7.68 A prosecution must be preceded by the service (and breach) of an abatement notice served under the EPA 1990. The local authority is under a duty to serve the abatement notice once it has determined that a statutory nuisance exists. In the authors' view, such costs are generally recoverable where an appeal against an abatement notice fails.[1]

1 See paras **2.33–2.40**.

Are costs which are incurred in connection with the service of the abatement notice recoverable on conviction of the defendant?

7.69 There appears to be no direct authority on this point. Where there has been an unsuccessful appeal against the abatement notice and the local authority has already recovered such costs, there cannot be any entitlement to recover costs where this would result in double recovery.

7.70 Where there has been no abatement notice appeal, the better view is that the costs associated with the service of the abatement notice are not recoverable. They are not incurred as a result of the offence – the *breach* of the abatement notice – and hence are not costs incurred in the criminal proceedings.

SECTION 5 COSTS OF A CIVIL APPEAL TO THE HIGH COURT AND A CRIMINAL APPEAL TO THE DIVISIONAL COURT OR CRIMINAL COURT OF APPEAL

Civil appeal to the High Court[1]

7.71 The general provisions governing the award of costs on a civil appeal to the High Court are found in the Civil Procedure Rules 1998 ('CPR'), Part 44.[2] The court has a discretion as to who should pay costs, how much should be paid and when costs are to be paid; the general rule is that the unsuccessful party will be ordered to pay the costs of the successful party, but the court may make a different order.[3]

1 This would arise from an appeal against an abatement notice.
2 The rules relating to costs in the High Court are fairly lengthy. Only a summary of the main principles is given here.
3 CPR, Pt 44, r 44.3(1) and (2).

7.72 In deciding what order (if any) to make about costs, the court must have regard to all the circumstances. These circumstances will include the conduct of the parties,[1] whether a party has succeeded on part of his case (even if he has not been wholly successful), and any admissible offer to settle the case that may have been made.[2]

1 For further guidance on the conduct of the parties, see CPR, Pt 44, r 44.3(5).
2 CPR, Pt 44, r 44.3(4).

7.73 Guidance is also provided on how the court should approach the amount of costs to be awarded.[1] In contrast to criminal proceedings, the court is under no express duty to consider the means of a party.

1   CPR, Pt 44, r 44.5(3).

Criminal appeal[1] to the Divisional Court

7.74 Appeals on a point or points of law are made to the Divisional Court. The appeal is known as an appeal by way of case stated: see Chapter 5, paras **5.122–5.125**. The Divisional Court has a general discretion to award costs of and incidental to proceedings before it to be paid by one party to the other under the SCA 1981. However, no power to award costs out of central (public) funds can be implied into that section.[2]

1   This would arise as an appeal from a prosecution for an order under EPA 1990, s 82, or an appeal against a prosecution for non-compliance with a nuisance order or local authority abatement notice.
2   *Steele Ford & Newton v Criminal Prosecution Service (No 2)* [1994] 1 AC 22.

7.75 A public authority acting as prosecutor is not entitled to an award of costs out of central (public) funds in respect of proceedings in a criminal cause or matter in the Divisional Court,[1] although a private prosecutor (such as the complainant in proceedings under section 82 of the EPA 1990) or a defendant may be awarded from public funds such amount as the court considers reasonably sufficient to compensate him for expenses properly incurred in the proceedings.[2]

1   POA 1985, ss 17(1), (2), (6)(c).
2   POA 1985, s 17(1) (prosecutor's costs); POA 1985, s 16(5), (6) (defendant's costs).

SECTION 6 APPLICATION FOR COSTS: EVIDENCE AND PROCEDURE IN THE MAGISTRATES' AND CROWN COURT

Evidence

7.76 In both civil and criminal proceedings, the courts have emphasised that when dealing with costs it is incumbent upon the parties to have available all the necessary information on the relevant day.[1]

1   *R v West London Magistrates' Court, ex p Kyprianou* [1992–1993] Env LR D21; *R v Northallerton Magistrates' Court, ex p Dove* [1999] Crim LR 760.

7.77 A party intending to make an application for costs should prepare a schedule of costs for the proceedings in question. It is suggested that schedule should set out broad headings under which costs have been incurred (for example, experts' fees, solicitors' fees,[1] and so forth) and then under each heading at least the following:

(i)   a description of the work done (including, where possible, a description of the relationship between the work and the issue in the proceedings)
(ii) the sum claimed (showing a breakdown of net and VAT) in respect of each item of work
(iii) the basis for calculating each sum claimed: time taken, hourly charge rate, seniority of person charging.

7.77 *Costs and compensation*

1   There is a rebuttable presumption that a complainant will be liable to pay his solicitor's costs and that, therefore, those costs are costs properly incurred by him in the proceedings. The presumption may be rebutted where one party raises a genuine issue as to the other party's liability to meet his solicitor's costs: *Hazlett v Sefton Metropolitan Borough Council* [1999] Env LR 416.

7.78 Where an item of costs is likely to be contentious, it is prudent to ensure that the costs schedule sets out this item separately. In this way, should the court be unwilling to award costs in respect of that item, it can simply be 'severed' from the rest of the schedule without prejudicing the prospect of recovering other items of costs.

7.79 A standard form costs schedule is found in Appendix A.

7.80 Any party resisting an application for costs should also prepare relevant evidence. In criminal proceedings, this will usually involve producing evidence of the relevant party's means. In such proceedings, the court should be satisfied that the defendant has the means and ability to pay before it makes an order for costs against him. By making provision for payment by instalments the court may properly require the defendant to pay an amount of costs which, if payable as a lump sum or over a relatively short period of time, would otherwise be excessive having regard to his means.[1] It is recommended that all relevant documentation should be produced, including bank statements and accounts where possible.[2]

1   See *R v Olliver and Olliver* (1989) 11 Cr App Rep (S) 10, CA, discussed at para 6-29 of *Archbold: Criminal Pleading, Evidence and Practice* (2008 edn).
2   The burden on a defendant to produce evidence of financial hardship should not be taken lightly: see by way of analogy, *Kent County Council v Brockman* [1996] 1 PLR 1.

7.81 In both criminal and civil proceedings, correspondence between the parties' representatives is often relevant to costs issues. It may provide evidence of a party's reasonable or unreasonable conduct (as the case may be). For example, where one party has suggested agreeing a common stance on a particular issue and the other party unreasonably refused to accept that offer, this may have costs consequences where dispute on that issue resulted in costs being incurred unnecessarily.'Without prejudice save as to costs' correspondence may also be relied upon, and the court has expressly endorsed the use of such letters in the context of statutory nuisance actions.[1]

1   *Taylor v Walsall District Property and Investment Co* [1998] Env LR 600.

Procedure

7.82 Issues as to costs are usually left until the conclusions of the proceedings as a whole.[1]

1   In criminal proceedings there is no obligation upon the defence to apply for costs on the same day that charges are dismissed though it is usual to do so. Costs should usually be left until the conclusion of the entire proceedings: see *R v Liverpool Magistrate's Court, ex p Abiaka* (1999) 163 JP 497.

7.83 A schedule of costs should be served in advance on the party to the proceedings against whom the costs application may be made to give that party a proper opportunity to consider the costs claimed and make representation on them if appropriate. A party wishing to dispute all or part of the costs should give proper notice of the objections to the other side, if possible, or at least make it plain to the court what these objections are.¹ The courts have indicated that it should be routine practice for any dispute about particular items of costs to be raised between the parties in advance and if possible resolved in advance of any costs hearing.² If the court itself is contemplating any unusual or unconventional order potentially adverse to one of the parties, then it should alert the relevant party and his representatives to that possibility.³

1   *R v Associated Octel Ltd* [1997] 1 Cr App Rep (S) 435, CA. In practice, usually it is only the defendant who may be held liable for the prosecution's costs.
2   *Taylor v Walsall District Property Investment Co* [1998] Env LR 600.
3   *R v Northallerton Magistrates' Court, ex p Dove* (1999) 163 JP 657, [2000] 1 Cr App Rep (S) 136.

7.84   Similarly, where on appeal against conviction the prosecutor intends to ask the Crown Court to interfere with the costs order of the court below, he should set that out in detail and in writing to the appellant *well before the case is listed for hearing in the Crown Court* so that the appellant has a fair chance to address his mind to the issue. Where this is not done, the appellant can expect the Crown Court not to interfere with the costs order made in the court below.¹

1   *Johnson v RSPCA* (2000) 164 JP 345 at 353G–354A per Schiemann LJ.

7.85   Whenever a financial order (whether costs or fine) is being considered by the court, it is essential that the parties are given a fair opportunity to adduce relevant information and make any submissions. It must be emphasised, however, that parties should be ready to deal with costs at the conclusion of the trial: fairness need not extend to granting an adjournment in favour of a poorly prepared litigant.¹ In particular, where the defendant does not make disclosure of his means, the court may draw reasonable inferences about his means from the evidence which it has heard and from all the circumstances of the case. However, although the court is not obliged to make inquiries of its own initiative,² a defendant who fails to disclose his means may nonetheless successfully appeal the level of fine and costs where he can show, in the light of his means, that the level is excessive.³

1   *R v West London Magistrates' Court, ex p Kyprianou* [1992–1993] Env LR D21.
2   *R v Northallerton Magistrates' Court, ex p Dove* (1999) 163 JP 657, [2000] 1 Cr App Rep (S) 136.
3   *R v Whitter* [1999] Env LR D21, CA.

7.86   The usual procedure is for the party making the costs application to make his submissions first, setting out what it is he is applying for and the grounds for the application, including the evidence upon which he is relying. The other party should then be given an opportunity to respond, which will usually be followed by a brief reply by the party applying for its costs. It has become quite common for a party seeking its costs to make its application in the briefest of terms and then make a lengthy reply once it has heard what the other party has to say on the costs issue. In these circumstances, the party against whom the costs application is being made should insist on a reply to any grounds for costs raised by the applicant which were not set out when the application was first made. Failure to give such an opportunity may make the costs award vulnerable to challenge.¹

1   *Berkeley v Secretary of State for the Environment* [1998] Env LR 741, CA (costs decision).

SECTION 7 CHALLENGING A COSTS ORDER

Costs order made in the magistrates' court

7.87 There is no right of appeal to the Crown Court against a magistrates' costs order alone.[1] Where a party seeks to challenge only an order for costs he must do so by an appeal by way of case stated[2] or judicial review[3] to the Divisional Court. Whichever procedure is adopted, the challenge can only be brought where the decision can be characterised as involving some error of legal principle in the approach which the magistrates' court took to the costs decision. The order cannot be challenged on its merits alone.

1 MCA 1980, s 108(3)(b); *R v Bow Street Stipendiary Magistrate, ex p Screen Multimedia Ltd* (1998) Times, 28 January; *R v Northallerton Magistrates' Court, ex p Dove* (1999) 163 JP 657, [2000] 1 Cr App Rep (S) 136. For the extent to which the Crown Court on appeal against sentence or conviction may interfere with the costs order of the magistrates' court, see *Johnson v RSPCA* (2000) 164 JP 345, para **7.39**.
2 For example *Liverpool City Council v Worthington* (1998) Times, 16 June, DC Simon Brown LJ and Hooper J (transcript reference CO/1677/98).
3 *R v Tottenham Justices, ex p Joshi* [1982] 1 WLR 631, DC.

Costs order made in the Crown Court

7.88 A costs order made by the Crown Court in statutory nuisance proceedings cannot be appealed to the Criminal Court of Appeal.[1]

1 The Criminal Appeal Act 1968, ss 9 and 50 confers a limited right of appeal against costs orders but these provisions would not encompass statutory nuisance proceedings.

SECTION 8 COMPENSATION AND DAMAGES

Awards of compensation in criminal proceedings

7.89 Where a party is convicted of an offence before the magistrates' court or Crown Court, the court may make a compensation order in respect of any personal injury, loss or damage which results from the offence in question.[1] The power to make a compensation order is thus available to the magistrates' court or the Crown Court following a defendant's conviction for failure to comply with an abatement notice or the making of an order under section 82(2) of the EPA 1990.[2]

1 Powers of Criminal Courts (Sentencing) Act 2000, s 130(1).
2 *Bottross v London Borough of Hammersmith and Fulham* [1995] Env LR 217.

Who may benefit from a compensation order?

7.90 Any person who has suffered personal injury, loss or damage as a result of the breach of the abatement notice or the nuisance to which the EPA 1990 section 82 proceedings related may benefit from a compensation order. The order should in terms relate to a specific 'victim' of the offence.

7.91 When examining causation the court does not apply strict rules of causation and foreseeability as it would to claims in contract or negligence.[1]

Provided it can fairly be said that the offence for which the defendant has been convicted either directly or indirectly caused the harm in question, that should be sufficient. There must, however, be some evidence upon which a finding of causation can rest.[2]

1 See *R v Thomson Holidays Ltd* (1974) 58 Cr App Rep 429, where it was observed that as the section allows a compensation order to be made in respect of offences formally taken into account, it cannot be necessary for the court to be appraised of the detailed facts of an offence before making a compensation order.
2 *R v Derby* (1990) 12 Cr App Rep (S) 502.

What type of harm may be covered by the order?

7.92 The order may cover personal injury, loss or damage. The personal injury element of the order may cover an amount to compensate for detriment to a person's health, including modest amounts for stress and anxiety[1] caused by the nuisance. As for loss and damage, the order may compensate for expenses incurred as a result of the nuisance and for any loss in value of property. In housing cases, for example, a court may award compensation for damage caused to things such as furniture, clothes, curtains and carpets as a result of the damp state of premises, or expenses incurred in cleaning mould of walls or carrying out repairs to property. Expenses and costs incurred in related civil proceedings should not be regarded as 'loss' for the purposes of making a compensation order.[2]

1 *Archbold: Criminal Pleading, Evidence and Practice* (2008 edn) para 5-415; *Blackstone's Criminal Practice* (2008), E18.2. See *Bond v Chief Constable of Kent* (1983) 4 Cr App Rep (S) 324, DC (terror occasioned by an attack on the victim's house); *R v Thompson Holidays Ltd* [1974] QB 592 ('tension' caused by a holiday company's failure to provide holiday amenities promised). There must be some evidence that the person concerned did experience stress and anxiety: *R v Vaughn* (1990) 12 Cr App Rep (S) 46, CA.
2 *Hammerton Cars Ltd v London Borough of Redbridge* [1974] 2 All ER 216.

7.93 The court can award a sum to compensate for personal injury, loss or damage suffered only as a result of the offence for which the defendant is convicted.[1] Where the period between the expiry of the EPA 1990 section 82 notice and the date the information was laid is no more than six months, the magistrates may take into account the injury, loss or damage due to the continuation of the nuisance from the date specified in the information to the date of the hearing. However, where the period between the expiry of the section 82(6) notice and the laying of the information is greater than six months, the magistrates' court may only take into account the injury, loss or damage caused by the continuation of the nuisance from six months before the laying of the information to the date of the hearing.[2]

1 And any offence formally taken into account. This is not usually relevant in the present context.
2 *R v Liverpool Crown Court, ex p Cooke* [1996] 1 WLR 700. For the 'six-month rule' for laying an information in criminal proceedings see paras **5.31–5.33**. For the six month rule proceedings under EPA 1990, s 82 see paras **6.42–6.43**.

7.94 The size of a compensation order made by a magistrates' court is limited by statute.[1] There is no such express limit on the powers of the Crown Court.

1 The aggregate amount in any order must not exceed £5,000: Powers of Criminal Courts (Sentencing) Act 2000, s 131.

7.95 *Costs and compensation*

When is it appropriate for the court to make a compensation order?

7.95 The court has a discretion whether or not to make a compensation order. The power to make an order should usually be exercised only in simple and straightforward cases where the issues can be dealt with fairly quickly, and statutory nuisance cases are no exception to this general rule.[1] Whether or not the particular case is sufficiently simple is a question for the magistrates' court (or Crown Court, as the case may be) to decide in the first instance.

1 See, eg: *Davenport v Walsall Metropolitan Borough Council* [1997] Env LR 24.

7.96 It will often be the case that the party who would benefit from the compensation order has available to them a civil remedy for damages which they are pursuing or could pursue in the county court. The availability of such a remedy and the difficulty in obtaining redress through the civil courts is a matter that the court in criminal proceedings should take into account when deciding whether the case is an appropriate one for the exercise of its discretion to make a compensation order.[1] However, the availability of a civil claim in damages is not an essential pre-requisite to the making of a compensation order, nor does the absence of a civil remedy mean that a compensation order must be made.[1] It follows that in some cases where the court refuses to make a compensation order, the 'victim' of the nuisance will have no other means of redress in damages.[2]

1 *Herbert v London Borough of Hammersmith and Fulham* (1991) 90 HLR 299; *Davenport v Walsall Metropolitan Borough Council* [1997] Env LR 24, at 34 and 42.
2 Powers of Criminal Courts (Sentencing) Act 2000, s 134 contains provisions on the approach to be taken to the assessment of damages in a subsequent civil claim where a compensation order has been made in respect of the same matter.

7.97 A compensation order may be made either in addition to or instead of a fine. Where the court considers that it would be appropriate to impose both, but the defendant has insufficient means to pay both an appropriate fine and appropriate compensation, the court must give preference to compensation (although it may impose a fine as well).[1] It has been suggested that if the compensation order is itself large enough to be punitive, a fine should not be imposed. If on the other hand the order is relatively small, then a fine may be added for punitive effect.[2]

1 Powers of Criminal Courts (Sentencing) Act 2000, s 130(1).
2 *R v Liverpool Crown Court, ex p Cooke* [1996] 4 All ER 589 at 595h.

7.98 The order itself should be realistic and the court should have regard to the defendant's means when setting the amount to be paid.[1] It should be precise in its terms, stating the offence and 'victim' to which it relates, the amount to be paid and the instalments, if payment is to be made by instalments.[2]

1 Where the local authority is the defendant, issues of 'means' are unlikely to arise.
2 *R v Miller* [1976] Crim LR 694.

Evidence and procedure

7.99 Where ever possible, the parties should agree with each other and the court as to the procedure to be adopted where a compensation order is to be sought by the prosecution. In practice, the question of compensation is left until after the decision whether or not to convict the defendant has been given. It is

Section 8 Compensation and damages 7.104

usual at that time for the parties to address the court on the appropriateness of making a compensation order, the amount of any order that should be made, and the evidence produced to support the award. Where an offence is proven or where the accused pleads guilty, the issue of compensation can be raised after the plea is entered.

7.100 Evidence in support of a compensation order should set out clearly the personal injury, loss and damage which it is claimed resulted from the offence. Where personal injury is in issue, a medical report should be produced if possible. Where other loss or damage is claimed, this should be itemised and quantified where appropriate, and evidence of any expenditure, such as receipts, should be produced. It will be important to establish clearly the state of affairs before and after the offence in question.

7.101 Since the power to make a compensation order should only be exercised in simple cases, a balance needs to be struck between the need to present the court with a straightforward claim and the need to provide sufficiently detailed evidence. The extent to which issues such as causation and the value of any damage are agreed between the parties will be a significant factor when the court makes its decision about whether the case is a suitable one for a compensation order to be made. Where compensation for personal injury is being sought, up-to-date medical evidence should be produced. Where the claim for personal injury is complex and a substantial sum of money is contemplated, the usual course will be for the matter to be left to the county court should the victim wish to pursue civil proceedings.[1]

1   *R v Cooper* [1982] Crim LR 308.

7.102 The court should first decide whether the case is one which is simple enough for a compensation order to be made. It should make this decision having heard submissions from both sides and considered any other information put before it.[1] It will usually not be an appropriate case in which to make a compensation order if extensive cross examination or lengthy oral evidence is required.

1   It has been suggested that there is usually no need for the court to hear oral evidence or cross-examination before making its decision *Davenport v Walsall Metropolitan Borough Council* [1997] Env LR 24 at 32. In the authors' view, this suggestion should be treated with caution. In many cases justice will require evidence to be tested: see para **7.104**.

7.103 Where the court decides that a compensation order is not appropriate, it must state it reasons for so deciding.[1] Where it decides that such an order is appropriate, it should go on to consider the appropriate amount.

1   Powers of Criminal Courts (Sentencing) Act 2000, s 130(3).

7.104 A compensation order made by the Magistrates' Court must not exceed £5,000[1]. The Crown Court has a wide discretion to order such amount as it considers appropriate, having regard to any evidence and to any representations that are made by or on behalf of the accused or the prosecutor.[2] However, where there is a serious dispute as to whether or not any personal injury, loss or damage has been suffered by a person and the amount which should be made the subject of an order, the court should receive evidence to determine liability and not act simply on representations made by the parties. Justice demands that the defendant should have a proper opportunity to test the grounds upon which the order is to be made against him.[3]

7.104 *Costs and compensation*

1   Powers of Criminal Courts (Sentencing) Act 2000, s 131.
2   Powers of Criminal Courts (Sentencing) Act 2000, s 130(4).
3   *R v Horsham Justices, ex p Richards* [1985] 2 All ER 1114.

Challenging an award of compensation

7.105 A compensation order made by the magistrates' court may be appealed to the Crown Court as part of an appeal against sentence. It should be borne in mind that the Crown Court's sentencing powers will then be 'at large,' and the appellant risks having a heavier sentence imposed upon him than was imposed by the magistrates.

7.106 A challenge to a magistrates' court compensation order on the grounds that there has been some error of law may be made by way of case stated to the Divisional Court. Any challenge to a compensation order made by the Crown Court must be made on appeal by way of case stated to the Divisional Court.[1]

1   SCA 1981, s 28.

Relevance of damages awarded in related civil claims

7.107 Specific provision is made to address the situation in which a compensation order is made and the beneficiary subsequently makes a claim for civil damages in respect of the injury, loss or damage to which the compensation order relates.[1] In these circumstances, although the civil damages must be calculated without reference to the amount of the compensation order, the beneficiary can only recover from the award of civil damages a sum equal to the aggregate of (i) the amount by which the damages exceed the compensation order and (ii) a sum equal to the amount of any ordered compensation which is not in fact paid.[2]

1   Powers of Criminal Courts (Sentencing) Act 2000, s 134.
2   Powers of Criminal Courts (Sentencing) Act 2000, s 134(2) The latter sum can only be recovered with the permission of the court.

Varying a compensation order

7.108 The magistrates' court has the power to vary or discharge a compensation order in a number of circumstances, such as where the offender has suffered a reduction in his means.[1] In the present context, the need to vary an order will rarely arise.[2]

1   See generally Powers of Criminal Courts (Sentencing) Act 2000, s133.
2   The majority of compensation orders are made against local authorities in housing cases following a conviction under EPA 1990, s 82.

Damages for interference with human rights

7.109 Under section 6 of the Human Rights Act 1998 (HRA 1998), it is unlawful for a public authority (subject to section 7(1) to act in a way which is incompatible with a person's rights under the European Convention of Human Rights (ECHR).[1] Where the court finds that an act (or proposed act) of a public authority is unlawful, it *may* grant such relief or remedy, or make such order within its powers as it considers just and appropriate.[2] This may include an award of damages where the court has power to award damages or compensation in civil proceedings.[3] Where, therefore, a local authority exercising its powers under the statutory nuisance regime of the EPA 1990 infringes the human rights of a person,[4] there is potential for that person to claim damages for the local authority's breach of section 6 of the HRA 1998.[5]

1   To the extent that the ECHR is given effect in domestic law by virtue of HRA 1998, Sch 1. The right to an effective remedy (ECHR art 13) is not incorporated in HRA 1998, Sch 1, although the government in parliamentary debates indicated its view that the courts may have regard to art 13 when considering HRA 1998, s 8 (judicial remedies): see 583 HL Official Report (5th Series), col 477 (18 November 1997).
2   HRA 1998, s 8(1).
3   HRA 1998, s 8(2). Importantly, where proceedings are commenced by the local authority and the defendant claims that the public authority has acted in breach of his Convention rights, he may rely upon his Convention rights whenever the act in question took place: see HRA 1998, ss 22(4) and 7(1)(b). In other words, he may rely upon that act as a shield, but not as a sword even if it took place before the HRA 1998 came into force.
4   'Person' may include a legal person.
5   The traditional approach to reviewing the exercise of a public authority's powers in judicial review has focused on the decision-making process. Where a claimant alleges that his human rights have been interfered with in breach of HRA 1998, s 6, the court may also consider the outcome of the decision or act, and not only the process by which that decision was made: see, for example, *R (SB) v Denbeigh High School* [2007] 1 AC 100 (HL) at [30].

7.110 In the present context, the most significant rights under the ECHR are:[1]

- *Article 6* – the right to a fair trial. An important aspect of this article is the right to a fair and public hearing within a reasonable time by an independent and impartial tribunal established by law. This right exists in the context of a determination of civil rights and obligations (such as an abatement notice appeal) and in the determination of any criminal charge (such as a criminal charge of failing to comply with an abatement notice).
- *Article 7* – no punishment without law. An important feature of this right is the prohibition on retrospective criminalisation. This may have implications, for example, in cases where the abatement notice, breach of which may give rise to criminal penalties, is poorly drafted.
- *Article 8* – the right to private life and the home. This is an important Convention right in the context of environmental pollution. It imposes an obligation on public bodies to ensure effective protection and respect for the home, which may in certain circumstances impose positive obligations on the public authority to act in a certain way to ensure that article 8 rights are properly protected.
- *Article 1 of the First Protocol* – the right to protection of the enjoyment of property. An important aspect of this right is the protection it may afford against interference with property rights in the public interest without adequate safeguards such as compensation (though the availability of compensation is not a pre-requisite for lawful interference with this right).

1   See paras **2.03–2.10**.

7.111 Some important qualifications on the HRA 1998 are set out below.

Damages are not available in the magistrates' court or Crown Court

7.112 As matters stand, a person will not be able to claim damages in proceedings in the magistrates' court or Crown Court, because neither of these courts has the power to award damages or compensation 'in civil proceedings.'

7.112 *Costs and compensation*

Therefore, any claim for damages will have to be brought in the civil courts, in practice, the High Court.[1]

1 Although the county court, in principle, may be able to make awards of damages under the HRA 1998, in the present context an action for damages alone would usually be brought by way of judicial review alleging that the public authority was in breach of the HRA 1998. Accordingly, the action would have to be commenced in the High Court.

There is no right to damages for breaches of Convention rights

7.113 As the power to award damages in discretionary, there is no *right* to damages in every case, even if the person's Convention rights have been infringed. The drafting of section 8 of the HRA 1998 strongly suggests that damages are intended to be a residual remedy. Under the section, no award of damages is to be made under the HRA 1998 unless, taking into account all of the circumstances of the case, the court is satisfied that the award is necessary to afford 'just satisfaction'[1] to the victim of the breach. Before deciding whether to award damages, the court must in particular have regard to any other relief or remedy[2] made or granted in relation to the act in question (by that or any other court) and the consequences of any decision (of that or any other court) in relation to that act.[3] Thus, the quashing of the abatement notice may of itself be sufficient remedy in most usual cases.[4]

1 ECHR, art 41 empowers the ECtHR to award 'just satisfaction to the injured party' for violations of his human rights.
2 It has been observed by some commentators that there appears to be no clear authority at ECtHR level requiring that compensation be available for all violations of Convention rights, if other remedies exist: Leigh and Lustergarten *'Making Rights Real: the Courts, Remedies, and the Human Rights Act'* (1999) 58 CLJ 509 at 527, 528. See also *Fose v Minister of Safety and Security* (1997) 2 BHRC 434 (Constitutional Court of South Africa).
3 HRA 1998, s 8(3). It is unclear what is meant by 'the consequences' of any decision, though the potential for 'opening the floodgates' to other claims may be an important factor in the court's decision.
4 See also *Rights Brought Home: the Human Rights Bill* (Cm 3782) p 9. The court must 'take into account' the principles applied by the European Court of Human Rights

The court must 'take into account' the principles applied by the European Court of Human Rights

7.114 In determining whether to award damages and if so, the amount of an award, the court must 'take into account' the principles applied by the ECtHR in relation to remedies under the ECHR.[1] As to those principles, it has been said that '... in truth [they] amount to little more than equitable assessments of the facts of the individual case.'[2]

1 HRA 1998, s 8(4).
2 Lester and Pannick (eds) *Human Rights Law and Practice* (2nd edn, 2004) para 2.8.4. The learned editors note in this respect that 'the case law of the ECtHR lacks coherence and advocates and judges are in danger of spending time attempting to identify principles that do not exist'.

7.115 *When might claims for damages for breaches of Convention rights arise?* It is not within the scope of this book to embark upon a detailed analysis of the principles to be applied to claims for damages for Breach of Convention Rights. The relevant principles to be considered were discussed by the Court of Appeal in *Anufrijeva v LB Southwark*.[1] It is clear that the approach under the HRA 1998 is not to be confined by reference to domestic cases that have taken a restrictive approach to claims for damages against local authorities.[2] The

Section 8 Compensation and damages 7.116

approach of the domestic courts should be as liberal as that of the European Court of Human Rights.³

1   [2003] EWCA Civ 1406 at [44] to [78]; [2004] QB 1124, followed in *Re P* [2007] EWCA Civ 2, [2007] HRLR 14.
2   See for example *X (Minors) v Bedfordshire County Council* [1995] 2 AC 633, *Stovin v Wise and Norfolk County Council* [1996] AC 923. For an example of the restrictive approach taken in the context of environmental regulation, see *Chung Tak Lam v Brennan* [1997] 3 PLR 22, and the authorities cited and discussed at 33H–35C by Potter LJ. The case concerned an action for damages for failure to take enforcement action under the EPA 1990 and the Town and Country Planning Act 1990 against paint fumes which were being discharged into the claimant's backyard. The Court of Appeal upheld an order of the first instance judge who had struck out the claim as disclosing no cause of action. For recognition of the impact of the Human Rights Act in this context, see *Kane v New Forest DC*[2002] 1 WLR 312, where the Court of Appeal refused to strike out a personal injury claim alleging negligence against a local authority arising from the exercise of its planning powers. The majority of the Court (May and Dyson LJJ) held that a principle of blanket immunity from action in such cases was not consistent with the case law of the European Court of Human Rights.
3   *Anufrijeva* at [57].

7.116 In the Author's view the instances of successful claims for damages in the statutory nuisance field are likely to be rare. A number of examples of issues which may have the potential to give rise to a claim for damages can be given:

- An unsuspended abatement notice is quashed on appeal. Where an immediately effective abatement notice with which there has been compliance is quashed on appeal, there may be grounds for claiming damages for breaches of article 6¹ and article 1 of the first protocol.² Whilst the mere fact that the abatement notice has been quashed may not of itself assist in showing that there has been a breach of a Convention right,³ there may be a claim under the HRA 1998 where court takes a different view to the local authority as to whether the notice should have been suspended and the local authority has failed to carry out a balancing exercise.⁴
- The local authority fails to serve an abatement notice on a nuisance causing activity. Where a nuisance is interfering with a person's use and enjoyment of their home, article 8 rights may be relevant.⁵ The ECtHR has held that in cases of severe environmental pollution affecting people's homes, there may be a positive duty on the local authority to provide effective protection for article 8 rights, which may include a duty to take enforcement action.⁶ Thus where a local authority fails to take effective action against a nuisance causing activity, a third party whose enjoyment of his home has been interfered with may have a claim for damages for breach of article 8 against the authority. In most cases, the existence of the procedure under section 82 of the EPA 1990 will prevent a claim for damages arising. However, where the technical or other resources, or powers to enter premises and obtain information, only lie with the local authority, then such a claim might arise.
- The local authority has information or the power to acquire information relevant to a nuisance affecting a person's enjoyment of their home but has chosen not to release that information. In these circumstances, article 8 may give rise to a positive obligation to release the information in question,⁷ and failure to do so may give rise to a claim in damages.

1   See paras **3.38–3.44**; paras **4.17–4.22**; paras **4.83–4.84** and paras **4.127–4.133** for a discussion of ECHR, art 6 in the present context.
2   See *Sporrong and Lünnroth v Sweden* (1982) 5 EHRR 35; *Pine Valley Developments v Ireland* (1991) 14 EHRR 319.

7.116 *Costs and compensation*

3   And see *Iatridis v Greece* (1999) 30 EHRLR 97; *Katte Klitsche de la Grange v Italy* (1994) 19 EHRR 368.
4   See paras **3.43–3.44**.
5   Note that ECHR, art 8 gives rise to a *qualified* right to respect for private and family life and the home. Intereference with the right may be justified where it is lawful and proportionate to a legitimate aim under art 8(2).
6   *Lopez Ostra v Spain* (1994) 20 EHRR 277.
7   See *Guerra v Italy* (1998) 26 EHRR 357.

Chapter 8

Noise and Smell

NOISE: INTRODUCTION

8.01 Noise is unwanted sound. It can damage hearing, generate stress and interfere with sleep; it can be prejudicial to health.[1] It can cause annoyance; this is a nuisance if the community, through its local authorities and courts, regards it as unacceptable. The then Lord Chief Justice Lord Bingham observed in *Brighton and Hove Council v Ocean Coachworks (Brighton) Ltd*[2] that:

> 'It is very well known that exposure to excessive noise can become intolerable to those exposed to it and even be injurious to health.'

The Office for National Statistics[3] recorded that complaints about noisy neighbours had increased fivefold in the 20 years to 20 07. Loud music and dogs were the most frequent complaints. There are, in addition to the statutory nuisance regime, other powers, which should particularly be noted in this context. The Noise Act 1996 provides a fast track procedure for night-time noise from dwellings and licensed premises.[4] Sections 60–62 of the Control of Pollution Act 1974 makes specific provision, and exemptions, for construction activities.[5] Specific provisions are now made for audible intruder alarms under the Clean Neighbourhoods and Environment Act 20 07.[6]

1 See Environmental Health Criteria 12, 1.1.3 (World Health Organisation Geneva, 1980).
2 DC [20 01] Env LR 4 p 77.
3 'Social Trends' 20 07.
4 See paras **9.101–9.108**.
5 See paras **1.67** and **9.109–9.135**.
6 See para **9.140**.

8.02 Opinions differ markedly about the acceptability of noises. The factors set out in Chapter 1 are notoriously difficult to balance. It is often a matter of degree or place. The then Lord Chancellor observed:

> '... interference with ... one's quiet ... whether or not that may be denominated a nuisance must undoubtedly depend greatly on the circumstances of the place where the thing actually complained of occurred'.[1]

1 *St Helen's Smelting Co v Tipping* (1865) 11 HL Cas 642.

8.03 An important question is whether the noise generating activity is out of the ordinary. The noises of everyday living emanating from an inadequately soundproofed dwelling cannot be a nuisance to neighbours.[1] Whereas the crowing of cockerels, kept in much larger numbers than usual for a farm, in a predominantly residential area were held to be a nuisance in *Leeman v Montagu*.[2] Occasionally it is straightforward. Thus in *Manley v New Forest District Council*[3] Newman J was able to note of the aptly named 'Howling Dog Kennels' that:

> 'Each morning and evening in the Fawley road area of Hythe ... there can be heard the sounds of the Siberian Tundra namely pack howling by Siberian Huskies marking out their territory. They are otherwise apparently relatively

8.03 *Noise and smell*

quiet dogs. Keen as they are to mark as a pack to mark out their territory the volume of the howling is loud enough to cover distances of up to one mile across the Siberian wastes. The neighbours in Fawley Road are rather more proximate ... The visitor to the Four Seasons Hotel 16 metres away from the pack, must regularly have occasion, when unexpectedly awakened to pause and consider whether he has not dramatically overshot his intended destination.'

1 *Baxter v London Borough of Camden* [2000] Env LR 112, HL.
2 [1936] 2 All ER 1677.
3 [1999] PLR 36, [2000] EHLR 113.

8.04 The range of circumstances that have been considered to be a nuisance is large. The judgments can be difficult. A classic statement of the approach of the courts to nuisances applied by Kindersley V-C[1] to the noise of church bells is that of Knight Bruce V-C in *Walter v Selfe*:[2]

'Ought this inconvenience to be considered, in fact, as more than fanciful, or as one of mere delicacy or fastidiousness; as an inconvenience materially interfering with ... ordinary comfort ... not merely according to elegant and dainty modes and habits of living; but according to plain sober and simple notions among the English people?'

It follows therefore that, as Callan J said:

'This branch of the law pays no regard to the special needs of invalids'.[3]

1 *Soltau v De Held* (1851) 2 Sim NS 133.
2 (1851) 15 Jur 416.
3 *Bloodworth v Cormack* [1949] NZLR 1058.

8.05 Unresolved conflicts can lead to violence. This underlines the wisdom of Megarry J in resolving a dispute between a restaurant playing music and a nearby house, when he said:

'It is the home rather than the meal table which must prevail. A home in which sleep is possible is a necessity, whereas loud music as an accompaniment, is for those who enjoy it, relatively a luxury'.[1]

This illustrates the way in which British judges have often instinctively adopted the approach of the European Convention on Human Rights, which gives everyone a right to respect for their home (article 8). This right is now incorporated into domestic law[2].

Megarry J's comment might be made about air conditioning and other equipment often causing great distress to those living nearby. There is no need to present evidence from those actually occupying properties to prove a nuisance; evidence from environmental health officers, even over a short period of time, may suffice[3].

1 *Hampstead and Garden Suburban Properties v Diomedous* [1968] 3 All ER 545.
2 See HRA 1998, ss 3, 6 and Schedule.
3 *Cooke v Adatia* (DC) (1988) 153 JP 129 W*estminster v McDonald* (DC) [2003] EWHC 2698 (Admin) 11, 13 'no more than ten minutes' 17and 23.

QUANTIFICATION

8.06 The courts early recognised the value in principle of objective quantification of sound levels. Thus Lord Widgery said in 1976:[1]

'This case ... throws up for the first time the very interesting question of whether ... the decibel cannot be used for the purposes of precision in cases such as the present (music from a juke box) ... the justices ... can as well describe that which is to be done as a reduction of noise volume to below so many decibels instead of using the time honoured formula of "abate the nuisance".'

Such measurements are, however, by no means necessary for a finding of a noise nuisance[2]. Nor is there is any obligation on a local authority to attend a noise creator's premises to 'advise individuals or assist them in reducing noise or giving them advice on how noise restrictions should be complied with'[3]. This does not mean that it cannot do so if it has sufficient resources; it simply means that it is no defence to an abatement notice or prosecution for non compliance that it has not done so.

1   *R v Fenny Stratford Justices, ex p Watney Mann (Midlands) Ltd* 1 [1976] WLR 1101.
2   *Lewisham v Hall* [2002] EWHC 960 (Admin), W*estminster v McDonald* (DC) [2003] EWHC 2698 (Admin) at 12, 17.
3   *Tewkesbury v Deacon* [2003] EWHC 2544 (Admin) 20

8.07   *Ex p Watney Mann*[1] also illustrates the importance of identifying the location at which measurements are to be taken. They had not been so identified. The court nuisance order failed for uncertainty. As Watkins J observed '... at any one of different places it could produce a different reading.'

1   [1976] 1 WLR 1107.

8.08   The Divisional Court has[1] upheld a requirement to reduce noise from tyre squeal as measured at any point along the boundary of a motor racing circuit:

'1   To a level not exceeding 50 dB at 1,000Hz ...
2   To a level not exceeding 45 dB at 1000 Hz before 9am or after 6pm on any day ...

All Sound Pressure Level measurements specified above are to be taken in the open air with a Type 1 sound level meter set on fast response and measured using 1/3 octave filters.'

The terms of the notice were held to do no more or less than give particulars of the abatement requirement under section 80(1)(a) and did not amount to a requirement for unspecified works or steps. The fact that the notice used the word '*steps*' to describe the required result did not indicate that in reality the authority were insisting on a particular means of abating the nuisance. The criticism based on the use of the word '*steps*' that they failed to specify the steps was 'barren and technical.'[2] The notice was valid.

1   *Sevenoaks v Brands Hatch Leisure Group* [2001] Env LR 5 p 86.
2   See Laws LJ at paras 20, 25 and 26 of the transcript.

8.09   Where particular means are required by the authority they do not have to be described at inordinate length. Thus Lord Wheatley[1] saw nothing vague or uncertain in requirements to:

'Fit all pneumatic breakers in use with effective exhaust silencers

Fit all pneumatic breakers in use with dampered tool bits

Use only suitably silenced compressors

8.09 *Noise and smell*

Keep all outside panels on air compressors closed while the said compressors are in operation

Ensure that there are no leaks in air lines used in conjunction with the said compressors and breakers.'

1   *Strathclyde Regional Council v Tudhope* [1983] JPL 536 High Court of Justiciary (in the context of Control of Pollution 1974, s 58).

8.10   A requirement to keep a door closed

'*except when it necessarily has to be opened from time to time for the moving of vehicles into and from the workshop or for other genuine business reasons*'.

was held by the then Lord Chief Justice[1] to be sufficiently clear to those who would have to abide by it in the running of a vehicle workshop.

1   *Brighton and Hove Council v Ocean Coachworks Brighton Ltd* [20 01] Env LR 4 p 77 per Lord Bingham.

Guidance[1]

8.11   Guidance has been published by a number of international, governmental and technical bodies. Much discussion focuses on the objective quantification and measurement of sound. Many methods of comparison between different sounds have been devised. A variety of attempts have been made to construct systems which enable an objective correlation to be made between measured sound and likely annoyance or harm to health.

1   See Appendix H for relevant extracts.

8.12   Some important documents which may be encountered and are worth examining, include the following:

World Health Organization Publications

8.13   WHO recommendations found in Environmental Health Criteria 12 1980[1] have been widely used as a basis in the UK as a starting point for government guidance. That document is a report of the collective views of an international group of experts published under the joint sponsorship of the United Nations Environment Programme and the World Health Organization (WHO). It discusses the properties, measurement, effects of, and protection against, noise. It recommends maximum standards for outdoor daytime noise and bedroom night-time noise. A more recent publication is 'Guidelines for Community Noise'[2].

1   World Health Organization, Geneva 1980 (ISBN 92 4 154072 9).
2   Ed Berglund, Lindvall and Schwela, WHO Geneva. It is the outcome of an expert task force of April 1999 and based on 'Community Noise' prepared for WHO in 1995 and published by Stockholm University and Karolinska University.

Planning Policy Guidance Note 24 1994 (PPG 24)

8.14   PPG 24 is guidance for England issued by the then Department of the Environment (DoE) (now Department for Communities and Local government ('DCLG'). It sets out the approach which the government wishes local planning authorities to adopt in their consideration of planning applications for noise generating and noise sensitive developments. It introduces a concept of Noise

Exposure Categories for the assessment of proposed residential development. It advises on the use of conditions and illustrates this with model conditions. It is not directed towards the assessment of statutory nuisances from existing noise sources. But it gives an important indication of some values which the Government considers to be of national application.[1]

1   The distinction between the planning and statutory nuisance regimes was emphasised by Turner J in *R v Kennet District Council, ex p Somerfield Property Co Ltd* [1999] JPL 361.

British Standard Method for Rating Industrial Noise Affecting Mixed Residential and Industrial Areas BS 4142 1997 (BS 4142)[1]

8.15 BS 4142 is the current revised edition of a document of the British Standards Institute first published in 1967. It describes both a method of determining the level of a noise of an industrial nature, and procedures for assessing the likelihood of complaints from residential neighbours. Interestingly although the noise level from the Alton Towers amusement park was at a level at which complaints were likely the court held in *Roper v Tussaud*[2] that there was no nuisance because of the history and grant of planning permission.

1   ISBN 0 580 2830 0 3.
2   [20 07] Env LR 31.

British Standard Code of Practice for Sound Insulation and Noise Reduction for Buildings 1999 (BS 8233)[1]

8.16 BS 8233 concentrates on construction techniques. It has an extremely useful bibliography which provides leads for specific problems. It also sets out quantitative recommendations for maximum noise levels in a variety of types of buildings.

1   ISBN 0 580 330 09 5.

Environment Agency Horizontal Guidance Note IPPC H3 (Parts 1 and 2)

8.17 H3 Parts 1 and 3 were prepared for the issuing of permits and drafting of conditions for those installations subject to the Integrated Pollution Prevention and Control regime of EC Directive 96/61/EC and the Pollution Prevention and Control Act 1999. They are thus directed to industrial enterprises. They have however much interesting technical material which may have a relevance in wider contexts. For example H3 Part 2 has a useful discussion at Section 3.4 of noise control techniques and provides in Appendix 5 information sheets about each type; these may be helpful in assessing assertions about 'best practicable means'. This is not merely dryly technical; it includes such sensible observations as that warning communities about noisy activities may enable people to schedule noise sensitive activities[1].

1   H3 Part 2 Section 3.4.5.

Limitations of quantitative methods

8.18 Such methods and guidance can be useful tools. They enable like to be compared with like. All such systems, however, present fundamental difficulties:

8.18 *Noise and smell*

- they are not capable of measuring some of the most important factors affecting annoyance[1]
- they can involve expensive equipment not readily affordable, or useable, by active citizens or community groups
- local authorities are often reluctant to make available financial and staff resources, particularly during antisocial hours, to carry out necessary monitoring
- experts engaged by commercial noise generators may have ample resources but choose carefully, and to the advantage of their clients, the times, locations and variables which they measure
- in practice, these systems tend to be used to measure only a few of the relevant measurable variables for a small part of the relevant time
- nonetheless, human nature is such that some decision-makers are prone to attach the same weight to the limited measurements presented to them as if they were a comprehensive quantification of all relevant factors.

1 They cannot, for example, measure the importance and value to the community of an activity, the difficulty of avoiding the propagation of noise in carrying it out or conventional attitudes to it.

8.19 Quantitative methods and systems must be regarded as the servants not the masters of decision-makers. Guidance must be used with common sense. Experts must not be approached with uncritical reverence. Sensible decision makers like to have them 'on tap' rather than 'on top'. Prudence, however, suggests that a good understanding of the range of quantitative techniques and guidance should be sought not only by those who wish to use it but also by those who may have to counter its misuse.

BACKGROUND TO TECHNOLOGY

8.20 Sounds are transmitted as longitudinal pressure waves[1]. A sound wave has several measurable properties. These include intensity,[2] pressure,[3] particle velocity and particle displacement. Machines cannot tell which sounds are unwanted. They can, however, measure intensity and frequency of sounds. Perceived loudness is a function of both intensity and frequency. The simplest method of measurement is that of the sound pressure level (SPL) through a filter or network of filters that represent the frequency response of the human ear.

1 This discussion is not intended as a substitute for experts' analyses but rather as an aid to understanding them.
2 Intensity increases at twice the rate that pressure does.
3 Pressure increases at half the rate that intensity does.

8.21 Differences in noise levels are expressed in decibels (dB). These are conventionally the logarithmic ratio between the sound pressure level measured and a reference level of 20 micro Pascals.[1] The measurements have to be weighted to reflect the human ear's response. The effect of low and high frequencies have to be adjusted in relation to medium frequencies. The most commonly used weighting is the A weighting; sound measured on this scale is expressed in dBAs.

1 Pascal is the *Systeme Internationale* (SI) unit of pressure.

8.22 The scale is logarithmic. A doubling of the sound pressure[1] level will be reflected only in an increase of 6 dB. A doubling of distance from a noise source will lead to a reduction of 6 dB. A doubling or halving of perceived loudness will, however, only occur with a change of 10 dbA. An increase of 3 dbA on its own, however, is generally considered to be just noticeable.

1   A doubling of the sound *intensity* would only lead to an increase of 3 dB. Pressure increases at half the rate that intensity does.

8.23 It is important to remember that the fact that a noise source is no louder than the existing noise sources in an area does not mean that noise will not increase. It will. First the cumulative effect of a number of additional sources none of which are higher than the original sound level may be substantial. The phenomenon is sometimes referred to as 'noise creep.' Second the nature of the noise may be different. Thus music was a nuisance even though not measurably louder than agricultural activities[1].

1   *Godfrey v Conwy BC* (DC) [20 01] Env LR 38 p 674 applying the same approach as in *Murdoch v Glacier Metal Company* [1998] Env LR 732.

NOISE INDICES

8.24 Commonly recorded measurements (usually taken over a period of time) are:

LA Max

8.25 LA Max is the maximum level reached during an *individual* noise event. It is an important measurement for assessing likely sleep disturbance.[1]

1   The World Health Organisation Task Force on Community Noise recommended in 1993 [EUR/ICP/RUD 163,1141g para 1.3] that guidelines to avoid sleep disturbance from community noise should be expressed in terms of maximum noise levels (LA max) as well as equivalent noise level (LAeq). WHO's 'Guidelines for Community Noise' and BS 8233 1999 recommend an LAmax of 45dBA for sleeping.

LA90

8.26 LA 90 is the level exceeded for 90% of the time (n dBA L90 T), which is often used as the *background* level against which to compare introduced noise source. A record of 65 dBA L90 18h, for example, indicates that for 90% of a period of 18 hours a noise level of 65 decibels or above was measured by an A weighted meter.

LA10

8.27 LA 10 is the level exceeded for 10% of the time (n dBA L10 T), which is often taken as the *upper level of fluctuating* noise such as traffic noise.'T' represents the period over which measurements were taken.

LAeq

8.28 The *equivalent continuous* sound level is recorded as LAeq n T. It is the sound level which a notionally steady sound would have if it had the same energy as a fluctuating sound over the measured period. This index is increasingly used. It has the advantage that it can be used to describe many different types of noise. However, it also has the *disadvantage which averages often have*; the calculation of notional steady sound may not the reflect the significance on people's lives

8.28 *Noise and smell*

which infrequent events may very well have. Thus, for example, Concorde may fly overhead only once during an hour. That one flight may cause a noise which reaches 110 dBA Lmax; such a noise is very loud and many would be awakened by it. But otherwise the general noise level during that hour might not exceed 60 dBA.[1] The equivalent continuous sound level for that hour would be a somewhat higher than 60 dBA; but it would not begin to approach 110 dBA. Sometimes the period over which noise is measured is reduced;[2] this can reduce but not eliminate this inherent weakness of this method. It could exacerbate the problem if the periods chosen did not include the noisiest events. This official note of caution is worth some reflection:

> 'Take care that all sample measurements are representative of the period of interest'.[3]

1   The World Health Organisation Task Force on Community Noise recommended in 1993 (EUR/ICP/RUD 163,1141g para 1.3) that guidelines to avoid sleep disturbance from community noise should be expressed in terms of maximum noise levels (LA max) as well as equivalent noise level (LAeq) and maximum number of noise events. See above on LAMax.
2   Thus in BS 4142 (1997) para 6.2 the time reference period for day measurements is one hour and for night measurements five minutes.
3   BS 4142 (1997) para 6.1.

8.29   It is worth understanding the quantitative techniques; but they are worse than worthless if they are not applied with common sense.

QUALITATIVE FACTOR ADJUSTMENTS

8.30   Some features are generally recognised as likely to make a noise more annoying than its level would suggest. Sometimes a quantitative adjustment to the measured noise level is recommended. Then the *rating* level, as the adjusted measured level is known, is used for comparison with standards. Thus the following features add 5 dB to the measured level in one methodology for industrial noise:[1]

- distinguishable, discrete notes (such as whines, hums, hisses or screeches)
- distinct impulses (such as bangs, clicks, clatters, or thumps)
- noticeable irregularity.

1   BS 4142 (1997), para 8.2.

8.31   It is important to remember that this adjustment is arbitrary; it reflects a judgment on the part of the authors of the particular methodology. It might well be that some features would make a noise as annoying as a noise without them that was more than 5 dB louder (or contrariwise less than 5 dBA louder). Insofar as it is an appropriate adjustment to make for industrial noise it will be appropriate to make it for noise of a similar type from non-industrial premises. Thus mechanical air extraction systems are frequent source of noise at industrial premises; they are also an increasingly frequent source of noise from hotel, restaurant and office premises.

TIMES AND SEASONS

8.32   Different expectations and conventions are associated with different times of day.[1] Three main periods are used in England and Wales. The period between 070 0-080 0hrs and 180 0hrs Monday to Friday and 070 0-080 0hrs to 130 0hrs Saturday is usually treated as the ordinary working day to which periods the noisiest activities of activity should be confined. The period between 230 0 and 070 0hrs[2] is usually treated as a sensitive period when people should be able to expect levels of noise which do not interfere with sleep. The remaining periods of time (which include weekday evenings, Saturday afternoon and the whole of Sunday[3]) are treated as hybrid periods. Bank holidays are usually treated as Sundays.

1   See eg, *Boynton v Helena Rubinstein Ltd* (1960) 176 Estates Gazette 443 (hoist not permitted except between 9am and 6pm).
2   See eg (1) PPG 24 para 12 which characterises these hours as 'the hours when people are normally sleeping' (2) BS 8233 (1999), para 7.3 and (3) the terms of the injunction in *London Borough of Hammersmith v Magnum Automated Forecourts Ltd* [1978] 1 WLR 50, CA, restraining taxi cab centre between 11pm and 7am.
3   Bank holidays are usually treated as Sundays.

8.33 The hybrids are treated as periods when noisy activities for some purposes are acceptable; for example, lawnmowers are accepted in this country during weekend days and often in early evenings. The principle seems to be that some necessary or desirable activities can with advantage be undertaken outside the ordinary working day. Householders do not all employ servants who can carry out necessary but noisy domestic activities during the ordinary working day. Social and cultural activities must inevitably be undertaken outside the working day. Such activities do not usually involve continuous noise on a regular basis over a long period of time. A degree of local informal control can be exercised through pressure of community disapproval of inconsiderate neighbours. By contrast building, engineering, manufacturing and other commercial activities can readily be carried out during the ordinary working day. They tend to be continuous over long periods of time. They are much less susceptible to informal local control.

8.34 The growing availability, marketing and use by people at their homes of noisy powered equipment for indoor and outdoor work (such as lawn mowing, hedge trimming and DIY) is creating an increasing problem. The noise is unpredictable and uncoordinated. One stops. Another starts. One family goes away on Saturday, but it is on Sunday that their neighbour chooses to mow his lawn. There may be merit in local authorities establishing guidelines in their development plans and supplementary planning documents which facilitate the coordination and predictability of such activities. Most local authorities never think of doing so. No doubt those who first do so will face cheap criticism in the media for oppressive bureaucracy. That criticism must be balanced against the legitimate interests of those who presently have to put up with what is to them oppressive noise.

SOME IMPORTANT MAXIMUM LEVELS

8.35 Two quantitative standards expressed in dBA Leq have considerable governmental support. The first is a maximum desirable daytime outdoor living area level of 55 dBA Leq.[1] The origin of this standard is the 1980 World Health Organisation (WHO) publication *Environmental Health Criteria 12* (EH 12) 'Noise'.[2] Paragraph 1.1.3.5 of the document explains that it is derived mainly from studies of annoyance from aircraft and road traffic noise. The general view expressed is that:

8.35 *Noise and smell*

'in residential areas [at this level] ... there will be few people *seriously* annoyed by noise; [our emphasis]

The more recent WHO publication 'Guidelines for Community Noise' gives a figure of 50dBA[3] for outdoor living areas to avoid *moderate* annoyance for most people.

1   This is similar, but not identical, to the Greater London Council (GLC) guideline for parks and gardens of 55 dBA L10 [GLC Scientific Branch: GLC Guidelines for environmental noise and vibration. Bulletin No 96 item 6, June 1976] This guideline was acknowledged with apparent approbation in para 8.1 of the British Standards Institute publication BS 8233:1987 'Sound Insulation and Noise Reduction for Buildings.' It is now considered too high to be a desirable noise climate for balconies and gardens (see 7.6.1.2 BS 8233, 1999; the desirable maximum is 50 dBA. Leq).
2   Geneva : ISBN 92 4 154072 9.
3   Table 4.1 p 65.

8.36 The guidance cautions however that:

'Some residents may consider this level too high, especially as substantially lower levels currently prevail in many suburban and rural areas'.

8.37 The 55dB maximum desirable level has been taken as the starting point for the planning assessment of acceptability in noise terms of potential housing sites in PPG 24.[1] For gardens and balconies, however, BS 8233 (1999)[2] now recommends as a desirable maximum 50 dBA Leq.

1   See PPG 24, Annex 2 para 4, explaining Annex 1, Table attached to para 10.
2   Para 7.6.1.2.

8.38 The second maximum standard is that of 35 dBA Leq within bedrooms for night-time. This is the recommended maximum 'to preserve the restorative process of sleep.'[1] This has been taken as the starting point for PPG 24's assessment of potential housing sites.[2] Many people consider it necessary to health or desirable to sleep with an open window. Even a partially open single glazed window substantially reduces noise levels. The degree of attenuation from a partially open window is often said to be 10-15 dBA.[3] If a large ill-fitting window is partially open the degree of attenuation may well be at the bottom of the range. Thus an external noise of 45 dBA Leq would on that basis correspond in those circumstances to an internal level of 35 dBA Leq.

1   WHO EH 12, para 1.1.3.3.
2   See PPG 24 and Annex 2 para 5, explaining Annex 1, Table attached to para 10.
3   See *Transportation Noise Reference Book*, ed by Paul Nelson: Butterworths 1987.

8.39 Other recommended limits which may be encountered include those set out in BS 8233:1999 at paragraph 7.3 and Table 5 for steady intrusive noises:

- **In bedrooms**
    - good noise limits of 30 d BA Leq with 45 dBA Lmax[1]
    - reasonable noise limits of 35 dBA Leq with 45 dBA Lmax.[2]
- **In living rooms**
    - a good noise limit of 30 d BA Leq
    - a reasonable noise limit of 40 dBA Leq.

1   Measured with F time-weighting.
2   Measured with F time-weighting.

BS 4142 INDUSTRIAL NOISES

8.40 The British Standards Institute have published a method for 'Rating industrial noise affecting mixed residential and industrial areas'[1] involving a comparison of the background noise level and the noise under consideration adjusted to take account of certain annoying features.[2] The methodology is based upon an assessment of the likelihood of complaints. The measured (or calculated) background noise level LAeq is subtracted from the adjusted noise level LAeq of the source under consideration.[3] As the difference increases, the likelihood of complaints increases:

- difference of around 10 dB indicates that complaints are likely
- difference of around 5 dB is of marginal significance.

1 BS 4142, 3 edn 1997, ISBN 0 580 28300 3.
2 'The rating level', see BS 4142, paras 8.1 and 8.2.
3 BS 4142, para 9. The noise under consideration is measured over one hour if it is daytime or five minutes if it is night-time (see para 6.2).

8.41 Sometimes experts appointed by generators of noise quote the above but do not appreciate the significance of the following

- If the rating level is *more* than *10 dB below* the measured background noise level then this a positive indication that complaints are unlikely

The often omitted statement indicates that complaints may well be received even though the level of the noise under consideration is lower than the background noise.

8.42 This illustrates one of the important limitations of such quantitative methods. A noise may be distinguishable and disturbing even though its level is not significantly greater than (or is lower than) the background level. It may have characteristics which make it noticeable and disturbing. BS 4142 seeks to take this factor into account to some extent by adjusting the measured noise level by adding 5 dB if it has such features. Such adjustments reduce but do not overcome the problem. BS 8233: 1999 acknowledges that:

> 'Low frequency noise can be disturbing or fatiguing to occupants, but may not have much effect on the dBA or NR[1] value'.[2]

1 NR is Noise Rating. It is an index of noise used for rating ventilation systems. There is no direct relationship between NR and dBA; a broad equivalence is expressed in the formula NR = dBA-6.
2 BS 8233 (1999), para 7.4.

8.43 Another problem of this methodology is that it is based upon likelihood of complaints. The Foreword to BS 4142 states:

> '... in general there will be a relationship between the incidence of complaints and the level of general community annoyance ...'

8.44 This statement should be viewed with considerable caution. Many factors other than disturbance influence propensity to complain. Most people would think that it was pointless to complain if nothing was likely to change as a result of a complaint. It may not be easy to identify the appropriate person to whom complaints should be directed. The British are phlegmatic and reluctant to create or run the risk of appearing to create 'scenes.' The WHO in EH 12[1] warns that:

8.44 *Noise and smell*

'the scientific basis for ... [criteria relating noise exposure and complaint potential] is rather fragmentary and surveys have indicated that the correlation between noise exposure and individual complaint behaviour is low'.

1   At para 1.1.3.5.

8.45 The Foreword to BS 4142 itself recognises some of its limitations. It is general and may not cover all situations. It acknowledges that among the factors which will influence the likelihood of complaints are the nature of the neighbourhood. It must be treated as no more than a potentially useful tool and always applied with common sense.

SMELL

8.46 Smell will be treated briefly. It has probably become less of a problem in the 21st century than it was in the 19th century. It seems to cause fewer complaints than noise. Improvements in sanitation, sewerage infrastructure, mechanised transportation and remote industrialisation of food production has no doubt played a part. It remains nonetheless a potentially serious nuisance for those living downwind of manufacturing industry or in close proximity to hot food outlets. Sensitive handling may be needed to deal with the irritation that can be caused by barbecues or by pungent domestic cooking smells whether vented into shared or neighbouring buildings.

8.47 The assessment of smell might seem to be so subjective that its acceptability must always be a matter of opinion in respect of which no quantitative analysis is possible. Both structured analysis and technical guidance might superficially seem unlikely to be useful. It is not, however, so. The Environment Agency[1] has published a working draft of guidance for regulation 'IPPC H4: Horizontal Guidance for Odour'. Like many such technical documents it has not passed beyond the stage of being a 'working draft document' despite being produced five years ago.[2] The Introduction of H4 recognises that the field of odour management and control is wide and continually evolving. It acknowledges that more debate is needed. But it pragmatically recognises nonetheless the value of providing some guidance for those decisions which have to be made and cannot wait for the outcome of further research.

1   In a joint publication with the Scottish Environment Protection Agency 'SEPA' and the Environment and Heritage Service of Northern Ireland 'EHS(NI)'.
2   In 2002.

8.48 Three important phenomena within the common experience of humankind are recognised in H4. First, even the smallest concentrations and amounts of some substances[1] can create powerful smells. Second, what may be pleasant in small quantities may become in large quantities or great frequency extremely unpleasant[2]. Third, ordinary people may reasonably become hypersensitive to smells that have over a period of time been a nuisance through past quantity or frequency. Thereafter lesser amounts or frequencies of that smell (which, absent the history of past exposure to greater amounts or frequencies, would not have been reasonably regarded as a nuisance) may be unacceptable[3].

Smell **8.50**

1   H4 Part 1 App 10.
2   However all odours have the potential to be offensive and can cause annoyance if exposure is frequent or at high concentrations' H4 Part 1 App 1 p 29.
3   H4 Part 1 App 6 p 55: 'Where an odour has generated a high level of complaints over a prolonged period of time, the population may become hypersensitive to that odour. As such, even if the levels of odour were to be reduced to what would be an acceptable level in other areas may still give rise to justifiable complaints'.

8.49 The relative pleasantness or offensiveness of a smell is sometimes described as its 'hedonic tone'. It can be expressed in units named after a researcher 'Dravnieks'. Panels of individuals with ordinary responses have assessed various substances in laboratory conditions. Tables have been drawn up of the concentrations at which substances become, in isolation, identifiable[1] and of their relative pleasantness or offensiveness (expressed in positive and negative numbers respectively[2]). For example, while roses are +3.08, cat's urine is -3.64.

1   H4 Part 1 App 10 Table A10.3.
2   H4 Part 1 App 10 Table A10.2 .

8.50 The Guidance offers a template[1] for Odour Management Plans (OMP). The extent to which an industrial enterprise has devised and implemented an OMP may be important in determining compliance with the best practicable means test.

1   H4 Part 1 App 7.

Chapter 9

Other Powers Dealing with Problems Akin to Nuisance

INTRODUCTION

9.01 This Chapter provides an overview of other powers available in England and Wales[1] to local authorities and (in some cases) the Environment Agency to deal with problems akin to nuisance. It should be noted that many of these powers were amended by the Clean Neighbourhoods and Environment Act 2005.

1   Much, of course, is also applicable in Scotland either directly or through similar provisions of Scottish legislation.

LAND ADVERSELY AFFECTING THE AMENITY OF AN AREA – TOWN AND COUNTRY PLANNING ACT 1990 SECTION 215

The statutory provisions

9.02 Section 215 of the Town and Country Planning Act 1990 (TCPA 1990) provides that if it appears to the local planning authority that the amenity of a part of their area, or of an adjoining area, is adversely affected by the condition of land in their area, they may serve on the owner and occupier of the land a notice.[1] That notice shall require such steps for remedying the condition of the land as may be specified in the notice to be taken within such period as may be so specified.[2] The notice is to state the period at the end of which it shall take effect.[3] The period must not be less than 28 days after service of the notice.[4] Best practice guidance on the use of section 215 by local authorities has been issued by the Government[5].

1   TCPA 1990, s 215(1).
2   TCPA 1990, s 215(2).
3   TCPA 1990, s 215(3).
4   TCPA 1990, s 215(4).
5   Town and Country Planning Act 1990 Section 215: Best Practice Guidance (January 2005).

9.03 It is a criminal offence if any owner or occupier of the land *on whom the notice was served* fails to take the steps required by the notice within the period specified.[1] Specific provisions address the situation of an owner or occupier who ceases to be the owner or occupier before the period for compliance has expired. In simple terms, these provisions allow the previous owner or occupier to require the new owner or occupier (as the case may be) to be brought before the court. In the case of a person served with a section 215 notice as an occupier and who has subsequently given up occupancy but not been replaced with a new occupant, the existing owner of the premises may be brought before the court.[2] In either case, where it can be shown that failure to comply with the notice within the requisite period was attributable in whole or part to the new or existing owner or occupier of the premises (as the case may be) then the new or existing owner or occupier of the premises may be convicted of an offence.[3] If

9.03 *Other powers dealing with problems akin to nuisance*

the person served with the notice also proves that he took all reasonable steps to ensure compliance with the notice, he shall be acquitted.[4] Conviction under section 216 carries a fine.[5]

1   TCPA 1990, s 216(2).
2   See TCPA 1990, s 216(3), (4).
3   TCPA 1990, s 216(5)(b)(i).
4   TCPA 1990, s 216(5)(b)(ii).
5   At the time of writing the penalties are level 3 (£1000) for the first offence and one-tenth of level 3 (£100) per day for a continuing offence.

9.04 The recipient of a section 215 notice and any person having an interest in the land may appeal to the magistrates' court against the notice.[1] The magistrates on determining the appeal shall give directions for giving effect to their determination, including directions for varying the notice in favour of the appellant or quashing the notice;[2] or they may dismiss the appeal. They may also correct any defect, error in informality in the notice if satisfied that the defect, error or informality is not material.[3]

1   TCPA 1990, s 217.
2   TCPA 1990, s 217(5).
3   TCPA 1990, s 217(4).

9.05 The grounds of appeal are as follows:[1]

(a) that the amenity of no part of the area of the local planning authority or of an adjoining area is adversely affected by the condition of the land to which the notice relates
(b) that the condition of the land to which the notice relates is 'attributable to, and such as results in the ordinary course of events from, the carrying on of operations or a use of land which is not in contravention of Part III of TCPA 1990
(c) the requirements of the notice exceed what is necessary for preventing the condition of the land adversely affecting the amenity of any part of the area of the local planning authority, or of any adjoining area
(d) the time period allowed for compliance with the notice's requirements is unreasonably short.

1   TCPA 1990, s 217(1)(a)–(d).

9.06 The operation of the notice is suspended pending the outcome of the appeal.[1] The local authority or the recipient of the notice may appeal to the Crown Court against the magistrates' court's decision.[2]

1   TCPA 1990, s 217(3).
2   TCPA 1990, s 218.

9.07 The local authority has power to carry out works to ensure compliance with a section 215 notice and recover the costs of doing so. Exercise of these powers is not dependent on a successful prosecution for breach of a notice.[1]

1   See generally, TCPA 1990, s 219.

Practical points

What is the meaning of 'affecting the amenity of the area'?

9.08 'Amenity' has been held to mean the pleasant circumstances, features or advantages[1] of the area or the visual appearance and the pleasure of its

Land adversely affecting the amenity of an area 9.12

enjoyment,[2] expressing '... that element in the appearance and layout of town and country which makes for a comfortable and pleasant life rather than mere existence.'[3] Thus, it can be seen that a wide range of conditions of land will potentially fall within the provisions of section 215 of the TCPA 1990.[4] The condition of such land may, but often will not, amount to a statutory nuisance under section 79(1) of the EPA 1990.[5] It does not matter[6] for the purposes of section 215 of the TCPA 1990 whether the condition of the land results from building operations on the land or the use or neglect of it.[7]

1   *Re Ellis and Ruislip-Northwood Urban District Council* [1920] 1 KB 343; *FFF Estates Ltd v London Borough of Hackney* [1981] QB 503, CA.
2   *Cartwright v Post Office* [1968] 2 QB 439.
3   *Re Parramatta City Council, ex p Tooth & Co Ltd* (1955) 55 SR (NSW) 282 at 306, 308, cited by Mynors in 'Property in need of maintenance: section 65 notices' [1988] JPL 154 at 158.
4   Some local authorities may in the future feel more comfortable using TCPA 1990, s 215 instead of statutory nuisance powers where they are concerned about the effect of the contaminated land exception on the exercise of their powers under EPA 1990, Pt III.
5   See also *Coventry City Council v Cartwright* [1975] 2 All ER 99.
6   Subject to the 'ordinary course of events' defence: see paras **9.15–9.17**.
7   See for example *Britt v Buckinghamshire County Council* [1964] 1 QB 77 at 90 (a case under TCPA 1947, s 33(1) but the principle remains sound under TCPA 1990, s 215).

9.09   A number of examples of conditions of land 'affecting the amenity of the area' can be given. The procedure[1] has been used in respect of dilapidated houses,[2] gardens which have become seriously overgrown or squalid,[3] untidy scrap metal yards[4] and land used for the storage of scrap cars.[5]

1   Or that under the predecessors to TCPA 1990, s 215 namely TCPA 1971, s 65.
2   See facts in *Miles v Secretary of State for the Environment* (11 August 2000, unreported) CA; (4 June 1999, unreported), QBD, cited in *Monen v SSTLGR* [2002] EWHC 81 Admin.
3   See facts of *R v Preston Crown Court, ex p Jolly* (7 April 2000, unreported) Henry LJ.
4   *R v Oxford Crown Court, ex p Smith* (1989) 154 LGR 458.
5   *Britt v Buckinghamshire County Council* [1964] 1 QB 77 (a case under TCPA 1947, s 33(1)).

Is a section 215 notice personal or does it run with the land?

9.10   This issue is important, because if the notice is personal to the recipient then a fresh notice would need to be served on any subsequent owner or occupier of the premises against whom the local planning authority wished to take action, notwithstanding service of a notice on the erstwhile owner or occupier.

9.11   In the authors' view, a notice served under section 215 of the TCPA 1990 is a personal notice; it does not run with the land. This appears to be the position because it is the recipient of the notice who is to be prosecuted for non-compliance with the notice under section 216. The immediate subsequent owner or occupier *may* be liable if it can be proven that any default in compliance by the recipient was attributable to that subsequent owner or occupier. However, liability only extends to the person who took ownership or occupancy from the party served with the notice. Liability does not extend further down the chain of owners or occupiers. Furthermore, there is no specific provision for registering section 215 notices.[1]

1   Contrast TCPA 1990, s 188 in respect of enforcement and stop notices.

9.12   In the authors' view therefore, local planning authorities are advised to serve a fresh notice where there is a new owner or occupier on the land.

9.13 *Other powers dealing with problems akin to nuisance*

Is a section 215 notice discharged once it had been complied with?

9.13 Although the position is not free from doubt, it would appear that once a section 215 notice has been complied with, it is discharged. A fresh notice should therefore be served to deal with any subsequent problems on the land, even if they are of a similar nature to those matters covered in the previous notice. The TCPA 1990 has made specific provision for planning enforcement notices under Part VII of the 1990 Act to remain in force even after compliance with their terms.[1] There is no such provision in respect of a section 215 notice.[2]

1   TCPA 1990, s 181, which applies to notices under TCPA 1990, Pt VII.
2   TCPA 1990, s 215 is located in Pt VIII.

In what proceedings can the legality of a section 215 notice be challenged?

9.14 The legality of a notice cannot be challenged in any proceedings whatsoever (such as judicial review) to the extent that such a challenge raises arguments that can be raised under the grounds of appeal contained in section 217(1)(a)[1] and (b)[2] of the TCPA 1990.[3] Save for this restriction, where the recipient of the notice is prosecuted, it appears that he may raise the legality of the notice as a defence to the prosecution.[4] Where the notice is sought to be challenged on other grounds, the challenge may be brought by way of judicial review.[5]

1   Condition of land does not adversely affect amenity.
2   The 'ordinary course of events' defence: see below for discussion on this.
3   See the preclusive provisions of TCPA 1990, s 285(3).
4   *R v Oxford Crown Court, ex p Smith* (1989) 154 LGR 458.
5   See by way of analogy with enforcement notices *Davey v Spelthorne Borough Council* [1984] AC 262 at 272D–H.

The 'ordinary course of events' ground of appeal

9.15 Under section 217(1)(b) of the TCPA 1990 the recipient of the notice or any person having an interest in the land to which the notice relates may appeal on the ground that the condition of the land to which the notice relates is attributable to, and as such results in the ordinary course of events from, the carrying on of operations or a use of land which is not in contravention of Part III of the Act.

9.16 Part III of the TCPA 1990 concerns control over development. In simple terms, to satisfy the last part of section 217(1)(b) the appellant must show that the use or operations of land to which its condition is attributable either has the benefit of planning consent or permitted development rights, or does not involve development.

9.17 However, the appeal will only succeed if the appellant can also show that the condition of the land results 'in the ordinary course of events' from such use or operations. In other words, where the use or operations would ordinarily result in the land being in the condition it is in, his appeal will succeed. But where the use or operations have resulted in the land being in the condition it is in but would not ordinarily have done so, the appeal will fail. Thus, the owner

Housing standards: Housing Act 2004 **9.22**

of a squalid garden, which has become an eyesore, cannot usually claim that its condition is an ordinary consequence of the land's use as a garden: land used as gardens does not ordinarily become squalid and an eyesore.[1]

1   To what extent can the nature of the area be considered? Take an example of an area plagued with vandalism and fly-tipping. Can it be claimed that the rubbish dumped and broken fences in the garden are simply the ordinary consequence of having a garden in such an area?

HOUSING STANDARDS: HOUSING ACT 2004

9.18 Sections 1-54 of Part 1 of the Housing Act 2004 make provision for housing standards and their enforcement. These provisions replace Part VI of the Housing Act 1985 and the previous system based on the test of fitness for human habitation contained in Section 604 of that Act.

9.19 Part 1 of the 2004 Act introduced the Housing Health and Safety Rating System (HSSRS), and evidence based system for assessing housing conditions. Sections 2 and 4 of the Act provide for regulations to be made prescribing hazards, methods for the assessment of their seriousness, and the manner and extent of inspections of housing to determine whether Category 1 or 2 hazards exist[1]. The act imposes a duty on local authorities to take enforcement action where a Category 1 hazard exists and a discretion to take action where a Category 2 hazard exists[2].

1   HA 2004, s 5.
2   HA 2004, s 6.

9.20 If a local authority considers that a Category 1 hazard exists the following types of enforcement action are available to it.

(a)   serving an improvement notice under section 11
(b)   making a prohibition order under section 20
(c)   serving a hazard awareness notice under section 48
(d)   taking emergency remedial action under section 40
(e)   making an emergency prohibition order under section 43
(f)   making a demolition order under Subsections (1) or (2) of Section 265 of the Housing Act 1985.

9.21 A Category 1 hazard is of a description described by regulations made by the Secretary of the State[1].

1   HA 2004, s 2(1). For details of the HHSRS see the Housing, Health and Safety Rating System (England) Regulations 2005, SI 2005/3208.

9.22 An improvement notice under this section is a notice requiring the person on whom it is served to take such remedial action in respect of the hazard concerned as is specified in the notice[1]. Remedial action is defined as action (whether in the form of carrying out works or otherwise) which, in the opinion of the local housing authority, will remove or reduce the hazard[2]. However as a minimum it must ensure that the hazard ceases to be a Category 1 hazard, but may extend beyond such action[3].

1   HA 2004, s 11(2).
2   HA 2004, s 11(8).
3   HA 2004, s 11(5).

9.23 *Other powers dealing with problems akin to nuisance*

9.23 An improvement notice must specify[1]:

(a) whether the notice is served under section 11 or 12
(b) the nature of the hazard and the residential premises on which it exists,
(c) the deficiency giving rise to the hazard,
(d) the premises in relation to which remedial action is to be taken in respect of the hazard and the nature of that remedial action
(e) the date when the remedial action is to be started
(f) the period within which the remedial action is to be completed or the period within which each part of it is to be completed.

1   HA 2004, s 13(2).

9.24 The notice may not require any remedial action to be started earlier than the 28th day after that on which the notice is served[1]. It must also contain information about the right of appeal against the decision and the period within which an appeal may be made[2]. The decision referred to is not specified but in the authors' view must mean the decision to issue the improvement notice.

1   HA 2004, s 13(3).
2   HA 2004, s 13(4).

Appeals against improvement notices

9.25 A person upon whom an improvement notice is served may appeal to a residential property tribunal against the notice. There are two specific grounds of appeal:

(a) that one or more other persons, as an owner or owners of the premises, ought to take the action concerned or pay the whole or part of the cost of taking that action[1]
(b) that making a prohibition order, serving a hazard awareness notice, or making a demolition order is the best course of action in relation to the hazard in respect of which the notice was served[2].

1   HA 2004, Sch 1, para 11.
2   HA 2004, Sch 1, para 12.

9.26 The provisions setting out these specific grounds of appeal do not affect the generality of the right to an appeal to against the notice[1]. Therefore it would appear that a number of other grounds may be raised by the appeal against the notice. For example, by analogy with the repealed regime under the Housing Act 2004 relating housing repair notices which these provisions replaced, the lawfulness or validity of the council's decision to serve the notice[2], the extent of the works required and the tine for completion of the works are all matters which may be raised on appeal.

1   HA 2004, Sch 1, para 10.
2   *Wandsworth London Borough Council v Winder* [1985] AC 461; *Elliot v Brighton Borough Council* (1980) 258 Estates Gazette 441.

9.27 An appeal against an improvement notice must be made within the period of 21 days beginning with the date on which the improvement notice was served. On appeal the Tribunal may by order confirm, quash or vary the improvement notice[1].

1   HA 2004, Sch 1, para 14. See generally Sch 1, Pt 3 for other provisions in respect of appeals.

Execution of works by the local authority

9.28 The local housing authority may by agreement with the person on whom an improvement notice is served take any action which that person is required to take in pursuance of the notice[1]. Any action taken by the local housing authority under paragraph 1 is to be taken at the expense of the person on whom the notice is served[2]. In the absence of agreement, the local authority may nevertheless execute the work themselves if the notice is not complied with[3], or if reasonable progress is not being made towards compliance[4]. Provision is made for powers of entry. It is an offence to obstruct a person in performance of anything which they are required or authorised to do under the provisions concerned with improvement notices[5].

1 HA 2004, Sch 3, para 1.
2 HA 2004, Sch 3, para 2.
3 HA 2004, Sch 3, para 3.
4 See n 3 above.
5 HA 2004, s 241 and Sch 3, para 5.

9.29 Provision is made for notice to be given of the authority's intention to enter the premises for the purpose of taking remedial action in relation to a hazard[1] and for the local authority to recover the costs of taking such action[2].

1 HA 2004, Sch 3, para 4.
2 HA 2004, Sch 3, para 6. See Part 3 of Schedule 3 for detailed provisions relating to the recovery of these expenses.

Failure to comply with the notice

9.30 A person on whom an improvement notice was served commits an offence if he fails to comply with it. Note that this offence differs from the previous offence under the repealed section 198A of the Housing Act 1985 which made it an offence where a person having control of premises *intentionally* fails to comply with a housing repair notice. The new provisions make the offence one of strict liability.

'FLY TIPPING' – ENVIRONMENTAL PROTECTION ACT 1990 SECTION 59

The statutory provisions

9.31 Section 59 of the EPA 1990 creates a specific power for the Environment Agency to deal with unlawfully deposited waste. The powers in section 59 are available to both the Environment Agency and to any waste collection authority.[1] They apply to deposits of 'controlled waste' made in contravention of section 33(1) of the EPA (see para **9.38**).

1 Normally the district, metropolitan or city council.

9.32 The EPA 1990 provides for the service of a section 59 notice on the occupier requiring him to:
  (a) Remove the waste from the land within a period set out in the notice but not less than 21 days from the service of the notice, and/or
  (b) Take specified steps to reduce or eliminate the effects of the waste within a specified period (again no sooner than 21 days from service).

9.33 *Other powers dealing with problems akin to nuisance*

9.33 As to 'controlled waste,' this term is defined in section 75 of the EPA 1990 as household, industrial or commercial waste. These broad definitions are added to by the Controlled Waste Regulations 1992[1] and Waste Management Licensing Regulations 1994.[2] The law on this has become rather complex because of the need to comply with European law. An outline follows.

1   SI 1992/558. These regulations are important in defining what types of waste are household waste (and therefore may be disposed of within the curtilage of dwelling concerned without breaching EPA 1990, s 33).
2   SI 1994/1056.

9.34 The Waste Framework Directive[1] provides a definition of waste which is now applied in the present context. In simple terms, no waste shall be regarded as household, industrial or commercial waste (and therefore controlled waste) unless it is 'Directive Waste'.[2] Directive Waste means any substance or object in the categories set out in Schedule 4 of the Waste Management Licensing Regulations 1994[3] which the producer or holder of that waste 'discards or intends to discard.' In fact the substances or objects list is very broad indeed including, for example, materials contaminated or soiled (for example, packing materials or containers), unusable parts (for example, reject batteries), products for which the holder has no further use. The list ends with the catch-all category of '... any materials, substances or products not contained in the above categories'! The meaning of 'discard' is therefore crucial to the determination of what is waste.

1   75/442/EC, as amended by Directive 91/156/EC.
2   Controlled Waste Regulations 1992, SI 1992/558, reg 7A.
3   SI 1994/1056.

9.35 The meaning of 'discard' has often been considered by both domestic and European courts. The sensible words of Carnwath J in *Mayer Parry Recycling Ltd v Environment Agency*[1] after considering the then previous decisions of the European Court of Justice[2] have not been the last word but remain a good starting point:

> 'The general concept is reasonably clear. The term "discard" is used in a broad sense equivalent to "get rid of"; but is coloured by the examples of waste given in Annex I[3] and the Waste Catalogue,[4] which indicate that it is concerned generally with materials which have ceased to be required for their original purpose, normally because they are unsuitable, unwanted or surplus to requirements.'

1   [1999] Env LR 489.
2   In particular *Criminal proceedings against Tombesi* [1997] ECR I-3561 and *Inter-Environnement Wallonie v Région Wallonne* [1997] ECR I-7411.
3   Annex I is the Directive list of waste reproduced in Waste Management Licensing Regulations 1994, SI 1994/1056, Sch 4.
4   This is a non-definitive list of types of waste produced by the European Commission (see Commission Decision (EC) 20 December 1993).

9.36 The European Court of Justice has however repeatedly emphasised that the meaning of discard should not be interpreted restrictively.[1] The definition gives rise to many problems particularly in respect of materials which are being recycled or re-used in some way.[2] However, in the majority of cases with which section 59 of the EPA 1990 will be concerned a simple analysis will be more than sufficient to demonstrate that controlled waste is involved. For example, unwanted or worn out cars, car batteries, tyres and old beds which are dumped on land would be 'controlled waste.'

1   See eg *Van de Walle v Texaco Belgium* Case C-1/03 [2005] All ER(EC) 1139 at para 45.
2   See eg *ARCO Chemie Nederland v M v V and EPON* Case C-418/97 [2003] Env LR 40 [2002] QB 646 and the most recent observations of Carnwath LJ in the Court of Appeal in *R (on the application of OSS Group Limited) v Environment Agency* [2007] EWCA Civ 611.

9.37 As to section 33(1) of the EPA 1990, this provision creates a number of criminal offences in relation to waste. The key provision, as far as the power under section 59 is concerned, is section 33(1)(a) which states:

'a person shall not ... deposit controlled waste or knowingly cause or knowingly permit controlled waste to be deposited in or on any land unless a waste management licence authorising the deposit is in force and that deposit is in accordance with the licence'

9.38 There are certain exceptional deposits of controlled waste which are permissible – for example, disposals of household waste within the curtilage of the domestic dwelling from which it arose or deposits which fall within an exception to the need for a waste management licence. It is clear that the term 'deposit' covers temporary as well as permanent or final deposits.[1]

1   See *R v Metropolitan Stipendiary Magistrate ex p London Waste Regulation Authority* [1993] 3 All ER 113. Thus EPA 1990, ss 33, 59 may apply even though the person concerned insists that they intended to move the waste at some later date.

Procedure under the EPA 1990, section 59

Appeal against the notice

9.39 The provisions for service of a section 59 notice are contained in section 160 of the EPA 1990.[1] Any person who receives a section 59 notice has 21 days to appeal against it to the magistrates' court.[2] The magistrates must quash the notice if the appellant establishes that:

(a)   The appellant neither deposited the waste nor knowingly caused or knowingly permitted the deposit,[3] or
(b)   There is a material defect in the notice.[4]

1   See Chapter 3.
2   The appeal is made by making a complaint to the magistrates' court. See by analogy appeals against a statutory nuisance abatement notices, Chapter 4, above.
3   On the meaning of 'knowingly permit' in this context see *Kent County Council v Beaney* [1991] 5 Env Law 89 where the court held that knowledge and permission could be inferred where it was obvious the landowner must have known what was going on. This could be important in the context of EPA 1990, s 59 where a landowner is aware of fly tipping and does not prevent it (eg by fencing, notices, ditches etc) or even where he does not admit his knowledge.
4   EPA 1990, s 59(3).

9.40 Section 59 of the EPA 1990 does not set out other grounds for appeal but states that '... in any other case [the court] shall either modify the requirement or dismiss the appeal.' This indicates that appeals might also be brought against the requirements included in the notice or the time schedule set out in it. Any notice is suspended during the appeal and the court is permitted to change the timetable, where it merely modifies the notice or dismisses the appeal entirely, to give the appellant a reasonable time to comply.[1]

1   EPA 1990, s 59(4).

9.41 *Other powers dealing with problems akin to nuisance*

Criminal enforcement

9.41 Section 59 notices may be enforced by either criminal prosecution for non-compliance with the requirements of the notice[1] or by the Environment Agency or waste collection authority exercising its powers to clean up the waste. Where the latter course of action is taken, the costs reasonably incurred in cleaning up are recoverable from the person served with the notice.[2]

1   EPA 1990, s 59(5) makes it an offence punishable by a fine of up to level 5 (£5,000) and a further fine of up to £500 per day for each day of continued non-compliance with the notice – until the Environment Agency or waste collection authority exercises its own clean up powers.
2   EPA 1990, s 59(6).

9.42 There are separate clean up powers[1] for the Environment Agency or waste collection authority to clean up where it is necessary to do so forthwith in order to remove or prevent pollution of land, water or air or harm to human health.[2] These powers may also be used where there is no occupier of the land or the occupier was not responsible for the deposit.[3] Where these 'forthwith' powers are used the cost may only be recovered from the occupier, unless the occupier proves that he did not deposit the waste nor did he knowingly cause or knowingly permit its deposit. In any other case the cost may be recovered if the Environment Agency or waste collection authority can show that the person was responsible for the deposit.[4] Where the clean up powers are exercised the waste removed belongs to the authority and can be disposed by them.

1   EPA 1990, s 59(7).
2   These terms are defined broadly in EPA 1990, s 29 and include, eg, offence to any of man's senses, harm to the health of living organisms or other interference with ecological systems.
3   This includes knowingly causing or knowingly permitting the deposit.
4   This includes making the deposit or knowingly causing or knowingly permitting the deposit.

POWERS CONCERNED WITH LITTER, RUBBISH AND REFUSE

9.43 A variety of powers allow public authorities to deal with the problem of litter, rubbish and refuse.

Litter

9.44 Particular areas (for example, around a shopping precinct or takeaway food shop) may be badly affected by litter. There is a discrete legal framework dealing with litter.[1]

1   Litter Act 1983 and EPA 1990, Pt IV.

9.45 A non-exhaustive definition of litter is provided by section 98 of the Environmental Protection Act 1990.[1] According to that section, litter can include 'the discarded ends of cigarettes, cigars and like products' and 'discarded chewing-gum and the discarded remains of other products designed for chewing'. The *Oxford English Dictionary*[2] says that it includes 'odds and ends or discarded material lying about . . . refuse or rubbish discarded in an open or public place.' It has been held in a case pre-dating the current legislation that a car was capable of being litter.[3] It may include dog faeces in public parks, beaches used for recreation, picnic sites and car parks for the purposes of Part IV of the EPA 1990[4] (which includes litter offences and clearance duties).

1   Inserted by the Clean Neighbourhoods and Environment Act 2005, s 27.
2   *The New Shorter Oxford English Dictionary* (1993) vol 1, p 1606.
3   *Vaughan v Briggs* [1960] 2 All ER 473.
4   See Litter (Animal Droppings) Order 1991, SI 1991/961.

9.46 In broad terms, the litter controls are limited to land to which there is public access and principally that within public ownership.

The litter offence: EPA 1990, section 87[1]

9.47 It is an offence to throw down, drop or deposit any litter in any place in the area of a principal litter authority, which is open to the air.[2] The perpetrator must have left the material there: no offence would be committed if someone dropped litter and then picked it up.[3]

1   As amended by the Clean Neighbourhoods and Environment Act 2005, s 18.
2   Before section 87 was amended by the Clean Neighbourhoods and Environment Act, in relation to private land it contained a requirement for the place to have been designated a litter control area by the local authority Such a requirement has now been removed.
3   See *Vaughan v Briggs* [1960] 2 All ER 473.

9.48 Under the amended provision, there is no requirement to prove that the material is thrown down, dropped or deposited in circumstances as to cause, contribute to or tend to lead to the defacement by litter of the place where it was deposited. The principal litter authorities are set out in section 86, and include all county and district councils. An area is not 'open to the air' for the purposes of section 87 of the EPA 1990 if the public do not have access to it. A place is treated as 'open to the air' notwithstanding that it is covered if it is open to the air on at least one side.[1] It is a defence to show that the deposit was lawful.[2]

1   EPA 1990, s 86(13). Similar words under the original section 87 were considered in relation to 'carding' of telephone boxes with cards advertising the services of prostitutes in *Felix v DPP* [1998] Crim LR 657. The court held that a telephone box with a door and a roof was not a public open space and therefore the litter offence was not committed.
2   EPA 1990, s 87(2); the deposit was authorised by law or done with the consent of the owner, occupier or other person having control of the place into which the thing was deposited.

9.49 The offence carries a maximum penalty of a level 4 fine.[1] Problems in bringing prosecutions may arise because of identification.[2] Litter wardens may be appointed by district or London Borough councils. A litter warden may issue a fixed penalty notice to anyone whom the warden believes has committed an offence under section 87 of the EPA 1990. The amount payable under the fixed penalty notice is that specified by the particular principal litter authority.[3]

1   Currently £2,500.
2   As Bates notes in *Waste Law* (2nd edn, 1997) there is no power for a member of the public or litter warden to obtain the name and address of a suspect or arrest them. A police constable will have a power of arrest under Police and Criminal Evidence Act 1984, s 25.
3   EPA 1990, s 88(6A).

Litter clearance duties

9.50 Litter clearance duties are imposed on local authorities and some other statutory bodies in respect of public land in the open air. There are specific duties imposed in areas where street litter control notices have been issued because of recurrent litter problems.

9.51 The duty to keep land in the open air clear of litter and refuse (so far as it is practicable to do so) applies to:

9.51 *Other powers dealing with problems akin to nuisance*

(a) highways maintainable at public expense. This will include pavements as well as roadways.[1] The duty normally lies with the district or London Borough council but may be transferred to the relevant highway authority[2]
(b) land in the open air to which the public have access with or without making payment[3]
(c) Crown land, which is subject to the duty in respect of land to which the public has access either with or without payment[4] – the duty applies to the Crown Estate Commissioners or the Minister in charge of the relevant Government department
(d) land of designated statutory undertakers to which the public has access either with or without payment[5]
(e) land of universities, colleges and state maintained or grant assisted schools[6] which is in the open air – the duty falls on the governing body.[7]

The nature of the duty is to keep the relevant area clear of litter, so far as is practicable. Considerable guidance on the nature and meaning of this duty is given in the statutory code of practice.[8]

1 EPA 1990, s 98.
2 EPA 1990, s 86(11).
3 This is known as 'relevant land' and excludes land held as an education authority (eg schools) and land below the mean high water mark: EPA 1990, s 89(1) and the Litter (Relevant Land of Principal Litter Authorities and Relevant Crown Land) Order 1991, SI 1991/476.
4 Again land below the mean high water mark is excluded rather significantly in this case as most of the foreshore belongs to the Crown.
5 Litter (Statutory Undertakers) (Designation and Relevant Land) Order 1991, SI 1991/1043, has included transport undertakers – railways, harbours, airports, canals etc but significantly not the utilities. Water utilities in particular who own substantial areas of land to which the public has access.
6 See the Litter (Designated Educational Institutions) Order 1991, SI 1991/561.
7 Any principal litter authority (except a county council in England) designates litter control areas in respect of certain types of land set out in the Litter Control Areas Order 1991, SI 1991/1325. The types of land include public car parks, shopping centres, industrial estates, camping sites and picnic areas. Orders may only be made where litter or refuse is detrimental to the amenity of the locality. There are procedures for making the order to ensure that landowners and occupiers affected are consulted.
8 EPA 1990, s 89(3) and Code of Practice on Litter and Refuse. The Code designates various standards of cleanliness for different categories of land and practical measures for compliance with the duty.

9.52 The litter clearance duties are enforceable either by litter abatement notices[1] issued by principal litter authorities[2] or litter abatement actions brought by private individuals.[3] The abatement notice procedure may require the land to be cleared of litter or refuse within a certain time or prohibit the land from becoming defaced by litter or refuse. There are appeal rights to the magistrates against litter abatement notices. It is a criminal offence to fail to comply with a litter abatement notice. In certain cases the litter authority may carry out the works in the notice and recover their costs.[4]

1 EPA 1990, s 92.
2 Except county councils in England.
3 EPA 1990, s 91.
4 In litter control areas and in respect of educational land: EPA 1990, s 92(9), (10).

9.53 Litter abatement actions may be brought by any 'person aggrieved'[1] on the ground that litter or refuse defaces an area subject to a litter clearance duty. These actions will be particularly important where the local authority is responsible for the failure to comply with their litter clearance duty. The complainant must first give five days' written notice of his intention to being proceedings to the person or body who is subject to the duty. If the problem is not then resolved a complaint is made to the magistrates' court. The court may make a litter abatement order and may order the defendant to pay the complainant's costs.[2] As with a litter notice, it is a criminal offence to fail to comply with an abatement order.

1   See by way of analogy, the meaning of 'person aggrieved' under EPA 1990, s 82 in Chapter 6 above.
2   EPA 1990, s 91(12).

Litter Clearing Notices

9.54   In respect of any land in its area that is open to the air, a principal litter authority has a power to serve a litter clearing notice on the owner or occupier of the land.[1] This power therefore enables the litter authority to act against private landowners. Such a notice can require the person on whom it is served to clear the land of the litter or refuse. If the litter authority is satisfied that the land is likely to become defaced by litter or refuse, they can also require such a notice to require the owner or occupier to take reasonable steps to prevent it becoming defaced.[2]

1   EPA 1990, s 92A.
2   EPA 1990, s 92A(3).

9.55   An appeal against litter clearing notices may be made to the magistrates' court. The notices may be enforced by an order from the magistrates' court. It is a criminal offence to fail to comply with such an order.

Street litter control notices

9.56   Principal litter authorities[1] may issue litter control notices in order to prevent accumulations of litter or refuse in and around any street or adjacent open land. Notices may impose requirements on occupiers of premises to keep the area specified in the notice clear of litter and refuse.[2] The notice may relate to commercial or retail premises for the sale of food or drink for consumption off the premises (for example, takeaway food shops, off licences and so forth) or premises where food and drink is consumed in the open air on land that is not part of a street or service stations or places of entertainment or places with outside cash dispensers.

1   Except county councils in England.
2   EPA 1990, ss 93, 94.

Litter and the Public Health Act 1936 section 78

9.57   One of the more obscure provisions on litter nuisance is in section 78 of the Public Health Act 1936 (PHA 1936). This applies to courts, yards or passages which are used in common by the occupiers of two or more buildings but are not highways which are not regularly swept and kept clean and free from rubbish or other accumulations. Local authorities have powers to sweep and cleanse the relevant area and recover their costs from the occupiers of premises served by the area.[1]

1   Disputes may be resolved in the magistrates' court: PHA 1936, s 78(2).

9.58 *Other powers dealing with problems akin to nuisance*

Abandoned shopping trolleys – EPA 1990 section 99 and Schedule 4

9.58 The particular problem of abandoned shopping trolleys being left in car parks or streets often some distance from the supermarket or shop to which they belong has now been addressed directly by legislation.

9.59 Section 99 and Schedule 4 of the EPA 1990 applies to shopping trolleys[1] and luggage trolleys.[2] Local authorities can chose to apply the provisions of the Act by resolution.[3] There are procedures for the making of the resolution and in particular for consultation with those affected. The effect of such a resolution is that a designated local authority officer can collect any trolley which appears to be abandoned on any land in the open air and take it to a collection point.[4] If the trolley is on land which appears to be occupied (someone's garden for example), then either the occupier must consent to its removal, or not object to its removal after written notice has been given to him.[5] The local authority must keep the trolley for at least six weeks and give notice to the apparent owner of the trolley so that he may collect it.[6] Where the local authority is satisfied that a person who within the six-week period claims to be the owner is the owner of the trolley, they shall deliver it to him provided that he pays on demand such charge as the local authority requires.[7] Where the trolley is not claimed and the authority has made reasonable inquiries to ascertain who owns it, the trolley may be disposed of or sold.[8]

1 Provided by a shop for customers to carry goods bought in the shop.
2 Provided by a railway, road transport undertaking (eg coach or bus station) or airport.
3 EPA 1990, s 99(1).
4 EPA 1990, Sch 4, para 2(1).
5 EPA 1990, Sch 4, para 2(2).
6 EPA 1990, Sch 4, para 3(1)(a).
7 EPA 1990, Sch 4, para 3(4).
8 EPA 1990, Sch 4, para 3(1)(b), (5).

Rubbish and refuse – Refuse Disposal (Amenity) Act 1978 sections 2 and 6 and Public Health Act 1961 section 34

9.60 These provisions address the issue of rubbish, refuse or other matter on land in the open air.[1] There are clear overlaps with section 59 of the EPA 1990 – although these powers are available to district councils whereas EPA 1990, section 59 powers are vested in the Environment Agency or waste collection authority.

1 Whether or not the public have access to the land in question.

9.61 Under section 2(1)(b) of the Refuse Disposal (Amenity) Act 1978 it is a criminal offence to abandon[1] without lawful authority any matter (other than a motor vehicle[2]) on land in the open or land forming part of the highway, being a thing which the defendant has brought onto the land for the purpose of abandoning it there.[3] The burden of proof relating to abandonment may shift to the defendant in any criminal proceedings, if the prosecution can establish that the matter was left by the defendant in circumstances or for such a time that it may reasonably be assumed that it has been abandoned.[4]

1 Abandon is not defined in the Refuse Disposal (Amenity) Act 1978; Bates *Waste Law* (2nd edn) suggests that this means to leave completely and finally with no intention to retrieve: *Ellerman's Wilson Line Ltd v Webster* [1952] 1 Lloyds Rep 179.

Powers concerned with litter, rubbish and refuse **9.65**

2 There is a separate offence relating to motor vehicles or parts of motor vehicles; see Refuse Disposal (Amenity) Act 1978, s 2(1)(a).
3 Refuse Disposal (Amenity) Act 1978, s 2(1)(b) punishable with a fine of up to level 4 (£2,500) and/or up to 51 weeks imprisonment.
4 See also the powers of a local authority (normally the district or London Borough in England or county or county borough in Wales) to remove any matter abandoned without lawful authority on open land or land forming part of the highway and recover the costs of removal: Refuse Disposal (Amenity) Act 1978, s 6. For powers of entry, see 1978 Act, s 8.

9.62 Section 34 of the PHA 1961 creates a power for a local authority to remove rubbish on land in the open air[1] which is seriously detrimental to the amenity of the neighbourhood. At least 28 days' prior notice must be given to the owner and occupier of the land requiring the removal of the specified rubbish. Any person served with a notice has the right to serve a counter notice stating that he will remove the rubbish himself.[2] Alternatively, the recipient of the notice may appeal to the magistrates' court on the grounds that the authority should not take action under section 34 (for example, if they allege the rubbish is not seriously detrimental to the amenity of the neighbourhood) or the steps proposed in the notice are unreasonable.[3]

1 But not at a licensed waste site: PHA 1961, s 34(5).
2 If this happens then the local authority may not exercise any power under PHA 1961, s 34 unless the person who served the counter notice fails to clear the land or make reasonable progress towards completing this work: s 34(2).
3 PHA 1961, s 34(2)(b).

Waste on the highway: Highways Act 1980 sections 149 and 151

9.63 Section 149 of the Highways Act 1980 (HA 1980) gives the highway authority a power to deal with anything deposited on the highway which constitutes a nuisance. Unless it is a danger to users of the highway,[1] the procedure is that a notice is served on the person who deposited it requiring its removal. If the removal does not take place the highways authority may seek an order from the magistrates authorising the authority to remove and dispose of the thing in question.

1 In which case the highways authority may remove it forthwith and recover their expenses from the person who deposited it or claims it belongs to them: HA 1980, s 149(3)(a). Alternatively, they may seek an order from the magistrates' court for an order allowing them to dispose of it to try and recoup their expenses – any shortfall may be recovered from the person who deposited it: HA 1980, s 149(3)(b).

9.64 Under section 151 of the HA 1980, a highway authority may serve the owner or occupier of the land adjoining a street which is a highway maintainable at public expense a notice requiring works to be carried out to prevent soil or refuse from that land from falling, or being washed or carried, on to the street or into any sewer or gully in it in such quantities as to obstruct the street or choke the sewer or gully.[1]

1 HA 1980, s 151.

9.65 There are rights of appeal against such notices to the magistrates' court.[1] Non-compliance with a section 151 notice is a criminal offence.[2]

1 HA 1980, s 151(2).
2 HA 1980, s 151(3).

9.66 *Other powers dealing with problems akin to nuisance*

DEMOLITION WASTE – BUILDING ACT 1984 SECTION 79

9.66 The problem of unsightly collapsed buildings or demolition sites is addressed in section 79(2) of the Building Act 1984. This creates a power for local authorities[1] to deal with rubbish or other material resulting from or exposed by the demolition or collapse of a building or structure, which is on the site of the building, or structure, or on adjoining land. Where the authority consider that by reason of the rubbish or material the site or land is seriously detrimental to the amenities of the neighbourhood, they may serve a notice on the owner of the land requiring steps to be taken for the clearance of the land.

1   District or London Borough councils in England and county or county boroughs in Wales.

9.67 There is an appeal against such a notice to the magistrates' court.[1] Non-compliance with such a notice is a criminal offence.[2] Where the notice is not complied with the authority may enter on the land, execute the works required by the notice and recover the costs thereof.[3]

1   BA 1984, s 83(3).
2   With a fine of up to level 4 (£2,500) and a continuing daily fine for non compliance after conviction of up to £2 per day.
3   BA 1984, s 83(3).

ABANDONED VEHICLES: REFUSE DISPOSAL (AMENITY) ACT 1978 SECTIONS 2 AND 3

9.68 The issue of abandoned vehicles has received its own specific treatment in the Refuse Disposal (Amenity) Act 1978. In broad terms, the provisions focus on the removal of abandoned vehicles and their disposal.

9.69 Under section 2(1)(a) of the Refuse Disposal (Amenity) Act 1978 it is an offence to abandon on any land in the open air, or on any other land forming part of a highway, a motor vehicle[1] or anything which formed part of a motor vehicle and was removed from it in the course of dismantling the vehicle on the land. The circumstances of the vehicle being left or the duration of time that has passed since it was left will be relevant in determining whether or not the vehicle has been abandoned.[2]

1   The Refuse Disposal (Amenity) Act 1978, s 11 defines a motor vehicle as mechanically propelled vehicle intended or adapted for use on the road (whether or not it is capable of this use) and includes a trailer for such a vehicle, any chassis or body of a vehicle.
2   Abandon is not defined in the Refuse Disposal (Amenity) Act 1978 but Bates *Waste Law* (2nd edn) suggests that this means to leave completely and finally with no intention to retrieve: *Ellerman's Wilson Line Ltd v Webster* [1952] 1 Lloyds Rep 179.

9.70 Under section 3 of the Refuse Disposal (Amenity) Act 1978 local authorities[1] have duty to remove vehicles that appear to have been abandoned in the open air or on other land which forms part of the highway. The duty to remove is subject to provisions for the giving of notice and obtaining consent of the occupier of land where the land on which the vehicle has been abandoned is occupied.[2] Specific provision is made for the disposal of removed vehicles.[3]

1   District or London Borough councils in England and county or county boroughs in Wales.
2   Unless they consider that it ought to be destroyed in which case they must fix a notice to the vehicle giving seven days, warning of its removal and destruction: Refuse Disposal (Amenity) Act 1978, s 3(5).
3   Refuse Disposal (Amenity) Act 1978, s 4.

Nuisance Parking: Part II Clean Neighbourhoods and Environment Act 2005

9.71 The problem caused by vehicles being placed on public highways in order to be sold or to be repaired is addressed by sections 3 and 4 of the Clean Neighbourhoods and Environment Act 2005. The Act introduced two new offences: that of exposing vehicles for sale on a road and repairing vehicles on a road. The offences are only targeted at businesses: for each offence it is a defence to prove that the actions were not carried out in the course of either a vehicles sales or repair business.[1]

1 Clean Neighbourhoods and Environment Act 2005, ss 3(2), 4(3).

MISCELLANEOUS PUBLIC HEALTH POWERS

9.72 This section includes various miscellaneous and, in some cases, somewhat arcane powers to deal with problems akin to nuisance.

Defective closets

9.73 Section 45 of the PHA 1936 provides a power for a local authority to serve a notice on the occupier or owner of a building[1] which has a defective closet.[2] The closet may be within a building or serve a building. The power only arises where the closet is in such a state as to be prejudicial to health or a nuisance. The notice may require works or cleansing to be carried out, but may not require reconstruction of the closet. Local authorities have powers to enter premises and examine the condition of sanitary conveniences.[3]

1 Not defined in the PHA 1936 but the section does not apply to workplaces covered by the Workplace (Health, Safety and Welfare) Regulations 1992, SI 1992/3004, namely all workplaces except those in reg 3 – eg, ships, mines or construction sites. The regulations include rules for the provision and maintenance of sanitary and washing facilities (regs 20, 21).
2 Closet is defined as including a privy: PHA 1936, s 90.
3 PHA 1936, ss 48 and 287 (entry powers).

9.74 In so far as the notice requires works to be carried out, a right of appeal exists to the magistrates' court.[1] In so far as the notice requires steps to be carried out other than the execution of works, there appears to be no appeal against the notice, although on any prosecution for non-compliance with such a notice it is open to the defendant to question the reasonableness of the local authority's requirements or their decision to address the notice to him and not the owner or occupier of the building, as the case may be.[2]

1 PHA 1936, ss 45(2), 290(3).
2 PHA 1936, s 45(3).

9.75 Where a notice which requires works has not been complied with the local authority may carry out the works required by a notice and recover their costs of doing so.[1] It is a criminal offence to fail to comply with a notice.[2]

1 PHA 1936, s 290(6). A charge may be placed on the premises where an owner is the recipient of the notice – PHA 1936, s 291.
2 Maximum fine is level 1 (£200) for notices which require steps other than works, with a continuing daily fine of up to £2 per day for each day of non-compliance following the first conviction: PHA 1936, s 45(3). In any proceedings under section 45 the defendant may argue that the notice's requirements or the local authority's decision to serve the notice on him rather than another person are or is unreasonable: PHA 1936, s 45(3). Where the notice requires works which are not complied with, the maximum fine is level 4 (£2,500): PHA 1936, s 290(6).

9.76 *Other powers dealing with problems akin to nuisance*

9.76 The PHA 1936 also provides duties for the maintenance of water and earth closets[1] and for the proper use and maintenance of sanitary conveniences shared between the members of two or more families.[2] Where earth closets are provided local authorities now have powers to require them to be replaced with water closets (providing there is a sufficient water supply).[3]

1   PHA 1936, s 51 states the occupier of the building must, for example, in the case of a water closet maintain the flushing apparatus and a sufficient water supply.
2   PHA 1936, s 52.
3   Building Act 1984, s 66.

9.77 Where a building is without sufficient closets or the closets provided are in such a state as to be prejudicial to health or a nuisance (and cannot be put right without reconstruction) then the local authority shall serve a notice on the owner requiring him to provide additional or new toilets.[1]

1   Building Act 1984, s 64; this section does not apply to factories or workplaces, though s 65 of the 1984 Act makes similar provision for workplaces.

Cesspools

9.78 A cesspool has been defined as including a settlement tank or other tank for the reception or disposal of foul water from buildings.[1] This might cover a cesspit; for example, a container receiving waste from a house or perhaps a unit receiving farm waste water or slurry from an agricultural building.

1   It need not be specially designed for such a purpose. A pit in a field into which sewage is discharged could be a cesspool: *Wincanton RDC v Parsons* (1905) 74 LJKB 533.

9.79 Section 50 of the PHA 1936 provides powers for local authorities to deal with cesspools, the contents of which are soaking away or overflowing. The local authority has power to serve a notice on the person by whose act, default or sufferance the soakage or overflow occurred or continued, requiring them to carry out works, or take other steps including the periodic emptying of the cesspool as may be necessary for preventing the soakage or overflow.

9.80 There is a right of appeal to the magistrates' court against the notice.[1] Where a notice which requires works has not been complied with the local authority may carry out the works required by a notice and recover their costs of doing so.[2] It is a criminal offence to fail to comply with a notice.[3]

1   PHA 1936, s 290(3).
2   PHA 1936, s 290(6). A charge may be placed on the premises where an owner is the recipient of the notice – PHA 1936, s 291.
3   Maximum fine is level 1 (£200) for notices which require steps other than works, with a continuing daily fine of up to £2 per day for each day of non-compliance following the first conviction: PHA 1936, s 50(3). In any proceedings under section 50 the defendant may argue that the local authority's requirements are unreasonable: PHA 1936, s 50(3). Where the notice requires works which are not complied with, the maximum fine is level 4 (£2,500): PHA 1936, s 290(6).

Drainage problems and defects

9.81 The section 59 of the Building Act 1984 includes powers for local authorities to deal with private sewers, cesspools, drains, soil pipes and so forth where they are defective in some respect. The powers extend to where these facilities are insufficient or defective or are prejudicial to health or a nuisance.[1] The power also apply to disused cesspools, private sewers or drains which are prejudicial to health or a nuisance. A notice may be served on the owner[2] requiring the execution of necessary works for renewal, repair or cleansing of the relevant appliance, or for filling up, removing or rendering innocuous the appliance if it is disused.[3]

1   Building Act 1984, s 59(1)(a)–(d).
2   Where a private sewer was used by several properties all the owners connected to the sewer should be served with the notice under s 59: *Swansea City Council v Jenkins* (1994) 158 JP 952.
3   Building Act 1984, s 59(1).

9.82 Where a water closet, drain or soil pipe is constructed or repaired so as to be prejudicial to health or a nuisance the person undertaking the work shall be guilty of a criminal offence unless he can show that reasonable care would not have avoided the problem.[1]

1   Building Act 1984, s 63.

Public Health Act byelaws

9.83 The PHA 1936 includes powers for byelaws to be made by local authorities for the prevention of nuisance[1] and removal of offensive matter or liquid.[2] Byelaws may cover:

(a) Nuisances arising from snow, filth, dust, ashes and rubbish
(b) Animals which are kept so as to be prejudicial to health
(c) The removal or carriage of any faecal, offensive or noxious matter or liquid

1   PHA 1936, s 81.
2   PHA 1936, s 82.

Filthy or verminous premises

9.84 Section 83 of the PHA 1936 creates powers to deal with premises which are filthy or infested with vermin. Where a local authority is satisfied that premises[1] are in such a filthy or unwholesome condition as to be prejudicial to health or are verminous[2] they may give notice to the owner or occupier requiring them to take steps necessary to remedy the condition of the premises.[3] The notice may require among other things the removal of wallpaper and the interior surface of walls to be painted, papered, distempered or whitewashed.[4]

1   Mines, quarries and factories are outside the ambit of this power.
2   Vermin is defined in PHA 1936, s 90 in its application to insects as including eggs, larvae and pupae.
3   PHA 1936, s 83(1).
4   For the detail of these provisions and the choice of methods see PHA 1936, s 83(1A).

9.85 Notices are enforced by prosecution[1] and/or by the local authority carrying out the necessary works and recovering their expenses.[2] There are special provisions relating to the use of gas to deal with vermin,[3] and powers for filthy or verminous articles in any premises.[4]

1   Maximum fine is level 1 (£200) with a continuing daily fine of up to £2 per day for each day of non-compliance following the first conviction. In any proceedings the defendant may argue that the notice's requirements are unreasonable: PHA 1936, s 83(2).
2   PHA 1936, s 83(2).
3   PHA 1936, s 83(3).
4   PHA 1936, s 84.

9.86 *Other powers dealing with problems akin to nuisance*

Notifiable diseases

9.86 The Public Health (Control of Disease) Act 1984 is concerned with the control of certain notifiable diseases.¹ It is primarily concerned with the notification of disease and measures to stop it spreading, for example, requiring infected persons to stop work, exclusion of infected children from schools and public places and so on. There are also provisions relating to infected premises.²

1 See Public Health Control of Disease Act 1984, s 10 – cholera, plague, relapsing fever, smallpox, typhus are covered, and other diseases covered by the Public Health (Infectious Diseases) Regulations 1988, SI 1988/1546, including meningitis, diphtheria, mumps and measles.
2 See Public Health Control of Disease Act 1984, ss 29–32.

Defective and dangerous premises

9.87 Premises which are in such a state as to be prejudicial to health or a nuisance may be dealt under procedures contained in section 76 of the Building Act 1984. The power to use these procedures arises where unreasonable delay in remedying the defects would result from using the EPA 1990 Part III provisions.¹

1 Building Act 1984, s 76(1).

9.88 The Building Act 1984 sets out procedures for serving a notice on the same person who would be liable under the EPA 1990 Part III setting out the defects and stating that the authority themselves intend to remedy the defects.¹ Nine days after the service of a Building Act 1984 section 76 notice the local authority may carry out the necessary works and recover their reasonable expenses.² There is a procedure for the person served to serve a counter notice saying that they will carry out the works; in which case the local authority are precluded from doing any works so long as the works are commenced within a reasonable time and reasonable progress is made with them.³

1 Building Act 1984, s 76(1).
2 Building Act 1984, s 76(2).
3 Building Act 1984, s 76(3).

9.89 In any proceedings by the local authority to recover their expenses¹ the court shall inquire whether the premises were so defective as to be prejudicial to health or a nuisance, or whether unreasonable delay would have resulted from the local authority's exercise of powers under the EPA 1990 Part III.² Where the local authority were not justified in concluding that the premises were in such a state or that such unreasonable delay would have resulted, they will not recover their costs.³ Where the defendant proves that he served a counter-notice, the court shall inquire whether the defendant failed to begin the works within a reasonable time or failed to make reasonable progress with the works.⁴ Where such failure is not established, the local authority shall not recover its expenses.⁵

1 Proceedings for expense recovery will be in the county court and are governed by Building Act 1984, ss 107–110.
2 Building Act 1984, s 76(4)(a).
3 Building Act 1984, s 76(4)(b)(i).
4 Building Act 1984, s 76(4)(b).
5 Building Act 1984, s 76(4)(b)(ii).

9.90 Sections 77 and 78 of the Building Act 1984 confer powers for dealing with buildings or structures in a dangerous condition or where a building is used to carry such loads as to be dangerous. It seems that this may be the appropriate power to deal with many types of housing and building problems that may fall outside statutory nuisance, for example dangerously steep or uneven stairs, a balcony without any railings, electrical wiring defects, a gas leak and exposed hot pipes.

9.91 Under section 77 of the Building Act 1984 the local authority may apply to the magistrates' court for an order. Where the danger arises from the condition of the building, the order may require the owner to carry out works necessary to obviate the danger or, if the owner elects, to demolish part or all of the building.[1] Where the danger arises from the overloading of the building the order may restrict the building's use until any necessary works have been executed.[2] It is criminal offence to fail to comply with an order made under section 77.[3] Where the notice is not complied with, the local authority may enter on the land and carry out the works ordered and recover their expenses from the person who is in default.[4]

1   Building Act 1984, s 77(1)(a).
2   Building Act 1984, s 77(1)(b).
3   Building Act 1984, s 77(2).
4   Building Act 1984, s 77(2).

9.92 Section 78 of the Building Act 1984 sets out the procedure where immediate action is needed to remove the danger. Under the section the local authority may take such action as they consider necessary to remove the danger, and need only give notice of their intention to do so where this is reasonably practicable.[1] No court order is required. There are provisions for the local authority to recover the expenses reasonably incurred in carrying out the works.[2]

1   Building Act 1984, s 78(1), (2).
2   Building Act 1984, s 78(3).

9.93 It appears that powers under section 78 of the Building Act 1984 may well be used in conjunction with section 77 – with urgent steps only being taken under section 78 and other works (perhaps a longer term solution) under section 77.

Ditches ponds, gutters and sewers[1]

9.94 The PHA 1936 contained certain powers specifically dealing with ponds, ditches and the like.[2] Parish councils and local authorities have powers to deal with ponds, pools, ditches, gutters or other places containing or used for the collection of water, filth or matter likely to be prejudicial to health.[3] There are special provisions relating to foul and offensive watercourses or ditches near to local authority boundaries.[4]

1   See also discussion of statutory nuisance in respect of these matters in Chapter 1.
2   Many of these powers may now be obsolete in practice as the Environment Agency now has a wide range of powers to deal with water quality and pollution issues, principally under the Water Resources Act 1991.
3   PHA 1936, s 260. These powers must not be used to interfere with private rights or sewage disposal works.
4   PHA 1936, s 261.

9.95 *Other powers dealing with problems akin to nuisance*

Animals and animal establishments

9.95 Animals and animal establishments can be a cause of considerable nuisance and neighbour concern. They may of course constitute a statutory nuisance by virtue of noise, smell or threat of disease. There are a series of licensing provisions relating to animals. In all cases they are not concerned directly with the impact on the amenity of the neighbourhood but rather with animal welfare. In many cases issues of amenity (such as noise, smell, traffic implications and so on) will have been addressed when planning permission was sought for the activity. However, although not directed at issues of nuisance these provisions may coincidentally have the effect of addressing nuisances, as the absence of a licence or breach of its terms may be a basis for closure of the establishment. Animal boarding establishments (for example, catteries and kennels),[1] kennels for breeding dogs,[2] zoos,[3] pet shops[4] and riding establishments (for example, riding schools or stables)[5] may all require licensing under relevant legislation.

1 Animal Boarding Establishments Act 1963.
2 Breeding of Dogs Acts 1973 and 1991 and Breeding and Sale of Dogs (Welfare) Act 1999.
3 Zoo Licensing Act 1981. Section 4 of the 1981 Act goes some way to allowing refusal of a zoo licence on grounds to do with effects on neighbours. It allows refusal where the zoo would injuriously affect the health and safety of persons living in the neighbourhood of the zoo.
4 Pet Animals Act 1951.
5 Riding Establishments Act 1970.

Pests and vermin

9.96 The problem of pests and vermin may be addressed in a number of ways: it may be a statutory nuisance,[1] or it may fall within powers to deal with filthy and verminous premises under the PHA 1936.[2] However, the particular issue of infestation by rats and mice is addressed by the Prevention of Damage by Pests Act 1949. Local authorities have powers under the 1949 Act to serve notices on owners or occupiers of premises requiring them to take reasonable steps for the destruction of the mice or rats on the land or otherwise keeping it free from mice or rats, where it appears to the local authority, that in the case of any land, that such steps should be taken.[3]

1 For example, under EPA 1990, s 79(1)(a).
2 See para **9.84**.
3 Prevention of Damage by Pests Act 1949, s 4(1).

9.97 There are provisions for appeals against notices served under the 1949 Act and for the enforcement of the notice by criminal prosecution or the local authority carrying out the specified works and recovering their expenses.[1]

1 Prevention of Damage by Pests Act 1949, s 5. The 1949 Act includes powers of entry for inspection and carrying out works: see s 22.

Dog fouling

9.98 The problem of dogs fouling land to which the public has access has caused considerable public concern, particularly in urban areas, partly because of the effect on the local amenity and concerns about public health. The statutory regime dealing with this issue under the Dogs (Fouling of Land) Act 1996 was repealed by the Clean Neighbourhoods and Environment Act 2005. Under section 64 of the Act local authority's no longer have power to make byelaws in relation to fouling of land by dogs and associated issues relating to dog control. However, byelaws in force at the time of the coming into force of the 2005 Act remain unaffected.[1]

1 Clean Neighbourhoods and Environment Act 2005, s 64(2).

9.99 Chapter 1 of Part 6 of the 2005 Act introduced a new system of dog control orders and fixed penalty notices where offences relating to control of dogs as set out in those orders are breached. Dog control orders can be made by local authorities. The offences that can be provided for in a dog control order are set out in the Dog Control Order (Prescribed Offences and Penalties etc) Regulations 2006.[1]

1 The Dog Control Order (Prescribed Offences and Penalties etc) Regulations 2006, SI 2006/1059.

Smoke from crop residue burning

9.100 The smoke and ash from burning crop residues and particularly stubble after harvest was a major cause of nuisance for some years. This has now been addressed in section 152 of the EPA 1990 and the Crop Residues (Restrictions on Burning) Regulations 1991,[1] which prohibit all crop residue burning except in very limited circumstances.

1 SI 1991/1399 and (No 2) SI 1991/1590.

NIGHT-TIME NOISE IN DWELLINGS: NOISE ACT 1996

9.101 The Noise Act 1996 (NA 1996) as amended by the Clean Neighbourhoods and Environment Act 2005 addresses night time noise from dwellings and licensed premises which affects another dwelling. It applies to the area of every local authority in England and Wales. The Act arose from a review of legislation by government which felt that the powers under the EPA 1990 Part III needed to be strengthened by amendment.[1] It provides a fast system for local authorities to deal with night time noise. Direction for the purposes of the Act and guidance on its provisions are found in Department of the Environment circular 8/97.[2]

1 For example, extending and clarifying powers of seizure of noise-making equipment.
2 Welsh Office circular 41/97. In June 2006 a consultation was launched on draft guidance on the Noise Act 1996 as amended by the Clean Neighbourhoods and Environment Act 2005, but at the time of writing such guidance remains in draft.

9.102 Where a local authority receives a complaint from an person present in a dwelling between the hours of 11pm and 7am that excessive noise is being emitted from another dwelling or licensed premises ('the offending dwelling'), they must take reasonable steps to investigate the complaint.[1] If after an investigation the council officer dealing with the case is satisfied that noise is being omitted from the offending dwelling and the noise if measured from within the complainant's dwelling would or might exceed 'the permitted level,' he may serve a warning notice about the noise.[2] It is for that officer to decide whether to assess the noise from within or outside the complainant's dwelling and whether to use any measuring equipment when reaching his view.[3] The 'permitted level' is set by the Secretary of State in directions given under the NA 1996.[4]

1 NA 1996, s 2(1), (2), (6).
2 NA 1996, s 2(4).

9.102 *Other powers dealing with problems akin to nuisance*

3   NA 1996, s 2(5).
4   NA 1996, s 5. The current levels are found in the Annex to Department of the Environment circular 8/97 (Welsh Office circular 41/97).

9.103 The formal requirements of a warning notice are found in section 3 of the NA 1996. The notice gives warning that any person who is responsible for noise which is emitted from the offending dwelling or premises during the period specified in the notice may be guilty of an offence.[1] The person responsible is the person to whose act default or sufferance the emission of the noise is wholly or partly responsible.[2] The period specified in the notice must begin not earlier that 10 minutes after the notice is served and end the following 7 am.[3]

1   NA 1996, s 3(1)(b). For other requirements of the notice, see also s 3(1)(a), (4).
2   NA 1996, s 3(5).
3   NA 1996, s 3(2).

9.104 The person responsible is guilty of an offence where noise that exceeds the permitted level (as measured from within the complainant's dwelling) is emitted from the offending dwelling during the period specified in the notice.[1]

1   NA 1996, s 4.

9.105 Where a warning notice has been served under section 3 in respect of noise emitted from premises, and noise has been emitted which exceeds the permitted level, the person responsible is guilty of an offence under section 4A of the NA 1996. The maximum fine for such an offence is level 5 on the standard scale: this differs from an offence under section 4 where the maximum fine is level 3. Furthermore, where the noise has been emitted from a licensed premises the defence of reasonable excuse is not available.[1]

1   Such a defence is available under the Noise Act 1996, s 4(2) (in respect of noise emitted from dwellings).

9.106 Approved measuring devices and techniques are set out in the relevant circular.[1] The offence may be dealt with by way of fixed penalty notice rather than formal prosecution.[2]

1   NA 1996, s 6; Department of the Environment Office circular 8/97 (Welsh Office circular 41/97).
2   NA 1996, s 8.

9.107 The NA 1996 also confers powers of entry and seizure of offending equipment.[1] The power can be exercised where an officer of the local authority has reason to believe that a warning notice has been served in respect of noise emitted from a dwelling and that at any time in the period specified in that notice the noise emitted from the dwelling (as measured from within the complainant's dwelling) has exceeded the permitted level.[2] Where he is so satisfied, a person duly authorised to do so may enter the dwelling from which the noise is emitted and seize and remove any equipment which it appears to him is being or has been used in the emission of the noise.[3] If required to do so, the person entering the dwelling to confiscate equipment must produce written authority to do so.[4]

1   NA 1996, s 10.
2   NA 1996, s 10(1).
3   NA 1996, s 10(2). Powers in relation to seized equipment are found in the Schedule to the Act.
4   NA 1996, s 10(3).

9.108 Specific provisions deal with the obstruction of someone duly authorised to enter premises and the obtaining of a warrant of entry.[1]

1   See NA 1996, s 10(4)–(6) and (8).

CONTROL OF NOISE FROM CONSTRUCTION AND ENGINEERING WORKS: CONTROL OF POLLUTION ACT 1974 SECTIONS 60 AND 61

9.109 Sections 60 and 61 of the Control of Pollution Act 1974 (COPA 1974) create a system of regulation of noise often associated with construction or engineering works.[1] The works covered are set out in section 60(1) and include:

(a) Erection, construction, alteration, repair or maintenance of buildings, structures or roads
(b) Breaking up or opening or boring under any road or adjacent land in connection with construction, inspection, maintenance or removal of works
(c) Demolition or dredging work, and
(d) Any work of engineering construction

1   The section appears wide enough, and is frequently used, to control noisy DIY works. There is no requirement that the works should be carried out for profit or by a building contractor. It also covers builders' works whether or not they take place on a construction site. Noise from demolition works or civil engineering (eg road construction or resurfacing) are also within the ambit of COPA 1974.

9.110 Where a local authority consider that works under section 60(1) of the COPA 1974 are being or are going to be carried out on any premises then they may serve a section 60 notice controlling the way in which the works are to be done.[1]

1   COPA 1974, s 60(2).

9.111 A notice under section 60 of the COPA 1974 may specify the plant or equipment to be used, or not to be used; the times during which works may be carried out; the noise levels which may be emitted or created at a specified point on the premises, or which may be emitted during particular specified hours; and may also provide for any change of circumstances.[1] The notice may specify the time within which it is to be complied with, and it may require the execution of such works or the talking of such steps as may be necessary for the purpose of the notice or as may be specified in the notice.[2]

1   COPA 1974, s 60(3).
2   COPA 1974, s 60(5).

9.112 The notice is to be served on any person carrying out or going to carry out the works and also on such other person who appears to be responsible for or to have control over the works.[1]

1   COPA 1974, s 60(6).

9.113 There is a right of appeal against the notice to the magistrates' court within 21 days from the service of the notice.[1]

1   COPA 1974, s 60(7).

9.114 *Other powers dealing with problems akin to nuisance*

Appeals under section 60(7): Control of Noise (Appeals) Regulations 1975

9.114 Appeals are governed by the Control of Noise (Appeals) Regulations 1975.[1] The appeal may be made on grounds that:[2]

(a) the notice is not justified by the terms of COPA 1974, section 60
(b) there has been some informality, defect or error in, or in connection with, the notice
(c) the requirements of the notice are unreasonable or unnecessary or the authority has unreasonably refused to accept compliance with alternative requirements
(d) the time or times specified in the notice are not reasonably sufficient for the purpose
(e) the notice should have been served on some person instead of the appellant, being a person who is carrying out or is going to carry out the works or has control over or is responsible for the carrying out of the works
(f) the notice might lawfully have been served on some one else in addition to the appellant, being a person who is carrying out or is going to carry out the works or has control over or is responsible for the carrying out of the works and that it would have been equitable for it to have been served on that person
(g) the authority has not had regard to some or all of the matters mentioned in section 60(4) of the COPA 1974.[3]

In the case of grounds (e) and (f) the appellant shall serve a copy of the notice of appeal on that other person.[4]

1 SI 1975/2116 (as amended).
2 See Control of Noise (Appeals) Regulations 1975, SI 1975/216, reg 5.
3 COPA 1974, s 60(4) sets out specific matters to which the local authority are expressly required to have regard when acting under s 60. They are: any relevant Code of Practice (see Control of Noise (Code of Practice for Construction and Open Sites) (England) Order 2002 SI 2002/461;the need to ensure that best practicable means are used to minimise noise; the desirability in the interests of the recipients of the notice, of specifying other plant, machinery or methods; and the need to protect persons in the locality from the effects of the noise.
4 Control of Noise (Appeals) Regulations 1975, SI 1975/2116, reg 5(4).

9.115 On appeal the magistrates' court has broad powers to quash the section 60 notice, vary it as it thinks fit (but only in favour of the appellant) or dismiss the appeal.

Suspension of section 60 notices upon appeal

9.116 An appeal against a COPA 1974 section 60 notice may suspend the operation of the notice. The notice may be automatically suspended where:

(a) the noise to which the notice relates is noise caused in the course of the performance of some duty imposed by law on the appellant or
(b) compliance with the notice would involve any person in expenditure on the carrying out of the works before the hearing of the appeal.[1]

1 Control of Noise (Appeals) Regulations 1975, SI 1975/2116, reg 10(1).

9.117 Automatic suspension will not occur where the notice contains a statement by the local authority that it shall not be suspended and certain conditions are fulfilled. The local authority must be satisfied that:[1]

Control of noise from construction and engineering works **9.121**

(a) the noise to which the notice relates is injurious to health
(b) is likely to be of such a short duration that suspension of the notice would render the notice of no practical effect or
(c) the expenditure to comply with the notice before any appeal has been decided would not be disproportionate to any public benefit derived from compliance with the notice.

1   See Control of Noise (Appeals) Regulations 1975, SI 1975/2116, reg 10(2).

9.118   The provisions are thus similar to those existing for the suspension of local authority abatement notices under the EPA 1990, and raise similar issues in respect of article 6 of the ECHR.[1]

1   See above, Chapter 3.

Effect of section 60 notice on a prosecution for failure to comply with a statutory nuisance abatement notice

9.119   A COPA 1974 section 60 notice may provide a defence to a prosecution under section 80(4) of the EPA 1990 for failing to comply with a local authority abatement notice. Where:

(a) the local authority abatement notice is in respect of a statutory nuisance falling within section 79(1)(g) or (ga)[1] and
(b) the offence consists in contravening a notice which requires the abatement of the nuisance or prohibits or restricts its occurrence or recurrence[2]

then it is a defence to prove that the alleged offence was covered by a notice served under section 60 of the COPA 1974.[3] It is important to note that the defence is not available in any proceedings under section 82 of the EPA 1990.[4]

1   Ie noise emitted from premises or noise from any vehicle, machinery or equipment in the street.
2   Ie a notice served imposing requirements under EPA 1990, s 80(1)(a). The defence is not available where the prosecution is in respect of a failure to carry out works or steps, as such requirements are imposed under EPA 1990, s 80(1)(b). A s 60 notice may also provide a defence to High Court proceedings under s 81(5): see EPA 1990, s 81(6).
3   EPA 1990, s 80(9)(a).
4   See Chapter 6.

Section 60 offences

9.120   It is an offence to breach any requirement of a COPA 1974 section 60 notice without reasonable excuse.[1] The offence is summary only with a maximum fine of level 5 on the standard scale.[2] If the offence continues after initial conviction a further daily fine may be incurred. It is a defence to show compliance with a section 61 consent (see paragraph **9.122** below).

1   COPA 1974, s 60(8). See further Chapter 5 above.
2   Currently £5,000.

Prior consent for noise from construction works: Control of Pollution Act 1974 section 61

9.121   Where a person is planning to carry out works covered by section 60 of COPA 1974, they may seek prior consent from the local authority in respect of those works under section 61. The consent may cover the works in question, the methods of carrying them out, and the steps proposed to minimise noise from

9.121 *Other powers dealing with problems akin to nuisance*

the works.¹ It is a defence to a prosecution for breach of a section 60 notice to show that the works were carried out in accordance with such a consent.² Specific provisions set out the powers and duties of the local authority in determining an application for a section 61 consent and the making of an appeal against a non-determination, refusal, or conditional approval of such an application.³

1   COPA 1974, s 63(3).
2   COPA 1974, s 61(8).
3   See COPA 1974, s 61(4)–(7A), and the Control of Noise (Appeals) Regulations 1975, SI 1975/2116, (as amended).

Effect of a section 61 consent on a prosecution for failure to comply with a statutory nuisance abatement notice

9.122 On a prosecution for failure to comply with a local authority abatement notice, it is a defence to prove that the alleged offence is covered by a consent granted under section 61 of the COPA 1974 where:

(a) the local authority abatement notice is in respect of a statutory nuisance falling within section 79(1)(g) or (ga),¹ and
(b) the offence consists in contravening a notice which requires the abatement of the nuisance or prohibits or restricts its occurrence or recurrence.²

1   Ie noise emitted from premises or noise from any vehicle, machinery or equipment in the street.
2   Ie a notice served imposing requirements under EPA 1990, s 80(1)(a). The defence is not available where the prosecution is in respect of a failure to carry out works or steps, as such requirements are imposed under EPA 1990, s 80(1)(b).

9.123 A section 61 consent will not provide any defence to any proceedings brought under section 82 of the EPA 1990, and any consent must contain an express statement to that effect.¹

1   COPA 1974, s 61(9).

NOISE ABATEMENT ZONES: CONTROL OF POLLUTION ACT 1974 SECTIONS 63–66¹

9.124 In areas which a already generally noisy, it can be difficult to establish that any additional noise constitutes a statutory nuisance. The creation and regulation of noise abatement zones (NAZs) in areas which are already noisy potentially overcomes these problems, by allowing local authorities to control noise from premises which is above a registered level, and, in certain circumstances, to require a reduction in the noise emanating from premises. NAZs have not proved popular with local authorities – although with rising concern about noise in the environment, particularly in cities, they may yet prove to be useful tools.

1   COPA 1974, ss 63–66 are described below. In addition, there are specific powers to deal with new building within a noise abatement zone (s 67) and noise from plant or machinery (s 68).

The NAZ order

9.125 A local authority may by order designate all or any part of its area a noise abatement zone.¹ The order, referred to in the COPA 1974 as noise abatement order but in this text as a 'NAZ order', must specify the classes of

Noise abatement zones: Control of Pollution Act 1974 ss 63–66 **9.129**

premises to which it applies. Schedule 1 to COPA 1974 sets out the procedure for making a NAZ order. This requires publicity of the proposal and notification to all affected owners, tenants and occupiers.

1   COPA 1974, s 63(1).

The noise level register

9.126 Once the NAZ order has been made the local authority compile a register of noise levels from all of the premises within the NAZ which are of any class covered by the order.[1] The methods to be used for measuring and calculating noise levels are set out in regulations.[2] The register is to be kept available for public inspection.[3]

1   See generally, COPA 1974, s 64.
2   Control of Noise (Measurement and Register) Regulations 1976, SI 1976/37.
3   COPA 1974, s 64(7).

9.127 The local authority on recording any measurement on the noise level register must serve a copy of that record on the owner and occupier of the relevant premises. Any person on whom a copy of such a record is may appeal against the record to the Secretary of State within 28 days of service.[1] Appeals are governed by the relevant regulations.[2]

1   COPA 1974, s 64(3).
2   Control of Noise (Appeals) Regulations 1975, SI 1975/2116.

Noise exceeding the registered level

9.128 If, in the absence of written consent from the local authority, noise in respect of any premises exceeds the level of noise entered in the register in respect of those premises, then the person responsible is guilty of a summary offence.[1] If the magistrates on convicting a person consider that the offence is likely to continue or recur, they may order him to carry out works necessary to prevent the recurrence or continuation of the offence. It is a further offence to fail, without reasonable excuse, to comply with the court's order.[2] The local authority may execute the works ordered if the person ordered does not carry them out.[3] The magistrates' court may also order the local authority to carry out the works themselves.[4]

1   COPA 1974, s 74(1), (5).
2   COPA 1974, s 65(6).
3   COPA 1974, s 69(1). The local authority may recover the necessary costs of doing so: COPA 1974, s 69(3)(b).
4   COPA 1974, s 65(7).

9.129 It is not an offence to exceed the registered noise level in respect of any premises where the local authority has given its written consent. Consents may be conditional as to the amount by which that level may be exceeded, or the period or periods during which the noise level may be increased.[1] Any consent must be noted in the register.[2] Specific provisions deal with the procedure for applying for consents and the making of appeals against the local authority's decision or its failure to determine the appeal within the required time.[3]

1   COPA 1974, s 65(2).
2   COPA 1974, s 65(2).
3   See COPA 1974, s 65(3), (4) and the Control of Noise (Appeals) Regulations 1975, SI 1975/2116.

9.130 *Other powers dealing with problems akin to nuisance*

Noise level reduction within noise abatement zones

9.130 There are additional powers to reduce noise levels from premises covered by NAZ orders. The local authority may serve a noise reduction notice where it appears to the authority that:

(a) the noise from premises to which a NAZ order applies is not acceptable having regard to the purposes for which the order was made and
(b) the reduction in the noise level is practicable at reasonable cost and would afford a public benefit.

9.131 The noise reduction notice must specify the reduced level of noise and state that the noise emanating from the premises must not exceed this level without the consent of the local authority. The notice may also set out steps to be taken by the recipient to achieve that purpose.[1] The notice must be served on the person responsible, that is, the person to whose act, default or sufferance the noise is attributable.[2] The noise reduction notice must also include a period for compliance which must be no less than six months from the date of its service.[3] Noise reduction notices are to be included in the noise level register.[4]

1 COPA 1974, s 66(2).
2 COPA 1974, ss 66(1), (2) and 73.
3 COPA 1974, s 66(3).
4 COPA 1974, s 66(6).

9.132 Provision is made for appeals against noise reduction notices within three months of the date of service.[1] The same provisions apply to the suspension of section 66 notices as apply to notices under section 60 of COPA 1974.[2] It is an offence to contravene the terms of a noise reduction notice without reasonable excuse.[3] Where the proceedings are in respect of noise caused in the course of a trade or business a defence of best practicable means is available.[4]

1 COPA 1974, s 66(7); Control of Noise (Appeals) Regulations 1975, SI 1975/2116.
2 See above; and Control of Noise (Appeals) Regulations 1975, reg 10. See also Chapter 3 for a discussion of issues arising under the HRA 1998 concerning suspended notices.
3 COPA 1974, s 66(8).
4 COPA 1974, s 66(9).

9.133 Local authorities may execute any works required by a noise reduction notice and recover its costs of so doing from the person to whom the notice applies.[1]

1 COPA 1974, s 69.

Relationship between noise abatement zones and statutory nuisance

9.134 On a prosecution for failure to comply with a local authority abatement notice where:

(a) the local authority abatement notice is in respect of a statutory nuisance falling within section 79(1)(g) or (ga)[1] and
(b) the offence consists in contravening a notice which requires the abatement of the nuisance or prohibits or restricts its occurrence or recurrence[2]

it shall be a defence to prove either:

(i) that the alleged offence is covered by a consent granted under section 65 of the COPA 1974 or
(ii) that the alleged offence was committed at a time that the relevant premises were subject to a noise reduction notice under section 66 of the COPA 1974 and the level of noise was not such as to contravene that notice.[3]

1 Ie noise emitted from premises or noise from any vehicle, machinery or equipment in the street.
2 Ie a notice served imposing requirements under EPA 1990, s 80(1)(a). The defence is not available where the prosecution is in respect of a failure to carry out works or steps, as such requirements are imposed under EPA 1990, s 80(1)(b).
3 See EPA 1990, s 80(9)(a), (b). There is a similar defence in respect of new buildings liable to abatement order under COPA 1974, s 67: EPA 1990, s 80(9)(c).

9.135 Neither a section 65 consent nor a section 66 order will provide any defence to any proceedings brought under section 82 of the EPA 1990.[1]

1 A consent under COPA 1974, s 65 must state that it does not constitute a defence to any proceedings under EPA 1990, s 82: see COPA 1974, s 65(8).

LOUDSPEAKERS AND STREET NOISE: CONTROL OF POLLUTION ACT 1974 SECTION 62

9.136 COPA 1974 section 62 is designed to prohibit at certain times and, in some cases at all times, the use of loud speakers in a street. A street is defined as including a highway and any other road, footway, square or court which is for the time being open to the public.[1] The section is aimed particularly at the use of loudspeakers by street traders and shops. Section 62(1) sets out the general rule, which is subject to exceptions, that loudspeakers shall not be operated in the street between 9 pm and 8am for any purpose; or at any other time for the purpose of advertising any entertainment, trade, or business.[2]

1 COPA 1974, s 62(1).
2 The Secretary of State may amend the times stated in COPA 1974, s 62(1) by order: see COPA 1974, s 62(1A), (1B).

9.137 The exceptions to the general rule are set out in sections 62(2) and (3) of the COPA 1974. They relate, amongst other things, to the emergency services, water or sewerage undertakers (for example, notifying customers of an impending loss of water supply or that drinking water should be boiled), local authorities and travelling showmen at pleasure fairs, and loudspeakers on vehicles carrying passengers (for example, open top buses), and vehicles being used to sell perishable commodities (such as ice cream or fish).[1]

1 Readers are referred to the specific wording of COPA 1974, s 62 for the details of the provisions contained therein.

9.138 It is an offence under the COPA 1974 to operate or permit the operation of a loudspeaker in breach of section 62(1).

9.139 A regime to allow the local authority to grant consents for the use of loudspeakers in contravention of s 62(1) of the COPA 1974 has been introduced by the Noise and Statutory Nuisance Act 1993.[1]

1 Noise and Statutory Nuisance Act 1993, s 8, and Sch 2. The provisions are only applicable where the local authority has resolved to apply them.

9.140 *Other powers dealing with problems akin to nuisance*

AUDIBLE INTRUDER ALARMS

9.140 Part 7 of the Clean Neighbourhoods and Environment Act 2005 gives local authority powers to designate alarm notification areas to ensure that keyholders are contactable to address the problem of burglar alarms being activated without being attended to. These provisions are not yet in force at the time of writing.

NOISE CODES OF PRACTICE: CONTROL OF POLLUTION ACT 1974 SECTION 71

9.141 The Secretary of State has power under section 71 of the COPA 1974 to approve codes of practice in order to give guidance on methods of minimising noise. A small number of codes of practice have been issued under orders made under this section covering a very limited range of noise sources:

- Control of Noise (Code of Practice on Noise from Ice Cream Van Chimes Etc) Order 1981[1]
- Control of Noise (Code of Practice on Noise from Audible Intruder Alarms) Order 1981[2]
- Control of Noise (Code of Practice on Noise from Model Aircraft) Order 1981[3]
- Control of Noise (Code of Practice for Construction and Open Sites) Orders 2002.[4]

1 SI 1981/1828.
2 SI 1981/1829.
3 SI 1981/1830.
4 SI 2002/461.

9.142 These codes are of particular importance in determining whether best practicable means are being used: a matter which is significant under a number of provisions of COPA 1974 and the EPA 1990.[1]

1 See in particular COPA 1974, ss 60(4), 66(9) and the Control of Noise (Appeals) Regulations 1975, SI 1975/2116; EPA 1990, ss 80(4), 82(8); Statutory Nuisance (Appeals) Regulations 1995, SI 1995/2644.

NOISE FROM VEHICLES

9.143 The issue of noise from vehicles has now been addressed to some extent by statutory nuisance.[1] Vehicle noise is also covered by other legislation. The Road Vehicles (Construction and Use) Regulations 1986[2] include regulations concerning the specification of exhaust systems and silencers, and a general requirement prohibiting the use of a vehicle on a road in such manner as to cause excessive noise which could have been avoided by reasonable care.[3]

1 See EPA 1990, s 79(1)(ga), and Chapter 1.
2 SI 1986/1078.
3 See Road Vehicles (Construction and Use) Regulations 1986, SI 1986/1078, reg 97.

ANTI-SOCIAL BEHAVIOUR ORDERS

9.144 The anti-social behaviour order regime established by the Anti-Social Behaviour Act 2003 is outside the scope of this work. However, it should be noted that many of the problems outlined above in this Chapter, in particular those relating to nuisance caused by noise, could potentially be controlled by the imposition of an anti-social behaviour order under that Act. Section 40 and 41 of that Act give local authorities the power to close down premises to prevent noise that is causing a public nuisance. The premises covered by these sections are licensed premises, such as pubs and clubs. Under this clause, local authorities can issue a closure order requiring the manager to shut the premises for up to 24 hours. It makes breach of this order an offence, with the maximum penalty upon summary conviction being three months in prison and/or a fine of up to £20,000. These sections came into force in November 2005.

Chapter 10
Other Environmental Regimes

INTRODUCTION

10.01 This Chapter is concerned with the relationship between statutory nuisance controls under the Environmental Protection Act 1990 (EPA 1990), Part III and other forms of regulation in England and Wales[1] of the problem area concerned. At its most basic level this deals with the degree to which statutory nuisance powers overlap with other environmental legislation. Although the detail of other environmental legislation is beyond the scope of this work environmental law has developed a series of discrete specialist systems for regulating waste[2] and contaminated land,[3] water,[4] air pollution,[5] pollution from major processes[6] and radioactive substances.[7] The general principle, to which there are exceptions, is that there should not be overlap between specialist systems of regulation and statutory nuisances. The overlap issue is important as the regulatory body may differ between the specialist regime and statutory nuisance. Furthermore, the presence of the duties to investigate suspected nuisances and serve an abatement notice if a nuisance is located[8] is in contrast to the normal discretion conferred by most other statutory environmental regulation.

1 Much, of course, is also applicable in Scotland either directly or through similar provisions of Scottish legislation.
2 Principally under EPA 1990, Pt II.
3 EPA 1990, Pt IIA, as inserted by Environment Act 1995, Pt II.
4 Principally under Water Resources Act 1991, Pt III.
5 See Clean Air Act 1993, Environment Act 1995, Pt IV and Pollution Prevention and Control Act 1999).
6 Major processes are defined currently in the Environmental Protection (Prescribed Processes and Substances) Regulations 1991, SI 1991/472, for regulation under EPA 1990, Pt I. This legislation is to be phased out in stages and replaced by the Pollution Prevention and Control Act 1999. This was due to be completed by 20 07 but at the time of writing the above regulations were still in force.
7 Radioactive Substances Act 1993, and for major nuclear sites Nuclear Installations Act 1965.
8 See Chapters 2 and 3.

EPA 1990, PART I

10.02 The provisions of the EPA 1990, Part I have been prospectively repealed by the Pollution Prevention and Control Act 1999[1] from a day to be appointed. The provisions of the EPA, Part I have been undergoing a process of replacement by regulations made under the 1999 Act implementing the system known as integrated pollution prevention and control. It had been anticipated that this process would be complete by 20 07 and Part I repealed. However, although the process is advanced,[2] it is ongoing and Part I has not been repealed as at the time of writing. Consequently, Part I is analysed in the following paragraphs. However, the regulations under the Pollution Prevention and Control Act 1999 are now the starting point for the purposes of Pollution Control.

1 See s 6 and Sch 3.
2 It is beyond the scope of this book to analyse the detail of this change, which is being made by a large number of separate regulations.

10.03 *Other environmental regimes*

10.03 The EPA 1990, Part I combines two largely distinct environmental regulation systems. Firstly, it includes integrated pollution control (IPC) which regulates pollution from the most polluting processes,[1] known as Part A processes, and is concerned with pollution to the environmental media of air, water and land. The Environment Agency regulates the 40 0 0 or so processes falling within integrated pollution control in England and Wales. The controls are based around the need for an authorisation before a process may be undertaken[2] and the imposition of conditions in the authorisation. The conditions in an IPC authorisation are based on a number of key considerations[3] but most crucially that the *best available techniques not entailing excessive cost* (BATNEEC) are adopted to prevent, minimise and render harmless pollution[4] and that taking all pollution from the process the *best practicable environmental option* (BPEO) is adopted.[5]

1 These are defined and listed in the Environmental Protection (Prescribed Processes and Substances) Regulations 1991, SI 1991/472.
2 EPA 1990, s 6.
3 See EPA 1990, s 7.
4 See EPA 1990, s 7(2) in respect of BATNEEC as basis for setting express conditions and s 7(4) for BATNEEC as an implied general condition for operation of the process.
5 See EPA 1990, s 7(6).

10.04 The second system of regulation contained in EPA 1990, Part I is air pollution control (APC). The regulator in this case is the local authority and once again the system is based around a list of processes,[1] Part B processes. The system of regulation is only concerned with emissions to the atmosphere but in other respects is very similar to that operated by the Environment Agency in respect of IPC.[2] Emissions to water are then covered by the Environment Agency under the Water Resources Act 1991.

1 Also listed in the Environmental Protection (Prescribed Processes and Substances) Regulations 1991, SI 1991/472.
2 Authorisations are required and conditions will be attached applying the BATNEEC principle; although BPEO does not apply as pollution to only one environmental medium is regulated.

10.05 The enforcement of the systems of control are based around a series of criminal offences[1] and enforcement and authorisation variation and revocation notices.[2] It is a criminal offence to operate a prescribed process without authorisation or in breach of authorisation conditions.[3]

1 See EPA 1990, s 23.
2 See EPA 1990, ss 10, 12–14.
3 EPA 1990, s 23(1) punishable by a fine of up to £20,0 0 0 on summary conviction and/or three months' imprisonment and on indictment punishable with an unlimited fine and/or imprisonment of up to two years.

The statutory provisions on the relationship with EPA 1990, Part I

10.06 There are express statutory provisions governing the relationship of Parts I and III of the EPA 1990. Part I of the EPA 1990 regulates not only integrated pollution control processes (by the Environment Agency) but also air pollution control by local authorities. Section 79(10) of the EPA 1990 prevents a local authority (unless it has the consent of the Secretary of State) from using EPA 1990, Part III in respect of a nuisance falling within the smoke, dust, steam, smell or other effluvia and accumulation or deposit, artificial light and noise categories of nuisance,[1] if proceedings might be instituted under Part I.[2]

However, the matters covered by EPA 1990, Part I in the case of air pollution control are limited to emissions to air, so any other matter which gives rise to a nuisance (for example accumulations or deposits of waste) remains within EPA 1990, Part III. Furthermore, the section does not prevent the use of section 82 by private individuals in respect of EPA 1990, Part I prescribed processes. In the absence of evidence of breach of authorisation conditions it is likely that any operator would submit that compliance with their authorisation amounted to the best practicable means and this might be difficult to rebut.

1　EPA 1990, s 79(1)(b), (d), (e).
2　In fact the exact wording is that 'a local authority shall not ... institute summary proceedings' under EPA 1990, Pt III in respect of the matters covered by Pt I. There is an argument that that summary proceedings would only commence following non-compliance with an abatement notice. It seems more likely that the intention was for all of the local authority statutory nuisance procedures to be excluded.

POLLUTION PREVENTION AND CONTROL ACT 1999

10.07 The Pollution Prevention and Control Act 1999 and Pollution Prevention and Control (England and Wales) Regulations 2000[1] implement the Integrated Pollution and Prevention Control Directive (96/61/EC). This introduces a system of process based pollution control which will replace EPA 1990 Part I over a phased period of implementation, as described above. In addition it introduces some new processes to pollution control for the first time[2] and also requires some waste operations to shift from waste management licensing regulation[3] to integrated pollution prevention and control (IPPC). Control is based on permits (and permit conditions) for installations carrying on processes listed in Schedule 1 to the 2000 Regulations. Permits are based on a number of principles[4] including the adoption of the best available techniques, waste minimisation, energy efficiency, accident prevention and site restoration on closure of the process. All IPC processes are covered by the IPPC system and the government has also chosen to use the 1999 Act and 2000 Regulations to cover air pollution control although the system of regulation for APC processes is limited to emissions to air and does not have the full ramifications of IPPC. This will allow EPA 1990 Part I to be phased out entirely. Under IPPC installations will usually be regulated by the Environment Agency[5] but some IPPC processes are subject to local authority control[6] with complex provisions for interaction with the Agency. Air pollution control is a matter for local authorities.[7]

1　SI 2000/1973.
2　For example substantial intensive farming operations.
3　Under EPA 1990, Pt II.
4　See Pollution Prevention and Control (England and Wales) Regulations 2000, SI 2000/1973, regs 7–9.
5　Part A(1) processes in Sch 1 to the 2000 Regulations.
6　Part A(2) processes in Sch 1 to the 2000 Regulations.
7　Part B processes in Sch 1 to the 2000 Regulations.

10.08 The Pollution Prevention and Control (England and Wales) Regulations 2000 provide for enforcement of the regime by a series of criminal offences[1] and powers and duties to serve notices or vary or revoke permits.[2] In outline the new system requires operators of installations and mobile plant where the processes covered are carried on to obtain a permit from the Environment Agency or in some cases the local authority and to comply with all permit conditions in the operation of the process.

10.08 *Other environmental regimes*

1 SI 2000/1973, Pt VII. For example operating a process without a permit or in breach of permit conditions is punishable by a fine of up to £20,000 on summary conviction and/or three months' imprisonment and on indictment punishable with an unlimited fine and/or imprisonment of up to five years.
2 SI 2000/1973, Pts II and III.

The statutory provisions on the relationship with Pollution Prevention and Control Act 1999 and Pollution Prevention and Control (England and Wales) Regulations 2000

10.09 The definition of pollution for the purposes of the Pollution Prevention and Control (England and Wales) Regulations 2000[1] includes many matters which might be statutory nuisances including offence to any of man's senses, noise, heat or vibration as well as emissions.

1 SI 2000/1973.

10.10 The Pollution Prevention and Control Act 1999 and Pollution Prevention and Control (England and Wales) Regulations 2000[1] have amended the EPA 1990, Part III.[2] The relationship is very similar to that already operating with EPA 1990, Part I except that noise nuisances are now within the area of overlap. The amendments now provide that no local authority (without the consent of the Secretary of State) shall institute summary proceedings in respect of a nuisance arising from smoke, dust, steam, smell or other effluvia, noise emitted from premises or noise caused by a vehicle, machinery or equipment in the street,[3] if proceedings in respect of that alleged nuisance might be brought under the 1999 Act or 2000 Regulations. This last point is important. Installations under the 2000 Regulations may be covered by integrated pollution prevention and control[4] in which case all types of pollution including noise are regulated under the 1999 Act and 2000 Regulations. Other processes are controlled only for the purposes of air pollution control under the 2000 Regulations[5] and for that noise control will not be possible under the new legislation and will remain a matter for statutory nuisance. As for the provisions governing the relationship with EPA 1990, Part I there is nothing to prevent the use of section 82 of the EPA 1990 by private individuals in respect of pollution prevention and control regulated installations and mobile plant.[6]

1 SI 2000/1973.
2 Pollution Prevention and Control Act 1999, s 6, Sch 2 and Pollution Prevention and Control (England and Wales) Regulations 2000, SI 2000/1973, Sch 10.
3 EPA 1990, s 79(1)(b), (d), (e), (g) and (ga).
4 Known as A1 and A2 in the 2000 Regulations.
5 Known as B processes in the 2000 Regulations.
6 See comments above at paras **1.95–1.104** on how such an overlap might be dealt with.

RADIOACTIVE SUBSTANCES ACT 1993

10.11 The Radioactive Substances Act 1993 creates an exclusive system of control over radioactivity, which arises from substances, articles or premises. It requires registration of premises (or mobile apparatus) where radioactive substances are to be used[1] and prior authorisation of the disposal or accumulation of radioactive substances.[2] The Environment Agency operates the controls under the 1993 Act. Under section 40 and Schedule 3 of the 1993 Act no account shall be taken of any radioactivity in the operation of any of the powers or duties in the EPA 1990, Part III. Thus, if complaint was made that premises were prejudicial to health because of radioactive contamination this lies outside the EPA 1990, Part III. Action might be taken by the Environment Agency under a number of powers contained in the 1993 Act.³

1   Radioactive Substances Act 1993, s 6, subject to various exemptions in s 8.
2   Radioactive Substances Act 1993, ss 13, 14.
3   See eg Radioactive Substances Act 1993, ss 21, 22, 30.

CONTAMINATED LAND REGIME UNDER EPA 1990 PART IIA

10.12 The Environment Act 1995, Part II inserted a new Part IIA into the EPA 1990, which came into force finally on 1 April 2000 and is supplemented by regulations and statutory guidance.¹ This Part is concerned entirely with the issue of contaminated land. It provides for identification of contaminated land and if appropriate its remediation. The system includes complex provisions on the meaning of contaminated land, clean up standards and who should be responsible for dealing with the contamination. The provisions of Part IIA were extended, with effect from 4 August 2006, to address land which is contaminated by virtue of radioactive substances.² In some ways the EPA 1990, Part IIA system bears resemblance to the EPA 1990, Part III. Local authorities are under a duty to inspect their area for contaminated land.³ Identified sites are normally the responsibility of the local authority; although some sites, known as special sites, are regulated by the Environment Agency.⁴ Once identified there is normally a duty to serve a remediation notice on the persons responsible for the site.⁵ The notice will set out steps to be taken and timetable. An appeal lies to the Secretary of State.⁶ The notice may be enforced by summary criminal penalty⁷ and/or the enforcing authority carrying out the works and recovering their costs.⁸ The contaminated land legislation is a framework of rules which are elaborated in both regulations and substantial statutory guidance.⁹ This provides detailed rules which must be applied by local authorities and the Environment Agency in for example defining contaminated land, determining clean up standards or establishing and apportioning liability.

1   Contaminated Land (England) Regulations 2006, SI 2006/1380, and DEFRA Circular 01/2006.
2   See Radioactive Contaminated Land (Enabling Powers) (England) Regulations 2005, SI 2005/3467, and the Radioactive Contaminated Land (Modification of Enactments) (England) Regulations 2006, SI 2006/1379
3   EPA 1990, s 78B.
4   See Contaminated Land (England) Regulations 2006, SI 2006/380.
5   Called appropriate persons in EPA 1990, Pt IIA and defined in s 78F. Occasionally the duty is disapplied see EPA 1990, s 78H.
6   EPA 1990, s 78L as amended by Clean Neighbourhoods and Environment Act 2005, s 104. If the notice is served by a local authority in Wales or by the Environment Agency in relation to land in Wales the appeal lies to the National Assembly for Wales
7   EPA 1990, s 78M.
8   EPA 1990, s 78N and 78P.
9   The guidance is annexed to DEFRA Circular 01/2006.

Statutory provisions on the relationship of EPA 1990, Part IIA and Part III

10.13 Until the coming into force of the EPA 1990, Part IIA (inserted by Part II of the Environment Act 1995) on the 1 April 2000 statutory nuisance was (along with the planning system,¹ some of the water pollution legislation² and section 215 of the Town and Country Planning Act 1990³) the key regulation for

10.13 *Other environmental regimes*

contaminated land. Land subject to contamination might have fallen within section 79(1)(a) of the EPA 1990 as premises[4] which were prejudicial to health or a nuisance or section 79(1)(e) as any accumulation or deposit (referring to the contaminants) which was prejudicial to health or a nuisance.

1   Through the use of planning conditions and obligations on the grant of planning permission for re-development of contaminated land: see Planning Policy Statement Note 23: Planning and Pollution Control.
2   In particular Water Resources Act 1991, s 161 providing clean up powers to the Environment Agency where controlled waters (see Water Resources Act 1991, s 104; the definition includes rivers, streams, canals, most lakes and ponds, estuaries and coastal waters and, of particular significance to contaminated land, groundwater) are being or are likely to be polluted.
3   Providing local authorities with powers to deal with land adversely affecting the local amenity, see paras **9.02–9.17**.
4   Premises include land: EPA 1990, s 79(7).

10.14 However, since the coming into force of EPA 1990 Part IIA, section 79(1A) states that 'no matter shall be a statutory nuisance to the extent that it consists of land or is caused by land being in a contaminated state'. This is discussed in Chapter 1. In the DETR Circular (No 2/20 0 0) issued under EPA 1990, Part IIA the government explained this exclusion of land from both the EPA 1990, Part IIA and Part III in para 53:

> 'The effect of this distinction is to ensure the statutory nuisance regime cannot be used to circumvent the statutory guidance under EPA Part IIA on what constitutes "significant harm" and "significant possibility". The Government considers that the Part IIA guidance sets out the right level of protection for human health and the environment from land contamination. It would therefore be in appropriate to leave in place another system which could, in theory, be used to impose regulatory requirements on a different basis.'

10.15 The Circular then explained there is one exception to this general rule of avoiding overlap between the EPA 1990, Parts IIA and III and indeed creating a regulatory gap and this arises where an abatement notice under section 80(1) of the EPA 1990 or a court order under section 82(2) has already been issued as at the implementation date and is still in force. There is authority that abatement notices can remain in force against the recipient indefinitely[1] even if issued under legislation preceding the EPA 1990.[2] Presumably, however, these principles only apply to notices or court orders that have some element which remains in force. This may be because the notice simply requires the recipient to refrain from creating a nuisance or because, although the notice is one that specifies works to be undertaken, not all of those works have been satisfactorily completed.

1   See *Wellingborough District Council v Gordon* [1991] JPL 874.
2   Eg Control of Pollution Act 1974 and *Aitken v South Hams District Council* [1994] 3 All ER 40 0 overruling *R v Folkestone Magistrates' Court, ex p Kibble* [1993] Crim LR 704.

10.16 The new DEFRA Circular 1/20 06 puts it somewhat differently and does not discuss the exception:

> '55   Until the implementation of the Part 2A contaminated land regime, the statutory nuisance system under Part 3 of the 1990 Act was the main regulatory mechanism for enforcing the remediation of contaminated land.
>
> 56   Parliament considered that the Part 2A regime, as explained in the statutory guidance, sets out the right level of protection for human health and

the environment from the effects of land contamination. It judged it inappropriate to leave in place the possibility of using another, less precisely defined, system which could lead to the imposition of regulatory requirements on a different basis.

57 From the entry into force of the contaminated land regime in April 2000, most land contamination issues were therefore removed from the scope of the statutory nuisance regime. This is the effect of an amendment to the definition of a statutory nuisance in section 79 of the 1990 Act, consisting of the insertion of sections 79(1A) and (1B); this amendment was made by paragraph 89 of Schedule 22 to the Environment Act 1995. Any matter which would otherwise have been a statutory nuisance will no longer be treated as such, to the extent that it consists of, or is caused by, land "being in a contaminated state" ...'

10.17 It is interesting to note in summary form the statutory guidance on meaning of significant harm and significant risk of significant harm:

'Harm' is to be regarded as significant only if it is of the following types:

- death, disease, serious injury, genetic mutation, birth defects or the impairment of reproductive functions (disease is to be taken to mean an unhealthy condition of the body or a part of it and can include, for example, cancer, liver dysfunction or extensive skin ailments. Mental dysfunction is included only insofar as it is attributable to the effects of a pollutant on the body of the person concerned
- for locations protected under the Wildlife and Countryside Act 1981, the Conservation (Natural Habitats etc) Regulations 1994, Planning Policy Statement (PPS 9) and National Parks and Access to the Countryside Act 1949, an irreversible adverse change, or in some other substantial adverse change, in the functioning of the ecological system within any substantial part of a protected location or harm which affects any species of special interest within that location and which endangers the long-term maintenance of the population of that species at that location and in the case of a protected location which is a European Site (or a candidate Special Area of Conservation or a potential Special Protection Area), harm which is incompatible with the favourable conservation status of natural habitats at that location or species typically found there
- a substantial diminution in yield or other substantial loss in the value of crops resulting from death, disease or other physical damage such that a substantial proportion of the crops are dead or otherwise no longer fit for their intended purpose
- death, serious disease or serious physical damage to domestic pets such that a substantial proportion of the animals are dead or otherwise no longer fit for their intended purpose
- structural failure, substantial damage or substantial interference with any right of occupation of a building.

10.18 In assessing 'risk' local authorities are to assess the possibility of harm, and its significance by reference to:

- the effects of the contamination and
- fundamental principles of risk assessment.

10.19 *Other environmental regimes*

10.19 'Risk assessment' involves an actual determination of:

- the contaminants present and their concentration
- their tendency to migrate
- the geo-technical ground conditions in the locality (how might they contribute to the movement of the contaminant)
- the likely effects of an escape or migration and in particular, how quickly harm may be suffered after exposure to the contaminant.

10.20 Substances, the routes by which they move and the entity which may be affected are described in terms of 'source-pathway-target' – 'pollution linkage'. The more severe the harm, the greater its degree, the shorter the timescale for it to occur or the greater the vulnerability of the target the more significant is the risk – 'significant pollution linkage'.

WATER POLLUTION CONTROLS: WATER RESOURCES ACT 1991 PART III

10.21 This section considers the relationship between the statutory nuisance controls and the specialist water pollution legislation contained primarily in the Water Resources Act 1991. This Act provides for a series of criminal offences[1] prohibiting pollution of controlled waters combined with a system of discharge consents permitting water pollution subject to conditions.[2] In addition to the criminal offences the Environment Agency has power to serve works notices ordering works to prevent water pollution, clean it up and restore the environment.[3]

1 Water Resources Act 1991, s 85.
2 Consents may be obtained from the Environment Agency: see Water Resources Act 1991, s 88, Sch 10.
3 Water Resources Act 1991, ss 161A–161D.

10.22 There is no explicit statutory relationship between the Water Resources Act 1991 controls over water pollution and the EPA 1990, Part III. The effect of this absence of express statutory guidance is that there is an overlap between statutory nuisance and water pollution control by way of prosecution under section 85 of the Water Resources Act 1991, works notices or the system of discharge consents. Matters have, however, now become complicated by the contaminated land provisions in section 79(1A) and (1B) of the EPA 1990 noted above. These are considered separately below.

10.23 It is possible to envisage water pollution or related activities giving rise to statutory nuisances in a number of ways. The cause of a discharge to water may also give rise to a statutory nuisance. A sewage treatment plant may be causing a smell or noise. In these cases there is no overlap as the water pollution legislation is to regulate pollution to waters not air and the statutory nuisance regime is the proper way for the smell or noise issues to be considered. The pollution may, however, lead to a statutory nuisance by leaving deposits on land which could be a nuisance under section 79(1)(a) of the EPA 1990 (premises including land, in such a state as to be prejudicial to health or a nuisance) or section 79(1)(e) of the EPA 1990 (accumulations or deposits which are prejudicial to health or a nuisance). This possibility was specifically approved by Carnwath J in *R v Carrick District Council, ex p Shelley*[1] (see paras

10.24–10.25) in relation to sewage debris washing on to a beach from a sewage treatment works.

1   [1996] Env LR 273.

Overlaps between water legislation and statutory nuisance: the *Shelley* case

10.24 In general terms the overlap between water pollution legislation was considered by Carnwath J in *R v Carrick District Council, ex p Shelley*.[1] This case was decided before the amendments as a result of the implementation of the EPA 1990, Part IIA, considered below. In this case a beach was being affected by sewage related debris from two sewage outfalls operated by South West Water. Residents of a nearby village complained to the local authority and asked that action be taken under the EPA 1990, Part III. At this time both sewage outfalls were authorised under discharge consents which the National Rivers Authority had sought to vary. Appeals to the Secretary of State had been entered against the variations under Schedule 10 of the Water Resources Act 1991 and had been outstanding for some two years. The relevant committee of Carrick District Council considered the issue of the sewage debris and decided to continue monitoring the situation but to take no formal action under the EPA 1990, Part III. That decision was challenged by the residents by means of judicial review. Carnwath J held that the statutory nuisance provisions applied independently of the Water Resources Act 1991 and that the sewage debris might be a deposit or accumulation under section 79(1)(e) of the EPA 1990. Carnwath J noted:

> 'I did not understand there to be any serious argument but that significant deposits on a public beach of sewage related debris such as condoms and sanitary towels are capable in principle of amounting a to a statutory nuisance even without specific evidence of injury to health.'

1   [1996] Env LR 273.

10.25 Carrick District Council was under a duty if a statutory nuisance existed to serve an abatement notice (section 80(1) of the EPA 1990). The approach of the council was legally flawed as they did not consider directly whether a nuisance existed or not but instead resolved it was not appropriate to take action. The application for judicial review, therefore, was successful.

WASTE MANAGEMENT LICENSING UNDER EPA 1990 PART II

10.26 Waste activities are regulated principally by the EPA 1990, Part II system of waste management licensing. This requires that those who treat, keep or dispose of controlled waste[1] or are brokers for waste should have a waste management licence and carry on the activity in accordance with the licence.[2] There are many exemptions to the need for a waste management licence;[3] for example the spreading of certain wastes (such as waste soil or sewage sludge) on agricultural land. However, waste licences are needed for the key waste activities, waste sorting and transfer, many recycling depots including scrap yards and landfill sites. There are complex provisions in EPA 1990, Part II for obtaining waste licences, their variation and termination by surrender. The Act

10.26 *Other environmental regimes*

also provides a range of enforcement mechanisms including clean up powers for the Environment Agency[4] and criminal offences. Even where no waste management licence is needed section 34 of the EPA 1990 imposes a duty of care relating to waste, breach of which is a crime. In outline this requires the holder of waste to take reasonable steps to prevent its escape and to pass it on lawfully. This will usually require a transfer (with a description in a waste transfer note) to someone holding a waste management licence or who is a registered waste carrier.[5]

1   Controlled waste is defined as household, industrial, commercial or any such waste: EPA 1990, s 75 and Controlled Waste Regulations 1992, SI 1992/588. The term is now interpreted in accordance with EC Directive 91/156/EC. For issues as to the meaning of waste see eg *Van de Walle v Texaco Belgium* Case C-1/03 [20 05] All ER(EC) 1139 , *ARCO Chemie Nederland v M v V and EPON* Case C-418/97 [20 03] Env LR 40 [20 02] QB 646 and the recent observations of Carnwath LJ in the Court of Appeal in *R(on the application of OSS Group Limited) v Environment Agency* [20 07] EWCA Civ 611. See also paras **9.36–9.38**.
2   EPA 1990, s 33 and Waste Management Licensing Regulations 1994, SI 1994/1056.
3   Waste Management Licensing Regulations 1994, SI 1994/1056, Sch 3.
4   In respect of licensed sites see EPA 1990, s 42 and in respect of unauthorised waste deposits see EPA 1990, s 59, paras **9.31–9.42**.
5   Control of Pollution (Amendment) Act 1989.

Statutory nuisance and waste management licensing

10.27 There is no express statutory relationship between the EPA 1990, Part II and Part III. It seems, therefore, that the regimes overlap and operate independently in the same way as for water pollution subject to the contaminated land amendments. For example, a waste transfer station will have a waste management licence under the EPA 1990, Part II and the Waste Management Licensing Regulations 1994.[1] The operation of the site creates a noise nuisance for those living nearby. Statutory nuisance might be used to address this problem. Similarly with smell or vermin from a landfill site. The noise, smell or vermin issues may of course also be addressed directly or indirectly by the conditions of the waste licence, for example, by requiring newly deposited waste to be covered or limiting hours of operation. Where waste related activities are authorised by waste management licence then the general issue of the impact of the licence on whether a nuisance exists arises. Some waste activities are, however, regulated under the Pollution Prevention and Control Act 1999 and in these cases there are specific express statutory provisions concerning the overlap between these statutes and the EPA 1990, Part III. Finally, where waste has resulted in land becoming contaminated then the provisions of the EPA 1990 Part IIA and its relationship with the EPA 1990, Part III discussed extensively above at paras **10.12–10.20** must be considered.

1   SI 1994/1056.

CLEAN AIR ACT 1993

10.28 The Clean Air Act 1993 is a consolidating statute bringing together provisions relating to atmospheric pollution principally from the Clean Air Acts 1956 and 1968 and from the Control of Pollution Act 1974. The Clean Air Acts developed a system of controlling atmospheric emissions principally by focussing on the visibility of smoke. Since the Acts developed in response to the toxic urban smogs of the 1950s the provisions have become of less importance as many industrial emissions have become the subject of specialist pollution control systems, such as integrated pollution prevention and control under the Pollution Prevention and Control Act 1999. Nevertheless, the Clean Air Act 1993 remains an important tool for dealing with domestic and some industrial and commercial sources of air pollution.

10.29 Statutory nuisance may cover a range of atmospheric emissions including smoke, dust, steam, smell or other effluvia. The Clean Air Act 1993 does not regulate noise or smell.[1] The relationship between the Clean Air Act 1993 and the EPA 1990 is largely governed by the limitations on the definition of statutory nuisance in s 79 of the EPA 1990. The legislation is drafted so as to avoid overlaps between the two Acts.

1 At least directly; smell might be associated with smoke, steam, effluvia etc. See eg, *Griffiths v Pembrokeshire County Council* [20 0 0] Env LR 622.

Clean Air Act 1993: Key provisions and their relationship with the EPA 1990 Part III

10.30 The first set out of key provisions in the Clean Air Act 1993 relate to the control of dark smoke emissions.[1] Part I of the 1993 Act controls dark smoke from chimneys attached to buildings (domestic or commercial), chimneys serving furnaces of any fixed boiler or industrial plant (but not from a building) and from industrial or trade premises (and not from a chimney at all). The relationship with statutory nuisance is governed by section 79(3) of the EPA 1990 which excludes dark smoke emissions falling within these cases from statutory nuisance. This means that the EPA 1990, Part III remains relevant for smoke which is not dark but or is nevertheless an emission or which falls outside the categories indicated above. This might include, for example, smoke from domestic bonfires. Where a matter lies outside the EPA 1990, Part III local authorities may be able to take action under the Clean Air Act 1993.[2]

1 Dark smoke is defined as smoke as dark or darker than shade 2 on the Ringelmann Chart.
2 Criminal offences are created under Clean Air Act 1993, ss 1, 2.

10.31 Part III of the Clean Air Act 1993 governs smoke control areas where the use of particular smokeless fuels is required in private dwellings. Section 79(3) of the EPA 1990 states that smoke from chimneys (regardless of its colour or density) from private dwellings is outside the statutory nuisance system. Any remedies will lie under the smoke control order and Clean Air Act 1993.[1]

1 Clean Air Act 1993, s 20.

10.32 Fumes and gases from all premises except private dwellings are excluded from the EPA 1990, Part III.[1] It seems the reason for this exclusion lies in the Clean Air Act 1993[2] which permits the Secretary of State to make regulations concerning fume and gas emissions, but in fact none have been made.

1 EPA 1990, s 79(4).
2 Clean Air Act 1993, s 47 and its similar predecessor provision in the Clean Air Act 1968.

10.33 The remaining overlaps cover three specific sources of atmospheric pollution – steam trains,[1] colliery spoilbanks[2] and vessels.[3]

1 1 Smoke, dust, steam, smell or other effluvia from steam railway locomotives are excluded from the EPA Part III: EPA 1990, s 73(3)(5). There are special clean air controls in the Clean Air Act 1993, s 43.

10.33 *Other environmental regimes*

2   Smoke, grit or dust from burning mine or quarry refuse from coal or shale coal mines or quarries is excluded from EPA 1990, Part III: Clean Air Act 1993, s 42.
3   Smoke, grit or dust from any vessel is also excluded both from waters not navigable by sea going ships (eg canals or rivers) and all waters within UK territory and within any port, harbour, river, estuary, haven, dock, canal or other place where charges may be levied for its use. See the Clean Air Act 1993 s 44.

Aircraft noise

10.34 Noise from any aircraft except for model aircraft is exempted from the statutory nuisance system.[1] No distinction is drawn between aircraft in the air and on the ground at airports. In this context it is important to note that under the EPA 1990, Part III noise includes vibration. Moreover, section 76 of the Civil Aviation Act 1982 provides that no action lies in common law nuisance by reason only of the flight of an aircraft over any property so long as the provisions of any air navigation order[2] have been complied with and there has been no breach of section 81 of the 1982 Act.[3] The level of noise emitted by civil aircraft is the subject of strict regulation.[4] There are also provisions in the 1982 Act for air navigation orders to control noise and vibration caused by aircraft on aerodromes. No common law action for nuisance may be brought so long as there is compliance with the relevant air navigation order.[5] The Secretary of State can designate certain airports in order to apply requirements as to noise and vibration[6] by limiting flight times or numbers of flights or giving other directions as avoiding, limiting or mitigating noise and vibration concerned with take off and landing. The Secretary of State can control times when flights are allowed.[7] The Secretary of State can also make schemes for designated airports to make grants towards the cost of insulating buildings in the vicinity of the airport from noise. The European Court of Human Rights at Strasbourg did seem at one point willing to hold the UK regime on aircraft noise at Heathrow as incompatible with the Convention, but the Grand Chamber of the Court drew back from that position.[8]

1   EPA 1990, s 79(6) excluding noise from aircraft from s 79(1)(g).
2   Eg the Rules of the Air Regulations 1996 inter alia control low level flying. See also *Farley v Skinner* [20 01] UKHL 49, [20 02] 2 AC 732.
3   This governs dangerous flying.
4   See EC Directive 92/14/EEC and Civil Aviation Act 1982, s 78.
5   See the Air Navigation (General) Regulations 20 06, SI 20 06/60.
6   Civil Aviation Act 1982, s 78(1). Heathrow, Gatwick and Stansted airports are so designated.
7   The Secretary of State's proposals for limitations on night flights at Heathrow was the subject of a number of judicial reviews: see *R v Secretary of State for Transport, ex p London Borough of Richmond-upon-Thames* [1994] 1 WLR 74.
8   *Hatton v United Kingdom* (20 02) 34 EHRR 1, (20 03) 37 EHRR 28.

10.35 Military aircraft and airports are, furthermore, the subject of Crown immunity under section 11 of the Crown Proceedings Act 1947 although the Ministry of Defence operates an ex gratia noise compensation scheme for those living near to military airfields. Damages have however been awarded at common law for nuisance from military aircraft.[1]

1   *Dennis v Ministry of Defence* [20 03] EWHC 793, QB, [20 03] EWHC LR 34 p 741.

CROWN PROPERTY

10.36 The Crown has traditionally had immunity from many types of proceedings and this immunity has been applied in the context of statutory nuisance.[1] However, since the introduction of the EPA 1990, Part III the position has changed. By virtue of section 159 of the EPA 1990 '... the provisions of this section, the provisions of this Act and of regulations and orders made under it shall bind the Crown.'[2] This means that if a nuisance is arising on Crown property, for example noise from an army barracks, then action may be taken under the EPA 1990, Part III. However, section 159 of the EPA 1990 does state that no contravention of the EPA 1990 shall make the Crown criminally liable, but instead the High Court may make a declaration on the application of a local or public authority declaring unlawful any act or omission of the Crown which contravenes the EPA 1990.[3] The Secretary of State may certify that particular Crown premises in respect of powers of entry under the EPA 1990 may be granted immunity in the interests of national security.[4]

1 *Nottingham No 1 Area Hospital Management Committee v Owen* [1958] 1 QB 50 concerning smoke emissions from a chimney at a hospital.
2 Moreover EPA 1990, s 159(3) states that the EPA 1990 applies to persons in public service as it does to other private individuals. So if an individual is responsible for creating a statutory nuisance then this allows them to be pursued in the normal way.
3 EPA 1990, s 159(2).
4 EPA 1990, s 159(4).

10.37 These provisions are relatively easy to interpret in relation to sections 79 to 81 of the EPA 1990, – local authorities are subject to the normal duties under the EPA 1990, Part III and the procedures applicable to Crown premises will remain identical up to the point at which an abatement notice is not complied with by the Crown. Then instead of a prosecution the appropriate remedy would be through the High Court. Section 82 proceedings brought by a private citizen, however, present difficulties. They are criminal or quasi-criminal. Access to the High Court is only given expressly to local and public authorities. It is tentatively suggested, therefore, that magistrates have part, but only part, of their section 82 powers. They can make a nuisance order. They cannot fine under section 82(2) when making a nuisance order against the Crown or under section 82(8) for non- compliance with one. An inference that access to the High Court for a declaration was excluded by the express mention of a specific limited right of access might be difficult to justify in the context of article 6[1] of the ECHR especially where the nuisance affected homes, which are protected by article 8 of the ECHR. Section 3(1) of the Human Rights Act 1998 imposes a duty of convergent construction,[2] so far as possible, to interpret legislation in a way which is consistent with ECHR rights.

1 See the discussion of article 6 of ECHR, paras **3.38–3.42**, particularly in relation to the suspension of abatement notices.
2 The felicitous phrase used by Sedley LJ of the similar duty in respect of European Union laws in *R v Durham County Council, ex p Huddleston* [20 0 0] 1 WLR 1484, CA.

Appendices – Contents

Appendix A Forms and Draft Notices	**295**
Draft abatement notices types: I, II, III and IV	296
Draft notice of proceedings under section 82	302
Court Forms (Magistrates' Courts (Forms) Rules 1981	303
Form 98 Complaint	303
Form1 Information	303
Pre-trial review standard questionnaire	304
Draft costs schedule	307
Appendix B Material Relating to Statutory Nuisance	**309**
Environmental Protection Act 1990, ss 79–82, 84, 157–160, Sch 3	309
Statutory Nuisance (Appeals) Regulations 1995, SI 1995/2644	330
Clean Air Act 1993, s 64	333
Control of Pollution Act 1974, ss 60, 61, 66, 67	335
Noise Act 1996	339
Statutory Nuisances (Insects) Regulations 2006, SI 2006/770	352
Statutory Nuisances (Artificial Lighting) (Designation of Relevant Sports) (England) Order 2006, SI 2006/781	354
Appendix C Material Relating to Magistrates' Court, Crown Court and High Court Proceedings	**357**
Magistrates' Courts Act 1980, ss 40, 53, 64, 101, 108–111, 123, 127	357
Magistrates' Courts Rules 1981, SI 1981/552, rr 4, 14, 16, 34, 43, 99	360
Supreme Court Act 1981, s 48	362
Criminal Appeal Act 1968, s 50	363
Criminal Appeal Rules 1968, SI 1968/1262, r 10	364
Criminal Procedure Rules 2005, SI 2005/384, rr 1, 2, 3, 7.1–7.3, 21, 24, 37, 63.1–63.5, 63.9, 64	364
Practice Note (Magistrates: Clerk and Authorised Legal Adviser) [2000] 4 All ER 895	383
Practice Note (Justices' Clerks) [1954] 1 WLR 213	385
Appendix D Material Relating to Evidence	**387**
Civil Evidence Act 1995, ss 1–16, Sch 2	387
Magistrates' Courts (Hearsay Evidence in Civil Proceedings) Rules 1999, SI 1999/681	394
Police and Criminal Evidence Act 1984, ss 67, 76, 78	397
Appendix E Material Relating to Sentencing and Costs	**401**
Courts Act 1971, s 52	401
Prosecution of Offences Act 1985, ss 16–21	401
Supreme Court Act 1981, ss 28, 48, 51	410
Practice Direction (Costs in Criminal Proceedings) [2004] 2 All ER; [2004] 1 WLR 2657, Pts I–VI, VII.1, VII.3, VIII, IX	413
Criminal Procedure Rules 2005, SI 2005/384, rr 78.1–78.7	421
Powers of the Criminal Courts (Sentencing) Act 2000, ss 130, 131, 134	424

Appendices – Contents

Appendix F   Human Rights — **427**
Human Rights Act 1998, ss 1–13, 19, 21, 22, Sch 1, arts 2, 6, 7, 8, First Protocol, art 1 — 427

Appendix G   Miscellaneous Statutory Material — **439**
Local Government Act 1972, s 222 — 439
Local Government (Miscellaneous Provisions) Act 1976, s 16 — 439
Environmental Information Regulations 2004, SI 2004/3391 — 440

Appendix H   Guidance Relating to Noise and Smell — **455**
PPG 24, Planning Policy Guidance: Planning and Noise, paras 1–27, Glossary, Annexes 1, 2, 5 — 455
WHO Environmental Health Criteria 12 Noise (1980) — 471
WHO Environmental Health Criteria Document on Community Noise — 480
WHO Guidelines for Community Noise — 491
Noise – DEFRA Guidance on sections 69 to 81 and section 86 of the Clean Neighbourhoods and Environment Act 2005 — 494
Statutory Nuisance from Insects and Light – DEFRA Guidance on sections 101 to 103 of the Clean Neighbourhoods and Environment Act 2005 — 502
Nuisance Parking Offences and Abandoned Vehicles – DEFRA Guidance — 526
Environment Agency Technical Guidance Note IPPC H4 – Draft Horizontal Guidance for Odour, Introduction, Apps 1, 2, 6, 7, 10 — 537

Appendix A

Forms and Draft Notices

Draft Abatement Notices: types I, II, III and IV

Modern variant bases from which to draft abatement notice

Before drafting a notice read the relevant parts of the book. Then exercise your own judgment about which parts of the base to use and how to adapt them by deletion, substitution, addition and alteration.

Type I:
- (a) Not to be suspended
- (b) Reg 3(2) not applicable
- (c) Article 6 wording included

Type II:
- (a) Not to be suspended
- (b) Reg 3(2) applicable
- (c) Article 6 wording included

Type III:
- (a) To be suspended
- (b) Reg 3(2) applicable
- (c) Article 6 makes no difference

Type IV:
- (a) To be suspended
- (b) Reg 3(2) not applicable
- (c) Suspension caused by Article 6

Appendix A

Draft Abatement Notice Type I
   (a) Not to be suspended
   (b) Reg 3(2) not applicable
   (c) Article 6 wording included

Before drafting a notice read the relevant parts of the book. Then exercise your own judgment about which parts of the base to use and how to adapt them by deletion, substitution, addition and alteration.

ABATEMENT NOTICE IN RESPECT OF STATUTORY NUISANCE

ENVIRONMENTAL PROTECTION ACT 1990 PART III ("THE ACT")

To: [The Company Secretary of Satanbars Limited]

Of: [Inferno House, Dante Street, Milltown, Barsetshire BA 1 4UY]

TAKE NOTICE that the [*Barchester District Council*] ("the Council") is satisfied of [the existence] [likely] [occurrence] [recurrence] of a statutory nuisance under Section 79(1) of the Act at the premises known as:

[*Jezebel's Joint, 1 Gomorrah Road, Smuttown*]

within the district of the Council

The nuisance is:

[*noise from amplified music emitted from the premises*]

You are:

[*the person responsible for the nuisance*] [(owner)(occupier) of the premises]

What you are required to do:

(A) [to abate the nuisance and thereafter neither to cause, permit nor otherwise allow its recurrence]

[The following works or steps are required:

(B) [Describe any works or steps which are required eg]

[*keep all rear windows facing the courtyard of the Missionaries Hospital closed at all times that amplified music is being played*]

Time for compliance:

(A) [within one week]

(B) [within one week]

from the date of service of this notice

WARNING:

(1) If without reasonable excuse you contravene or fail to comply with any requirement of this notice you will be committing an offence under section 80(4) of the Act. On summary conviction fines on Level 5 may be imposed. Further fines up to one tenth of that level may be imposed for

Forms and draft notices

each day on which the offence continues after conviction. Fines up to £20,000[1] may be imposed in respect of industrial, trade or business premises.

(2) If you fail to comply with this notice the Council may abate the nuisance and do whatever is required to achieve compliance.

1 Note that the maximum fine in Scotland is £40,000 (see Chapter 5).

STATUTORY NUISANCE (APPEALS) REGULATIONS

RIGHT OF APPEAL: You may appeal against this notice to a magistrates' court within 21 days beginning with the date of the service of this notice. The grounds of appeal prescribed in the Regulations are [reproduced overleaf] [attached].

The Council considers after balancing your interests and the interests of those adversely affected by the nuisance that the notice should not be suspended pending the determination of any appeal because [[eg] *of the risk to health/ the effect on elderly people's homes*].

If an appeal is made, therefore,

THIS NOTICE WILL NOT BE SUSPENDED PENDING DETERMINATION OF AN APPEAL

Signed on behalf of the Council:

Dated:

Draft Abatement Notice Type II
  (a) Not to be suspended
  (b) Reg 3(2) applicable
  (c) Article 6 wording included

Before drafting a notice read the relevant parts of the book. Then exercise your own judgment about which parts of the base to use and how to adapt them by deletion, substitution, addition and alteration.

ABATEMENT NOTICE IN RESPECT OF STATUTORY NUISANCE

ENVIRONMENTAL PROTECTION ACT 1990 PART III ("THE ACT")

To: [The Company Secretary of Satanbars Limited]

Of: [Inferno House, Dante Street, Milltown, Barsetshire BA 1 4UY]

TAKE NOTICE that the [*Barchester District Council*] ("the Council") is satisfied of [the existence] [likely] [occurrence] [recurrence] of a statutory nuisance under Section 79(1) of the Act at the premises known as:

[*Jezebel's Joint, 1 Gomorrah Road, Smuttown*]

within the district of the Council

The nuisance is:

[*noise from amplified music emitted from the premises*]

Appendix A

You are:

[*the person responsible for the nuisance*] [(owner)(occupier) of the premises]

What you are required to do:

(A) [to abate the nuisance and thereafter neither to cause, permit, nor otherwise allow its recurrence]

[The following works or steps are required:

(B) [Describe any works or steps which are required eg]

[*triple glaze the rear window adjoining the courtyard of the Missionaries' Hospital keep that window closed at all times that amplified music is being played*]

Time for compliance:

(A) [within two months]

(B) [within two months]

from the date of service of this notice

WARNING:

(1) If without reasonable excuse you contravene or fail to comply with any req- uirement of this notice you will be committing an offence under section 80(4) of the Act. On summary conviction fines on Level 5 may be imposed. Further fines up to one tenth of that level may be imposed for each day on which the offence continues after conviction. Fines up to £20,000[1] may be imposed in respect of industrial, trade or business premises.
(2) If you fail to comply with this notice the Council may abate the nuisance and do whatever is required to achieve compliance.

1   Note that the maximum fine in Scotland is £40,000 (see Chapter 5).

STATUTORY NUISANCE (APPEALS) REGULATIONS

RIGHT OF APPEAL: You may appeal against this notice to a magistrates court within 21 days beginning with the date of the service of this notice. The grounds of appeal prescribed in the Regulations are [reproduced overleaf] [attached].

Paragraph 2 of regulation 3 applies but the Council considers that the nuisance to which this notice relates
   [AT LEAST ONE OF (a) (b) or (c) MUST APPLY]
   [(a) (is injurious to health)
   (b) (is likely to be of limited duration so that suspension would render it of no practical effect)
   (c) (in respect of which the expenditure on works would not be disproportionate to the public benefits to be expected in the period before the appeal is determined)]

and that after balancing your interests and the interests of those adversely affected by the nuisance that the notice should not be

Forms and draft notices

suspended pending the determination of any appeal because [[eg] *of the risk to health/ the effect on people's homes*]

If an appeal is made, therefore,

THIS NOTICE WILL NOT BE SUSPENDED PENDING DETERMINATION OF AN APPEAL

Signed on behalf of the Council:

Dated:

Draft Abatement Notice Type III
(a) To be suspended
(b) Reg 3(2) applicable
(c) Article 6 makes no difference

Before drafting a notice read the relevant parts of the book. Then exercise your own judgment about which parts of the base to use and how to adapt them by deletion, substitution, addition and alteration.

ABATEMENT NOTICE IN RESPECT OF STATUTORY NUISANCE

ENVIRONMENTAL PROTECTION ACT 1990 PART III ("THE ACT")

To: [The Company Secretary of Satanbars Limited]

Of: [Inferno House, Dante Street, Milltown, Barsetshire BA 1 4UY]

TAKE NOTICE that the [*Barchester District Council*] ("the Council") is satisfied of [the existence] [likely] [occurrence] [recurrence] of a statutory nuisance under Section 79(1) of the Act at the premises known as:

[*Jezebel's Joint, 1 Gomorrah Road, Smuttown*]

within the district of the Council

The nuisance is:

[*noise from amplified music emitted from the premises*]

You are:

[*the person responsible for the nuisance*] [(owner)(occupier) of the premises]

What you are required to do:

(A) [to abate the nuisance and thereafter neither cause, permit nor otherwise allow its recurrence]

[The following works or steps are required:

(B) [Describe any works or steps which are required] eg

[*triple glaze all the rear windows of the premises adjoining the courtyard of the Missionaries' Hospital*

299

Appendix A

keep all those windows closed at all times that amplified music is being played]

Time for compliance:

(A) [within two months]

(B) [within two months]

from the date of service of this notice or, if an appeal is made, the end of any period of suspension.

WARNING:

(1) If without reasonable excuse you contravene or fail to comply with any requirement of this notice you will be committing an offence under section 80(4) of the Act. On summary conviction fines on Level 5 may be imposed. Further fines up to one tenth of that level may be imposed for each day on which the offence continues after conviction. Fines up to £20,000[1] may be imposed in respect of industrial, trade or business premises.

(2) If you fail to comply with this notice the Council may abate the nuisance and do whatever is required to achieve compliance.

1   Note that the maximum fine in Scotland is £40,000 (see Chapter 5).

STATUTORY NUISANCE (APPEALS) REGULATIONS

RIGHT OF APPEAL: You may appeal against this notice to a magistrates' court within 21 days beginning with the date of the service of this notice. The grounds of appeal prescribed in the Regulations are [reproduced overleaf] [attached]

Signed on behalf of the Council:

Dated:

Draft Abatement Notice Type IV
   (a)   To be suspended
   (b)   Reg 3(2) not applicable
   (c)   Suspension caused by Article 6

Before drafting a notice read the relevant parts of the book. Then exercise your own judgment about which parts of the base to use and how to adapt them by deletion, substitution, addition and alteration.

ABATEMENT NOTICE IN RESPECT OF STATUTORY NUISANCE

ENVIRONMENTAL PROTECTION ACT 1990 PART III ("THE ACT")

To: [The Company Secretary of Satanbars Limited]

Of: [Inferno House, Dante Street, Milltown, Barsetshire BA 1 4UY]

TAKE NOTICE that the [*Barchester District Council*] ("the Council") is satisfied of [the existence] [likely] [occurrence] [recurrence] of a statutory nuisance under section 79(1) of the Act at the premises known as:

Forms and draft notices

[*Jezebel's Joint, 1 Gomorrah Road, Smuttown*]

within the district of the Council

The nuisance is:

[*noise from amplified music emitted from the premises*]

You are:

[*the person responsible for the nuisance*] [(owner)(occupier)of the premises]

What you are required to do:

(A) [to abate the nuisance and thereafter neither to cause, permit nor otherwise allow its recurrence]

[The following works or steps are required:

(B) [Describe any works or steps which are required eg]

[*triple glaze the rear window adjoining the courtyard of the Missionaries' Hospital*

keep that window closed at all times that amplified music is being played]

Time for compliance:

(A) [*within two months*]

(B) [*within two months*]

from the date of service of this notice or, if an appeal is made, the date when the magistrates' court determines[1] any appeal.

1   An Article 6(1) compliant determination will have been made by the magistrates even if it is the subject of a successful appeal to the Crown Court or Divisional Court. There is therefore no Article 6(1) ECHR reason to suspend the notice thereafter.

WARNING:

(1) If without reasonable excuse you contravene or fail to comply with any requirement of this notice you will be committing an offence under section 80(4) of the Act. On summary conviction fines on Level 5 may be imposed. Further fines up to one tenth of that level may be imposed for each day on which the offence continues after conviction. Fines up to £20,000 may be imposed in respect of industrial, trade or business premises.

(2) If you fail to comply with this notice the Council may abate the nuisance and do whatever is required to achieve compliance.

STATUTORY NUISANCE (APPEALS) REGULATIONS

RIGHT OF APPEAL: You may appeal against this notice to a magistrates' court within 21 days beginning with the date of the service of this notice. The grounds of appeal prescribed in the Regulations are [reproduced overleaf] [attached].

Signed on behalf of the Council:

Dated:

Appendix A

Draft notice of proceedings under section 82

EXAMPLE 1: LETTER OF INTENTION TO START PROCEEDINGS UNDER SECTION 82 EPA 1990

TO: [NAME & ADDRESS OF PERSON TO BE SERVED]

Dear Sir/Madam

I live at 32 Blissful Street, Sleepytown, which is next door to your bar.

The sound system in your bar is giving me grief. It is out of order for you to play it so loudly that it can be clearly heard in the baby's room and in my bedroom until the early hours.

Unless you stop it I shall go to the magistrates' court to get an order under section 82 of the Environmental Protection Act 1990 to get you to stop making so much noise.

Yours faithfully

EXAMPLE 2: LETTER OF INTENTION TO START PROCEEDINGS UNDER SECTION 82 EPA 1990

TO: [NAME & ADDRESS OF PERSON TO BE SERVED]

Dear Sir/Madam

I am writing on behalf of my client who is a tenant at flat 33, Parwood House, New Road, Townsville, of which the local authority are the landlords.

This letter is to give you formal notice of my client's intention to commence proceedings for a nuisance order under section 82 Environmental Protection Act 1990 because of the state of the flat. The complaint arises because the roof and window frames are leaking and there is inadequate ventilation. This is making living conditions very difficult for my client and his young family and is affecting their health. I enclose a surveyor's report setting out the defects in the flat.

Unless the nuisance is abated or we hear from you with firm proposals to remedy the situation, we are instructed to start proceedings after 21 days from the giving of this notice.

I look forward to hearing from you as a matter of urgency.

Yours faithfully

Forms and draft notices

Court Forms (Magistrates' Courts (Forms) Rules 1981):

Form 98
Complaint

(Magistrates' Courts Act 1980, s 52; Magistrates' Courts Rules 1981, r 4)

.... Magistrates' Court (*Code*)

Date: ....

Defendant: ....

Address: ....

Matter of complaint: (*short particulars and statute*)

The complaint of: ....

Address: .... Telephone No. ....

who (upon oath) states that the defendant was responsible for the matter of complaint of which particulars are given above.

Taken (and sworn) before me

.... Justice of the Peace

.... (Justices' Clerk)

Form 1
Information

(Magistrates' Court Acts 1980, s 1; Magistrates' Courts Rules 1981, r 4)

.... Magistrates' Court (*Code*)

Date: ....

Accused: ....

Address: ....

Alleged offence: ....(*short particulars and statute*)

The information of: ....

Address: .... Telephone No. ....

who (upon oath) states that the accused committed the offence of which particulars are given above.

Taken (and sworn) before me

.... Justice of the Peace

.... (Justices' Clerk)

Appendix A

Pre-trial review standard form questionnaire:
CASE NO.
BEFORE:

....

MAGISTRATES' COURT
BETWEEN:

(Complainant)-V-(Local Authority)

In order to assist the court you are asked to complete this form and return it within fourteen days to the clerk of the court and send a copy of it at the same time to the other party in this matter. If you are not able to return this form within fourteen days you should write to the clerk of the court and copied to the other party explaining your reasons and when you expect to be able to complete the form.

COMPLAINANT/APPELLANT [COMPLETED BY THE COURT]	DEFENDANT/LOCAL AUTHORITY [COMPLETED BY THE COURT]
Name:	Name:
Address:	Address:

Name and address of complainant's solicitors, or if no solicitors acting, the address for service of any documentation relating to this matter.

Name and address of local authority solicitors, or if no solicitors acting, the address for service of any documentation relating to this matter.

Name:	Name:
Address:	Address:

Tel. No.	Tel. No.
Fax No.	Fax No.
Ref No.	Ref No.

1. Do the grounds of appeal need clarification or further particularisation?   YES/NO

2. For the complainant (i.e. appellant) only:

(a) Do you intend to apply for permission to amend the grounds of your appeal?   YES/NO

(b) If so, are proposed amendments attached to this form?   YES/NO

Forms and draft notices

If you propose to add further grounds the court will wish to know why these grounds were not included in the original grounds of appeal and why it is that you now seek permission to add them.

3. Do you wish the case to come before a stipendiary magistrate?
   YES/NO/NO PREFERENCE

4. If your answer to 3 was 'YES' or 'NO' give your brief reasons:

5. Will you be asking the court to make a site visit?   YES/NO

6. Is it agreed between the parties that a site visit is necessary?
   YES/NO

7. If 'YES' to 5 or 6 give your brief reasons why a site visit is thought to be necessary.

8. How many witnesses (other than expert witnesses) do you intend to call?

9. Do you intend to provide witnesses statements?   YES/NO

10. When will these statements be ready?

11. If you do not intend to produce witness statements prior to the hearing please explain your reasons.

At the pre-trial hearing you will be expected to have a note of any dates that your witnesses may be unavailable and the reason for their unavailability.

12. Will you be calling expert evidence?   YES/NO

13. If 'YES' to (9) identify the expert witness(es) and area(s) of expertise.

Appendix A

14. Have the parties agreed a timetable for the exchange of expert and rebuttal reports to be filed before the trial date?   YES/NO

15. If 'YES' to 14 what periods have been agreed:

For exchange of expert reports?

For exchange of any reports in progress?

16. Have the parties agreed to prepare before the trial date a schedule of matters agreed/not agreed?   YES/NO

17. Will the parties prepare an agreed court bundle?   YES/NO

18. Is it likely that legal authorities will be cited?   YES/NO

19. If 'YES' to (18) will copies of the authorities and a skeleton argument be supplied to the clerk of the court three clear working days before the date for trial?   YES/NO

20. Time estimate of length of trial hearing

21. Is there any special equipment that will be required at the trial hearing, e.g. video recorder, TV?   YES/NO

22. If 'YES' to 21 is its admission agreed by the other side?   YES/NO

23. If 'YES' to 21 identify the equipment and state whether you intend producing it yourself.

24. Do you think that a pre-trial review would be useful? If so, to deal with what matters?

25. State any other matters that you consider may be of assistance to the court in preparing for the trial hearing.

© Gregart 2000

Forms and draft notices

Draft Costs Schedule

STANDARD FORM COSTS SCHEDULE: CASE WITH LAWYERS' FEES

[INSERT NAME OF COURT]

[INSERT NAME OF CASE]

1. Solicitors' costs

Fee earner: [NAME]   [POSITION]   [HOURLY RATE]

Work done: £

2. Expert Witnesses' costs

Witness (1):   [NAME]   [POSITION]   [HOURLY RATE]

Work done:[1] £

3. Other witnesses

Witness(1):   [NAME]

Expenses:[2] £

4. Other expenses

[court fees] £

Others [give brief description] £

TOTAL £

Amount of VAT £

GRAND TOTAL £

The costs estimated above do not exceed the costs which the [PARTY] is liable to pay in respect of the work which this estimate covers.

In the case of costs claimed by salaried officers of the [LOCAL AUTHORITY], these costs are attributable to the [OFFENCE COMMITTED/THE NUISANCE CAUSED] and do not arise from any routine inspections.

Dated   Signed   Position

1   This may include work in relation to evidence not used at trial and the costs of salaried officers of the local authority: see Chapter 7.
2   Non-expert witnesses will usually only recover limited amounts for attendance.

Appendix A

STANDARD FORM COSTS SCHEDULE: LITIGANT IN PERSON

[INSERT NAME OF COURT]

[INSERT NAME OF CASE]

[PARTY]'s Schedule of Costs

1. Litigant's expenses

Expenses incurred:

[e.g. travel expenses] £

2. Witnesses' expenses

Witness(1):   [NAME]

Expenses:[1] £

3. Other expenses

[court fees] £

Others [give brief description] £

TOTAL £

Amount of VAT £

GRAND TOTAL £

Dated   Signed

1   Non-expert witnesses will usually only recover limited amounts for attendance.

Appendix B

Material Relating to Statutory Nuisance

Environmental Protection Act 1990

(Up to date as at 1 October 2007 in relation to England and Wales. The addition of categories fa (insects) and fb (artificial light), and consequential amendments, made by the Clean Neighbourhoods and Environment Act 2005 for England and Wales have not yet been made for Scotland. The Public Health Etc. (Scotland) Bill is likely to make such additions for Scotland. Other variations for Scotland are shown in italics and square brackets.)

79 Statutory nuisances and inspections therefor

(1) Subject to subsections (1A) to (6A) below, the following matters constitute "statutory nuisances" for the purposes of this Part, that is to say—
- (a) any premises in such a state as to be prejudicial to health or a nuisance;
- (b) smoke emitted from premises so as to be prejudicial to health or a nuisance;
- (c) fumes or gases emitted from premises so as to be prejudicial to health or a nuisance;
- (d) any dust, steam, smell or other effluvia arising on industrial, trade or business premises and being prejudicial to health or a nuisance;
- (e) any accumulation or deposit which is prejudicial to health or a nuisance;
- (f) any animal kept in such a place or manner as to be prejudicial to health or a nuisance;
- (fa) any insects emanating from relevant industrial, trade or business premises and being prejudicial to health or a nuisance;
- (fb) artificial light emitted from premises so as to be prejudicial to health or a nuisance;
- (g) noise emitted from premises so as to be prejudicial to health or a nuisance;
- (ga) noise that is prejudicial to health or a nuisance and is emitted from or caused by a vehicle, machinery or equipment in a street [or in Scotland, road];
- (h) any other matter declared by any enactment to be a statutory nuisance;

and it shall be the duty of every local authority to cause its area to be inspected from time to time to detect any statutory nuisances which ought to be dealt with under section 80 below [or sections 80 and 80A below] and, where a complaint of a statutory nuisance is made to it by a person living within its area, to take such steps as are reasonably practicable to investigate the complaint.

(1A) No matter shall constitute a statutory nuisance to the extent that it consists of, or is caused by, any land being in a contaminated state.

Appendix B

(1B) Land is in a "contaminated state" for the purposes of subsection (1A) above if, and only if, it is in such a condition, by reason of substances in, on or under the land, that—
- (a) harm is being caused or there is a possibility of harm being caused; or
- (b) pollution of controlled waters is being, or is likely to be, caused;

and in this subsection "harm", "pollution of controlled waters" and "substance" have the same meaning as in Part IIA of this Act.

[(1B) Land is in a "contaminated state" for the purposes of sub section (1A) above if, and only if, it is in such a condition, by reason of substances in, on or under the land, that–
- *(a) significant harm is being caused or there is a significant possibility of such harm being caused; or*
- *(b) significant pollution of the water environment is being caused or there is a significant possibility of such pollution being caused;*

and in this subsection "harm", "pollution" in relation to the water environment, "substance" and "the water environment" have the same meanings as in Part IIA of this Act.][1]

(2) Subsection (1)(b), (fb) and (g) above do not apply in relation to premises—
- (a) occupied on behalf of the Crown for naval, military or air force purposes or for the purposes of the department of the Secretary of State having responsibility for defence, or
- (b) occupied by or for the purposes of a visiting force;

and "visiting force" means any such body, contingent or detachment of the forces of any country as is a visiting force for the purposes of any of the provisions of the Visiting Forces Act 1952.

(3) Subsection (1)(b) above does not apply to—
- (i) smoke emitted from a chimney of a private dwelling within a smoke control area,
- (ii) dark smoke emitted from a chimney of a building or a chimney serving the furnace of a boiler or industrial plant attached to a building or for the time being fixed to or installed on any land,
- (iii) smoke emitted from a railway locomotive steam engine, or
- (iv) dark smoke emitted otherwise than as mentioned above from industrial or trade premises.

(4) Subsection (1)(c) above does not apply in relation to premises other than private dwellings.

(5) Subsection (1)(d) above does not apply to steam emitted from a railway locomotive engine.

(5A) Subsection (1)(fa) does not apply to insects that are wild animals included in Schedule 5 to the Wildlife and Countryside Act 1981 (animals which are protected), unless they are included in respect of section 9(5) of that Act only.

(5B) Subsection (1)(fb) does not apply to artificial light emitted from—
- (a) an airport;
- (b) harbour premises;
- (c) railway premises, not being relevant separate railway premises;

Material relating to statutory nuisance

(d) tramway premises;
(e) a bus station and any associated facilities;
(f) a public service vehicle operating centre;
(g) a goods vehicle operating centre;
(h) a lighthouse;
(i) a prison.

(6) Subsection (1)(g) above does not apply to noise caused by aircraft other than model aircraft.

(6A) Subsection (1)(ga) above does not apply to noise made—
(a) by traffic,
(b) by any naval, military or air force of the Crown or by a visiting force (as defined in subsection (2) above), or
(c) by a political demonstration or a demonstration supporting or opposing a cause or campaign.

(6B) Subsection (1)(gb) above does not apply in relation to smoke, fumes or gases emitted from the exhaust system of a vehicle.

(7) In this Part—
"airport" has the meaning given by section 95 of the Transport Act 2000;
"associated facilities" , in relation to a bus station, has the meaning given by section 83 of the Transport Act 1985;
"bus station" has the meaning given by section 83 of the Transport Act 1985;]
"chimney" includes structures and openings of any kind from or through which smoke may be emitted;
"dust" does not include dust emitted from a chimney as an ingredient of smoke;
"equipment" includes a musical instrument;
"fumes" means any airborne solid matter smaller than dust;
"gas" includes vapour and moisture precipitated from vapour;
"goods vehicle operating centre", in relation to vehicles used under an operator's licence, means a place which is specified in the licence as an operating centre for those vehicles, and for the purposes of this definition "operating centre" and "operator's licence" have the same meaning as in the Goods Vehicles (Licensing of Operators) Act 1995;
"harbour premises" means premises which form part of a harbour area and which are occupied wholly or mainly for the purposes of harbour operations, and for the purposes of this definition "harbour area" and "harbour operations" have the same meaning as in Part 3 of the Aviation and Maritime Security Act 1990;
"industrial, trade or business premises" means premises used for any industrial, trade or business purposes or premises not so used on which matter is burnt in connection with any industrial, trade or business process, and premises are used for industrial purposes where they are used for the purposes of any treatment or process as well as where they are used for the purposes of manufacturing;
"lighthouse" has the same meaning as in Part 8 of the Merchant Shipping Act 1995;
"local authority" means, subject to subsection (8) below,—
(a) in Greater London, a London borough council, the Common Council of the City of London and, as respects the Temples,

Appendix B

> the Sub-Treasurer of the Inner Temple and the Under-Treasurer of the Middle Temple respectively;
> (b) in England outside Greater London, a district council;
> (bb) in Wales, a county council or county borough council;
> (c) the Council of the Isles of Scilly; and
> (d) in Scotland, a district or islands council or a council constituted under section 2 of the Local Government etc (Scotland) Act 1994;

"noise" includes vibration;
"person responsible"—
> (a) in relation to a statutory nuisance, means the person to whose act, default or sufferance the nuisance is attributable;
> (b) in relation to a vehicle, includes the person in whose name the vehicle is for the time being registered under the Vehicle Excise and Registration Act 1994 and any other person who is for the time being the driver of the vehicle;
> (c) in relation to machinery or equipment, includes any person who is for the time being the operator of the machinery or equipment;

"prejudicial to health" means injurious, or likely to cause injury, to health;
"premises" includes land and, subject to subsection (12) and, in relation to England and Wales section 81A(9) below, any vessel;
"prison" includes a young offender institution;
"private dwelling" means any building, or part of a building, used or intended to be used, as a dwelling;
"private dwelling" means any building, or part of a building, used or intended to be used, as a dwelling;
"public service vehicle operating centre", in relation to public service vehicles used under a PSV operator's licence, means a place which is an operating centre of those vehicles, and for the purposes of this definition "operating centre", "PSV operator's licence" and "public service vehicle" have the same meaning as in the Public Passenger Vehicles Act 1981;
"railway premises" means any premises which fall within the definition of "light maintenance depot", "network", "station" or "track" in section 83 of the Railways Act 1993;
"relevant separate railway premises" has the meaning given by subsection (7A);
"road" has the same meaning as in Part IV of the New Roads and Street Works Act 1991;
"smoke" includes soot, ash, grit and gritty particles emitted in smoke;
"street" means a highway and any other road, footway, square or court that is for the time being open to the public;
"tramway premises" means any premises which, in relation to a tramway, are the equivalent of the premises which, in relation to a railway, fall within the definition of "light maintenance depot", "network", "station" or "track" in section 83 of the Railways Act 1993;
and any expressions used in this section and in [the Clean Air Act 1993] have the same meaning in this section as in that Act and [section 3 of the Clean Air Act 1993] shall apply for the interpretation of the expression "dark smoke" and the operation of this Part in relation to it.

(7A) Railway premises are relevant separate railway premises if–

Material relating to statutory nuisance

   (a) they are situated within–
      (i) premises used as a museum or other place of cultural, scientific or historical interest, or
      (ii) premises used for the purposes of a funfair or other entertainment, recreation or amusement, and
   (b) they are not associated with any other railway premises.

(7B) For the purposes of subsection (7A)–
   (a) a network situated as described in subsection (7A)(a) is associated with other railway premises if it is connected to another network (not being a network situated as described in subsection (7A)(a));
   (b) track that is situated as described in subsection (7A)(a) but is not part of a network is associated with other railway premises if it is connected to track that forms part of a network (not being a network situated as described in subsection (7A)(a));
   (c) a station or light maintenance depot situated as described in subsection (7A)(a) is associated with other railway premises if it is used in connection with the provision of railway services other than services provided wholly within the premises where it is situated.

In this subsection "light maintenance depot", "network", "railway services", "station" and "track" have the same meaning as in Part 1 of the Railways Act 1993.

(8) Where, by an order under section 2 of the Public Health (Control of Disease) Act 1984, a port health authority has been constituted for any port health district or in Scotland where by an order under section 172 of the Public Health (Scotland) Act 1897 a port local authority or a joint port local authority has been constituted for the whole or part of a port, the port health authority, port local authority or joint port local authority, as the case may be shall have by virtue of this subsection, as respects its district, the functions conferred or imposed by this Part in relation to statutory nuisances other than a nuisance falling within paragraph (fb), (g)or (ga) of subsection (1) above and no such order shall be made assigning those functions; and "local authority" and "area" shall be construed accordingly.

(9) In this Part "best practicable means" is to be interpreted by reference to the following provisions—
   (a) "practicable" means reasonably practicable having regard among other things to local conditions and circumstances, to the current state of technical knowledge and to the financial implications;
   (b) the means to be employed include the design, installation, maintenance and manner and periods of operation of plant and machinery, and the design, construction and maintenance of buildings and structures;
   (c) the test is to apply only so far as compatible with any duty imposed by law;
   (d) the test is to apply only so far as compatible with safety and safe working conditions, and with the exigencies of any emergency or unforeseeable circumstances;

and, in circumstances where a code of practice under section 71 of the Control of Pollution Act 1974 (noise minimisation) is applicable, regard shall also be had to guidance given in it.

Appendix B

(10) A local authority shall not without the consent of the Secretary of State institute summary proceedings under this Part in respect of a nuisance falling within paragraph (b),(d) or (e), (fb) or (g) and, in relation to Scotland, paragraph (ga), of subsection (1) above if proceedings in respect thereof might be instituted *under Part I² or* under regulations under section 2 of the Pollution Prevention and Control Act 1999.

(11) The area of a local authority which includes part of the seashore shall also include for the purposes of this Part the territorial sea lying seawards from that part of the shore; and subject to subsection (12) and, in relation to England and Wales, section 81A] below, this Part shall have effect, in relation to any area included in the area of a local authority by virtue of this subsection—
  (a) as if references to premises and the occupier of premises included respectively a vessel and the master of a vessel; and
  (b) with such other modifications, if any, as are prescribed in regulations made by the Secretary of State.

(12) A vessel powered by steam reciprocating machinery is not a vessel to which this Part of this Act applies.

1   Words in italics and square brackets apply to Scotland only.
2   Words in italics repealed as from a day to be appointed by the Pollution Prevention and Control Act 1999, s 6(2), Sch 3.

80 Summary proceedings for statutory nuisances

(1) Subject to subsection (2A) where a local authority is satisfied that a statutory nuisance exists, or is likely to occur or recur, in the area of the authority, the local authority shall serve a notice ("an abatement notice") imposing all or any of the following requirements—
  (a) requiring the abatement of the nuisance or prohibiting or restricting its occurrence or recurrence;
  (b) requiring the execution of such works, and the taking of such other steps, as may be necessary for any of those purposes,

and the notice shall specify the time or times within which the requirements of the notice are to be complied with.

(2) Subject to section 80A(1) below, the abatement notice shall be served—
  (a) except in a case falling within paragraph (b) or (c) below, on the person responsible for the nuisance;
  (b) where the nuisance arises from any defect of a structural character, on the owner of the premises;
  (c) where the person responsible for the nuisance cannot be found or the nuisance has not yet occurred, on the owner or occupier of the premises.

(2A) Where a local authority is satisfied that a statutory nuisance falling within paragraph (g) of section 79(1) above exists, or is likely to occur or recur, in the area of the authority, the authority shall—
  (a) serve an abatement notice in respect of the nuisance in accordance with subsections (1) and (2) above; or
  (b) take such other steps as it thinks appropriate for the purpose of persuading the appropriate person to abate the nuisance or prohibit or restrict its occurrence or recurrence.

(2B) If a local authority has taken steps under subsection (2A)(b) above and either of the conditions in subsection (2C) below is satisfied, the authority shall serve an abatement notice in respect of the nuisance.

(2C) The conditions are—
  (a) that the authority is satisfied at any time before the end of the relevant period that the steps taken will not be successful in persuading the appropriate person to abate the nuisance or prohibit or restrict its occurrence or recurrence;
  (b) that the authority is satisfied at the end of the relevant period that the nuisance continues to exist, or continues to be likely to occur or recur, in the area of the authority.

(2D) The relevant period is the period of seven days starting with the day on which the authority was first satisfied that the nuisance existed, or was likely to occur or recur.

(2E) The appropriate person is the person on whom the authority would otherwise be required under subsection (2A)(a) above to serve an abatement notice in respect of the nuisance.

(3) A person served with an abatement notice may appeal against the notice to a magistrates' court or in Scotland, the sheriff within the period of twenty-one days beginning with the date on which he was served with the notice.

(4) If a person on whom an abatement notice is served, without reasonable excuse, contravenes or fails to comply with any requirement or prohibition imposed by the notice, he shall be guilty of an offence.

(5) Except in a case falling within subsection (6) below, a person who commits an offence under subsection (4) above shall be liable on summary conviction to a fine not exceeding level 5 on the standard scale together with a further fine of an amount equal to one-tenth of that level for each day on which the offence continues after the conviction.

(6) A person who commits an offence under subsection (4) above on industrial, trade or business premises shall be liable on summary conviction to a fine not exceeding £20,000.

[*(6) A person who commits an offence under subsection (4) above on industrial, trade or business premises shall be liable on summary conviction to a fine not exceeding £40,000.*][1]

(7) Subject to subsection (8) below, in any proceedings for an offence under subsection (4) above in respect of a statutory nuisance it shall be a defence to prove that the best practicable means were used to prevent, or to counteract the effects of, the nuisance.

(8) The defence under subsection (7) above is not available—
  (a) in the case of a nuisance falling within paragraph (a),(d),(e),(f), (fa) or (g) of section 79(1) above except where the nuisance arises on industrial, trade or business premises;
  (aza) in the case of a nuisance falling within paragraph (fb) of section 79(1) above except where—
    (i) the artificial light is emitted from industrial, trade or business premises, or

Appendix B

> (ii) the artificial light (not being light to which sub-paragraph (i) applies) is emitted by lights used for the purpose only of illuminating an outdoor relevant sports facility;
>
> (aa) in the case of a nuisance falling within paragraph (ga) of section 79(1) above except where the noise is emitted from or caused by a vehicle, machinery or equipment being used for industrial, trade or business purposes;
>
> (b) in the case of a nuisance falling within paragraph (b) of section 79(1) above except where the smoke is emitted from a chimney; and
>
> (c) in the case of a nuisance falling within paragraph (c) or (h) of section 79(1) above.

(8A) For the purposes of subsection (8)(aza) a relevant sports facility is an area, with or without structures, that is used when participating in a relevant sport, but does not include such an area comprised in domestic premises.

(8B) For the purposes of subsection (8A) "relevant sport" means a sport that is designated for those purposes by order made by the Secretary of State, in relation to England, or the National Assembly for Wales, in relation to Wales.

A sport may be so designated by reference to its appearing in a list maintained by a body specified in the order.

(8C) In subsection (8A) "domestic premises" means—
  (a) premises used wholly or mainly as a private dwelling, or
  (b) land or other premises belonging to, or enjoyed with, premises so used.

(9) In proceedings for an offence under subsection (4) above in respect of a statutory nuisance falling within paragraph (g)or (ga) of section 79(1) above where the offence consists in contravening requirements imposed by virtue of subsection (1)(a) above it shall be a defence to prove—
  (a) that the alleged offence was covered by a notice served under section 60 or a consent given under section 61 or 65 of the Control of Pollution Act 1974 (construction sites, etc); or
  (b) where the alleged offence was committed at a time when the premises were subject to a notice under section 66 of that Act (noise reduction notice), that the level of noise emitted from the premises at that time was not such as to a constitute a contravention of the notice under that section; or
  (c) where the alleged offence was committed at a time when the premises were not subject to a notice under section 66 of that Act, and when a level fixed under section 67 of that Act (new buildings liable to abatement order) applied to the premises, that the level of noise emitted from the premises at that time did not exceed that level.

(10) Paragraphs (b) and (c) of subsection (9) above apply whether or not the relevant notice was subject to appeal at the time when the offence was alleged to have been committed.

1   Words in italics and square brackets apply to Scotland only.

80A Abatement notice in respect of noise in the street

(1) In the case of a statutory nuisance within section 79(1)(ga) above that—
- (a) has not yet occurred, or
- (b) arises from noise emitted from or caused by an unattended vehicle or unattended machinery or equipment,

the abatement notice shall be served in accordance with subsection (2) below.[1]

(2) The notice shall be served—
- (a) where the person responsible for the vehicle, machinery or equipment can be found, on that person;
- (b) where that person cannot be found or where the local authority determines that this paragraph should apply, by fixing the notice to the vehicle, machinery or equipment.

(3) Where—
- (a) an abatement notice is served in accordance with subsection (2)(b) above by virtue of a determination of the local authority, and
- (b) the person responsible for the vehicle, machinery or equipment can be found and served with a copy of the notice within an hour of the notice being fixed to the vehicle, machinery or equipment,

a copy of the notice shall be served on that person accordingly.

(4) Where an abatement notice is served in accordance with subsection (2)(b) above by virtue of a determination of the local authority, the notice shall state that, if a copy of the notice is subsequently served under subsection (3) above, the time specified in the notice as the time within which its requirements are to be complied with is extended by such further period as is specified in the notice.

(5) Where an abatement notice is served in accordance with subsection (2)(b) above, the person responsible for the vehicle, machinery or equipment may appeal against the notice under section 80(3) above as if he had been served with the notice on the date on which it was fixed to the vehicle, machinery or equipment.

(6) Section 80(4) above shall apply in relation to a person on whom a copy of an abatement notice is served under subsection (3) above as if the copy were the notice itself.

(7) A person who removes or interferes with a notice fixed to a vehicle, machinery or equipment in accordance with subsection (2)(b) above shall be guilty of an offence, unless he is the person responsible for the vehicle, machinery or equipment or he does so with the authority of that person.

(8) A person who commits an offence under subsection (7) above shall be liable on summary conviction to a fine not exceeding level 3 on the standard scale.

81 Supplementary provisions

(1) [Subject to subsection (1A) below, where] more than one person is responsible for a statutory nuisance section 80 above shall apply to each of those persons whether or not what any one of them is responsible for would by itself amount to a nuisance.

Appendix B

[(1A) In relation to a statutory nuisance within section 79(1)(ga) above for which more than one person is responsible (whether or not what any one of those persons is responsible for would by itself amount to such a nuisance), section 80(2)(a) above shall apply with the substitution of "any one of the persons" for "the person".

(1B) In relation to a statutory nuisance within section 79(1)(ga) above caused by noise emitted from or caused by an unattended vehicle or unattended machinery or equipment for which more than one person is responsible, section 80A above shall apply with the substitution—
  (a) in subsection (2)(a), of "any of the persons" for "the person" and of "one such person" for "that person",
  (b) in subsection (2)(b), of "such a person" for "that person",
  (c) in subsection (3), of "any of the persons" for "the person" and of "one such person" for "that person",
  (d) in subsection (5), of "any person" for "the person", and
  (e) in subsection (7), of "a person" for "the person" and of "such a person" for "that person".]

(2) Where a statutory nuisance which exists or has occurred within the area of a local authority, or which has affected any part of that area, appears to the local authority to be wholly or partly caused by some act or default committed or taking place outside the area, the local authority may act under section 80 above as if the act or default were wholly within that area, except that any appeal shall be heard by a magistrates' court [or in Scotland, the sheriff] having jurisdiction where the act or default is alleged to have taken place.

(3) Where an abatement notice has not been complied with the local authority may, whether or not they take proceedings for an offence [or, in Scotland, whether or not proceedings have been taken for an offence,] under section 80(4) above, abate the nuisance and do whatever may be necessary in execution of the notice.

[(3A) The power under subsection (3) above shall, where the matter to be abated is a statutory nuisance by virtue of section 79(1)(g) above, include power to seize and remove any equipment which it appears to the authority is being or has been used in the emission of the noise in question.

(3B) A person who wilfully obstructs any person exercising, by virtue of subsection (3A) above, the power conferred by subsection (3) above shall be liable, on summary conviction, to a fine not exceeding level 3 on the standard scale.

(3C) Schedule 1 to the Antisocial Behaviour etc. (Scotland) Act 2004 (asp 8) shall have effect in relation to equipment seized by virtue of subsection (3A) above as it does in relation to equipment seized under section 47(2) of that Act, subject to the following modifications—
  (a) in paragraph 1(a), "noise offence" means an offence under section 80(4) above in respect of a statutory nuisance falling within section 79(1)(g) above; and
  (b) in paragraph 1(b), "seized equipment" means equipment seized by virtue of subsection (3A) above.][1]

(4) Any expenses reasonably incurred by a local authority in abating, or preventing the recurrence of, a statutory nuisance under subsection (3)

Material relating to statutory nuisance

above may be recovered by them from the person by whose act or default the nuisance was caused and, if that person is the owner of the premises, from any person who is for the time being the owner thereof; and the court [or sheriff] may apportion the expenses between persons by whose acts or defaults the nuisance is caused in such manner as the court consider [or sheriff considers] fair and reasonable.

(5) If a local authority is of opinion that proceedings for an offence under section 80(4) above would afford an inadequate remedy in the case of any statutory nuisance, they may, subject to subsection (6) below, take proceedings in the High Court [or, in Scotland, in any court of competent jurisdiction] for the purpose of securing the abatement, prohibition or restriction of the nuisance, and the proceedings shall be maintainable notwithstanding the local authority have suffered no damage from the nuisance.

(6) In any proceedings under subsection (5) above in respect of a nuisance falling within paragraph (g)[or (ga)] of section 79(1) above, it shall be a defence to prove that the noise was authorised by a notice under section 60 or a consent under section 61 (construction sites) of the Control of Pollution Act 1974.

(7) The further supplementary provisions in Schedule 3 to this Act shall have effect.

1   Words in italics and square brackets apply to Scotland only.

81A Expenses recoverable from owner to be a charge on premises

(1) Where any expenses are recoverable under section 81(4) above from a person who is the owner of the premises there mentioned and the local authority serves a notice on him under this section—
  (a) the expenses shall carry interest, at such reasonable rate as the local authority may determine, from the date of service of the notice until the whole amount is paid, and
  (b) subject to the following provisions of this section, the expenses and accrued interest shall be a charge on the premises.

(2) A notice served under this section shall—
  (a) specify the amount of the expenses that the local authority claims is recoverable,
  (b) state the effect of subsection (1) above and the rate of interest determined by the local authority under that subsection, and
  (c) state the effect of subsections (4) to (6) below.

(3) On the date on which a local authority serves a notice on a person under this section the authority shall also serve a copy of the notice on every other person who, to the knowledge of the authority, has an interest in the premises capable of being affected by the charge.

(4) Subject to any order under subsection (7)(b) or (c) below, the amount of any expenses specified in a notice under this section and the accrued interest shall be a charge on the premises—
  (a) as from the end of the period of twenty-one days beginning with the date of service of the notice, or
  (b) where an appeal is brought under subsection (6) below, as from the final determination of the appeal,
until the expenses and interest are recovered.

Appendix B

(5) For the purposes of subsection (4) above, the withdrawal of an appeal has the same effect as a final determination of the appeal.

(6) A person served with a notice or copy of a notice under this section may appeal against the notice to the county court within the period of twenty-one days beginning with the date of service.

(7) On such an appeal the court may—
    (a) confirm the notice without modification,
    (b) order that the notice is to have effect with the substitution of a different amount for the amount originally specified in it, or
    (c) order that the notice is to be of no effect.

(8) A local authority shall, for the purpose of enforcing a charge under this section, have all the same powers and remedies under the Law of Property Act 1925, and otherwise, as if it were a mortgagee by deed having powers of sale and lease, of accepting surrenders of leases and of appointing a receiver.

(9) In this section—
    "owner", in relation to any premises, means a person (other than a mortgagee not in possession) who, whether in his own right or as trustee for any other person, is entitled to receive the rack rent of the premises or, where the premises are not let at a rack rent, would be so entitled if they were so let, and
    "premises" does not include a vessel.

(10) This section does not apply to Scotland.

[81B Payment of expenses by instalments]

[(1) Where any expenses are a charge on premises under section 81A above, the local authority may by order declare the expenses to be payable with interest by instalments within the specified period, until the whole amount is paid.

(2) In subsection (1) above—
    "interest" means interest at the rate determined by the authority under section 81A(1) above, and
    "the specified period" means such period of thirty years or less from the date of service of the notice under section 81A above as is specified in the order.

(3) Subject to subsection (5) below, the instalments and interest, or any part of them, may be recovered from the owner or occupier for the time being of the premises.

(4) Any sums recovered from an occupier may be deducted by him from the rent of the premises.

(5) An occupier shall not be required to pay at any one time any sum greater than the aggregate of—
    (a) the amount that was due from him on account of rent at the date on which he was served with a demand from the local authority together with a notice requiring him not to pay rent to his landlord without deducting the sum demanded, and
    (b) the amount that has become due from him on account of rent since that date.]

[(6) This section does not apply to Scotland.]

82 Summary proceedings by persons aggrieved by statutory nuisances

(1) A magistrates' court may act under this section on a complaint [or, in Scotland, the sheriff may act under this section on a summary application,] made by any person on the ground that he is aggrieved by the existence of a statutory nuisance.

(2) If the magistrates' court [or, in Scotland, the sheriff] is satisfied that the alleged nuisance exists, or that although abated it is likely to recur on the same premises [or, in the case of a nuisance within section 79(1)(ga) above, in the same street][or, in Scotland, road], the court [or the sheriff] shall make an order for either or both of the following purposes—
   (a) requiring the defendant [or, in Scotland, defender] to abate the nuisance, within a time specified in the order, and to execute any works necessary for that purpose;
   (b) prohibiting a recurrence of the nuisance, and requiring the defendant [or defender], within a time specified in the order, to execute any works necessary to prevent the recurrence;

and[, in England and Wales,] may also impose on the defendant a fine not exceeding level 5 on the standard scale.

(3) If the magistrates' court [or the sheriff] is satisfied that the alleged nuisance exists and is such as, in the opinion of the court [or of the sheriff], to render premises unfit for human habitation, an order under subsection (2) above may prohibit the use of the premises for human habitation until the premises are, to the satisfaction of the court [or of the sheriff], rendered fit for that purpose.

(4) Proceedings for an order under subsection (2) above shall be brought—
   (a) except in a case falling within [paragraph (b),(c) or (d) below], against the person responsible for the nuisance;
   (b) where the nuisance arises from any defect of a structural character, against the owner of the premises;
   (c) where the person responsible for the nuisance cannot be found, against the owner or occupier of the premises.
   [(d) in the case of a statutory nuisance within section 79(1)(ga) above caused by noise emitted from or caused by an unattended vehicle or unattended machinery or equipment, against the person responsible for the vehicle, machinery or equipment.]

(5) [Subject to subsection (5A) below, where] more than one person is responsible for a statutory nuisance, subsections (1) to (4) above shall apply to each of those persons whether or not what any one of them is responsible for would by itself amount to a nuisance.

[(5A) In relation to a statutory nuisance within section 79(1)(ga) above for which more than one person is responsible (whether or not what any one of those persons is responsible for would by itself amount to such a nuisance), subsection (4)(a) above shall apply with the substitution of "each person responsible for the nuisance who can be found" for "the person responsible for the nuisance".

Appendix B

(5B) In relation to a statutory nuisance within section 79(1)(ga) above caused by noise emitted from or caused by an unattended vehicle or unattended machinery or equipment for which more than one person is responsible, subsection (4)(d) above shall apply with the substitution of "any person" for "the person".]

(6) Before instituting proceedings for an order under subsection (2) above against any person, the person aggrieved by the nuisance shall give to that person such notice in writing of his intention to bring the proceedings as is applicable to proceedings in respect of a nuisance of that description and the notice shall specify the matter complained of.

(7) The notice of the bringing of proceedings in respect of a statutory nuisance required by subsection (6) above which is applicable is—
   (a) in the case of a nuisance falling within paragraph (g)[or (ga)] of section 79(1) above, not less than three days' notice; and
   (b) in the case of a nuisance of any other description, not less than twenty-one days' notice;

but the Secretary of State may, by order, provide that this subsection shall have effect as if such period as is specified in the order were the minimum period of notice applicable to any description of statutory nuisance specified in the order.

(8) A person who, without reasonable excuse, contravenes any requirement or prohibition imposed by an order under subsection (2) above shall be guilty of an offence and liable on summary conviction to a fine not exceeding level 5 on the standard scale together with a further fine of an amount equal to one-tenth of that level for each day on which the offence continues after the conviction.

(9) Subject to subsection (10) below, in any proceedings for an offence under subsection (8) above in respect of a statutory nuisance it shall be a defence to prove that the best practicable means were used to prevent, or to counteract the effects of, the nuisance.

(10) The defence under subsection (9) above is not available—
   (a) in the case of a nuisance falling within paragraph (a),(d),(e),(f) or (g) of section 79(1) above except where the nuisance arises on industrial, trade or business premises;
   [(aa) in the case of a nuisance falling within paragraph (ga) of section 79(1) above except where the noise is emitted from or caused by a vehicle, machinery or equipment being used for industrial, trade or business purposes;]
   (b) in the case of a nuisance falling within paragraph (b) of section 79(1) above except where the smoke is emitted from a chimney;
   (c) in the case of a nuisance falling within paragraph (c) or (h) of section 79(1) above; and
   (d) in the case of a nuisance which is such as to render the premises unfit for human habitation.

(11) If a person is convicted of an offence under subsection (8) above, a magistrates' court [or the sheriff] may, after giving the local authority in whose area the nuisance has occurred an opportunity of being heard, direct the authority to do anything which the person convicted was required to do by the order to which the conviction relates.

Material relating to statutory nuisance

(12) Where on the hearing of proceedings for an order under subsection (2) above it is proved that the alleged nuisance existed at the date of the making of the complaint [or summary application], then, whether or not at the date of the hearing it still exists or is likely to recur, the court [or the sheriff] shall order the [defendant or defender (or defendants or defenders] in such proportions as appears fair and reasonable) to pay to the person bringing the proceedings such amount as the court [or the sheriff] considers reasonably sufficient to compensate him for any expenses properly incurred by him in the proceedings.

(13) If it appears to the magistrates' court [or to the sheriff] that neither the person responsible for the nuisance nor the owner or occupier of the premises [or (as the case may be) the person responsible for the vehicle, machinery or equipment] can be found the court [or the sheriff] may, after giving the local authority in whose area the nuisance has occurred an opportunity of being heard, direct the authority to do anything which the court [or the sheriff] would have ordered that person to do.

84 Termination of Public Health Act controls over offensive trades etc

(1) Where a person carries on, in the area or part of the area of any local authority—
  (a) in England or Wales, a trade which—
    (i) is an offensive trade within the meaning of section 107 of the Public Health Act 1936 in that area or part of that area, and
    (ii) constitutes a prescribed process designated for local control for the carrying on of which an authorisation is required under section 6 of this Act; or
  (b) in Scotland, a business which—
    (i) is mentioned in section 32(1) of the Public Health (Scotland) Act 1897 (or is an offensive business by virtue of that section) in that area or part of that area; and
    (ii) constitutes a prescribed process designated for local control for the carrying on of which an authorisation is required under the said section 6,

subsection (2) below shall have effect in relation to that trade or business as from the date on which an authorisation is granted under section 6 of this Act or, if that person has not applied for such an authorisation within the period allowed under section 2(1) above for making aplications under that section, as from the end of the period.

(2) Where this subsection applies in relation to the trade or business carried on by any person—
  (a) nothing in section 107 of the Public Health Act 1936 or in section 32 of the Public Health (Scotland) Act 1897 shall apply in relation to it, and
  (b) no byelaws or further byelaws made under section 108(2) of the said Act of 1936, or under subsection (2) of the said section 32, with respect to a trade or business of that description shall apply in relation to it;

but without prejudice to the continuance of, and imposition of any penalty in, any proceedings under the said section 107 or the said section 32 which were instituted before the date as from which this subsection has effect in relation to the trade or business.

Appendix B

(3) Subsection (2)(b) above shall apply in relation to the trade of fish frying as it applies in relation to an offensive trade.

(4) When the Secretary of State considers it expedient to do so, having regard to the operation of Part I and the preceding provisions of this Part of this Act in relation to offensive trades or businesses, he may by order repeal—
  (a) sections 107 and 108 of the Public Health Act 1936; and
  (b) section 32 of the Public Health (Scotland) Act 1897;

and different days may be so appointed in relation to trades or businesses which constitute prescribed processes and those which do not.

(5) In this section—
  "prescribed process" has the same meaning as in Part I of this Act; and
  "offensive trade" or "trade" has the same meaning as in section 107 of the Public Health Act 1936.

157 Offences by bodies corporate

(1) Where an offence under any provision of this Act committed by a body corporate is proved to have been committed with the consent or connivance of, or to have been attributable to any neglect on the part of, any director, manager, secretary or other similar officer of the body corporate or a person who was purporting to act in any such capacity, he as well as the body corporate shall be guilty of that offence and shall be liable to be proceeded against and punished accordingly.

(2) Where the affairs of a body corporate are managed by its members, subsection (1) above shall apply in relation to the acts or defaults of a member in connection with his functions of management as if he were a director of the body corporate.

158 Offences under Parts I, II, IV, VI, etc due to fault of others

Where the commission by any person of an offence under Part I, II, IV, or VI, or section 140, 141 or 142 above is due to the act or default of some other person, that other person may be charged with and convicted of the offence by virtue of this section whether or not proceedings for the offence are taken against the first-mentioned person.

159 Application to Crown

(1) Subject to the provisions of this section, the provisions of this Act and of regulations and orders made under it shall bind the Crown.

(2) No contravention by the Crown of any provision of this Act or of any regulations or order made under it shall make the Crown criminally liable; but the High Court or, in Scotland, the Court of Session may, on the application of any public or local authority charged with enforcing that provision, declare unlawful any act or omission of the Crown which constitutes such a contravention.

(3) Notwithstanding anything in subsection (2) above, the provisions of this Act and of regulations and orders made under it shall apply to

Material relating to statutory nuisance

persons in the public service of the Crown as they apply to other persons.

(4) If the Secretary of State certifies that it appears to him, as respects any Crown premises and any powers of entry exercisable in relation to them specified in the certificate that it is requisite or expedient that, in the interests of national security, the powers should not be exercisable in relation to the premises, those powers shall not be exercisable in relation to those premises; and in this subsection "Crown premises" means premises held or used by or on behalf of the Crown.

(5) Nothing in this section shall be taken as in any way affecting Her Majesty in her private capacity; and this subsection shall be construed as if section 38(3) of the Crown Proceedings Act 1947 (interpretation of references in that Act to Her Majesty in her private capacity) were contained in this Act.

(6) References in this section to regulations or orders are references to regulations or orders made by statutory instrument.

(7) For the purposes of this section in its application to Part II and Part IV the authority charged with enforcing the provisions of those Parts in its area is—
- (a) in the case of Part II, any waste regulation authority, and
- (b) in the case of Part IV, any principal litter authority.

160 Service of notices

(1) Any notice required or authorised by or under this Act to be served on or given to an inspector may be served or given by delivering it to him or by leaving it at, or sending it by post to, his office.

(2) Any such notice required or authorised to be served on or given to a person other than an inspector may be served or given by delivering it to him, or by leaving it at his proper address, or by sending it by post to him at that address.

(3) Any such notice may—
- (a) in the case of a body corporate, be served on or given to the secretary or clerk of that body;
- (b) in the case of a partnership, be served on or given to a partner or a person having the control or management of the partnership business.

(4) For the purposes of this section and of section 7 of the Interpretation Act 1978 (service of documents by post) in its application to this section, the proper address of any person on or to whom any such notice is to be served or given shall be his last known address, except that—
- (a) in the case of a body corporate or their secretary or clerk, it shall be the address of the registered or principal office of that body;
- (b) in the case of a partnership or person having the control or the management of the partnership business, it shall be the principal office of the partnership;

and for the purposes of this subsection the principal office of a company registered outside the United Kingdom or of a partnership carrying on business outside the United Kingdom shall be their principal office within the United Kingdom.

Appendix B

(5) If the person to be served with or given any such notice has specified an address in the United Kingdom other than his proper address within the meaning of subsection (4) above as the one at which he or someone on his behalf will accept notices of the same description as that notice, that address shall also be treated for the purposes of this section and section 7 of the Interpretation Act 1978 as his proper address.

(6) The preceding provisions of this section shall apply to the sending or giving of a document as they apply to the giving of a notice.

SCHEDULE 3 STATUTORY NUISANCES: SUPPLEMENTARY PROVISIONS

APPEALS TO MAGISTRATES' COURT

1(1) This paragraph applies in relation to appeals under section 80(3) against an abatement notice to a magistrates' court.

(2) An appeal to which this paragraph applies shall be by way of complaint for an order and the Magistrates' Courts Act 1980 shall apply to the proceedings.

(3) An appeal against any decision of a magistrates' court in pursuance of an appeal to which this paragraph applies shall lie to the Crown Court at the instance of any party to the proceedings in which the decision was given.

(4) The Secretary of State may make regulations as to appeals to which this paragraph applies and the regulations may in particular—
- (a) include provisions comparable to those in section 290 of the Public Health Act 1936 (appeals against notices requiring the execution of works);
- (b) prescribe the cases in which an abatement notice is, or is not, to be suspended until the appeal is decided, or until some other stage in the proceedings;
- (c) prescribe the cases in which the decision on appeal may in some respects be less favourable to the appellant than the decision from which he is appealing;
- (d) prescribe the cases in which the appellant may claim that an abatement notice should have been served on some other person and prescribe the procedure to be followed in those cases.

APPEALS TO SHERIFF

1A(1) This paragraph applies in relation to appeals to the sheriff under section 80(3) against an abatement notice.

(2) An appeal to which this paragraph applies shal be by way of a summary application.

(3) The Secretary of State may make regulations as to appeals to which this paragraph applies and the regulations may in particular include or prescribe any of the matters referred to in sub-paragraphs (4)(a) to (d) of paragraph 1 above.

POWERS OF ENTRY ETC

2(1) Subject to sub-paragraph (2) below, any person authorised by a local authority may, on production (if so required) of his authority, enter any premises at any reasonable time—
   (a) for the purpose of ascertaining whether or not a statutory nuisance exists; or
   (b) for the purpose of taking any action, or executing any work, authorised or required by Part III.

(2) Admission by virtue of sub-paragraph (1) above to any premises used wholly or mainly for residential purposes shall not except in an emergency be demanded as of right unless twenty-four hours notice of the intended entry has been given to the occupier.

(3) If it is shown to the satisfaction of a justice of the peace on sworn information in writing—
   (a) that admission to any premises has been refused, or that refusal is apprehended, or that the premises are unoccupied or the occupier is temporarily absent, or that the case is one of emergency, or that an application for admission would defeat the object of the entry; and
   (b) that there is reasonable ground for entry into the premises for the purpose for which entry is required,

the justice may by warrant under his hand authorise the local authority by any authorised person to enter the premises, if need be by force.

(4) An authorised person entering any premises by virtue of sub-paragraph (1) or a warrant under sub-paragraph (3) above may—
   (a) take with him such other persons and such equipment as may be necessary;
   (b) carry out such inspections, measurements and tests as he considers necesary for the discharge of any of the local authority's functions under Part III; and
   (c) take away such samples or articles as he considers necessary for that purpose.

(5) On leaving any unoccupied premises which hehas entered by virtue of sub-paragraph (1) above or a warrant under sub-paragraph (3) above the authorised person shall leave them as effectually secured against trespassers as he found them.

(6) A warrant issued in pursuance of sub-paragraph (3) above shall continue in force until the purpose for which the entry is required has been satisfied.

(7) Any reference in this paragraph to an emergency is a reference to a case where the person requiring entry has reasonable cause to believe that circumstances exist which are likely to endanger life or health and that immediate entry is necessary to verify the existence of those circumstances or to ascertain their cause and to effect a remedy.

(8) In the application of this paragraph to Scotland, a reference to a justice of the peace or to a justice includes a reference to the sheriff.

Appendix B

2A(1) Any person authorised by a local authority may on production (if so required) of his authority—
- (a) enter or open a vehicle, machinery or equipment, if necessary by force, or
- (b) remove a vehicle, machinery or equipment from a street or, in Scotland, road to a secure place,

for the purpose of taking any action, or executing any work, authorised by or required under Part III in relation to a statutory nuisance within section 79(1)(ga) above caused by noise emitted from or caused by the vehicle, machinery or equipment.

(2) On leaving any unattended vehicle, machinery or equipment that he has entered or opened under sub-paragraph (1) above, the authorised person shall (subject to sub-paragraph (3) below) leave it secured against interference or theft in such manner and as effectually as he found it.

(3) If the authorised person is unable to comply with sub-paragraph (2) above, he shall for the purpose of securing the unattended vehicle, machinery or equipment either—
- (a) immobilise it by such means as he considers expedient, or
- (b) remove it from the street to a secure place.

(4) In carrying out any function under sub-paragraph (1), (2) or (3) above, the authorised person shall not cause more damage than is necessary.

(5) Before a vehicle, machinery or equipment is entered, opened or removed under sub-paragraph (1) above, the local authority shall notify the police of the intention to take action under that sub-paragraph.

(6) After a vehicle, machinery or equipment has been removed under sub-paragraph (1) or (3) above, the local authority shall notify the police of its removal and current location.

(7) Notification under sub-paragraph (5) or (6) above may be given to the police at any police station in the local authority's area or, in the case of the Temples, at any police station of the City of London Police.

(8) For the purposes of section 81(4) above, any expenses reasonably incurred by a local authority under sub-paragraph (2) or (3) above shall be treated as incurred by the authority under section 81(3) above in abating or preventing the recurrence of the statutory nuisance in question.

OFFENCES RELATING TO ENTRY

3(1) A person who wilfully obstructs any person acting in the exercise of any powers conferred by paragraph 2 or 2A above shall be liable, on summary conviction, to a fine not exceeding level 3 on the standard scale.

(2) If a person discloses any information relating to any trade secret obtained in the exercise of any powers conferred by paragraph 2 above he shall, unless the disclosure was made in the performance of his duty or with the consent of the person having the right to disclose the information, be liable, on summary conviction, to a fine not exceeding level 5 on the standard scale.

DEFAULT POWER

4(1) This paragraph applies to the following functions of a local authority, that is to say its duty under section 79 to cause its area to be inspected to detect any statutory nuisance which ought to be dealt with under section 80 or sections 80 and 80A and its powers under paragraph 2 or 2A above.

(2) If the Secretary of State is satisfied that any local authority has failed, in any respect, to discharge the function to which this paragraph applies which it ought to have discharged, he may make an order declaring the authority to be in default.

(3) An order made under sub-paragraph (2) above which declares an authority to be in default may, for the purpose of remedying the default, direct the authority ("the defaulting authority") to perform the function specified in the order and may specifiy the manner in which and the time or times within which the function is to be performed by the authority.

(4) If the defaulting authority fails to comply with any direction contained in such an order the Secretary of State may, instead of enforcing the order by mandamus, make an order transferring to himself the function of the authority specified in the order.

(5) Where the function of a defaulting authority is transferred under sub-paragraph (4) above, the amount of any expenses which the Secretary of State certifies were incurred by him in performing the function shall on demand be paid to him by the defaulting authority.

(6) Any expenses required to be paid by a defaulting authority under sub-paragraph (5) above shall be defrayed by the authority in like manner, and shall be debited to the like account, as if the function had not been transferred and the expenses had been incurred by the authority in performing them.

(7) The Secretary of State may by order vary or revoke any order previously made by him under this paragraph.

(8) Any order under this paragraph may include such incidental, supplemental and transitional provisions as the Secretary of State considers appropriate.

(9) This paragraph does not apply to Scotland.

PROTECTION FROM PERSONAL LIABILITY

5 Nothing done by, or by a member of, a local authority or by an officer of or other person authorised by a local authority shall, if done in good faith for the purpose of executing Part III, subject them or any of them personally to any action, liability, claim or demand whatsoever (other than any liability under section 17 or 18 of the Audit Commission Act 1998 (powers of district auditor and court)).

Appendix B

STATEMENT OF RIGHT OF APPEAL IN NOTICES

6 Where an appeal against a notice served by a local authority lies to a magistrates' court or, in Scotland, the sheriff by virtue of section 80, it shall be the duty of the authority to include in such a notice a statement indicating that such an appeal lies as aforesaid and specifying the time within which it must be brought.

Statutory Nuisance (Appeals) Regulations 1995, SI 1995/2644

[As amended by SI 2006/771 and SI 2007/117.]

1 Citation, commencement and interpretation

(1) These Regulations may be cited as the Statutory Nuisance (Appeals) Regulations 1995 and shall come into force on 8th November 1995.

(2) In these Regulations—
"the 1974 Act" means the Control of Pollution Act 1974;
"the 1990 Act" means the Environmental Protection Act 1990; and
"the 1993 Act" means the Noise and Statutory Nuisance Act 1993.

2 Appeals under section 80(3) of the 1990 Act

(1) The provisions of this regulation apply in relation to an appeal brought by any person under section 80(3) of the 1990 Act (appeals to magistrates) against an abatement notice served upon him by a local authority.

(2) The grounds on which a person served with such a notice may appeal under section 80(3) are any one or more of the following grounds that are appropriate in the circumstances of the particular case—
  (a) that the abatement notice is not justified by section 80 of the 1990 Act (summary proceedings for statutory nuisances);
  (b) that there has been some informality, defect or error in, or in connection with, the abatement notice, or in, or in connection with, any copy of the abatement notice served under section 80A(3)(certain notices in respect of vehicles, machinery or equipment);
  (c) that the authority have refused unreasonably to accept compliance with alternative requirements, or that the requirements of the abatement notice are otherwise unreasonable in character or extent, or are unnecessary;
  (d) that the time, or where more than one time is specified, any of the times, within which the requirements of the abatement notice are to be complied with is not reasonably sufficient for the purpose;
  (e) where the nuisance to which the notice relates—
    (i) is a nuisance falling within section 79(1)(a),(d),(e),(f), (fa) or (g) of the 1990 Act and arises on industrial, trade, or business premises, or
    (ii) is a nuisance falling within section 79(1)(b) of the 1990 Act and the smoke is emitted from a chimney, or
    (iii) is a nuisance falling within section 79(1)(ga) of the 1990 Act and is noise emitted from or caused by a vehicle, machinery

or equipment being used for industrial, trade or business purposes, or
(iv) is a nuisance falling within section 79(1)(fb) of the 1990 Act and—
(aa) the artificial light is emitted from industrial, trade or business premises, or
(bb) the artificial light (not being light to which sub-paragraph (aa) applies) is emitted by lights used for the purpose only of illuminating an outdoor relevant sports facility (within the meaning given by section 80(8A) of the 1990 Act),

that the best practicable means were used to prevent, or to counteract the effects of, the nuisance;

(f) that, in the case of a nuisance under section 79(1)(g) or (ga) of the 1990 Act (noise emitted from premises), the requirements imposed by the abatement notice by virtue of section 80(1)(a) of the Act are more onerous than the requirements for the time being in force, in relation to the noise to which the notice relates, of—
 (i) any notice served under section 60 or 66 of the 1974 Act (control of noise on construction sites and from certain premises), or
 (ii) any consent given under section 61 or 65 of the 1974 Act (consent for work on construction sites and consent for noise to exceed registered level in a noise abatement zone), or
 (iii) any determination made under section 67 of the 1974 Act (noise control of new buildings);

(g) that, in the case of a nuisance under section 79(1)(ga) of the 1990 Act (noise emitted from or caused by vehicles, machinery or equipment), the requirements imposed by the abatement notice by virtue of section 80(1)(a) of the Act are more onerous than the requirements for the time being in force, in relation to the noise to which the notice relates, of any condition of a consent given under paragraph 1 of Schedule 2 to the 1993 Act (loudspeakers in streets or roads);

(h) that the abatement notice should have been served on some person instead of the appellant, being—
 (i) the person responsible for the nuisance, or
 (ii) the person responsible for the vehicle, machinery or equipment, or
 (iii) in the case of a nuisance arising from any defect of a structural character, the owner of the premises, or
 (iv) in the case where the person responsible for the nuisance cannot be found or the nuisance has not yet occurred, the owner or occupier of the premises;

(i) that the abatement notice might lawfully have been served on some person instead of the appellant being—
 (i) in the case where the appellant is the owner of the premises, the occupier of the premises, or
 (ii) in the case where the appellant is the occupier of the premises, the owner of the premises,

and that it would have been equitable for it to have been so served;

Appendix B

  (j) that the abatement notice might lawfully have been served on some person in addition to the appellant, being—
   (i) a person also responsible for the nuisance, or
   (ii) a person who is also owner of the premises, or
   (iii) a person who is also an occupier of the premises, or
   (iv) a person who is also the person responsible for the vehicle, machinery or equipment,
and that it would have been equitable for it to have been so served.

(3) If and so far as an appeal is based on the ground of some informality, defect or error in, or in connection with, the abatement notice, or in, or in connection with, any copy of the notice served under section 80A(3), the court shall dismiss the appeal if it is satisfied that the informality, defect or error was not a material one.

(4) Where the grounds upon which an appeal is brought include a ground specified in paragraph (2)(i) or (j) above, the appellant shall serve a copy of his notice of appeal on any other person referred to, and in the case of any appeal to which these regulations apply he may serve a copy of his notice of appeal on any other person having an estate or interest in the premises, vehicle, machinery or equipment in question.

(5) On the hearing of the appeal the court may—
  (a) quash the abatement notice to which the appeal relates, or
  (b) vary the abatement notice in favour of the appellant in such manner as it thinks fit, or
  (c) dismiss the appeal;

and an abatement notice that is varied under sub-paragraph (b) above shall be final and shall otherwise have effect, as so varied, as if it had been so made by the local authority.

(6) Subject to paragraph (7) below, on the hearing of an appeal the court may make such order as it thinks fit—
  (a) with respect to the person by whom any work is to be executed and the contribution to be made by any person towards the cost of the work, or
  (b) as to the proportions in which any expenses which may become recoverable by the authority under Part III of the 1990 Act are to be borne by the appellant and by any other person.

(7) In exercising its powers under paragraph (6) above the court—
  (a) shall have regard, as between an owner and an occupier, to the terms and conditions, whether contractual or statutory, of any relevant tenancy and to the nature of the works required, and
  (b) shall be satisfied before it imposes any requirement thereunder on any person other than the appellant, that that person has received a copy of the notice of appeal in pursuance of paragraph (4) above.

3 Suspension of notice

(1) Where—
  (a) an appeal is brought against an abatement notice served under section 80 or section 80A of the 1990 Act, and—
  (b) either—

(i) compliance with the abatement notice would involve any person in expenditure on the carrying out of works before the hearing of the appeal, or
(ii) in the case of a nuisance under section 79(1)(g) or (ga) of the 1990 Act, the noise to which the abatement notice relates is noise necessarily caused in the course of the performance of some duty imposed by law on the appellant, and
(c) either paragraph (2) does not apply, or it does apply but the requirements of paragraph (3) have not been met,

the abatement notice shall be suspended until the appeal has been abandoned or decided by the court.

(2) This paragraph applies where—
(a) the nuisance to which the abatement notice relates—
(i) is injurious to health, or
(ii) is likely to be of a limited duration such that suspension of the notice would render it of no practical effect, or
(b) the expenditure which would be incurred by any person in the carrying out of works in compliance with the abatement notice before any appeal has been decided would not be disproportionate to the public benefit to be expected in that period from such compliance.

(3) Where paragraph (2) applies the abatement notice—
(a) shall include a statement that paragraph (2) applies, and that as a consequence it shall have effect notwithstanding any appeal to a magistrates' court which has not been decided by the court, and
(b) shall include a statement as to which of the grounds set out in paragraph (2) apply.

4 Revocations

. . .

Clean Air Act 1993

64 General provisions as to interpretation

(1) In this Act, except so far as the context otherwise requires,—

"authorised officer" means any officer of a local authority authorised by them in writing, either generally or specially, to act in matters of any specified kind or in any specified matter;

"building regulations" means, as respects Scotland, any statutory enactments, byelaws, rules and regulations or other provisions under whatever authority made, relating to the construction, alteration or extension of buildings;

"caravan" means a caravan within the meaning of Part I of the Caravan Sites and Control of Development Act 1960, disregarding the amendment made by section 13(2) of the Caravan Sites Act 1968, which usually and for the time being is situated on a caravan site within the meaning of that Act;

"chimney" includes structures and openings of any kind from or through which smoke, grit, dust or fumes may be emitted, and, in particular, includes flues, and references to a chimney of a building include

Appendix B

references to a chimney which serves the whole or a part of a building but is structurally separate from the building;

"dark smoke" has the meaning given by section 3(1);

"day" means a period of twenty-four hours beginning at midnight;

"domestic furnace" means any furnace which is—
   (a) designed solely or mainly for domestic purposes, and
   (b) used for heating a boiler with a maximum heating capacity of less than 16.12 kilowatts;

"fireplace" includes any furnace, grate or stove, whether open or closed;

"fixed boiler or industrial plant" means any boiler or industrial plant which is attached to a building or is for the time being fixed to or installed on any land;

"fumes" means any airborne solid matter smaller than dust;

"industrial plant" includes any still, melting pot or other plant used for any industrial or trade purposes, and also any incinerator used for or in connection with any such purposes;

"local authority" means—
   (a) in England . . ., the council of a district or a London borough, the Common Council of the City of London, the Sub-Treasurer of the Inner Temple and the Under Treasurer of the Middle Temple;
   (aa) in Wales, the council of a county or county borough;
   (b) in Scotland, a council constituted under section 2 of the Local Government etc (Scotland) Act 1994;

"owner", in relation to premises—
   (a) as respects England and Wales, means the person for the time being receiving the rackrent of the premises, whether on his own account or as agent or trustee for another person, or who would so receive the rackrent if the premises were let at a rackrent; and
   (b) as respects Scotland, means the person for the time being entitled to receive or who would, if the premises were let, be entitled to receive, the rents of the premises and includes a trustee, factor, or person entitled to act as the legal representative of a person under disability by reason of nonage or mental or other incapacity and, in the case of public or municipal property, includes the persons to whom the management of the property is entrusted;

"port health authority" means, as respects Scotland, a port local authority constituted under Part X of the Public Health (Scotland) Act 1897 and includes a reference to a joint port health authority constituted under that Part;

"practicable" means reasonably practicable having regard, amongst other things, to local conditions and circumstances, to the financial implications and to the current state of technical knowledge, and "practicable means" includes the provision and maintenance of plant and its proper use;

"premises" includes land;

"smoke" includes soot, ash, grit and gritty particles emitted in smoke; and

"vessel" has the same meaning as "ship" in the Merchant Shipping Act 1995.

(2) Any reference in this Act to the occupier of a building shall, in relation to any building different parts of which are occupied by different persons, be read as a reference to the occupier or other person in control of the part of the building in which the relevant fireplace is situated.

(3) In this Act any reference to the rate of emission of any substance or any reference which is to be understood as such a reference shall, in relation to any regulations or conditions, be construed as a reference to the quantities of that substance which may be emitted during a period specified in the regulations or conditions.

(4) In this Act, except so far as the context otherwise requires,"private dwelling" means any building or part of a building used or intended to be used as such, and a building or part of a building is not to be taken for the purposes of this Act to be used or intended to be used otherwise than as a private dwelling by reason that a person who resides or is to reside in it is or is to be required or permitted to reside in it in consequence of his employment or of holding an office.

(5) In considering for the purposes of this Act whether any and, if so, what works are reasonably necessary in order to make suitable provision for heating and cooking in the case of a dwelling or are reasonably necessary in order to enable a building to be used for a purpose without contravention of any of the provisions of this Act, regard shall be had to any difficulty there may be in obtaining, or in obtaining otherwise than at a high price, any fuels which would have to be used but for the execution of the works.

(6) Any furnaces which are in the occupation of the same person and are served by a single chimney shall, for the purposes of sections 5 to 12, 14 and 15, be taken to be one furnace.

Control of Pollution Act 1974

60 Control of noise on construction sites

(1) This section applies to works of the following description, that is to say—
- (a) the erection, construction, alteration, repair or maintenance of buildings, structures or roads;
- (b) breaking up, opening or boring under any road or adjacent land in connection with the construction, inspection, maintenance or removal of works;
- (c) demolition or dredging work; and
- (d) (whether or not also comprised in paragraph (a), (b) or (c) above) any work of engineering construction.

(2) Where it appears to a local authority that works to which this section applies are being, or are going to be, carried out on any premises, the local authority may serve a notice imposing requirements as to the way in which the works are to be carried out and may if it thinks fit publish notice of the requirements in such way as appears to the local authority to be appropriate.

(3) The notice may in particular—
- (a) specify the plant or machinery which is or is not to be used;
- (b) specify the hours during which the works may be carried out;

Appendix B

    (c) specify the level of noise which may be emitted from the premises in question or at any specified point on those premises or which may be so emitted during specified hours; and
    (d) provide for any change of circumstances.

(4) In acting under this section the local authority shall have regard—
    (a) to the relevant provisions of any code of practice issued under this Part of this Act;
    (b) to the need for ensuring that the best practicable means are employed to minimise noise;
    (c) before specifying any particular methods or plant or machinery, to the desirability in the interests of any recipients of the notice in question of specifying other methods or plant or machinery which would be substantially as effective in minimising noise and more acceptable to them;
    (d) to the need to protect any persons in the locality in which the premises in question are situated from the effects of noise.

(5) A notice under this section shall be served on the person who appears to the local authority to be carrying out, or going to carry out, the works, and on such other persons appearing to the local authority to be responsible for, or to have control over, the carrying out of the works as the local authority thinks fit.

(6) A notice under this section may specify the time within which the notice is to be complied with, and may require the execution of such works, and the taking of such other steps, as may be necessary for the purpose of the notice, or as may be specified in the notice.

(7) A person served with a notice under this section may appeal against the notice to a magistrates' court within twenty-one days from the service of the notice.

(8) If a person on whom a notice is served under this section without reasonable excuse contravenes any requirement of the notice he shall be guilty of an offence against this Part of this Act.

61 Prior consent for work on construction sites

(1) A person who intends to carry out works to which the preceding section applies may apply to the local authority for a consent under this section.

(2) Where approval under building regulations . . . , or in Scotland a building warrant under section 9 of the Building (Scotland) Act 2003 (asp 8), is required for the carrying out of the works, the application under this section must be made at the same time as, or later than, the request for the approval under building regulations or, as the case may be, the application for a building warrant under the said Act of 2003.

(3) An application under this section shall contain particulars of—
    (a) the works, and the method by which they are to be carried out; and
    (b) the steps proposed to be taken to minimise noise resulting from the works.

(4) If the local authority considers that the application contains sufficient information for the purpose and that, if the works are carried out in accordance with the application, it would not serve a notice under the

preceding section in respect of those works, the local authority shall give its consent to the application.

(5) In acting under this section a local authority shall have regard to the considerations set out in subsection (4) of the preceding section and shall have power to—
  (a) attach any conditions to a consent; and
  (b) limit or qualify a consent to allow for any change in circumstances; and
  (c) limit the duration of a consent;

and any person who knowingly carries out the works, or permits the works to be carried out, in contravention of any conditions attached to a consent under this section shall be guilty of an offence against this Part of this Act.

(6) The local authority shall inform the applicant of its decision on the application within twenty-eight days from receipt of the application; and if the local authority gives its consent to the application it may if it thinks fit publish notice of the consent, and of the works to which it relates, in such way as appears to the local authority to be appropriate.

(7) If—
  (a) the local authority does not give a consent within the said period of twenty-eight days; or
  (b) the local authority gives its consent within the said period of twenty-eight days but attaches any condition to the consent or limits or qualifies the consent in any way,

the applicant may appeal to a magistrates' court within twenty-one days from the end of that period.

(8) In any proceedings for an offence under section 60(8) of this Act it shall be a defence to prove that the alleged contravention amounted to the carrying out of the works in accordance with a consent given under this section.

(9) A consent given under this section shall contain a statement to the effect that the consent does not of itself constitute any ground of defence against any proceedings instituted under . . . . . . section 82 of the Environmental Protection Act 1990 . . ..

(10) Where a consent has been given under this section and the works are carried out by a person other than the applicant for the consent, it shall be the duty of the applicant to take all reasonable steps to bring the consent to the notice of that other person; and if he fails to comply with this subsection he shall be guilty of an offence against this Part of this Act.

66 Reduction of noise levels

(1) If it appears to the local authority—
  (a) that the level of noise emanating from any premises to which a noise abatement order applies is not acceptable having regard to the purposes for which the order was made; and
  (b) that a reduction in that level is practicable at reasonable cost and would afford a public benefit,

the local authority may serve a notice on the person responsible.

(2) The notice shall require that person—
   (a) to reduce the level of noise emanating from the premises to such level as may be specified in the notice;
   (b) to prevent any subsequent increase in the level of noise emanating from those premises without the consent of the local authority; and
   (c) to take such steps as may be specified in the notice to achieve those purposes.

(3) A notice under this section (in this Part of this Act referred to as a "noise reduction notice") shall specify a time, not being less than six months from the date of service of the notice, within which the noise level is to be reduced to the specified level and, where the notice specifies any steps necessary to achieve that purpose, within which those steps shall be taken.

(4) A noise reduction notice may specify particular times, or particular days, during which the noise level is to be reduced, and may require the noise level to be reduced to different levels for different times or days.

(5) A notice under this section shall take effect whether or not a consent under the preceding section authorises a level of noise higher than that specified in the notice.

(6) The local authority shall record particulars of a noise reduction notice in the noise level register.

(7) A person who is served with a noise reduction notice may, within three months of the date of service, appeal to a magistrates' court against the notice.

(8) A person who without reasonable excuse contravenes a noise reduction notice shall be guilty of an offence against this Part of this Act.

(9) In proceedings for an offence under the preceding subsection in respect of noise caused in the course of a trade or business, it shall be a defence to prove that the best practicable means had been used for preventing, or for counteracting the effect of, the noise.

67 New buildings, etc

(1) Where it appears to the local authority—
   (a) that a building is going to be constructed and that a noise abatement order will apply to it when it is erected; or
   (b) that any premises will, as the result of any works, become premises to which a noise abatement order applies,

the local authority may, on the application of the owner or occupier of the premises or a person who satisfies the authority that he is negotiating to acquire an interest in the premises or on its own initiative, determine the level of noise which will be acceptable as that emanating from the premises.

(2) The local authority shall record in the noise level register the level of noise determined under this section for any premises.

(3) The local authority shall give notice of its intention to the applicant or, in the case of a decision made on its own initiative, to the owner or the occupier of the premises, and the recipient of the notice may appeal

Material relating to statutory nuisance

to the Secretary of State against that decision within three months of the date on which the local authority notifies him of that decision; and it shall be the duty of the local authority to act in accordance with the decision of the Secretary of State on the appeal.

(4) If within the period of two months beginning with the date when the local authority receives an application in pursuance of subsection (1) of this section, the authority has not given notice to the applicant of its decision on the application, the authority shall be deemed to have given him notice on the expiration of that period that it has decided not to make a determination in pursuance of the application; and the applicant may accordingly appeal against the decision to the Secretary of State in pursuance of the preceding subsection.

(5) Where at any time after the coming into force of a noise abatement order any premises become premises to which the order applies as a result of the construction of a building or as a result of any works carried out on the premises but no level of noise has been determined under this section as respects the premises, section 66 of this Act shall apply as if—
  (a) paragraph (b) of subsection (1) were omitted; and
  (b) three months were substituted for six months in subsection (3); and
  (c) subsection (9) were omitted.

Noise Act 1996

SUMMARY PROCEDURE FOR DEALING WITH NOISE AT NIGHT

1 Application of sections 2 to 9

Sections 2 to 9 apply to the area of every local authority in England and Wales.

2 Investigation of complaints of noise at night

(1) A local authority in England and Wales may, if they receive a complaint of the kind mentioned in subsection (2), arrange for an officer of the authority to take reasonable steps to investigate the complaint.

(2) The kind of complaint referred to is one made by any individual present in a dwelling during night hours (referred to in this Act as "the complainant's dwelling") that excessive noise is being emitted from—
  (a) another dwelling (referred to in this group of sections as "the offending dwelling"), or
  (b) any premises in respect of which a premises licence or a temporary event notice has effect (referred to in this group of sections as "the offending premises").

(3) A complaint under subsection (2) may be made by any means.

(4) If an officer of the authority is satisfied, in consequence of an investigation under subsection (1), that—
  (a) noise is being emitted from the offending dwelling or the offending premises during night hours, and

Appendix B

(b) the noise, if it were measured from within the complainant's dwelling, would or might exceed the permitted level,

he may serve a notice about the noise under section 3.

(5) For the purposes of subsection (4), it is for the officer of the authority dealing with the particular case—
- (a) to decide whether any noise, if it were measured from within the complainant's dwelling, would or might exceed the permitted level, and
- (b) for the purposes of that decision, to decide whether to assess the noise from within or outside the complainant's dwelling and whether or not to use any device for measuring the noise.

(6) In this group of sections, "night hours" means the period beginning with 11 pm and ending with the following 7 am.

(7) Where a local authority receive a complaint under subsection (2) and the offending dwelling is, or the offending premises are, within the area of another local authority, the first local authority may act under this group of sections as if the offending dwelling or the offending premises were within their area.

(7A) In this group of sections—
"premises licence" has the same meaning as in the Licensing Act 2003 (c 17);
"temporary event notice" has the same meaning as in the Licensing Act 2003 (and is to be treated as having effect in accordance with section 171(6) of that Act).

(8) In this section and sections 3 to 9, "this group of sections" means this and those sections.

3 Warning notices

(1) A notice under this section (referred to in this Act as "a warning notice") must—
- (a) state that an officer of the authority considers—
  - (i) that noise is being emitted from the offending dwelling or the offending premises during night hours, and
  - (ii) that the noise exceeds, or may exceed, the permitted level, as measured from within the complainant's dwelling, and
- (b) give warning—
  - (i) in a case where the complaint is in respect of a dwelling, that any person who is responsible for noise which is emitted from the offending dwelling in the period specified in the notice and which exceeds the permitted level, as measured from within the complainant's dwelling, may be guilty of an offence;
  - (ii) in a case where the complaint is in respect of other premises, that the responsible person in relation to the offending premises may be guilty of an offence if noise which exceeds the permitted level, as measured from within the complainant's dwelling, is emitted from the premises in the period specified in the notice.

Material relating to statutory nuisance

(2) The period specified in a warning notice must be a period—
   (a) beginning not earlier than ten minutes after the time when the notice is served, and
   (b) ending with the following 7 am.

(3) In a case where the complaint is in respect of a dwelling, a warning notice must be served—
   (a) by delivering it to any person present at or near the offending dwelling and appearing to the officer of the authority to be responsible for the noise, or
   (b) if it is not reasonably practicable to identify any person present at or near the dwelling as being a person responsible for the noise on whom the notice may reasonably be served, by leaving it at the offending dwelling.

(3A) In a case where the complaint is in respect of other premises, a warning notice must be served by delivering it to the person who appears to the officer of the authority to be the responsible person in relation to the offending premises at the time the notice is delivered.

(4) A warning notice must state the time at which it is served.

(5) For the purposes of this group of sections, a person is responsible for noise emitted from a dwelling if he is a person to whose act, default or sufferance the emission of the noise is wholly or partly attributable.

(6) For the purposes of this group of sections, the responsible person in relation to premises at a particular time is—
   (a) where a premises licence has effect in respect of the premises—
      (i) the person who holds the premises licence if he is present at the premises at that time,
      (ii) where that person is not present at the premises at that time, the designated premises supervisor under the licence if he is present at the premises at that time, or
      (iii) where neither of the persons mentioned in sub-paragraphs (i) and (ii) is present at the premises at that time, any other person present at the premises at that time who is in charge of the premises;
   (b) where a temporary event notice has effect in respect of the premises—
      (i) the premises user in relation to that notice if he is present at the premises at that time, or
      (ii) where the premises user is not present at the premises at that time, any other person present at the premises at that time who is in charge of the premises.

4 Offence where noise from a dwelling exceeds permitted level after service of notice

(1) If a warning notice has been served in respect of noise emitted from a dwelling, any person who is responsible for noise which—
   (a) is emitted from the dwelling in the period specified in the notice, and
   (b) exceeds the permitted level, as measured from within the complainant's dwelling,

is guilty of an offence.

Appendix B

(2) It is a defence for a person charged with an offence under this section to show that there was a reasonable excuse for the act, default or sufferance in question.

(3) A person guilty of an offence under this section is liable on summary conviction to a fine not exceeding level 5 on the standard scale.

4A Offence where noise from other premises exceeds permitted level after service of notice
- (1) If—
  - (a) a warning notice has been served under section 3 in respect of noise emitted from premises,
  - (b) noise is emitted from the premises in the period specified in the notice, and
  - (c) the noise exceeds the permitted level, as measured from within the complainant's dwelling,

  the responsible person in relation to the offending premises at the time at which the noise referred to in paragraph (c) is emitted is guilty of an offence.
- (2) A person guilty of an offence under this section is liable on summary conviction to a fine not exceeding level 5 on the standard scale.

5 Permitted level of noise

(1) For the purposes of this group of sections, the appropriate person may by directions in writing determine the maximum level of noise (referred to in this group of sections as "the permitted level") which may be emitted during night hours from any dwelling or other premises.

(2) The permitted level is to be a level applicable to noise as measured from within any other dwelling in the vicinity by an approved device used in accordance with any conditions subject to which the approval was given.

(3) Different permitted levels may be determined for different circumstances, and the permitted level may be determined partly by reference to other levels of noise.

(4) The appropriate person may from time to time vary his directions under this section by further directions in writing.

6 Approval of measuring devices

(1) For the purposes of this group of sections, the appropriate person may approve in writing any type of device used for the measurement of noise; and references in this group of sections to approved devices are to devices of a type so approved.

(2) Any such approval may be given subject to conditions as to the purposes for which, and the manner and other circumstances in which, devices of the type concerned are to be used.

(3) In proceedings for an offence under section 4 or 4A, a measurement of noise made by a device is not admissible as evidence of the level of noise unless it is an approved device and any conditions subject to which the approval was given are satisfied.

Material relating to statutory nuisance

7 Evidence

(1) In proceedings for an offence under section 4 or 4A, evidence—
 (a) of a measurement of noise made by a device, or of the circumstances in which it was made, or
 (b) that a device was of a type approved for the purposes of section 6, or that any conditions subject to which the approval was given were satisfied,

may be given by the production of a document mentioned in subsection (2).

(2) The document referred to is one which is signed by an officer of the local authority and which (as the case may be)—
 (a) gives particulars of the measurement or of the circumstances in which it was made, or
 (b) states that the device was of such a type or that, to the best of the knowledge and belief of the person making the statement, all such conditions were satisfied;

and if the document contains evidence of a measurement of noise it may consist partly of a record of the measurement produced automatically by a device.

(3) In proceedings for an offence under section 4, evidence that noise, or noise of any kind, measured by a device at any time was noise emitted from a dwelling may be given by the production of a document—
 (a) signed by an officer of the local authority, and
 (b) stating that he had identified that dwelling as the source at that time of the noise or, as the case may be, the noise of that kind.

(3A) In proceedings for an offence under section 4A, evidence that noise, or noise of any kind, measured by a device at any time was noise emitted from any other premises may be given by the production of a document—
 (a) signed by an officer of the local authority, and
 (b) stating that he had identified those premises as the source at that time of the noise or, as the case may be, noise of that kind.

(4) For the purposes of this section, a document purporting to be signed as mentioned in subsection (2), (3)(a) or (3A)(a) is to be treated as being so signed unless the contrary is proved.

(5) This section does not make a document admissible as evidence in proceedings for an offence unless a copy of it has, not less than seven days before the hearing or trial, been served on the person charged with the offence.

(6) This section does not make a document admissible as evidence of anything other than the matters shown on a record produced automatically by a device if, not less than three days before the hearing or trial or within such further time as the court may in special circumstances allow, the person charged with the offence serves a notice on the prosecutor requiring attendance at the hearing or trial of the person who signed the document.

8 Fixed penalty notices

(1) Where an officer of a local authority who is authorised for the purposes of this section has reason to believe that a person is

Appendix B

committing or has just committed an offence under section 4 or 4A, he may give that person a notice (referred to in this Act as a "fixed penalty notice") offering him the opportunity of discharging any liability to conviction for that offence by payment of a fixed penalty.

(2) A fixed penalty notice may be given to a person—
 (a) by delivering the notice to him, or
 (b) if it is not reasonably practicable to deliver it to him, by leaving the notice, addressed to him, at the offending dwelling or the offending premises (as the case may be).

(3) Where a person is given a fixed penalty notice in respect of such an offence—
 (a) proceedings for that offence must not be instituted before the end of the period of fourteen days following the date of the notice, and
 (b) he cannot be convicted of that offence if he pays the fixed penalty before the end of that period.

(4) A fixed penalty notice must give such particulars of the circumstances alleged to constitute the offence as are necessary for giving reasonable information of the offence.

(5) A fixed penalty notice must state—
 (a) the period during which, because of subsection (3)(a), proceedings will not be taken for the offence,
 (b) the amount of the fixed penalty, and
 (c) the person to whom and the address at which the fixed penalty may be paid.

(6) Payment of the fixed penalty may (among other methods) be made by pre-paying and posting to that person at that address a letter containing the amount of the penalty (in cash or otherwise).

(7) Where a letter containing the amount of the penalty is sent in accordance with subsection (6), payment is to be regarded as having been made at the time at which that letter would be delivered in the ordinary course of post.

8A Amount of fixed penalty

(1) This section applies in relation to a fixed penalty payable to a local authority in pursuance of a notice under section 8.

(2) In the case of an offence under section 4 the amount of the fixed penalty—
 (a) is the amount specified by the local authority in relation to the authority's area, or
 (b) if no amount is so specified, is £100.

(2A) In the case of an offence under section 4A the amount of the fixed penalty is £500.

(3) The local authority may make provision for treating the fixed penalty as having been paid if a lesser amount is paid before the end of a period specified by the authority.

Material relating to statutory nuisance

(4) The appropriate person may by regulations make provision in connection with the powers conferred on local authorities under subsections (2)(a) and (3).

(5) Regulations under subsection (4) may (in particular)—
   (a) require an amount specified under subsection (2)(a) to fall within a range prescribed in the regulations;
   (b) restrict the extent to which, and the circumstances in which, a local authority can make provision under subsection (3).

(6) The appropriate person may by order substitute a different amount for the amount for the time being specified in subsection (2)(b) or 2A.

8B Fixed penalty notices: power to require name and address

(1) If an officer of a local authority who is authorised for the purposes of section 8 proposes to give a person a fixed penalty notice, the officer may require the person to give him his name and address.

(2) A person commits an offence if—
   (a) he fails to give his name and address when required to do so under subsection (1), or
   (b) he gives a false or inaccurate name or address in response to a requirement under that subsection.

(3) A person guilty of an offence under subsection (2) is liable on summary conviction to a fine not exceeding level 3 on the standard scale.

9 Section 8: supplementary

(1) If a form for a fixed penalty notice is specified in an order made by the appropriate person, a fixed penalty notice must be in that form.

(2) If a fixed penalty notice is given to a person in respect of noise emitted from a dwelling in any period specified in a warning notice—
   (a) no further fixed penalty notice may be given to that person in respect of noise emitted from the dwelling during that period, but
   (b) that person may be convicted of a further offence under section 4 in respect of noise emitted from the dwelling after the fixed penalty notice is given and before the end of that period.

(2A) If a fixed penalty notice is given to a person in respect of noise emitted from other premises in any period in a warning notice—
   (a) no further fixed penalty notice may be given to that person in respect of noise emitted from the premises during that period, but
   (b) that person may be convicted of a further offence under section 4A in respect of noise emitted from the premises after the fixed penalty notice is given and before the end of that period.

(3) *Repealed by the Clean Neighbourhoods and Environment Act 2005, Schedule 5, Part 7.*

(3A) The Secretary of State may, when making an order under subsection (3) above, substitute different penalties as regards enforcement action zones designated under section 29 (enforcement action zones) of the London Local Authorities Act 2007 (c. ii).

(4) A local authority may use any sums it receives under section 8 (its "penalty receipts") only for the purpose of functions of its that are qualifying functions.

Appendix B

(4A) The following are qualifying functions for the purposes of this section—
- (a) functions under this Act,
- (aa) functions under Chapter 1 of Part 7 of the Clean Neighbourhoods and Environment Act 2005;
- (ab) functions under sections 79 to 82 of the Environmental Protection Act 1990 (statutory nuisances) in connection with statutory nuisances falling with section 79(1)(g) or (ga) (noise) of that Act;
- (b) functions of a description specified in regulations made by the appropriate person.

(4B) Regulations under subsection (4A)(b) may (in particular) have the effect that a local authority may use its penalty receipts for the purposes of any of its functions.

(4C) A local authority must supply the appropriate person with such information relating to the use of its penalty receipts as the Secretary of State may require.

(4D) The appropriate person may by regulations—
- (a) make provision for what a local authority is to do with its penalty receipts—
  - (i) pending their being used for the purposes of qualifying functions of the authority;
  - (ii) if they are not so used before such time after their receipt as may be specified by the regulations;
- (b) make provision for accounting arrangements in respect of a local authority's penalty receipts.

(4E) The provision that may be made under subsection (4D)(a)(ii) includes (in particular) provision for the payment of sums to a person (including the appropriate person) other than the local authority.

(4F) Before making regulations under this section, the appropriate person must consult—
- (a) the local authorities to which the regulations are to apply, and
- (b) such other persons as the appropriate person considers appropriate.

(4G) The powers to make regulations conferred by this section are, for the purposes of subsection (1) of section 100 of the Local Government Act 2003, to be regarded as included among the powers mentioned in subsection (2) of that section.

(4H) Regulations under this section relating to local authorities in England may—
- (a) make provision in relation to—
  - (i) all local authorities,
  - (ii) particular local authorities, or
  - (iii) particular descriptions of local authority;
- (b) make different provision in relation to different local authorities or descriptions of local authority.

(5) In proceedings for an offence under section 4 or 4A, evidence that payment of a fixed penalty was or was not made before the end of any period may be given by the production of a certificate which—
- (a) purports to be signed by or on behalf of the person having responsibility for the financial affairs of the local authority, and

Material relating to statutory nuisance

(b) states that payment of a fixed penalty was made on any date or, as the case may be, was not received before the end of that period.

SEIZURE, ETC OF EQUIPMENT USED TO MAKE NOISE UNLAWFULLY

10 Powers of entry and seizure etc

(1) The power conferred by subsection (2) may be exercised where an officer of a local authority has reason to believe that—
   (a) a warning notice has been served in respect of noise emitted from a dwelling or other premises, and
   (b) at any time in the period specified in the notice, noise emitted from the dwelling or other premises has exceeded the permitted level, as measured from within the complainant's dwelling.

(2) An officer of the local authority, or a person authorised by the authority for the purpose, may enter the dwelling or other premises from which the noise in question is being or has been emitted and may seize and remove any equipment which it appears to him is being or has been used in the emission of the noise.

(3) A person exercising the power conferred by subsection (2) must produce his authority, if he is required to do so.

(4) If it is shown to a justice of the peace on sworn information in writing that—
   (a) a warning notice has been served in respect of noise emitted from a dwelling or other premises,
   (b) at any time in the period specified in the notice, noise emitted from the dwelling or other premises has exceeded the permitted level, as measured from within the complainant's dwelling, and
   (c) entry of an officer of the local authority, or of a person authorised by the authority for the purpose, to the dwelling or other premises has been refused, or such a refusal is apprehended, or a request by an officer of the authority, or of such a person, for admission would defeat the object of the entry,

the justice may by warrant under his hand authorise the local authority, by any of their officers or any person authorised by them for the purpose, to enter the dwelling or other premises, if need be by force.

(5) A person who enters any dwelling or other premises under subsection (2), or by virtue of a warrant issued under subsection (4), may take with him such other persons and such equipment as may be necessary; and if, when he leaves, the dwelling is, or the premises are, unoccupied, must leave it or them as effectively secured against trespassers as he found it or them.

(6) A warrant issued under subsection (4) continues in force until the purpose for which the entry is required has been satisfied.

(7) The power of a local authority under section 81(3) of the Environmental Protection Act 1990 to abate any matter, where that matter is a statutory nuisance by virtue of section 79(1)(g) of that Act (noise emitted from premises so as to be prejudicial to health or a

Appendix B

nuisance), includes power to seize and remove any equipment which it appears to the authority is being or has been used in the emission of the noise in question.

(8) A person who wilfully obstructs any person exercising any powers conferred under subsection (2) or by virtue of subsection (7) is liable, on summary conviction, to a fine not exceeding level 3 on the standard scale.

(9) The Schedule to this Act (which makes further provision in relation to anything seized and removed by virtue of this section) has effect.

GENERAL

11 Interpretation and subordinate legislation

(1) In this Act, "local authority" means—
   (a) in Greater London, a London borough council, the Common Council of the City of London and, as respects the Temples, the Sub-Treasurer of the Inner Temple and the Under-Treasurer of the Middle Temple respectively,
   (b) outside Greater London—
      (i) any district council,
      (ii) the council of any county so far as they are the council for any area for which there are no district councils,
      (iii) in Wales, the council of a county borough, and
   (c) the Council of the Isles of Scilly.

(2) In this Act—
   (a) "dwelling" means any building, or part of a building, used or intended to be used as a dwelling,
   (b) references to noise emitted from a dwelling include noise emitted from any garden, yard, outhouse or other appurtenance belonging to or enjoyed with the dwelling.

(2A) In this Act "appropriate person" means—
   (a) the Secretary of State, in relation to England;
   (b) the National Assembly for Wales, in relation to Wales.

(3) The power to make an order or regulations under this Act is exercisable by statutory instrument which (except in the case of an order under section 14 or an order or regulations made solely by the national Assembly for Wales) shall be subject to annulment in pursuance of a resolution of either House of Parliament.

12 Protection from personal liability

(1) A member of a local authority or an officer or other person authorised by a local authority is not personally liable in respect of any act done by him or by the local authority or any such person if the act was done in good faith for the purpose of executing powers conferred by, or by virtue, of this Act.

(2) Subsection (1) does not apply to liability under section 17 or 18 of the Audit Commission Act 1998 (powers of district auditor and court).

13 Expenses

There is to be paid out of money provided by Parliament any increase attributable to this Act in the sums payable out of money so provided under any other enactment.

14 Short title, commencement and extent

(1) This Act may be cited as the Noise Act 1996.

(2) This Act is to come into force on such day as the Secretary of State may by order appoint, and different days may be appointed for different purposes.

(3) This Act does not extend to Scotland.

(4) In its application to Northern Ireland this Act has effect with the following modifications—
- (a) for any reference to a local authority there is substituted a reference to a district council,
- (b) for any reference to the area of a local authority there is substituted a reference to the district of a district council,
- (c) for any reference to the Secretary of State there is substituted a reference to the Department of the Environment for Northern Ireland,
- (d) any reference to an enactment includes reference to an enactment comprised in Northern Ireland legislation,
- (e) in section 10(4) for the words "sworn information" there is substituted the words "a complaint made on oath and",
- (f) in section 11 for subsection (3) there is substituted—

"(3) The power to make orders under this Act shall be exercisable by statutory rule for the purposes of the Statutory Rules (Northern Ireland) Order 1979, and any orders made under this Act shall (except in the case of an order under section 14) be subject to negative resolution within the meaning assigned by section 41(6) of the Interpretation Act (Northern Ireland) 1954 as if they were statutory instruments within the meaning of that Act.",

- (g) in section 12 for subsection (2) there is substituted—

"(2) Subsection (1) does not apply to liability under section 81 or 82 of the Local Government Act (Northern Ireland) 1972 (powers of local government auditor and court).",

- (h) the following provisions are omitted—
  - (i) section 10(7),
  - (ii) in section 10(8) the words "or by virtue of subsection (7)",
  - (iii) section 11(1),
  - (iv) in the Schedule, paragraph 1(a)(ii) and the word "and" immediately before it,
  - (v) in the Schedule, in paragraph 1(b), the words "or section 81(3) of the Environmental Protection Act 1990 (as so extended)".

SCHEDULE POWERS IN RELATION TO SEIZED EQUIPMENT

Section 10

INTRODUCTORY

1 In this Schedule—

(a) a "noise offence" means—
  (i) in relation to equipment seized under section 10(2) of this Act, an offence under section 4 of this Act, and
  (ii) in relation to equipment seized under section 81(3) of the Environmental Protection Act 1990 (as extended by section 10(7) of this Act), an offence under section 80(4) of that Act in respect of a statutory nuisance falling within section 79(1)(g) of that Act,
(b) "seized equipment" means equipment seized in the exercise of the power of seizure and removal conferred by section 10(2) of this Act or section 81(3) of the Environmental Protection Act 1990 (as so extended),
(c) "related equipment", in relation to any conviction of or proceedings for a noise offence, means seized equipment used or alleged to have been used in the commission of the offence,
(d) "responsible local authority", in relation to seized equipment, means the local authority by or on whose behalf the equipment was seized.

RETENTION

2(1) Any seized equipment may be retained—
  (a) during the period of twenty-eight days beginning with the seizure, or
  (b) if it is related equipment in proceedings for a noise offence instituted within that period against any person, until—
    (i) he is sentenced or otherwise dealt with for the offence or acquitted of the offence, or
    (ii) the proceedings are discontinued.

(2) Sub-paragraph (1) does not authorise the retention of seized equipment if—
  (a) a person has been given a fixed penalty notice under section 8 of this Act in respect of any noise,
  (b) the equipment was seized because of its use in the emission of the noise in respect of which the fixed penalty notice was given, and
  (c) that person has paid the fixed penalty before the end of the period allowed for its payment.

FORFEITURE

3(1) Where a person is convicted of a noise offence the court may make an order ("a forfeiture order") for forfeiture of any related equipment.

(2) The court may make a forfeiture order whether or not it also deals with the offender in respect of the offence in any other way and without regard to any restrictions on forfeiture in any enactment.

(3) In considering whether to make a forfeiture order in respect of any equipment a court must have regard—
  (a) to the value of the equipment, and
  (b) to the likely financial and other effects on the offender of the making of the order (taken together with any other order that the court contemplates making).

Material relating to statutory nuisance

(4) A forfeiture order operates to deprive the offender of any rights in the equipment to which it relates.

CONSEQUENCES OF FORFEITURE

4(1) Where any equipment has been forfeited under paragraph 3, a magistrates' court may, on application by a claimant of the equipment (other than the person in whose case the forfeiture order was made) make an order for delivery of the equipment to the applicant if it appears to the court that he is the owner of the equipment.

(2) No application may be made under sub-paragraph (1) by any claimant of the equipment after the expiry of the period of six months beginning with the date on which a forfeiture order was made in respect of the equipment.

(3) Such an application cannot succeed unless the claimant satisfies the court—
   (a) that he had not consented to the offender having possession of the equipment, or
   (b) that he did not know, and had no reason to suspect, that the equipment was likely to be used in the commission of a noise offence.

(4) Where the responsible local authority is of the opinion that the person in whose case the forfeiture order was made is not the owner of the equipment, it must take reasonable steps to bring to the attention of persons who may be entitled to do so their right to make an application under sub-paragraph (1).

(5) An order under sub-paragraph (1) does not affect the right of any person to take, within the period of six months beginning with the date of the order, proceedings for the recovery of the equipment from the person in possession of it in pursuance of the order, but the right ceases on the expiry of that period.

(6) If on the expiry of the period of six months beginning with the date on which a forfeiture order was made in respect of the equipment no order has been made under sub-paragraph (1), the responsible local authority may dispose of the equipment.

RETURN ETC OF SEIZED EQUIPMENT

5 If in proceedings for a noise offence no order for forfeiture of related equipment is made, the court (whether or not a person is convicted of the offence) may give such directions as to the return, retention or disposal of the equipment by the responsible local authority as it thinks fit.

6(1) Where in the case of any seized equipment no proceedings in which it is related equipment are begun within the period mentioned in paragraph 2(1)(a)—
   (a) the responsible local authority must return the equipment to any person who—
      (i) appears to them to be the owner of the equipment, and

Appendix B

(ii) makes a claim for the return of the equipment within the period mentioned in sub-paragraph (2), and
(b) if no such person makes such a claim within that period, the responsible local authority may dispose of the equipment.

(2) The period referred to in sub-paragraph (1)(a)(ii) is the period of six months beginning with the expiry of the period mentioned in paragraph 2(1)(a).

(3) The responsible local authority must take reasonable steps to bring to the attention of persons who may be entitled to do so their right to make such a claim.

(4) Subject to sub-paragraph (6), the responsible local authority is not required to return any seized equipment under sub-paragraph (1)(a) until the person making the claim has paid any such reasonable charges for the seizure, removal and retention of the equipment as the authority may demand.

(5) If—
(a) equipment is sold in pursuance of—
(i) paragraph 4(6),
(ii) directions under paragraph 5, or
(iii) this paragraph, and
(b) before the expiration of the period of one year beginning with the date on which the equipment is sold any person satisfies the responsible local authority that at the time of its sale he was the owner of the equipment,

the authority is to pay him any sum by which any proceeds of sale exceed any such reasonable charges for the seizure, removal or retention of the equipment as the authority may demand.

(6) The responsible local authority cannot demand charges from any person under sub-paragraph (4) or (5) who they are satisfied did not know, and had no reason to suspect, that the equipment was likely to be used in the emission of noise exceeding the level determined under section 5.

Statutory Nuisances (Insects) Regulations 2006, SI 2006/770

Title, commencement and application

1 These Regulations—
(a) may be cited as the Statutory Nuisances (Insects) Regulations 2006;
(b) come into force on 6th April 2006;
(c) apply in England only.

'Relevant industrial etc. premises': further exclusions

2 For the purposes of paragraph (d) of section 79(7C) of the Environmental Protection Act 1990, there is prescribed land in respect of which any payment is made under any of the schemes mentioned in the Schedule to these Regulations.

Schedule Schemes

Scheme	Legislation
Countryside Stewardship Scheme	The Countryside Stewardship Regulations 2000 (SI 2000/3048)
Entry Level Pilot Scheme	The Entry Level Agri-Environment Scheme (Pilot) (England) Regulations 2003 (SI 2003/838)
Environmental Stewardship Scheme	The Environmental Stewardship (England) Regulations 2005 (SI 2005/621)
Environmentally Sensitive Areas Scheme	The Environmentally Sensitive Areas (Stage I) Designation Order 2000 (SI 2000/3049)
	The Environmentally Sensitive Areas (Stage II) Designation Order 2000 (SI 2000/3050)
	The Environmentally Sensitive Areas (Stage III) Designation Order 2000 (SI 2000/3051)
	The Environmentally Sensitive Areas (Stage IV) Designation Order 2000 (SI 2000/3052)
Farm Woodland Premium Scheme	The Farm Woodland Scheme 1988 (SI 1988/1291)
	The Farm Woodland Premium Scheme 1992 (SI 1992/905)
	The Farm Woodland Premium Scheme 1997 (SI 1997/829)
Habitat Scheme	The Habitat (Water Fringe) Regulations 1994 (SI 1994/1291)
	The Habitat (Salt-Marsh) Regulations 1994 (SI 1994/1293)
	The Conservation (Natural Habitats, &c.) Regulations 1994 (SI 1994/2716)
Nitrate Sensitive Areas Scheme	The Farm Waste Grant (Nitrate Vulnerable Zones) (England and Wales) Scheme 1996 (SI 1996/908)
	The Farm Waste Grant (Nitrate Vulnerable Zones) (England) Scheme 2000 (SI 2000/2890)
	The Farm Waste Grant (Nitrate Vulnerable Zones) (England) (No.2) Scheme 2000 (SI 2000/2911)

Appendix B

	The Farm Waste Grant (Nitrate Vulnerable Zones) (England) Scheme 2003 (SI 2003/562)
Organic Farming Scheme	The Organic Farming (Aid) Regulations 1994 (SI 1994/1721)
	The Organic Farming Regulations 1999 (SI 1999/590)
	The Organic Farming (England Rural Development Programme) Regulations 2001 (SI 2001/432)
	The Organic Farming (England Rural Development Programme) Regulations 2003 (SI 2003/1235)

Statutory Nuisances (Artificial Lighting) (Designation of Relevant Sports) (England) Order 2006, SI 2006/781

Title, commencement and application

1 This Order—
   (a) may be cited as the Statutory Nuisances (Artificial Lighting) (Designation of Relevant Sports) (England) Order 2006;
   (b) comes into force on 6th April 2006;
   (c) applies in England only.

Designation of a "relevant sport"

2 A sport appearing in the list of sports set out in the Schedule to this Order is designated as a "relevant sport" for the purposes of section 80(8A) of the Environmental Protection Act 1990.

Schedule List of sports
   1   American Football
   2   Archery
   3   Association Football
   4   Athletics
   5   Australian Rules Football
   6   Badminton
   7   Baseball
   8   Basketball
   9   Biathlon
   10 Bobsleigh
   11 Bowls
   12 Camogie
   13 Cricket
   14 Croquet
   15 Curling
   16 Cycling
   17 Equestrian Sports
   18 Gaelic Football
   19 Golf
   20 Gymnastics

Material relating to statutory nuisance

21 Handball
22 Hockey
23 Horse Racing
24 Hurling
25 Ice Hockey
26 Ice Skating
27 Lacrosse
28 Luge
29 Modern Pentathlon
30 Motor Cycling
31 Motor Sports
32 Netball
33 Polo
34 Roller Sports
35 Rounders
36 Rowing
37 Rugby League
38 Rugby Union
39 Shooting
40 Skateboarding
41 Skiing
42 Softball
43 Swimming (including Diving)
44 Tennis
45 Triathlon
46 Tug of War
47 Volleyball

Appendix C

Material Relating to Magistrates' Court, Crown Court and High Court Proceedings

Magistrates' Courts Act 1980

53 Procedure on hearing

(1) On the hearing of a complaint, the court shall, if the defendant appears, state to him the substance of the complaint.

(2) The court, after hearing the evidence and the parties, shall make the order for which the complaint is made or dismiss the complaint.

(3) Where a complaint is for an order for the payment of a sum recoverable summarily as a civil debt, or for the variation of the rate of any periodical payments ordered by a magistrates' court to be made, or for such other matter as may be prescribed, the court may make the order with the consent of the defendant without hearing evidence.

64 Power to award costs and enforcement of costs

(1) On the hearing of a complaint, a magistrates' court shall have power in its discretion to make such order as to costs—
   (a) on making the order for which the complaint is made, to be paid by the defendant to the complainant;
   (b) on dismissing the complaint, to be paid by the complainant to the defendant,

as it thinks just and reasonable; but if the complaint is for an order for the periodical payment of money, or for the revocation, revival or variation of such an order, or for the enforcement of such an order, the court may, whatever adjudication it makes, order either party to pay the whole or any part of the other's costs.

(2) The amount of any sum ordered to be paid under subsection (1) above shall be specified in the order, or order of dismissal, as the case may be.

(3) Subject to subsection (4) below, costs ordered to be paid under this section shall be enforceable as a civil debt.

[(4) Any costs awarded on a complaint for a maintenance order, or for the enforcement, variation, discharge or revival of such an order, against the person liable to make payments under the order shall be enforceable as a sum ordered to be paid by a magistrates' court maintenance order.]

(5) The preceding provisions of this section shall have effect subject to any other Act enabling a magistrates' court to order a successful party to pay the other party's costs.

Appendix C

101 Onus of proving exceptions, etc

Where the defendant to an information or complaint relies for his defence on any exception, exemption, proviso, excuse or qualification, whether or not it accompanies the description of the offence or matter of complaint in the enactment creating the offence or on which the complaint is founded, the burden of proving the exception, exemption, proviso, excuse or qualification shall be on him; and this notwithstanding that the information or complaint contains an allegation negativing the exception, exemption, proviso, excuse or qualification.

108 Right of appeal to the Crown Court

(1) A person convicted by a magistrates' court may appeal to the Crown Court—
    (a) if he pleaded guilty, against his sentence;
    (b) if he did not, against the conviction or sentence.

[(1A) [Section 14] of the [Powers of Criminal Courts Sentencing Act 2000] (under which a conviction of an offence for which . . . an order for conditional or absolute discharge is made is deemed not to be a conviction except for certain purposes) shall not prevent an appeal under this section, whether against conviction or otherwise.]

(2) A person sentenced by a magistrates' court for an offence in respect of which . . . an order for conditional discharge has been previously made may appeal to the Crown Court against the sentence.

(3) In this section "sentence" includes any order made on conviction by a magistrates' court, not being—
    (a) . . .
    (b) an order for the payment of costs;
    (c) an order under [section 37(1)] of the [Animal Welfare Act 2006] (which enables a court to order the destruction of an animal); or
    (d) an order made in pursuance of any enactment under which the court has no discretion as to the making of the order or its terms;

[and also includes a [declaration of relevance within the meaning of section 23 of the Football Spectators Act 1989].

(4) Subsection (3)(d) above does not prevent an appeal against a surcharge imposed under [section 161A of the Criminal Justice Act 2003.]

109 Abandonment of appeal

(1) Where notice to abandon an appeal has been duly given by the appellant—
    (a) the court against whose decision the appeal was brought may issue process for enforcing that decision, subject to anything already suffered or done under it by the appellant; and
    (b) the said court may, on the application of the other party to the appeal, order the appellant to pay to that party such costs as appear to the court to be just and reasonable in respect of expenses properly incurred by that party in connection with the appeal before notice of the abandonment was given to that party.

(2) In this section "appeal" means an appeal from a magistrates' court to the Crown Court, and the reference to a notice to abandon an appeal is a reference to a notice shown to the satisfaction of the magistrates' court to have been given in accordance with [rules of court].

110 Enforcement of decision of the Crown Court

After the determination by the Crown Court of an appeal from a magistrates' court the decision appealed against as confirmed or varied by the Crown Court, or any decision of the Crown Court substituted for the decision appealed against, may, without prejudice to the powers of the Crown Court to enforce the decision, be enforced—
  (a) by the issue by the court by which the decision appealed against was given of any process that it could have issued if it had decided the case as the Crown Court decided it;
  (b) so far as the nature of any process already issued to enforce the decision appealed against permits, by that process;

and the decision of the Crown Court shall have effect as if it had been made by the magistrates' court against whose decision the appeal is brought.

111 Statement of case by magistrates' court

(1) Any person who was a party to any proceeding before a magistrates' court or is aggrieved by the conviction, order, determination or other proceeding of the court may question the proceeding on the ground that it is wrong in law or is in excess of jurisdiction by applying to the justices composing the court to state a case for the opinion of the High Court on the question of law or jurisdiction involved; but a person shall not make an application under this section in respect of a decision against which he has a right of appeal to the High Court or which by virtue of any enactment passed after 31st December 1879 is final.

(2) An application under subsection (1) above shall be made within 21 days after the day on which the decision of the magistrates' court was given.

(3) For the purpose of subsection (2) above, the day on which the decision of the magistrates' court is given shall, where the court has adjourned the trial of an information after conviction, be the day on which the court sentences or otherwise deals with the offender.

(4) On the making of an application under this section in respect of a decision any right of the applicant to appeal against the decision to the Crown Court shall cease.

(5) If the justices are of opinion that an application under this section is frivolous, they may refuse to state a case, and, if the applicant so requires, shall give him a certificate stating that the application has been refused; but the justices shall not refuse to state a case if the application is made by or under the direction of the Attorney General.

(6) Where justices refuse to state a case, the High Court may, on the application of the person who applied for the case to be stated, make an order of mandamus requiring the justices to state a case.

Appendix C

123 Defect in process

(1) No objection shall be allowed to any information or complaint, or to any summons or warrant to procure the presence of the defendant, for any defect in it in substance or in form, or for any variance between it and the evidence adduced on behalf of the prosecutor or complainant at the hearing of the information or complaint.

(2) If it appears to a magistrates' court that any variance between a summons or warrant and the evidence adduced on behalf of the prosecutor or complainant is such that the defendant has been misled by the variance, the court shall, on the application of the defendant, adjourn the hearing.

127 Limitation of time

(1) Except as otherwise expressly provided by any enactment and subject to subsection (2) below, a magistrates' court shall not try an information or hear a complaint unless the information was laid, or the complaint made, within 6 months from the time when the offence was committed, or the matter of complaint arose.

(2) Nothing in—
   (a) subsection (1) above; or
   (b) subject to subsection (4) below, any other enactment (however framed or worded) which, as regards any offence to which it applies, would but for this section impose a time-limit on the power of a magistrates' court to try an information summarily or impose a limitation on the time for taking summary proceedings,

shall apply in relation to any indictable offence.

(3) Without prejudice to the generality of paragraph (b) of subsection (2) above, that paragraph includes enactments which impose a time-limit that applies only in certain circumstances (for example, where the proceedings are not instituted by or with the consent of the Director of Public Prosecutions or some other specified authority).

(4) Where, as regards any indictable offence, there is imposed by any enactment (however framed or worded, and whether falling within subsection (2)(b) above or not) a limitation on the time for taking proceedings on indictment for that offence no summary proceedings for that offence shall be taken after the latest time for taking proceedings on indictment.

Magistrates' Courts Rules 1981, SI 1981/552

4 Information and complaint

[Revoked by implication on the coming into force of the Criminal Procedure Rules 2005, SI 2005/384, as specified by Part 2, r 2.1.]

14 Order of evidence and speeches: complaint

[Revoked by implication on the coming into force of the Criminal Procedure Rules 2005, SI 2005/384, as specified by Part 2, r 2.1.]

16 [Record of Adjudication]

[Revoked by implication on the coming into force of the Criminal Procedure Rules 2005, SI 2005/384, as specified by Part 2, r 2.1.]

APPEAL TO MAGISTRATES' COURT

34 Appeal to be by complaint

Where under any enactment an appeal lies to a magistrates' court against the decision or order of a local authority or other authority, or other body or person, the appeal shall be by way of complaint for an order.

43 Service of copy of order

Where a magistrates' court makes, revokes, discharges, suspends, revives, alters or varies a [magistrates' court maintenance order] or order enforceable as a [magistrates' court maintenance order] or allows time or further time for payment of a lump sum under any such order or orders payment of a lump sum under any such order to be paid by instalments or varies any such order for payment by instalments the court shall cause a copy of its order to be served on the defendant by delivering it to him or by sending it by post in a letter addressed to him at his last known or usual place of abode.

99 Service of summons, etc

(1) Service of a summons issued by a justice of the peace on a person other than a corporation may be effected—
  (a) by delivering it to the person to whom it is directed; or
  (b) by leaving it for him with some person at his last known or usual place of abode; or
  (c) by sending it by post in a letter addressed to him at his last known or usual place of abode.

(2) ...

(3) Service for the purposes of the Act of 1980 of a summons issued by a justice of the peace on a corporation may be effected by delivering it at, or sending it by post to, the registered office of the corporation, if that office is in the United Kingdom, or, if there is no registered office in the United Kingdom, any place in the United Kingdom where the corporation trades or conducts its business.

(4) Paragraph (3) shall have effect in relation to a document (other than a summons) issued by a justice of the peace as it has effect in relation to a summons so issued, but with the substitution of references to England and Wales for the references to the United Kingdom.

(5) Any summons or other document served in manner authorised by the preceding provisions of this rule shall, for the purposes of any enactment other than the Act of 1980 or these Rules requiring a summons or other document to be served in any particular manner, be deemed to have been as effectively served as if it had been served in that manner; and nothing in this rule shall render invalid the service of a summons or other document in that manner.

(6) Sub-paragraph (c) of paragraph (1) shall not authorise the service by post of—
  (a) a summons requiring the attendance of any person to give evidence or produce a document or thing; or
  (b) a summons issued under any enactment relating to the liability of members of the naval, military or air forces of the Crown for the

Appendix C

maintenance of their [husbands, wives or civil partners, as the case may be,] and children, whether legitimate or illegitimate.

(7) In the case of a summons issued on an application for an order under section 16 or 17(1) of the Act of 1978 (powers of court to make orders for the protection of a party to a marriage or a child of the family) service of the summons shall not be effected in manner authorised by sub-paragraph (b) or (c) of paragraph (1) unless a justice of the peace is satisfied by evidence on oath that prompt personal service of the summons is impracticable and allows service to be effected in such manner.

(8) Where this rule or any other of these Rules provides that a summons or other document may be sent by post to a person's last known or usual place of abode that rule shall have effect as if it provided also for the summons or other document to be sent in the manner specified in the rule to an address given by that person for that purpose.

(9) This rule shall not apply to a judgment summons.

Supreme Court Act 1981

48 Appeals to Crown Court

(1) The Crown Court may, in the course of hearing any appeal, correct any error or mistake in the order or judgment incorporating the decision which is the subject of the appeal.

(2) On the termination of the hearing of an appeal the Crown Court—
- (a) may confirm, reverse or vary [any part of the decision appealed against, including a determination not to impose a separate penalty in respect of an offence]; or
- (b) may remit the matter with its opinion thereon to the authority whose decision is appealed against; or
- (c) may make such other order in the matter as the court thinks just, and by such order exercise any power which the said authority might have exercised.

(3) Subsection (2) has effect subject to any enactment relating to any such appeal which expressly limits or restricts the powers of the court on the appeal.

(4) [Subject to section 11(6) of the Criminal Appeal Act 1995, if] the appeal is against a conviction or a sentence, the preceding provisions of this section shall be construed as including power to award any punishment, whether more or less severe than that awarded by the magistrates' court whose decision is appealed against, if that is a punishment which that magistrates' court might have awarded.

(5) This section applies whether or not the appeal is against the whole of the decision.

(6) In this section "sentence" includes any order made by a court when dealing with an offender, including—
- (a) a hospital order under [Part III of the Mental Health Act 1983], with or without [a restriction order, and an interim hospital order under [that Act]]; and
- (b) a recommendation for deportation made when dealing with an offender.

[(7) The fact that an appeal is pending against an interim hospital order under [the said Act of 1983] shall not affect the power of the magistrates' court that made it to renew or terminate the order or to deal with the appellant on its termination; and where the Crown Court quashes such an order but does not pass any sentence or make any other order in its place the Court may direct the appellant to be kept in custody or released on bail pending his being dealt with by that magistrates' court.

(8) Where the Crown Court makes an interim hospital order by virtue of subsection (2)—
- (a) the power of renewing or terminating the order and of dealing with the appellant on its termination shall be exercisable by the magistrates' court whose decision is appealed against and not by the Crown Court; and
- (b) that magistrates' court shall be treated for the purposes of [section 38(7) of the said Act of 1983](absconding offenders) as the court that made the order.]

Criminal Appeal Act 1968

50 Meaning of "sentence"

[(1) In this Act "sentence", in relation to an offence, includes any order made by a court when dealing with an offender including, in particular—
- (a) a hospital order under Part III of the Mental Health Act 1983, with or without a restriction order;
- (b) an interim hospital order under that Part;
- [(bb) a hospital direction and a limitation direction under that Part;]
- (c) a recommendation for deportation;
- [(ca) a confiscation order under Part 2 of the Proceeds of Crime Act 2002;
- (cb) an order which varies a confiscation order made under Part 2 of the Proceeds of Crime Act 2002 if the varying order is made under section 21, 22 or 29 of that Act (but not otherwise);]
- (d) a confiscation order under the [Drug Trafficking Act 1994] other than one made by the High Court;
- (e) a confiscation order under Part VI of the Criminal Justice Act 1988;
- (f) an order varying a confiscation order of a kind which is included by virtue of paragraph (d) or (e) above;
- (g) an order made by the Crown Court varying a confiscation order which was made by the High Court by virtue of [section 19 of the Act of 1994]; and
- (h) a declaration of relevance, within the meaning of [section 23 of the Football Spectators Act 1989][; and
- (i) an order under section 129(2) of the Licensing Act 2003 (forfeiture or suspension of personal licence).]

[(1A) [Section 14 of the Powers of Criminal Courts (Sentencing) Act 2000] (under which a conviction of an offence for which . . . an order for conditional or absolute discharge is made is deemed not to be a conviction except for certain purposes) shall not prevent an appeal under this Act, whether against conviction or otherwise.]

Appendix C

(2) Any power of the criminal division of the Court of Appeal to pass a sentence includes a power to make a recommendation for deportation in cases where the court from which the appeal lies had power to make such a recommendation.

[(3) An order under section 17 of the Access to Justice Act 1999 is not a sentence for the purposes of this Act.]

Criminal Appeal Rules 1968, SI 1968/1262

10 Abandonment of proceedings

[Revoked by implication on the coming into force of the Criminal Procedure Rules 2005, SI 2005/384, as specified by Part 2, r 2.1.]

Criminal Procedure Rules 2005, SI 2005/384

PART 1
THE OVERRIDING OBJECTIVE

1.1 The overriding objective

(1) The overriding objective of this new code is that criminal cases be dealt with justly.

(2) Dealing with a criminal case justly includes—
   (a) acquitting the innocent and convicting the guilty;
   (b) dealing with the prosecution and the defence fairly;
   (c) recognising the rights of a defendant, particularly those under Article 6 of the European Convention on Human Rights;
   (d) respecting the interests of witnesses, victims and jurors and keeping them informed of the progress of the case;
   (e) dealing with the case efficiently and expeditiously;
   (f) ensuring that appropriate information is available to the court when bail and sentence are considered; and
   (g) dealing with the case in ways that take into account—
      (i) the gravity of the offence alleged,
      (ii) the complexity of what is in issue,
      (iii) the severity of the consequences for the defendant and others affected, and
      (iv) the needs of other cases.

1.2 The duty of participants in a criminal case

(1) Each participant, in the conduct of each case, must—
   (a) prepare and conduct the case in accordance with the overriding objective;
   (b) comply with these Rules, practice directions and directions made by the court; and
   (c) at once inform the court and all parties of any significant failure (whether or not that participant is responsible for that failure) to take any procedural step required by these Rules, any practice direction or any direction of the court. A failure is significant if it might hinder the court in furthering the overriding objective.

(2) Anyone involved in any way with a criminal case is a participant in its conduct for the purposes of this rule.

1.3 The application by the court of the overriding objective

The court must further the overriding objective in particular when–
  (a) exercising any power given to it by legislation (including these Rules);
  (b) applying any practice direction; or
  (c) interpreting any rule or practice direction.

PART 2
UNDERSTANDING AND APPLYING THE RULES

2.1 When the Rules apply

(1) In general, the Criminal Procedure Rules apply–
  (a) in all criminal cases in magistrates' courts and in the Crown Court; and
  (b) in all cases in the criminal division of the Court of Appeal.

(2) If a rule applies only in one or two of those courts, the rule makes that clear.

(3) The Rules apply on and after 4th April, 2005, but do not affect any right or duty existing under the rules of court revoked by the coming into force of these Rules.

(4) The rules in Part 33 apply in all cases in which the defendant is charged on or after 6 November 2006 and in other cases if the court so orders.

(5) The rules in Part 14 apply in cases in which one of the events listed in sub-paragraphs (a) to (d) of rule 14.1(1) takes place on or after 2nd April 2007. In other cases the rules of court replaced by those rules apply.

(6) The rules in Part 28 apply in cases in which an application under rule 28.3 is made on or after 2nd April 2007. In other cases the rules replaced by those rules apply.

[(7) The rules in Parts 65, 66, 67, 68, 69 and 70 apply where an appeal, application or reference, to which one of those Parts applies, is made on or after 1st October 2007. In other cases the rules replaced by those rules apply.]

[Note. The rules replaced by these Rules are revoked when these Rules come into force by provisions of the Courts Act 2003, the Courts Act 2003 (Commencement No 6 and Savings) Order 2004 and the Courts Act 2003 (Consequential Amendments) Order 2004. These Rules reproduce the substance of all the rules they replace.]

2.2 Definitions

(1) In these Rules, unless the context makes it clear that something different is meant:
  "business day" means any day except Saturday, Sunday, Christmas Day, Boxing Day, Good Friday, Easter Monday or a bank holiday;

Appendix C

"court" means a tribunal with jurisdiction over criminal cases. It includes a judge, recorder, District Judge (Magistrates' Court's), lay justice and, when exercising their judicial powers, the Registrar of Criminal Appeals, a justices' clerk or assistant clerk;
"court officer" means the appropriate member of the staff of a court;
"live link" means an arrangement by which a person can see and hear, and be seen and heard by, the court when that person is not in court;
"Practice Direction" means the Lord Chief Justice's Consolidated Criminal Practice Direction, as amended[; and]
"public interest ruling" means a ruling about whether it is in the public interest to disclose prosecution material under sections 3(6), 7A(8) or 8(5) of the Criminal Procedure and Investigations Act 1996.

(2) Definitions of some other expressions are in the rules in which they apply.

2.3 References to Acts of Parliament and to Statutory Instruments

In these Rules, where a rule refers to an Act of Parliament or to subordinate legislation by title and year, subsequent references to that Act or to that legislation in the rule are shortened: so, for example, after a reference to the Criminal Procedure and Investigations Act 1996 that Act is called "the 1996 Act"; and after a reference to the Criminal Procedure and Investigations Act 1996 (Defence Disclosure Time Limits) Regulations 1997 those Regulations are called "the 1997 Regulations".

2.4 The glossary

The glossary at the end of the Rules is a guide to the meaning of certain legal expressions used in them.

PART 3
CASE MANAGEMENT

3.1 The scope of this Part

This Part applies to the management of each case in a magistrates' court and in the Crown Court (including an appeal to the Crown Court) until the conclusion of that case.

[Note. Rules that apply to procedure in the Court of Appeal are in Parts 65 to 73 of these Rules.]

3.2 The duty of the court

(1) The court must further the overriding objective by actively managing the case.

(2) Active case management includes–
   (a) the early identification of the real issues;
   (b) the early identification of the needs of witnesses;
   (c) achieving certainty as to what must be done, by whom, and when, in particular by the early setting of a timetable for the progress of the case;

Material relating to magistrates' court, Crown & High Court proceedings

    (d) monitoring the progress of the case and compliance with directions;
    (e) ensuring that evidence, whether disputed or not, is presented in the shortest and clearest way;
    (f) discouraging delay, dealing with as many aspects of the case as possible on the same occasion, and avoiding unnecessary hearings;
    (g) encouraging the participants to co-operate in the progression of the case; and
    (h) making use of technology.

(3) The court must actively manage the case by giving any direction appropriate to the needs of that case as early as possible.

3.3 The duty of the parties

Each party must–
    (a) actively assist the court in fulfilling its duty under rule 3.2, without or if necessary with a direction; and
    (b) apply for a direction if needed to further the overriding objective.

3.4 Case progression officers and their duties

(1) At the beginning of the case each party must, unless the court otherwise directs–
    (a) nominate an individual responsible for progressing that case; and
    (b) tell other parties and the court who he is and how to contact him.

(2) In fulfilling its duty under rule 3.2, the court must where appropriate–
    (a) nominate a court officer responsible for progressing the case; and
    (b) make sure the parties know who he is and how to contact him.

(3) In this Part a person nominated under this rule is called a case progression officer.

(4) A case progression officer must–
    (a) monitor compliance with directions;
    (b) make sure that the court is kept informed of events that may affect the progress of that case;
    (c) make sure that he can be contacted promptly about the case during ordinary business hours;
    (d) act promptly and reasonably in response to communications about the case; and
    (e) if he will be unavailable, appoint a substitute to fulfil his duties and inform the other case progression officers.

3.5 The court's case management powers

(1) In fulfilling its duty under rule 3.2 the court may give any direction and take any step actively to manage a case unless that direction or step would be inconsistent with legislation, including these Rules.

(2) In particular, the court may–
    (a) nominate a judge, magistrate, justices' clerk or assistant to a justices' clerk to manage the case;
    (b) give a direction on its own initiative or on application by a party;

Appendix C

    (c) ask or allow a party to propose a direction;
    (d) for the purpose of giving directions, receive applications and representations by letter, by telephone or by any other means of electronic communication, and conduct a hearing by such means;
    (e) give a direction without a hearing;
    (f) fix, postpone, bring forward, extend or cancel a hearing;
    (g) shorten or extend (even after it has expired) a time limit fixed by a direction;
    (h) require that issues in the case should be determined separately, and decide in what order they will be determined; and
    (i) specify the consequences of failing to comply with a direction.

(3) A magistrates' court may give a direction that will apply in the Crown Court if the case is to continue there.

(4) The Crown Court may give a direction that will apply in a magistrates' court if the case is to continue there.

(5) Any power to give a direction under this Part includes a power to vary or revoke that direction.

[Note. Depending upon the nature of a case and the stage that it has reached, its progress may be affected by other Criminal Procedure Rules and by other legislation. The note at the end of this Part lists other rules and legislation that may apply.]

3.6 Application to vary a direction

(1) A party may apply to vary a direction if–
    (a) the court gave it without a hearing;
    (b) the court gave it at a hearing in his absence; or
    (c) circumstances have changed.

(2) A party who applies to vary a direction must–
    (a) apply as soon as practicable after he becomes aware of the grounds for doing so; and
    (b) give as much notice to the other parties as the nature and urgency of his application permits.

3.7 Agreement to vary a time limit fixed by a direction

(1) The parties may agree to vary a time limit fixed by a direction, but only if–
    (a) the variation will not–
        (i) affect the date of any hearing that has been fixed, or
        (ii) significantly affect the progress of the case in any other way;
    (b) the court has not prohibited variation by agreement; and
    (c) the court's case progression officer is promptly informed.

(2) The court's case progression officer must refer the agreement to the court if he doubts the condition in paragraph (1)(a) is satisfied.

3.8 Case preparation and progression

(1) At every hearing, if a case cannot be concluded there and then the court must give directions so that it can be concluded at the next hearing or as soon as possible after that.

(2) At every hearing the court must, where relevant–

Material relating to magistrates' court, Crown & High Court proceedings

(a) if the defendant is absent, decide whether to proceed nonetheless;
(b) take the defendant's plea (unless already done) or if no plea can be taken then find out whether the defendant is likely to plead guilty or not guilty;
(c) set, follow or revise a timetable for the progress of the case, which may include a timetable for any hearing including the trial or (in the Crown Court) the appeal;
(d) in giving directions, ensure continuity in relation to the court and to the parties' representatives where that is appropriate and practicable; and
(e) where a direction has not been complied with, find out why, identify who was responsible, and take appropriate action.

3.9 Readiness for trial or appeal

(1) This rule applies to a party's preparation for trial or (in the Crown Court) appeal, and in this rule and rule 3.10 trial includes any hearing at which evidence will be introduced.

(2) In fulfilling his duty under rule 3.3, each party must–
   (a) comply with directions given by the court;
   (b) take every reasonable step to make sure his witnesses will attend when they are needed;
   (c) make appropriate arrangements to present any written or other material; and
   (d) promptly inform the court and the other parties of anything that may–
      (i) affect the date or duration of the trial or appeal, or
      (ii) significantly affect the progress of the case in any other way.

(3) The court may require a party to give a certificate of readiness.

3.10 Conduct of a trial or an appeal

In order to manage the trial or (in the Crown Court) appeal, the court may require a party to identify–
   (a) which witnesses he intends to give oral evidence;
   (b) the order in which he intends those witnesses to give their evidence;
   (c) whether he requires an order compelling the attendance of a witness;
   (d) what arrangements, if any, he proposes to facilitate the giving of evidence by a witness;
   (e) what arrangements, if any, he proposes to facilitate the participation of any other person, including the defendant;
   (f) what written evidence he intends to introduce;
   (g) what other material, if any, he intends to make available to the court in the presentation of the case;
   (h) whether he intends to raise any point of law that could affect the conduct of the trial or appeal; and
   (i) what timetable he proposes and expects to follow.

3.11 Case management forms and records

(1) The case management forms set out in the Practice Direction must be used, and where there is no form then no specific formality is required.

Appendix C

(2) The court must make available to the parties a record of directions given.

[Note. Case management may be affected by the following other rules and legislation:

Criminal Procedure Rules

Parts 10.4 and 27.2: reminders of right to object to written evidence being read at trial

Part 12.2: time for first appearance of accused sent for trial

Part 13: dismissal of charges sent or transferred to the Crown Court

Part 14: the indictment

Part 15: preparatory hearings in serious fraud and other complex or lengthy cases

Parts 21–26: the rules that deal with disclosure

Parts 27–36: the rules that deal with evidence

Part 37: summary trial

Part 38: trial of children and young persons]

PART 7
COMMENCING PROCEEDINGS IN MAGISTRATES' COURTS

7.1 Information and complaint

(1) An information may be laid or complaint made by the prosecutor or complainant in person or by his counsel or solicitor or other person authorised in that behalf.

(2) Subject to any provision of the Magistrates' Courts Act 1980 and any other enactment, an information or complaint need not be in writing or on oath.

[Note. Formerly rule 4(1) and (2) of the Magistrates' Courts Rules 1981. As to the form of an information, see rules 7.2 and 7.3.]

7.2 Statement of offence

(1) Every [written charge issued by a public prosecutor and every information, summons or warrant laid in or issued by], a magistrates' court shall be sufficient if it–
   (a) describes the offence with which the accused is charged, or of which he is convicted, in ordinary language avoiding as far as possible the use of technical terms; and
   (b) gives such particulars as may be necessary to provide reasonable information about the nature of the charge.

(2) It shall not be necessary for any of those documents to–
   (a) state all the elements of the offence; or
   (b) negative any matter upon which the accused may rely.

(3) If the offence charged is one created by or under any Act, the description of the offence shall contain a reference to the section of the Act, or, as the case may be, the rule, order, regulation, bylaw or other instrument creating the offence.

[Note. Section 1 of the Magistrates' Courts Act 1980 provides for the laying of an information in a magistrates' court. Section 29 of the Criminal Justice Act 2003 provides for the issue of a written charge and requisition by a public prosecutor. These rules derive in part from rules 4(3) and 100 of the Magistrates' Courts Rules 1981.]

7.3 Information or written charge to be for one offence only

(1) Subject to any Act passed after 2nd October 1848, a magistrates' court shall not proceed to the trial of an information or written charge that charges more than one offence.

(2) Nothing in this rule shall prohibit two or more informations or written charges being set out in one document.

(3) If, notwithstanding paragraph (1), it appears to the court at any stage in the trial of an information[or written charge] that the information[or written charge] charges more than one offence, the court shall call upon the prosecutor to elect on which offence he desires the court to proceed, whereupon the offence or offences on which the prosecutor does not wish to proceed shall be struck out of the information[or written charge]; and the court shall then proceed to try that information[or written charge] afresh.

(4) If a prosecutor who is called upon to make an election under paragraph (3) fails to do so, the court shall dismiss the information[or written charge].

(5) Where, after an offence has or offences have been struck out of the information[or written charge] under paragraph (3), the accused requests an adjournment and it appears to the court that he has been unfairly prejudiced, it shall adjourn the trial.

[Note. Formerly rule 12 of the Magistrates' Courts Rules 1981.]

PART 21
ADVANCE INFORMATION

21.1 Scope of procedure for furnishing advance information

This Part applies in respect of proceedings against any person ("the accused") for an offence triable either way.

[Note. Formerly rule 2 of the Magistrates' Courts (Advance Information) Rules 1985.]

21.2 Notice to accused regarding advance information

As soon as practicable after a person has been charged with an offence in proceedings in respect of which this Part applies or a summons has been served on a person in connection with such an offence, the prosecutor shall provide him with a notice in writing explaining the effect of rule 21.3 and setting out the address at which a request under that section may be made.

Appendix C

[Note. Formerly rule 3 of the Magistrates' Courts (Advance Information) Rules 1985.]

21.3 Request for advance information

(1) If, in any proceedings in respect of which this Part applies, either before the magistrates' court considers whether the offence appears to be more suitable for summary trial or trial on indictment or, where the accused has not attained the age of 18 years when he appears or is brought before a magistrates' court, before he is asked whether he pleads guilty or not guilty, the accused or a person representing the accused requests the prosecutor to furnish him with advance information, the prosecutor shall, subject to rule 21.4, furnish him as soon as practicable with either–
   (a) a copy of those parts of every written statement which contain information as to the facts and matters of which the prosecutor proposes to adduce evidence in the proceedings; or
   (b) a summary of the facts and matters of which the prosecutor proposes to adduce evidence in the proceedings.

(2) In paragraph (1) above, "written statement" means a statement made by a person on whose evidence the prosecutor proposes to rely in the proceedings and, where such a person has made more than one written statement one of which contains information as to all the facts and matters in relation to which the prosecutor proposes to rely on the evidence of that person, only that statement is a written statement for purposes of paragraph (1) above.

(3) Where in any part of a written statement or in a summary furnished under paragraph (1) above reference is made to a document on which the prosecutor proposes to rely, the prosecutor shall, subject to rule 21.4, when furnishing the part of the written statement or the summary, also furnish either a copy of the document or such information as may be necessary to enable the person making the request under paragraph (1) above to inspect the document or a copy thereof.

[Note. Formerly rule 4 of the Magistrates' Courts (Advance Information) Rules 1985.]

21.4 Refusal of request for advance information

(1) If the prosecutor is of the opinion that the disclosure of any particular fact or matter in compliance with the requirements imposed by rule 21.3 might lead to any person on whose evidence he proposes to rely in the proceedings being intimidated, to an attempt to intimidate him being made or otherwise to the course of justice being interfered with, he shall not be obliged to comply with those requirements in relation to that fact or matter.

(2) Where, in accordance with paragraph (1) above, the prosecutor considers that he is not obliged to comply with the requirements imposed by rule 21.3 in relation to any particular fact or matter, he shall give notice in writing to the person who made the request under that section to the effect that certain advance information is being withheld by virtue of that paragraph.

[Note. Formerly rule 5 of the Magistrates' Courts (Advance Information) Rules 1985.]

21.5 Duty of court regarding advance information

(1) Subject to paragraph (2), where an accused appears or is brought before a magistrates' court in proceedings in respect of which this Part applies, the court shall, before it considers whether the offence appears to be more suitable for summary trial or trial on indictment, satisfy itself that the accused is aware of the requirements which may be imposed on the prosecutor under rule 21.3

(2) Where the accused has not attained the age of 18 years when he appears or is brought before a magistrates' court in proceedings in respect of which this rule applies, the court shall, before the accused is asked whether he pleads guilty or not guilty, satisfy itself that the accused is aware of the requirements which may be imposed on the prosecutor under rule 21.3.

[Note. Formerly rule 6 of the Magistrates' Courts (Advance Information) Rules 1985.]

21.6 Adjournment pending furnishing of advance information

(1) If, in any proceedings in respect of which this Part applies, the court is satisfied that, a request under rule 21.3 having been made to the prosecutor by or on behalf of the accused, a requirement imposed on the prosecutor by that section has not been complied with, the court shall adjourn the proceedings pending compliance with the requirement unless the court is satisfied that the conduct of the case for the accused will not be substantially prejudiced by non-compliance with the requirement.

(2) Where, in the circumstances set out in paragraph (1) above, the court decides not to adjourn the proceedings, a record of that decision and of the reasons why the court was satisfied that the conduct of the case for the accused would not be substantially prejudiced by non-compliance with the requirement shall be entered in the register kept under rule 6.1.

[Note. Formerly rule 7 of the Magistrates' Courts (Advance Information) Rules 1985.]

PART 24
DISCLOSURE OF EXPERT EVIDENCE

24.1 Requirement to disclose expert evidence

(1) Following–
   (a) a plea of not guilty by any person to an alleged offence in respect of which a magistrates' court proceeds to summary trial;
   (b) the committal for trial of any person;
   (c) the transfer to the Crown Court of any proceedings for the trial of a person by virtue of a notice of transfer given under section 4 of the Criminal Justice Act 1987;
   (d) the transfer to the Crown Court of any proceedings for the trial of a person by virtue of a notice of transfer served on a magistrates' court under section 53 of the Criminal Justice Act 1991;
   (e) the sending of any person for trial under section 51 of the Crime and Disorder Act 1998;

Appendix C

    (f) the preferring of a bill of indictment charging a person with an offence under the authority of section 2(2)(b) of the Administration of Justice (Miscellaneous Provisions) Act 1933; or

    (g) the making of an order for the retrial of any person,

if any party to the proceedings proposes to adduce expert evidence (whether of fact or opinion) in the proceedings (otherwise than in relation to sentence) he shall as soon as practicable, unless in relation to the evidence in question he has already done so or the evidence is the subject of an application for leave to adduce such evidence in accordance with section 41 of the Youth Justice and Criminal Evidence Act 1999–

    (i) furnish the other party or parties and the court with a statement in writing of any finding or opinion which he proposes to adduce by way of such evidence,[and notify the expert of this disclosure,] and

    (ii) where a request in writing is made to him in that behalf by any other party, provide that party also with a copy of (or if it appears to the party proposing to adduce the evidence to be more practicable, a reasonable opportunity to examine) the record of any observation, test, calculation or other procedure on which such finding or opinion is based and any document or other thing or substance in respect of which any such procedure has been carried out.

(2) A party may by notice in writing waive his right to be furnished with any of the matters mentioned in paragraph (1) and, in particular, may agree that the statement mentioned in paragraph (1)(a) may be furnished to him orally and not in writing.

(3) In paragraph (1), "document" means anything in which information of any description is recorded.

[Note. Formerly rule 3 of the Magistrates' Courts (Advance Notice of Expert Evidence) Rules 1997 and rule 3 of the Crown Court (Advance Notice of Expert Evidence) Rules 1987. For the equivalent requirement in Crown Court proceedings under Part 2 of the Proceeds of Crime Act 2002 see rule 57.9. Part 33 contains rules about the duties of an expert and the content of an expert's report..]

24.2 Withholding evidence

(1) If a party has reasonable grounds for believing that the disclosure of any evidence in compliance with the requirements imposed by rule 24.1 might lead to the intimidation, or attempted intimidation, of any person on whose evidence he intends to rely in the proceedings, or otherwise to the course of justice being interfered with, he shall not be obliged to comply with those requirements in relation to that evidence.

(2) Where, in accordance with paragraph (1), a party considers that he is not obliged to comply with the requirements imposed by rule 24.1 with regard to any evidence in relation to any other party, he shall give notice in writing to that party to the effect that the evidence is being withheld and the grounds for doing so.

[Note. Formerly rule 4 of the Magistrates' Courts (Advance Notice of Expert Evidence) Rules 1997 and rule 4 of the Crown Court (Advance Notice of Expert Evidence) Rules 1987. For the equivalent exception in

Material relating to magistrates' court, Crown & High Court proceedings

Crown Court proceedings under Part 2 of the Proceeds of Crime Act 2002 see rule 57.10.]

24.3 Effect of failure to disclose

A party who seeks to adduce expert evidence in any proceedings and who fails to comply with rule 24.1 shall not adduce that evidence in those proceedings without the leave of the court.

[Note. Formerly rule 5 of the Magistrates' Courts (Advance Notice of Expert Evidence) Rules 1997 and rule 5 of the Crown Court (Advance Notice of Expert Evidence) Rules 1987.]

PART 37
SUMMARY TRIAL

37.1 Order of evidence and speeches: information

(1) On the summary trial of an information, where the accused does not plead guilty, the prosecutor shall call the evidence for the prosecution, and before doing so may address the court.

(2) At the conclusion of the evidence for the prosecution, the accused may address the court, whether or not he afterwards calls evidence.

(3) At the conclusion of the evidence, if any, for the defence, the prosecutor may call evidence to rebut that evidence.

(4) At the conclusion of the evidence for the defence and the evidence, if any, in rebuttal, the accused may address the court if he has not already done so.

(5) Either party may, with the leave of the court, address the court a second time, but where the court grants leave to one party it shall not refuse leave to the other.

(6) Where both parties address the court twice the prosecutor shall address the court for the second time before the accused does so.

[Note. Formerly rule 13 of the Magistrates' Courts Rules 1981.]

37.2 Procedure on information where accused is not legally represented

(1) The court shall explain to an accused who is not legally represented the substance of the charge in simple language.

(2) If an accused who is not legally represented, instead of asking a witness in support of the charge questions by way of cross-examination, makes assertions, the court shall then put to the witness such questions as it thinks necessary on behalf of the accused and may for this purpose question the accused in order to bring out or clear up any point arising out of such assertions.

[Note. Formerly rule 13A of the Magistrates' Courts Rules 1981.]

37.3 Adjournment of trial of information

(1) Where in the absence of the accused a magistrates' court adjourns the trial of an information, the court officer shall give to the accused notice in writing of the time and place at which the trial is to be resumed.

Appendix C

(2) . . .

[Note. [This rule derives in part from] rule 15 of the Magistrates' Courts Rules 1981.]

37.4 Formal admissions

Where under section 10 of the Criminal Justice Act 1967 a fact is admitted orally in court by or on behalf of the prosecutor or defendant for the purposes of the summary trial of an offence the court shall cause the admission to be written down and signed by or on behalf of the party making the admission.

[Note. Formerly rule 71 of the Magistrates' Courts Rules 1981.]

37.5 Notice of intention to cite previous convictions

Service on any person of a notice of intention to cite previous convictions under section 104 of the Magistrates' Courts Act 1980 or section 13 of the Road Traffic Offenders Act 1988 may be effected by delivering it to him or by sending it by post in a registered letter or by recorded delivery service, or by first class post addressed to him at his last known or usual place of abode.

[Note. Formerly rule 72 of the Magistrates' Courts Rules 1981.]

37.6 Application to change a plea of guilty

[(1) The defendant must apply as soon as practicable after becoming aware of the grounds for making an application to change a plea of guilty, and may only do so before the final disposal of the case, by sentence or otherwise.

(2) Unless the court otherwise directs, the application must be in writing and it must—
  (a) set out the reasons why it would be unjust for the guilty plea to remain unchanged;
  (b) indicate what, if any, evidence the defendant wishes to call;
  (c) identify any proposed witness; and
  (d) indicate whether legal professional privilege is waived, specifying any material name and date.

(3) The defendant must serve the written application on—
  (a) the court officer; and
  (b) the prosecutor.]

37.7 Preservation of depositions where offence triable either way is dealt with summarily

[The magistrates' court officer for the magistrates' court by which any person charged with an offence triable either way has been tried summarily shall preserve for a period of three years such depositions as have been taken.]

[Note. Formerly rule 22 of the Magistrates' Courts Rules 1981.]

37.8 Order of evidence and speeches: complaint

[(1) On the hearing of a complaint, except where the court determines under section 53(3) of the Magistrates' Courts Act 1980 to make the order with the consent of the defendant without hearing evidence, the complainant shall call his evidence, and before doing so may address the court.

(2) At the conclusion of the evidence for the complainant the defendant may address the court, whether or not he afterwards calls evidence.

(3) At the conclusion of the evidence, if any, for the defence, the complainant may call evidence to rebut that evidence.

(4) At the conclusion of the evidence for the defence and the evidence, if any, in rebuttal, the defendant may address the court if he has not already done so.

(5) Either party may, with the leave of the court, address the court a second time, but where the court grants leave to one party it shall not refuse leave to the other.

(6) Where the defendant obtains leave to address the court for a second time his second address shall be made before the second address, if any, of the complainant.]

[Note. Formerly rule 14 of the Magistrates' Courts Rules 1981. For criminal proceedings commenced by complaint see rules 50.3 (variation or discharge of certain orders), 53.1 (review of compensation order) and 55.2 (removal of driving disqualification).]

PART 63
APPEAL TO THE CROWN COURT

63.1 Application of this Part

This Part shall apply to any appeal under section 108(1) of the Magistrates' Courts Act 1980 (conviction and sentence), section 45(1) of the Mental Health Act 1983 (hospital or guardianship order in the absence of conviction), paragraph 11 of Schedule 3 to the Powers of the Criminal Courts (Sentencing) Act 2000 (re-sentencing on failure to comply with supervision order and section 14A(5A) of the Football Spectators Act 1989 (failure to make football banning order)).

[[Note. This rule derives in part from] rule 6 of the Crown Court Rules 1982. See also direction V.52 of the Practice Direction.]

63.2 Notice of appeal

(1) An appeal shall be commenced by the appellant's giving notice of appeal in accordance with the following provisions of this rule.

(2) The notice required by the preceding paragraph shall be in writing and shall be given to a court officer for the magistrates' court and to any other party to the appeal.

(3) Notice of appeal shall be given not later than 21 days after the making of, or failure to make, the decision appealed against and, for this purpose, where the court has adjourned the trial of an information after conviction, that day shall be the day on which the court sentences or otherwise deals with the offender:

Provided that, where a court exercises its power to defer sentence under section 1(1) of the Powers of the Criminal Courts (Sentencing) Act 2000,

Appendix C

that day shall, for the purposes of an appeal against conviction, be the day on which the court exercises that power.

(4) A notice of appeal shall state the grounds of appeal.

(5) The time for giving notice of appeal may be extended, either before or after it expires, by the Crown Court, on an application made in accordance with paragraph (6).

(6) An application for an extension of time shall be made in writing, specifying the grounds of the application and sent to a Crown Court officer.

(7) Where the Crown Court extends the time for giving notice of appeal, the Crown Court officer shall give notice of the extension to–
  (a) the appellant; and
  (b) the magistrates' court officer,

and the appellant shall give notice of the extension to any other party to the appeal.

[[Note. This rule derives in part from] rule 7 of the Crown Court Rules 1982.]

63.3 Documents to be sent to Crown Court

(1) The magistrates' court officer shall as soon as practicable send to the Crown Court officer any notice of appeal to the Crown Court given to the magistrates' court officer.

(2) The magistrates' court officer shall send to the Crown Court officer, with the notice of appeal, a copy of the extract of the magistrates' court register relating to that decision or proceedings, and details of the last known addresses of the parties to the appeal.

(3) Where any person, having given notice of appeal to the Crown Court, has been granted bail for the purposes of the appeal the magistrates' court officer shall before the day fixed for the hearing of the appeal send to the Crown Court officer a copy of the record made in pursuance of section 5 of the Bail Act 1976.

(4) Where a notice of appeal is given in respect of a hospital order or guardianship order made under section 37 of the Mental Health Act 1983 (powers of courts to order hospital admission or guardianship), a magistrates' court officer for the court from which the appeal is brought shall send with the notice to the Crown Court officer any written evidence considered by the court under section 37(2) of the 1983 Act.

(5) Where a notice of appeal is given in respect of an appeal against conviction by a magistrates' court the magistrates' court officer shall send with the notice to the Crown Court officer any admission of facts made for the purposes of the summary trial under section 10 of the Criminal Justice Act 1967 (proof by formal admission).

(6) Where a notice of appeal is given in respect of an appeal against sentence by a magistrates' court, and where that sentence was a custodial sentence, the magistrates' court officer shall send with the notice to the Crown Court officer a statement of whether the magistrates'

court obtained and considered a pre-sentence report before passing such sentence.

[[Note. This rule derives in part from] rule 74 of the Magistrates' Courts Rules 1981.]

63.4 Entry of appeal and notice of hearing

On receiving notice of appeal, the Crown Court officer shall enter the appeal and give notice of the time and place of the hearing to–
(a) the appellant;
(b) any other party to the appeal; and
(c) the magistrates' court officer.

[Note. Formerly rule 8 of the Crown Court Rules 1982.]

63.5 Abandonment of appeal - notice

(1) Without prejudice to the power of the Crown Court to give leave for an appeal to be abandoned, an appellant may abandon an appeal by giving notice in writing, in accordance with the following provisions of this rule, not later than the third day before the day fixed for hearing the appeal.

(2) The notice required by the preceding paragraph shall be given–
   (a) to the magistrates' court officer;
   (b) to the Crown Court officer; and
   (c) to any other party to the appeal.

(3) For the purposes of determining whether notice of abandonment was given in time there shall be disregarded any Saturday, Sunday and any day which is specified to be a bank holiday in England and Wales under section 1(1) of the Banking and Financial Dealings Act 1971.

[Note. Formerly rule 11 of the Crown Court Rules 1982.]

63.9 Disqualifications

A justice of the peace shall not sit in the Crown Court on the hearing of an appeal in a matter on which that justice adjudicated.

[[Note. This rule derives in part from] rule 5 of the Crown Court Rules 1982.]

PART 64
APPEAL TO THE HIGH COURT BY WAY OF CASE STATED

64.1 Application to a magistrates' court to state a case

(1) An application under section 111(1) of the Magistrates' Courts Act 1980 shall be made in writing and signed by or on behalf of the applicant and shall identify the question or questions of law or jurisdiction on which the opinion of the High Court is sought.

(2) Where one of the questions on which the opinion of the High Court is sought is whether there was evidence on which the magistrates' court could come to its decision, the particular finding of fact made by the magistrates' court which it is claimed cannot be supported by the evidence before the magistrates' court shall be specified in such application.

Appendix C

(3) Any such application shall be sent to a court officer for the magistrates' court whose decision is questioned.

[Note. Formerly rule 76 of the Magistrates' Courts Rules 1981. As to the procedure to be followed in the High Court, see Part 52 of the Civil Procedure Rules 1998.]

64.2 Consideration of a draft case by a magistrates' court

(1) Within 21 days after receipt of an application made in accordance with rule 64.1, a court officer for the magistrates' court whose decision is questioned shall, unless the justices refuse to state a case under section 111(5) of the Magistrates' Courts Act 1980, send a draft case in which are stated the matters required under rule 64.6 (content of case stated) to the applicant or his legal representative and shall send a copy thereof to the respondent or his legal representative.

(2) Within 21 days after receipt of the draft case under paragraph (1), each party may make representations thereon. Any such representations shall be in writing and signed by or on behalf of the party making them and shall be sent to the magistrates' court officer.

(3) Where the justices refuse to state a case under section 111(5) of the 1980 Act and they are required by a mandatory order of the High Court under section 111(6) to do so, this rule shall apply as if in paragraph (1)–
   (a) for the words "receipt of an application made in accordance with rule 64.1" there were substituted the words "the date on which a mandatory order under section 111(6) of the 1980 Act is made"; and
   (b) the words "unless the justices refuse to state a case under section 111(5) of the 1980 Act" were omitted.

[Note. Formerly rule 77 of the Magistrates' Courts Rules 1981.]

64.3 Preparation and submission of final case to a magistrates' court

(1) Within 21 days after the latest day on which representations may be made under rule 64.2, the justices whose decision is questioned shall make such adjustments, if any, to the draft case prepared for the purposes of that rule as they think fit, after considering any such representations, and shall state and sign the case.

(2) A case may be stated on behalf of the justices whose decision is questioned by any 2 or more of them and may, if the justices so direct, be signed on their behalf by the justices' clerk.

(3) Forthwith after the case has been stated and signed a court officer for the court shall send it to the applicant or his legal representative, together with any statement required by rule 64.4.

[Note. Formerly rule 78 of the Magistrates' Courts Rules 1981.]

64.4 Extension of time limits by a magistrates' court

(1) If a magistrates' court officer is unable to send to the applicant a draft case under rule 64.2(1) within the time required by that paragraph, he shall do so as soon as practicable thereafter and the provisions of that rule shall apply accordingly; but in that event a court officer shall attach

Material relating to magistrates' court, Crown & High Court proceedings

to the draft case, and to the final case when it is sent to the applicant or his legal representative under rule 64.3(3), a statement of the delay and the reasons for it.

(2) If a magistrates' court officer receives an application in writing from or on behalf of the applicant or the respondent for an extension of the time within which representations on the draft case may be made under rule 64.2(2), together with reasons in writing for it, the justices' clerk may, by notice in writing sent to the applicant, or respondent as the case may be, by the magistrates' court officer, extend the time and the provisions of that paragraph and of rule 64.3 shall apply accordingly; but in that event the court officer shall attach to the final case, when it is sent to the applicant or his legal representative under rule 64.3(3), a statement of the extension and the reasons for it.

(3) If the justices are unable to state a case within the time required by rule 64.3(1), they shall do so as soon as practicable thereafter and the provisions of that rule shall apply accordingly; but in that event a court officer shall attach to the final case, when it is sent to the applicant or his legal representative under rule 64.3(3), a statement of the delay and the reasons for it.

[Note. Formerly rule 79 of the Magistrates' Courts Rules 1981.]

64.5 *[Revoked by the Criminal Procedure (Amendment) Rules 2007, SI 2007/699]*

64.6 Content of case stated by a magistrates' courts

(1) A case stated by the magistrates' court shall state the facts found by the court and the question or questions of law or jurisdiction on which the opinion of the High Court is sought.

(2) Where one of the questions on which the opinion of the High Court is sought is whether there was evidence on which the magistrates' court could come to its decision, the particular finding of fact which it is claimed cannot be supported by the evidence before the magistrates' court shall be specified in the case.

(3) Unless one of the questions on which the opinion of the High Court is sought is whether there was evidence on which the magistrates' court could come to its decision, the case shall not contain a statement of evidence.

[Note. Formerly rule 81 of the Magistrates' Courts Rules 1981.]

64.7 Application to the Crown Court to state a case

(1) An application under section 28 of the Supreme Court Act 1981 to the Crown Court to state a case for the opinion of the High Court shall be made in writing to a court officer within 21 days after the date of the decision in respect of which the application is made.

(2) The application shall state the ground on which the decision of the Crown Court is questioned.

(3) After making the application, the applicant shall forthwith send a copy of it to the parties to the proceedings in the Crown Court.

Appendix C

(4) On receipt of the application, the Crown Court officer shall forthwith send it to the judge who presided at the proceedings in which the decision was made.

(5) On receipt of the application, the judge shall inform the Crown Court officer as to whether or not he has decided to state a case and that officer shall give notice in writing to the applicant of the judge's decision.

(6) If the judge considers that the application is frivolous, he may refuse to state a case and shall in that case, if the applicant so requires, cause a certificate stating the reasons for the refusal to be given to him.

(7) If the judge decides to state a case, the procedure to be followed shall, unless the judge in a particular case otherwise directs, be the procedure set out in paragraphs (8) to (12) of this rule.

(8) The applicant shall, within 21 days of receiving the notice referred to in paragraph (5), draft a case and send a copy of it to the Crown Court officer and to the parties to the proceedings in the Crown Court.

(9) Each party to the proceedings in the Crown Court shall, within 21 days of receiving a copy of the draft case under paragraph (8), either–
  (a) give notice in writing to the applicant and the Crown Court officer that he does not intend to take part in the proceedings before the High Court;
  (b) indicate in writing on the copy of the draft case that he agrees with it and send the copy to a court officer; or
  (c) draft an alternative case and send it, together with the copy of the applicant's case, to the Crown Court officer.

(10) The judge shall consider the applicant's draft case and any alternative draft case sent to the Crown Court officer under paragraph (9)(c).

(11) If the Crown Court so orders, the applicant shall, before the case is stated and delivered to him, enter before the Crown Court officer into a recognizance, with or without sureties and in such sum as the Crown Court considers proper, having regard to the means of the applicant, conditioned to prosecute the appeal without delay.

(12) The judge shall state and sign a case within 14 days after either–
  (a) the receipt of all the documents required to be sent to a court officer under paragraph (9); or
  (b) the expiration of the period of 21 days referred to in that paragraph,

whichever is the sooner.

(13) A case stated by the Crown Court shall state the facts found by the Crown Court, the submissions of the parties (including any authorities relied on by the parties during the course of those submissions), the decision of the Crown Court in respect of which the application is made and the question on which the opinion of the High Court is sought.

(14) Any time limit referred to in this rule may be extended either before or after it expires by the Crown Court.

(15) If the judge decides not to state a case but the stating of a case is subsequently required by a mandatory order of the High Court, paragraphs (7) to (14) shall apply to the stating of the case save that–

(a) in paragraph (7) the words "If the judge decides to state a case" shall be omitted; and
(b) in paragraph (8) for the words "receiving the notice referred to in paragraph (5)" there shall be substituted the words "the day on which the mandatory order was made".

[Note. Formerly rule 26 of the Crown Court Rule 1982.]

Practice Note (Magistrates: Clerk and Authorised Legal Adviser) [2000] 4 All ER 895

QUEEN'S BENCH DIVISION

2 OCTOBER 2000

Magistrates—clerk and authorised legal adviser—functions and responsibilites

Lord Woolf CJ made the following statement at the sitting of the court.

1. A justices' clerk is responsible for: (a) the legal advice tendered to the justices within the area; (b) the performance of any of the functions set out below by any member of his/her staff acting as legal adviser; (c) ensuring that competent advice is available to justices when the justices' clerk is not personally present in court; and (d) the effective delivery of case management and the reduction of unnec- essary delay.

2. Where a person other than the justices' clerk (a 'legal adviser'), who is authorised to do so, performs any of the functions referred to in this direction he/she will have the same responsibilities as the justices' clerk. The legal adviser may consult the justices' clerk or other person authorised by the justices' clerk for that purpose before tendering advice to the bench. If the justices' clerk or that person gives any advice directly to the bench, he/she should give the parties or their advocates an opportunity of repeating any relevant submissions prior to the advice being given.

3. It shall be the responsibility of the legal adviser to provide the justices with any advice they required to properly perform their functions whether or not the justices had requested that advice, on: (i) questions of law (including European Court of Human Rights jurisprudence and those matters set out in section 2(1) of the Human Rights Act 1998); (ii) questions of mixed law and fact; (iii) matters of practice and procedure; (iv) the range of penalties available; (v) any relevant decisions of the superior courts or other guidelines; (vi) other issues relevant to the matter before the court; and (vii) the appropriate decision-making structure to be applied in any given case. In addition to advising the justices it shall be the legal adviser's responsibility to assist the court, where appropriate, as to the formulation of reasons and the recording of those reasons.

4. A justices' clerk or legal adviser must not play any part in making findings of fact but may assist the bench by reminding them of the evidence, using any notes of the proceedings for this purpose.

Appendix C

5. A justices' clerk or legal adviser may ask questions of witnesses and the parties in order to clarify the evidence and any issues in the case.

6. A legal adviser has a duty to ensure that every case is conducted fairly.

7. When advising the justices the justices' clerk or legal adviser, whether or not previously in court, should: (i) ensure that he/she is aware of the relevant facts; (ii) provide the parties with the information necessary to enable the parties to make any representations they wish as to the advice before it is given.

8. At any time, justices are entitled to receive advice to assist them in discharging their responsibilities. If they are in any doubt as to the evidence which has been given, they should seek the aid of their legal adviser, referring to his/her notes as appropriate. This should ordinarily be done in open court. Where the justices request their adviser to join them in the retiring room, this request should be made in the presence of the parties in court. Any legal advice given to the justices other than in open court should be clearly stated to be provisional and the adviser should subsequently repeat the substance of the advice in open court and give the parties an opportunity to make any representations they wish on that provisional advice. The legal adviser should then state in open court whether the provisional advice is confirmed or if it is varied the nature of the variation.

9. The performance of a legal adviser may be appraised by a person authorised by the magistrates' courts committee to do so. For that purpose the appraiser may be present in the justices' retiring room. The content of the appraisal was confidential, but the fact that an appraisal has taken place, and the presence of the appraiser in the retiring room, should be briefly explained in open court.

10. The legal adviser is under a duty to assist unrepresented parties to present their case, but must do so without appearing to become an advocate for the party concerned.

11. The role of legal advisers in fine default proceedings or any other proceedings for the enforcement of financial orders, obligations or penalties is to assist the court. They must not act in an adversarial or partisan manner. With the agreement of the justices a legal adviser may ask questions of the defaulter to elicit information which the justices will require to make an adjudication, for example to facilitate his or her explanation for the default. A legal adviser may also advise the justices in the normal way as to the options open to them in dealing with the case. It would be inappropriate for the legal adviser to set out to establish wilful refusal or neglect or any other type of culpable behaviour, to offer an opinion on the facts, or to urge a particular course of action upon the justices. The duty of impartiality is the paramount consideration for the legal adviser at all times, and this takes precedence over any role he or she may have as a collecting officer. The appointment of other staff to 'prosecute' the case for the collecting officer is not essential to ensure compliance with the law, including the [Human Rights Act 1998]. Whether to make such appointments is a matter for the justices' chief executive.

12. The *Practice Direction* (*magistrates: clerk's functions*) [1981] 2 All ER 831, [1981] 1 WLR 1163 is revoked. *Practice Direction* (*justices: clerks*) [1954] 1 All ER 230, [1954] 1 WLR 213 remains in force.

13. This practice direction is issued with the concurrence of the President of the Family Division.

Practice Note (Justices' Clerks) [1954] 541 All ER 230; [1954] 1 WLR 213

Justices—Clerk—Presence in retiring room while justices consider decision—Matrimonial proceedings

15 January 1954. The following judgment was delivered.

LORD MERRIMAN P. In a statement made in the Divisional Court of the Queen's Bench Division on 16 November 1953 ([1953] 2 All ER 1306) about clerks to justices being present when the justices have retired to consider their decision, Lord Goddard CJ said (ibid, 1307) that the ruling of that court did not apply to justices when exercising jurisdiction in matrimonial cases as they were then subject to the directions and control of this Division. Before making any pronouncement in response to several requests for a ruling by this court on the subject, I wished to consult the judges of this Division. I now have their authority to say that they agree with the statement I am about to make. I am also authorised by Lord Simonds LC to say that he approves of it. Vaisey J also asks me to say that he agrees with it.

I wish to say at the outset that it rarely happens that an allegation of undue interference by the clerk in the decision of a complaint under the Summary Jurisdiction (Separation and Maintenance) Acts, 1895 to 1949, is made a ground of appeal to this Divisional Court. Nevertheless, it is at least as important in cases of this class as in cases of other classes dealt with by courts of summary jurisdiction that the decision should be that of the justices themselves and not that of the justices and their clerk, and that, not only should this be so in fact, but that nothing should be done to give the parties or the public the impression that the clerk is influencing the decision. I am, therefore, in complete agreement with Lord Goddard CJ that it should not be regarded as a matter of course that, if justices retire to consider their decision, the clerk should retire with them. Moreover, whether the justices invite the clerk to retire with them or send for him in the course of their deliberations, I agree that the clerk should always return to his place in court as soon as the justices release him, leaving them to complete their deliberations alone. Bearing in mind that domestic proceedings are often lengthy and may involve points of law in relation to the complaint itself or to the amount of maintenance, and that this court insists that a proper note of the evidence must be kept, and that, in the event of an appeal, justices must be prepared to state the reasons for their decision, I recognise that more often than not justices may properly wish to refresh their recollection of the evidence by recourse to the clerk's note, or to seek his advice about the law, before coming to their decision.

Having regard to the high standard of care which is generally shown by courts of summary jurisdiction in dealing with these domestic

Appendix C

proceedings. I do not think it is necessary for me to say more than that I am confident that justices taking part in them may be trusted to act, and to ensure that they appear to act, on the fundamental principle that they alone are the judges.

Appendix D

Material Relating to Evidence

Civil Evidence Act 1995

1 Admissibility of hearsay evidence

(1) In civil proceedings evidence shall not be excluded on the ground that it is hearsay.

(2) In this Act—
   (a) "hearsay" means a statement made otherwise than by a person while giving oral evidence in the proceedings which is tendered as evidence of the matters stated; and
   (b) references to hearsay include hearsay of whatever degree.

(3) Nothing in this Act affects the admissibility of evidence admissible apart from this section.

(4) The provisions of sections 2 to 6 (safeguards and supplementary provisions relating to hearsay evidence) do not apply in relation to hearsay evidence admissible apart from this section, notwithstanding that it may also be admissible by virtue of this section.

2 Notice of proposal to adduce hearsay evidence

(1) A party proposing to adduce hearsay evidence in civil proceedings shall, subject to the following provisions of this section, give to the other party or parties to the proceedings—
   (a) such notice (if any) of that fact, and
   (b) on request, such particulars of or relating to the evidence,

as is reasonable and practicable in the circumstances for the purpose of enabling him or them to deal with any matters arising from its being hearsay.

(2) Provision may be made by rules of court—
   (a) specifying classes of proceedings or evidence in relation to which subsection (1) does not apply, and
   (b) as to the manner in which (including the time within which) the duties imposed by that subsection are to be complied with in the cases where it does apply.

(3) Subsection (1) may also be excluded by agreement of the parties; and compliance with the duty to give notice may in any case be waived by the person to whom notice is required to be given.

(4) A failure to comply with subsection (1), or with rules under subsection (2)(b), does not affect the admissibility of the evidence but may be taken into account by the court—
   (a) in considering the exercise of its powers with respect to the course of proceedings and costs, and
   (b) as a matter adversely affecting the weight to be given to the evidence in accordance with section 4.

Appendix D

3 Power to call witness for cross-examination on hearsay statement

Rules of court may provide that where a party to civil proceedings adduces hearsay evidence of a statement made by a person and does not call that person as a witness, any other party to the proceedings may, with the leave of the court, call that person as a witness and cross-examine him on the statement as if he had been called by the first-mentioned party and as if the hearsay statement were his evidence in chief.

4 Considerations relevant to weighing of hearsay evidence

(1) In estimating the weight (if any) to be given to hearsay evidence in civil proceedings the court shall have regard to any circumstances from which any inference can reasonably be drawn as to the reliability or otherwise of the evidence.

(2) Regard may be had, in particular, to the following—
  (a) whether it would have been reasonable and practicable for the party by whom the evidence was adduced to have produced the maker of the original statement as a witness;
  (b) whether the original statement was made contemporaneously with the occurrence or existence of the matters stated;
  (c) whether the evidence involves multiple hearsay;
  (d) whether any person involved had any motive to conceal or misrepresent matters;
  (e) whether the original statement was an edited account, or was made in collaboration with another or for a particular purpose;
  (f) whether the circumstances in which the evidence is adduced as hearsay are such as to suggest an attempt to prevent proper evaluation of its weight.

5 Competence and credibility

(1) Hearsay evidence shall not be admitted in civil proceedings if or to the extent that it is shown to consist of, or to be proved by means of, a statement made by a person who at the time he made the statement was not competent as a witness.

For this purpose "not competent as a witness" means suffering from such mental or physical infirmity, or lack of understanding, as would render a person incompetent as a witness in civil proceedings; but a child shall be treated as competent as a witness if he satisfies the requirements of section 96(2)(a) and (b) of the Children Act 1989 (conditions for reception of unsworn evidence of child).

(2) Where in civil proceedings hearsay evidence is adduced and the maker of the original statement, or of any statement relied upon to prove another statement, is not called as a witness—
  (a) evidence which if he had been so called would be admissible for the purpose of attacking or supporting his credibility as a witness is admissible for that purpose in the proceedings; and
  (b) evidence tending to prove that, whether before or after he made the statement, he made any other statement inconsistent with it is admissible for the purpose of showing that he had contradicted himself.

Material relating to evidence

Provided that evidence may not be given of any matter of which, if he had been called as a witness and had denied that matter in cross-examination, evidence could not have been adduced by the cross-examining party.

6 Previous statements of witnesses

(1) Subject as follows, the provisions of this Act as to hearsay evidence in civil proceedings apply equally (but with any necessary modifications) in relation to a previous statement made by a person called as a witness in the proceedings.

(2) A party who has called or intends to call a person as a witness in civil proceedings may not in those proceedings adduce evidence of a previous statement made by that person, except—
 (a) with the leave of the court, or
 (b) for the purpose of rebutting a suggestion that his evidence has been fabricated.

This shall not be construed as preventing a witness statement (that is, a written statement of oral evidence which a party to the proceedings intends to lead) from being adopted by a witness in giving evidence or treated as his evidence.

(3) Where in the case of civil proceedings section 3, 4 or 5 of the Criminal Procedure Act 1865 applies, which make provision as to—
 (a) how far a witness may be discredited by the party producing him,
 (b) the proof of contradictory statements made by a witness, and
 (c) cross-examination as to previous statements in writing,

this Act does not authorise the adducing of evidence of a previous inconsistent or contradictory statement otherwise than in accordance with those sections.

This is without prejudice to any provision made by rules of court under section 3 above (power to call witness for cross-examination on hearsay statement).

(4) Nothing in this Act affects any of the rules of law as to the circumstances in which, where a person called as a witness in civil proceedings is cross-examined on a document used by him to refresh his memory, that document may be made evidence in the proceedings.

(5) Nothing in this section shall be construed as preventing a statement of any description referred to above from being admissible by virtue of section 1 as evidence of the matters stated.

7 Evidence formerly admissible at common law

(1) The common law rule effectively preserved by section 9(1) and (2)(a) of the Civil Evidence Act 1968 (admissibility of admissions adverse to a party) is superseded by the provisions of this Act.

(2) The common law rules effectively preserved by section 9(1) and (2)(b) to (d) of the Civil Evidence Act 1968, that is, any rule of law whereby in civil proceedings—
 (a) published works dealing with matters of a public nature (for example, histories, scientific works, dictionaries and maps) are admissible as evidence of facts of a public nature stated in them,

Appendix D

    (b) public documents (for example, public registers, and returns made under public authority with respect to matters of public interest) are admissible as evidence of facts stated in them, or
    (c) records (for example, the records of certain courts, treaties, Crown grants, pardons and commissions) are admissible as evidence of facts stated in them,

shall continue to have effect.

(3) The common law rules effectively preserved by section 9(3) and (4) of the Civil Evidence Act 1968, that is, any rule of law whereby in civil proceedings—
    (a) evidence of a person's reputation is admissible for the purpose of proving his good or bad character, or
    (b) evidence of reputation or family tradition is admissible—
        (i) for the purpose of proving or disproving pedigree or the existence of a marriage, or
        (ii) for the purpose of proving or disproving the existence of any public or general right or of identifying any person or thing,

shall continue to have effect in so far as they authorise the court to treat such evidence as proving or disproving that matter.

Where any such rule applies, reputation or family tradition shall be treated for the purposes of this Act as a fact and not as a statement or multiplicity of statements about the matter in question.

(4) The words in which a rule of law mentioned in this section is described are intended only to identify the rule and shall not be construed as altering it in any way.

8 Proof of statements contained in documents

(1) Where a statement contained in a document is admissible as evidence in civil proceedings, it may be proved—
    (a) by the production of that document, or
    (b) whether or not that document is still in existence, by the production of a copy of that document or of the material part of it,

authenticated in such manner as the court may approve.

(2) It is immaterial for this purpose how many removes there are between a copy and the original.

9 Proof of records of business or public authority

(1) A document which is shown to form part of the records of a business or public authority may be received in evidence in civil proceedings without further proof.

(2) A document shall be taken to form part of the records of a business or public authority if there is produced to the court a certificate to that effect signed by an officer of the business or authority to which the records belong.

For this purpose—
    (a) a document purporting to be a certificate signed by an officer of a business or public authority shall be deemed to have been duly given by such an officer and signed by him; and

Material relating to evidence

(b) a certificate shall be treated as signed by a person if it purports to bear a facsimile of his signature.

(3) The absence of an entry in the records of a business or public authority may be proved in civil proceedings by affidavit of an officer of the business or authority to which the records belong.

(4) In this section—
"records" means records in whatever form;
"business" includes any activity regularly carried on over a period of time, whether for profit or not, by any body (whether corporate or not) or by an individual;
"officer" includes any person occupying a responsible position in relation to the relevant activities of the business or public authority or in relation to its records; and
"public authority" includes any public or statutory undertaking, any government department and any person holding office under Her Majesty.

(5) The court may, having regard to the circumstances of the case, direct that all or any of the above provisions of this section do not apply in relation to a particular document or record, or description of documents or records.

10 Admissibility and proof of Ogden Tables

(1) The actuarial tables (together with explanatory notes) for use in personal injury and fatal accident cases issued from time to time by the Government Actuary's Department are admissible in evidence for the purpose of assessing, in an action for personal injury, the sum to be awarded as general damages for future pecuniary loss.

(2) They may be proved by the production of a copy published by Her Majesty's Stationery Office.

(3) For the purposes of this section—
   (a) "personal injury" includes any disease and any impairment of a person's physical or mental condition; and
   (b) "action for personal injury" includes an action brought by virtue of the Law Reform (Miscellaneous Provisions) Act 1934 or the Fatal Accidents Act 1976.

11 Meaning of "civil proceedings"

In this Act "civil proceedings" means civil proceedings, before any tribunal, in relation to which the strict rules of evidence apply, whether as a matter of law or by agreement of the parties.

References to "the court" and "rules of court" shall be construed accordingly.

12 Provisions as to rules of court

(1) Any power to make rules of court regulating the practice or procedure of the court in relation to civil proceedings includes power to make such provision as may be necessary or expedient for carrying into effect the provisions of this Act.

Appendix D

(2) Any rules of court made for the purposes of this Act as it applies in relation to proceedings in the High Court apply, except in so far as their operation is excluded by agreement, to arbitration proceedings to which this Act applies, subject to such modifications as may be appropriate.

Any question arising as to what modifications are appropriate shall be determined, in default of agreement, by the arbitrator or umpire, as the case may be.

13 Interpretation

In this Act—

"civil proceedings" has the meaning given by section 11 and "court" and "rules of court" shall be construed in accordance with that section;

"document" means anything in which information of any description is recorded, and "copy", in relation to a document, means anything onto which information recorded in the document has been copied, by whatever means and whether directly or indirectly;

"hearsay" shall be construed in accordance with section 1(2);

"oral evidence" includes evidence which, by reason of a defect of speech or hearing, a person called as a witness gives in writing or by signs;

"the original statement", in relation to hearsay evidence, means the underlying statement (if any) by—
 (a) in the case of evidence of fact, a person having personal knowledge of that fact, or
 (b) in the case of evidence of opinion, the person whose opinion it is; and

"statement" means any representation of fact or opinion, however made.

14 Savings

(1) Nothing in this Act affects the exclusion of evidence on grounds other than that it is hearsay.

This applies whether the evidence falls to be excluded in pursuance of any enactment or rule of law, for failure to comply with rules of court or an order of the court, or otherwise.

(2) Nothing in this Act affects the proof of documents by means other than those specified in section 8 or 9.

(3) Nothing in this Act affects the operation of the following enactments—
 (a) section 2 of the Documentary Evidence Act 1868 (mode of proving certain official documents);
 (b) section 2 of the Documentary Evidence Act 1882 (documents printed under the superintendence of Stationery Office);
 (c) section 1 of the Evidence (Colonial Statutes) Act 1907 (proof of statutes of certain legislatures);
 (d) section 1 of the Evidence (Foreign, Dominion and Colonial Documents) Act 1933 (proof and effect of registers and official certificates of certain countries);

(e) section 5 of the Oaths and Evidence (Overseas Authorities and Countries) Act 1963 (provision in respect of public registers of other countries).

15 Consequential amendments and repeals

(1) The enactments specified in Schedule 1 are amended in accordance with that Schedule, the amendments being consequential on the provisions of this Act.

(2) The enactments specified in Schedule 2 are repealed to the extent specified.

16 Short title, commencement and extent

(1) This Act may be cited as the Civil Evidence Act 1995.

(2) The provisions of this Act come into force on such day as the Lord Chancellor may appoint by order made by statutory instrument, and different days may be appointed for different provisions and for different purposes.

[(3) Subject to subsection (3A), the provisions of this Act shall not apply in relation to proceedings begun before commencement.]

[(3A) Transitional provisions for the application of the provisions of this Act to proceedings begun before commencement may be made by rules of court or practice directions.]

(4) This Act extends to England and Wales.

(5) Section 10 (admissibility and proof of Ogden Tables) also extends to Northern Ireland. As it extends to Northern Ireland, the following shall be substituted for subsection (3)(b)— "(b) "action for personal injury" includes an action brought by virtue of the Law Reform (Miscellaneous Provisions)(Northern Ireland) Act 1937 or the Fatal Accidents (Northern Ireland) Order 1977."

(6) The provisions of Schedules 1 and 2 (consequential amendments and repeals) have the same extent as the enactments respectively amended or repealed.

SCHEDULE 2
REPEALS

Section 15(2)

Chapter	Short title	Extent of repeal
1938 c 28	Evidence Act 1938	Sections 1 and 2
		Section 6(1) except the words from 'Proceedings' to 'references'
		Section 6(2)(b)
1968 c 64	Civil Evidence Act 1968	Part I

Appendix D

Chapter	Short title	Extent of repeal
1971 c 33	Armed Forces Act 1971	Section 26
1972 c 30	Civil Evidence Act 1972	Section 1
	Section 2(1) and (2)	
	In section 2(3)(b), the words from "by virtue of section 2" to "out-of-court statements)"	
	In section 3(1), the words "Part I of the Civil Evidence Act 1968 or"	
	In section 6(3), the words "1 and", in both places where they occur	
1975 c 63	Inheritance (Provision for Family and Dependants) Act 1975	Section 21
1979 c 2	Customs and Excise Management Act 1979	Section 75A(6)(a) Section 118A(6)(a)
1980 c 43	Magistrates' Courts Act 1980	In Schedule 7, paragraph 75
1984 c 28	County Courts Act 1984	In Schedule 2, paragraphs 33 and 34
1985 c 54	Finance Act 1985	Section 10(7)
1986 c 21	Armed Forces Act 1986	Section 3
1988 c 39	Finance Act 1988	Section 127(5)
1990 c 26	Gaming (Amendment) Act 1990	In the Schedule, paragraph 2(7)
1994 c 9	Finance Act 1994	Section 22(2)(a)
	In Schedule 7, paragraph 1(6)(a)	
1994 c 23	Value Added Tax Act 1994	Section 96(6) and (7)
		In Schedule 11, paragraph 6(6)(a)
1995 c 4	Finance Act 1995	In Schedule 4, paragraph 38

Magistrates' Courts (Hearsay Evidence in Civil Proceedings) Rules 1999, SI 1999/681

1 Citation and commencement

These Rules may be cited as the Magistrates' Courts (Hearsay Evidence in Civil Proceedings) Rules 1999 and shall come into force on 1st April 1999.

2 Application and interpretation

(1) In these Rules, the "1995 Act" means the Civil Evidence Act 1995.

(2) In these Rules—
"hearsay evidence" means evidence consisting of hearsay within the meaning of section 1(2) of the 1995 Act;
"hearsay notice" means a notice under section 2 of the 1995 Act.

(3) These Rules shall apply to hearsay evidence in civil proceedings in magistrates' courts.

3 Hearsay notices

(1) Subject to paragraphs (2) and (3), a party who desires to give hearsay evidence at the hearing must, not less than 21 days before the date fixed for the hearing, serve a hearsay notice on every other party and file a copy in the court by serving it on the [designated officer for the court].

(2) Subject to paragraph (3), the court or the justices' clerk may make a direction substituting a different period of time for the service of the hearsay notice under paragraph (1) on the application of a party to the proceedings.

(3) The court may make a direction under paragraph (2) of its own motion.

(4) A hearsay notice must—
 (a) state that it is a hearsay notice;
 (b) identify the proceedings in which the hearsay evidence is to be given;
 (c) state that the party proposes to adduce hearsay evidence;
 (d) identify the hearsay evidence;
 (e) identify the person who made the statement which is to be given in evidence; and
 (f) state why that person will not be called to give oral evidence.

(5) A single hearsay notice may deal with the hearsay evidence of more than one witness.

4 Power to call witness for cross-examination on hearsay evidence

(1) Where a party tenders as hearsay evidence a statement made by a person but does not propose to call the person who made the statement to give evidence, the court may, on application, allow another party to call and cross-examine the person who made the statement on its contents.

(2) An application under paragraph (1) must—
 (a) be served on the justices' clerk with sufficient copies for all other parties;
 (b) unless the court otherwise directs, be made not later than 7 days after service of the hearsay notice; and
 (c) give reasons why the person who made the statement should be cross-examined on its contents.

Appendix D

(3) On receipt of an application under paragraph (1), the justices' clerk must—
  (a) unless the court otherwise directs, allow sufficient time for the applicant to comply with paragraph (4);
  (b) fix the date, time and place and endorse them on the copies of the application filed by the applicant; and
  (c) return the copies to the applicant forthwith.

(4) Subject to paragraphs (5) and (6), on receipt of the copies from the justices' clerk under paragraph (3)(c), the applicant must serve a copy on every other party giving not less than 3 days' notice of the hearing of the application.

(5) The court or the justices' clerk may give directions as to the manner in which service under paragraph (4) is to be effected and may, subject to giving notice to the applicant, alter or dispense with the notice requirement under paragraph (4) if the court or the [designated officer's], as the case may be, considers it is in the interests of justice to do so.

(6) The court may hear an application under paragraph (1) ex parte if it considers it is in the interests of justice to do so.

(7) Subject to paragraphs (5) and (6), where an application under paragraph (1) is made, the applicant must file with the court a statement at or before the hearing of the application that service of a copy of the application has been effected on all other parties and the statement must indicate the manner, date, time and address at which the document was served.

(8) The court must notify all parties of its decision on an application under paragraph (1).

5 Credibility and previous inconsistent statements

(1) If—
  (a) a party tenders as hearsay evidence a statement made by a person but does not call the person who made the statement to give oral evidence, and
  (b) another party wishes to attack the credibility of the person who made the statement or allege that the person who made the statement made any other statement inconsistent with it,

that other party must notify the party tendering the hearsay evidence of his intention.

(2) Unless the court or the justices' clerk otherwise directs, a notice under paragraph (1) must be given not later than 7 days after service of the hearsay notice and, in addition to the requirements in paragraph (1), must be served on every other party and a copy filed in the court.

(3) If, on receipt of a notice under paragraph (1), the party referred to in paragraph (1)(a) calls the person who made the statement to be tendered as hearsay evidence to give oral evidence, he must, unless the court otherwise directs, notify the court and all other parties of his intention.

(4) Unless the court or the justices' clerk otherwise directs, a notice under paragraph (3) must be given not later than 7 days after the service of the notice under paragraph (1).

Material relating to evidence

6 Service

(1) Where service of a document is required by these Rules it may be effected, unless the contrary is indicated—
- (a) if the person to be served is not known by the person serving to be acting by solicitor—
  - (i) by delivering it to him personally, or
  - (ii) by delivering at, or by sending it by first-class post to, his residence or his last known residence, or
- (b) if the person to be served is known by the person serving to be acting by solicitor—
  - (i) by delivering the document at, or sending it by first-class post to, the solicitor's address for service,
  - (ii) where the solicitor's address for service includes a numbered box at a document exchange, by leaving the document at that document exchange or at a document exchange which transmits documents on every business day to that document exchange, or
  - (iii) by sending a legible copy of the document by facsimile transmission to the solicitor's office.

(2) In this rule,"first-class post" means first-class post which has been pre-paid or in respect of which pre-payment is not required.

(3) A document shall, unless the contrary is proved, be deemed to have been served—
- (a) in the case of service by first-class post, on the second business day after posting,
- (b) in the case of service in accordance with paragraph (1)(b)(ii), on the second business day after the day on which it is left at the document exchange, and
- (c) in the case of service in accordance with paragraph (1)(b)(iii), where it is transmitted on a business day before 4 pm, on that day and in any other case, on the next business day.

(4) In this rule,"business day" means any day other than—
- (a) a Saturday, Sunday, Christmas Day or Good Friday; or
- (b) a bank holiday under the Banking and Financial Dealings Act 1971, in England and Wales.

7 Amendment to the Justices' Clerks Rules 1970

The Justices' Clerks Rules 1970 shall be amended by the insertion, after paragraph 18 of the Schedule, of the following paragraph—
"19 The giving, variation or revocation of directions in accordance with rules 3(2), 4(5), 5(2) and (4) of the Magistrates' Courts (Hearsay Evidence in Civil Proceedings) Rules 1999.".

Police and Criminal Evidence Act 1984

67 Codes of practice—supplementary

(1) In this section, "code" means a code of practice under section 60, 60A or 66.

(2) The Secretary of State may at any time revise the whole or any part of a code.

Appendix D

(3) A code may be made, or revised, so as to—
 (a) apply only in relation to one or more specified areas,
 (b) have effect only for a specified period,
 (c) apply only in relation to specified offences or descriptions of offender.

(4) Before issuing a code, or any revision of a code, the Secretary of State must consult—
 [(a) the Association of Police Authorities,
 (b) the Association of Chief Police Officers of England, Wales and Northern Ireland,]
 (c) the General Council of the Bar,
 (d) the Law Society of England and Wales,
 (e) the Institute of Legal Executives, and
 (f) such other persons as he thinks fit.

(5) A code, or a revision of a code, does not come into operation until the Secretary of State by order so provides.

(6) The power conferred by subsection (5) is exercisable by statutory instrument.

(7) An order bringing a code into operation may not be made unless a draft of the order has been laid before Parliament and approved by a resolution of each House.

(7A) An order bringing a revision of a code into operation must be laid before Parliament if the order has been made without a draft having been so laid and approved by a resolution of each House.

(7B) When an order or draft of an order is laid, the code or revision of a code to which it relates must also be laid.

(7C) No order or draft of an order may be laid until the consultation required by subsection (4) has taken place.

(7D) An order bringing a code, or a revision of a code, into operation may include transitional or saving provisions.

(8) . . .

(9) Persons other than police officers who are charged with the duty of investigating offences or charging offenders shall in the discharge of that duty have regard to any relevant provision of a code.

(9A) Persons on whom powers are conferred by—
 (a) any designation under section 38 or 39 of the Police Reform Act 2002 (c. 30) (police powers for police authority employees), or
 (b) any accreditation under section 41 of that Act (accreditation under community safety accreditation schemes),

shall have regard to any relevant provision of a code in the exercise or performance of the powers and duties conferred or imposed on them by that designation or accreditation.

(10) A failure on the part—
 (a) of a police officer to comply with any provision of a code;
 (b) of any person other than a police officer who is charged with the duty of investigating offences or charging offenders to have

Material relating to evidence

regard to any relevant provision of a code in the discharge of that duty, or
(c) of a person designated under section 38 or 39 or accredited under section 41 of the Police Reform Act 2002 (c 30) to have regard to any relevant provision of a code in the exercise or performance of the powers and duties conferred or imposed on him by that designation or accreditation.

shall not of itself render him liable to any criminal or civil proceedings.

(11) In all criminal and civil proceedings any code shall be admissible in evidence; and if any provision of a code appears to the court or tribunal conducting the proceedings to be relevant to any question arising in the proceedings it shall be taken into account in determining that question.

(12) In this section "criminal proceedings" includes—
(a) proceedings in the United Kingdom or elsewhere before a court-martial constituted under the Army Act 1955, the Air Force Act 1955 or the Naval Discipline Act 1957;
(b) proceedings before the Courts-Martial Appeal Court; and
(c) proceedings before a Standing Civilian Court.

76 Confessions

(1) In any proceedings a confession made by an accused person may be given in evidence against him in so far as it is relevant to any matter in issue in the proceedings and is not excluded by the court in pursuance of this section.

(2) If, in any proceedings where the prosecution proposes to give in evidence a confession made by an accused person, it is represented to the court that the confession was or may have been obtained—
(a) by oppression of the person who made it; or
(b) in consequence of anything said or done which was likely, in the circumstances existing at the time, to render unreliable any confession which might be made by him in consequence thereof,

the court shall not allow the confession to be given in evidence against him except in so far as the prosecution proves to the court beyond reasonable doubt that the confession (notwithstanding that it may be true) was not obtained as aforesaid.

(3) In any proceedings where the prosecution proposes to give in evidence a confession made by an accused person, the court may of its own motion require the prosecution, as a condition of allowing it to do so, to prove that the confession was not obtained as mentioned in subsection (2) above.

(4) The fact that a confession is wholly or partly excluded in pursuance of this section shall not affect the admissibility in evidence—
(a) of any facts discovered as a result of the confession; or
(b) where the confession is relevant as showing that the accused speaks, writes or expresses himself in a particular way, of so much of the confession as is necessary to show that he does so.

(5) Evidence that a fact to which this subsection applies was discovered as a result of a statement made by an accused person shall not be

Appendix D

admissible unless evidence of how it was discovered is given by him or on his behalf.

(6) Subsection (5) above applies—
- (a) to any fact discovered as a result of a confession which is wholly excluded in pursuance of this section; and
- (b) to any fact discovered as a result of a confession which is partly so excluded, if the fact is discovered as a result of the excluded part of the confession.

(7) Nothing in Part VII of this Act shall prejudice the admissibility of a confession made by an accused person.

(8) In this section "oppression" includes torture, inhuman or degrading treatment, and the use or threat of violence (whether or not amounting to torture).

[(9) Where the proceedings mentioned in subsection (1) above are proceedings before a magistrates' court inquiring into an offence as examining justices this section

shall have effect with the omission of
- (a) in subsection (1) the words "and is not excluded by the court in pursuance of this section", and
- (b) subsections (2) to (6) and (8).]

78 Exclusion of unfair evidence

(1) In any proceedings the court may refuse to allow evidence on which the prosecution proposes to rely to be given if it appears to the court that, having regard to all the circumstances, including the circumstances in which the evidence was obtained, the admission of the evidence would have such an adverse effect on the fairness of the proceedings that the court ought not to admit it.

(2) Nothing in this section shall prejudice any rule of law requiring a court to exclude evidence.

[(3) This section shall not apply in the case of proceedings before a magistrates' court inquiring into an offence as examining justices.]

Appendix E

Material Relating to Sentencing and Costs

Courts Act 1971

52 Award of costs where information or complaint is not proceeded with

(1), (2)...

(3) Where—
  (a) ...
  (b) a complaint is made to a justice of the peace [acting in any local justice area] but the complaint is not proceeded with,

a magistrates' court for that area may make such order as to costs to be paid ... by the complainant to the defendant as it thinks just and reasonable.

(4) An order under subsection (3) above shall specify the amount of the costs ordered to be paid.

(5) ... for the purpose of enforcement an order under subsection (3) above made in relation to a complaint which is not proceeded with shall be treated as if it were an order made under [section 64 of the Magistrates' Courts Act 1980] (power to award, and enforcement of, costs in civil proceedings).

Prosecution of Offences Act 1985

16 Defence costs

(1) Where—
  (a) an information laid before a justice of the peace for any area, charging any person with an offence, is not proceeded with;
  (b) a magistrates' court inquiring into an indictable offence as examining justices determines not to commit the accused for trial;
  (c) a magistrates' court dealing summarily with an offence dismisses the information;

that court or, in a case falling within paragraph (a) above, a magistrates' court for that area, may make an order in favour of the accused for a payment to be made out of central funds in respect of his costs (a "defendant's costs order").

(2) Where—
  (a) any person is not tried for an offence for which he has been indicted or [sent] for trial; or
  [(aa) a notice of transfer is given under [a relevant transfer provision] but a person in relation to whose case it is given is not tried on a charge to which it relates; or]
  (b) any person is tried on indictment and acquitted on any count in the indictment;

Appendix E

the Crown Court may make a defendant's costs order in favour of the accused.

(3) Where a person convicted of an offence by a magistrates' court appeals to the Crown Court under section 108 of the Magistrates' Courts Act 1980 (right of appeal against conviction or sentence) and, in consequence of the decision on appeal—
  (a) his conviction is set aside; or
  (b) a less severe punishment is awarded;

the Crown Court may make a defendant's costs order in favour of the accused.

(4) Where the Court of Appeal—
  (a) allows an appeal under Part I of the Criminal Appeal Act 1968 against—
    (i) conviction;
    (ii) a verdict of not guilty by reason of insanity; or
    [(iii) a finding under the Criminal Procedure (Insanity) Act 1964 that the appellant is under a disability, or that he did the act or made the omission charged against him;]
  [(aa) directs under section 8(1B) of the Criminal Appeal Act 1968 the entry of a judgment and verdict of acquittal;]
  (b) on an appeal under that Part against conviction—
    (i) substitutes a verdict of guilty of another offence;
    (ii) in a case where a special verdict has been found, orders a different conclusion on the effect of that verdict to be recorded; or
    (iii) is of the opinion that the case falls within paragraph (a) or (b) of section 6(1) of that Act (cases where the court substitutes a finding of insanity or unfitness to plead); or
  (c) on an appeal under that Part against sentence, exercises its powers under section 11(3) of that Act (powers where the court considers that the appellant should be sentenced differently for an offence for which he was dealt with by the court below); the court may make a defendant's costs order in favour of the accused.

[(4A) The court may also make a defendant's costs order in favour of the accused on an appeal under section 9(11) of the Criminal Justice Act 1987 (appeals against orders or rulings at preparatory hearings).]

(5) Where—
  (a) any proceedings in a criminal cause or matter are determined before a Divisional Court of the Queen's Bench Division;
  (b) the House of Lords determines an appeal, or application for leave to appeal, from such a Divisional Court in a criminal cause or matter;
  (c) the Court of Appeal determines an application for leave to appeal to the House of Lords under Part II of the Criminal Appeal Act 1968; or
  (d) the House of Lords determines an appeal, or application for leave to appeal, under Part II of that Act;

the court may make a defendant's costs order in favour of the accused.

(6) A defendant's costs order shall, subject to the following provisions of this section, be for the payment out of central funds, to the person in

Material relating to sentencing and costs

whose favour the order is made, of such amount as the court considers reasonably sufficient to compensate him for any expenses properly incurred by him in the proceedings.

(7) Where a court makes a defendant's costs order but is of the opinion that there are circumstances which make it inappropriate that the person in whose favour the order is made should recover the full amount mentioned in subsection (6) above, the court shall—
   (a) assess what amount would, in its opinion, be just and reasonable; and
   (b) specify that amount in the order.

(8) . . .

(9) Subject to subsection (7) above, the amount to be paid out of central funds in pursuance of a defendant's costs order shall—
   (a) be specified in the order, in any case where the court considers it appropriate for the amount to be so specified and the person in whose favour the order is made agrees the amount; and
   (b) in any other case, be determined in accordance with regulations made by the Lord Chancellor for the purposes of this section.

(10) Subsection (6) above shall have effect, in relation to any case falling within subsection (1)(a) or (2)(a) above, as if for the words "in the proceedings" there were substituted the words "in or about the defence".

(11) Where a person ordered to be retried is acquitted at his retrial, the costs which may be ordered to be paid out of central funds under this section shall include—
   (a) any costs which, at the original trial, could have been ordered to be so paid under this section if he had been acquitted; and
   (b) if no order was made under this section in respect of his expenses on appeal, any sums for the payment of which such an order could have been made.

[(12) In subsection (2)(aa)"relevant transfer provision" means—
   (a) section 4 of the Criminal Justice Act 1987, or
   (b) section 53 of the Criminal Justice Act 1991.]

17 Prosecution costs

(1) Subject to subsection (2) below, the court may—
   (a) in any proceedings in respect of an indictable offence; and
   (b) in any proceedings before a Divisional Court of the Queen's Bench Division or the House of Lords in respect of a summary offence;

order the payment out of central funds of such amount as the court considers reasonably sufficient to compensate the prosecutor for any expenses properly incurred by him in the proceedings.

(2) No order under this section may be made in favour of—
   (a) a public authority; or
   (b) a person acting—
      (i) on behalf of a public authority; or
      (ii) in his capacity as an official appointed by such an authority.

Appendix E

(3) Where a court makes an order under this section but is of the opinion that there are circumstances which make it inappropriate that the prosecution should recover the full amount mentioned in subsection (1) above, the court shall—
- (a) assess what amount would in its opinion, be just and reasonable; and
- (b) specify that amount in the order.

(4) Subject to subsection (3) above, the amount to be paid out of central funds in pursuance of an order under this section shall—
- (a) be specified in the order, in any case where the court considers it appropriate for the amount to be so specified and the prosecutor agrees the amount; and
- (b) in any other case, be determined in accordance with regulations made by the Lord Chancellor for the purposes of this section.

(5) Where the conduct of proceedings to which subsection (1) above applies is taken over by the Crown Prosecution Service, that subsection shall have effect as if it referred to the prosecutor who had the conduct of the proceedings before the intervention of the Service and to expenses incurred by him up to the time of intervention.

(6) In this section "public authority" means—
- (a) a police force within the meaning of section 3 of this Act;
- (b) the Crown Prosecution Service or any other government department;
- (c) a local authority or other authority or body constituted for purposes of—
  - (i) the public service or of local government; or
  - (ii) carrying on under national ownership any industry or undertaking or part of an industry or undertaking; or
- (d) any other authority or body whose members are appointed by Her Majesty or by any Minister of the Crown or government department or whose revenues consist wholly or mainly of money provided by Parliament.

18 Award of costs against accused

(1) Where—
- (a) any person is convicted of an offence before a magistrates' court;
- (b) the Crown Court dismisses an appeal against such a conviction or against the sentence imposed on that conviction; or
- (c) any person is convicted of an offence before the Crown Court;

the court may make such order as to the costs to be paid by the accused to the prosecutor as it considers just and reasonable.

(2) Where the Court of Appeal dismisses—
- (a) an appeal or application for leave to appeal under Part I of the Criminal Appeal Act 1968; or
- (b) an application by the accused for leave to appeal to the House of Lords under Part II of that Act [or
- (c) an appeal or application for leave to appeal under section 9(11) of the Criminal Justice Act 1987;]

it may make such order as to the costs to be paid by the accused, to such person as may be named in the order, as it considers just and reasonable.

Material relating to sentencing and costs

[(2A) Where the Court of Appeal reverses or varies a ruling on an appeal under Part 9 of the Criminal Justice Act 2003, it may make such order as to the costs to be paid by the accused, to such person as may be named in the order, as it considers just and reasonable.]

(3) The amount to be paid by the accused in pursuance of an order under this section shall be specified in the order.

(4) Where any person is convicted of an offence before a magistrates' court and—
   (a) under the conviction the court orders payment of any sum as a fine, penalty, forfeiture or compensation; and
   (b) the sum so ordered to be paid does not exceed £5;

the court shall not order the accused to pay any costs under this section unless in the particular circumstances of the case it considers it right to do so.

(5) Where any person under [the age of eighteen] is convicted of an offence before a magistrates' court, the amount of any costs ordered to be paid by the accused under this section shall not exceed the amount of any fine imposed on him.

(6) Costs ordered to be paid under subsection (2) [or (2A)] above may include the reasonable cost of any transcript of a record of proceedings made in accordance with rules of court made for the purposes of section 32 of the Act of 1968.

19 Provision for orders as to costs in other circumstances

(1) The Lord Chancellor may by regulations make provision empowering magistrates' courts, the Crown Court and the Court of Appeal, in any case where the court is satisfied that one party to criminal proceedings has incurred costs as a result of an unnecessary or improper act or omission by, or on behalf of, another party to the proceedings, to make an order as to the payment of those costs.

(2) Regulations made under subsection (1) above may, in particular—
   (a) allow the making of such an order at any time during the proceedings;
   (b) make provision as to the account to be taken, in making such an order, of any other order as to costs . . . which has been made in respect of the proceedings [or any grant of representation for the purposes of the proceedings which has been made under the Legal Aid Act 1988] [or any grant of a right to representation funded by the Legal Services Commission as part of the Criminal Defence Service];
   (c) make provision as to the account to be taken of any such order in the making of any other order as to costs in respect of the proceedings; and
   (d) contain provisions similar to those in section 18(4) and (5) of this Act.

(3) The Lord Chancellor may by regulations make provision for the payment out of central funds, in such circumstances and in relation to such criminal proceedings as may be specified, of such sums as appear to the court to be reasonably necessary—

Appendix E

> (a) to compensate any witness in the proceedings[, and any other person who in the opinion of the court necessarily attends for the purpose of the proceedings otherwise than to give evidence,] for the expense, trouble or loss of time properly incurred in or incidental to his attendance;
> (b) to cover the proper expenses of an interpreter who is required because of the accused's lack of English;
> (c) to compensate a duly qualified medical practitioner who—
>   (i) makes a report otherwise than in writing for the purpose of section 30 of the Magistrates' Courts Act 1980 [section 11 of the Powers of Criminal Courts (Sentencing) Act 2000] (remand for medical examination); or
>   (ii) makes a written report to a court in pursuance of a request to which section 32(2) of the Criminal Justice Act 1967 (report by medical practitioner on medical condition of offender) applies;
>   for the expenses properly incurred in or incidental to his reporting to the court.
> [(d) to cover the proper fee or costs of a person appointed by the Crown Court under section 4A of the Criminal Procedure (Insanity) Act 1964 to put the case for the defence.]
> [(e) to cover the proper fee or costs of a legal representative appointed under section 38(4) of the Youth Justice and Criminal Evidence Act 1999 (defence representation for purposes of cross-examination) and any expenses properly incurred in providing such a person with evidence or other material in connection with his appointment.]

[(3A) In subsection (3)(a) above "attendance" means attendance at the court or elsewhere.]

(4) The Court of Appeal may order the payment out of central funds of such sums as appear to it to be reasonably sufficient to compensate an appellant who is not in custody and who appears before it on, or in connection with, his appeal under Part I of the Criminal Appeal Act 1968.

(5) The Lord Chancellor may by regulations provide that any provision made by or under this Part which would not otherwise apply in relation to any category of proceedings in which an offender is before a magistrates' court or the Crown Court shall apply in relation to proceedings of that category, subject to any specified modifications.

[19A Costs against legal representatives etc]

[(1) In any criminal proceedings—
  (a) the Court of Appeal;
  (b) the Crown Court; or
  (c) a magistrates' court,

may disallow, or (as the case may be) order the legal or other representative concerned to meet, the whole of any wasted costs or such part of them as may be determined in accordance with regulations.

(2) Regulations shall provide that a legal or other representative against whom action is taken by a magistrates' court under subsection (1) may appeal to the Crown Court and that a legal or other representative

Material relating to sentencing and costs

against whom action is taken by the Crown Court under subsection (1) may appeal to the Court of Appeal.

(3) In this section—
"legal or other representative", in relation to any proceedings, means a person who is exercising a right of audience, or a right to conduct litigation, on behalf of any party to the proceedings;
"regulations" means regulations made by the Lord Chancellor; and
"wasted costs" means any costs incurred by a party—
   (a) as a result of any improper, unreasonable or negligent act or omission on the part of any representative or any employee of a representative; or
   (b) which, in the light of any such act or omission occurring after they were incurred, the court considers it is unreasonable to expect that party to pay.]

[19B Provision for award of costs against third parties]

[(1) The Lord Chancellor may by regulations make provision empowering magistrates' courts, the Crown Court and the Court of Appeal to make a third party costs order if the condition in subsection (3) is satisfied.

(2) A " third party costs order" is an order as to the payment of costs incurred by a party to criminal proceedings by a person who is not a party to those proceedings (" the third party").

(3) The condition is that–
   (a) there has been serious misconduct (whether or not constituting a contempt of court) by the third party, and
   (b) the court considers it appropriate, having regard to that misconduct, to make a third party costs order against him.

(4) Regulations made under this section may, in particular–
   (a) specify types of misconduct in respect of which a third party costs order may not be made;
   (b) allow the making of a third party costs order at any time;
   (c) make provision for any other order as to costs which has been made in respect of the proceedings to be varied on, or taken account of in, the making of a third party costs order;
   (d) make provision for account to be taken of any third party costs order in the making of any other order as to costs in respect of the proceedings.

(5) Regulations made under this section in relation to magistrates' courts must provide that the third party may appeal to the Crown Court against a third party costs order made by a magistrates' court.

(6) Regulations made under this section in relation to the Crown Court must provide that the third party may appeal to the Court of Appeal against a third party costs order made by the Crown Court.]

20 Regulations

(1) The Lord Chancellor may make regulations for carrying this Part into effect and the regulations may, in particular, make provision as to—
   (a) the scales or rates of payments of any costs payable out of central funds in pursuance of any costs order, the circumstances in which

Appendix E

and conditions under which such costs may be allowed and paid and the expenses which may be included in such costs; and
(b) the review, as respects costs payable out of central funds in pursuance of any costs order, of any decision on taxation, or determination of the amount, of the costs;

and any provision made by or under this Part enabling any sum to be paid out of central funds shall have effect subject to any such regulations.

(2) The Lord Chancellor may by regulations make provision for the recovery of sums paid [by the Legal Aid Board [Legal Services Commission] or out of] central funds in cases where—
(a) a costs order has been made against a [person]; and
(b) the person in whose favour the order was made is a legally assisted person or a person in whose favour a defendant's costs order or, as the case may be, an order under section 17 of this Act has been made.

(3) Regulations made under subsection (1) above may provide that rates or scales of allowances payable out of central funds under a costs order shall be determined by the Lord Chancellor with the consent of the Treasury.

(4) Regulations made under subsection (2) above may, in particular—
(a) require the person mentioned in paragraph (a) of that subsection to pay sums due under the costs order in accordance with directions given by the Lord Chancellor (either generally or in respect of the particular case); and
(b) enable the Lord Chancellor to enforce those directions in cases to which they apply.

(5) ...

(6) Any regulations under this Part may contain such incidental and supplemental provisions as the Lord Chancellor considers appropriate.

(7) Before making any regulations under section 19(1) of this Act which affect the procedure of any court, the Lord Chancellor shall so far as is reasonably practicable consult any rule committee by whom, or on whose advice, rules of procedure for the court may be made or whose concurrence is required to any such rules.

(8) In this section "costs order" means—
(a) an order made under or by virtue of this Part for payment to be made—
  (i) out of central funds; or
  (ii) by a party to proceedings; or
(b) an order made in a criminal case by the House of Lords for the payment of costs by a party to proceedings.

21 Interpretation, etc

(1) In this Part—
["accused" and "appellant", in a case where section 44A of the Criminal Appeal Act 1968 (death of convicted person) applies, include the person approved under that section;]

Material relating to sentencing and costs

"defendant's costs order" has the meaning given in section 16 of this Act;

. . .

["legally assisted person", in relation to any proceedings, means a person to whom representation under the Legal Aid Act 1988 [a right to representation funded by the Legal Services Commission as part of the Criminal Defence Service] has been granted for the purposes of the proceedings;]

"proceedings" includes—
   (a) proceedings in any court below; and
   (b) in relation to the determination of an appeal by any court, any application made to that court for leave to bring the appeal; and

"witness" means any person properly attending to give evidence, whether or not he gives evidence or is called at the instance of one of the parties or of the court, but does not include a person attending as a witness to character only unless the court has certified that the interests of justice required his attendance.

(2) Except as provided by or under this Part no costs shall be allowed on the hearing or determination of, or of any proceedings preliminary or incidental to, an appeal to the Court of Appeal under Part I of the Criminal Appeal Act 1968.

(3) Subject to rules of court made under section 53(1) of the Supreme Court Act 1981 (power by rules to distribute business of Court of Appeal between its civil and criminal divisions), the jurisdiction of the Court of Appeal under this Part, or under regulations made under this Part, shall be exercised by the criminal division of that Court; and references in this Part to the Court of Appeal shall be construed as references to that division.

(4) For the purposes of sections 16 and 17 this Act, the costs of any party to proceedings shall be taken to include the expense of compensating any witness for the expenses, trouble or loss of time properly incurred in or incidental to his attendance.

[(4A) Where one party to any proceedings is a legally assisted person then—
   (a) for the purposes of sections 16 and 17 of this Act, his costs shall be taken not to include either the expenses incurred on his behalf by the Legal Aid Board or the Lord Chancellor or, if he is liable to make a contribution under section 23 of the Legal Aid Act 1988, any sum paid or payable by way of contribution [the cost of representation funded for him by the Legal Services Commission as part of the Criminal Defence Service]; and
   (b) for the purposes of sections 18 and 19 of this Act, his costs shall be taken to include the expenses incurred on his behalf by the Legal Aid Board or the Lord Chancellor (without any deduction on account of any contribution paid or payable under section 23 of the Legal Aid Act 1988) but, if he is liable to make such a contribution his costs shall be taken not to include any sum paid or payable by way of contribution [, 19 and 19A of this Act, his costs shall be taken to include the cost of representation funded

Appendix E

for him by the Legal Services Commission as part of the Criminal Defence Service].]

(5) Where, in any proceedings in a criminal cause or matter or in either of the cases mentioned in subsection (6) below, an interpreter is required because of the accused's lack of English, the expenses properly incurred on his employment shall not be treated as costs of any party to the proceedings.

(6) The cases are—
   (a) where an information charging the accused with an offence is laid before a justice of the peace for any area but not proceeded with and the expenses are incurred on the employment of the interpreter for the proceedings on the information; and
   (b) where the accused is [sent] for trial but [proceedings against the accused are transferred to the Crown Court for trial but the accused is] not tried and the expenses are incurred on the employment of the interpreter for the proceedings in the Crown Court.

Supreme Court Act 1981

28 Appeals from Crown Court and Inferior Courts

(1) Subject to subsection (2), any order, judgment or other decision of the Crown Court may be questioned by any party to the proceedings, on the ground that it is wrong in law or is in excess of jurisdiction, by applying to the Crown Court to have a case stated by that court for the opinion of the High Court.

(2) Subsection (1) shall not apply to—
   (a) a judgment or other decision of the Crown Court relating to trial on indictment; or
   (b) any decision of that court under [. . .] the Local Government (Miscellaneous Provisions) Act 1982 which, by any provision of any of those Acts, is to be final.

(3) Subject to the provisions of this Act and to rules of court, the High Court shall, in accordance with section 19(2), have jurisdiction to hear and determine—
   (a) any application, or any appeal (whether by way of case stated or otherwise), which it has power to hear and determine under or by virtue of this or any other Act; and
   (b) all such other appeals as it had jurisdiction to hear and determine immediately before the commencement of this Act.

(4) In subsection (2)(a) the reference to a decision of the Crown Court relating to trial on indictment does not include a decision relating to an order under section 17 of the Access to Justice Act 1999.

48 Appeals to Crown Court

(1) The Crown Court may, in the course of hearing any appeal, correct any error or mistake in the order or judgment incorporating the decision which is the subject of the appeal.

(2) On the termination of the hearing of an appeal the Crown Court—

Material relating to sentencing and costs

    (a) may confirm, reverse or vary [any part of the decision appealed against, including a determination not to impose a separate penalty in respect of an offence]; or
    (b) may remit the matter with its opinion thereon to the authority whose decision is appealed against; or
    (c) may make such other order in the matter as the court thinks just, and by such order exercise any power which the said authority might have exercised.

(3) Subsection (2) has effect subject to any enactment relating to any such appeal which expressly limits or restricts the powers of the court on the appeal.

(4) [Subject to section 11(6) of the Criminal Appeal Act 1995, if] the appeal is against a conviction or a sentence, the preceding provisions of this section shall be construed as including power to award any punishment, whether more or less severe than that awarded by the magistrates' court whose decision is appealed against, if that is a punishment which that magistrates' court might have awarded.

(5) This section applies whether or not the appeal is against the whole of the decision.

(6) In this section "sentence" includes any order made by a court when dealing with an offender, including—
    (a) a hospital order under [Part III of the Mental Health Act 1983], with or without [a restriction order, and an interim hospital order under [that Act]]; and
    (b) a recommendation for deportation made when dealing with an offender.

[(7) The fact that an appeal is pending against an interim hospital order under [the said Act of 1983] shall not affect the power of the magistrates' court that made it to renew or terminate the order or to deal with the appellant on its termination; and where the Crown Court quashes such an order but does not pass any sentence or make any other order in its place the Court may direct the appellant to be kept in custody or released on bail pending his being dealt with by that magistrates' court.

(8) Where the Crown Court makes an interim hospital order by virtue of subsection (2)—
    (a) the power of renewing or terminating the order and of dealing with the appellant on its termination shall be exercisable by the magistrates' court whose decision is appealed against and not by the Crown Court; and
    (b) that magistrates' court shall be treated for the purposes of [section 38(7) of the said Act of 1983](absconding offenders) as the court that made the order.]

[51 Costs in civil division of Court of Appeal, High Court and county courts]

[(1) Subject to the provisions of this or any other enactment and to rules of court, the costs of and incidental to all proceedings in—
    (a) the civil division of the Court of Appeal;

Appendix E

    (b) the High Court; and
    (c) any county court,

shall be in the discretion of the court.

(2) Without prejudice to any general power to make rules of court, such rules may make provision for regulating matters relating to the costs of those proceedings including, in particular, prescribing scales of costs to be paid to legal or other representatives [or for securing that the amount awarded to a party in respect of the costs to be paid by him to such representatives is not limited to what would have been payable by him to them if he had not been awarded costs].

(3) The court shall have full power to determine by whom and to what extent the costs are to be paid.

(4) In subsections (1) and (2)"proceedings" includes the administration of estates and trusts.

(5) Nothing in subsection (1) shall alter the practice in any criminal cause, or in bankruptcy.

(6) In any proceedings mentioned in subsection (1), the court may disallow, or (as the case may be) order the legal or other representative concerned to meet, the whole of any wasted costs or such part of them as may be determined in accordance with rules of court.

(7) In subsection (6), "wasted costs" means any costs incurred by a party—
    (a) as a result of any improper, unreasonable or negligent act or omission on the part of any legal or other representative or any employee of such a representative; or
    (b) which, in the light of any such act or omission occurring after they were incurred, the court considers it is unreasonable to expect that party to pay.

(8) Where—
    (a) a person has commenced proceedings in the High Court; but
    (b) those proceedings should, in the opinion of the court, have been commenced in a county court in accordance with any provision made under section 1 of the Courts and Legal Services Act 1990 or by or under any other enactment,

the person responsible for determining the amount which is to be awarded to that person by way of costs shall have regard to those circumstances.

(9) Where, in complying with subsection (8), the responsible person reduces the amount which would otherwise be awarded to the person in question—
    (a) the amount of that reduction shall not exceed 25 per cent; and
    (b) on any taxation of the costs payable by that person to his legal representative, regard shall be had to the amount of the reduction.

(10) The Lord Chancellor may by order amend subsection (9)(a) by substituting, for the percentage for the time being mentioned there, a different percentage.

Material relating to sentencing and costs

(11) Any such order shall be made by statutory instrument and may make such transitional or incidental provision as the Lord Chancellor considers expedient.

(12) No such statutory instrument shall be made unless a draft of the instrument has been approved by both Houses of Parliament.

(13) In this section "legal or other representative", in relation to a party to proceedings, means any person exercising a right of audience or right to conduct litigation on his behalf.]

Practice Direction (Costs in Criminal Proceedings) [2004] 2 All ER 1070; [2004] 1 WLR 2657

Practice Note

(criminal law costs)

COURT OF APPEAL (CRIMINAL DIVISION)

18 MAY 2004

Lord Woolf CJ gave the following direction at the sitting of the court.

PART I: INTRODUCTION

SCOPE

I.1.1 This direction shall have effect in magistrates' courts, the Crown Court, the Administrative Court and the Court of Appeal (Criminal Division) where the court, in the exercise of its discretion, considers an award of costs in criminal proceedings or deals with Criminal Defence *2659 Service ("CDS") funded work and recovery of defence costs orders. The provisions in this practice direction will take effect from 18 May 2004.

THE POWER TO AWARD COSTS

I.2.1 The powers enabling the court to award costs in criminal proceedings are primarily contained in Part II of the Prosecution of Offences Act 1985 ("the Act") (sections 16, 17 and 18), the Access to Justice Act 1999 (in relation to funded clients) and in regulations made under those Acts including the Costs in Criminal Cases (General) Regulations 1986, as amended ("the General Regulations"). References in this direction are to the Prosecution of Offences Act 1985 and those Regulations unless otherwise stated. Schedule 1 below sets out details of the relevant regulations.

I.2.2 Section 16 of the Act makes provision for the award of defence costs out of central funds. Section 17 provides for an award of costs to a private prosecutor out of central funds. Section 18 gives power to order a convicted defendant or unsuccessful appellant to pay costs to the prosecutor. Section 19(1) of the Act and regulation 3 of the General Regulations provide for awards of costs between parties and section 19A provides for the court to disallow or order a legal or other representative of a party to the proceedings to meet wasted costs.

Appendix E

I.2.3 The Supreme Court also has the power under its inherent jurisdiction over officers of the court to order a solicitor personally to pay costs thrown away. It may also give directions relating to CDS funded costs and recovery of defence costs orders.

EXTENT OF ORDERS FOR COSTS FROM CENTRAL FUNDS

I.3.1 Where a court orders that the costs of a defendant, appellant or private prosecutor should be paid from central funds, the order will be for such amount as the court considers sufficient reasonably to compensate the party for expenses incurred by him in the proceedings. This will include the costs incurred in the proceedings in the lower courts unless for good reason the court directs that such costs are not included in the order, but it cannot include expenses incurred which do not directly relate to the proceedings themselves, such as loss of earnings. Where the party in whose favour the costs order is made is CDS funded, he will only recover his personal costs: see section 21(4A)(a). Schedule 2 below sets out the extent of availability of costs from central funds and the relevant statutory authority.

AMOUNT OF COSTS TO BE PAID

I.4.1 Except where the court has directed, in an order for costs out of central funds, that only a specified sum shall be paid, the amount of costs to be paid shall be determined by the appropriate officer of the court. The court may however order the disallowance of costs out of central funds not properly incurred or direct the determining officer to consider whether or not specific items have been properly incurred. The court may also make observations regarding CDS funded costs. The procedures to be followed when such circumstances arise are set out in this direction.

I.4.2 Where the court orders an offender to pay costs to the prosecutor, orders one party to pay costs to another party, disallows or orders a legal or *2660 other representative to meet any wasted costs, the order for costs must specify the sum to be paid or disallowed.

I.4.3 Where the court is required to specify the amount of costs to be paid it cannot delegate the decision. Wherever practicable those instructing advocates should provide the advocate with details of costs incurred at each stage in the proceedings. The court may however require the appropriate officer of the court to make enquiries to inform the court as to the costs incurred and may adjourn the proceedings for enquiries to be made if necessary. Special provisions apply in relation to recovery of defence costs orders as to which see Part XI below.

Part II: Defence costs from central funds

IN A MAGISTRATES' COURT

II.1.1 Where an information laid before a justice of the peace charging a person with an offence is not proceeded with, a magistrates' court enquiring into an indictable offence as examining justices determines not to commit the accused for trial, or a magistrates' court dealing summarily with an offence dismisses the information, the court may make a defendant's costs order. An order under section 16 of the Act may also be made in relation to breach of bind-over proceedings in a magistrates' court or the Crown Court: regulation 14(4) of the General Regulations. As is the case with the Crown Court (see below) such an order should normally be made unless there are positive reasons for not doing so. For example, where the defendant's own conduct has brought suspicion on himself and has misled the prosecution into thinking that the case against him was stronger than it was, the defendant can be left to pay his own costs. In the case of a partial acquittal the court may make a part order: details are at paras II.2.1 and II.2.2 below.

II.1.2 Whether to make such an award is a matter in the discretion of the court in the light of the circumstances of each particular case.

IN THE CROWN COURT

II.2.1 Where a person is not tried for an offence for which he has been indicted, or in respect of which proceedings against him have been sent for trial or transferred for trial, or has been acquitted on any count in the indictment, the court may make a defendant's costs order in his favour. Such an order should normally be made whether or not an order for costs between the parties is made, unless there are positive reasons for not doing so. For example, where the defendant's own conduct has brought suspicion on himself and has misled the prosecution into thinking that the case against him was stronger than it was, the defendant can be left to pay his own costs. The court when declining to make a costs order should explain, in open court, that the reason for not making an order does not involve any suggestion that the defendant is guilty of any criminal conduct but the order is refused because of the positive reason that should be identified.

II.2.2 Where a person is convicted of some count(s) in the indictment and acquitted on other(s) the court may exercise its discretion to make a defendant's costs order but may order that only part of the costs incurred be paid. The court should make whatever order seems just having regard to the relative importance of the two charges and the conduct of the parties generally. Where the court considers that it would be inappropriate that the *2661 defendant should recover all of the costs properly incurred, the amount must be specified in the order.

II.2.3 The Crown Court may make a defendant's costs order in favour of a successful appellant: see section 16(3) of the Act.

IN THE ADMINISTRATIVE COURT

II.3.1 The court may make a defendant's costs order on determining proceedings in a criminal cause or matter.

IN THE COURT OF APPEAL (CRIMINAL DIVISION)

II.4.1 A successful appellant under Part I of the Criminal Appeal Act 1968 may be awarded a defendant's costs order. Orders may also be made on an appeal against an order or ruling at a preparatory hearing (section 16(4A)), to cover the costs of representing an acquitted

Appendix E

defendant in respect of whom there is an Attorney Generals' reference under section 36 of the Criminal Justice Act 1972 (see section 36(5), (5A) of the 1972 Act) and in the case of aperson whose sentence is reviewed under section 36 of the Criminal Justice Act 1988: see section 36 of, and paragraph 11 of Schedule 3 to, the 1988 Act.

II.4.2 On determining an application for leave to appeal to the House of Lords under Part II of the Criminal Appeal Act 1968, whether by prosecutor or by defendant, the court may make a defendant's costs order.

II.4.3 In considering whether to make such an order the court will have in mind the principles applied by the Crown Court in relation to acquitted defendants: see paras II.2.1 and II.2.2 above.

Part III: Private prosecutor's costs from central funds

III.1.1 There is no power to order the payment of costs out of central funds of any prosecutor who is a public authority, a person acting on behalf of a public authority, or acting as an official appointed by a public authority as defined in the Act. In the limited number of cases in which a prosecutor's costs may be awarded out of central funds, an application is to be made by the prosecution in each case. An order should be made save where there is good reason for not doing so, for example, where proceedings have been instituted or continued without good cause. This provision applies to proceedings in respect of an indictable offence or proceedings before the Administrative Court in respect of a summary offence. Regulation 14(1) of the General Regulations extends it to certain committals for sentence rom a magistrates' court.

Part IV: Costs of witness, interpreter or medical evidence

IV.1 The costs of attendance of a witness equired by the accused, a private prosecutor or the court, or of an nterpreter required because of the accused's lack of English or of an ral report by a medical practitioner are allowed out of central funds nless the court directs otherwise: see section 20(3) of the Act and regulation 16(1) of the General Regulations. If, and only if, the court makes such a direction can the expense of the witness be claimed as a disbursement out of CDS funds. A witness includes any person properly attending to give evidence whether or not he gives evidence *2662 or is called, but it does not include a character witness unless the court has certified that the interests of justice require his attendance.

IV.2 The Crown Court may order the payment out of central funds of such sums as appear to be sufficient reasonably to compensate any medical practitioner for the expenses, trouble or loss of time properly incurred in preparing and making a report on the mental condition of a person accused of murder: see section 34(5) of the Mental Health (Amendment) Act 1982.

Part V: Disallowance of costs out of central funds

V.1.1 Where the court makes an order for costs out of central funds, it must: (a) direct the appropriate authority to disallow the costs incurred in respect of any items if it is plain that those costs were not properly incurred; such costs are not payable under sections 16(6) and 17(1) of the Act, and it may: (b) direct the appropriate authority to consider or investigate on determination any items which may have been improperly incurred. Costs not properly incurred include costs in respect of work unreasonably done, e g, if the case has been conducted unreasonably so as to incur unjustified expense, or costs have been wasted by failure to conduct proceedings with reasonable competence and expedition. In a plain case it will usually be more appropriate to make a wasted costs order under section 19A of the Act: see Part VIII below. The precise terms of the order for costs and of any direction must be entered in the court record.

V.1.2 Where the court has in mind that a direction in accordance with para V.1.1(a) or (b) might be given it must inform any party whose costs might be affected, or his legal representative, of the precise terms thereof and give a reasonable opportunity to show cause why no direction should be given. If a direction is given under para V.1.1(b) the court should inform the party concerned of his rights to make representations to the appropriate authority.

V.1.3 The appropriate authority may consult the court on any matter touching upon the allowance or disallowance of costs. It is not appropriate for the court to make a direction under para V.1.1(a) when so consulted.

Part VI: Award of costs against offenders and appellants

VI.1.1 A magistrates' court or the Crown Court may make an order for costs against a person convicted of an offence before it or in dealing with it in respect of certain orders as to sentence specified in regulation 14(3) of the General Regulations The Crown Court may make an order against an unsuccessful appellant and against a person committed by a magistrates' court in respect of the proceedings specified in regulation 14(1), (2). The court may make such order payable to the prosecutor as it considers just and reasonable: section 18(1) of the Act.

VI.1.2 In a magistrates' court where the defendant is ordered to pay a sum not exceeding £5 by way of fine, penalty, forfeiture or compensation the court must not make a costs order unless in the particular circumstances of the case it considers it right to do so: section 18(4) of the Act. Where the defendant is under 18 the amount of any costs awarded against him by a magistrates' court shall not exceed the amount of any fine imposed on him: section 18(5).

*2663

VI.1.3 The Court of Appeal (Criminal Division) may order an unsuccessful appellant to pay costs to such person as may be named in the order. Such costs may include the costs of any transcript obtained for the proceedings in the Court of Appeal: section 18(2), (6) of the Act.

VI.1.4 An order should be made where the court is satisfied that the offender or appellant has the means and the ability to pay.

VI.1.5 The amount must be specified in the order by the court.

Appendix E

VI.1.6 The Administrative Court is not covered by section 18 of the Act but it has complete discretion over all costs between the parties in relation to proceedings before it.

VI.1.7 An order under section 18 of the Act includes Legal Services Commission ("LSC") funded costs: see section 21(4A)(b) of the Act.

Part VII: Award of costs between the parties

VII.1 COSTS INCURRED AS A RESULT OF UNNECESSARY OR IMPROPER ACT OR OMISSION

VII.1.1 A magistrates' court, the Crown Court and the Court of Appeal (Criminal Division) may order the payment of any costs incurred as a result of any unnecessary or improper act or omission by or on behalf of any party to the proceedings as distinct from his legal representative: section 19 of the Act and regulation 3 of the General Regulations.

VII.1.2 The court must hear the parties and may then order that all or part of the costs so incurred by one party shall be paid to him by the other party.

VII.1.3 Before making such an order the court must take into account any other order as to costs and the order must specify the amount of the costs to be paid. The court is entitled to take such an order into account when making any other order as to costs in the proceedings: regulation 3(2)–(4) of the General Regulations. The order can extend to LSC costs incurred on behalf of any party: section 21(4A)(b) of the Act.

VII.1.4 In a magistrates' court no order may be made which requires a convicted person under 18 to pay an amount by way of costs which exceeds the amount of any fine imposed upon him: regulation 3(5) of the General Regulations.

VII.1.5 Such an order is appropriate only where the failure is that of the defendant or of the prosecutor. Where the failure is that of the legal representative(s) Parts VIII and IX (below) apply.
VII.3 Award of costs against third parties

VII.3.1 The magistrates' court, the Crown Court and the Court of Appeal may make a third party costs order if there has been serious misconduct (whether or not constituting a contempt of court) by a third party and the court considers it appropriate, having regard to that misconduct, to make a third party costs order against him. A "third party costs order" is an order as to the payment of costs incurred by a party to criminal proceedings by a person who is not a party to those proceedings ("the third party"): Prosecution of Offences Act 1985, section 19B, as inserted by section 93 of the Courts Act 2003.

VII.3.2 The Lord Chancellor may make Regulations: (1) specifying types of conduct in respect of which a third party costs order may not be made; (2) allowing the making of a third party costs order at any time; (3) making provision for any other order as to costs which has been made in respect of the proceedings to be varied on, or taken account of in, the making of a third party costs order; (4) making provision for account to be taken of any third party costs order in the making of any other order as to costs in respect of the proceedings.

VII.3.4 Regulations will provide that the third party may appeal to the Crown Court against a third party costs order made by a magistrates' court and to the Court of Appeal against a third party costs order made by the Crown Court.

VII.3.5 These provisions came into force on 1 February 2004.

Part VIII: Costs against legal representatives-wasted costs

VIII.1.1 Section 19A of the Act allows a magistrates' court, the Crown Court or the Court of Appeal (Criminal Division) to disallow or order the legal or other representative to meet the whole or any part of the wasted costs. The order can be made against any person exercising a right of audience or a right to conduct litigation (in the sense of acting for a party to *2667 the proceedings). "Wasted costs" are costs incurred by a party (which includes an LSC funded party) as a result of any improper, unreasonable or negligent act or omission on the part of any representative or his employee, or which, in the light of any such act or omission occurring after they were incurred, the court considers it unreasonable to expect that party to pay: section 19A(3) of the Act; section 89(8) of the Proceeds of Crime Act 2002.

VIII.1.2 The judge has a much greater and more direct responsibility for costs in criminal proceedings than in civil and should keep the question of costs in the forefront of his mind at every stage of the case and ought to be prepared to take the initiative himself without any prompting from the parties.

VIII.1.3 Regulation 3B of the General Regulations requires the court to specify the amount of the wasted costs and before making the order to allow the legal or other representative and any party to the proceedings to make representations. In making the order the court must take into account any other orders for costs and must take the wasted costs order into account when making any other order as to costs. The court should also give reasons for making the order and must notify any interested party (which includes the CDS fund and central funds determining authorities) of the order and the amount.

VIII.1.4 udges contemplating making a wasted costs order should bear in mind the guidance given by the Court of Appeal in re A Barrister (Wasted Costs Order) (No 1 of 1991) [1993] QB 293. The guidance, which is set out below, is to be considered together with all the statutory and other rules and recommendations set out by Parliament and in this practice direction. (i) There is a clear need for any judge or court intending to exercise the wasted costs jurisdiction to formulate carefully and concisely the complaint and grounds upon which such an order may be sought. These measures are draconian and, as in contempt proceedings, the grounds must be clear and particular. (ii) Where necessary a transcript of the relevant part of the proceedings under discussion should be available and in accordance with the rules a transcript of any wasted cost hearing must be made. (iii) A defendant involved in a case where such proceedings are contemplated should be present if, after discussion with counsel, it is thought that his interest may be affected and he should certainly be present and represented if the matter might affect the course of his trial. Regulation 3B(2) of the

Appendix E

General Regulations, as inserted by the Costs in Criminal Cases (General) (Amendment) Regulations 1991, furthermore requires that before a wasted costs order is made "the court shall allow the legal or other representative and any party to the proceedings to make representations". There may be cases where it may be appropriate for counsel for the Crown to be present. (iv) A three stage test or approach is recommended when a wasted costs order is contemplated: (a) Has there been an improper, unreasonable or negligent act or omission? (b) As a result have any costs been incurred by a party? (c) If the answers to (a) and (b) are "yes", should the court exercise its discretion to disallow or order the representative to meet the whole or any part of the relevant costs, and if so what specific sum is involved? (v) It is inappropriate to propose any settlement that the representative might forgo fees. The complaint should be formally stated by the judge and the representative invited to make his own comments. After any other party has been heard the judge should give his formal ruling. Discursive conversations *2668 may be unfair and should certainly not take place. The judge must specify the sum to be allowed or ordered. Alternatively the relevant available procedure should be substituted should it be impossible to fix the sum: see para VIII.1.7 below.

VIII.1.5 The Court of Appeal has given further guidance in re P (A Barrister) [2001] 1 Cr App R 207 as follows: (i) The primary object is not to punish but to compensate, albeit as the order is sought against a non party, it can from that perspective be regarded as penal. (ii) The jurisdiction is a summary jurisdiction to be exercised by the court which has "tried the case in the course of which the misconduct was committed". (iii) Fairness is assured if the lawyer alleged to be at fault has sufficient notice of the complaint made against him and a proper opportunity to respond to it. (iv) Because of the penal element a mere mistake is not sufficient to justify an order: there must be a more serious error. (v) Although the trial judge can decline to consider an application in respect of costs, for example on the ground that he or she is personally embarrassed by an appearance of bias, it will only be in exceptional circumstances that it will be appropriate to pass the matter to another judge, and the fact that, in the proper exercise of his judicial function, a judge has expressed views in relation to the conduct of a lawyer against whom an order is sought, does not of itself normally constitute bias or the appearance of bias so as to necessitate a transfer. (vi) If the allegation is one of serious misconduct or crime the standard of proof will be higher but otherwise it will be the normal civil standard of proof.

VIII.1.6 Though the court cannot delegate its decision to the appropriate authority, it may require the appropriate officer of the court to make enquiries and inform the court as to the likely amount of costs incurred.

VIII.1.7 The court may postpone the making of a wasted costs order to the end of the case if it appears more appropriate to do so, for example, because the likely amount is not readily available, there is a possibility of conflict between the legal representatives as to the apportionment of blame, or the legal representative concerned is unable to make full representations because of a possible conflict with the duty to the client.

VIII.1.8 A wasted costs order should normally be made regardless of

Material relating to sentencing and costs

the fact that the client of the legal representative concerned is CDS funded. However where the court is minded to disallow substantial costs out of the CDS fund, it may, instead of making a wasted costs order, make observations to the determining authority that work may have been unreasonably done: see para X.1.1 below. This practice should only be adopted where the extent and amount of the costs wasted is not entirely clear.

THE ADMINISTRATIVE COURT

VIII.2.1 In the Administrative Court where the court is considering whether to make an order under section 51(6) of the Supreme Court Act 1981 (a wasted costs order) it will do so in accordance with CPR r 48.7 which contains similar provisions as to giving the legal representative a reasonable opportunity to attend a hearing to give reasons why the court should not make such an order. In addition to the power to make a wasted costs order, the Administrative Court has powers in relation to misconduct under CPR r 44.14 which enable the court to make an order against a party *2669 or his legal representative where it appears to the court that the conduct of a party or his legal representative before or during the proceedings which gave rise to the summary or detailed assessment proceedings was unreasonable or improper.

Part IX: Awards of costs against solicitors under the court's inherent jurisdiction

IX.1.1 In addition to the power under regulation 3 of the General Regulations to order that costs improperly incurred be paid by a party to the proceedings and the power to make wasted costs orders under section 19A of the Act, the Supreme Court (which includes the Crown Court) may, in the exercise of its inherent jurisdiction over officers of the court, order a solicitor personally to pay costs thrown away by reason of a serious dereliction on the part of the solicitor of his duty to the court.

IX.1.2 No such order may be made unless reasonable notice has been given to the solicitor of the matter alleged against him and he is given a reasonable opportunity of being heard in reply.

IX.1.3 This power should be used only in exceptional circumstances not covered by the statutory powers.

Criminal Procedure Rules 2005, SI 2005/384

PART 78
COSTS ORDERS AGAINST THE PARTIES

78.1 Crown Court's jurisdiction to award costs in appeal from magistrates' court

(1) Subject to the provisions of section 109(1) of the Magistrates' Courts Act 1980 (power of magistrates' courts to award costs on abandonment of appeals from magistrates' courts), no party shall be entitled to recover any costs of any proceedings in the Crown Court from any other party to the proceedings except under an order of the Court.

Appendix E

(2) Subject to the following provisions of this rule, the Crown Court may make such order for costs as it thinks just.

(3) No order for costs shall be made on the abandonment of an appeal from a magistrates' court by giving notice under rule 63.5.

(4) Without prejudice to the generality of paragraph (2), the Crown Court may make an order for costs on dismissing an appeal where the appellant has failed to proceed with the appeal or on the abandonment of an appeal not being an appeal to which paragraph (3) applies.

[Note. Formerly rule 12 of the Crown Court Rules 1982. See also the relevant provisions of the Prosecution of Offences Act 1985 and the Costs in Criminal Cases (General) Regulations 1986. As to costs in restraint or receivership proceedings under Part 2 of the Proceeds of Crime Act 2002 see rules 61.19 to 61.22.]

78.2 Crown Court's jurisdiction to award costs in magistrates' court proceedings from which appeal is brought

Where an appeal is brought to the Crown Court from the decision of a magistrates' court and the appeal is successful, the Crown Court may make any order as to the costs of the proceedings in the magistrates' court which that court had power to make.

[Note. Formerly rule 13 of the Crown Court Rules 1982. See also the relevant provisions of the Prosecution of Offences Act 1985 and the Costs in Criminal Cases (General) Regulations 1986.]

78.3 Taxation of Crown Court costs

(1) Where under these Rules the Crown Court has made an order for the costs of any proceedings to be paid by a party and the Court has not fixed a sum, the amount of the costs to be paid shall be ascertained as soon as practicable by the Crown Court officer (hereinafter referred to as the taxing authority).

(2) On a taxation under the preceding paragraph there shall be allowed the costs reasonably incurred in or about the prosecution and conviction or the defence, as the case may be.

[Note. Formerly rule 14 of the Crown Court Rules 1982. See also the relevant provisions of the Prosecution of Offences Act 1985 and the Costs in Criminal Cases (General) Regulations 1986.]

78.4 Review of Crown Court costs by taxing authority

(1) Any party dissatisfied with the taxation of any costs by the taxing authority under rule 78.3 may apply to the taxing authority to review his decision.

(2) The application shall be made by giving notice to the taxing authority and to any other party to the taxation within 14 days of the taxation, specifying the items in respect of which the application is made and the grounds of objection.

(3) Any party to whom notice is given under the preceding paragraph may within 14 days of the service of the notice deliver to the taxing authority answers in writing to the objections specified in that notice to

Material relating to sentencing and costs

the taxing authority and, if he does, shall send copies to the applicant for the review and to any other party to the taxation.

(4) The taxing authority shall reconsider his taxation in the light of the objections and answers, if any, of the parties and any oral representations made by or on their behalf and shall notify them of the result of his review.

[Note. Formerly rule 15 of the Crown Court Rules 1982. See also the relevant provisions of the Prosecution of Offences Act 1985 *and the* Costs in Criminal Cases (General) Regulations 1986.*]*

78.5 Further review of Crown Court costs by Taxing Master

(1) Any party dissatisfied with the result of a review of taxation under rule 78.4 may, within 14 days of receiving notification thereof, request the taxing authority to supply him with reasons in writing for his decision and may within 14 days of the receipt of such reasons apply to the Chief Taxing Master for a further review and shall, in that case, give notice of the application to the taxing authority and to any other party to the taxation, to whom he shall also give a copy of the reasons given by the taxing authority.

(2) Such application shall state whether the application wishes to appear or be represented, or whether he will accept a decision given in his absence and shall be accompanied by a copy of the notice given under rule 78.4, of any answer which may have been given under paragraph (3) thereof and of the reasons given by the taxing authority for his decision, together with the bill of costs and full supporting documents.

(3) A party to the taxation who receives notice of an application under this rule shall inform the Chief Taxing Master whether he wishes to appear or be represented at a further review, or whether he will accept a decision given in his absence.

(4) The further review shall be conducted by a Taxing Master and if the applicant or any other party to the taxation has given notice of his intention to appear or be represented, the Taxing Master shall inform the parties (or their agents) of the date on which the further review will take place.

(5) Before reaching his decision the Taxing Master may consult the judge who made the order for costs and the taxing authority and, unless the Taxing Master otherwise directs, no further evidence shall be received on the hearing of the further review; and no ground of objection shall be valid which was not raised on the review under rule 78.4.

(6) In making his review, the Taxing Master may alter the assessment of the taxing authority in respect of any sum allowed, whether by increase or decrease.

(7) The Taxing Master shall communicate the result of the further review to the parties and to the taxing authority.

Appendix E

[Note. Formerly rule 16 of the Crown Court Rules 1982. See also the relevant provisions of the Prosecution of Offences Act 1985 and the Costs in Criminal Cases (General) Regulations 1986.]

78.6 Appeal to High Court judge after review of Crown Court costs

(1) Any party dissatisfied with the result of a further review under rule 78.5 may, within 14 days of receiving notification thereof, appeal by originating summons to a judge of the Queen's Bench Division of the High Court if, and only if, the Taxing Master certifies that the question to be decided involves a point of principle of general importance.

(2) On the hearing of the appeal the judge may reverse, affirm or amend the decision appealed against or make such other order as he thinks appropriate.

[Note. Formerly rule 17 of the Crown Court Rules 1982. See also the relevant provisions of the Prosecution of Offences Act 1985 and the Costs in Criminal Cases (General) Regulations 1986.]

78.7 Supplementary provisions on Crown Court costs

(1) On a further review or an appeal to a judge of the High Court the Taxing Master or judge may make such order as he thinks just in respect of the costs of the hearing of the further review or the appeal, as the case may be.

(2) The time set out by rules 78.4, 78.5 and 78.6 may be extended by the taxing authority, Taxing Master or judge of the High Court on such terms as he thinks just.

[Note. Formerly rule 18 of the Crown Court Rules 1982. See also the relevant provisions of the Prosecution of Offences Act 1985 and the Costs in Criminal Cases (General) Regulations 1986.]

Powers of the Criminal Courts (Sentencing) Act 2000

PART VI
FINANCIAL PENALTIES AND ORDERS

130 Compensation orders against convicted persons

(1) A court by or before which a person is convicted of an offence, instead of or in addition to dealing with him in any other way, may, on application or otherwise, make an order (in this Act referred to as a " compensation order") requiring him—
- (a) to pay compensation for any personal injury, loss or damage resulting from that offence or any other offence which is taken into consideration by the court in determining sentence; or
- (b) to make payments for funeral expenses or bereavement in respect of a death resulting from any such offence, other than a death due to an accident arising out of the presence of a motor vehicle on a road;

but this is subject to the following provisions of this section and to section 131 below.

(2) Where the person is convicted of an offence the sentence for which is fixed by law or falls to be imposed under 110(2) or 111(2) above, section 51A(2) of the Firearms Act 1968[, section 225, 226, 227 or 228 of the Criminal Justice Act 2003 or section 29(4) or (6) of the Violent Crime Reduction Act 2006], subsection (1) above shall have effect as if the words " instead of or" were omitted.

(3) A court shall give reasons, on passing sentence, if it does not make a compensation order in a case where this section empowers it to do so.

(4) Compensation under subsection (1) above shall be of such amount as the court considers appropriate, having regard to any evidence and to any representations that are made by or on behalf of the accused or the prosecutor.

(5) In the case of an offence under the Theft Act 1968 or Fraud Act 2006, where the property in question is recovered, any damage to the property occurring while it was out of the owner's possession shall be treated for the purposes of subsection (1) above as having resulted from the offence, however and by whomever the damage was caused.

(6) A compensation order may only be made in respect of injury, loss or damage (other than loss suffered by a person's dependants in consequence of his death) which was due to an accident arising out of the presence of a motor vehicle on a road, if—
- (a) it is in respect of damage which is treated by subsection (5) above as resulting from an offence under the Theft Act 1968 or Fraud Act 2006; or
- (b) it is in respect of injury, loss or damage as respects which—
  - (i) the offender is uninsured in relation to the use of the vehicle; and
  - (ii) compensation is not payable under any arrangements to which the Secretary of State is a party.

(7) Where a compensation order is made in respect of injury, loss or damage due to an accident arising out of the presence of a motor vehicle on a road, the amount to be paid may include an amount representing the whole or part of any loss of or reduction in preferential rates of insurance attributable to the accident.

(8) A vehicle the use of which is exempted from insurance by section 144 of the Road Traffic Act 1988 is not uninsured for the purposes of subsection (6) above.

(9) A compensation order in respect of funeral expenses may be made for the benefit of any one who incurred the expenses.

(10) A compensation order in respect of bereavement may be made only for the benefit of a person for whose benefit a claim for damages for bereavement could be made under section 1A of the Fatal Accidents Act 1976; and the amount of compensation in respect of bereavement shall not exceed the amount for the time being specified in section 1A(3) of that Act.

(11) In determining whether to make a compensation order against any person, and in determining the amount to be paid by any person under such an order, the court shall have regard to his means so far as they appear or are known to the court.

Appendix E

(12) Where the court considers—
- (a) that it would be appropriate both to impose a fine and to make a compensation order, but
- (b) that the offender has insufficient means to pay both an appropriate fine and appropriate compensation,

the court shall give preference to compensation (though it may impose a fine as well).

131 Limit on amount payable under compensation order of magistrates' court

(1) The compensation to be paid under a compensation order made by a magistrates' court in respect of any offence of which the court has convicted the offender shall not exceed £5,000.

(2) The compensation or total compensation to be paid under a compensation order or compensation orders made by a magistrates' court in respect of any offence or offence taken into consideration in determining sentence shall not exceed the difference (if any) between—
- (a) the amount or total amount which under subsection (1) above is the maximum for the offence or offences of which the offender has been convicted; and
- (b) the amount or total amounts (if any) which are in fact ordered to be paid in respect of that offence or those offences.

134 Effect of compensation order on subsequent award of damages in civil proceedings

(1) This section shall have effect where a compensation order, or a service compensation order or award, has been made in favour of any person in respect of any injury, loss or damage and a claim by him in civil proceedings for damages in respect of the injury, loss or damage subsequently falls to be determined.

(2) The damages in the civil proceedings shall be assessed without regard to the order or award, but the plaintiff may only recover an amount equal to the aggregate of the following—
- (a) any amount by which they exceed the compensation; and
- (b) a sum equal to any portion of the compensation which he fails to recover,

and may not enforce the judgment, so far as it relates to a sum such as is mentioned in paragraph (b) above, without the leave of the court.

(3) In this section a " service compensation order or award" means—
- (a) an order requiring the payment of compensation under paragraph 11 of Schedule 5A to the Army Act 1955, of Schedule 5A to the Air Force Act 1955 or of Schedule 4A to the Naval Discipline Act 1957; or
- (b) an award of stoppages payable by way of compensation under any of those Acts.

Appendix F

Human Rights

Human Rights Act 1998

1 The Convention Rights

(1) In this Act "the Convention rights" means the rights and fundamental freedoms set out in—
- (a) Articles 2 to 12 and 14 of the Convention,
- (b) Articles 1 to 3 of the First Protocol, and
- (c) [Article 1 of the Thirteenth Protocol],

as read with Articles 16 to 18 of the Convention.

(2) Those Articles are to have effect for the purposes of this Act subject to any designated derogation or reservation (as to which see sections 14 and 15).

(3) The Articles are set out in Schedule 1.

(4) The Secretary of State may by order make such amendments to this Act as he considers appropriate to reflect the effect, in relation to the United Kingdom, of a protocol.

(5) In subsection (4) "protocol" means a protocol to the Convention—
- (a) which the United Kingdom has ratified; or
- (b) which the United Kingdom has signed with a view to ratification.

(6) No amendment may be made by an order under subsection (4) so as to come into force before the protocol concerned is in force in relation to the United Kingdom.

2 Interpretation of Convention rights

(1) A court or tribunal determining a question which has arisen in connection with a Convention right must take into account any—
- (a) judgment, decision, declaration or advisory opinion of the European Court of Human Rights,
- (b) opinion of the Commission given in a report adopted under Article 31 of the Convention,
- (c) decision of the Commission in connection with Article 26 or 27(2) of the Convention, or
- (d) decision of the Committee of Ministers taken under Article 46 of the Convention,

whenever made or given, so far as, in the opinion of the court or tribunal, it is relevant to the proceedings in which that question has arisen.

(2) Evidence of any judgment, decision, declaration or opinion of which account may have to be taken under this section is to be given in proceedings before any court or tribunal in such manner as may be provided by rules.

Appendix F

(3) In this section "rules" means rules of court or, in the case of proceedings before a tribunal, rules made for the purposes of this section—
- (a) by the Lord Chancellor or the Secretary of State, in relation to any proceedings outside Scotland;
- (b) by the Secretary of State, in relation to proceedings in Scotland; or
- (c) by a Northern Ireland department, in relation to proceedings before a tribunal in Northern Ireland—
  - (i) which deals with transferred matters; and
  - (ii) for which no rules made under paragraph (a) are in force.

3 Interpretation of legislation

(1) So far as it is possible to do so, primary legislation and subordinate legislation must be read and given effect in a way which is compatible with the Convention rights.

(2) This section—
- (a) applies to primary legislation and subordinate legislation whenever enacted;
- (b) does not affect the validity, continuing operation or enforcement of any incompatible primary legislation; and
- (c) does not affect the validity, continuing operation or enforcement of any incompatible subordinate legislation if (disregarding any possibility of revocation) primary legislation prevents removal of the incompatibility.

4 Declaration of incompatibility

(1) Subsection (2) applies in any proceedings in which a court determines whether a provision of primary legislation is compatible with a Convention right.

(2) If the court is satisfied that the provision is incompatible with a Convention right, it may make a declaration of that incompatibility.

(3) Subsection (4) applies in any proceedings in which a court determines whether a provision of subordinate legislation, made in the exercise of a power conferred by primary legislation, is compatible with a Convention right.

(4) If the court is satisfied—
- (a) that the provision is incompatible with a Convention right, and
- (b) that (disregarding any possibility of revocation) the primary legislation concerned prevents removal of the incompatibility,

it may make a declaration of that incompatibility.

(5) In this section "court" means—
- (a) the House of Lords;
- (b) the Judicial Committee of the Privy Council;
- (c) the Courts-Martial Appeal Court;
- (d) in Scotland, the High Court of Justiciary sitting otherwise than as a trial court or the Court of Session;
- (e) in England and Wales or Northern Ireland, the High Court or the Court of Appeal
- [(f) the Court of Protection, in any matter being dealt with by the President of the Family Division, the Vice-Chancellor or a puisne judge of the High Court].

Human rights

(6) A declaration under this section ("a declaration of incompatibility")—
  (a) does not affect the validity, continuing operation or enforcement of the provision in respect of which it is given; and
  (b) is not binding on the parties to the proceedings in which it is made.

5 Right of Crown to intervene

(1) Where a court is considering whether to make a declaration of incompatibility, the Crown is entitled to notice in accordance with rules of court.

(2) In any case to which subsection (1) applies—
  (a) a Minister of the Crown (or a person nominated by him),
  (b) a member of the Scottish Executive,
  (c) a Northern Ireland Minister,
  (d) a Northern Ireland department,

is entitled, on giving notice in accordance with rules of court, to be joined as a party to the proceedings.

(3) Notice under subsection (2) may be given at any time during the proceedings.

(4) A person who has been made a party to criminal proceedings (other than in Scotland) as the result of a notice under subsection (2) may, with leave, appeal to the House of Lords against any declaration of incompatibility made in the proceedings.

(5) In subsection (4)—
  "criminal proceedings" includes all proceedings before the Courts-Martial Appeal Court; and
  "leave" means leave granted by the court making the declaration of incompatibility or by the House of Lords.

6 Acts of public authorities

(1) It is unlawful for a public authority to act in a way which is incompatible with a Convention right.

(2) Subsection (1) does not apply to an act if—
  (a) as the result of one or more provisions of primary legislation, the authority could not have acted differently; or
  (b) in the case of one or more provisions of, or made under, primary legislation which cannot be read or given effect in a way which is compatible with the Convention rights, the authority was acting so as to give effect to or enforce those provisions.

(3) In this section "public authority" includes—
  (a) a court or tribunal, and
  (b) any person certain of whose functions are functions of a public nature,

but does not include either House of Parliament or a person exercising functions in connection with proceedings in Parliament.

(4) In subsection (3) "Parliament" does not include the House of Lords in its judicial capacity.

Appendix F

(5) In relation to a particular act, a person is not a public authority by virtue only of subsection (3)(b) if the nature of the act is private.

(6) "An act" includes a failure to act but does not include a failure to—
   (a) introduce in, or lay before, Parliament a proposal for legislation; or
   (b) make any primary legislation or remedial order.

7 Proceedings

(1) A person who claims that a public authority has acted (or proposes to act) in a way which is made unlawful by section 6(1) may—
   (a) bring proceedings against the authority under this Act in the appropriate court or tribunal, or
   (b) rely on the Convention right or rights concerned in any legal proceedings,

but only if he is (or would be) a victim of the unlawful act.

(2) In subsection (1)(a) "appropriate court or tribunal" means such court or tribunal as may be determined in accordance with rules; and proceedings against an authority include a counterclaim or similar proceeding.

(3) If the proceedings are brought on an application for judicial review, the applicant is to be taken to have a sufficient interest in relation to the unlawful act only if he is, or would be, a victim of that act.

(4) If the proceedings are made by way of a petition for judicial review in Scotland, the applicant shall be taken to have title and interest to sue in relation to the unlawful act only if he is, or would be, a victim of that act.

(5) Proceedings under subsection (1)(a) must be brought before the end of—
   (a) the period of one year beginning with the date on which the act complained of took place; or
   (b) such longer period as the court or tribunal considers equitable having regard to all the circumstances,

but that is subject to any rule imposing a stricter time limit in relation to the procedure in question.

(6) In subsection (1)(b) "legal proceedings" includes—
   (a) proceedings brought by or at the instigation of a public authority; and
   (b) an appeal against the decision of a court or tribunal.

(7) For the purposes of this section, a person is a victim of an unlawful act only if he would be a victim for the purposes of Article 34 of the Convention if proceedings were brought in the European Court of Human Rights in respect of that act.

(8) Nothing in this Act creates a criminal offence.

(9) In this section "rules" means—
   (a) in relation to proceedings before a court or tribunal outside Scotland, rules made by the Lord Chancellor or the Secretary of State for the purposes of this section or rules of court,
   (b) in relation to proceedings before a court or tribunal in Scotland, rules made by the Secretary of State for those purposes,

Human rights

    (c) in relation to proceedings before a tribunal in Northern Ireland—
        (i) which deals with transferred matters; and
        (ii) for which no rules made under paragraph (a) are in force,
  rules made by a Northern Ireland department for those purposes,

and includes provision made by order under section 1 of the Courts and Legal Services Act 1990.

(10) In making rules, regard must be had to section 9.

(11) The Minister who has power to make rules in relation to a particular tribunal may, to the extent he considers it necessary to ensure that the tribunal can provide an appropriate remedy in relation to an act (or proposed act) of a public authority which is (or would be) unlawful as a result of section 6(1), by order add to—
    (a) the relief or remedies which the tribunal may grant; or
    (b) the grounds on which it may grant any of them.

(12) An order made under subsection (11) may contain such incidental, supplemental, consequential or transitional provision as the Minister making it considers appropriate.

(13) "The Minister" includes the Northern Ireland department concerned.

8 Judicial remedies

(1) In relation to any act (or proposed act) of a public authority which the court finds is (or would be) unlawful, it may grant such relief or remedy, or make such order, within its powers as it considers just and appropriate.

(2) But damages may be awarded only by a court which has power to award damages, or to order the payment of compensation, in civil proceedings.

(3) No award of damages is to be made unless, taking account of all the circumstances of the case, including—
    (a) any other relief or remedy granted, or order made, in relation to the act in question (by that or any other court), and
    (b) the consequences of any decision (of that or any other court) in respect of that act,

the court is satisfied that the award is necessary to afford just satisfaction to the person in whose favour it is made.

(4) In determining—
    (a) whether to award damages, or
    (b) the amount of an award,

the court must take into account the principles applied by the European Court of Human Rights in relation to the award of compensation under Article 41 of the Convention.

(5) A public authority against which damages are awarded is to be treated—
    (a) in Scotland, for the purposes of section 3 of the Law Reform (Miscellaneous Provisions)(Scotland) Act 1940 as if the award were made in an action of damages in which the authority has

Appendix F

been found liable in respect of loss or damage to the person to whom the award is made;
(b) for the purposes of the Civil Liability (Contribution) Act 1978 as liable in respect of damage suffered by the person to whom the award is made.

(6) In this section—
"court" includes a tribunal;
"damages" means damages for an unlawful act of a public authority; and
"unlawful" means unlawful under section 6(1).

9 Judicial acts

(1) Proceedings under section 7(1)(a) in respect of a judicial act may be brought only—
  (a) by exercising a right of appeal;
  (b) on an application (in Scotland a petition) for judicial review; or
  (c) in such other forum as may be prescribed by rules.

(2) That does not affect any rule of law which prevents a court from being the subject of judicial review.

(3) In proceedings under this Act in respect of a judicial act done in good faith, damages may not be awarded otherwise than to compensate a person to the extent required by Article 5(5) of the Convention.

(4) An award of damages permitted by subsection (3) is to be made against the Crown; but no award may be made unless the appropriate person, if not a party to the proceedings, is joined.

(5) In this section—
"appropriate person" means the Minister responsible for the court concerned, or a person or government department nominated by him;
"court" includes a tribunal;
"judge" includes a member of a tribunal, a justice of the peace and a clerk or other officer entitled to exercise the jurisdiction of a court;
"judicial act" means a judicial act of a court and includes an act done on the instructions, or on behalf, of a judge; and
"rules" has the same meaning as in section 7(9).

10 Power to take remedial action

(1) This section applies if—
  (a) a provision of legislation has been declared under section 4 to be incompatible with a Convention right and, if an appeal lies—
    (i) all persons who may appeal have stated in writing that they do not intend to do so;
    (ii) the time for bringing an appeal has expired and no appeal has been brought within that time; or
    (iii) an appeal brought within that time has been determined or abandoned; or
  (b) it appears to a Minister of the Crown or Her Majesty in Council that, having regard to a finding of the European Court of Human Rights made after the coming into force of this section in proceedings against the United Kingdom, a provision of

legislation is incompatible with an obligation of the United Kingdom arising from the Convention.

(2) If a Minister of the Crown considers that there are compelling reasons for proceeding under this section, he may by order make such amendments to the legislation as he considers necessary to remove the incompatibility.

(3) If, in the case of subordinate legislation, a Minister of the Crown considers—
   (a) that it is necessary to amend the primary legislation under which the subordinate legislation in question was made, in order to enable the incompatibility to be removed, and
   (b) that there are compelling reasons for proceeding under this section,

he may by order make such amendments to the primary legislation as he considers necessary.

(4) This section also applies where the provision in question is in subordinate legislation and has been quashed, or declared invalid, by reason of incompatibility with a Convention right and the Minister proposes to proceed under paragraph 2(b) of Schedule 2.

(5) If the legislation is an Order in Council, the power conferred by subsection (2) or (3) is exercisable by Her Majesty in Council.

(6) In this section "legislation" does not include a Measure of the Church Assembly or of the General Synod of the Church of England.

(7) Schedule 2 makes further provision about remedial orders.

11 Safeguard for existing human rights

A person's reliance on a Convention right does not restrict—
   (a) any other right or freedom conferred on him by or under any law having effect in any part of the United Kingdom; or
   (b) his right to make any claim or bring any proceedings which he could make or bring apart from sections 7 to 9.

12 Freedom of expression

(1) This section applies if a court is considering whether to grant any relief which, if granted, might affect the exercise of the Convention right to freedom of expression.

(2) If the person against whom the application for relief is made ("the respondent") is neither present nor represented, no such relief is to be granted unless the court is satisfied—
   (a) that the applicant has taken all practicable steps to notify the respondent; or
   (b) that there are compelling reasons why the respondent should not be notified.

(3) No such relief is to be granted so as to restrain publication before trial unless the court is satisfied that the applicant is likely to establish that publication should not be allowed.

(4) The court must have particular regard to the importance of the Convention right to freedom of expression and, where the proceedings

Appendix F

relate to material which the respondent claims, or which appears to the court, to be journalistic, literary or artistic material (or to conduct connected with such material), to—
- (a) the extent to which—
   - (i) the material has, or is about to, become available to the public; or
   - (ii) it is, or would be, in the public interest for the material to be published;
- (b) any relevant privacy code.

(5) In this section—
"court" includes a tribunal; and
"relief" includes any remedy or order (other than in criminal proceedings).

13 Freedom of thought, conscience and religion

(1) If a court's determination of any question arising under this Act might affect the exercise by a religious organisation (itself or its members collectively) of the Convention right to freedom of thought, conscience and religion, it must have particular regard to the importance of that right.

(2) In this section "court" includes a tribunal.

19 Statements of compatibility

(1) A Minister of the Crown in charge of a Bill in either House of Parliament must, before Second Reading of the Bill—
- (a) make a statement to the effect that in his view the provisions of the Bill are compatible with the Convention rights ("a statement of compatibility"); or
- (b) make a statement to the effect that although he is unable to make a statement of compatibility the government nevertheless wishes the House to proceed with the Bill.

(2) The statement must be in writing and be published in such manner as the Minister making it considers appropriate.

21 Interpretation, etc

(1) In this Act—
"amend" includes repeal and apply (with or without modifications);
   "the appropriate Minister" means the Minister of the Crown having charge of the appropriate authorised government department (within the meaning of the Crown Proceedings Act 1947);
"the Commission" means the European Commission of Human Rights;
"the Convention" means the Convention for the Protection of Human Rights and Fundamental Freedoms, agreed by the Council of Europe at Rome on 4th November 1950 as it has effect for the time being in relation to the United Kingdom;
"declaration of incompatibility" means a declaration under section 4;
"Minister of the Crown" has the same meaning as in the Ministers of the Crown Act 1975;
"Northern Ireland Minister" includes the First Minister and the deputy First Minister in Northern Ireland;
"primary legislation" means any—

Human rights

    (a) public general Act;
    (b) local and personal Act;
    (c) private Act;
    (d) Measure of the Church Assembly;
    (e) Measure of the General Synod of the Church of England;
    (f) Order in Council—
        (i) made in exercise of Her Majesty's Royal Prerogative;
        (ii) made under section 38(1)(a) of the Northern Ireland Constitution Act 1973 or the corresponding provision of the Northern Ireland Act 1998; or
        (iii) amending an Act of a kind mentioned in paragraph (a),(b) or (c);
    and includes an order or other instrument made under primary legislation (otherwise than by the National Assembly for Wales, a member of the Scottish Executive, a Northern Ireland Minister or a Northern Ireland department) to the extent to which it operates to bring one or more provisions of that legislation into force or amends any primary legislation;

"the First Protocol" means the protocol to the Convention agreed at Paris on 20th March 1952;

"the Sixth Protocol" means the protocol to the Convention agreed at Strasbourg on 28th April 1983;

"the Eleventh Protocol" means the protocol to the Convention (restructuring the control machinery established by the Convention) agreed at Strasbourg on 11th May 1994;

"remedial order" means an order under section 10;

"subordinate legislation" means any—
    (a) Order in Council other than one—
        (i) made in exercise of Her Majesty's Royal Prerogative;
        (ii) made under section 38(1)(a) of the Northern Ireland Constitution Act 1973 or the corresponding provision of the Northern Ireland Act 1998; or
        (iii) amending an Act of a kind mentioned in the definition of primary legislation;
    (b) Act of the Scottish Parliament;
    (c) Act of the Parliament of Northern Ireland;
    (d) Measure of the Assembly established under section 1 of the Northern Ireland Assembly Act 1973;
    (e) Act of the Northern Ireland Assembly;
    (f) order, rules, regulations, scheme, warrant, byelaw or other instrument made under primary legislation (except to the extent to which it operates to bring one or more provisions of that legislation into force or amends any primary legislation);
    (g) order, rules, regulations, scheme, warrant, byelaw or other instrument made under legislation mentioned in paragraph (b),(c),(d) or (e) or made under an Order in Council applying only to Northern Ireland;
    (h) order, rules, regulations, scheme, warrant, byelaw or other instrument made by a member of the Scottish Executive,[Welsh Ministers, the First Minister for Wales, the Counsel General to the Welsh Assembly Government,] a Northern Ireland Minister or a Northern Ireland department in exercise of prerogative or

Appendix F

other executive functions of Her Majesty which are exercisable by such a person on behalf of Her Majesty;

"transferred matters" has the same meaning as in the Northern Ireland Act 1998; and

"tribunal" means any tribunal in which legal proceedings may be brought.

(2) The references in paragraphs (b) and (c) of section 2(1) to Articles are to Articles of the Convention as they had effect immediately before the coming into force of the Eleventh Protocol.

(3) The reference in paragraph (d) of section 2(1) to Article 46 includes a reference to Articles 32 and 54 of the Convention as they had effect immediately before the coming into force of the Eleventh Protocol.

(4) The references in section 2(1) to a report or decision of the Commission or a decision of the Committee of Ministers include references to a report or decision made as provided by paragraphs 3, 4 and 6 of Article 5 of the Eleventh Protocol (transitional provisions).

(5) Any liability under the Army Act 1955, the Air Force Act 1955 or the Naval Discipline Act 1957 to suffer death for an offence is replaced by a liability to imprisonment for life or any less punishment authorised by those Acts; and those Acts shall accordingly have effect with the necessary modifications.

22 Short title, commencement, application and extent

(1) This Act may be cited as the Human Rights Act 1998.

(2) Sections 18, 20 and 21(5) and this section come into force on the passing of this Act.

(3) The other provisions of this Act come into force on such day as the Secretary of State may by order appoint; and different days may be appointed for different purposes.

(4) Paragraph (b) of subsection (1) of section 7 applies to proceedings brought by or at the instigation of a public authority whenever the act in question took place; but otherwise that subsection does not apply to an act taking place before the coming into force of that section.

(5) This Act binds the Crown.

(6) This Act extends to Northern Ireland.

(7) Section 21(5), so far as it relates to any provision contained in the Army Act 1955, the Air Force Act 1955 or the Naval Discipline Act 1957, extends to any place to which that provision extends.

SCHEDULE I

ARTICLE 2
RIGHT TO LIFE

1 Everyone's right to life shall be protected by law. No one shall be deprived of his life intentionally save in the execution of a sentence of a court following his conviction of a crime for which this penalty is provided by law.

2 Deprivation of life shall not be regarded as inflicted in contravention of this Article when it results from the use of force which is no more than absolutely necessary:
- (a) in defence of any person from unlawful violence;
- (b) in order to effect a lawful arrest or to prevent the escape of a person lawfully detained;
- (c) in action lawfully taken for the purpose of quelling a riot or insurrection.

ARTICLE 6
RIGHT TO A FAIR TRIAL

1 In the determination of his civil rights and obligations or of any criminal charge against him, everyone is entitled to a fair and public hearing within a reasonable time by an independent and impartial tribunal established by law. Judgment shall be pronounced publicly but the press and public may be excluded from all or part of the trial in the interest of morals, public order or national security in a democratic society, where the interests of juveniles or the protection of the private life of the parties so require, or to the extent strictly necessary in the opinion of the court in special circumstances where publicity would prejudice the interests of justice.

2 Everyone charged with a criminal offence shall be presumed innocent until proved guilty according to law.

3 Everyone charged with a criminal offence has the following minimum rights:
- (a) to be informed promptly, in a language which he understands and in detail, of the nature and cause of the accusation against him;
- (b) to have adequate time and facilities for the preparation of his defence;
- (c) to defend himself in person or through legal assistance of his own choosing or, if he has not sufficient means to pay for legal assistance, to be given it free when the interests of justice so require;
- (d) to examine or have examined witnesses against him and to obtain the attendance and examination of witnesses on his behalf under the same conditions as witnesses against him;
- (e) to have the free assistance of an interpreter if he cannot understand or speak the language used in court.

ARTICLE 7
NO PUNISHMENT WITHOUT LAW

1 No one shall be held guilty of any criminal offence on account of any act or omission which did not constitute a criminal offence under national or international law at the time when it was committed. Nor shall a heavier penalty be imposed than the one that was applicable at the time the criminal offence was committed.

2 This Article shall not prejudice the trial and punishment of any person for any act or omission which, at the time when it was committed, was criminal according to the general principles of law recognised by civilised nations.

ARTICLE 8
RIGHT TO RESPECT FOR PRIVATE AND FAMILY LIFE

1 Everyone has the right to respect for his private and family life, his home and his correspondence.

2 There shall be no interference by a public authority with the exercise of this right except such as is in accordance with the law and is necessary in a democratic society in the interests of national security, public safety or the economic well-being of the country, for the prevention of disorder or crime, for the protection of health or morals, or for the protection of the rights and freedoms of others.

THE FIRST PROTOCOL
ARTICLE 1

Protection of property

Every natural or legal person is entitled to the peaceful enjoyment of his possessions. No one shall be deprived of his possessions except in the public interest and subject to the conditions provided for by law and by the general principles of international law.

The preceding provisions shall not, however, in any way impair the right of a State to enforce such laws as it deems necessary to control the use of property in accordance with the general interest or to secure the payment of taxes or other contributions or penalties.

Appendix G

Miscellaneous Statutory Material

Local Government Act 1972

222 Power of local authorities to prosecute or defend legal proceedings

(1) Where a local authority consider it expedient for the promotion or protection of the interests of the inhabitants of their area—
   (a) they may prosecute or defend or appear in any legal proceedings and, in the case of civil proceedings, may institute them in their own name, and
   (b) they may, in their own name, make representations in the interests of the inhabitants at any public inquiry held by or on behalf of any Minister or public body under any enactment.

(2) In this section "local authority" includes the Common Council [and the London Fire and Emergency Planning Authority].

Local Government (Miscellaneous Provisions) Act 1976

16 Power of local authorities to obtain particulars of persons interested in land

(1) Where, with a view to performing a function conferred on a local authority by any enactment, the authority considers that it ought to have information connected with any land, the authority may serve on one or more of the following persons, namely—
   (a) the occupier of the land; and
   (b) any person who has an interest in the land either as freeholder, mortgagee or lessee or who directly or indirectly receives rent for the land; and
   (c) any person who, in pursuance of an agreement between himself and a person interested in the land, is authorised to manage the land or to arrange for the letting of it,

a notice specifying the land and the function and the enactment which confers the function and requiring the recipient of the notice to furnish to the authority, within a period specified in the notice (which shall not be less than fourteen days beginning with the day on which the notice is served), the nature of his interest in the land and the name and address of each person whom the recipient of the notice believes is the occupier of the land and of each person whom he believes is, as respects the land, such a person as is mentioned in the provisions of paragraphs (b) and (c) of this subsection.

(2) A person who—
   (a) fails to comply with the requirements of a notice served on him in pursuance of the preceding subsection; or
   (b) in furnishing any information in compliance with such a notice makes a statement which he knows to be false in a material

Appendix G

particular or recklessly makes a statement which is false in a material particular,

shall be guilty of an offence and liable on summary conviction to a fine not exceeding [level 5 on the standard scale].

Environmental Information Regulations 2004, SI 2004/3391

PART 1 INTRODUCTORY

1 Citation and commencement

These Regulations may be cited as the Environmental Information Regulations 2004 and shall come into force on 1st January 2005.

2 Interpretation

(1) In these Regulations—

"the Act" means the Freedom of Information Act 2000;

"applicant", in relation to a request for environmental information, means the person who made the request;

"appropriate records authority", in relation to a transferred public record, has the same meaning as in section 15(5) of the Act;

"the Commissioner" means the Information Commissioner;

"the Directive" means Council Directive 2003/4/EC on public access to environmental information and repealing Council Directive 90/313/EEC;

"environmental information" has the same meaning as in Article 2(1) of the Directive, namely any information in written, visual, aural, electronic or any other material form on—

(a) the state of the elements of the environment, such as air and atmosphere, water, soil, land, landscape and natural sites including wetlands, coastal and marine areas, biological diversity and its components, including genetically modified organisms, and the interaction among these elements;

(b) factors, such as substances, energy, noise, radiation or waste, including radioactive waste, emissions, discharges and other releases into the environment, affecting or likely to affect the elements of the environment referred to in (a);

(c) measures (including administrative measures), such as policies, legislation, plans, programmes, environmental agreements, and activities affecting or likely to affect the elements and factors referred to in (a) and (b) as well as measures or activities designed to protect those elements;

(d) reports on the implementation of environmental legislation;

(e) cost-benefit and other economic analyses and assumptions used within the framework of the measures and activities referred to in (c); and

(f) the state of human health and safety, including the contamination of the food chain, where relevant, conditions of human life, cultural sites and built structures inasmuch as they are or may be affected by the state of the elements of the environment referred to in (a) or, through those elements, by any of the matters referred to in (b) and (c);

Miscellaneous statutory material

"historical record" has the same meaning as in section 62(1) of the Act;
"public authority" has the meaning given by paragraph (2);
"public record" has the same meaning as in section 84 of the Act;
"responsible authority", in relation to a transferred public record, has the same meaning as in section 15(5) of the Act; "Scottish public authority" means–
(a) a body referred to in section 80(2) of the Act; and
(b) insofar as not such a body, a Scottish public authority as defined in section 3 of the Freedom of Information (Scotland) Act 2002;
"transferred public record" has the same meaning as in section 15(4) of the Act; and
"working day" has the same meaning as in section 10(6) of the Act.

(2) Subject to paragraph (3), "public authority" means–
   (a) government departments;
   (b) any other public authority as defined in section 3(1) of the Act, disregarding for this purpose the exceptions in paragraph 6 of Schedule 1 to the Act, but excluding–
      (i) any body or office-holder listed in Schedule 1 to the Act only in relation to information of a specified description; or
      (ii) any person designated by Order under section 5 of the Act;
   (c) any other body or other person, that carries out functions of public administration; or
   (d) any other body or other person, that is under the control of a person falling within sub-paragraphs (a), (b) or (c) and–
      (i) has public responsibilities relating to the environment;
      (ii) exercises functions of a public nature relating to the environment; or
      (iii) provides public services relating to the environment.

(3) Except as provided by regulation 12(10) a Scottish public authority is not a "public authority" for the purpose of these Regulations.

(4) The following expressions have the same meaning in these Regulations as they have in the Data Protection Act 1998[1], namely–
   (a) "data" except that for the purposes of regulation 12(3) and regulation 13 a public authority referred to in the definition of data in paragraph (e) of section 1(1) of that Act means a public authority within the meaning of these Regulations;
   (b) "the data protection principles";
   (c) "data subject"; and
   (d) "personal data".

(5) Except as provided by this regulation, expressions in these Regulations which appear in the Directive have the same meaning in these Regulations as they have in the Directive.

3 Application

(1) Subject to paragraphs (3) and (4), these Regulations apply to public authorities.

(2) For the purposes of these Regulations, environmental information is held by a public authority if the information–

Appendix G

(a) is in the authority's possession and has been produced or received by the authority; or
(b) is held by another person on behalf of the authority.

(3) These Regulations shall not apply to any public authority to the extent that it is acting in a judicial or legislative capacity.

(4) These Regulations shall not apply to either House of Parliament to the extent required for the purpose of avoiding an infringement of the privileges of either House.

(5) Each government department is to be treated as a person separate from any other government department for the purposes of Parts 2, 4 and 5 of these Regulations.

PART 2 ACCESS TO ENVIRONMENTAL INFORMATION HELD BY PUBLIC AUTHORITIES

4 Dissemination of environmental information

(1) Subject to paragraph (3), a public authority shall in respect of environmental information that it holds–
   (a) progressively make the information available to the public by electronic means which are easily accessible; and
   (b) take reasonable steps to organize the information relevant to its functions with a view to the active and systematic dissemination to the public of the information.

(2) For the purposes of paragraph (1) the use of electronic means to make information available or to organize information shall not be required in relation to information collected before 1st January 2005 in non-electronic form.

(3) Paragraph (1) shall not extend to making available or disseminating information which a public authority would be entitled to refuse to disclose under regulation 12.

(4) The information under paragraph (1) shall include at least–
   (a) the information referred to in Article 7(2) of the Directive; and
   (b) facts and analyses of facts which the public authority considers relevant and important in framing major environmental policy proposals.

5 Duty to make available environmental information on request

(1) Subject to paragraph (3) and in accordance with paragraphs (2), (4), (5) and (6) and the remaining provisions of this Part and Part 3 of these Regulations, a public authority that holds environmental information shall make it available on request.

(2) Information shall be made available under paragraph (1) as soon as possible and no later than 20 working days after the date of receipt of the request.

(3) To the extent that the information requested includes personal data of which the applicant is the data subject, paragraph (1) shall not apply to those personal data.

(4) For the purposes of paragraph (1), where the information made available is compiled by or on behalf of the public authority it shall be up to date, accurate and comparable, so far as the public authority reasonably believes.

(5) Where a public authority makes available information in paragraph (b) of the definition of environmental information, and the applicant so requests, the public authority shall, insofar as it is able to do so, either inform the applicant of the place where information, if available, can be found on the measurement procedures, including methods of analysis, sampling and pre-treatment of samples, used in compiling the information, or refer the applicant to a standardised procedure used.

(6) Any enactment or rule of law that would prevent the disclosure of information in accordance with these Regulations shall not apply.

6 Form and format of information

(1) Where an applicant requests that the information be made available in a particular form or format, a public authority shall make it so available, unless–
- (a) it is reasonable for it to make the information available in another form or format; or
- (b) the information is already publicly available and easily accessible to the applicant in another form or format.

(2) If the information is not made available in the form or format requested, the public authority shall–
- (a) explain the reason for its decision as soon as possible and no later than 20 working days after the date of receipt of the request for the information;
- (b) provide the explanation in writing if the applicant so requests; and
- (c) inform the applicant of the provisions of regulation 11 and of the enforcement and appeal provisions of the Act applied by regulation 18.

7 Extension of time

(1) Where a request is made under regulation 5, the public authority may extend the period of 20 working days referred to in the provisions in paragraph (2) to 40 working days if it reasonably believes that the complexity and volume of the information requested means that it is impracticable either to comply with the request within the earlier period or to make a decision to refuse to do so.

(2) The provisions referred to in paragraph (1) are–
- (a) regulation 5(2);
- (b) regulation 6(2)(a); and
- (c) regulation 14(2).

(3) Where paragraph (1) applies the public authority shall notify the applicant accordingly as soon as possible and no later than 20 working days after the date of receipt of the request.

8 Charging

(1) Subject to paragraphs (2) to (8), where a public authority makes environmental information available in accordance with regulation 5(1)

Appendix G

the authority may charge the applicant for making the information available.

(2) A public authority shall not make any charge for allowing an applicant—
- (a) to access any public registers or lists of environmental information held by the public authority; or
- (b) to examine the information requested at the place which the public authority makes available for that examination.

(3) A charge under paragraph (1) shall not exceed an amount which the public authority is satisfied is a reasonable amount.

(4) A public authority may require advance payment of a charge for making environmental information available and if it does it shall, no later than 20 working days after the date of receipt of the request for the information, notify the applicant of this requirement and of the amount of the advance payment.

(5) Where a public authority has notified an applicant under paragraph (4) that advance payment is required, the public authority is not required—
- (a) to make available the information requested; or
- (b) to comply with regulations 6 or 14,

unless the charge is paid no later than 60 working days after the date on which it gave the notification.

(6) The period beginning with the day on which the notification of a requirement for an advance payment is made and ending on the day on which that payment is received by the public authority is to be disregarded for the purposes of determining the period of 20 working days referred to in the provisions in paragraph (7), including any extension to those periods under regulation 7(1).

(7) The provisions referred to in paragraph (6) are—
- (a) regulation 5(2);
- (b) regulation 6(2)(a); and
- (c) regulation 14(2).

(8) A public authority shall publish and make available to applicants—
- (a) a schedule of its charges; and
- (b) information on the circumstances in which a charge may be made or waived.

9 Advice and assistance

(1) A public authority shall provide advice and assistance, so far as it would be reasonable to expect the authority to do so, to applicants and prospective applicants.

(2) Where a public authority decides that an applicant has formulated a request in too general a manner, it shall—
- (a) ask the applicant as soon as possible and in any event no later than 20 working days after the date of receipt of the request, to provide more particulars in relation to the request; and
- (b) assist the applicant in providing those particulars.

(3) Where a code of practice has been made under regulation 16, and to the extent that a public authority conforms to that code in relation to

Miscellaneous statutory material

the provision of advice and assistance in a particular case, it shall be taken to have complied with paragraph (1) in relation to that case.

(4) Where paragraph (2) applies, in respect of the provisions in paragraph (5), the date on which the further particulars are received by the public authority shall be treated as the date after which the period of 20 working days referred to in those provisions shall be calculated.

(5) The provisions referred to in paragraph (4) are–
- (a) regulation 5(2);
- (b) regulation 6(2)(a); and
- (c) regulation 14(2).

10 Transfer of a request

(1) Where a public authority that receives a request for environmental information does not hold the information requested but believes that another public authority or a Scottish public authority holds the information, the public authority shall either–
- (a) transfer the request to the other public authority or Scottish public authority; or
- (b) supply the applicant with the name and address of that authority,

and inform the applicant accordingly with the refusal sent under regulation 14(1).

(2) Where a request is transferred to a public authority, for the purposes of the provisions referred to in paragraph (3) the request is received by that public authority on the date on which it receives the transferred request.

(3) The provisions referred to in paragraph (2) are–
- (a) regulation 5(2);
- (b) regulation 6(2)(a); and
- (c) regulation 14(2).

11 Representations and reconsideration

(1) Subject to paragraph (2), an applicant may make representations to a public authority in relation to the applicant's request for environmental information if it appears to the applicant that the authority has failed to comply with a requirement of these Regulations in relation to the request.

(2) Representations under paragraph (1) shall be made in writing to the public authority no later than 40 working days after the date on which the applicant believes that the public authority has failed to comply with the requirement.

(3) The public authority shall on receipt of the representations and free of charge–
- (a) consider them and any supporting evidence produced by the applicant; and
- (b) decide if it has complied with the requirement.

(4) A public authority shall notify the applicant of its decision under paragraph (3) as soon as possible and no later than 40 working days after the date of receipt of the representations.

Appendix G

(5) Where the public authority decides that it has failed to comply with these Regulations in relation to the request, the notification under paragraph (4) shall include a statement of—
- (a) the failure to comply;
- (b) the action the authority has decided to take to comply with the requirement; and
- (c) the period within which that action is to be taken.

PART 3 EXCEPTIONS TO THE DUTY TO DISCLOSE ENVIRONMENTAL INFORMATION

12 Exceptions to the duty to disclose environmental information

(1) Subject to paragraphs (2), (3) and (9), a public authority may refuse to disclose environmental information requested if—
- (a) an exception to disclosure applies under paragraphs (4) or (5); and
- (b) in all the circumstances of the case, the public interest in maintaining the exception outweighs the public interest in disclosing the information.

(2) A public authority shall apply a presumption in favour of disclosure.

(3) To the extent that the information requested includes personal data of which the applicant is not the data subject, the personal data shall not be disclosed otherwise than in accordance with regulation 13.

(4) For the purposes of paragraph (1)(a), a public authority may refuse to disclose information to the extent that—
- (a) it does not hold that information when an applicant's request is received;
- (b) the request for information is manifestly unreasonable;
- (c) the request for information is formulated in too general a manner and the public authority has complied with regulation 9;
- (d) the request relates to material which is still in the course of completion, to unfinished documents or to incomplete data; or
- (e) the request involves the disclosure of internal communications.

(5) For the purposes of paragraph (1)(a), a public authority may refuse to disclose information to the extent that its disclosure would adversely affect—
- (a) international relations, defence, national security or public safety;
- (b) the course of justice, the ability of a person to receive a fair trial or the ability of a public authority to conduct an inquiry of a criminal or disciplinary nature;
- (c) intellectual property rights;
- (d) the confidentiality of the proceedings of that or any other public authority where such confidentiality is provided by law;
- (e) the confidentiality of commercial or industrial information where such confidentiality is provided by law to protect a legitimate economic interest;
- (f) the interests of the person who provided the information where that person—
  - (i) was not under, and could not have been put under, any legal obligation to supply it to that or any other public authority;

(ii) did not supply it in circumstances such that that or any other public authority is entitled apart from these Regulations to disclose it; and
(iii) has not consented to its disclosure; or
(g) the protection of the environment to which the information relates.

(6) For the purposes of paragraph (1), a public authority may respond to a request by neither confirming nor denying whether such information exists and is held by the public authority, whether or not it holds such information, if that confirmation or denial would involve the disclosure of information which would adversely affect any of the interests referred to in paragraph (5)(a) and would not be in the public interest under paragraph (1)(b).

(7) For the purposes of a response under paragraph (6), whether information exists and is held by the public authority is itself the disclosure of information.

(8) For the purposes of paragraph (4)(e), internal communications includes communications between government departments.

(9) To the extent that the environmental information to be disclosed relates to information on emissions, a public authority shall not be entitled to refuse to disclose that information under an exception referred to in paragraphs (5)(d) to (g).

(10) For the purposes of paragraphs (5)(b), (d) and (f), references to a public authority shall include references to a Scottish public authority.

(11) Nothing in these Regulations shall authorise a refusal to make available any environmental information contained in or otherwise held with other information which is withheld by virtue of these Regulations unless it is not reasonably capable of being separated from the other information for the purpose of making available that information.

13 Personal data

(1) To the extent that the information requested includes personal data of which the applicant is not the data subject and as respects which either the first or second condition below is satisfied, a public authority shall not disclose the personal data.

(2) The first condition is–
 (a) in a case where the information falls within any of paragraphs (a) to (d) of the definition of "data" in section 1(1) of the Data Protection Act 1998, that the disclosure of the information to a member of the public otherwise than under these Regulations would contravene–
  (i) any of the data protection principles; or
  (ii) section 10 of that Act (right to prevent processing likely to cause damage or distress) and in all the circumstances of the case, the public interest in not disclosing the information outweighs the public interest in disclosing it; and
 (b) in any other case, that the disclosure of the information to a member of the public otherwise than under these Regulations would contravene any of the data protection principles if the exemptions in section 33A(1) of the Data Protection Act 1998 (which relate to manual data held by public authorities) were disregarded.

Appendix G

(3) The second condition is that by virtue of any provision of Part IV of the Data Protection Act 1998 the information is exempt from section 7(1) of that Act and, in all the circumstances of the case, the public interest in not disclosing the information outweighs the public interest in disclosing it.

(4) In determining whether anything done before 24th October 2007 would contravene any of the data protection principles, the exemptions in Part III of Schedule 8 to the Data Protection Act 1998 shall be disregarded.

(5) For the purposes of this regulation a public authority may respond to a request by neither confirming nor denying whether such information exists and is held by the public authority, whether or not it holds such information, to the extent that–
- (a) the giving to a member of the public of the confirmation or denial would contravene any of the data protection principles or section 10 of the Data Protection Act 1998 or would do so if the exemptions in section 33A(1) of that Act were disregarded; or
- (b) by virtue of any provision of Part IV of the Data Protection Act 1998, the information is exempt from section 7(1)(a) of that Act.

14 Refusal to disclose information

(1) If a request for environmental information is refused by a public authority under regulations 12(1) or 13(1), the refusal shall be made in writing and comply with the following provisions of this regulation.

(2) The refusal shall be made as soon as possible and no later than 20 working days after the date of receipt of the request.

(3) The refusal shall specify the reasons not to disclose the information requested, including–
- (a) any exception relied on under regulations 12(4), 12(5) or 13; and
- (b) the matters the public authority considered in reaching its decision with respect to the public interest under regulation 12(1)(b) or, where these apply, regulations 13(2)(a)(ii) or 13(3).

(4) If the exception in regulation 12(4)(d) is specified in the refusal, the authority shall also specify, if known to the public authority, the name of any other public authority preparing the information and the estimated time in which the information will be finished or completed.

(5) The refusal shall inform the applicant–
- (a) that he may make representations to the public authority under regulation 11; and
- (b) of the enforcement and appeal provisions of the Act applied by regulation 18.

15 Ministerial certificates

(1) A Minister of the Crown may certify that a refusal to disclose information under regulation 12(1) is because the disclosure–
- (a) would adversely affect national security; and
- (b) would not be in the public interest under regulation 12(1)(b).

(2) For the purposes of paragraph (1)–
- (a) a Minister of the Crown may designate a person to certify the matters in that paragraph on his behalf; and

(b) a refusal to disclose information under regulation 12(1) includes a response under regulation 12(6).

(3) A certificate issued in accordance with paragraph (1)–
 (a) shall be conclusive evidence of the matters in that paragraph; and
 (b) may identify the information to which it relates in general terms.

(4) A document purporting to be a certificate under paragraph (1) shall be received in evidence and deemed to be such a certificate unless the contrary is proved.

(5) A document which purports to be certified by or on behalf of a Minister of the Crown as a true copy of a certificate issued by that Minister under paragraph (1) shall in any legal proceedings be evidence (or, in Scotland, sufficient evidence) of that certificate.

(6) In paragraphs (1), (2) and (5), a "Minister of the Crown" has the same meaning as in section 25(3) of the Act.

PART 4 CODE OF PRACTICE AND HISTORICAL RECORDS

16 Issue of a code of practice and functions of the Commissioner

(1) The Secretary of State may issue, and may from time to time revise, a code of practice providing guidance to public authorities as to the practice which it would, in the Secretary of State's opinion, be desirable for them to follow in connection with the discharge of their functions under these Regulations.

(2) The code may make different provision for different public authorities.

(3) Before issuing or revising any code under this regulation, the Secretary of State shall consult the Commissioner.

(4) The Secretary of State shall lay before each House of Parliament any code issued or revised under this regulation.

(5) The general functions of the Commissioner under section 47 of the Act and the power of the Commissioner to give a practice recommendation under section 48 of the Act shall apply for the purposes of these Regulations as they apply for the purposes of the Act but with the modifications specified in paragraph (6).

(6) For the purposes of the application of sections 47 and 48 of the Act to these Regulations, any reference to–
 (a) a public authority is a reference to a public authority within the meaning of these Regulations;
 (b) the requirements or operation of the Act, or functions under the Act, includes a reference to the requirements or operation of these Regulations, or functions under these Regulations; and
 (c) a code of practice made under section 45 of the Act includes a reference to a code of practice made under this regulation.

17 Historical and transferred public records

(1) Where a request relates to information contained in a historical record other than one to which paragraph (2) applies and the public

Appendix G

authority considers that it may be in the public interest to refuse to disclose that information under regulation 12(1)(b), the public authority shall consult–
  (a) the Lord Chancellor, if it is a public record within the meaning of the Public Records Act 1958; or
  (b) the appropriate Northern Ireland Minister, if it is a public record to which the Public Records Act (Northern Ireland) 1923 applies,

before it decides whether the information may or may not be disclosed.

(2) Where a request relates to information contained in a transferred public record, other than information which the responsible authority has designated as open information for the purposes of this regulation, the appropriate records authority shall consult the responsible authority on whether there may be an exception to disclosure of that information under regulation 12(5).

(3) If the appropriate records authority decides that such an exception applies–
  (a) subject to paragraph (4), a determination on whether it may be in the public interest to refuse to disclose that information under regulation 12(1)(b) shall be made by the responsible authority;
  (b) the responsible authority shall communicate its determination to the appropriate records authority within such time as is reasonable in all the circumstances; and
  (c) the appropriate records authority shall comply with regulation 5 in accordance with that determination.

(4) Where a responsible authority is required to make a determination under paragraph (3), it shall consult–
  (a) the Lord Chancellor, if the transferred public record is a public record within the meaning of the Public Records Act 1958; or
  (b) the appropriate Northern Ireland Minister, if the transferred public record is a public record to which the Public Records Act (Northern Ireland) 1923 applies,

before it determines whether the information may or may not be disclosed.

(5) A responsible authority which is not a public authority under these Regulations shall be treated as a public authority for the purposes of–
  (a) the obligations of a responsible authority under paragraphs (3)(a) and (b) and (4); and
  (b) the imposition of any requirement to furnish information relating to compliance with regulation 5.

PART 5 ENFORCEMENT AND APPEALS, OFFENCES, AMENDMENT AND REVOCATION

18 Enforcement and appeal provisions

(1) The enforcement and appeals provisions of the Act shall apply for the purposes of these Regulations as they apply for the purposes of the Act but with the modifications specified in this regulation.

(2) In this regulation, "the enforcement and appeals provisions of the Act" means–

Miscellaneous statutory material

(a) Part IV of the Act (enforcement), including Schedule 3 (powers of entry and inspection) which has effect by virtue of section 55 of the Act; and

(b) Part V of the Act (appeals).

(3) Part IV of the Act shall not apply in any case where a certificate has been issued in accordance with regulation 15(1).

(4) For the purposes of the application of the enforcement and appeals provisions of the Act–
  (a) for any reference to–
    (i) "this Act" there shall be substituted a reference to "these Regulations"; and
    (ii) "Part I" there shall be substituted a reference to "Parts 2 and 3 of these Regulations";
  (b) any reference to a public authority is a reference to a public authority within the meaning of these Regulations;
  (c) for any reference to the code of practice under section 45 of the Act (issue of a code of practice by the Secretary of State) there shall be substituted a reference to any code of practice issued under regulation 16(1);
  (d) in section 50(4) of the Act (contents of decision notice)–
    (i) in paragraph (a) for the reference to "section 1(1)" there shall be substituted a reference to "regulation 5(1)"; and
    (ii) in paragraph (b) for the references to "sections 11 and 17" there shall be substituted references to "regulations 6, 11 or 14";
  (e) in section 56(1) of the Act (no action against public authority) for the words "This Act does not confer" there shall be substituted the words "These Regulations do not confer";
  (f) in section 57(3)(a) of the Act (appeal against notices served under Part IV) for the reference to "section 66" of the Act (decisions relating to certain transferred public records) there shall be substituted a reference to "regulations 17(2) to (5)";
  (g) in paragraph 1 of Schedule 3 to the Act (issue of warrants) for the reference to "section 77" (offence of altering etc. records with intent to prevent disclosure) there shall be substituted a reference to "regulation 19"; and
  (h) in paragraph 8 of Schedule 3 to the Act (matters exempt from inspection and seizure) for the reference to "information which is exempt information by virtue of section 23(1) or 24(1)" (bodies and information relating to national security) there shall be substituted a reference to "information whose disclosure would adversely affect national security".

(5) In section 50(4)(a) of the Act (contents of decision notice) the reference to confirmation or denial applies to a response given by a public authority under regulation 12(6) or regulation 13(5).

(6) Section 53 of the Act (exception from duty to comply with decision notice or enforcement notice) applies to a decision notice or enforcement notice served under Part IV of the Act as applied to these Regulations on any of the public authorities referred to in section 53(1)(a); and in section 53(7) for the reference to "exempt information"

Appendix G

there shall be substituted a reference to "information which may be refused under these Regulations".

(7) Section 60 of the Act (appeals against national security certificate) shall apply with the following modifications–
- (a) for the reference to a certificate under section 24(3) of the Act (national security) there shall be substituted a reference to a certificate issued in accordance with regulation 15(1);
- (b) subsection (2) shall be omitted; and
- (c) in subsection (3), for the words, "the Minister did not have reasonable grounds for issuing the certificate" there shall be substituted the words "the Minister or person designated by him did not have reasonable grounds for issuing the certificate under regulation 15(1)".

(8) A person found guilty of an offence under paragraph 12 of Schedule 3 to the Act (offences relating to obstruction of the execution of a warrant) is liable on summary conviction to a fine not exceeding level 5 on the standard scale.

(9) A government department is not liable to prosecution in relation to an offence under paragraph 12 of Schedule 3 to the Act but that offence shall apply to a person in the public service of the Crown and to a person acting on behalf of either House of Parliament or on behalf of the Northern Ireland Assembly as it applies to any other person.

(10) Section 76(1) of the Act (disclosure of information between Commissioner and ombudsmen) shall apply to any information obtained by, or furnished to, the Commissioner under or for the purposes of these Regulations.

19 Offence of altering records with intent to prevent disclosure

(1) Where–
- (a) a request for environmental information has been made to a public authority under regulation 5; and
- (b) the applicant would have been entitled (subject to payment of any charge) to that information in accordance with that regulation,

any person to whom this paragraph applies is guilty of an offence if he alters, defaces, blocks, erases, destroys or conceals any record held by the public authority, with the intention of preventing the disclosure by that authority of all, or any part, of the information to which the applicant would have been entitled.

(2) Subject to paragraph (5), paragraph (1) applies to the public authority and to any person who is employed by, is an officer of, or is subject to the direction of, the public authority.

(3) A person guilty of an offence under this regulation is liable on summary conviction to a fine not exceeding level 5 on the standard scale.

(4) No proceedings for an offence under this regulation shall be instituted–
- (a) in England and Wales, except by the Commissioner or by or with the consent of the Director of Public Prosecutions; or
- (b) in Northern Ireland, except by the Commissioner or by or with the consent of the Director of Public Prosecutions for Northern Ireland.

Miscellaneous statutory material

(5) A government department is not liable to prosecution in relation to an offence under paragraph (1) but that offence shall apply to a person in the public service of the Crown and to a person acting on behalf of either House of Parliament or on behalf of the Northern Ireland Assembly as it applies to any other person.

20 Amendment

(1) Section 39 of the Act is amended as follows.

(2) In subsection (1)(a), for "regulations under section 74" there is substituted "environmental information regulations".

(3) After subsection (1) there is inserted–

"(1A) In subsection (1) "environmental information regulations" means–
  (a) regulations made under section 74, or
  (b) regulations made under section 2(2) of the European Communities Act 1972 for the purpose of implementing any Community obligation relating to public access to, and the dissemination of, information on the environment.".

21 Revocation

The following are revoked–
  (a) The Environmental Information Regulations 1992 and the Environmental Information (Amendment) Regulations 1998 except insofar as these apply to Scottish public authorities; and
  (b) The Environmental Information Regulations (Northern Ireland) 1993 and the Environmental Information (Amendment) Regulations (Northern Ireland) 1998.

Appendix H

Guidance Relating to Noise and Smell

PPG 24 (September 1994)

PLANNING POLICY GUIDANCE: PLANNING AND NOISE

Planning policy guidance notes set out the Government's policies on different aspects of planning. Local authorities must take their content into account in preparing their development plans. They may be material to decisions on individual planning applications and appeals.

This PPG gives guidance to local authorities in England on the use of their planning powers to minimise the adverse impact of noise and builds on the advice previously contained in DOE Circular 10/73. It:
— outlines the considerations to be taken into account in determining planning applications both for noise-sensitive developments and for those activities which will generate noise;
— introduces the concept of noise exposure categories for residential development, encourages their use and recommends appropriate levels for exposure to different sources of noise; and
— advises on the use of conditions to minimise the impact of noise.

Introduction

1 Noise can have a significant effect on the environment and on the quality of life enjoyed by individuals and communities. The aim of this guidance is to provide advice on how the *planning system* can be used to minimise the adverse impact of noise without placing unreasonable restrictions on development or adding unduly to the costs and administrative burdens of business. It builds upon the principles established in Circular 10/73 'Planning and Noise', and takes account of the recommendations of the Noise Review Working Party which reported in October 1990 (HMSO, ISBN 0 11 752343 7). It outlines some of the main considerations which local planning authorities should take into account in drawing up development plan policies and when determining planning applications for development which will either generate noise or be exposed to existing noise sources.

General principles

2 The impact of noise can be a material consideration in the determination of planning applications. The planning system has the task of guiding development to the most appropriate locations. It will be hard to reconcile some land uses, such as housing, hospitals or schools, with other activities which generate high levels of noise, but the planning system should ensure that, wherever practicable, noise-sensitive developments are separated from major sources of noise (such as road, rail and air transport and certain types of industrial development). It is equally important that new development involving noisy activities should, if possible, be sited away from noise-sensitive land uses. Development

Appendix H

plans provide the policy framework within which these issues can be weighed but careful assessment of all these factors will also be required when individual applications for development are considered. Where it is not possible to achieve such a separation of land uses, local planning authorities should consider whether it is practicable to control or reduce noise levels, or to mitigate the impact of noise, through the use of conditions or planning obligations.

Noise policies in development plans

3 Where the development plan is material to the development proposal, section 54A of the *Town and Country Planning Act 1990* (inserted by section 26 of the *Planning and Compensation Act 1991*) requires applications and appeals to be determined in accordance with the plan, unless material considerations indicate otherwise. Development plans should give developers and local communities a degree of certainty about the areas in which particular types of development will be acceptable and those in which special measures may be required in order to mitigate the impact of noise. Policies on noise should take account of the guidance in the rest of this note and in the Annexes: it will generally be appropriate for these policies to be set out in Part II of Unitary Development Plans and in district local plans. But in some cases (when dealing with strategic issues such as development of, or near, major aerodromes, for example) it may be necessary to include some noise policies in Part I of UDPs and in structure plans.

4 Where noise policies apply to the plan area as a whole, they should be set out in the same way as other general policies. Area-specific noise policies may be useful in some circumstances and, in such cases, the relevant boundaries should be illustrated on the proposals map. However, it will generally be inappropriate for a proposals map to show detailed noise contours as noise emissions may change significantly over time (eg, in the case of an aerodrome, operational changes may lead to significant variations in the impact of the noise on those living in the area).

5 Plans should contain policies designed to ensure, as far as is practicable, that noise-sensitive developments are located away from existing sources of significant noise (or programmed development such as new roads) and that potentially noisy developments are located in areas where noise will not be such an important consideration or where its impact can be minimised. It may also be appropriate for local planning authorities to adopt policies to avoid potentially noisy developments in areas which have remained relatively undisturbed by noise nuisance and are prized for their recreational and amenity value for this reason.

6 The Secretary of State considers that housing, hospitals and schools should generally be regarded as noise-sensitive development, but planning authorities may wish to includes other developments or uses within this definition, depending on local circumstances and priorities and, if so, these should be explained in the development plan.

7 Where it is particularly difficult to separate noise-sensitive development from noisy activities, plans should contain an indication of any general policies which the local planning authority propose to apply in respect of conditions or planning obligation.

Guidance relating to noise and smell

Noise exposure categories for residential development

8 This guidance introduces the concept of Noise Exposure Categories (NECs), ranging from A–D, to help local planning authorities in their consideration of applications for residential development near transport-related noise sources. Category A represents the circumstances which noise is unlikely to be a determining factor, while Category D relates to the situation in which development should normally be refused. Categories B and C deal with situations where noise mitigation measures may make development acceptable. Annex 1 illustrates this approach in more detail. It also explains why the NEC procedure cannot be used in the reverse context for proposals which would introduce new noise sources into areas of existing residential development.

9 The table in Annex 1 contains a recommended range of noise levels for each NEC covering day and night-time periods. However, in some cases it may be appropriate for local planning authorities to determine the range of noise levels which they wish to attribute to any or each of the NECs. For example, where there is a clear need for new residential development in an already noisy area some or all NECs might be increased by up to 3 dB(A) above the recommended levels. In other cases, a reduction of up to 3 dB(A) may be justified.

Development control

Noisy development

10 Much of the development which is necessary for the creation of jobs and the construction and improvement of essential infrastructure will generate noise. The planning system should not place unjustifiable obstacles in the way of such development. Nevertheless, local planning authorities must ensure that development does not cause an unacceptable degree of disturbance. They should also bear in mind that a subsequent intensification or change of use may result in greater intrusion and they may wish to consider the use of appropriate conditions.

11 Noise characteristics and levels can vary substantially according to their source and the type of activity involved. In the case of industrial development for example, the character of the noise should be taken into account as well as its level. Sudden impulses, irregular noise or noise which contains a distinguishable continuous tone will require special consideration. In addition to noise from aircraft landing and taking off, noise from aerodromes is likely to include activities such as engine testing as well as ground movements. The impact of noise from sport, recreation and entertainment will depend to a large extent on frequency of use and the design of facilities. More detailed advice on factors to consider in relation to the major noise source including roads, railways, airports, industrial and recreational noise and their measurement is given in Annex 3. Separate advice on the control of noise from mineral working sites is provided in Minerals Planning Guidance Note 11–'The Control of Noise at Surface Mineral Workings' (MPG11).

Noise-sensitive development

12 Local planning authorities should consider carefully in each case whether proposals for new noise-sensitive development would be incompatible with existing activities. Such development should not normally be

Appendix H

permitted in areas which are—or are expected to become—subject to unacceptably high levels of noise. When determining planning applications for development which will be exposed to an existing noise source, local planning authorities should consider both the likely level of noise exposure at the time of the application and any increase that may reasonably be expected in the foreseeable future, for example at an airport. Annex 3 gives guidance on the assessment of noise from different sources. Authorities will also wish to bear in mind that, while there will be sites where noise is significantly lower at night than during the day, other sites may be subjected to night-time noise, for example from traffic, at a level which is little below the daytime level. These sites warrant particular protection: noise-sensitive development should not normally be permitted where high levels of noise will continue throughout the night, especially during the hours when people are normally sleeping (23.00 to 07.00).

Measures to mitigate the impact of noise

13 A number of measures can be introduced to control the source of, or limit exposure to, noise. Such measures should be proportionate and reasonable and may include one or more of the following:
  (i)   **engineering**: reduction of noise at point of generation (eg by using quiet machines and/or quiet methods of working); containment of noise generated (eg by insulating buildings which house machinery and/or providing purpose-built barriers around the site); and protection of surrounding noise-sensitive buildings (eg by improving sound insulation in these buildings and/or screening them by purpose-built barriers);
  (ii) **lay-out**: adequate distance between source and noise-sensitive building or area; screening by natural barriers, other buildings, or non-critical rooms in a building;
  (iii) **administrative**: limiting operating time of source; restricting activities allowed on the site; specifying an acceptable noise limit.

[14] Early consultation with the applicant about the possible use of such measures is desirable and may enable them to be incorporated into the design of the proposal before it is formally submitted for determination. Alternatively it may be appropriate for a local planning authority to ensure that such measures are introduced by imposing conditions.

Conditions

15 The appropriate use of planning conditions can enable many development proposals to proceed where it would otherwise be necessary to refuse permission. General advice on the use of conditions is contained in DOE Circular 1/85. Conditions should only be imposed where they are
  *   necessary
  *   relevant to planning
  *   relevant to the development to be permitted
  *   enforceable
  *   precise
  *   reasonable in all other respects.

16 Some examples of model conditions are given in Annex 4, but local planning authorities should give careful consideration to the individual circumstances of each application before imposing any conditions. In particular, authorities should not use the opportunity presented by an

Guidance relating to noise and smell

application for minor development to impose conditions on an existing development which already enjoys planning permission. In the case of aerodromes, for example, limits on hours of operation and the number and type of aircraft may be applied to new aerodromes, but in the case of existing aerodromes they should only be sought where the proposed development is likely to have a material effect on use. Conditions which set noise limits raise particular issues on which detailed guidance is given in Annex 5.

17 Where it is proposed to grant permission for noise-sensitive development in areas of high ambient noise, planning conditions should be imposed to ensure that the effects of noise are mitigated as far as possible. For example, intervening buildings or structures (such as garages) may be designed to serve as noise barriers. In some cases sound insulation measures may be considered appropriate. (Such measures will mainly apply to windows: additional guidance is given in Annex 6.) However, it should be remembered that the sound level within a residential building is not the only consideration: most residents will also expect a reasonable degree of peaceful enjoyment of their gardens and adjacent amenity areas.

18 There will also be circumstances when it is acceptable—or even desirable in order to meet other planning objectives—to allow noise generating activities on land near or adjoining a noise-sensitive development. In such cases, local planning authorities should consider the use of conditions or planning obligations to safeguard local amenity. Care should be taken to keep the noisiest activities away from the boundary or to provide for measures to reduce the impact of noise. Authorities should also take into account the fact that the background noise level in some parts of suburban and rural areas is very low, and the introduction of noisy activities into such areas may be especially disruptive.

19 Where an authority's planning objectives cannot be achieved by imposing a planning condition (because, for example, they require the developer to make a financial contribution, or they relate to development, roads or buildings other than those covered by the planning application), it may be appropriate to enter into a planning obligation under section 106 of the *Town and Country Planning Act 1990* (as substituted by section 12 of the *Planning and Compensation Act 1991*). Advice on the use of such obligations is given in DOE Circular 16/91.

Designated areas and the countryside

20 Special consideration is required where noisy development is proposed in or near Sites of Special Scientific Interest (SSSIs). Proposals likely to affect SSSIs designated as internationally important under the EC Habitats or Birds Directives or the Ramsar Convention require extra scrutiny. Further advice will be given in a forthcoming PPG on Nature Conservation. Special consideration should also be given to development which would affect the quiet enjoyment of the National Parks, the Broads, Areas of Outstanding Natural Beauty or Heritage Coasts. The effect of noise on the enjoyment of other areas of landscape, wildlife and historic value should also be taken into account.

21 In some cases, noisy development may have a serious effect on the welfare of livestock on nearby farms. The degree to which different

Appendix H

species will be affected will vary, so, when considering applications which could affect livestock, local planning authorities may wish to consult the Ministry of Agriculture, Fisheries and Food (Land Use Planning Unit).

Environmental Assessment

22 EC Directive 85/337 requires environmental assessment (EA) for certain types of project to be carried out before planning permission is granted. It has been implemented for projects that require planning permission by the *Town and Country Planning (Assessment of Environmental Effects) Regulations 1988*. For a limited number of projects listed in Schedule 1 to the Regulations, such as major aerodromes, EA is required in every case; for a wider range of projects listed in Schedule 2 to the Regulations, including local roads, other new aerodromes, industrial estate development, disposal of non-toxic waste and mineral extraction, EA is required if the proposal is likely to have significant environmental effects. Where EA is required, the likely effects of noise will be one of the considerations to be dealt with in the environmental statement prepared by the developer and submitted to the local planning authority with the planning application.

Other statutory controls

23 Additional statutory powers to control noise exist outside the planning system. The granting of planning permission does not remove the need to comply with these controls. The major legislative instruments are:
   (i)   Part III of the *Environmental Protection Act 1990*, as amended by the *Noise and Statutory Nuisance Act 1993*, which requires local authorities to serve abatement notices where the noise emitted from any premises, or from vehicles, machinery and equipment in the street, constitutes a statutory nuisance; and
   (ii) Part III of the *Control of Pollution Act 1974*, which gives local authorities powers to control noise from construction sites, and also introduced the concept of the Noise Abatement Zone (NAZ).

Implementation of this legislation usually falls to the Environmental Health Department of a local authority.

24 Other means of tackling noise include:
   (i)   the *Noise at Work Regulations 1989*, which are enforced by inspectors of the Health and Safety Executive (HSE);
   (ii) the *Building Regulations 1991*, which impose standards for sound insulation between dwellings (see paragraph **25**); and
   (iii) the *Civil Aviation Act 1982*, which provides for noise mitigation measures at designated aerodromes.

Codes of Practice giving guidance on how to reduce or minimise noise from various activities have been produced, some of which have been approved as statutory codes under the *Control of Pollution Act 1974*. Certain noise producing appliances are subject to product standard controls.

25 More information on other noise control regimes is given in Annex 7. The bodies and authorities responsible for offering advice or for implementing these controls will often have expertise or experience

Guidance relating to noise and smell

which planning authorities may find helpful in assessing proposals for development. For example, in the case of proposals for noisy indoor or outdoor sports developments, authorities should liaise with the regional office of the Sports Council and with the governing body for the sport, who may be able to advise on ways of minimising the disturbance. In the case of landfill waste disposal sites, much of the advice contained in MPG11 'The Control of Noise at Surface Mineral Workings' will be relevant, but waste regulation authorities should in any case be consulted at an early stage to discuss the need for specific noise controls. Where development is proposed near an aerodrome, liaison with the aerodrome management will be essential. Annexes 3 and 7 give further guidance on some of these points.

26 In some cases it will be particularly important for local planning authorities to liaise with the relevant body because some part of the activity for which planning permission has been sought may be subject to another more appropriate means of control or licensing condition. The planning permission should not seek to duplicate such controls or conditions. For example, the Government considers that the Building Regulations are the most appropriate means of control for sound insulation between dwellings and local planning authorities should not therefore use planning conditions to control sound insulation in such cases.

Cancellation of advice

27 The following advice is hereby cancelled insofar as it relates to England:
— DOE Circular 10/73
— model planning conditions 5–10 in Appendix A to DOE Circular 1/85.

GLOSSARY

Below are explanations of terms as they are used in the PPG; they are not definitions.

Aerodrome: any area of land, water, or space on the roof of a building, which is commonly used to provide facilities for the landing and departure of aircraft–including types capable of descending or climbing vertically. The term is generic and embraces other terms such as airport, airfield and heliport. For a formal definition see the *Civil Aviation Act 1982*.

Decibel(dB): a unit of level derived from the logarithm of the ratio between the value of a quantity and a reference value. It is used to describe the level of many different quantities. For sound pressure level the reference quantity is 20 |gmPa, the threshold of normal hearing is in the region of 0 dB, and 140 dB is the threshold of pain. A change of 1 dB is only perceptible under controlled conditions.

dB(A): decibels measured on a sound level meter incorporating a frequency weighting (A weighting) which differentiates between sounds of different frequency (pitch) in a similar way to the human ear. Measurements in dB(A) broadly agree with people's assessment of loudness. A change of 3 dB(A) is the minimum perceptible under normal conditions, and a change of 10 dB(A) corresponds roughly to halving or doubling the loudness of a sound. The background noise level in a living room may be about 30 dB(A); normal conversation about 60 dB(A) at 1

Appendix H

metre; heavy road traffic about 80 dB(A) at 10 metres; the level near a pneumatic drill about 100 dB(A).

Hertz (Hz): unit of frequency, equal to one cycle per second. Frequency is related to the pitch of a sound.

LA10,T: the A weighted level of noise exceeded for 10% of the specified measurement period (T). It gives an indication of the upper limit of fluctuating noise such as that from road traffic. LA10,18h is the arithmetic average of the 18 hourly LA10,1hvalues from 06.00 to 24.00.

LA90,T: the A weighted noise level exceeded for 90% of the specified measurement period (T). In BS 4142: 1990 it is used to define background noise level.

LAeq,T: the equivalent continuous sound level–the sound level of a notionally steady sound having the same energy as a fluctuating sound over a specified measurement period (T). LAeq,T is used to describe many types of noise and can be measured directly with an integrating sound level meter. It is written as Leq in connection with aircraft noise.

LAmax: the highest A weighted noise level recorded during a noise event. The time weighting used (F or S) should be stated.

Noise and Number Index (NNI): A composite measure of exposure to aircraft noise that takes into account the average peak noise level and the number of aircraft in a specific period. Now generally superseded by Leq.

Noise index: a measure of noise over a period of time which correlates well with average subjective response.

Rating level: the noise level of an industrial noise source which includes an adjustment for the character of the noise. Used in BS 4142: 1990.

Rw: single number rating used to describe the sound insulation of building elements (also see Annex 6). It is defined in BS 5821: 1984.

ANNEX 1

NOISE EXPOSURE CATEGORIES FOR DWELLINGS

1 When assessing a proposal for residential development near a source of noise, local planning authorities should determine into which of the four noise exposure categories (NECs) the proposed site falls, taking account of both day and night-time noise levels. Local planning authorities should then have regard to the advice in the appropriate NEC, as below:

NEC

A Noise need not be considered as a determining factor in granting planning permission, although the noise level at the high end of the category should not be regarded as a desirable level.

B Noise should be taken into account when determining planning applications and, where appropriate, conditions imposed to ensure an adequate level of protection against noise.

C Planning permission should not normally be granted. Where it is considered that permission should be given, for example because there

Guidance relating to noise and smell

are no alternative quieter sites available, conditions should be imposed to ensure a commensurate level of protection against noise.

D Planning permission should normally be refused.

2 A recommended range of noise levels is given below for each of the NECs for dwellings exposed to noise from road, rail, air, and 'mixed sources'. Annex 2 provides a detailed explanation of how the boundaries of each of the NECs have been derived. Paragraph **9** of the main text explains that in some cases local planning authorities may be able to justify a range of NECs of up to 3 dB(A) above or below those recommended.

3 The NEC noise levels should not be used for assessing the impact of industrial noise on proposed residential development because the nature of this type of noise, and local circumstances, may necessitate individual assessment and because there is insufficient information on people's response to industrial noise to allow detailed guidance to be given. However, at a mixed noise site where industrial noise is present but not dominant, its contribution should be included in the noise level used to establish the appropriate NEC.

4 The NEC procedure is only applicable where consideration is being given to introducing residential development into an area with an existing noise source, rather than the reverse situation where new noise sources are to be introduced into an existing residential area. This is because the planning system can be used to impose conditions to protect incoming residential development from an existing noise source but, in general, developers are under no statutory obligation to offer noise protection measures to existing dwellings which will be affected by a proposed new noise source. Moreover, there would be no obligation on individuals with an interest in each dwelling affected to take up such an offer, and therefore no guarantee that all necessary noise protection measures would be put in place.

5 Thus, where new industrial or commercial development is proposed near a residential area the effect of the new noise source on the surrounding area will have to be assessed in accordance with existing procedures. In many cases where a new source of noise is to be introduced by a project that requires environmental assessment (EA) (see paragraph **22**), the effect of noise will be considered in this context; but it must be accepted that in these circumstances the options to control noise are likely to be more limited than where residential development is proposed in an area with an existing noise source. It must also be borne in mind that when dealing with new roads and aerodromes, schemes may exist to provide insulation in specified circumstances.

Other noise-sensitive development

6 Developments such as offices, hospitals and schools will contain buildings and activities which are noise-sensitive. But these developments are likely to occupy sizeable sites and to contain a proportion of buildings and activities which are less noise-sensitive. The NEC principle cannot therefore be sensibly applied to such developments and it will be more appropriate to refer to specific guidance on internal noise standards in respect of each activity. General information can be found in BS

Appendix H

8233: 1987. Information about guidance for health and hospital buildings is available from NHS Estates, an Executive Agency of the Department of Health, 1 Trevelyan Square, Boar Lane, Leeds LS1 6AE. The Department for Education publishes guidance for schools (see Annex 8).

Noise index and measurement positions

7 Traditionally, different indices have been used to describe noise from different sources, and limits have been set over different time periods. This has caused confusion, and this PPG follows the move towards consistency advocated in BS 7445: 1991 by expressing all noises in terms of LAeq,T. The recommended time periods a 07.00–23.00 and 23.00–07.00.

8 Values in the table below refer to noise levels measured on an open site at the position of the proposed dwellings, well away from any existing buildings, and 1.2m to 1.5m above the ground. The arithmetic average of recorded reading should be rounded up. Where that average falls on the boundary between NECs B and C it will be for the local planning authority to determine which is the more appropriate NEC for the proposal.

9 Levels of noise from road and rail traffic are often specified at one metre from a facade, and these facade levels should be assumed to be 3 dB(A) higher than levels measured away from any buildings, unless a more accurate figure is available. For road traffic noise in NECs C and D, LAeq,16h–LA10,18h −2 dB.

10 For aircraft, the noise levels refer to aircraft noise exposure contour values which are specified at 1.2m above the ground and published at 3 dB(A) intervals (each 3 dB(A) increment represents a doubling of noise energy). Because most aircraft noise originates from above, contours include the effects of ground reflection (see Note 2 below).

RECOMMENDED NOISE EXPOSURE CATEGORIES FOR NEW DWELLINGS NEAR EXISTING NOISE SOURCES

NOISE LEVELS[0] CORRESPONDING TO THE NOISE EXPOSURE CATEGORIES FOR NEW DWELLINGS LAeq,T dB

NOISE SOURCE	NOISE EXPOSURE CATEGORY			
	A	B	C	D
road traffic				
07.00–23.00	\h55	55–63	63–72	\g72
23.00–07.00[1]	\h45	45–57	57–66	\g66
rail traffic				
07.00–23.00	\h55	55–66	66–74	\g74
23.00–07.00[1]	\h45	45–59	59–66	\g66
air traffic[2]				
07.00–23.00	\h57	57–66	66–72	\g72
23.00–07.00[1]	\h48	48–57	57–66	\g66
mixed sources[3]				
07.00–23.00	\h55	55–63	63–72	\g72
23.00–07.00[1]	\h45	45–57	57–66	\g66

Guidance relating to noise and smell

Notes
0   **Noise levels:** the noise level(s) (LAeq,T/) used when deciding the NEC of a site should be representative of typical conditions.
1   **Night-time noise levels (23.00–07.00):** sites where individual noise events regularly exceed 82 dB LAmax (S time weighting) several times in any hour should be treated as being in NEC C, regardless of the LAeq,8h (except where the LAeq,8h already puts the site in NEC D).
2   **Aircraft noise:** daytime values accord with the contour values adopted by the Department of Transport which relate to levels measured 1.2m above open ground. For the same amount of noise energy, contour values can be up to 2 dB(A) higher than those of other sources because of ground reflection effects.
3   **Mixed sources:** this refers to any combination of road, rail, air and industrial noise sources. The 'mixed source' values are based on the lowest numerical values of the single source limits in the table. The 'mixed source' NEC8 should only be used where no individual noise source is dominant.

To check if any individual noise source is dominant (for the purposes of this assessment) the noise level from the individual sources should be determined and then combined by decibel addition (remembering first to subtract 2 dB(A) from any aircraft noise contour values). If the level of any one source then lies within 2 dB(A) of the calculated combined value, that source should be taken as the dominant one and the site assessed against the appropriate NEC for that source, rather than using the 'mixed source' NECs. If the dominant source is industrial noise see paragraph **19** of Annex 3.

If the contribution of the individual noise sources to the overall noise level cannot be determined by measurement and/or calculation, then the overall measured level should be used and the site assessed against the NECs for 'mixed sources'.

ANNEX 2

NOISE EXPOSURE CATEGORIES: EXPLANATION OF NOISE LEVELS

1 The following is an explanation of how the boundaries of each of the noise exposure categories (NECs) in the table in Annex 1 have been calculated or derived. Wherever possible figures have been based on research findings or figures contained in statutory regulations. However, the NEC table attempts to give guidance across a broad spectrum of situations and not all of these are covered by existing research work or regulations. In these instances assessments and interpolations have had to be made and these are also explained below.

2 The explanations under each heading make specific reference to each of the transport modes: road, rail, and air. However, separate explanations of 'mixed sources' are not given. The 'mixed source' values are based on the lowest numerical values of the single source limits in the table.

3 The values given in the NEC table are free-field levels, together with an addition of 2 dB(A) for ground reflection of air traffic noise. Details of correction factors to convert between facade levels and free-field where appropriate are given below. For night-time levels typical insulation values for window installations that are likely to be used in each NEC have been assumed. Because the insulation performance of different window installations is likely to vary, these values are nominal.

Noise levels at the boundary of NEC A and NEC B

DAYTIME

4 There is no recent, major, U.K.-based research from which to take figures for road or rail traffic. The level at the boundary of NEC A and

Appendix H

NEC B is therefore based on guidance provided by the World Health Organisation[1] that 'general daytime outdoor noise levels of less than 55 dB(A) Leq are desirable to prevent any significant community annoyance'. The figure of 55 dB(A) has been taken to be free-field and therefore no adjustments have been necessary for road and rail traffic noise levels before inserting them in the table. In respect of air traffic noise a considerable amount of research has been carried out.[2] 57 dB(A) Leq (previously 35 NNI) relates to the onset of annoyance as established by noise measurements and social surveys.

1 Environmental Health Criteria 12 — Noise. World Health Organisation, 1980.
2 Directorate of Operational Research and Analysis 'The Noise and Number Index' DORA Communication 7907, Second Edition, September 1981
Brooker, P et al 'United Kingdom Aircraft Noise Index Study: Final Report' Civil Aviation Authority DR Report 8402, January 1985
Critchley, JB and Ollerhead, JB 'The Use of Leq as an Aircraft Noise Index' Civil Aviation Authority DORA Report 9023, September 1990.

Night-Time

5 As for daytime, there is no recent, major, U.K.-based research from which to take figures for road or rail traffic. There has been research on the effects of aircraft noise, most recently on sleep disturbance[3], which looks at noise levels at which people are awoken from sleep. The night–time noise level at the boundary of NEC A and NEC B is based on the WHO guideline previously referred to[1] which states that for night-time: 'based on limited data available, a level of less than 35 dB(A) is recommended to preserve the restorative process of sleep' and this is considered more relevant when seeking to achieve the best practicable conditions for rest and sleep.

3 Report of a field study of aircraft noise and sleep disturbance. Department of Transport, 1992.
1 Environmental Health Criteria 12 — Noise. World Health Organisation, 1980.

6 For a site to fall within NEC A noise should not be a determining factor when granting planning permission. It follows that residents may reasonably expect to sleep with their windows open sufficiently to provide adequate ventilation. No guidance is given in the WHO document on the allowance to be made for the sound insulation qualities of a partially open window. This is usually taken to be 10–15 dB(A)[4] and for the purposes of the NEC table a reduction of 13 dB(A) from the facade level has been assumed. This would give a recommended maximum figure of 48 dB(A) at the facade. However, as the NEC figures are free-field a correction of -3 dB(A) is necessary giving 45 dB(A) in the table for road and rail noise. For air traffic noise 2 dB(A) has been added to 45 dB(A) to allow for ground reflection, making 47 dB(A). The level in the table of 48 dB(A) is the nearest aircraft dB(A) Leq contour value.

4 Transportation Noise Reference Book: Edited by Paul Nelson, published by Butterworths, 1987.

Noise levels at the boundary of NEC B and NEC C

Daytime

7 The daytime noise levels for all three transport modes at the boundary of NEC B and NEC C are based on the levels that trigger official grant schemes. For road traffic noise the trigger level is 68 dB $L_{A10,18h}$[5] at a

Guidance relating to noise and smell

facade. This has been converted to an LAeq,18h level by subtracting 3 dB, and to an LAeq,16h value by adding 1 dB, giving 66 dB LAeq,6h at a facade. Finally, this figure has been converted to a free-field level by subtracting 3 dB, thus arriving at 63 dB LAeq,16h in the table.

5   *Noise Insulation Regulations, 1975*: SI 1975:1763

8   For railway noise the proposed trigger level[6] is 68 dB LAeq,8h at a facade. This has been converted to 66 dB LAeq,16h free-field.

6   *Draft Noise Insulation (Railways and Other Guided Transport Systems) Regulations 1993*, issued for consultation October 1993.

9   For air traffic noise, 66 dB(A) Legeq,16h, previously 50 NNI, was the daytime criterion for noise insulation schemes at Heathrow, Gatwick and Stansted.

NIGHT-TIME

10   The night-time level at the boundary of NEC B and NEC C for road traffic is, like that at the boundary of NEC A and NEC B, based on the WHO figure of 35 dB(A). Because noise should be taken into account when determining planning applications in NEC B, it has been assumed that the minimum amelioration measure available to an occupant at night will be to close bedroom windows. Single glazed windows. provide insulation of about 25 dB(A).[7] Therefore, in order to achieve 35 dB(A) inside a bedroom, the facade level should not exceed 60 dB(A). This facade level requires a further 3 dB(A) adjustment to convert it to the free-field level of 57 dB(A) for road traffic at the boundary of NEC B and NEC C. For rail traffic, the level proposed to trigger the official grant scheme[6] has been adopted. This level is 63 dB LAeq,6h and it has been converted to 59 dB LAeq,8h free-field. For air traffic, the level proposed to trigger the recent grant scheme at Stansted airport[8] has been adopted. This level is the 57 dB(A3 Leq contour value.

7   Transportation Noise Reference Book: Edited by Paul Nelson, published by Butterworths, 1987 and Sound Control For Homes, published by the Building Research Establishment and CIRIA, 1993 [BRE report 238, CIRIA report 127].
6   *Draft Noise Insulation (Railways and Other Guided Transport Systems) Regulations 1993*, issued for consultation October 1993.
8   Department of Transport Consultation Paper: Proposed Stansted Noise Insulation Grants Scheme, September 1990.

Noise levels at the boundary of NEC C and NEC D

DAYTIME

11   The noise level at the boundary of NEC C and NEC D for road traffic is based on a Building Research Establishment (BRE) survey[9] which has shown that the insulation package supplied under the Noise Insulation Regulations is inadequate for road traffic noise levels of 78 dB LA10,18h and above at a facade. This figure is equivalent to a free-field level of 75 dB LA10,18h; which in turn is equivalent to 73 dB LAeq,16h. The 73 dB LAeq,16h has been reduced by 1 dB to 72 dB LAeq,16h in the table at the boundary of NEC C and NEC D, which is the maximum external level that the standard noise insulation package will reduce to an acceptable internal level.

9   Utley W. et al 'The effectiveness and acceptability of measures for insulating dwellings against traffic noise' (Journal of Sound and Vibration (1986) Vol 109(1), pages 1–18).

Appendix H

12 For rail traffic noise no reliable data are available on which to base the level at the boundary of NEC C and NEC D. However, there is some evidence[10] that noise from rail traffic causes less disturbance than noise from road traffic at the same level. Therefore, the level at the boundary of NEC C and NEC D has been set 2 dB higher than the free-field level for road traffic noise.

10 'Railway Noise and the Insulation of Dwellings' Mitchell Committee Report, published February 1991.

13 For air traffic noise the value put forward in Circular 10/73, which is now well established, has been used. This is 60 NNI or 72 dB LAeq,16h, including a 2 dB allowance for ground reflection.

NIGHT-TIME

14 The night-time levels at the boundary of NEC C and NEC D are, like those at the boundary of NEC A and NEC B, based on the WHO figure of 35 dB(A). The standard noise insulation package provides insulation of about 35 dB(A)[9]. Therefore at a facade level of 70 dB(A) or above the internal limit for a bedroom of 35 dB(A) may not be achieved. The level of 70 dB(A) has therefore been reduced by 1 dB(A) and a correction factor of 3 dB(A) applied to derive the free-field level of 66 dB(A) in the table at the boundary of NEC C and NEC D for road and rail noise. For air traffic noise the level of 66 dB(A) is the nearest aircraft dB(A) Leq contour value to provide equivalent protection.

9 Utley W. et al 'The effectiveness and acceptability of measures for insulating dwellings against traffic noise' Journal of Sound and Vibration (1986) Vol 109(1), pages 1–18).

ANNEX 5
SPECIFYING NOISE LIMITS

If a local planning authority wishes to impose a planning condition which will specify an acceptable noise limit from a new source, the following points should be considered.

1 Type of limit

Depending on circumstances, it may be appropriate to set either:
  (a) an absolute limit based on the average level of noise which should not be exceeded in a specified time period;
  (b) a relative limit based on the permitted increase in noise level with respect to the background level. This is the approach used in BS 4142:1990.

Generally, relative limits are not appropriate where the permitted increase in noise over background is substantial–eg 15 dB or more. Because background noise varies during the day, the background noise level determined should be representative of a typical quiet period during the working day.

Either type of limit may be a single value over the relevant period, or different values for, say, day and night. It may be appropriate to set an evening value as well where the noise source lends itself to fine control.

A noise limit which is close to the background level will be difficult to monitor and the advice given in BS 4142 should be followed. This is

Guidance relating to noise and smell

particularly important at quiet sites where the LAeq,T may be 10 dB or more above the LA90,T–even when the noise source is not operating.

The idea of setting an additional overriding maximum level is often attractive, but may be hard to enforce because with unattended monitoring stations it is difficult to exclude extraneous noises (which will increase the measured level). There may also be the administrative difficulty of dealing with occasional transient high noise levels from the site.

Where the noise will only be produced inside buildings and the maximum frequency spectrum levels are known, it may be appropriate to set a standard for the sound insulation of a building envelope rather than a noise limit at an external monitoring point.

2 Noise index

Because noises vary over time and have different characteristics many indices have been developed to describe noise levels. The equivalent continuous noise level over a time period T (LAeq,T) has emerged as the best general purpose index for environmental noise. For road traffic noise LA10,18h is still widely used; and to describe background noise LA90,T is appropriate. To describe the sound insulation of a component of a building envelope (eg a window) R^w (BS 5821: Part 3:1984) is appropriate. It is more difficult to specify the insulation of the whole building envelope because the value depends on different insulation values for the various building elements such as windows, walls and roof structure, as well as the type of noise source and its location.

These indices are explained in the Glossary. Additional information may be found in BS 7445: 1991.

3 Monitoring point(s)

Normally the noise limit will be chosen to protect the nearest noise-sensitive premises and the best position for the monitoring point(s) will often be outside the sensitive premises. However, this does not mean that the monitoring point must always be close to the premises. Normally noise limits refer only to noise from the source under consideration and not to the total measured value which may include, for example, traffic noise. In situations where extraneous noise makes monitoring difficult it may be easier to monitor a suitably adjusted level at the boundary of the site instead of outside the premises to be protected. This approach requires that the noise level at the boundary monitoring point is a reliable indicator of the level at the building to be protected and this may not be the case if the noise source is mobile. Monitoring points should be accessible to all parties concerned.

4 Meteorological conditions

The noise level measured at a monitoring point will be affected by wind speed and direction, and temperature gradients, particularly when the monitoring point is remote (\w30m) from the source. The size of these effects is hard to predict, and so measurements (or predictions) should be made under reasonably stable conditions. A suitable condition is a light wind with a vector component up to 2 m/s from source to receiver; his will increase the noise level by about 2 dB(A) compared with the no wind case.

Appendix H

This report contains the collective views of an international group of experts and does not necessarily represent the decisions or the stated policy of either the World Health Organization or the United Nations Environment Programme.

Environmental Health Criteria 12 NOISE Published under the joint sponsorship of the United Nations Environment Programme and the World Health Organization World Health OrganizationGeneva, 1980

List of abbreviations and symbols used in this document

AI	articulation index
c	speed of sound
CNEL	community noise equivalent level
CNR	composite noise rating
|SF	frequency
I	sound intensity
Lgo	day-night average-sound level
Lge	aircraft exposure level
Lpq	equivalent continuous sound pressure level
Lp or SPL	sound pressure level
Lo(A)	A-weighted sound pressure level
Lpn	mean peak perceived noise level
NEF	noise exposure forecast
NI	noiseness index
NIPTS	noise-induced permanent threshold shift
NITS	noise-induced threshold shift
NITTS	noise-induced temporary threshold shift
NNI	noise and number index
NPL	noise pollution level
p	root mean square pressure
Pe	mean square sound pressure
P	sound power
PNL	perceived noise level
SIL	speech interference level
SPL or Zp	sound pressure level

Guidance relating to noise and smell

TNEL total noise exposure level
TNI traffic noise index
WECPNL weighted equivalent continuous perceived noise level
|gl wavelength

WHO Task Group on Environmental Health Criteria for Noise

Members
Dr H. E. von Glerke, Department of the Air Force, Aerospace Medical Research Laboratory, Wright Patterson Air Force Base, OH, USA (*Chairman*)
Dr E. Gros, Institute for Hygiene and Occupational Medicine, University Clinic, Essen, Federal Republic of Germany
Professor L. L. Karagodina, F. F. Erisman Research Institute of Hygiene, Moscow, USSR (*Vice-Chairman*)
Professor G. E. Lambert, Médecin Inspecteur du Travail Region Midi-Pyrénées, Cité Administrative, Toulouse, France
Professor J. B. Ollerhead, Department of Transport Technology, University of Technology, Loughbrough, Leicester, England (*Rapporteur*)
Dr Y. Osada, The Institute of Public Health, Tokyo, Japan
Professor B. Paccagnella, Institute of Hygiene, University of Padita, Verona, Italy
Dr P. Rey, Institute of Social and Preventive Medicine, University of Geneva, Geneva, Switzerland
Professor R. Rylander, Department of Hygiene, University of Gothenburg, Gothenburg, Sweden (*Rapporteur*)
Professor W. J. Sulkowski, Institute of Occupational Medicine, Lodz, Poland
Ms A. Suter, Office of Noise Abatement and Control, United States Environmental Protection Agency, Washington DC, USA (*Rapporteur*)
Representatives of other organizations
Dr G. H. Coppée, International Labour Organisation, Geneva, Switzerland
Dr W. Hunter, Commission of the European Communities, Luxembourg
Dr A. Alexandre, Organisation for Economic Co-operation and Development, Paris, France
Mr L. Nielsen, International Organization for Standardization, Hellerup, Denmark
Observers
Ms G. Vindevogel, Ministry of Public Health and Family, Brussels, Belgium
Mr L. Backelandt, Ministry of Public Health and Family, Brussels, Belgium
Secretariat
Ms B. Goelzer, Scientist, Office of Occupational Health, World Health Organization, Geneva, Switzerland
Dr H. W. de Koning, Scientist, Control of Environmental Pollution and Hazards, World Health Organization, Geneva, Switzerland (*Secretary*)

Appendix H

Dr V. Krichagin, Environment and Occupational Health, WHO Regional Office for Europe, Copenhagen, Denmark

Dr J. Lang, National Institute for Research on Heat and Noise Technology, Vienna, Austria (*Temporary Adviser*)

A WHO Task Group on Environmental Health Criteria for Noise met in Brussels from 31 January to 4 February 1977. Dr. H. W. de Koning, Scientist, Control of Environmental Pollution and Hazards, Division of Environmental Health, WHO, opened the meeting on behalf of the Director General and expressed the appreciation of the Organization to the Government of Belgium for having made available the necessary financial support for the meeting. On behalf of the Government, the Group was welcomed by Professor Lafontaine, Director of the Institute for Hygiene and Epidemiology, Brussels. The Task Group reviewed and revised the second draft criteria document and made an evaluation of the health risks from exposure to noise.

The first draft of the criteria document was prepared by a study group that met in Geneva from 5–9 November 1973. Participants of the Group included: Dr. T. L. Henderson and Professor G. Jansen (Federal Republic of Germany); Dr A. F. Meyer (USA); Professor J. B. Ollerhead (United Kingdom, *Rapporteur*); Professor P. Rey (Switzerland, *Chairman*); Professor R. Rylander (Sweden); Professor W.J Sulkowski (Poland); Dr A. Annoni, Mr E. Hellen, and Mr B. Johansson (Consultant), International Labour Organisation (ILO); Dr A. Alexandre, Organisation for Economic Co-operation and Development (OECD): Dr A. Berlin, Commission of the European Communities (CEC); Professor L. A. Saenz, Scientific Committee on Problems of the Environment (SCOPE); Mr H.J. Cursahaney, International Civil Aviation Organization (ICAO); Dr M. Suess, World Health Organization Regional Office for Europe; and Dr G. Cleary and Dr G. E. Lambert, World Health Organization, Geneva, Certain sections of the first draft were later completed with the assistance of Dr A. Alexandre (OECD), Dr D. E. Broadbent (UK), Professor G. Jensen (FRG), and Professor W. D. Ward (USA).

The second draft was prepared by the Secretariat after comments had been received from the national focal points for the WHO Environmental Health Criteria Programme in Czechoslovakia, Federal Republic of Germany, Finland, Greece, Japan, New Zealand, Poland, Sweden, Thailand, United Kingdom, USSR, and USA, and from the International Labour Organisation, Commission of the European Communities, the Organisation for Economic Co-operation and Development, the International Civil Aviation Organization and the International Organization for Standardization. Many comments were also received from individual experts and commercial concerns including E. I. Du Pont de Nemours & Company, Wilmington, Delaware, USA, whose contributions are gratefully acknowledged.

The Secretariat particularly wishes to thank Dr. D. Hickish, Ford Motor Company Limited, Brentwood, Essex, England, Dr G. E. Lambert, Professor J. B. Ollerhead, Professor P. Rey, Professor R. Rylander, and Ms A. Suter for their most valued help in the final phases of the preparation of the document.

This document is based primarily on original publications listed in the reference section and every effort has been made to review all pertinent data and information available up to 1978. In addition, reference has often been made to the various publications on noise of the International Organization for Standardization that include the international standards for noise assessment (ISO, 1971; 1973a; 1975a). The following reviews and criteria documents have been referred to: Burns & Robinson (1970), Karagodina et al. (1972), Burns (1978), NIOSH (1978a), US Environmental Protection Agency (1978a), ILO (1976), Thiessen (1976), Rylander et al, (1978), and Health and Welfare, Canada (1979).

Details of the WHO Environmental Health Criteria Programme including some terms frequently used in the document may be found in the general introduction to the Environmental Health Criteria Programme published together with the environmental health criteria document on mercury (Environmental Health Criteria 1, Mercury, World Health Organization, Geneva, 1976) and now available as a reprint.

1. Summary and Recommendations for Further Studies

1.1 SUMMARY

1.1.1 Introduction

Noise can disturb man's work, rest, sleep, and communication; it can damage his hearing and evoke other psychological, physiological, and possibly pathological reactions. However, because of their complexity, their variability, and the interaction of noise with other environmental factors, the adverse health effects of noise do not lend themselves to a straightforward analysis.

Probably the most important issue is the industrial noise problem, and a need for noise control and hearing conservation programmes is widely recognized. Road traffic is the main source of community noise that may disturb large segments of the urban population. Also of worldwide concern is aircraft noise, which can significantly affect the mode of life of people living in the vicinity of airports.

1.1.2 Noise measurement

Sound is produced by the vibration of bodies or air molecules and is transmitted as a longitudinal wave motion. It is, therefore, a form of mechanical energy and is measured in energy-related units. The sound output of a source is measured in watts and the intensity of sound at a point in space is defined by the rate of energy flow per unit area, measured in watts per m^2. Intensity is proportional to the mean square of the sound pressure and, as the range of this variable is so wide, it is usual to express its value in decibels (dB)[a]. Because the effects of noise depend strongly upon frequency of sound pressure oscillation, spectrum analysis is important in noise measurement.

The perceived magnitude of sound is defined as loudness and its decibel equivalent is known as the loudness level. The loudness is a function of both intensity and frequency, and various procedures exist by which it may be estimated from physical measurements. The simplest methods involve the measurement of the sound pressure level (SPL)

Appendix H

through a filter or network of filters that represent the frequency response of the ear. Despite the existence of other slightly more accurate but more complex techniques, the A-weighted sound pressure level scale is gaining widespread acceptance and is recommended for general use[b]. Whatever procedure is used, such frequency-weighted measurements are referred to simply as sound (or noise) levels.

a   decibel = a measure on a logarithmic scale of a quantity such as sound pressure, sound power, or intensity with respect to a standard reference value (0.0002 microbars for sound pressure, 10^{-13}W for sound power, and 10^{-13}W/m² for intensity). Thus, for example, when the sound intensity increases by a factor of 1.26 $(=10^{0.1})$, it is said to have increased by 1 decibel (dB); 1 Bel equals 10 dB or a factor of 10 in intensity. The standard reference values are implied throughout this document unless otherwise stated.

b   To obtain a single number representing the sound level of a noise containing a wide range of frequencies in a manner representative of the ear's response, it is necessary to modify the effects of the low and high frequencies with respect to the medium frequencies. The A-filter is one particular frequency weighting and, when this is used, the resulting sound level is said to be A-weighted.

Measurements of sound level may be averaged over two distinctly different periods of time. Steady sound levels and instantaneous levels of variable sounds are measured on a very short time scale of 1 second or less. Variable sounds can be measured with a much longer average time, over periods of hours if necessary, and are expressed in terms of the equivalent continuous sound pressure level (Leq). This convenient measure of average noise exposure using the A-weighting correlates reasonably well with many human responses to noise and is recommended for general use.

Many noise indices have been developed for predicting human reaction to various noise levels. Some of these incorporate non-acoustic factors that influence the reaction. Although the use of such indices is not to be discouraged, it is desirable to adopt a uniform approach to noise measurement, whenever possible.

1.1.3 Effects of noise

1.1.3.1 Interference with communication

Although there appears to be no firm evidence, it is believed that interference with speech in occupational situations may lead to accidents due to an inability to hear warning shouts etc. In offices, schools, and homes, speech interference is a major source of annoyance. Many attempts have been made to develop a single index of such interference, based on the characteristics of the masking noise, that directly indicates the degree of interference with speech perception. Such indices involve a considerable degree of approximation. The following are the three most widely used:

Articulation index (AI). This is the most complicated index, since it takes into account the fact that some frequencies are more effective in masking speech than others. The frequency range from 250 to 7000 Hz is divided into 20 bands. The difference between the average speech peak level in each of these bands is calculated and the resulting numbers combined to give a single index.

Speech interference level (SIL). SIL was designed as a simplified substitute for the AI. It was originally defined as the average of the now obsolete octave-band SPLs in the 600–1200, 1200–2400, and 2400–4800 Hz octaves. At the present time, SIL, based upon the octave band levels at the preferred frequencies of 500, 1000, 2000, and 4000 Hz, is considered to provide a better estimate of the masking ability of a noise. As SIL does not take the actual speech level into account, the associated masking effect depends upon vocal effort and speaker-to-listener distance.

A-weighed sound level. This is also a convenient and fairly accurate index of speech interference.

It is usually possible to express the relationship between noise levels and speech intelligibility in a single diagram, based on the assumptions and empirical observations that for speaker-to-listener distances of about 1m:
  (a) speech spoken in relaxed conversation is 100% intelligible in background noise levels of about 45 dB(A), and can be understood fairly well in background levels of 55 dB(A); and
  (b) speech spoken with slightly more vocal effort can be understood well, when the noise level is 65 dB(A).

For outdoor speech communication, the |P`inverse square law|P' controls speech transmission over moderate distances, i.e., when the distance between speaker and listener is doubled, the level of the speech drops by approximately 6 dB. This relationship is less likely to apply indoors, where speech communication is affected by the reverberation characteristics of the room.

In cases where the speech signals are of paramount importance, e.g., in classrooms or conference rooms, or where listeners with impaired hearing faculties are involved, e.g., in homes for aged people, lower levels of background noise are desirable.

1.1.3.2 Hearing loss

Hearing loss can be either temporary or permanent. Noise-induced temporary threshold shift (NITTS) is a temporary loss of hearing acuity experienced after a relatively short exposure to excessive noise. Pre-exposure hearing is recovered fairly rapidly after cessation of the noise. Noise-induced permanent threshold shift (NIPTS) is an irreversible (sensorineural) loss of hearing that is caused by prolonged noise exposure. Both kinds of loss together with presbyacusis, the permanent hearing impairment that is attributed to the natural aging process, can be experienced simultaneously.

In the quantification of hearing damage, it is necessary to differentiate between NIPTS, hearing level (the audiometric level of an individual or group in relation to an accepted audiometric standard), and hearing impairment.

NIPTS is the hearing loss (i.e., the reduction of hearing level) attributable to noise exposure alone, disregarding losses due to aging. NIPTS occurs typically at high frequencies, usually with a maximum loss at

Appendix H

around 4000 Hz. Noise-induced hearing loss occurs gradually, usually over a period of years. Once there is considerable hearing loss at a particular frequency, the rate of loss usually diminishes. Audiometrically, noise-induced losses are similar to presbyacusis. Hearing loss due to prolonged excessive noise exposure is generally associated with destruction of the hair cells of the inner ear. The severity of hearing loss is correlated with both the location and the extent of damage in the organ of Corti.

'Hearing impairment' is usually defined as the hearing level at which individuals begin to experience difficulties in everyday life. It is assessed in terms of difficulty in understanding speech. The amount of loss at the speech frequencies has been used as a basis for compensation and varies from one country to another. The unweighted average of the losses, in dB, at 500, 1000, and 2000 Hz that is widely used for assessing noise-induced hearing impairment, is somewhat misleading since most hearing loss usually occurs at 2000 Hz and above. Consequently, there is an increased tendency to include the frequencies of 3000 and 4000 Hz in damage assessment formulae.

Attempts have been made to establish the levels of noise that are permanently damaging to the ear and to identify individual susceptibility to NIPTS on the basis of NITTS measurements. However, the validity of the connection between NITTS and NIPTS has not been agreed.

There is also some disagreement concerning the relationship between the relative ear-damaging capacity of the noise level and its duration. However, the hypothesis that the hearing damage associated with a particular noise exposure is related to the total energy of the sound (i.e., the integrated product of intensity and time) is rapidly gaining favour for practical purposes. Thus, noise should preferably be described in terms of equivalent continuous sound level, L_{gq}, measured in dB(A). For occupational noise, the level should be averaged over the entire 8-h shift (L_{gq} (8–h)).

Available data show that there is considerable variation in human sensitivity with respect to NIPTS. The hazardous nature of a noisy environment is therefore described in terms of 'damage risk'. This may be expressed as the percentage of people exposed to that environment who are expected to suffer noise-induced hearing impairment after appropriate allowance has been made for hearing losses due to other causes. It is now accepted that this risk is negligible at noise exposure levels of less than 75 dB(A) Leq (8–h) but increases with increasing levels. Based on national judgements concerning 'acceptable risk', many countries have adopted industrial noise exposure limits of 85 dB(A) \d 5dB(A) in their regulations and recommended practices.

The exposure to ototoxic drugs such as certain aminoglycosidic antibiotics however, can lower the threshold below which noise can damage the ear.

It is not yet clear whether the damage risk rules already mentioned can be extended to the very short durations of impulsive noise. Available evidence indicates that a considerable risk exists, when impulsive sound levels reach 130–160 dB, depending upon the temporal characteristics of the impulse.

Although there is a fairly wide range of individual variability, especially for high frequency stimuli, the threshold of pain for normal ears is in the region of 135–140 dB sound pressure level. Aural pain should always be considered to be an early warning sign of excessive noise exposure.

Wherever possible, problems of noise control should be tackled at source, i.e., by reducing the amount of noise produced. An acceptable alternative is to isolate people from the noise by the use of noise insulation, including soundproof enclosures, partitions, and acoustic barriers. If this is not possible, the risk can also be minimized by limiting the duration of exposure. Only in cases where these control measures are impracticable should personal ear protection be considered. These devices can and do provide useful protection but inherent problems include those of proper fitting and use, and a degree of discomfort.

If there us any risk of hearing damage, pre-employment and follow-up audiometric examinations of workers should be carried out to detect changes in hearing acuity that might indicate possible development of NIPTS, in order to initiate preventative action.

1.1.3.3 Disturbance of sleep

Noise intrusion can cause difficulty in falling asleep and can awaken people who are asleep. Detailed laboratory studies of the problem have been made by monitoring electroencephalographic (EEG) responses and changes in neurovegetative reactions during sleep.

Studies have indicated that the disturbance of sleep becomes increasingly apparent as ambient noise levels exceed about 35 dB(A) Leq. It has been found that the probability of subjects being awakened by a peak sound level of 40 dB(A) is 5%, increasing to 80% at 70 dB(A). Defining sleep disturbance in terms of EEG changes, the probability of disturbance increases from 10% at 40 dB(A) to 60% at 70 dB(A). It has also been observed that subjects who sleep well (based on psycho-motoric activity data) at 35 dB(A) Leq complain about sleep disturbance and have difficulty in falling asleep at 50 dB(A) Leq and even at 40 dB(A) Leq. Weak stimuli that are unexpected can still interfere with sleep.

Within a population, differences in sensitivity to noise occur related, for example, to age and sex. Adaptation has been observed only when noise stimuli are of low intensity. Even though sleep is more disturbed by noise rich in information, habituation to such noise has been observed. Based on the limited data available, a level of less than 35 dB(A) Leq is recommended to preserve the restorative process of sleep.

1.1.3.4 Stress

Noise produces different reactions along the hypothalamo-hypophyseal-adrenal axis including an increase in adenocorticotropic hormone (ACTH) release and an elevation of corticosteroid levels. Some of these reactions have been elicited in an acute form in laboratory experiments at rather moderate levels of noise.

Effects on the systemic circulation such as constriction of blood vessels have been produced under laboratory conditions and a high incidence of circulatory disturbances including hypertension has been found in noise-exposed workers. A tendency for blood pressure to be higher in

Appendix H

populations living in noisy areas around airports has been suggested but no conclusive evidence of this has been presented.

Noise affects the sympathetic division of the autonomic nervous system. Eye dilation, bradycardia, and increased skin conductance are proportional to the intensity of noise above 70 dB SPL, wihtout adaptation to the stimulus.

Other sympathetic disturbances, such as changes in gastrointestinal motility, can be produced by intense sound. Medical records of workers have shown that, in addition to a higher incidence of hearing loss, noise-exposed groups have a higher prevalence of peptic ulcer; however, a causal relationship has not been established.

More studies are required to determine the long-term health risks due to the action of noise on the autonomic nervous system.

1.1.3.5 Annoyance

Noise annoyance may be defined as a feeling of displeasure evoked by a noise. The annoyance-inducing capacity of a noise depends upon many of its physical characteristics including its intensity, spectral characteristics, and variations of these with time. However, annoyance reactions are sensitive to many nonacoustic factors of a social, psychological, or economic nature and there are considerable differences in individual reactions to the same noise.

Attempts to define criterias linking noise exposure and annoyance have led to the development of many methods for the measurement of both variables. In social surveys, questionaires are used to assess the annoyance felt by an individual in response to various types of noise. Much research has been aimed at the definition of suitable questions through which annoyance reactions could be quantified.

In the search for a suitable noise index, numerous noise and some nonacoustic variables were assembled in various ways to discover which combinations were most closely correlated with annoyance reactions. The resulting diverse indices were given such names as composite noise rating (CNR), community noise equivalent level (CNEL), noise and number index (NNI), and noise pollution level (NPL) among many others. In fact, many experts consider that, in terms of annoyance prediction ability, there is little practical difference between the various indices and that an appropriate index should be selected for the convenience with which it can be measured or calculated. For this reason, variants of the equivalent continuous A-weighted sound pressure level (L_{gq}) are being widely adopted for general use. These are conveniently applied to noise exposure patterns of all kinds, from multiple sources if necessary, and are reasonably well correlated both with annoyance and with other specific effects of noise.

Whatever noise scale is used to express noise exposure, it must be recognized that, at any level of noise annoyance, reactions will vary greatly because of psychosocial differences. A useful technique for accommodating the possible extent of individual variation is the use of a criterion curve showing the percentage of persons who will be annoyed as a function of noise level.

Such curves have been derived for a variety of noise conditions but mainly for those concerned with aircraft or road traffic noise. On the basis of these, it can be concluded that, in residential areas where the general daytime noise exposure is below 55 dB(A) Leqs there will be few people seriously annoyed by noise. This is recomended as a desirable noise exposure limit for the general community, even though it will be difficult to achieve in many urban areas. Some residents may consider this level too high, especially as substantially lower levels currently prevail in many suburban and rural areas.

Criteria relating noise exposure and complaint potential have found widespread application for environmental control purposes in some countries. However, the scientific basis for such criteria is rather fragmentary and surveys have indicated that the correlation between noise exposure and individual complaint behaviour is low. This may be explained in terms of the strong influence of psychosocial factors.

1.1.3.6 Effects on performance

The effects of noise on the performance of tasks has mainly been studied in the laboratory and, to some extent, in work situations, but, there have been few, if any, detailed studies of the effects of noise on human productivity in real-life situations. It is evident that when a task involves auditory signals of any kind, noise at an intensity sufficient to mask or interfere with the perception of these signals will intefere with the performance of the task.

Noise can act as a distracting stimulus, depending on how meaningful the stimulus might be, and may also affect the psychophysiological state of the individual. A novel event, such as the start of an unfamiliar noise will cause distraction and interfere with many kinds of tasks. Impulsive noise (such as sonic booms may produce disruptive effects as the result of startle responses which are more resistant to habituation.

Noise can change the state of alertness of an individual and may increase or decrease efficiency.

Performance of tasks involving motor or monotonous activities is not always degraded by noise. At the other extreme, mental activities involving vigilance, information gathering, and analytical processes appear to be particularly sensitive to noise. It has been suggested that, in industry, the most likely indicator of the effects of noise on performance would be an increase in accidents attributable to reduced vigilance.

1.1.3.7 Miscellaneous effects

Certain noises, especially impulsive ones, may induce a startle reaction. This consists of contraction of the flexor muscles of the limbs and the spine, a contraction of the orbital which can be recorded as an eye blink, and a focusing of attention towards the location of the noise. The startle reflex to acoustic stimulation has been observed in the 27–28 week fetus in *utero* as a change in the pulse rate.

It has been suggested that observed noise-induced equilibrium effects are due to the noise stimulating the vestibular apparatus, the receptors of which are part of the inner ear structure.

Although there is no clear evidence of a direct relationship between noise and fatigue, noise can be considered as an environmental stress

Appendix H

which, in conjunction with other environmental and host factors, may induce a chronic fatigue that could lead to non-specific health disorders.

1.1.4 Summary of recommended noise exposure limits

The equivalent continuous A-weighted sound pressure level Leq is recommended for use as a common measure of noise exposure. The measurement period should be related to the problem under study, for example in the case of occupational noise, Lgq (8–h) would be measured for a complete 8–h shift.

For the working environment, there is no identifiable risk of hearing damage in noise levels of less than 75 dB(A) Leq (8–h). For higher levels, there is an increasing predictable risk and this must be taken into account when setting occupational noise standards.

In other occupational and domestic environments, acceptable noise levels can be established on the basis of speech communication criteria. For good speech intelligibility indoors, background noise levels of less than 45 dB(A) Leq are required.

At night, sleep disturbance is the main consideration and available data suggest a bedroom noise limit of 35 dB(A) Leq.

Data from surveys of community noise annoyance lead to the recommendation that general daytime outdoor noise levels of less than 55 dB(A) Leq are desirable to prevent any significant community annoyance. This is consistent with speech communication requirements. At night, a lower level is desirable to meet sleep criteria; depending upon local housing conditions and other factors this would be in the order of 45 dB(A) Leq.

WHO REGIONAL OFFICE FOR EUROPE

THE ENVIRONMENTAL HEALTH CRITERIA DOCUMENT ON COMMUNITY NOISE

Report on the Task Force Meeting

Dusseldorf, Federal Republic of Germany

24–28 November 1992

This activity was organized by the WHO Regional Office for Europe to promote work aimed at achieving the following target in the health for all strategy.

TARGET 24

HUMAN ECOLOGY AND SETTLEMENTS

By the year 2000 cities, towns and rural communities throughout the Region should offer physical and social environments supportive to the health of their inhabitants.

ABSTRACT

Community noise has always been a major environmental pollutant which affects health through many pathways: sleep disturbances, behavioural disturbances, and even in some specific cases, hearing impairments.

The WHO European Office has convened, together with WHO/HQ, a meeting to review a document drafted by the Nordic Noise Group and providing the following elements: effects of noise on humans, evaluation of risks and recommendations for noise levels.

Recommendations for guideline values are given in order to mitigate effects of noise on health and to create environments suitable for healthy living. There is no guideline for sources.

The new version of the draft will then be reviewed before June 1993 and be presented to the next International Commission on Biological Effects of Noise (ICBEN) Conference before publication.

Keywords

ENVIRONMENTAL HEALTH
NOISE—adverse effects
EUROPE

Introduction

A Task Force composed of 18 participants from nine countries covering three Regions of the World Health Organization, viz. AMRO, EURO and SEARO, and two international organizations, was held in D\)sseldorf, Federal Republic of Germany, to review the draft document on community noise prepared by the Nordic Noise Group. The meeting was convened in collaboration with the City of D\)sseldorf.

Professor C. Jansen served as Chairperson, Dr B Rohrmann as Vice-Chairperson, and Professors B Berglund and Th Lindvall as Rapporteurs.

The scope and purpose of the meeting was to make an in-depth review of the criteria document on community noise. The document would largely be a revision of the earlier WHO document 'Noise', but would be expanded and supplemented to include physiology of hearing and related mechanisms on mental and behavioural effects of noise. Noise control and guidelines for noise levels in different environments would also be included. It would not deal with occupational noise.

Dr Saatkamp welcomed the participants on behalf of the Lord Mayor of D\)sseldorf, and expressed how happy the City of D\)sseldorf; which belongs to the Healthy Cities network, was to welcome this meeting.

The agenda was then discussed, changed and adopted. It was decided that the participants would be divided into four subgroups to discuss the various chapters.

The terms of reference of the working groups were to revise the chapters, make the modifications when it was possible, include the comments received by mail prior to the meeting and report to the plenary the remaining tasks which were to be performed.

Appendix H

The decisions and recommendations of the subgroups were then discussed in plenary and the changes and comments were, or would be, incorporated by Professors Berglund and Lindvall in the document on noise.

Comments

Some of the main comments received by mail and expressed by the participants can be summarized as follows.

—The scientific basis for each recommendation should be more precise.

—The following sections of the document needed to be updated: hearing damage, speech intelligibility, performance.

—The physical expression of the guidelines should be more consistent.

—Chapters on (a) hearing impairment in children and (b) economic aspects should be developed and expanded.

—When possible, better balance with regard to sources (other than aircraft noise) should be achieved.

—Reference list (bibliography) should be cleaned and updated.

—The draft issued from the meeting should be reviewed again by external reviewers (including ICBEN).

—The document should only deal with community noise.

—An executive summary would be required.

Table of contents

After discussion, it was agreed that the new table of contents would read as follows:
1. Summary
2. Scope of the document
3. Types of noise, basic definitions
4. Anatomy and physiology
5. Effects of noise on humans
   (5.1–6,4)
6. Economic aspects
7. Acoustic measurement issues
8. Evaluation of health risks (including principles for assessing effects)
9. Recommendations
   —guidelines values
   —research needs

It was agreed to have a review of the new draft by external reviewers, by mail in early 1993. The participants provided the secretariat with a list of potential reviewers.

Conclusions and recommendations

The main recommendations of the meeting will be included in the revised document which will be sent for final reviewing and are included as an annex to this report.

Guidance relating to noise and smell

The final draft should be ready for the ICBEN congress and if any major modification is proposed during the congress, it should then be included in the WHO publication.

A very warm thank you and due acknowledgement to the heavy work already performed has been forwarded to Professors Lindvall and Berglund.

ANNEX I RECOMMENDATIONS

The acoustic world around us continuously stimulates the auditory system. The brain selects relevant signals from the acoustic input, but the ear and the lower auditory system are continuously receiving stimuli. This fact does not necessarily imply disturbing and harmful effects. The auditory nerve provides activating impulses to the brain, which enables us to regulate the vigilance and wakefulness necessary for optimum performance. On the other hand, there are scientific reports on harmful effects on humans due to sensory deprivation, which would be the case, if the world around us became completely silent. Thus, it is harmful to have too much sound but also harmful to have too little sound in our environment. Therefore, too, humans should have the right to decide for themselves the quality of the acoustic environment to live in.

By tradition, the exposure to noise from various sources is most commonly expressed as the average sound intensity over a specific time period, such as 24 hours. This implies that the same level of chosen time can either consist of a larger number of events with a relatively low, indeed almost nonaudible level, or a few events with a high level. This technical concept does not agree with common experience on how environmental noise is experienced, nor with the neurophysiological characteristics of the human receptor system.

Human perception of the environment through vision, hearing, touch, smell and taste is characterized by a good discrimination of stimulus intensity differences and a decaying sensitivity to a continuous stimulus. Single events can only be discriminated up to a certain threshold, whereafter the exposure is interpreted as continuous, These characteristics are linked to conditions for survival in terms of discrimination of new and different stimuli with low probability and high information value indicating warnings.

Thus, it is relevant to consider the importance of the background level, the number of events, and the noise exposure level independently when assessing the effects of environmental noise on man.

Community noise studies have traditionally considered only noise from a single specific source, such as aircraft, road traffic or railways. In recent years, efforts have been made to compare the results from road traffic, aircraft, and railway surveys. Data from a number of sources suggest that aircraft noise might be more annoying than mad traffic noise which, in turn, might be more annoying than railway noise. But, without a clearer understanding of the mechanisms that sometimes creates differences in reactions to different sources, the extent to which the findings from individual studies can be extrapolated to other acoustical environments and community settings is at present unclear.

Appendix H

There may be some populations at greater risk for the harmful effects of noise. Young children (especially during language acquisition), the blind, and perhaps fetuses are examples of such populations. There are no definite conclusions on this topic but the reader should be alerted that guidelines in this report are developed for the population at large and have not addressed the topic of potentially more vulnerable groups.

1. Specific Effects

1.1 Interference with communications

Noise tends to interfere with auditory communication in which speech is a most important signal. However, it is also vital to be able to hear alarming and informative signals such as door bells, telephone signals, alarm clocks, fire alarms, etc, as well as sounds and signals involved in occupational tasks. The vast number of experimental data on noise effects on speech discrimination deals with that in lexical terms. Speech interference level starts from below 50 dB SPL for octave bands centered to the main speech frequencies of 0.5, 1, and 2 kHz, when communication distance grows beyond a few meters.

It is usually possible to express the relationship between noise levels and speech intelligibility in a single diagram, based on the assumptions and empirical observations that, for speaker-to-listener distance of about 1m; (a) speech spoken in relaxed conversation is 100% intelligible in background noise levels of about 45 dBA, and can be understood fairly well in background levels of 55 dBA; and (b) speech spoken with slightly more vocal effort can be understood well, when the noise level is 65 dBA.

With respect to interference with speech perception, a majority of the population belong to sensitive groups. Most sensitive are the elderly and persons with impaired hearing. Even slight hearing impairments in the high-frequency range may cause problems with speech perception in a noisy environment. From 40 years of age and up, people demonstrate impaired ability to interpret difficult, spoken messages with low linguistic redundancy compared to those aged between 20–30 years. It has also been shown that children before language acquisition has been completed have demonstrated more adverse effects to high noise levels and long reverberation times than young adults.

For outdoor speech communication, the 'inverse square law' applies for speech level over moderate distances, that is, when the distance between speaker and listener is doubled, the level of the speech drops by approximately 6 dB. This relationship is applicable to indoor conditions only up to a distance of about 2m. Speech communication is affected also by the reverberation characteristics of the room. Already reverberation times beyond 1 s can produce loss in speech discrimination. Even in a quiet environment a reverberation time below 0.6 s is desirable for an adequate speech intelligibility for sensitive groups. A longer reverberation time combined with background noise makes speech perception still more difficult/straining.

In cases where the speech signal perception is of paramount importance, for example in classrooms or conference rooms, or where listeners with impaired hearing are involved, for example, in homes for the elderly, lower background levels of noise are desirable. To ensure satisfactory speech communication the signal-to-noise relationship should always exceed approximately zero dB (for details see Chapter 8: Acoustic Measurement Issues).

For sensitive groups or when listening to complicated messages (at school, listening to foreign languages, telephone conversation) the signal-to-noise ratio should be at least 10 dB. This means that in classrooms, one should strive for as low background level as possible. For sensitive groups this would mean that with a background level of 35 dBA, the message should be at least 45 dBA.

1.2 Noise-induced hearing loss

High-level noise exposure giving rise to noise-induced hearing deficits is by no means restricted to occupational situations. Such levels can also occur in open air concerts, discotheques, motor sports, shooting ranges, and dwellings in terms of noise from loudspeakers or oilier leisure activities. Other sources are also important such as music played back in headphones and impulse noise from toys and fireworks. It has also been argued that community noise exposure would be a contributing factor to hearing deficits with increasing age. The existence of such a 'socioacusis' waits for final scientific verification since so many other factors and agents are also influencing hearing.

Hearing disability may be assessed in terms of difficulty in understanding speech. The amount of loss at various speech frequencies has been used as a basis for monetary compensation and varies from one country to another. The unweighted average of the losses, in dB at 500, 1000 and 2000 Hz, that is widely used for assessing noise-induced hearing impairment, is somewhat misleading since noise-induced hearing deficits usually occur at 2000 Hz and above. Commonly, frequencies of 3000, 4000, and 6000 Hz are also included in damage assessment formulae.

There is some disagreement concerning the relationship between the relative ear-damaging capacity of the noise level and its duration. However, the hypothesis that the hearing damage associated with a particular noise exposure is related to the total energy of the sound (ie, the product of intensity and time) is used for practical purposes. Thus, from a hearing-deficit point of view, noise is primarily described in terms of equivalent continuous sound level, Leq, measured in dBA. For occupational noise, the level is usually averaged over the entire 8-h shift [leq (8-h)], and 40 h per week.

Available data show that there is considerable variation in human sensitivity with respect to hearing impairment. The hazardous nature of a noisy environment is therefore described in terms of 'damage risk'. This may be expressed as the percentage of people exposed to that environment who are expected to suffer noise-induced hearing impairment after appropriate allowance has been made for hearing losses due to other causes, mainly aging. It is generally believed that this risk is negligible at noise exposure levels of less than 75 dBAleq (8-h) but increases with increasing levels. The threshold value below which noise can damage hearing, may be even lower due to the exposure combined with intake of ototoxic drugs and chemicals.

Appendix H

It is not yet clear whether the damage risk rules can be extended to the very short durations of impulsive noise. Available evidence indicates that an increasing risk exists, when impulsive sound levels reach 130-150 dB peak. Available evidence also indicates that addition of impulsive noise on a steady noise increases the risk for damage. It is not yet clear to what extent impulse noises and low-frequency noises should be given extra consideration in damage risk calculations.

1.3 Sleep-disturbance effects

Sleep disturbance due to continuous, as well as intermittent noise, has been demonstrated by electrophysiological and behavioural methods. The more intense the background noise is, the more disturbing is its effect on sleep. Measurable effects start from about 30 dBAL q. Physiological sleep effects include changes the pattern of sleep stage, especially a reduction in the proportion of REM-sleep. Subjective effects have also been identified such as difficulties in failing asleep, subjective sleep quality, and adverse after-effects like headache and tiredness. The sensitive groups will mainly include elderly persons, shift workers, persons who are especially vulnerable due to physical or mental disorders, and other individuals who have sleeping difficulties.

Sleep disturbance increases with increased maximum noise level. Even if the total equivalent noise level is fairly low, a small number of noise events avoid sleep disturbance should be expressed in terms of equivalent noise level as well as maximum levels, and number of noise events. It should be noted that the low frequency noise, for example, from ventilation systems, can disturb rest and sleep even at low intensity.

Where noise is continuous, the equivalent noise level should not exceed 30 dBA indoors, if negative effects on sleep are to be avoided. In the presence of a large proportion of low frequency noise a still lower guideline value is recommended. It should be noted that the adverse effect of noise partly depends on the nature of the source.

If the noise is not continuous, the maximum level is best correlated to sleep disturbances. Effects have been observed at individual exposures of 45 dBA or even less. It is especially important to limit the noise events exceeding 45 dBa where the background level is low; to protect sensitive persons a still lower guideline value would be preferred.

Measures reducing disturbance during the first part of the night are believed to be most effective for the ability of falling asleep. In noise exposure control, one should consider at the same time the equivalent noise level, the levels of the noise peaks and the number of noise events.

1.4 Cardiovascular and psychophysiological effects

Effects on the systemic circulation such as constriction of blood vessels have been produced under laboratory and field conditions. Many studies have shown blood pressure to be higher in noise-exposed workers and in populations living in noisy areas around airports, and on noisy streets than in control populations, while other investigations indicate no blood pressure effects. The overall evidence suggests that a weak association exists between long-term noise exposure and blood pressure elevation or hypertension. Other psychophysiological effects, such as gastro-intestinal motility, are less clear. More research is required in order to

Guidance relating to noise and smell

estimate the long-term cardiovascular and psychophysiological risks due to noise. In view of the equivocal findings, no guideline values may be given.

1.5 Performance effects

The effect of noise on the performance of tasks has mainly been studied in the laboratory and to some extent in work situations, but, there have been few, if any, detailed studies of the effects of noise on human productivity in community situations. It is evident that when a task involves auditory signals of any kind, noise at an intensity sufficient to mask or interfere with the perception of these signals will interfere with the performance of the task. There are consistent after effects of noise in cognitive performance (eg, proofreading, persistence on challenging puzzles).

Noise can act as a distracting stimulus, depending on how meaningful the stimulus might be, and may also affect the psychophysiological state of the individual. A novel event, such *as* the start of an unfamiliar noise will cause distraction and interfere with many kinds of tasks. Impulsive noise (such as sonic booms) may produce disruptive effects as the result of startle responses which are more resistant to habituation.

Performance of tasks involving motor or monotonous activities is not always degraded by once Mental activities involving sustained attention to multiple cues, high load in working memory, and complex analytical processes are sensitive to noise. Some accidents may be an indicator of performance deficits as well.

Chronic exposure to noise during early childhood appears to damage reading acquisition. Evidence indicates that the longer the exposure, the greater the damage. There is no sufficient information on these effects to set specific acoustic guideline values. It is clear, however, that daycare centres and schools should not be located near major noise sources, such as highways, airports, and industrial sites.

1.6 Annoyance responses

Noise annoyance may be defined as a feeling of displeasure evoked by a noise. The annoyance-inducing capacity of a noise depends upon many of its physical characteristics including its intensity, spectral characteristics, and variations of these with time. However, annoyance reactions are sensitive to many non-acoustic factors of a social, psychological, or economic nature and then are considerable differences in individual reactions to the same noise.

Annoyance is affected by the equivalent noise level, the highest noise level of a noise event, the number of such events, and the time of the day. The method for combining these effects has been extensively studied. The data are not inconsistent with the simple, physically based equivalent energy theory, which is represented by the Leq index.

Community annoyance varies with activity (speech communication, relaxation to radio arid TV, etc.). The threshold of annoyance for steady continuous noise is around 50 dBAleq. Few people are seriously annoyed during the day time at noise levels below around 55 dBALeq. Noise levels during the evening and night should be 5 to 10 dB lower

Appendix H

than during the day. It is emphasized that for intermittent noise it is necessary to take into account the maximum level and the number of noise events. GuideLines or noise abatement measures also should take into account residential outdoor activities.

1.7 Effects on social behaviour

The effects of environmental noise may be evaluated by assessing interference with different activities. For many community noises, the most important interference seams to be interference with rest/recreation/watching television. There is fairly consistent evidence that noise above 80 dBA causes reduced helping behaviour. Loud noise also increases aggressive behaviour in individuals predisposed to aggressiveness.

There is concern that exposure to high levels of chronic noise could contribute to susceptibility to helplessness in school children. Guidelines on these issues must await further research.

2. Specific environments

A noise measure based only on energy summation expressed as the conventional equivalent measure, Leq, is not enough for the characterization of most noise environments. It is equally important to measure and display the maximum values of the noise fluctuations, preferably combined with a measure of the number of noise events. If the noise includes a large proportion of low frequency components, still lower values than the recommended guideline values below will be needed.

Where prominent low-frequency components are present, they should be assessed with appropriate octave or one/third octave instruments. However, the difference between dBlin (or dBC) and dBA will give crude information about the contributions of low frequency sounds. If the difference is more than 20 dB, it is recommended to perform a frequency analysis of the noise. It should be noted that a large proportion of low frequency components in the noise may increase considerably the adverse effect.

2.1 Dwellings

For dwellings the critical effects are sleep distrubance, annoyance and speech interference. Specifically, for bedrooms the critical effect is sleep disturbance. Recommended guideline values for bedrooms inside are 30 dBA Leq for steady-state continuous noise and 45 dBa Lmax. Lower levels may be annoying depending on the nature of the noise source. The maximum level should be measured with the instrument set at 'fast'. To protect the majority of people from being seriously annoyed during the daytime the noise level from steady, continuous noise on balconies, terraces, and in outdoor living areas should not exceede 55 dBA Leq.

To protect the majority of people from being moderately annoyed during the daytime, the noise level should not exceed 50 dBALeq. Where it is practical and feasible the lower noise level should be considered the maximum desirable noise level for decisions in relation to new development.

At nighttime outside noise levels should not exceed 45 dBA Leq, so that people may sleep with bedroom windows open. This value has been obtained by assuming that the noise reduction from outside to inside with the window open is 15 dB.

2.2 Schools and PreSchools

For schools, the critical effects are speech interference, disturbance of information extraction (eg, comprehension and reading acquisition), message communication, and annoyance. To be able to hear and understand spoken messages in classrooms, the noise level should not exceed 35 dBA Leq during teaching sessions. For hearing impaired children, a still lower level may be needed. The reverberation time in the classroom should be about 0.6 s, and preferably lower for hearing impaired children.

For assembly halls and cafeterias in school buildings, the reverberation time should be less than 1 s. For outdoor playgrounds the noise level from external sources should not exceed 55 dBA Leq.

For preschools, the same critical effects and guideline values apply as for schools. In bedrooms in preschools during sleeping hours, the guideline values for bedrooms in dwellings replace those of schools.

2.3 Hospitals

For most spaces in hospitals, the critical effects are sleep disturbance, annoyance, and communication interference, including warning signals. Since patients have less ability to cope with stress, the equivalent sound level should not exceed 35 dBA Leq, in most rooms in which patients are being treated, observed or resting. Attention should be given to the noise levels in intensive care units and operating theatres. Guideline values must await future research.

Momentary sounds during night time should not exceed the guideline value recommended for equivalent noise by more than 10 dBA with the instrument set at 'fast'. For ward rooms in hospitals, the recommended guideline values should be 30 dBA Leq together with 40 dBA Lmax. The maximum level should be measured with the instrument set at 'fast'.

2A Concert Halls, Outdoor concerts and discotheques

There is widespread concern about the effect of loud music on young people who frequently attend concerts and discotheques. The sound level is typically in excess of 100 dBA leq. This level could lead to significant hearing impairment, especially in later life.

Noise exposure for employees of these venues should be controlled by established occupational standards. Ideally the same standards should apply to the patrons of these premises as some people may be exposed to high noise levels from other sources during the day. However, the basis for recommending guideline values for patrons is still inconclusive. But the concern for protecting young people's hearing warrants provisional guidelines. It is therefore recommended that patrons should not be exposed to sound pressure levels greater than 100 dBA Leq during a 4-hr period.

2.5 Sounds played back in headphones

The same critical effects and guideline values apply for sounds played back in headphones as for exposure to music in concert halls, outdoor

Appendix H

concerts, and discotheques. The exposure should not be greater than when converted to equivalent free-field level.

2.6 Impulsive sounds from Toys and Fireworks

To avoid hearing deficits, performers and audience should not be exposed to more than 140 dB peak. The instrument should be set at 'impulse'.

2.7 Outdoors in Parkland and Conservation Areas

Existing large quiet outdoor areas should be preserved and the signal to noise ratio kept low.

ANNEX 2 TEMPORARY ADVISERS

AUSTRALIA

Mr JA Lambert, Department of Environment and Land Management, Noise Abatement Branch, *Adelaide*

CANADA

Dr Sharon M Abel, Hearing Research Laboratory, Mount Sinai Hospital, *Toronto*

FEDERAL REPUBLIC OF GERMANY

Professor Gerd Jansen, University of D\)sseldorf, Institute of Occupational and Social Medicine, *D\)sseldorf*

Professor Bernd Rohrmann, Facultät PPE, Universität Mannheim, *Mannheim*

FINLAND

Dr Tapani Jauhiainen, University of Helsinki, *Helsinki*

Ms Sirkka-Liisa Pakklcida, Ministry of the Environment, Chairman of the Secretariat, Nordic Noise Group of the Nordic Council of Ministers, *Helsinki*

FRANCE

Mr M Vallet, INRTS, *Bron*

POLAND

Professor Henry K Mi.kolajczyk, Head, Department of Physical Hazards, Institute of Occupational Medicine, *Lodz*

SWEDEN

Professor Birgitta Berglund, Department of Psychology, Stockholm University, *Stockholm*

Professor Dr Med Th Lindvall, National Institute of Environmental Medicine, Karolinska Institute, Department of Hygiene, *Stockholm*

UNITED KINGDOM

Dr Jan H Flindell, Institute of Sound and Vibration Research, The University of Southampton, *Southampton*

U.S.A.

Professor Gary W Evans, Department of Design and Environment Analysis, Cornell University, *New York*

Dr Laurence D Fechter, Associate Professor of Toxicological Sciences and Otolaryngology, School of Hygiene and Public Health, Department of Environmental Health Sciences, Johns Hopkins University, *Maryland*

Dr Shirley J Thompson, University of South Carolina, Department of Epidemiology and Biostatistics, *South Carolina*

REPRESENTATIVES OF OTHER ORGANIZATIONS

Commission of the European Communities

Dr H Muller, Directorate DGXI/B/3, Commission of European Communities, *Brussels*

HEALTHY CITIES DUSSELDORF

Dr Boschck. Health Department of D\)sseldorf, *D\)sseldorf*

Mr Jost Bové, Coordinator, Healthy Cities Project, *D\)sseldorf*

Mr Paul Saatkamp, Head, Department for Youth, Health and Social Welfare, *D\)sseldorf*

WORLD HEALTH ORGANIZATION

HEADQUARTERS

Mr Eric Giroult, Manager, Environmental Health in Rural and Urban Development and Housing

REGIONAL OFFICE FOR EUROPE

Mr Xavier Bonnefoy, Regional Adviser, Environmental Health Planning/Ecology

Mrs Annette Enevoldsen, Programme Assistant, Environmental Health Planning/Ecology

WHO GUIDELINES FOR COMMUNITY NOISE

Edited by Birgitta Berglund, Thomas Lindvall and Dietrich H Schwela

This WHO document on the Guidelines for Community Noise is the outcome of the WHO-expert task force meeting held in London, United Kingdom, in April 1999. It bases on the document entitled 'Community Noise' that was prepared for the World Health Organization and published in 1995 by the Stockholm University and Karolinska Institute.

[. . .]

4.4 WHO Guideline Values

The WHO guideline values in Table 4.1 are organized according to specific environments. When multiple adverse health effects are identified for a given environment, the guideline values are set at the level of the lowest adverse health effect (the critical health effect). An adverse health effect of noise refers to any temporary or long-term

Appendix H

deterioration in physical, psychological or social functioning that is associated with niose exposure. The guideline values represent the sound pressure levels that effect the most exposed receiver in the listed environment.

The time base for LAeq for 'daytime' and 'night-time' is 16h and 8h, respectively. No separate time base is given for evenings alone, but typically, guideline values should be 5–10dB lower than for a 12h daytime period. Other time bases are recommended for schools, preschools and playgrounds, depending on activity.

The available knowledge of the adverse effects of noise on health is sufficient to propose guideline values for community noise for the following:
   a. Annoyance.
   b. Speech intelligibility and communication interference.
   c. Disturbance of information extraction.
   d. Sleep disturbance.
   e. Hearing impairment.

The different critical health effects are relevant to specific environments, and guideline values for community noise are proposed for each environment. These are:
   a. Dwellings, including bedrooms and outdoor living areas.
   b. Schools and preschools, including rooms for sleeping and outdoor playgrounds.
   c. Hospitals, including ward and treatment rooms.
   d. Industrial, commercial shopping and traffic areas, including public addresses, indoors and outdoors.
   e. Ceremonies, festivals and entertainment events, indoors and outdoors.
   f. Music and other sounds through headphones.
   g. Impulse sounds from toys, fireworks and firearms.
   h. Outdoors in parkland and conservation areas.

It is not enough to characterize the noise environment in terms of noise measures or indices based only on energy summation (e.g. LAeq), because different critical health effects require different descriptions. Therefore, it is important to display the maximum values of the noise fluctuations, preferably combined with a measure of the number of noise events. A separate characterization of noise exposures during night-time would be required. For indoor environments, reverberation time is also an important factor. If the noise includes a large proportion of low frequency components, still lower guideline values should be applied.

Supplementary to the guideline values given in Table 4.1, precautionary recommendations are given in Section 4.2 and 4.3 for vulnerable groups, and for noise of a certain character (e.g. low frequency components, low background noise), respectively. In Section 3.10, information is given regarding which critical effects and specific environments are considered relevant for vulnerable groups, and what precautionary noise protection would be needed in comparison to the general population.

Table 4.1: Guideline values for community noise in specific environments

Specific environment	Critical health effect(s)	LAeq [dB]	Time base [hours]	LAmax, fast [dB]
Outdoor living area	Serious annoyance, daytime and evening	55	16	–
	Moderate annoyance, daytime and evening	50	16	–
Dwelling indoors	Speech intelligibility and moderate annoyance, daytime and evening	35	16	
Inside bedrooms	Sleep disturbance, night-time	30	8	45
Outside bedrooms	Sleep disturbance, window open (outdoor values)	45	8	60
School classrooms and preschools, indoors	Speech intelligibility, disturbance of information extraction, message communication	35	during class	–
Preschool bedrooms, indoors	Sleep disturbance	30	sleeping time	45
School, playground, outdoors	Annoyance (external source)	55	during play	–
Hospital, ward rooms, indoors	Sleep disturbance, night-time	30	8	40
	Sleep disturbance, daytime and evenings	30	16	–
Hospitals, treatment rooms, indoors	Interference with rest and recovery	#1		
Industrial, commercial shopping and traffic areas, indoors and outdoors	Hearing impairment	70	24	110
Ceremonies, festivals and entertainment events	Hearing impairment (patrons:<5 times/year)	100	4	110

Appendix H

Specific environment	Critical health effect(s)	LAeq [dB]	Time base [hours]	LAmax, fast [dB]
Public addresses, indoors and outdoors	Hearing impairment	85	1	110
Music through headphones/ earphones	Hearing impairment (free-field value)	85 #4	1	110
Impulse sounds from toys, fireworks and firearms	Hearing impairment (adults)	–	–	140 #2
	Hearing impairment (children)	–	–	120 #2
Outdoors in parkland and conservation areas	Disruption of tranquility	#3		

#1: as low as possible;
#2: peak sound pressure (not LAmax, fast), measured 100mm from the ear;
#3: existing quiet outdoor areas should be preserved and the ratio of intruding noise to natural background sound should be kept low;
#4: under headphones, adapted to free-field values.

NOISE – DEFRA GUIDANCE ON SECTIONS 69 TO 81 AND SECTION 86 OF THE CLEAN NEIGHBOURHOODS AND ENVIRONMENT ACT 2005

Overview

This document provides guidance on the provisions in the Clean Neighbourhoods and Environment Act 2005 that apply to audible intruder alarms and abatement notices issued under Section 79 (1) (g) (Noise) of the Environmental Protection Act 1990.

Audible Intruder Alarms

General Principles

1 Sections 69 to 81 introduce new powers for local authorities to deal with audible intruder alarms (which do not include fire alarms) in their areas and the annoyance they may cause. A local authority may designate its area (or part(s) of it) as an 'alarm notification area'. The occupier or (if none) the owner (the 'responsible person') in respect of any premises (residential or non-residential, actually occupied or vacant) that are fitted with an audible intruder alarm in the designated area must nominate a key-holder for those premises and notify the local authority of the contact details of that key-holder.

The authority can then turn in the first instance to that key-holder for assistance in silencing an alarm where necessary1. It is a summary offence to fail to nominate, or to fail to notify the local authority of the

Guidance relating to noise and smell

details of, a key-holder or a replacement key-holder within the specified time.

2 The provisions set out the steps that must be followed by a local authority wishing to designate an area as an alarm notification area. In particular, an authority must advertise its intention to designate, consider representations on the proposal, and send notice of any decision to designate to all premises in the affected area. A local authority has the power to withdraw a designation if it wishes, again subject to a requirement to publicise any decision to do so and to send a notice of such a decision to all premises in the affected area.

3 This part of the Act also provides local authorities with powers to enter premises in order to silence alarms where keyholders cannot be reached, or where the alarm is not in an alarm notification area. Local authorities do not need to designate an alarm notification area before using these powers of entry.

A local authority can, for example, continue to use a voluntary database of key-holder details if it wishes, without the sanctions that those who fail to register key-holders face under the 2005 Act. These new provisions do not affect the use of powers under the Environmental Protection Act 1990 and the Noise Act 1996 where relevant, although the former applies to alarms causing a nuisance, and the latter to alarms exceeding a permitted level further to receipt of complaints. These powers of entry apply to audible intruder alarms sounding for 20 minutes continuously or 1 hour intermittently, and likely to cause annoyance to those in the vicinity.

1 Section 23 of the London Local Authority Act 1991 and the unimplemented section 9 of, and Schedule 3 to, the Noise and Statutory Nuisance Act 1993 (both repealed by Schedule 5 of the Clean Neighbourhoods and Environment Act 2005) required key-holder details to be registered with the police, who do not have the authority to enter premises to deactivate an alarm.

Detailed Guidance

Section 69 – Designation of alarm notification areas

4 Section 69 empowers a local authority to designate all or any part(s) of its area as an 'alarm notification area'. If a local authority proposes to designate such an area, it must arrange for notice of the proposal to be published in a newspaper circulating in the area stating that representations may be made to the authority by a specified date at least 28 days hence. The local authority must consider any representations about the proposal which it receives before the specified date.

5 If a local authority then decides to go ahead and designate an area as an alarm notification area, it must arrange for notice of the decision to be published in a newspaper circulating in the same area, and send a copy of the notice to the address of all premises in the area. The notice must state the date on which the designation takes effect, and this date must be at least 28 days hence. If a local authority decides not to designate an area as an alarm notification area after all, it must arrange for notice of that decision to be published in a newspaper circulating in the area.

6 The requirement to notify all premises in an area of a designation is intended to ensure that people whose premises in that area are fitted with an audible intruder alarm are aware of their obligations to nominate

Appendix H

a key-holder and notify the council of his details, and that it is a criminal offence not to comply. It is *not*, however, necessary for a local authority to arrange to notify newcomers (people or businesses) who move into the designated area after the initial notification. Local authorities might choose to consider taking steps to ensure that newcomers to a designated area are aware of the requirement to notify the local authority of nominated key holders, which could include notifying landlords and estate agents, but it is not a requirement of the Act and it might well be overly burdensome.

7 For the initial notification it is not essential to use a dedicated mail-shot. Many councils have mechanisms for undertaking area-based communications, such as the distribution of newsletters, council tax bills, and magazines, and it is sufficient to include the notification in an existing mailing exercise. A notification sent out with these mail-shots should take the form of a separate insert. Forward planning should allow designation of alarm notification areas to be undertaken at minimal additional cost.

8 The requirement in section 69 is for the local authority to send details of the proposed designation to all addresses in the relevant area. The Department's legal advice is that (unless a local authority had failed on a large scale to observe the notification requirements) it would probably not be accepted as a defence for a person accused of failing to notify the local authority of an intruder alarm to argue in court that he had not received notification of the designation at his premises.

Section 70 – Withdrawal of designation

9 Section 70 allows a local authority which has designated an area as an alarm notification area to withdraw the designation, but it must do so in its entirety – it cannot modify a designation this way.

In terms of publicising its decision, the local authority need only arrange for notice of the decision to be published in a newspaper circulating in the area, and to send a copy of the notice to the address of all premises in the area, stating the date on which withdrawal of designation takes effect.

Sections 71 and 72 – Notification and nomination of key-holders

10 Sections 71 and 72 require the 'responsible person' (defined in section 81(1) as the occupier, or if there is no occupier, the owner of the premises) to nominate a key-holder and to notify the local authority in writing, within the required period, of the name, address and telephone number of the key-holder. If the alarm was installed before designation took effect, the required period for notification is 28 days from the date on which designation came into force. If the alarm was installed on or after the commencement of designation, the required time period is within 28 days of the date on which its installation was completed. It is an offence to fail to nominate a key-holder or to fail to notify the local authority of the relevant details within the time limit. The maximum penalty on conviction is a fine not exceeding level 3 on the standard scale (currently £1,000).

Section 72 sets out the requirements that must be met by key-holders

11 A person may only be nominated as a key-holder if he holds keys to gain access to the part of the premises in which the controls for the alarm are situated; is normally resident or situated in the vicinity of the

premises; knows how to silence the alarm; and agrees to be a nominated key-holder. Premises with a twenty-minute cut-out included on their alarm are not excluded from the requirement to register key-holders in an alarm notification area.

12 For residential premises, a key-holder must be either an individual who is not the occupier of the premises, or a key-holding company (i.e. which holds keys and can be contacted at any time of day). For non-residential premises, a key-holder can be the responsible person (i.e. can include the occupier or (if none) the owner of the premises), someone acting on behalf of the responsible person if the responsible person is not an individual, or a keyholding company.

13 The arrangements within key-holding companies are likely to vary considerably, and there may be occasions when, for example, a company responsible for a central telephone number is not the same as the company actually holding the keys. Local authorities are not expected to make enquiries about the precise status of key-holding companies (or individuals), provided that they are satisfied that the contact number they have will enable someone holding the keys to be contacted rapidly if the need arises.

14 If the responsible person becomes aware that a key-holder no longer satisfies one or more of the requirements, the responsible person must nominate another person as a key-holder within 28 days of becoming aware of the fact, and it is again an offence if he fails to do so. Local authorities should be able to demonstrate culpability in such cases if they wish to take proceedings to prosecute or issue a fixed penalty notice. Where it is in dispute that the responsible person has known for 28 days that the registered key-holder no longer satisfies the requirements under the 2005 Act, a written warning to the responsible person at least 28 days before taking such action should be sufficient to demonstrate culpability if the key-holder then fails to nominate a new key-holder in the meantime.

Transferring police data to local authorities

15 Some local authorities in London took the opportunity to adopt the section 23 provisions on audible intruder alarms (now to be repealed by the 2005 Act) contained in the London Local Authorities Act 1991, which required key-holder details to be registered with the police.

16 The Clean Neighbourhoods and Environment Act 2005 does not require the police to transfer any such data held. Local authorities and the police should seek their own legal advice on data protection issues, but as a general rule data should be transferred only with the consent of the key-holder. This would also provide an ideal opportunity to ensure that data that are held are up to date and accurate, a requirement under Schedule 1 of the Data Protection Act 1998. It should be noted that the information Commissioner does not regard non-response as consent.

17 The Association of Chief Police Officers' Police Response to Security Systems (www.acpo.police.uk/asp/policies/Data/police_response_to_ security_systems_policy_april05.doc) requires those with Type A intruder alarms (that upon activation alert the police) to register at least two key holders with the Alarm Receiving Centre/Remote Video

Appendix H

Response Centre. Those with Type A intruder alarms will still have to nominate and register a key holder with the local authority within the required period should they live in an alarm notification area. Should the police be unsuccessful in contacting a key holder to deactivate a misfiring intruder alarm, they can contact the local authority (should they not already have been contacted) to inform them of the situation. The local authority will be able to use the powers under the Clean Neighbourhoods and Environment Act 2005 to enter the premises without force, or with force if necessary and once a warrant has been obtained, to deactivate the alarm.

Data protection issues

18 Local authorities will need to make arrangements to maintain databases of nominated key-holders. These databases will need to be maintained in accordance with the Data Protection Act 1998. This Act allows local authorities to keep information for as long as is relevant for the purposes of the database or register. When the information changes, such as when a key-holder steps down, that information will no longer be relevant and should not be kept. The key issue is that the data must not be disseminated to third parties without the consent of the key-holder and the responsible person, apart from in exceptional circumstances – legal advice should be sought before this is considered.

19 The liability for notifying the local authority of key-holder details, including amendments, falls to the 'responsible person', i.e. the occupier, or, where there is no occupier, the owner of premises on which an audible intruder alarm is installed. Local authorities may wish to make it as easy as possible for the responsible person to keep key-holder details up to date by, for example, providing an internet-based system on which to register key-holder details.

Sections 73 to 76 – fixed penalty notices

Note: This section covers the basic principles of fixed penalty notices for offences relating to intruder alarms under section 71. However, detailed information on their use is provided in the separate guidance available on fixed penalty notices; authorised officers and persons accredited under Community Safety Accreditation Schemes are strongly advised to consult this guidance when using the fixed penalty notice provisions.

Sections 77 to 79 – powers of entry

20 These sections provide local authorities with additional powers to deal with sounding intruder alarms causing likely annoyance to those in the vicinity. These powers are not linked to designated areas, and can be used by a local authority to silence a problem alarm anywhere in its area.

21 Section 77 gives to an authorized officer of a local authority a power to enter premises without force in order to silence an audible intruder alarm where the following conditions are met: that the alarm has been sounding continuously for more than twenty minutes or intermittently for more than one hour (it is sufficient to rely on witnesses for this purpose); that it is likely to give persons living or working in the vicinity reasonable cause for annoyance; and where, in a designated area, the authority has first taken reasonable steps to get the nominated key-holder to silence the alarm. The officer must show evidence of his authority to effect entry

Guidance relating to noise and smell

if required.

22 Once on the premises, an authorized officer can take whatever steps are necessary to silence the alarm. This might include, for example, disabling the externally mounted alarm, but would not include picking a lock to enter.

23 Section 78 empowers a justice of the peace to issue a warrant authorising the use of force to enter premises to which an authorised officer has a right of entry under section 77. Before issuing a warrant a justice of the peace must be satisfied that the conditions in section 77 above have been met, and that the local authority cannot gain entry without the use of force. Before applying for a warrant, the authorised officer must leave a notice (of the local authority's own design) at the premises stating that he is satisfied that the alarm is likely to give reasonable cause of annoyance to those living or working in the vicinity, and that an application will be made for a warrant to authorise entry to the premises using reasonable force if necessary in order to silence the alarm. The officer must show evidence of the warrant if required. There is no minimum time period between leaving a notice and applying for a warrant.

24 Under section 79 an officer may take any steps he thinks necessary for the purpose of silencing the alarm, and take with him such other persons and equipment as he thinks necessary for the purpose of silencing the alarm. The officer and any accompanying persons must not cause more damage or disturbance than is necessary in order to silence the alarm.

25 If the premises are unoccupied or (where the premises are occupied) the occupier of the premises is temporarily absent, the officer must leave a notice (of the local authority's own design) at the premises stating what action has been taken on the premises under this section and section 77 or 78, and leave the premises (so far as is reasonably practicable) as effectively secured against entry as he found them. The officer is expressly not required to re-set the alarm.

26 Any expenses reasonably incurred by the local authority in connection with entering the premises, silencing the alarm, leaving a notice and securing the premises may be recovered by the authority from the responsible person. Such expenses include the cost of steps taken to silence the alarm before the premises are entered, such as the cost of calling out an engineer. An example of this would be where the alarm is deactivated by the responsible person after steps have been taken to prepare entry to the premises, but before the local authority has entered the premises. Administrative and court costs may also be reclaimed.

27 A warrant under section 78 stays in force until the alarm has been silenced, and for as long as is necessary thereafter to leave a notice at the premises and, where practicable, to secure the premises.

28 The local authority, its authorized officers, and accompanying persons are not to be subject to any action, liability, claim or demand in respect of anything done under section 77, 78 or 79 provided it was done in good faith.

Appendix H

Section 81 – Interpretation

29 Section 81 defines the terms used in this part of the Act as follows:
- 'alarm notification area' means an area in respect of which a designation under section 69 has effect;
- 'local authority' means, in England, a district council; a county council for an area for which there is no district council; a London borough council; the Common Council of the City of London, and the Council of the Isles of Scilly; and in Wales, a county or county borough council;
- 'the occupier' in respect of premises means a person occupying the premises, or, if the premises are unoccupied, a person entitled to occupy the premises (other than the owner). The fact that a person is occupying premises is to be disregarded for the purposes of this definition if the premises comprise a building that is being erected, constructed, altered, improved, maintained, cleaned or repaired; the person is occupying the premises in connection with that erection, construction, etc., and the person is doing so by virtue of a written licence to occupy granted for less than four weeks. In such situations another occupier (if any) or (if none) the owner is the responsible person.
- 'premises' does not include a vehicle;
- 'the responsible person' in respect of premises means the occupier, or if there is no occupier, the owner.

Repeals

30 Section 23 of the London Local Authorities Act 1991 on audible intruder alarms – which could be adopted by London local authorities – is repealed.

Other Relevant Legislation/documents

31 Other relevant legislation/documents
- *S 79(1)(g) of the Environmental Protection Act 1990* – places a duty on local authorities to take reasonably practicable steps to investigate 'noise emitted from premises so as to be prejudicial to health or a nuisance'. Section 80(1) requires a local authority to issue an abatement notice if satisfied that e.g. an audible intruder alarm is causing, or may cause, a statutory nuisance. Where an abatement notice is not complied with, local authorities may enter the premises to abate the nuisance (e.g. by silencing an alarm). Section 80(2A) enables a local authority to take such other steps (e.g under the Clean Neighbourhoods and Environment Act 2005) as it thinks appropriate to persuade the appropriate person to abate the nuisance within a seven day period without serving an abatement notice. An abatement notice should be served after the seven day period if the local authority thinks that a statutory nuisance still exists, or is likely to occur or recur.
- *Guidance on section 86 of the Clean Neighbourhoods and Environment Act 2005: Deferral of duty to serve an abatement notice.*
- *Code of Practice on Audible Intruder Alarms* (1982) (statutory code of practice)

Guidance relating to noise and smell

- *Noise Act 1996* – the night noise offence of emitting excessive noise from a dwelling (extended to licensed premises by section 84 of, and Schedule 1 to, the Clean Neighbourhoods and Environment Act 2005) between the hours of 11pm and 7am may arise as much by virtue of an intruder alarm as by virtue of other sources of noise, such as that from hi-fis. Following the service of a Warning Notice, the person responsible may be liable to a fixed penalty or summary prosecution. Elements of the alarm, in particular its sounder, may be removed (i.e. seized) by a local authority officer acting under a warrant if necessary.

Deferral of duty to serve abatement notice

32 Section 86 of the Clean Neighbourhoods and Environment Act amends section 80 of the Environmental Protection Act 1990 by addition of a new subsection (2A) so as to enable a local authority to defer the issue of an abatement notice in the case of a statutory nuisance under section 79(1)(g) of the 1990 Act (i.e. that caused by noise emitted from premises). The deferral can be for up to seven days while the local authority takes appropriate steps to persuade the person on whom it would otherwise be serving the notice to abate the nuisance or prohibit or restrict its occurrence or recurrence.

33 This new provision only applies *after* a local authority has completed its investigation of a complaint and has concluded that it is satisfied that a statutory nuisance exists. It does not affect practices and procedures for investigating complaints at an earlier stage, including cases where there are a number of factors to consider before being satisfied that a statutory nuisance exists or is likely to occur or recur.

34 There is no obligation on the authority to pursue this alternative route – it may still proceed by issuing an abatement notice straightaway if it so chooses. Whenever a local authority decides to use the power to defer service of an abatement notice it should record the reasons for doing so.

35 If the authority does defer and the nuisance is not abated by the end of the seven-day period (or if the authority concludes before then that it will not be abated within that period), the authority must in most circumstances proceed to serve an abatement notice under section 80(1) in any event.

Why are these changes being introduced?

36 Currently, local authorities are required to issue an abatement notice once they are satisfied (see 10.33 above) that a statutory nuisance exists or may occur or recur. There is no provision for the exercise of discretion as to whether or not to take this action, even if the local authority suspects that 'best practicable means' may be in place (only the courts can rule on whether 'best practicable means' are in place).

In some circumstances an informal approach will engender greater co-operation and a faster resolution of a noise nuisance. Sometimes it can be counterproductive and/or unnecessary to issue an abatement notice – for example, the notice may provoke one party to withdraw from negotiations, actually aggravate a situation, or enable the person responsible to avoid having to abate the problem by, for example, holding a one-off noisy party). The option to defer serving an abatement notice

Appendix H

for up to seven days in order to pursue specific steps may support resolution without recourse to a formal abatement notice. It may also be more effective to use other means of enforcement, such as the Noise Act 1996 in cases of night noise from dwellings.

Issuing a Warning Notice under the Noise Act 1996 can often be a more effective means for dealing with one-off occurrences of night noise.

How will the changes work?

37 In cases where the local authority wishes to use the seven day deferral power, it will usually be appropriate to advise the person responsible for the nuisance in writing that a noise nuisance exists or is likely to occur or recur, and of the decision to defer service of an abatement notice provided the nuisance is dealt with within seven days. The local authority may also inform the noisemaker that if the nuisance continues after seven days of the notification of deferral, an abatement notice will be served. Outlining the consequences of an abatement notice in this initial letter advising of the decision to defer is recommended.

38 If during the course of the seven days the nuisance is abated or adequately restricted, the local authority should write to the person responsible and advise that the nuisance has been satisfactorily dealt with and that no further action will be taken under the Environmental Protection Act 1990 in regard to the specific nuisance referred to in the first letter, provided no recurrence occurs.

39 If the local authority is satisfied that a statutory nuisance continues to exist, or is likely to occur or recur, after the seven day deferral period, an abatement notice must be served requiring the abatement of the nuisance or prohibiting or restricting its occurrence or recurrence.

STATUTORY NUISANCE FROM INSECTS AND ARTIFICIAL LIGHT – DEFRA GUIDANCE ON SECTIONS 101 TO 103 OF THE CLEAN NEIGHBOURHOODS AND ENVIRONMENT ACT 2005

Overview

1 This guidance covers sections 101, 102 and 103 of the Clean Neighbourhoods and Environment Act 2005, which amend sections 79, 80 and 82 of the Environmental Protection Act 1990 to extend the statutory nuisance regime to include two new statutory nuisances:
- statutory nuisance from insects; and
- statutory nuisance from artificial light.

2 This guidance is aimed at local authorities, particularly Environmental Health Practitioners who enforce nuisance legislation. It may also be useful to other agencies.

Central Principles

3 These changes extend the duty on local authorities to check their areas periodically for existing and potential statutory nuisances so as now to include such nuisances arising from insects and from artificial lighting. Local authorities must take reasonable steps to investigate

Guidance relating to noise and smell

complaints of such nuisances. Once satisfied that a statutory nuisance exists or may occur or recur, local authorities must issue an abatement notice (in accordance with section 80(1) and (2) of the 1990 Act) against, in the first instance, the person responsible for the nuisance or, where that person cannot be found or the nuisance has not yet occurred, the owner or occupier of the premises from which it emanates, requiring that the nuisance cease or be abated within a set timescale. (Where a nuisance arises from any defect of a structural character, the abatement notice must be served on the owner of the premises.)

4 It also becomes possible for persons aggrieved by these new statutory nuisances to take private proceedings in respect of them in the magistrates' court by way of section 82 of the 1990 Act.

5 The appeals procedure is as for the other statutory nuisances. An appeal against an abatement notice can be made to the Magistrates' Courts. As grounds for appeal, the claim of 'best practicable means' can be used against an abatement notice, or subsequently as a defence against liability for conviction for breaching or failing to comply with an abatement notice, for nuisances on industrial, trade or business premises. In the case of artificial light nuisance, this defence of 'best practicable means' also applies to all such lighting used for the outdoor illumination of 'relevant' sports (please see the proposed list under the healthy living and sports section). (In the case of smoke nuisance, it applies to any premises, but only where the smoke is emitted from a chimney.)

6 The defence of 'reasonable excuse' for breaching or failing to comply with an abatement notice remains available to all.

7 A statutory nuisance may also be capable of being a nuisance at common law (and, where reliance is on the 'nuisance' limb, *must* also be a nuisance at common law), in which case an operator may be the subject of proceedings in tort by persons aggrieved by a common law nuisance even if the operator can rely on the defence of 'best practicable means' against action for statutory nuisance.

Section 101

8 Section 101 adds to the descriptions of statutory nuisances listed in section 79(1) of the Environmental Protection Act 1990:

'(fa) any insects emanating from relevant industrial, trade or business premises and being prejudicial to health or a nuisance'.

9 This provision does not apply to insects from domestic premises or to insects listed in Schedule 5 to the Wildlife and Countryside Act 1981, unless they are included in that Schedule solely to prevent their trade or sale.

10 This measure is intended to provide local authorities with a remedy to nuisances from insect infestations (whether naturally occurring or caused by human activities) on 'relevant' industrial, trade or business premises. However, it is not meant to be used against most naturally occurring concentrations of insects on open land or in ways that would adversely affect biodiversity. Accordingly, subsection (5) inserts two new subsections (7C) and (7D) into section 79 of the Environmental Protection Act 1990 which exclude from the definition of 'relevant' industrial, trade and business premises:

Appendix H

(a) land used as arable, grazing, meadow or pasture land (but not structures placed on the land),
(b) land used as osier land, reed beds, or woodland,
(c) land used for market gardens, nursery grounds or orchards,
(d) land forming part of an agricultural unit (but not covered by (a) to (c)) and which is of a description specified in regulations,
(e) land included in a Site of Special Scientific Interest,

and land covered by, and the waters of, rivers, watercourses (except sewers and drains), lakes and ponds.

11 Land which falls under (d) above is described by regulations. These regulations prescribe the descriptions of land under s.79(7C)(d) of the Environmental Protection Act 1990 (introduced by s.101(5) of the Clean Neighbourhoods and Environment Act 2005), that form part of an agricultural unit and which are (in addition to the types of land already listed at s.79(7C) (a)-(c)) to be exempt from 'relevant industrial etc. premises' from which the new statutory nuisance from insects (s.79(1)(fa) Environmental Protection Act 1990) is capable of emanating.

Certain types of land are exempted from being capable of statutory nuisance from insects in order to safeguard endangered species, and protect biodiversity.

Section 102

12 Section 102 adds to the descriptions of statutory nuisances listed in section 79(1) of the 1990 Act

'(fb) artificial light emitted from premises so as to be prejudicial to health or a nuisance'.

13 However, this does not include artificial light emitted from the following premises. These are premises used for transport purposes and other premises where high levels of light are required for safety and security reasons, i.e.:
- Airports
- Harbours
- Railway premises
- Tramway premises
- Bus stations and associated facilities
- Public service vehicle operating centres
- Goods vehicle operating centres
- Lighthouses
- Prisons
- Premises occupied for Defence purposes

14 These premises are listed in a new subsection (5B) to section 79 of the Environmental Protection Act 1990 and are defined in subsection (7) and in new subsections (7A) and (7B) of that Act (inserted by subsections 102(4) to (6) of the Clean Neighbourhoods and Environment Act 2005). The exemption for Defence premises is made by section 102(3) of the 2005 Act, amending section 79(2) of the 1990 Act.

Section 103

15 Section 103 extends the defence of 'best practicable means' to these new statutory nuisances where either is emitted from industrial, trade or

Guidance relating to noise and smell

business premises or, in the case of light, also from relevant outdoor sports facilities which are not industrial etc. premises. Most artificially illuminated sports facilities will be regarded as businesses, and so will benefit thereby from the 'best practicable means' defence. However, there may be some that are not; perhaps local authority grounds or facilities run by amateur clubs.

16 The Statutory Nuisances (Artificial Lighting) (Designation of Relevant Sports) (England) Order 2006 designates the 'relevant sports' the facilities for which will be able to use the defence of 'best practicable means' in appealing against, or as a defence against prosecution for breaching or failing to comply with, an abatement notice for statutory nuisance from artificial light under s.79(1)(fb) Environmental Protection Act 1990.

Guidance on using the new powers
General
Assessing complaints of nuisance

17 Statutory nuisance from insects and statutory nuisance from artificial light from premises follow the same regime as for other statutory nuisances. That is, it is initially for an Environmental Health Practitioner to assess on the evidence available whether or not a statutory nuisance exists, or may occur or recur, on a case-by-case basis. Not least because it will depend on their effects, there are no objective and set levels of insect infestation or artificial light above which a statutory nuisance is or may be caused, and below which it is not.

18 'Nuisance' is not defined in statute, but is rather based on the common law concept of what is to be regarded as an unreasonable interference with someone's use of their own property; alternatively, a statutory nuisance may be something that is 'prejudicial to health' of other people; ultimately, it will be for the courts to decide whether a statutory nuisance exists, should an appeal be made against an abatement notice within the 21 day period from its being issued, or should an individual take a private action through the local magistrates' court under section 82 of the Environmental Protection Act 1990 (or, possibly, as a defence to prosecution for failure to observe an abatement notice). As for all statutory nuisances, when assessing a case of potential statutory nuisance the Environmental Health Practitioner should take account of a range of factors including:
- Duration
- Frequency
- Impact – i.e. material interference with use of property or personal well-being; actually or likely to be adverse to health
- Local environment
- Motive – i.e. unreasonable behaviour or normal user
- Sensitivity of the plaintiff – statutory nuisance relies on the concept of the average person, and is not designed to take account of unusual sensibilities

19 For statutory artificial light nuisance, technical parameters on obtrusive lighting, formulated by the International Commission on

Appendix H

Illumination (CIE) and Institution of Lighting Engineers from research into individual sensitivity to light, may help inform consideration of the level of sensitivity that might be considered that of the 'average person'.

20 Enforcement should be reasonable and proportionate. If, however, the Environmental Health Practitioner is satisfied that a statutory nuisance exists, or may occur or recur, an abatement order must be issued requiring that the nuisance cease or be abated within a set timescale.

Statutory Nuisance and Planning

21 Prevention is better than cure, and it is preferable to address potential statutory nuisances at the planning stage.

22 The Courts have ruled that lighting itself is not 'development'. However, planning permission is required for lighting if it alters the material appearance of a building. It has been possible since 1997 for local authorities to consider lighting as part of the planning process for new buildings, both residential and commercial. Local authorities can decide to regulate lighting under planning permission, and set planning obligations for lighting to prevent light pollution. In these circumstances, new lighting must adhere to the original planning permission of the building. These conditions cannot be applied retrospectively and can only be applied to buildings built after 1997.

23 However, the existence of planning permission does not mean that a statutory nuisance cannot then exist. Circumstances and local environments change. Statutory nuisance can occur whether or not planning permission is in place either expressly or implicitly permitting lighting.

Recording complaints

24 Complaints should be logged and recorded, as for any other complaint of statutory nuisance. It is highly likely that in future the Chartered Institute of Environmental Health and / or Defra will contact local authorities to request statistics so that the scale and nature of insect nuisance and light nuisance can be assessed and monitored in order to provide an evidence base for future policy development.

25 Logging and recording information, including geo-coding, may also assist local authorities to map and monitor statutory nuisances to inform their approach to meeting their duties.

Insects

Likely sources of insect nuisance

26 It is expected that the following sources will generate most complaints of insect nuisance:
- Poultry houses / farms (buildings on agricultural land are not exempt from statutory nuisance from insects, even though the land surrounding them may be)
- Sewage treatment works
- Manure / silage storage areas
- Animal housing
- Stagnant ditches and drains (i.e. containing putrid and anoxic water) (provided they are on relevant industrial etc. premises)
- Landfill sites / refuse tips

Guidance relating to noise and smell

- Waste transfer premises
- The commercial parts of mixed commercial / residential blocks of buildings (i.e. excluding the residential premises contained therein)
- Trade or business premises (e.g. contaminated goods, kitchen areas)
- Slaughterhouses
- Used car tyre recycling businesses

27 Local authorities have a duty, however, to take reasonable steps, where practicable, to investigate any complaints of insect nuisance.

28 It is probable that complaints will be received about insects from domestic premises. As indicated above, insects emanating from domestic premises are not covered by this extension of the statutory nuisance regime. Any problems caused by insects from domestic premises may, however, be capable of being dealt with under section 79(1)(a) of the Environmental Protection Act 1990 – 'any premises in such a state as to be prejudicial to health or a nuisance'.

29 This limb might be appropriate if, for example, the state of a domestic dwelling was such that it encouraged an infestation of insects that constituted a nuisance to neighbouring dwellings.

Assessing complaints of insect nuisance

30 Ascertaining the source of insect nuisance can sometimes be a difficult and lengthy process, as premises which have high levels of insect infestation may be mistaken for the source when they might themselves also be sufferers. There may be a temptation for some people to ascribe insect nuisance to businesses by virtue of them being likely sources. A participatory approach to determining the source is likely to help satisfactory outcomes.

31 Proper management and treatment programmes should be able to minimise most insect nuisance cases that arise. Noticing infestations in their early stages is important, to try and keep on top of the insect nuisance.

Insect Nuisance

32 The vast majority of insect species do not cause a nuisance, but are essential components of biodiversity and maintain ecosystems through pollination, soil maintenance and other functions.

33 There are also a number of insect species which can cause nuisance in sufficient quantities, or seasonally. Some may also pose a public health risk, although they may not be regarded as a public health pest in terms of environmental legislation, or a risk in animal husbandry. Such insects include mosquitoes (Culicidae), house flies (*Musca domestica* Linnaeus), lesser house flies (*Fannia canicularis* (Linnaeus)), etc.

34 There is a difference between insects arising from an activity on a business, trade or industrial premises, and natural occurrence of insect populations. It is *not* the intention for this measure to cause environmental damage to the ecosystem or biodiversity.

35 It should *not* be assumed that killing insects is necessarily the most appropriate way to cease or abate a nuisance. One of the intentions

Appendix H

behind the measure to introduce insect statutory nuisance is to capture statutory insect nuisance caused as a result of activity on premises, where control through the existing limb of 'any premises in such a state as to be prejudicial to health or a nuisance' would not be appropriate. Another intention is to control statutory insect nuisance at source, where such control will not cause unacceptable damage to the environment or biodiversity. If activity and conditions attract or provide breeding conditions for insects to such an extent that they constitute a statutory nuisance, then it is the activity and conditions which the Environmental Health Practitioner should address.

36 Environmental consequences – indirect as well as cumulative – of remedial action must be considered, such as the effects of insecticides, if used, on the environment, nature, bodies of water, etc. Insecticides should therefore be chosen with care and regard for the Pesticides Safety Precautions Scheme in their use.

37 An abatement notice once issued may be 'simple' and require abatement within a specified timescale. It may, but does not have to, specify works or other steps necessary to abate the nuisance or restrict its occurrence or recurrence.

Example of insect nuisance – species of house fly (*Musca domestica* Linnaeus). Lesser house fly (*Fannia canicularis* (Linnaeus)), blow flies (*Calliphora* spp and *Lucilia* spp).

38 Houseflies can be classed as public health pests or pests of animal husbandry. They are associated with conditions that exist in rotting, fermenting, or at least moist organic matter, preferably of a high protein content, such as those that could be present at a sewage works (though they are also a natural part of the biological process and may indicate good quality effluent and process if found on a filter works at a sewage treatment works). Houseflies are frequently found in association with man, either indoors or taking advantage of other human activities, as do many other species of insect.

39 Houseflies and other pests which occur in significant numbers to cause a pest problem are almost certainly being attracted to the site because of a breakdown in standards of hygiene. Occasionally, the problem may be localised, i.e. blow flies (*Calliphora* spp and *Lucilia* spp) may be attracted by a dead bird or rodent, or due to external causes, such as a nearby farm or cattle in an adjacent field. Thus the most important aspect of fly control is to trace the cause of the problem and correct it. Only then can preventative measures be undertaken.

40 Houseflies are significant vectors of disease. They can transmit intestinal worms, dysentery, gastro-enteritis, typhoid, cholera and tuberculosis. The larvae are capable of developing intestinally if ingested. They can contaminate foodstuffs, though this would usually occur only where there are poor hygiene standards. As they will feed indiscriminately on faecal matter and human food, their status as a vector is well noted.

41 There are no objective levels at which a statutory nuisance exists or may be caused. In general, in domestic premises, it is likely that the threshold will be very low and control actions might be taken in cases of few house flies. As a guideline, an occupier will normally experience

Guidance relating to noise and smell

some irritation if there are five or more 'flying' house flies present in any one room at any one time on three successive days. If house flies are monitored with baited traps, sticky ribbons, or spot cards a collection of more than 25 in any 48-hour period may indicate grounds for distress.

42 The complaint threshold density of houseflies at waste management sites may be 150 individuals per flypaper per 30 minutes.

43 However, as stated earlier, there are no objective levels for statutory nuisance. It does not, therefore, necessarily follow that fewer than five house flies in a room in a house, or 150 house flies per flypaper per 30 minutes at waste management sites, do not constitute a statutory nuisance, or that five or 150 necessarily do. Just as noise nuisance is not a matter of decibel levels, insect nuisance is not a matter of numbers of insects. Impact may also depend on, e.g., size of room, number of people / premises affected etc. House flies do not damage property.

44 Both house flies (*Musca domestica*) and lesser house flies (*Fannia canicularis*) occur throughout the UK. Both houseflies and lesser houseflies are common in homes, barns, stables, and poultry houses in spring, summer and autumn.

45 Lesser house fly larvae typically consume decaying organic matter and excrement, but have been known to develop in the intestinal tract of man and animals. In some areas, lesser house fly larvae are the predominant maggots found in chicken manure.

46 Adults may live as long as two months. Populations flourish during cool seasons, particularly spring, early summer, and late autumn. Peak numbers usually occur by July, after which dry, hot weather and parasitism causes populations to subside until autumn.

47 **Prevention**: Physical prevention is preferred to pesticide usage. It may be preferable to control / reduce harbourage and breeding material than to treat an infestation once it is established. Currently in the UK natural predation of house flies in poultry houses is based on indigenous species, such as the Carcinops beetle (though it may not be sufficient alone). Larvicides are also generally used, although adulticides should be the last line of defence. Elsewhere in Europe and America, poultry farmers are using specially bred parasitic wasps and predator flies as a control method.

48 Premises need to adopt an integrated approach to house fly control which includes building design, effective management and systematic monitoring of house fly populations.

49 For example, integrated fly control programmes for poultry houses tend to be based on (i) selective application of insecticides against the adult; (ii) early introduction of insecticide control measures in early spring before house flies appear, repeated as needed throughout the warm months, and (iii) leaving manure undisturbed throughout the warm months when house fly breeding may occur, removing it just once in early spring before house flies appear. Engaging the farmer in discussion about management practices that could be adopted may support satisfactory outcomes. There may, for example, be times when manure may be removed in the autumn for land spreading, or twice a year.

Appendix H

50 Ordinarily, house fly control from 1 to 2 km around sensitive sites will prevent ingress into a sensitive area (containing dwellings, for example). In cases where no local breeding area can be identified, adult house flies may be flying long distances (i.e. several miles) from infestation sources of, for example, refuse tips or animal houses. Good sanitation, and elimination of breeding areas, are necessary for good management. Chemical treatment is the last line of defence.

51 Spot cards can be used as a diagnostic tool. These are 3-inch by 5-inch white index cards which are attached to a house-fly resting surface. A minimum of five cards should be placed in a suspect animal facility and left in place for seven days. As a guide, a count of 100 or more faecal or vomit spots per card per week may be taken to indicate a high level of house fly activity and a need for control (although this is not to say that a count of, say, 99 would not indicate a high level of house fly activity and a need for control).

52 Physical prevention methods:
- Food and materials on which the house flies can lay their eggs should be removed, destroyed as a breeding medium, or isolated from the egglaying adult house fly.
- Wet manure should be removed at least twice weekly if necessary to break the breeding cycle.
- Wet straw should not pile up in or near buildings and, as one of the best fly breeding materials, is not recommended as bedding.
- Spilled feed should not be allowed to accumulate, and should be cleaned up at least twice a week.
- Windows and doors can be proofed with fly screens of approximately 1.5 mm mesh.
- Fly traps may be useful in some house fly control programmes if enough traps are used, placed correctly, and used both indoors and outdoors. House flies are attracted to white surfaces and baits that give off odours. Lesser house flies are shyer of traps.
- Dustbins, wheelie-bins, paladins and skips should have tight-fitting lids and be cleaned regularly. Dry and wet rubbish should be placed in plastic rubbish bags and sealed up. All waste receptacles should be located as far from building entrances as possible.
- For control at waste disposal sites, refuse should be deposited onto the same area as inorganic wastes to reduce the capacity of breeding resources, or covered with soil or other inorganic wastes of around 15 cm consistent thickness.

53 Electronic fly killers which can attract insects to an electrified grid by using an ultra-violet light source are not generally effective against houseflies. House flies are not particularly attracted to them and, although they may kill the occasional one, they cannot cope with large numbers. If they are used, one trap should be placed for every 30 feet of wall inside buildings, but not placed over or within five feet of food preparation areas. Recommended placement areas outdoors include near building entrances, in alleyways, beneath trees, and around animal sleeping areas and manure piles.

54 **Eradication – chemical**: Chemical treatment should be considered as a last resort, as it may only be treating the insects in the vicinity at the time of treatment and not the source, although most pesticides do have

Guidance relating to noise and smell

a residual effect and may work on particular species throughout their lifecycle. Given the considerable link to water at sewage treatment works for example, management of insects may be more beneficial than treatment, by reducing the need for pesticide usage.

The use of pesticides near water bodies is one of the most risky and heavily controlled areas of pesticide use, and the potential for pesticide use on linear water bodies that drain into rivers and streams must be minimised. Removal of breeding material and habitats can keep insects under control or at bay.

- For adult control, conventional knockdown or residual treatments will kill the majority of adult flies in spite of the development of high resistance levels in a number of housefly populations.
- Residual insecticides applied to the house flies' favoured resting areas will control landing flies in some situations, although they should not generally be applied to breeding areas, as insecticide breakdown can be rapid and resistance may be encouraged.
- In poultry houses, the use of mists, fogs or baits may be necessary for house fly control. Treatment in poultry stations should be carried out by a qualified pest controller. Insecticides to control maggots should not be applied to manure, which should be kept dry and removed only during the winter.
- When flies are a major pest in commercial egg production facilities, they can be controlled by applying adulticides, or larvicides, to suppress adult densities directly or indirectly. Residual wall sprays can be applied where the flies congregate. Resistance can develop more rapidly in house fly populations on farms on a continuous insecticide regime using a single chemical than on farms in which insecticides are alternated. Residual insecticides may be applied to favoured resting areas for house flies. Breeding areas should be avoided as spray targets as, where the insecticide breaks down in an area where eggs are developing, it may encourage increased resistance in the house fly population.
- Outdoors, house fly control can include the use of chemical treatments in the bottom of skips, and treatment of vertical walls adjacent to skips and other breeding sites, with microencapsulated or wettable powder formulation, and the use of fly baits near adult feeding sources. In areas like rubbish tips treatment should always be carried out by a pest control specialist.
- Indoors, house fly control can include automatic misters, fly paper, electrocuting and baited traps that can be used in milking parlours and other areas of low fly numbers.

Example of insect nuisance – fruit flies (Drosophila spp)

55 Fruit flies compromise several species of the genus Drosophila (family Drosophilidae). They are increasingly associated with commercial composting activities and vegetable producers, wholesalers, and packers who store waste and / or reject produce in the open, as they are attracted to ripened or fermenting fruit and vegetables. Dwellings that report high infestations are increasingly found near these commercial undertakings. Fruit flies can be a problem year-round in domestic kitchens. They can contaminate foodstuffs, but usually only where there are poor hygiene standards or exposed, ripe fruit. They do not carry

Appendix H

disease or cause structural damage to buildings. The sheer numbers that congregate can create a nuisance. As a guideline, an occupier will normally experience some distress if there are 50 or more 'flying' fruit flies present in any one room at any one time on three successive days.

56 Detecting domestic breeding areas for fruit flies involves finding the source(s) of attraction and breeding, which can require much thought and persistence. Potential breeding sites which are inaccessible (e.g., waste-disposals and drains) can be inspected by taping a clear plastic food storage bag over the opening overnight. If flies are breeding in these areas, the adults will emerge and be caught in the bag.

57 **Prevention**: The best way to prevent problems with fruit flies is to eliminate sources of attraction. Produce which has ripened should be covered rather than discarded in the open. A single rotting potato or onion can breed thousands of fruit flies, as can a waste or recycling bin which is not emptied or cleaned.

58 Where regular spillages of fruit juice or pulp inside buildings attract fruit flies, windows and doors should be equipped with tight-fitting (16 mesh) screens to help prevent adult fruit flies from entering from outdoors.

All spillages and accumulations of fruit and vegetable juice and pulp should still be cleaned up regularly and thoroughly.

59 **Eradication**: Once a structure is infested with fruit flies, all potential breeding areas must be located and eliminated. Unless the breeding sites are removed or cleaned, the problem will continue no matter how often insecticides are applied to control the adults. Once the source is eliminated the flies will try to find new potential breeding substrates, usually out of doors. Only if the source has been eliminated and flies given time to disperse should an aerosol insecticide be used to kill remaining flies.

Example of insect nuisance – cockroaches (*Periplaneta Americana* (Linnaeus), *Blattella germanica* (Linnaeus), *Blatta orientalis* (Linnaeus))

60 Cockroaches pose a public health risk. Cockroaches can also cause allergic reactions in susceptible individuals, e.g., asthmatics, house dust mite allergen sufferers, and individuals exposed to infestations for long periods of time. Perhaps the most important effect that cockroaches have on humans is allergies. Their presence may cause an occupier distress. They can contaminate a range of stored food products.

61 There are three main pest species: the American (*Periplaneta americana*), German (*Blattella germanica*) and Oriental (*Blatta orientalis*) Cockroaches. The German and Oriental species are common in the UK. Cockroaches are highly adaptable and extremely mobile, moving into new buildings via sewer pipes, ducts etc. The Oriental cockroach is the most common and largest of the two. It can climb rough surfaces such as brickwork and will congregate around water sources. The German cockroach is smaller, but is able to climb vertical smooth surfaces. They do not cause structural damage.

62 One way to confirm an infestation is by using a stick trap. These can be purchased from a pest control contractor.

63 **Prevention**: Good standards of hygiene alone cannot prevent a cockroach invasion or combat an existing infestation, but are a necessary component of any control strategy. Since most buildings cannot be instantly cooled or heated to the temperatures required to kill cockroaches (7oC or 46oC), and vacuuming them up may not appeal, the use of insecticidal bait gels, fumigants and sprays are at present the most common method employed to control cockroaches.

64 Prevention involves proofing. Cockroaches are nocturnal and they prefer warm dark spaces. Any cracks in walls, floors and ceilings or inaccessible void between and behind equipment should be eliminated.

65 **Eradication**: It is a legal requirement that any signs of cockroaches in a food business are controlled. Various insecticides can be used to control cockroaches. These are dangerous chemicals and must be applied only by a competent professional pest control operator.

66 The use of insecticidal bait gels and fumigating sprays is the most common method employed to control cockroaches. Increased public concerns regarding the safety of synthetic pesticides and their effect upon human health and the environment, together with the increasing problem of cockroach resistance to insecticides, have resulted in a demand for effective, environmentally positive methods of control.

Example of insect nuisance – moth flies or sewage filter flies (*Psychoda* spp and *Tinearia alternata* (Say)

67 Sewage filter flies (principally *Psychoda albipennis* Zetterstedt, but also some other species of *Psychoda* and *Tinearia alternata* (Say)) belong to the family Psychodidae, commonly known as moth flies. They like moist, organic or septic systems for egg laying, and are common in the vicinity of sewage works. The larvae are often considered beneficial as an essential part of the cycle that breaks down waste into water-soluble compounds. Because they tend to live in protected places, clouds of flies might be the first sign of infestation.

They do not bite or sting, but can be a nuisance, flying in the eyes, mouth and nostrils of people. Because of their points of origin, they can carry disease,although actual transmission is extremely unlikely. They do not pose a contamination risk to food. There are no objective levels at which sewage filter flies do or may cause a statutory nuisance. As a general guideline, they might cause an occupier distress if 50 or more 'flying' sewage filter flies are present in a room on three successive days, though obviously this indication will vary and depend on such factors as room size etc. Sewage filter flies have a relatively slow breeding cycle with about eight generations a-year. Most infestations take place during the summer months as the adults emerge.

68 Control of sewage filter flies requires locating and eliminating larval breeding sites, which may be difficult and require perseverance. One way to check potential individual breeding sites is to cover the entrance with plastic film taped to the floor or fixture. If sewage filter flies are breeding there, they will accumulate beneath the film within a day or two.

69 One way of eliminating sewage filter flies is to clean the breeding place to remove organic matter. For example, a slow-moving drain can be cleaned with a stiff brush or other tool. Drains that cannot be scrubbed

Appendix H

can be rinsed with water under high pressure, sterilised with boiling water, or treated with a bacterial agent to biodegrade the organic matter.

70 Household insecticides can be used to control adult sewage filter flies, but the effects will be very temporary unless the source of the larvae is also removed.

71 It is recommended that operators of sewage treatment works should have systems in place for treating beds with a larvicide where there is a risk of, or a measurable, nuisance, and checking for high concentrations of sewage filter flies. The timing and dosing of the filter beds is critical to effectiveness, and must be carefully managed to prevent the release of chemicals into waterways or an effect on the balance of organisms in the ecosystem. In some cases it may be best to limit treatment to knock down or surface treatments.

Insects emanating from filter beds are a source of food for various wild bird and bat species, which in turn as act as a natural means of pest control. Treatment at filter beds could be so effective that these species lose a useful source of food supply.

Example of insect nuisance – mosquitoes (Culicidae)

72 There are about 30 species of mosquito (family Culicidae) in the UK, occupying aquatic habits such as coastal salt waters, brackish inland waters, stagnant pools and water-filled hollows (including in trees and logs). There are four stages of life, eggs laid on water which hatch within a few hours; larva and pupa that are free swimming in water and must come to the surface to breath; and the winged adult.

73 The British climate is not currently suited to the transmission of tropical diseases, and low fevers which can be caused by mosquitoes in Southern and Central Europe have not been detected here. Malaria is the only human infection known to have been transmitted in this country by two species of mosquitoes of the genus *Anopheles* but it is *extremely* unlikely.

74 British mosquitoes can have a nuisance value. Their bites can cause severe skin eruption and localised pain, and severe infestations can cause much distress which is a valid reason for mosquito control. There are no objective levels at which a statutory nuisance may or does exist. As a general guideline, an occupier might feel irritation if five or more 'flying' mosquitoes are present in a room for three successive days. They do not damage property or pose a contamination risk to foodstuffs.

75 Prevention: Mosquito control should be aimed at both the larval and adult stages of life cycle, although as mosquitoes do not normally rest in buildings, control of adults can be impractical.

76 Larval control can be achieved through eliminating or changing the characteristics of larval sites, which might need to be achieved piecemeal and over a period of years.

77 Man-made containers of water such as old car tyres, empty pots, open sewers and drains containing putrid and anoxic water should, as far as is practicable, be drained and kept empty. Water can be channelled to increase flow. Cesspools, septic tanks and drains should be sealed. Rainwater butts and tanks should have close-fitting lids. Rivers,

Guidance relating to noise and smell

watercourses (other than those mentioned above), lakes and ponds are excluded from the nuisance definition and should not be drained.

78 Insecticides, repellents, vapourising mats, mosquito coils and fly screens may offer some personal protection from adult mosquitoes.

79 **Eradication**: Light oil or lecithin can be applied to water to reduce the surface tension and prevent larvae from obtaining oxygen. Such agents spread readily over large areas.

The technique should not be used where rivers, watercourses (other than open sewers and drains containing putrid and anoxic water), lakes or ponds may be affected. The Environment Agency should be consulted before use, as should the relevant Statutory Nature Conservation Agency if there is a Special Site of Scientific Interest in the local vicinity. The technique will also affect non-target species of insect living in the waterbody, many of which are the natural predators of the mosquito larvae. The removal of the more long-lived predators of the mosquitoes may result in an increased problem as the mosquitoes would be able to respond quickly to take advantage of the predator-free environment. Agents need to be appropriately approved as biocides.

80 Larvae can be attacked by applying formulations to larval sites which produce a crystal which breaks down into stomach poison.

81 Adult mosquitoes can be eliminated using 'knock-down' agents or residual insecticides.

Environmental impact

82 Insects rarely cause a significant health risk, and health risks where they do or may exist, are often associated with human habitation and waste, so significant damage to the environment should not be necessary. Environmental management should be the first option.

83 Any mitigating treatment should take account of factors including impact on health and well being; impact on the target and non-target species; impact on the environment including ground and water source contamination; cost; and efficacy.

Artificial Lighting

Likely sources of artificial light statutory nuisance.

84 In order to understand what may be termed a statutory nuisance in lighting, an understanding of some lighting terminology is required:

Light (or luminous flux) is a type of radiation and forms part of the electromagnetic spectrum visible to the eye. It is measured in *lumens (lm)* (N.B. *not* 'watts', which is only a measure of electrical consumption).

The amount of light falling on a surface is known as *illuminance* and is measured in *lumens per square metre* or *lux*.

While 'illuminance' is easy to calculate and measure and is therefore widely used, the eye does not see illuminance, but rather the light radiated or reflected *off* a surface which is known as *luminance*, or brightness. It is measured in *candelas per square metre (cd/m2)* and if the surface is glossy, can differ with the angle of view.

Appendix H

The term *candela (cd)* or (Kcd = 1000 cd) is by itself a measure of light *intensity*. Whether this light 'intensity' is seen as glare or not depends on the surrounding 'luminance', as can be noted when comparing a road lighting luminaire or floodlight lit during the day and again at night.

85 Local authorities have a duty to take reasonable steps, where practicable, to investigate any complaints of artificial light nuisance; it is expected that the following sources will generate most complaints:
- Domestic security lights
- Commercial security lights
- Healthy living and sports facilities (see below)
- Domestic decorative lighting
- Exterior lighting of buildings and decorative lighting of landscapes
- Laser shows / sky beams / light art

86 Christmas lights may also be the subject of complaint, and could be covered by statutory light nuisance, although this seems unlikely given their duration.

87 We anticipate that much artificial light nuisance will be caused by excessive levels of illuminance and glare, which is inappropriate to its need and which has been poorly designed, directed, operated and maintained. Simple remedies, such as re-aiming or screening, should be sufficient in many cases and, although light nuisance is not a matter of light levels *per se*, light meters are available and affordable for taking measurements in order to quantify the scale of the possible nuisance.

88 Efficient and high-quality lighting installations that help people to see where they are going and bring security to both themselves and their property can be designed so as to produce minimal impact on the environment. The management and maintenance of such lighting that limits both glare and dark shadows is also essential for people with a visual impairment.

89 We also anticipate a number of complaints on streetlights. However, these are not likely to qualify as artificial light statutory nuisance as they are unlikely to be located on 'premises'. They can, nevertheless, cause adverse affects and are discussed in more detail under 'Streetlights' below.

Statutory nuisance from artificial light and light pollution

90 Artificial light *nuisance* may be, but is not necessarily, the same as light *pollution*. Artificial light *nuisance* is a source of light that in the opinion of a trained public health professional, who makes an assessment on a case by case basis, interferes with someone's use of their property, and / or is or might be prejudicial to someone's health. Light *pollution* could be defined as any form of artificial light which shines outside the area it needs to illuminate, including light that is directed above the horizontal into the night sky creating sky glow (which impedes our views of the stars), or which creates a danger by glare. Although light pollution might affect the aesthetic beauty of the night sky and interfere with astronomy, it is not necessarily also a statutory nuisance. The statutory nuisance regime is not an appropriate tool with which to address light pollution *per se*.

Guidance relating to noise and smell

Domestic security lights

91 Those aggrieved by a neighbour's lighting should be encouraged to speak to their neighbour first where possible, perhaps with the aid of a mediation service. Mediation UK (www.mediationuk.org.uk) may be able to advise.

92 Inappropriate lighting can cause glare and dark shadows which may adversely affect drivers, cyclists and other road users, including pedestrians, and people with a visual impairment. Bad lighting can also produce shadows for those with criminal intent to hide in or behind. Many cases of artificial light nuisance can be solved through simple engineering techniques and consideration of function and effect. For example:

- The minimum level of illumination necessary to light a property should be used. Relatively high-powered lights are rarely necessary in domestic situations and, besides wasting energy and money, can cause glare, which can adversely affect road users or other passers-by. Excessive levels of illumination provide dark shadows for people, including those with criminal intent, to hide in or behind. Lighting that is shielded or angled down can actually improve rather than compromise security. There are agreed Standards for lighting levels, some of which are listed at the end of this document.
- Special optics or 'double asymmetric' luminaires – which are designed to ensure full flow of light over the lit area from each floodlight – can be aimed facing downwards while still spreading light over a wide distance (the lamp is usually fitted close to the back edge of the unit, not in the middle). The reflector becomes less visible to onlookers resulting in low glare to the surrounding locality.
- A separate switching detector can be used on some models to sense the movement of intruders on the property. Luminaires and detectors should be aimed to detect and light people on the property, not people or animals walking down the street. If lights detect everything that moves, they will switch on and off repeatedly and could be a source of statutory nuisance.
- Timers adjusted to the minimum can reduce the operation of the light.
- Bulkhead or porch lights are cheaper than security lights, use less energy, and have reduced glare so there are fewer shadows for those with criminal intent to hide in. Movement detectors on these lights are generally mounted lower and so are less susceptible to nuisance switching on and off. However, they tend, because they are lower, to be aimed more horizontally, capture movement over a wider range, and if not located with care can be interfered with.
- Vegetation may help screen the light at certain times of year provided the movement of vegetation itself does not trigger light, and it does not cause a 'high hedges' problem.

93 It is sometimes suggested that a complaint of artificial light nuisance could easily be mitigated by the use of curtains or blinds, even blackout curtains or blinds, by the complainant. It is for the Environmental Health Practitioner to exercise discretion over what is reasonable and what is not. It might be reasonable to expect a complainant to use curtains or

Appendix H

blinds of everyday standard if they are bothered by unwanted light in their home. It might not be reasonable to require a complainant to purchase and install blackout hangings which might be expensive, and/or impair that person's enjoyment of his property. Few would wish to have their curtains drawn on a hot summers night. It is not reasonable to leave the solution and cost of abatement to the complainant rather than the perpetrator.

94 Technical parameters on obtrusive lighting, formulated by the International Commission on Illumination (CIE) and Institution of Lighting Engineers (ILE) from research into individual sensitivity to light, may be helpful in considering the level of sensitivity that might be considered that of the 'average person' without unusual sensitivities. These parameters vary depending on whether the installation is in town or country (there are four suggested environmental zones), and there is a suggested curfew time of 23.00 after which lighting levels should be further restricted. However, there are no objective levels at which artificial light does or does not constitute a statutory nuisance.

95 It is sensible for abatement notices to be 'simple', requiring abatement and non-recurrence within a specified timescale. If the abatement notice is too detailed, it could be that the terms of the abatement notice may be fulfilled whilst the nuisance remains unabated.

96 A list of useful sources of further information and useful practical advice on the positioning of external lighting is listed at the end of this guidance.

Commercial security lights

97 Lighting used on commercial premises will be subject to the same controls as apply to domestic premises, i.e. it will be for the local authority to decide whether the lighting amounts to a statutory nuisance.

98 Commercial premises are more likely than domestic premises to use lighting which makes a material change to the external façade of the building. It may therefore be subject to planning permission. Planning Policy Statement 23 provides guidance for such applications, and can also be used when considering lighting schemes for new buildings. Planning policy falls within the remit of the Office of the Deputy Prime Minister.

100 Premises or apparatus used for the provision of electronic communication services need adequate lighting for operation and security purposes, to ensure the safety of their staff, and to protect the integrity of the telecommunications network. Statutory nuisance law recognises the need for industry to be able to carry out its usual functions without being compromised by inadequate security lighting. That need is protected by the defence of 'best practicable means'.

Exterior lighting of buildings and landscapes

101 Exterior lighting to enhance the appearance of buildings, monuments, trees and other civic features increasingly impacts on the street scene. Such installations can enhance and add interest to the surrounding environment provided they are properly designed. Such lighting systems should not be used also to provide e.g. street lighting and should generally be switched off overnight, following an agreed curfew time.

Guidance relating to noise and smell

Laser shows, sky beams, light art

102 In order to constitute an existing or potential statutory nuisance, laser shows, sky beams and light art would have materially to affect someone's use of his home and / or actually or potentially his health, assuming normal sensibilities. Local authorities already have the means to deal with nuisance lighting and are accountable to those within their areas. Local authorities should do their best to ensure that lighting under their control does not cause problems to the local community. Local authorities should also take into account whether laser shows / beams etc are a sustainable or wasteful use of energy. The Government expects local authorities to take reasonable steps to investigate and, where appropriate, resolve problems as a matter of good practice and consideration for the local environment and the community to which they are accountable.

Streetlights

103 Streetlights are not specifically exempt, but because of their location are unlikely to qualify, as generally speaking they are not found on 'premises'. It is, however, acknowledged that streetlights can have adverse affects on the local community.

104 Local authorities have a duty under section 17 of the Crime and Disorder Act 1998 to exercise their functions with due regard to the likely effect on crime and disorder in their areas, and to do what they reasonably can to prevent crime and disorder. Local authorities already have the means to deal with nuisance street lighting and are accountable to those within their areas. Local authorities should do their best to ensure that streetlights under their control do not cause problems to the local community. The Government expects local authorities to take reasonable steps to investigate and, where appropriate, resolve problems from streetlights as a matter of good practice and consideration for the local environment and the community to which they are accountable.

105 The Government supports good design, installation and maintenance practice to minimise problems where possible.

106 New technologies now allow much finer control of light distribution and reduced light directed towards the sky. Beneficial lighting can be achieved that is fit for purpose, provided roads are appropriately rather than over classified, and which minimises the impact on the environment through using modern light sources in combination with luminaires designed to appropriate, not unnecessarily high, lighting levels. The simply use of front and / or back shields can improve illumination on the road whilst reducing intrusion elsewhere. £300 million in Private Finance Initiative credits were made available to local authorities outside London in 2003/04 to help modernise street lighting. A further £85 million in Private Finance Initiative credits is being made available for local authorities in London for this purpose in addition to the support available through the Revenue Support Grant.

107 Guidance has been published by the Department for Transport and also the Institution of Lighting Engineers to help reduce light pollution and sky glow generally, and to promote good practice for street lighting maintenance. As most street lighting is alight throughout the night, the

Appendix H

obtrusive light levels to be adhered to should be those given for all night, i.e. after curfew. In addition, the Government's 'Lighting in the Countryside: Towards good practice' includes street lighting, and is applicable to towns as well as country. The Government will continue to work with the appropriate organisations to promote good practice in design, installation and maintenance to minimise problems where possible.

Licensed premises

108 Guidance issued by the Department for Culture, Media and Sport under section 182 of the Licensing Act 2003 advises that licensing authorities and responsible authorities should consider the impacts of licensed premises on those living in the vicinity, mainly concerning noise nuisance, light pollution, noxious smells and litter. The Guidance advises that lighting outside premises should be installed in a way that balances the need to prevent crime and disorder while having consideration for those living in the vicinity. Many licensed premises use decorative floodlighting to draw attention to their premises. Where possible premises should use carefully installed downlighting rather that uplighting, which can be both glaring and wasteful of light into the sky.

109 Licensed premises and licensing authorities will also want to consider any lighting schemes with regard to potential action under the statutory nuisance regime. As business premises, licensed premises will have the defence of best practicable means.

Lighting in the Countryside

110 The 1998 Transport White Paper *A New Deal for Transport – Better for Everyone* stated that 'where lighting is essential, it should be designed in such a way that nuisance is reduced and the effect on the night sky in the countryside minimised'. Exterior lighting in rural areas can have a particular impact.

111 **Lighting in the Countryside**: Towards Good Practice is accessible free of charge at www.odpm.gov.uk/planning// litc/index.htm (under Planning Advice and Guidance). This document continues to be a valuable guide for local authorities, highways planners and engineers, and members of the public. It demonstrates what can be done to lessen the adverse effects of external lighting, including street lighting. The advice is applicable in towns as well as the countryside.

The relationship between planning and statutory nuisance

112 It is clearly preferable, and a demonstration of good practice, to prevent a statutory nuisance from occurring in the first place. One approach is to identify it at the planning stage.

113 Well-designed public lighting increases the opportunity for surveillance at night and sends out positive messages about the management of an area, and can help to reduce crime and disorder. Detailed guidance on types of lighting is available at www.securedbydesign.com. Further advice on the planning system and crime prevention can be obtained from the publication '*Safer Places: The planning system and crime prevention*', by the Office of the Deputy Prime Minister (responsible for planning) and the Home Office (crime and disorder).

Guidance relating to noise and smell

114 Lighting installation proposals should be submitted to local authorities to assist them in determining planning permissions. Local authorities should carry out professional reviews of developments involving exterior lighting to minimise their impact by day and night. Planning permission for such developments should include requirements to ensure that the installation is maintained in a satisfactory manner; and that all screens, shields, baffles and aiming requirements etc imposed are maintained throughout the life of the installation.

115 The existence of a planning permission does not, however, mean that a statutory nuisance cannot exist. Statutory nuisance can exist whether a particular site has planning permission for the artificial light or not. Circumstances and local environments change, so, for example, artificial light that was not a nuisance before may become one.

Exemptions

116 Whilst the Government recognises that some premises are of strategic importance owing to their nature and importance to the community, and exterior lighting may be necessary to prevent crime, disorder and safety hazard, it is expected that exempted premises will take seriously their social responsibility to use artificial light responsibly and with consideration to local circumstances. Exempted premises are expected to maintain lighting systems that do not unduly affect the environment and neighbourhood. Lighting systems should be adequate for purpose, and not in excess of that requirement, so that impact is minimal whilst remaining compatible with the use and function of the facilities. Inappropriately designed installations may cause unnecessary distraction for drivers on adjacent highways and compromise safety for road users, pedestrians, and people with a visual impairment. The Government will consider further guidance on good practice use of artificial light if necessary.

117 Local authorities may still need to undertake an initial investigation of complaints made about artificial light from exempted premises in order to establish first whether or not that premises really is the source. Even though enforcement action for artificial light statutory nuisance from exempted premises cannot be taken under section 102, efforts should still be made to negotiate an acceptable solution on an informal basis. The exemptions are to protect the public interest and health and safety, not to condone the irresponsible, inconsiderate or unnecessary use of artificial light.

Best Practicable Means

118 The defence of having used 'best practicable means' to abate a nuisance is available as a ground of appeal against an abatement notice, and as a defence against prosecution for breaching or failing to comply with an abatement notice, for both these new statutory nuisances where they emanate from industrial, trade or business premises, and also, in the case of artificial lighting, from outdoor illuminated sports facilities (see below). It is for the courts to decide whether best practicable means are being used by the premises in question. Section 79(9) of the Environmental Protection Act 1990 requires that best practicable means is interpreted with reference to the following provisions:

Appendix H

(a) 'practicable' means reasonably practicable having regard among other things to local conditions and circumstances, to the current state of technical knowledge and to the financial implications;
(b) the means to be employed include the design, installation, maintenance and manner and periods of operation of plant and machinery, and the design, construction and maintenance of buildings and structures;
(c) the test is to apply only so far as compatible with any duty imposed by law;
(d) the test is to apply only so far as compatible with safety and safe working conditions, and with the exigencies of any emergency or unforeseeable circumstances'.

Healthy living and sports facilities

119 It is Government policy to increase participation in sport and provide better healthy living and sporting opportunities at every level. In order to help achieve this aim the Government has invested heavily in new and improved sports facilities, including the floodlighting of playing fields and other facilities.

120 Given the limited hours of daylight in Britain in the winter, floodlighting is essential if communities are to make maximum use of many sports grounds, and the Government will continue to promote their use. All new floodlighting schemes are subject to appraisal under the planning system, which aims to balance the interests of those who may object to new sources of bright light against the interest of those who will benefit from the lighting in terms of greater opportunity to participate in sport. Full details of the equipment to be used and estimated lighting levels, not only on the field of play, but also that trespassing onto surrounding properties, should all be submitted to the local authority to assist with planning permissions. Where planning permission is granted, it is usually accompanied by strict technical specifications designed to ensure that nuisance from the lighting is minimised.

121 Against this background, Defra would not normally expect local authorities to have to resort to a statutory nuisance abatement order to address complaints about light from illuminated outdoor sports facilities.

122 Any modern facility which is operating in accordance with approved standards will be able to rely on the statutory defence of 'best practicable means' (BPM). Most such facilities are likely to be regarded as businesses, and so benefit from this defence in any event under sections 80(8) and 82(10) of the Environmental Protection Act 1990, but to ensure that all are covered by this defence, section 80(8)(aza)(ii), (8A), (8B) and (8C) of the Environmental Protection Act 1990 (inserted by section 103(2)(b) and (3) of the Clean Neighbourhoods and Environment Act 2005) specifically extends the BPM defence to all outdoor relevant sports facilities.

123 There may be occasions when badly sited or defective floodlighting causes unnecessary hardship to individuals. In such cases a local authority may consider making use of statutory nuisance legislation. However, before concluding that it is satisfied that a statutory nuisance exists a local authority should make every effort to resolve the problem through discussion with those responsible for the lighting. For example,

Guidance relating to noise and smell

older floodlighting towers can be affected by wind which can change slightly the direction of the floodlights; such situations can be resolved by altering the fixings and repositioning the lights in their original position. Zero upward light can be achieved by using double asymmetric full horizontal cut-off luminaires. Additional shielding, suitably painted black, can provide further mitigation if required. An abatement notice should only be issued as a measure of last resort.

124 'Relevant sports facility' is defined in the new subsections 80 (8A), (8B) and (8C) of the Environmental Protection Act 1990. It is a facility used when participating in a relevant sport, and includes the playing area and related structures. However, sports facilities that are located in domestic premises, including land attached to such premises, are excluded. 'Relevant sports' will be listed in an Order. The following are designated as relevant sports (see section 16 above on the Statutory Nuisances (Artificial Lighting) (Designation of Relevant Sports) (England) Order 2006):

American Football, Archery, Association Football, Athletics, Australian Rules Football, Badminton, Basketball, Baseball, Biathlon, Bobsleigh, Bowls, Camogie, Cricket, Croquet, Curling, Cycling, Equestrian Sports, Gaelic Football, Golf, Gymnastics, Handball, Hockey, Horse Racing, Hurling, Ice Hockey, Ice Skating, Lacrosse, Lawn Tennis, Luge, Modern Pentathlon, Motor Cycling, Motor Sports, Netball, Polo, Roller Sports, Rounders, Rowing, Rugby League, Rugby Union, Shooting, Skateboarding, Skiing, Softball, Swimming and Diving, Trialthon, Tug of War, Volleyball.

Other relevant legislation/documents

INSECTS

Wildlife and Countryside Act 1981

LIGHT

Useful Web Sites:
- Institution of Lighting Engineers – www.ile.org.uk
- International Commission on Illumination (CIE) – www.cie.co.at
- Lighting Industry Federation – www.lif.co.uk
- Society of Light and Lighting – www.cibse.org.

UK Guidance
- *BS 5489-1: 2003 Code of Practice for the Design of Road Lighting – Part 1: Lighting of Roads and Public Amenity Areas*
- *BS EN 12193:1999 Light and Lighting Sports Lighting*
- *International Commission on Illumination – CIE – Standard S 015/E:2005 – Lighting of Outdoor Work Places* (will be the first standard to give the CIE 150 and ILE obtrusive light values in a special section on limiting obtrusive light and will become a British / European Standard in the near future)
- *Domestic Security Lighting, Friend or Foe* – Institution of Lighting Engineers (2001)
- *Environmental Considerations for Exterior Lighting* – Chartered Institution of Building Services Engineers (2003)

Appendix H

- *Guidance Notes for the Reduction of Obtrusive Light* – Institution of Lighting Engineers (2005)
- *Light Pollution* – Supplementary Planning Guidance – South Northamptonshire Council (1998)
- *Lighting in the Countryside – Towards Good Practice* – Department of Environment, Food and Rural Affairs, and Country Commission (1997)
- *Lighten our Darkness* – Royal Fine Arts Commission (1994)
- *Lighting the Environment* – A Guide to Good Urban Lighting – Chartered Institution of Building Services Engineers and Institution of Lighting Engineers (1995)
- *Low Energy Domestic Lighting* – Energy Saving Trust (2002)
- *Night Blight!* – Campaign to Protect Rural England (2003)
- *Road Lighting and the Environment* – Department of Transport (1993)
- *Starry, Starry Night* – British Astronomical Association, and Campaign for the Protection of Rural England (2000)

EU Guidance / Standards
- *BS EN 13201: 2003, Road Lighting, Part 2: Performance Standards* (EU document with a range of classified lighting levels for different roadway, pathway and conflict areas linked to traffic volumes)
- *PrEN 12464-2, Lighting of Work Places – Part 2: Outdoor Work Places* (EU document (out for voting January 2006) which will lay down lighting requirements – levels and uniformities – for various outdoor workplaces)

International Guidance
- *CIE Standard S 015/E:2005 – Lighting of Outdoor Work Places* – see above
- *Pub. No. 126: 1997 Guidelines for Minimising Sky Glow* – International Commission on Illumination
- *Pub. No. 150: 2003 Guide on the Limitation of the Effects of Obtrusive Light from Outdoor Lighting Installations* – International Commission on Illumination

Annex 1

SCHEMES

Scheme	Legislation
Environmental Stewardship Scheme	The Environmental Stewardship (England) Regulations 2005 (S.I. 2005/621)
Entry Level Pilot Scheme	The Entry Level Agri-Environment Scheme (Pilot) (England) Regulations 2003 (S.I. 2003/838)
Countryside Stewardship Scheme	The Countryside Stewardship Regulations 2000 (S.I. 2000/3048)
The Environmentally Sensitive Areas Scheme	The Environmentally Sensitive Areas (Stage I) Designation Order 2000 (S.I.2000/3049)

Guidance relating to noise and smell

Scheme	Legislation
	The Environmentally Sensitive Areas (Stage II) Designation Order 2000 (S.I.2000/3050)
	The Environmentally Sensitive Areas (Stage III) Designation Order 2000 (S.I.2000/3051)
	The Environmentally Sensitive Areas (Stage IV) Designation Order 2000 (S.I. 2000/3052)
Farm Woodland Premium Scheme	Farm Woodland Scheme 1988 (S.I. 1988/1291)
	Farm Woodland Premium Scheme 1992 (S.I. 1992/905)
	Farm Woodland Premium Scheme 1997 (S.I. 1997/829)
Organic Farming Scheme	Organic Farming (Aid) Scheme 1994 (S.I. 1994/1721)
	Organic Farming Regulations 1999 (S.I.1999/590)
	Organic Farming (ERDP) Regulations 2001 (S.I. 2001/432)
	Organic Farming (ERDP) Regulations 2003 (S.I. 2003/1235)
Nitrate Sensitive Areas Scheme	The Farm Waste Grant (Nitrate Vulnerable Zones) (England and Wales) Scheme 1996 (S.I. 1996/908)
	The Farm Waste Grant (Nitrate Vulnerable Zones) (England and Wales) Scheme 2000 (S.I. 2000/2890)
	The Farm Waste Grant (Nitrate Vulnerable Zones) (England and Wales) Scheme 2000 (S.I. 2000/2911)
	The Farm Waste Grant (Nitrate Vulnerable Zones) (England and Wales) Scheme 2003 (S.I. 2003/562)
Habitat Scheme	Conservation (Natural Habitats, &c) Regulations 1994 (S.I. 1994/2716)
	Habitat (Water Fringe) Regulations 1994 (S.I. 1994/1291)
	Habitat (Salt-Marsh) Regulations 1994 (S.I. 1994/1293

Appendix H

NUISANCE PARKING OFFENCES AND ABANDONED VEHICLES – DEFRA GUIDANCE

Overview

This document provides guidance on the nuisance parking provisions in sections 3 to 9 of the Clean Neighbourhoods and Environment Act 2005, and on abandoned vehicles legislation.

Nuisance Parking

General Principles

For the purpose of this guidance, the term 'nuisance parking' covers only those vehicles involved in the offences described in sections 3 and 4 of the Clean Neighbourhoods and Environment Act 2005 and is not intended to cover other parking infringements.

1 Some garages and businesses place cars for sale, for an extended period, on the street. This can cause a significant nuisance to local residents and takes up valuable car parking spaces. The same is true with vehicles that are repaired on the street, which can also look unsightly, can lead to damage of the local environment (for example when oil is spilled or leaked) and may also present a danger to passers by.

2 The offence of selling vehicles on the road is intended to target those people who run a business selling motor vehicles and use the road as a mock showroom. This behaviour is unfair to local residents who are thereby deprived of using the road themselves to park vehicles and go about their daily lives.

It is not intended to target individual private sellers of single vehicles, but the nuisance that is caused by the presence of numbers of vehicles being offered for sale by the same person or business. This is why the offence may only be committed where there are two or more vehicles being offered for sale for the purposes of a business.

It is recognised that a private individual may at one time or another have more than one car to sell and decide to offer them by parking them close together on a road, but it is anticipated that this will only happen on rare occasions: a person who can demonstrate that he is acting in such a capacity, and not for the purposes of a business, is not liable for conviction for the nuisance parking offence.

3 The offence of repairing a vehicle is also aimed primarily at those that act irresponsibly as part of a business and which are attempting to use the road as a mock workshop.

It is not intended to target private individuals who are carrying out minor work to their vehicles (unless the repairs cause unreasonable annoyance to persons in the vicinity), or those who carry out necessary work to vehicles by the side of the road in order to get them moving again after a breakdown or accident (such as breakdown organisations and mobile mechanics), provided the work is completed within 72 hours. It replaces a similar provision that applied in London only.

Guidance relating to noise and smell

Detailed Guidance

4 This part of the guidance gives a commentary on each relevant section and sub-section in the Clean Neighbourhoods and Environment Act.

Section 3 – Exposing vehicles for sale on a road

Section 3 (1) sets out the particulars of the offence: A person commits an offence if:
- a) he leaves two or more motor vehicles parked within 500m of each other on a road or roads where they are exposed or advertised for sale, or
- b) he causes two or more motor vehicles to be so left.

Section 3 (2) sets out a defence:

A person is not to be convicted of an offence under subsection (1) if he proves to the satisfaction of the court that he was not acting for the purposes of a business of selling motor vehicles.

Section 3 (3) sets out the penalty:

A person guilty of an offence under subsection (1) is liable on summary conviction to a fine not exceeding level 4 (currently £2,500) on the standard scale.

Section 3 (4) sets out the definitions of 'motor vehicle' and 'road'

The definition of **'road'** is defined in section 142 of the Road Traffic Regulation Act 1984:

'[in England and Wales] any length of highway or of any other road to which the public has access, and includes bridges over which a road passes.'

5 This is a wide definition and includes not only public rights of way, but also ways to which the public has access by permission of the landowner, rather than by right. It therefore includes access roads through estates that are owned by organisations such as housing associations or by the residents who live there. It covers both the carriageway and the footpath, but a car park would not normally come within the definition of a road as its function is to enable people to leave their vehicle.

6 The definition of **'motor vehicle'** is the same as used in the Refuse Disposal (Amenity) Act 1978 (section 11(1)):

'a mechanically propelled vehicle intended or adapted for use on roads, whether or not it is in a fit state for such use, and includes any trailer intended or adapted for use as an attachment to such a vehicle, any chassis or body, with or without wheels, appearing to have formed part of such a vehicle or trailer and anything attached to such a vehicle or trailer'

7 This definition covers cars, motorcycles the chassis of a car or motorcycle, a trailer and a caravan.

Section 4 – Repairing vehicles on a road

Section 4 (1) sets out the offence:

A person who carries out restricted works on a motor vehicle on a road is guilty of an offence.

Appendix H

Section 4 (2) defines the term 'restricted works' used in subsection (1):

'restricted works' –

'works for the repair, maintenance, servicing, improvement or dismantling of a motor vehicle or of any part of or accessory to a motor vehicle'

and

'works for the installation, replacement or renewal of any such part or accessory.'

Section 4 (3) sets out the circumstances in which a person is not to be convicted of an offence:

A person is not to be convicted of an offence under this section in relation to any works if he proves to the satisfaction of the court that the works were not carried out –
  (a) in the course of, or for the purposes of, a business of carrying out restricted works; or
  (b) for gain or reward.

Section 4 (4) sets out circumstances in which the defence set out in subsection (3) does not apply:

[The defence] does not apply where the carrying out of the works gave reasonable cause for annoyance to persons in the vicinity.

8 There is no legal definition of 'reasonable cause for annoyance' and interpretation of this provision will be for the courts. However, the concept of 'reasonableness' is one that will be familiar to local authorities.

9 **Section 4 (5)** sets out an additional defence, *both* elements of which must be demonstrated:

A person is not to be convicted of an offence under this section in relation to any works if he proves to the satisfaction of the court that the works carried out were works of repair which –
  (a) arose from an accident or breakdown in circumstances where repairs on the spot or elsewhere on the road were necessary; and
  (b) were carried out within 72 hours of the accident or breakdown or were within that period authorised to be carried out at a later time by the local authority for the area.

10 **Section 4 (6)** sets out the penalty:

A person guilty of an offence under this section is liable on summary conviction to a fine not exceeding level 4 (currently £2,500) on the standard scale.

11 Section 4 (7) sets out the definitions of 'motor vehicle', 'road' and 'local authority' used in section 4:

'motor vehicle' and **'road'** – have the same definitions as used in section 3 (4) – see page 5.

12 Local authorities can under this section authorise repairs to go on outside the initial 72 hour period. The definition of 'local authority' is as defined in section 9 as:
  (a) a district council in England;

Guidance relating to noise and smell

(b) a county council in England for an area for which there is no district council;
(c) a London borough council
(d) the Common Council of the City of London
(e) the Council of the Isles of Scilly;
(f) a county or county borough council in Wales

Section 5 – Liability of Directors

13 This section aims to ensure that directors and officers of companies (corporate bodies) and others who are in similar positions do not shirk the responsibilities of their business. It introduces personal liability for the offences for directors and officers and others acting or purporting to act in such a capacity. This is in addition to the company being liable. It applies to both new offences set out in sections 3 and 4.

14 **Section 5 (1)** sets out the extent of their liability:

Where an offence under section 3 or 4 committed by a body corporate is proved to have been committed with the consent or connivance of, or to have been attributable to any neglect on the part of –
(a) any director, manager, secretary or other similar officer of the body corporate, or
(b) a person who was purporting to act in such a capacity,

he as well as the body corporate is guilty of the offence and liable to be proceeded against and punished accordingly.

15 **Section 5 (2)** offers further clarification in relation to personal liability in the case of a company that is managed by its members where those members (or some of them) are treated as if they were the directors:

Where the affairs of a body corporate are managed by its members, subsection (1) applies in relation to the acts or defaults of a member in connection with his functions of management as if he were a director of the body.

Sections 6 to 9 – Fixed Penalty Notices

These sections provide for fixed penalty notices to be issued when an authorised officer believes that a nuisance vehicle offence has been committed. The fixed penalty is set at £100, and an authorised officer must be an employee of a local authority authorised in writing by that authority to issue fixed penalty notices. Guidance on fixed penalty notices is available separately, and it is strongly recommended that this is consulted before the provisions in these sections are made use of.

Other Relevant Legislation

16 There is other legislation that local authorities can use to tackle nuisance vehicles. This part of the guidance sets out two examples.

The Local Government (Miscellaneous Provisions) Act 1976

17 Section 7(1) of this Act gives a highway authority power to specify a highway, through a control order, whereupon any person is prohibited from 'selling' or 'offering to expose anything for sale ' on the designated highway. This includes selling from a stall or vehicle. Breaking such an order can lead to a maximum of a level 3 fine (currently £1,000) and a

Appendix H

£10 fine for each day a person convicted of the offence continues to sell, or offer or expose to sell, after the expiration of a seven-day period. Such a control order does not apply to a shop or petrol filling station or a market where a toll or rent is applicable. Stalls in a roadside lay-by offering refreshments are also exempted.

The Highways Act 1980

18 Section 137(1) makes it an offence to wilfully obstruct free passage along a highway. The penalty for such an offence is a maximum of a level 3 (currently £1,000) fine.

19 Section 147A(1) makes it an offence to use a stall, container or vehicle with the purpose of offering anything for sale. This does not include vehicles designed for itinerant trading with occupiers of premises, or if part of a market where tolls or rents are applicable (Level 3 fine).

20 Sections 148(c) and 149 make it an offence to deposit anything on the highway 'to the interruption of any user of the highway' (Level 3 fine). If such an offence occurrs the owner of the object may be issued with a notice to remove within a set time. If this notice is not complied with the local authority may apply to a magistrate's court for a removal and disposal order. If the object is considered a danger to users of the highway, or ought to be removed immediately, then the authority can remove the object immediately and reclaim expenses.

Abandoned Vehicles

This part provides guidance on the following legislation, as amended by sections 10–17 of the Clean Neighbourhoods and Environment Act 2005:
- Refuse Disposal (Amenity) Act 1978 – Sections 2–5;
- Road Traffic Regulation Act 1984 – Sections 99–103;
- Removal and Disposal of Vehicles Regulations 1986 (SI 1986/183)

It is intended as a guide for local authorities to use when exercising their duties regarding abandoned vehicles. It is not a replacement for the legislation and should be read in conjunction with the legislation and explanatory notes – some of which is accessible through the following links.
- www.opsi.gov.uk/acts/acts2005/20050016.htm
- www.opsi.gov.uk/acts/en2005/2005en16.htm
- www.opsi.gov.uk/si/si1989/Uksi_19890744_en_1.htm

Legislation pre-dating 1988 should be ordered through Her Majesty's Stationary Office at www.hmso.gov.uk

This guidance is issued by the Secretary of State and under section 4A of the Refuse Disposal (Amenity) Act 1978 and section 103(4) and (5) of the Road Traffic Regulation Act 1984. Local authorities must have regard to it when exercising their functions under sections 3 or 4 of the Refuse Disposal (Amenity) Act 1978 and sections 99 to 102 of the Road Traffic Regulation Act 1984.

Sections 11–13 and 15–17 of the Clean Neighbourhoods and Environment Act 2005 on abandoned vehicles were introduced with effect from 18 October 2005 (see S.I. 2005/2896).

Guidance relating to noise and smell

For ease of reference the legislation is covered under the following headings:
1   The offence of abandonment
2   The removal and custody of abandoned vehicles
3   The disposal of abandoned vehicles
4   Recovery of costs connected with removed vehicles
5   Powers of entry

1 The Offence of Abandonment

Section 2 of the Refuse Disposal (Amenity) Act 1978 (RDAA) makes it a criminal offence to abandon a motor vehicle[1] or anything that has formed part of a motor vehicle on any land in the open air or on any other land forming part of a highway. (It is also an offence to abandon anything else that has been brought on to land for the purposes of abandoning it).

23 A person found guilty of such an offence may be punished on summary conviction with a fine not exceeding level 4 on the standard scale (currently £2,500), or a term not exceeding three months imprisonment (possibly to be raised to 51 weeks), or both.

24 The Clean Neighbourhoods and Environment Act 2005 inserts a new section 2A into the RDAA, which allows an authorised officer of a local authority to issue a fixed penalty notice as an alternative to prosecution for the offence. The fixed penalty is set at £200, and an authorised officer must be an employee of a local authority authorised in writing by that authority to issue fixed penalty notices. *Guidance on fixed penalty notices is available separately, and it is strongly recommended that this is consulted before the provisions in these sections are made use of.*

1   In this Act, 'motor vehicle' means – 'a mechanically propelled vehicle intended or adapted for use on roads, whether or not it is in a fit state for such use, and includes any trailer intended or adapted for use as an attachment to such a vehicle, any chassis or body, with or without wheels, appearing to have formed part of such a vehicle or trailer and anything attached to such a vehicle or trailer' (s.11(1)). (Note: This includes Caravans).

2 Removal and custody of abandoned vehicles

25 This covers section 3 of the RDAA, section 99 of the Road Traffic Regulation Act 1984 and Part II of the Removal and Disposal of Vehicles Regulations 1986.

Note: As well as dealing with abandoned vehicles, the Road Traffic Regulations Act 1984 sets out powers to remove vehicles that are broken down or causing an obstruction. However, local authorities have powers to remove abandoned vehicles only. Those that are broken down or causing an obstruction should be removed by the Police (or – following the Traffic Management Act 2004 – by designated Traffic Officers).

The Duty

26 Where it appears to a local authority that a vehicle in its area is abandoned, it will be its duty to remove the vehicle. **This duty applies to all land in the open air or any land forming part of a highway.** However, in respect of such vehicles that are not on the carriageway, this duty does not apply where the costs of removing them to the nearest convenient carriageway is unreasonably high.

Appendix H

Best Value Performance Indicator 218 has required local authorities to record, since April 2005, the number of abandoned vehicles investigated within 24 hours of their being reported, and the number removed within 24 hours of the authority being legally entitled to do so. The changes to the abandoned vehicle legislation will mean that this indicator will be modified slightly to reflect the removal of the 24 hour notice. Revised guidance for this indicator can be found using the link: www.odpm.gov.uk/index.asp? id=1136106

Definition of 'abandoned'

27 There is no legal definition of 'abandoned' and this guidance does not seek to create one. Local authority officers have the freedom to use their discretion when making decisions on abandonment.

28 However, the following characteristics are generally common to abandoned vehicles and one or a combination of the following could assist a local authority officer in making a decision on abandonment.
   (a) **Untaxed, with**
   (b) **No current vehicle keeper on the Driver and Vehicle Licensing Agency's (DVLA) record**
   (c) **Stationary for a significant amount of time**
   (d) **Significantly damaged, run down or unroadworthy**
   (e) **Burned out**
   (f) **Lacking one or more of its number plates**
   (g) **Containing waste**

Category (d) could include vehicles with flat tyres, wheels removed or broken windows.

This is not an exhaustive list and a vehicle would not have to be displaying the full list to be considered abandoned.

29 However, a vehicle should not be considered abandoned solely on the grounds that it is not displaying a valid tax disc. Local authorities should use the DVLA's free on-line link to check keepership details and vehicle taxation status prior to taking action. This is available 24 hours-a-day, 365 days-a-year. DVLA can check vehicle details using either the registration number or the vehicle identity number (VIN).

The exception to the duty

30 A local authority shall not be required to remove an abandoned vehicle if the cost of removal to the nearest 'carriageway'[2] would be unreasonably high.

31 It is for the local authority to decide – on a case by case basis – whether the costs of removing a vehicle to the nearest carriageway (not to its final destination) are unreasonably high. In such cases the duty to remove the vehicle ceases to apply and the local authority is not required to take any further action. However, such circumstances should rarely occur and only when a vehicle has been abandoned on remote or hard to access areas, or where special and/or additional machinery is needed to aid removal. Local authorities have no power to charge for the costs they incur in exercising their duty, and occupiers should not therefore be charged for the removal of vehicles abandoned, for example, on hard surfaced residential areas (or associated grass verges) without their permission.

Guidance relating to noise and smell

32 Local authorities may, of course, remove abandoned vehicles at the request of the occupier in circumstances where the duty does not apply; in such cases they are free to make arrangements with the occupier to recover their costs.

2 'carriageway' means a way constituting or comprised in a highway, being a way (other than a cycle track) over which the public have a right of way for the passage of vehicles (Highways Act 1980, s.329(1)).

Notice requirements

33 Where a vehicle, which is deemed to be abandoned is on land that is occupied, the local authority must give the occupier 15 days notice that they propose to remove the vehicle. The local authority is not entitled to remove the vehicle if the occupier objects to the proposal within that period. However, if the occupier gives the local authority permission to remove the vehicle (e.g. if the vehicle was abandoned without their consent), the 15-day notice automatically lapses and the vehicle can be removed immediately.

34 The legislation does not define the term 'occupier'. The general rule is that if a term is not defined in the statute in which it is used, it is given its natural meaning. This will ultimately be for the local authority officer to decide. However the term 'occupier' has been previously defined as:
  (i) The tenant or licensee.
  (ii) Anyone who has legal possession of and control over the premises.

Full details of how this notice should be served and how a person can object can be found in regulations 8 and 9 of, and Schedule 2 to, the Removal and Disposal of Vehicles Regulations 1986. The regulations do not require the notice to be affixed to the vehicle and doing so can often lead to anti-social behaviour and arson.

35 Under a change introduced by the Clean Neighbourhoods and Environment Act, a 15-day notice is not required where a vehicle is abandoned on a 'road' (within the meaning of section 142 the Road Traffic Regulation Act 1984[3]). Section 142 defines a road as (in England and Wales) **'any length of highway or of any other road to which the public has access, and includes bridges over which a road passes.'**

This is a wide definition, and includes not only public rights of way, but also ways to which the public has access by permission of the landowner, rather than by right. It therefore includes access roads through estates that are owned by organisations such as housing associations or by the residents who live there.

It covers both the carriageway and the footpath, but a car park would not normally come within the definition of a road as its function is to enable people to leave their vehicle.

36 The Clean Neighbourhoods and Environment Act 2005 has removed the requirement to affix a 24-hour notice to a vehicle that is deemed fit for destruction. All such abandoned vehicles can now be removed immediately.

Appendix H

Manner and period during which occupier of land may object.

37 The period with which the occupier can object is 15 days from the day in which a notice is served on him.

Custody procedures

38 Local authorities can remove vehicles by towing, driving or by any other means necessary. A local authority authorised officer can also take any measures he may think necessary to enable him to remove or move it.

39 Local authorities shall deliver abandoned vehicles to the relevant disposal authorities in accordance with arrangements as may be agreed between the two and where vehicles are in the custody of a local authority, and should take all steps that are reasonably necessary for the safe custody of that vehicle.

40 No action can be taken against a local authority for damage resulting from not carrying out its abandoned vehicle duties. However, if the Secretary of State, after holding a local inquiry, is satisfied that the local authority has failed to carry out the duty, he may require the authority to take steps to carry that duty out.

3 Disposal of abandoned vehicles

41 This covers section 4 of the RDAA, sections 100 and 101 of the Road Traffic Regulations Act 1984 and part III of the Removal and Disposal of Vehicles Regulations 1986, as amended, and includes steps required to trace the owner of vehicles.

42 For certain types of abandoned vehicles, local authorities will be bound to take steps to trace the owner of a vehicle and, if successful, give them **7 days written** notice that the authority intends to dispose of the vehicle if it is not collected within that time. If the owner is traced, the local authority has the option of serving a fixed penalty as an alternative to prosecution.

43 On satisfying the local authority of ownership, the owner of a vehicle can remove the vehicle from custody after paying sums relating to removal and storage owed to the authority. Up to a year after a vehicle is sold by a local authority the owner can reclaim the sum of the proceeds of sale minus any removal, storage and disposal costs that may have accrued.

44 Local authorities have the power to dispose of abandoned vehicles that they have removed and are in their custody. **The local authority may dispose of an abandoned vehicle in 'such a manner as they think fit'.**

End of life vehicles should only be destroyed at one of the network of Authorised Treatment Facilities. Disposal can only take place in accordance with the following timescales:
    a)   In the case of a vehicle which in the opinion of the authority is in such a condition that it ought to be destroyed, at any time after its removal;
    b)   In the case of a vehicle, not falling within paragraph (a), which –
        i)   does not display a licence (i.e. tax disc) (whether current or otherwise and whether or not the vehicle is required to display a licence)

Guidance relating to noise and smell

and
  ii) does not display any registration mark (i.e. number plate) (whether indicating registration within or outside the United Kingdom).

At any time after its removal.

Note: The Clean Neighbourhoods and Environment Act 2005 has amended legislation relating to disposal of vehicles that do not display a current licence or registration mark, enabling them to be destroyed immediately after removal. A vehicle must satisfy both criteria in paragraph (b) in order to be disposed of immediately. There is no obligation to trace or inform the owner when a vehicle can be disposed of immediately under paragraphs (a) or (b).

  c) In any other case, at any time after the local authority have taken such steps as may be prescribed to find a person appearing to them to be the owner[4] of the vehicle and either –
  i) they have failed to find such a person; or
  ii) he has failed to comply with a notice served on him in the prescribed manner by the local authority requiring him to remove the vehicle within the prescribed period from their custody.

4 The owner of a vehicle is taken to also include the registered keeper as per the national record maintained by the Driver and Vehicle Licensing Agency (DVLA).

Steps to be taken to find the owners of certain vehicles

45 This is covered in detail in regulation 12 of the 1986 Regulations.

46 If the vehicle carries a GB registration mark (number plate) the local authority should find and send a written notice to the owner (having found the details from the DVLA database) declaring that their vehicle has been removed and is being held in their custody and that should they wish to reclaim it they should do so within **7 days** (in England) of the notice being served otherwise the vehicle will be disposed of.

47 The owner of a vehicle in custody can remove the vehicle after satisfying the local authority that he is the owner and paying any charges that are due.

Charges are set out in the Removal, Storage and Disposal of Vehicles (Prescribed Sums and Charges) Regulations 1989 (SI 1989/744), as amended. These can be viewed at: www.opsi.gov.uk

48 The owner of a vehicle, up to one year after the vehicle is sold by a local authority, can reclaim the value of the sale minus any charges that may be owed to the authority.

49 If more than one owner claims a vehicle that is in custody, or the proceeds of a sale of that vehicle, the local authority shall choose the one they 'think fit' and treat him as the owner for the purposes of enabling him to remove the vehicle from custody or to reclaim the costs of a sale.

50 Local authorities are empowered to provide plant and apparatus for the purpose of disposing of vehicles. Under the 'End of Life Vehicle Directive' vehicles will have to be de-polluted and disposed of at an Authorised Treatment Facility.

Appendix H

51 It is a legal requirement that information relating to the vehicle, ascertained through a DVLA check be given to the following relevant authorities following the disposal of a vehicle:
   a)   If the vehicle bore a GB registration mark, to the Secretary of State (i.e. DVLA), the chief officer of the police in whose area the vehicle was found and Hire Purchase Information Limited (HPI Ltd).
   b)   The appropriate police chief and Secretary of State where the vehicle bore a Northern Ireland registration mark.
   c)   The appropriate police chief of the local authority in which the vehicle was found, the Secretary of State, and HPI Ltd in the case of a Republic of Ireland registration mark.
   d)   The appropriate police chief in the case of a Channel Islands, Isle of Man, or other country not previously specified, registration mark.
   e)   The appropriate police chief and the local authority in whose area the vehicle was apparently abandoned (if it is not the local authority which did the disposing) if no registration mark is found or the vehicle has a foreign number plate.
   f)   Any person who appears to the local authority to be the owner of the vehicle immediately before it was disposed of.

4 Recovery of costs connected with removed vehicles

52 Before surrendering a vehicle to the owner, the local authority is entitled to charge the owner for removal and storage as prescribed in the **Removal, Storage, and Disposal of Vehicles (Prescribed Sums and Charges etc) Regulations 1989 as amended):**

www.opsi.gov.uk

53 These sums are different in London. London local authorities should refer to Section 4 of the London Local Authorities Act 2004.

www.opsi.gov.uk/acts/locact04/40001—c.htm#4

54 Any sum recoverable by virtue of this section shall be recoverable as a simple contract debt in any court or competent jurisdiction.

55 If a person is convicted of an offence under Section 2(1), the court may order him to pay any costs to the local authority for the removal, storage and disposal of the vehicle to which they are entitled.

5 Powers of Entry

56 This is covered under section 8 of the RDAA

57 Any person authorised in writing by the Secretary of State or a local authority may at any reasonable time enter any land for the purposes of investigating the need to carry out their removal of abandoned vehicle functions.

Guidance relating to noise and smell

ENVIRONMENT AGENCY TECHNICAL GUIDANCE NOTE IPPC H4 – INTEGRATED POLLUTION PREVENTION AND CONTROL (IPPC)

DRAFT HORIZONTAL GUIDANCE FOR ODOUR[1]
Part 1 – Regulation and Permitting

Preliminary Pages

Introduction

This guidance has been produced by the Environment Agency for England and Wales in collaboration with the Scottish Environment Protection Agency (SEPA) and the Northern Ireland Environment and Heritage Service (EHS). Together these are referred to as "the Agency" or "the Regulator" in this document.

This document has been released in the form of a working draft. Publication in final form will take place after wider consultation with industry, government departments, non-governmental organisations and other interested parties. Comments on this document and proposals for improved ways of working are particularly welcome during the consultation period.

The field of odour measurement and control is very wide in scope and is continually developing. There are a number of areas where it would be desirable to have more data than is currently available, however this has been balanced against the need to provide guidance at this time. The best information available to the Agency has been used in compiling this document and some aspects have been necessarily simplified. Any additional data which is supplied to the Agency as part of this consultation which is constructive and relevant to the content and purpose of this guidance note will be most welcome and will be considered in the post-consultation review.

The aim and scope of this guidance

This guidance aims to bring consistency to the overall approach to the regulation of odorous emissions by the Agency under IPPC. It brings together a number of aspects relating to the permitting and regulation of odour-generating activities and shows how these can be applied within the BAT framework of IPPC.

In England and Wales the Environment Agency will have regulatory responsibility for IPPC installations designated as A1 and Local Authorities will have responsibility for A2 activities. In Scotland and Northern Ireland there is no such distinction between A1 and A2 activities. Therefore SEPA will regulate all Part A installations in Scotland and, similarly, EHS will regulate all Part A installations in Northern Ireland. In both England & Wales and in Scotland legislation is in place to implement IPPC. In Northern Ireland the relevant legislation is in preparation and any queries should be directed to EHS.

In England and Wales guidance relating to odorous emissions from Part A2 and Part B activities can be found in the relevant Secretary of State's Process Guidance Notes or IPPC Sector Guidance Notes.

Guidance on odour control requirements which are specific to the **Waste Management Licensing** regime can be found in Reference 13. As an interim measure, the aforementioned reference should also be consulted with respect to those landfill operations which will be migrating to IPPC or PPC.

Odour Management at IPPC Intensive Livestock Installations describes the odour impact assessment requirements and odour management techniques for pig and poultry units (Reference 29).

This guidance consists of two parts:

Part 1 - this document - outlines the main considerations relating to the **Permitting and Regulation** of odour-generating activities. It is aimed primarily at the information needs of Regulators, but also contains information which will be of use to Applicants. This Note:
- describes the information relating to odorous releases that is required from the Operator for the purpose of making an application for an IPPC Permit
- describes the process of determination as it relates to odour
- provides background information relating to the human response to odours
- outlines the tools available for the assessment of the environmental impact of odour.

Part 2, "Odour Assessment & Control", is aimed equally at Regulators and Operators. It describes:
- a range of odour impact assessment methodologies
- the collection of odour samples
- the "measurement" of odour – using analytical and sensory techniques
- the control of odour by design, and by operational and management techniques
- the range of "end-of-pipe" odour abatement technologies available.

Part 2 forms a background to Part 1 and will assist in determining BAT for a given installation.

This document provides an overview of the subject. It should be used in conjunction with the appropriate Sector Guidance Note to determine BAT and appropriate Permit conditions for a specific installation, taking local factors into account.

---

[1] The Environment Agency expects to publish the final guidance documents in April 2008.

Appendix H

APPENDIX 1 - ATTRIBUTES & QUANTIFICATION OF ODOUR

APPENDIX 1 - Attributes and quantification of odorous releases

Describing odour

There are four interlinked (sensory) characteristics that are used to describe an odorous emission:

1. **Hedonic tone**
   This is a judgement of the relative pleasantness or unpleasantness of an odour made by assessors in an odour panel. The method for measuring hedonic tone is given in VDI 3882, Part 2 (Reference 18).

   Outside of a laboratory setting this parameter can be subject to substantial variation between individuals. Some odours may be pleasant when weak but unpleasant when strong, or when exposure is frequent. A list of "hedonic scores" is given in Appendix 10 – this is a ranking of everyday odours which can assist in determining relative offensiveness of different odours. (These are also referred to as "Dravnieks").

2. **Quality/Characteristics**
   This is a qualitative attribute which is expressed in terms of "descriptors", e.g. "fruity", "almond", "fishy". This can be of use when establishing an odour source from complainants' descriptions. Alternatively, it may be possible to identify key chemical components by a description of their specific odour. A list of descriptors is given in Appendix 10.

3. **Concentration**
   The "amount" of odour present in a sample of air. It can be expressed in terms of ppm, ppb or in mg m^{-3} of air for a single odorous compound. More usually a mixture of compounds are present and the concentration of the mixture can be expressed in odour units per cubic metre (ou_E).

4. **Intensity**
   Faint to strong. *Perceived intensity* – is the magnitude (strength) of *perception* of an odour. Intensity increases as concentration increases but the relationship is logarithmic. Increases or decreases in concentration of an odour do not always produce a corresponding proportional change in the odour strength as perceived by the human nose. This can be important for control where an odour has a strong intensity at low concentration as even a low residual odour may cause odour problems. The method for measuring intensity is given in VDI 3882, Part 1 (Reference 17).

Odour quality, hedonic tone and concentration influence the perceived odour intensity (and potential for annoyance), although the response to a particular odour will vary between individuals.

The most commonly used of the above attributes is concentration, but the hedonic tone (which is a consideration in "offensiveness") is also important. The following terms – detection threshold, recognition threshold and odour units - are largely used to describe concentration.

Detection threshold
The threshold of detection is the point at which the increasing concentration of an odour sample becomes strong enough to produce a first sensation of odour. As there is some variation amongst individuals, the definitive threshold value is a statistically derived value that represents an "average" response from 50% of trained observers. A list of odour threshold values is given in Appendix 10 for individual odorous compounds. Such values are expressed in ppm, ppb or in mg m^{-3} of air and are different for different substances

Mixtures of odorous compounds are treated in much the same way - the "strength" is considered in terms of the number of times that a sample of the mixture has to be diluted before it becomes just detectable to 50% of the panel of observers (this point is equivalent to one odour unit). The concentration of the original sample is expressed in terms of the number of dilutions or in odour units. Other ways of expressing the same thing are TON (Threshold Odour Number) or DTT (Dilutions To Threshold).

A number of different methodologies have been used over the years and so there can be incompatibility between the quoted threshold of detection (and hence the magnitude of one odour unit) for the same substance or mixture. This is most noticeable in the figures given for odour threshold values for single compounds in Appendix 10; they can vary by orders of magnitude between different publications, depending on the test method used. As a general rule, the more recent values are more reliable than older ones.

Guidance relating to noise and smell

APPENDIX 1 - ATTRIBUTES & QUANTIFICATION OF ODOUR

Recognition threshold

The concentration at which an odour becomes *recognisable* is not the same as the concentration at which it is detectable. Whilst the detection threshold is the point at which it can be ascertained that an odour is present, a higher concentration is usually required before the odour can be recognised, i.e. it can be categorised or described by a trained observer. The recognition threshold is generally about three times the detection threshold, although this may be higher outside of a laboratory setting.

Odour units

What is an odour unit?

An odour unit, as described above, is a measure of the concentration of a mixture of odorous compounds in a sample. It is determined by means of olfactometry (described in Part 2 of this Note).

The unit links a physiological response (the detection of odour by the nose) to exposure to a particular sample and expresses it in terms of a single number. The sample could be one of many odorous substances or mixture of substances, and so the odour unit will vary between test samples. A baseline value for the odour unit is defined in a standard method given in the draft CEN standard on olfactometry (Reference 19) using n-butanol. This is used to "calibrate" odour panel members. An odour unit as defined by the CEN standard is 1 ou_E. (European Odour Unit)

A considerable amount of work has been undertaken in the Netherlands on odour exposure and response but it should be noted when looking at earlier work that the pre-CEN odour unit differs from the European odour unit by a factor of 2 (one European odour unit equates to two Dutch odour units).

How "strong" is an odour unit?

The figures given here are generalised assumptions based upon laboratory-based experiments on perceived intensity. They are given here to provide some context to discussion of exposure to odours and guideline values.

- 1 ou_E m^{-3} is the point of detection
- 5 ou_E m^{-3} is a faint odour
- 10 ou_E m^{-3} is a distinct odour.

However, it is important to consider the following points to put this into the context of a non-laboratory situation:

- people are continuously exposed to a medley of "background" odours at different concentrations, and can often be unaware of them – individuals may develop a "tolerance", i.e. the receptors in the nose lose sensitivity and/or the mind may screen them out. In the laboratory the determination of the detection threshold is made against a background of non-odorous air and carefully controlled conditions. Normal background odours such as from traffic, grass cutting, plants, etc, ie the "normal" medley of "environmental" odours, amounts to anything from 5 to 40oum^{-3} (Reference 16, also see Section 2.5.1).
- The recognition threshold is often about three odour units, although it can be less for offensive substances and more if a person is distracted by other stimuli.
- A rapidly fluctuating odour is often more noticeable than a steady background at low concentration;

Offensiveness

Offensiveness is related to the "unpleasantness" of an odour. The perceived offensiveness of an odour will vary from person to person, and for any particular odour the offensiveness may vary according to concentration and the context within which the exposure takes place (for example, at meal times, or when feeling unwell). Historical events associated with a particular odour can also affect attitude.

The 1936 Public Health Act defined a number of "offensive" trades. Nearly all involved animal remains, or by-products. This Act has now been superseded, and many of these activities (where still undertaken) will not be A1 activities regulated by the Agency in England & Wales. They will however be regulated by SEPA in Scotland and EHS in Northern Ireland. It is still however a useful pointer to the types of compounds which could reasonably be considered to be amongst the more offensive. Sulphides and mercaptans for example may be present in the emissions from a range of other Agency-regulated processes where putrescible materials are handled or arise from anaerobic breakdown of materials.

The offensiveness of an odour will affect the concentration at which annoyance occurs and the degree of that annoyance. This is very relevant to regulation of odorous releases. Persistence and frequency of exposure are also important. Some odours will be offensive to nearly everybody, whilst others may be relatively inoffensive. However, <u>all</u> odours have the potential to be offensive and cause annoyance if exposure is frequent and at high concentration. See also Appendix 8 which gives a procedure for subjective testing that includes offensiveness as a category.

In addition to the Offensive Trades mentioned above, other sources of information which may help in determining how offensive a particular odour is, relative to other odours, are:

Appendix H

APPENDIX 1 - ATTRIBUTES & QUANTIFICATION OF ODOUR

- Hedonic Scores (also referred to as "Dravnieks").
  This is a list of <u>everyday odours,</u> based on data from the USA, which are ranked in terms of relative pleasantness and unpleasantness (see Reference 20). Less detailed information is available for industrial type odours. These are listed in Appendix 10, under the heading "hedonic scores", together with a description of how they were derived.
- UK and European odour ranking study
  A study has been undertaken in the Netherlands amongst people dealing with odour professionally (see Reference 15). This has subsequently been repeated amongst a similar group in the UK to identify any significant differences between the groups. Several hundred responses have been evaluated and work is currently underway with a much larger group.

Table A1.1 shows the ranking according to the UK results and compares these with the Dutch results and the USA hedonic (Dravnieks) scores. This shows that the rankings show good general agreement between nationalities for the purpose of determining the relative offensiveness of different <u>everyday and industrial odours</u>.

Table A1.1: Ranking table for everyday and industrial odours

Generic odours	Hedonic score Dravnieks,1994	Ranking	Ranking	Ranking	Ranking	Ranking	Ranking	Environmental odours
Descriptor	USA	UK median	UK mean	NL mean	NL mean	UK mean	UK Median	Descriptor
Roses	3.08	4	4.4	3.4	1.7	2.5	1	Bread Factory
Coffee	2.33	3	4.5	4.6	4.6	3.9	2	Coffee Roaster
Cinnamon	2.54	4	4.9	6	5.1	4.6	3	Chocolate Factory
Mowed lawn	2.14	4	4.9	6.4	8.1	7.7	6	Beer Brewery
Orange	2.86	4	5.2	5.8	9.8	8.5	8	Fragrance & Flavour Factory
Hay	1.31	7	6.9	7.5	9.4	9.2	8	Charcoal Production
Soap	0.96	8	7.8	7.3	14	10.3	9	Green Fraction composting
Brandy		9	8.8	7.8	9.8	10.5	9	Fish smoking
Raisins	1.56	8	8.8	7.9	9.6	11	10	Frozen Chips production
Beer	0.14	9	9.5	9.3	9.8	11.3	11	Sugar Factory
Cork	0.19	10	10	10.5	9.8	11.7	12	Car Paint Shop
Peanut Butter	1.99	10	10.4	11.1	12.8	12.6	12	Livestock odours
Vinegar	-1.26	14	13.3	14.8	11.2	12.7	13	Asphalt
Wet Wool	-2.28	14	14	14.1	13.2	14.2	15	Livestock Feed Factory
Paint	-0.75	15	14	14.4	13.2	14.3	14	Oil Refinery
Sauerkraut	-0.5	15	14.6	12.8	8.3	14.4	15	Car Park Bldg
Cleaning Agent	-1.69	15	14.7	12.1	12.9	16.1	17	Wastewater Treatment
Sweat	-2.53	18	16.6	17.2	15.7	17.3	18	Fat & Grease Processing
Sour Milk	-2.91	19	18	17.5		17.7	10	Creamery/milk products
Cat's Pee	-3.64	19	18.8	19.4		17.7	19	Pet Food Manufacture
						17.8	18	Brickworks (burning rubber)
					17	18.3	19	Slaughter House
					14.1	18.5	20	Landfill

The above outcome in terms of ranking has been used in Appendix 6 in considering the relative offensiveness of different odour types.

[. . .]

Guidance relating to noise and smell

APPENDIX 2 - FACTORS AFFECTING RESPONSE

APPENDIX 2 - Factors affecting human response

The aim of this Appendix

This Appendix underpins Sections 2 and 3 of this document, and aims to give an overview of:
- the terms used to describe an adverse response
- the chain of events which lead from a release of odour to annoyance
- the reasons for variation in response between individuals – why some are more sensitive than others, and
- how much odour is annoying – and how much is acceptable.

This is compiled from the best information that has been made available at the time of writing. It is acknowledged that more research on the response to odours would be desirable and this text will be reviewed should additional relevant data become available.

The characteristics of individuals which affect their response to odours

The sensitivity of the general population, and of individuals, to odours

Olfactory acuity (the ability to smell a certain odour) in the population follows a lognormal distribution. Two percent are predictably hypersensitive and 2 percent are insensitive. The insensitive range includes those who are unable to smell at all (anosmic) and those who are partially unable to smell (hyposmic). A person may be relatively insensitive to one smell and abnormally sensitive to another.

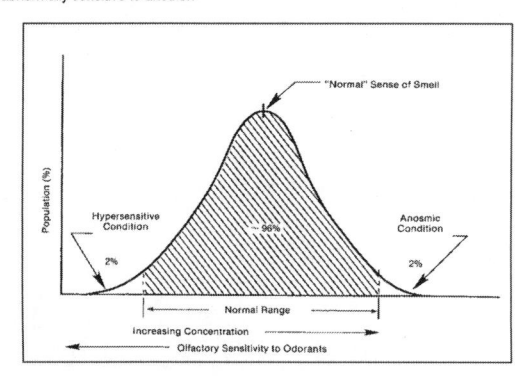

Figure A2.2: Diagram representing a frequency distribution of olfactory sensitivity

The non-specified values on the horizontal axis (e.g. ppb n-butanol at detection threshold) are typically expressed in log values (after log transformation).

Variation between individuals

There are a number of factors which affect the variation in response to odours between individuals. These can be broadly described as:
  (i) physical, and
  (ii) psychosocial

Physical:
The ability to detect odours varies with age; increasing age correlates with decreasing ability. Women tend to show a slightly heightened sensitivity compared with men at any given age. Smoking habits can affect olfactory sensitivity, with smokers being less sensitive than non-smokers.

Psychosocial:
Once a person detects an odour there are a number of factors which may affect the way in which he/she responds. These include the history of previous exposure, current state of health and perception of risks to health from emissions, economic dependence on the source, expectations, coping strategies, residential satisfaction and personality. See Reference 15 for more detailed information.

Appendix H

APPENDIX 2 - FACTORS AFFECTING RESPONSE

The following theories have been tested and confirmed by various researchers (Reference 15).

- Individuals with health complaints have a higher probability of experiencing annoyance than others at the same exposure level, (the link is the occurrence of annoyance, not a link between exposure to odour and prevalence of health complaints).
- Individuals who are anxious that odour is related to a health risk have a higher probability of experiencing odour-induced annoyance than those who are not anxious.
- Where an individual has a history of exposure and odour related annoyance it may lead to a long term heightened annoyance sensitivity, even a number of years after the high exposure has been abated.

Individuals with increased tolerance

There are three main divisions of individuals who can have an increased tolerance to particular odours (excluding those who have a decreased ability to detect odours) (Reference 15).

(i) Those who have a vested interest, i.e. individuals with an economic interest in the activity associated with the source of odour are less likely to experience annoyance than others and can tolerate a higher dose before they become annoyed.

(ii) Those who are accustomed to it – a higher dose can be tolerated better than by someone who is not accustomed to it, but not as much as those with a vested interest.

(iii) Those who either do not perceive the odour as a result of attention to other, more important, life matters or those who automatically develop a coping strategy.

Hypersensitive individuals

The most sensitive section of the population will be able to detect some odours at a concentration that lies below the threshold of detection for the majority of the population. Within this, further sub-sets can be identified:

(i) Those who have an acute awareness of an odour exposure situation: there is a difference between the level of odorant that *can* be detected and the level which *will* be detected, i.e. where the attention of the subject is focussed upon the sole objective of detecting odour as compared to someone who is distracted by other matters.

(ii) Those who have a medical condition which can produce a degree of hypersensitivity. In addition to the increased likelihood of annoyance in those with health problems, some medical conditions may increase sensitivity to odours in some individuals.

How much odour is annoying - and what is "acceptable"?

Complaints can serve as good indicators of an operational malfunction and the effectiveness of on-going control, but cannot provide a reliable estimation of the state of annoyance of a community. They are ungraded, all-or-nothing, responses and are not suitable for measuring small amounts of annoyance in a sensitive way. They only occur when a certain threshold of dissatisfaction has been exceeded.

Guideline values published by the World Health Organisation (see Appendix 5) indicate "acceptable" benchmark exposure levels, which are based on avoidance of annoyance, for a handful of single odorous substances, but equivalent benchmarks do not exist for mixtures of substances. This document, in Appendix 6, sets out a method for determining values for an acceptable ground level concentration for odorous mixtures which are tailored to particular installations, as required by the Regulations.

Dose-effect studies

The only realistic way of estimating the actual level of annoyance in a particular community resulting from exposure is by carrying out dose-effect studies locally. Such a study links the exposure (determined by mathematical modelling of emissions from the installation) to the level of annoyance (which is determined by a standardised questionnaire that disguises the purpose of the survey). Alternatively the response can be based on complaint records but this is less accurate, (Reference 15).

A number of these studies have been undertaken in Europe for different industry/process types using a common methodology and the information has been extrapolated for application to other populations with due regard for any particular local factors. Such studies are fairly limited at present, (Reference 15).

Exposure is usually quantified in terms of a frequency of occurrence over a year of hourly average concentrations above a certain limit odour concentration; e.g. 2 odour units per cubic metre ($ou_E \cdot m^{-3}$) as a 98-percentile of hourly averages of odour concentration for a year: $C_{98} = 2\ ou_E \cdot m^{-3}$. This is calculated from an estimated or measured odour emission from the source, and local meteorological ("worst case" is usually considered) and terrain input data, using an atmospheric dispersion model.

Guidance relating to noise and smell

APPENDIX 6 – INSTALLATION-SPECIFIC EXPOSURE CRITERIA

APPENDIX 6 - Installation-specific odour exposure "acceptability" criteria for mixed odours

[. . .]

Offensiveness of odour - some considerations (see also Appendix 1)
- Odours from some industry types such as chemical manufacture will vary across the sector and the nature of any odorous emission will be dependent upon the types of materials used and products manufactured.
- There may be a difference in the odour described by local residents and the odour as experienced at source. Odours can change in nature over distance (Section 3.1.4).
- For some types of process or activity there will be variation in odour intensity, and possibly character also, depending upon the stage of the cycle (e.g. livestock) or upon season (e.g. landfilling of putrescible wastes).

A list of "**hedonic scores**" is given in Appendix 10; these scores indicate *relative* "pleasantness" or "unpleasantness" based upon descriptions of what an odour smells like. These may assist in determining the relative offensiveness of an odour where it is not possible to categorise it in terms of an industry type or process.

Adjustments for local factors

In accordance with the PPC Regulations, installation-specific factors should be taken into account in determining emission limit values. These factors relate to both the technical characteristics of the plant and also local conditions:

When deriving installation-specific benchmarks for odour the following types of environmental factors should be considered:

Local conditions
- Where an odour has generated a high level of complaints over a prolonged period of time, the population may become hypersensitive to that odour. As such, even if the levels of odour were reduced to what would be an acceptable level in other areas may still give rise to justifiable complaints.
- This effect may be more pronounced in densely populated areas where the numbers of hypersensitive individuals would be greater.

There may be other relevant local factors in addition to the above. Local topography does not need to be taken into account in determining a benchmark as such, but it will need to be included in the input to a dispersion model when calculating the equivalent emission at source to meet the benchmark.

Technical aspects of the operation will need to be considered in determining BAT, but not in determining the installation-specific odour exposure criterion as the latter only considers the local receiving environment.

Where an adjustment is considered to be necessary, the indicative odour exposure criteria given in Table A6.1 can be adjusted upwards (ie less stringent) or downwards (more stringent). If the environment is considered to be insensitive the need to apply such criteria at all should be reconsidered.

As an example of an adjustment to reduce the level of exposure, the criteria given in Table A6.1 become:
  High Criterion: 1.0 ou_E m^{-3} as the 98th percentile of a year of hourly averages (from 1.5ou_E)
  Medium Criterion: 2.5 ou_E m^{-3} as the 98th percentile of a year of hourly averages (from 3ou_E)
  Low Criterion: 5.5 ou_E m^{-3} as the 98th percentile of a year of hourly averages (from 6ou_E)

The indicative odour exposure criteria are based upon a number of different populations but if an installation-specific criterion does not provide for "no reasonable cause for annoyance", for a specific population then it may need to be re-visited. However the degree to which BAT allows the installation-specific criterion to be met should be taken into account.

Other considerations
A number of other considerations may need to be taken into account.
- Where the receptors are remote from the source it would be unlikely that the Operator would need to go through the full process of calculating an installation-specific odour exposure criterion unless there is some other sensitivity, and the balance of costs and benefits would be expected to be less heavily weighted towards more expenditure when compared to a more sensitive location
- Under some circumstances where more local information is required in determining the level at which acceptability criteria should reasonably be set, it <u>may</u> be appropriate to undertake a survey of annoyance in the community. The methodology is described in Section 1 of Part 2 to this Note
- Where many complaints have been received, the calculated odour exposure criterion could be calibrated against a plot of locations of complaints around the source.

543

Appendix H

APPENDIX 6 - INSTALLATION-SPECIFIC EXPOSURE CRITERIA

Using exposure criteria - what it means in practice for regulation

The odour exposure criteria given in Table A6.1 have been derived from dose effect studies and describe ground level concentrations of different odour types which have been reported at interview by those exposed as being "acceptable" in the long term. The following description aims to explain what these criteria actually mean in terms of the odour to which those people interviewed were exposed and what it might mean where these criteria are used for planning or regulatory purposes.

What are odour exposure criteria?

Odour exposure criteria are a statistical means of linking the odour emission from a process to the impact (concentration) at ground level, in terms of probability of occurrence, taking frequency of occurrence into account. They are determined by mathematical dispersion modelling of source emission data and other local data.

They are probability-based and therefore are not absolute "limits"; they are merely indicative of an <u>average</u> concentration that is likely to occur for a specified percentage of the time over a year.

An example of the way an odour exposure criterion is set out might be:

$$x \ ou_E \ m^{-3} \text{ as a } 98^{th} \text{ percentile of a year of hourly means}$$

A 98th percentile value "x" of a year of hourly averaged concentrations means that hourly averaged concentrations will be less than or equal to x for 98% of the year. For 2% of the year, hourly averaged concentrations will be higher than or equal to x.

An odorous emission which is equivalent to the odour exposure criterion at ground level does not, therefore, mean that receptors do not experience odour at all.

Factors affecting response

The average concentration, duration and frequency of exposure (and also the type of odour) are important in determining the likely response of receptors. However the magnitude of the peaks is often the factor determining whether an acceptable situation becomes annoying to those exposed. The magnitude of the peaks may be a feature of the process (i.e. the emissions vary) or it may be related to the height and type of source (point sources can give much greater peak to mean ratios downwind than area sources) or to atmospheric conditions (see Appendix 4 – peak to mean ratios).

Using odour exposure criteria in Permitting

The aim should be to identify a criterion using this Appendix where the average exposure level is not likely to give reasonable cause for annoyance and, in the case of an existing process, the Operator should use BAT to get as close to this as possible.

There might be several reasons for excursions proving to be too frequent: (i.e. the average exposure is greater than the atmospheric dispersion modelling predicts, or the peaks are frequent and of high concentration)

- there might be particularly "difficult" topography which impairs dispersion and brings the plume to ground
- the meteorological data used may not adequately reflect the local situation, for example in a valley subject to inversion conditions, or it may be for a dissimilar area
- the emissions may be very variable and worst case has not been used in the calculations
- there may be fugitive emissions which have not been taken into account.

Other factors, such as the uncertainties in source measurement and in modelling, will also need to be considered in any assessment.

Odour exposure criteria <u>cannot be used directly as conditions</u> because compliance is impossible to determine as the measurement of odorants is very rarely possible at such dilute concentrations as are present in ambient air samples and in any case the exposure is averaged over a year.

The emission rate at source is used to calculate the actual ground level concentration. The actual ground level concentration should be compared with the desired ground level concentration which aims to give no reasonable cause for annoyance and the Operator should get as close to this level as possible using BAT. <u>It is however the emission rate which is used as a condition NOT the exposure benchmark itself.</u> Monitoring can then be undertaken to show compliance with the condition.

Continuous monitoring is possible for some odorous substances, but where mixtures are present olfactometry is usually the most suitable means of quantification, unless a suitable surrogate can be identified (see Section 2.5.2). Olfactometry is more expensive to undertake than some techniques, hence periodic monitoring – quarterly or half yearly (or according to risk) is usually specified for compliance purposes. A parallel means of ensuring that emissions are fairly constant between compliance checks is to impose a condition relating to a relevant process parameter, i.e. something that can be continuously or frequently checked and which is a surrogate for the emission concentration. This might be pH and circulation rate of scrubber liquor, or flow rate (back pressure) through a carbon bed, for example.

Guidance relating to noise and smell

APPENDIX 7 – ODOUR MANAGEMENT PLAN

APPENDIX 7 - Template for an Odour Management Plan

This Appendix should be read and interpreted in conjunction with:
- the information on application requirements given in the appropriate Sector Guidance Note and Application Forms
- Section 2.5 of this guidance, and any current requirements relating to the use of Permit conditions.

What is an Odour Management Plan?

An odour management plan is a working document for managing odour issues on the installation.

Whilst an odour management plan could be used to cover all aspects of odour management on an installation, in most cases it is likely to contain a description of foreseeable events which may lead to an increased odour impact at sensitive receptors and which are <u>outside the control of the Operator</u>, and for which it is agreed that it is not BAT to provide backup or alternative. It will also contain a description of the actions which will be taken in each case to minimise the impact.

The nature of those events and the subsequent actions should be agreed with the Agency at the time of drawing up the document. A means of recording the failure and demonstrating that the appropriate actions were indeed taken must be put in place by the Operator. It should be stressed that such events would be infrequent; if they occur regularly then BAT needs to be re-evaluated in the light of the degree of environmental impact.

In order to prepare the plan, the operator will need to consider:
- the activity which produces the odour and the point(s) of odour release (both intentional and unintentional)
- possible process or control failures or abnormal situations which could lead to an increased level of exposure
- the potential outcome of each failure scenario in respect of the likely odour impact on local sensitive receptors
- the actions which are to be taken to mitigate the effect of the odour release, and details of the persons responsible for the actions on the installation.

What should be included?

There are four main types of failure which may lead to an increase in emissions of offensive odour. These are:

- those which have potential to affect the process and the generation of odour
- those which affect the ability to abate/reduce odour
- those which affect the ability to contain odour (where releases are not normally permitted)
- those affecting dispersion between the source and sensitive receptors (for permitted release points such as vents, stacks or permitted open (area) sources.

Within all of these general headings there are causative factors which the operator could take actions to prevent and there may also be potential failure scenarios which are outside of his control and for which it has been agreed that it is not BAT to provide back-up or mitigation. For example it may not be BAT to provide a stand-by generator against the possibility of very infrequent power supply interruptions. It is the latter that will be of particular interest to the Regulator.

Examples of the issues which might need to be considered under the above headings are given in Table A7.1

A suggested template is given in Table A7.2

[. . .]

545

Appendix H

APPENDIX 10 - TABULATED INFORMATION

APPENDIX 10 - Tabulated information

Odour descriptors

Descriptors can help to establish the source of an odour and it is useful, when recording information from a complainant, to seek their description of the odour.

It should be noted that some commercial substances have odour characteristics which are very different to the pure form - for example, carbon disulphide (CS_2) has an ethereal (fruity) odour that is far more "pleasant" than the commercial grade which has a "rotten cabbage" smell resulting from the presence of impurities (mercaptans).

Table A10.1: Odour descriptors for commonly encountered compounds

Substance	Odour	Substance	Odour
Acetaldehyde	Apple, stimulant	Dimethyl sulphide	Rotten vegetable
Acetic acid	sour vinegar	Diphenylamine	Floral
Acetone	chemical/sweetish/solvent	Diphenyl sulphide	Burnt rubber
Acetonitrile	Ethereal	Ethanol	Pleasant, sweet
Acrylaldehyde	Burning fat	Ethyl acetate	Fragrant
Acrolein	Burnt sweet, pungent	Ethyl acrylate	Hot plastic, earthy
Acrylonitrile	Onion, garlic, pungent	Ethylbenzene	Aromatic
Aldehydes C9	Floral, waxy	Ethyl mercaptan	Garlic/onion, sewer, decayed cabbage, earthy
Aldehydes C10	Orange peel	Formaldehyde	Disinfectant, hay/straw-like, pungent
Allyl alcohol	Pungent, mustard like	Furfuryl alcohol	Ethereal
Allyl chloride	Garlic onion pungent	n-Hexane	Solvent
Amines	Fishy, pungent	Hydrogen sulphide	Rotten eggs
Ammonia	Sharp, pungent odour	Indole	Excreta
Aniline	Pungent	Iodoform	Antiseptic
Benzene	Solvent	Methanol	Medicinal, sweet
Benzaldehyde	Bitter almonds	Methyl ethyl ketone	Sweet
Benzyl acetate	Floral (jasmine), fruity	Methyl isobutyl ketone	Sweet
Benzyl chloride	Solvent	Methyl mercaptan	Skunk, sewer, rotten cabbage
Bromine	Bleach, pungent	Methyl methacrylate	Pungent, sulphide like
Sec-Butyl acetate	Fruity	Methyl sulphide	Decayed vegetables
Butyric acid	Sweat, body odour	Naphthalene	Moth balls
Camphor	Medicinal	Nitrobenzene	Bitter almonds
Caprylic acid	Animal like	Phenol	Sweet, tarry odour, carbolic acid
Carbon disulphide	Rotten vegetable	Pinenes	Resinous, woody, pine-like
Chlorine	Irritating, bleach, pungent	Propyl mercaptan	Skunk
Chlorobenzene	Moth balls	Putrescine	Decaying flesh
2-Chloroethanol	Faint, ethereal	Pyridine	Nauseating, burnt
Chloroform	Sweet	Skatole	Excreta, faecal odour
Chlorophenol	Medicinal	Styrene	Penetrating, rubbery, plastic
p-Cresol	Tar-like, pungent	Sulphur dioxide	Pungent, irritating odour
Cyclohexane	Sweetish when pure, pungent when contaminated	Thiocresol	Rancid, skunklike odour
Cyclohexanol	Camphor, methanol	Toluene	Floral, pungent, moth balls
Cyclohexanone	Acetone-like	Trichloroethylene	Solventy
Diamines	Rotten flesh	Triethylamine	Fishy, pungent
1,1-Dichloroethane	Ether-like	Valeric acid	Sweat, body odour, cheese
1,2-Dichloroethylene	Chloroform-like	Vinyl chloride	Faintly sweet
Diethyl ether	Pungent	Xylene	Aromatic, sweet
Dimethylacetamide	Amine, burnt, oily		

References The Royal Society of Chemistry, "Chemical Safety Data Sheets" Volumes 1 and 5.
Knowlton J and Pearce S, "Handbook of Cosmetic Science and Technology".
Leonardos G, Kendall D and Bernard N, "Odour threshold determinations of 53 odorant chemicals" JAPCA Volume 19, No 2, 1969.
Turk, "Atmospheric gases and vapors" Annals New York Academy of Sciences.

Guidance relating to noise and smell

APPENDIX 10 - TABULATED INFORMATION

Hedonic Scores (1)

This table is continued on the following page.

These scores are also referred to as "Dravnieks" and are derived from laboratory-based experiments. They give an indication of the relative pleasantness or unpleasantness of one odour when compared to another. When considering odours from industrial activities, the descriptors given in the previous table can be used. Alternatively refer to the European odour ranking survey results in Appendix 2.

Use of these scores

The higher the positive "score", the more "pleasant" the odour descriptor, and the greater the negative figure the more "unpleasant" the odour descriptor. The terms pleasant and unpleasant are used to indicate relative response rather than a sign of a positive or negative level of satisfaction. Zero cannot be considered to be neutral.

Table A10.2: Hedonic scores (1)

Description	Hedonic Score	Description	Hedonic Score	Description	Hedonic Score
Cadaverous (dead animal)	-3.75	Fishy	-1.98	Wet paper	-0.94
Putrid, foul, decayed	-3.74	Musty, earthy, mouldy	-1.94	Medicinal	-0.89
Sewer odour	-3.68	Sooty	-1.69	Chalky	-0.85
Cat urine	-3.64	Cleaning fluid	-1.69	Varnish	-0.85
Faecal (like manure)	-3.36	Kerosene	-1.67	Nail polish remover	-0.81
Sickening (vomit)	-3.34	Blood, raw meat	-1.64	Paint	-0.75
Urine	-3.34	Chemical	-1.64	Turpentine (pine oil)	-0.73
Rancid	-3.15	Tar	-1.63	Kippery-smoked fish	-0.69
Burnt rubber	-3.01	Disinfectant, carbolic	-1.60	Fresh tobacco smoke	-0.66
Sour milk	-2.91	Ether, anaesthetic	-1.54	Sauerkraut	-0.60
Stale tobacco smoke	-2.83	Burn, smoky	-1.53	Camphor	-0.55
Fermented (rotten) fruit	-2.76	Burnt paper	-1.47	Cardboard	-0.54
Dirty linen	-2.55	Oily, fatty	-1.41	Alcoholic	-0.47
Sweaty	-2.53	Bitter	-1.38	Crushed weeds	-0.21
Ammonia	-2.47	Creosote	-1.35	Garlic, onion	-0.17
Sulphurous	-2.45	Sour, vinegar	-1.26	Rope	-0.16
Sharp, pungent, acid	-2.34	Mothballs	-1.25	Beery	-0.14
Household gas	-2.30	Gasoline, solvent	-1.16	Burnt candle	-0.08
Wet wool, wet dog	-2.28	Animal	-1.13	Yeasty	-0.07
Mouse-like	-2.20	Seminal, sperm-like	-1.04	Dry, powdery	-0.07
Burnt milk	-2.19	New rubber	-0.96		
Stale	-2.04	Metallic	-0.94		

IPPC

Appendix H

APPENDIX 10 - TABULATED INFORMATION

Hedonic Scores (2)

Table A10.2: Hedonic scores (2)

Description	Hedonic Score	Description	Hedonic Score	Description	Hedonic Score
Cork	0.19	Crushed grass	1.34	Maple syrup	2.26
Black pepper	0.19	Celery	1.36	Pear	2.26
Musky	0.21	Green pepper	1.39	Caramel	2.32
Raw potato	0.26	Tea leaves	1.40	Coffee	2.33
Eggy (fresh eggs)	0.45	Aromatic	1.41	Meaty (cooked, good)	2.34
Mushroom	0.52	Raisins	1.56	Melon	2.41
Beany	0.54	Cooked vegetables	1.58	Popcorn	2.47
Geranium leaves	0.57	Clove	1.67	Minty, peppermint	2.50
Grainy (as grain)	0.63	Nutty	1.92	Lemon	2.50
Dill	0.87	Coconut	1.93	Fragrant	2.52
Woody, resinous	0.94	Grapefruit	1.95	Fried chicken	2.53
Soapy	0.96	Perfumery	1.96	Cinnamon	2.54
Laurel leaves	0.97	Peanut butter	1.99	Cherry	2.55
Eucalyptus	0.99	Spicy	1.99	Vanilla	2.57
Molasses	1.00	Banana	2.00	Pineapple	2.59
Incense	1.01	Almond	2.01	Apple	2.61
Malty	1.05	Sweet	2.03	Peach	2.67
Caraway	1.06	Buttery, fresh butter	2.04	Violets	2.68
Soupy	1.13	Grape juice	2.07	Fruity, citrus	2.72
Bark, birch bark	1.18	Honey	2.08	Chocolate	2.78
Anise (liquorice)	1.21	Cedarwood	2.11	Floral	2.79
Oak wood, cognac	1.23	Herbal, green, cut grass	2.14	Orange	2.86
Seasoning (for meat)	1.27	Cologne	2.16	Strawberry	2.93
Leather	1.30	Fresh green vegetables	2.19	Rose	3.08
Raw cucumber	1.30	Fruity, other than citrus	2.23	Bakery (fresh bread)	3.53
Hay	1.31	Lavender	2.25		

References
(Reference 20) Dravnieks A, Masurat T, Lamm R A, "Hedonics of Odours and Odour Descriptors": in *Journal of the Air Pollution Control Association,* July 1984, Vol. 34 No. 7, pp 752-755

(Reference 13) Guidance for the Regulation of Odour at Waste Management Facilities under the Waste Management Licensing Regulations, July 2001, Version 2.3

Guidance relating to noise and smell

APPENDIX 10 - TABULATED INFORMATION

Odour threshold values

The quality of odour detection threshold data can be poor. *"Odour measurement and control - an update"* (Woodfield and Hall 1994) (Reference 26) differentiates between chemicals for which threshold values have been determined by a recognised test method (dynamic dilution olfactometry), and those chemicals where threshold values have not been determined by a recognised test method. The data quality for compounds determined by recognised methods are more likely to approach the "true value". The table below contains those odour threshold values which have been determined using recognised test methodologies.

Table A10.3: Odour threshold values of common odorants

Compound	mg m^{-3}	ppm	Compound	mg m^{-3}	ppm
Acetic acid	0.043	0.016	2-Hydroxyethyl acetate	0.527	0.114
Acetic anhydride	0.0013	0.00029	Light fuel oil	0.053	
Acetone	13.9	4.58	3-Methylbutanal	0.0016	0.0004
Acrylic acid	0.0013	0.0004	2-Methyl-1-butanol	0.16	0.041
Amyl acetate	0.95	0.163	Methyldithiomethane	0.0011	0.00026
iso Amyl acetate	0.022	0.0038	2-Methyl 5-ethyl pyridine	0.032	0.006
Benzene	32.5	8.65	Methyl methacrylate	0.38	0.085
1,3-Butadiene	1.1	0.455	3-Methoxybutyl acetate	0.044	0.007
1-Butanol	0.09	0.03	1-Methoxypropan-2-ol	0.0122	0.003
2-Butanol	3.3	1	1-Methoxy-2-propylacetate	0.0075	0.0014
2-Butanone (MEK)	0.87	0.27	2-Methyl-1-pentanol	0.096	0.021
Butoxybutane	0.03	0.005	2-Methyl pentaldehyde	0.09	0.02
2-Butoxyethanol	0.0051	0.00097	4-Methyl-2-pentanone (MIBK)	0.54	0.121
2-Butoxyethyl acetate	0.045	0.0063	2-Methyl-2-propanol	71	21.46
Butoxypropanol	0.191	0.0324	α-Methyl styrene	0.021	0.003
Butyl acetate	0.047	0.0066	1-Nitropropane	28.2	7.09
2-(2-Butoxyethocy)ethanol	0.0092	0.0013	1-Octene	0.33	0.066
2,2-butoxyethoxyethyl acetate	0.015	0.0016	2-Octene	0.5	0.1
Carbon tetrachloride	280	40.73	2-Octyne	0.03	0.006
Carbon sulphide	0.0275	0.0102	2,4-Pentanedione	0.045	0.01
m-Cresol	0.0013	0.0003	1-Pentanol	0.02	0.0051
o-Cresol	0.0028	0.0005	Petroleum naptha	0.2	
p-Cresol	0.0029	0.0006	Phenyl ether	0.0021	0.0003
Cyclohexane	315	83.8	2-Picoline	0.014	0.0034
Cyclohexanone	0.083	0.019	Propanal	0.014	0.0054
Dichloromethane	3.42	0.912	2-Propanol	1.185	0.442
Diesel	0.06		2-Propen-1-ol	1.2	0.47
Dimethyl adipate	7.101	0.913	iso Propylamine	0.158	0.06
Dimethyl glutarate	1.212	0.169	Propylbenzene	0.048	0.009
Dimethyl succinate	0.992	0.152	Propylene-n-butylether	0.206	0.01
1,4-Dioxane	30.6	7.78	Propyl ether	0.024	0.0053
1,3-Dioxolane	56.3	17.02	Styrene	0.16	0.0344
Diphenylmethane	0.41	0.55	1,1,2,2-Tetrachloroethane	1.6	0.21
Ethoxypropanol	0.161	0.035	Toluene	0.644	0.16
Ethoxypropyl acetate	0.0052	0.0008	Trichloroethylene	8	1.36
Ethyl acetate	2.41	0.61	Trimethylamine	0.0026	0.001
Ethyl alcohol	0.28	0.136	Xylene (mixed)	0.078	0.016
2-Ethyl-1-butanol	0.07	0.015	2,3 Xylenol	0.0037	0.0007
2-Ethyl-1-hexanol	0.5	0.086	2,4 Xylenol	0.064	0.0117
2-Ethylhexyl acrylate	0.6	0.073			
2-Furaldehyde	0.25	0.058			
1-Hexanol	0.005	0.0011			
Hydrogen sulphide	0.00076	0.0005			

Other sources of threshold values

Compilation of odour threshold values in air and water, Central Institute for Nutrition and Food Research, TNO, Netherlands, June 1997. Editors: van Gembert L J; Nettenbrejer A H.

Compilation of odour and taste threshold values data, American Society for Testing and Materials, ASTM Data Series DS 48A. Editor: Fazzalari F A.

The documents listed above contain odour threshold values for a much wider range of substances. The fact that a document is listed does not necessarily mean that the values given are consistent with other documents and it is advisable to cross-check values with more than one source as there can be considerable variation. This list is not exhaustive and other published values exist.

IPPC

[. . .]

INDEX

Abandoned shopping trolleys
  litter, 9.58–9.59
Abandoned vehicles
  disposal, 9.68–9.70
Abandonment of appeals
  costs in Crown Court, 7.27–7.28
  costs in magistrates' court, 7.189
Abatement actions
  litter, 9.53
Abatement notices
  amendment, 3.56–3.58
  best practicable means, 3.45–3.52
  breach of, proceedings for
    and see Criminal proceedings
    appeals, 5.1116–5.125
    availability disclosure, 5.48–5.67
    categories of offence, 5.19–5.25
    conduct of trial, 5.68–5.102
    elements of offence, 5.03–5.04
    evidence, 5.39–5.47
    information, 5.26–5.38
    introduction, 5.01–5.02
    nature of offence, 5.05–5.18
    Newton procedure, 5.115
    sentencing, 5.103–5.114
  challenges against
    and see Challenging an abatement notice
    appeal, by, 4.05–4.151
    complaint to Ombudsman, by, 4.146–4.151
    introduction, 4.03–4.04
    judicial review, by, 4.135–4.145
  drafting
    formalities, 3.08
    guidance, 3.31–3.44
    introduction, 3.01–3.02
    principle, 3.04–3.07
    requirements, 3.09–3.22
  effect of breach
    generally, 2.33–2.43
    local authorities actions, 2.11–2.20
  formalities, 3.08
  guidance
    compliance with requirements of third party, 3.34
    description of nuisance, 3.24–3.25
    introduction, 3.23
    prohibition of recurrence, 3.24
    specifying steps or works required, 3.25–3.30
    suspension of notice, 3.35–3.37

Abatement notices – *contd*
  Human Rights Act 1998, and
    generally, 3.38–3.42
    practical advice, 3.43–3.44
  issue
    local authorities' powers, 2.32–2.49
    procedure, 3.03
  letters before notice, 3.53
  local authorities' powers, and
    effect of breach, 2.47–2.47
    generally, 2.32–2.43
    Ombudsman's decisions, 2.46
    power to restrict nuisance, 2.44–2.45
  noise from street, 3.74
  quashing, 3.56–3.58
  recipients
    act, default or sufferance, 3.65
    default of structural character, 3.68–3.73
    exceptions, 3.64
    introduction, 3.63
    owner, 3.66–3.67
  records of offers, 3.54–3.55
  requirements
    background, 3.10–3.12
    current position, 3.13–3.17
    introduction, 3.09
    restrictions, 3.18–3.21
    specified works, 3.22
  service, 3.77–3.80
  statutory authority, 3.59–3.62
  street noise, 3.74
  suspension, 2.53
  unlawful shifting of burden, 3.75
  variation, 2.83–2.85
  withdrawal, 2.63–2.85, 3.81
Accumulations
  best practicable means
    introduction, 1.49
    meaning, 1.83–1.94
  meaning, 1.46–1.50
  prejudicial to health, 1.03–1.05
Acts outside area
  local authorities' powers, and, 2.80
Adjournment of appeals
  costs in Crown Court, 7.28
  costs in magistrates' court, 7.17
Air pollution control (APC)
  enforcement, 10.04
  introduction, 10.03
Aircraft noise
  introduction, 10.34–10.35

551

Index

Amendment of grounds
  appeals against abatement notices,
    4.78–4.82
Amenity of area, land adversely affecting
  affecting amenity of area, 9.08–9.09
  appeals
    generally, 9.04
    grounds, 9.05
    suspension of notice, 9.06
  challenging, 9.14
  discharge, 9.13
  failure to comply, 9.03
  grounds of appeal
    generally, 9.05
    ordinary course of events, 9.15–9.17
  introduction, 9.01
  legality, 9.14
  local authority works, 9.07
  personal nature, 9.10–9.12
Animal establishments
  local authorities' powers, 9.94
Animals
  best practicable means
    introduction, 1.57, 1.59
    meaning, 1.83–1.94
  meaning, 1.50–1.59
  local authorities' powers, 9.94
  prejudicial to health, 1.04–1.05
Appeals
  abatement notice, against
    and see below
    appeals from, 4.124–4.133
    burden of proof, 4.105–4.107
    conduct of trial, 4.99–4.103
    courts' powers, 4.110–4.123
    date of facts, 4.108–4.109
    evidence, 4.93–4.98
    form, 4.08–4.11
    generally, 4.05–4.07
    grounds, 4.35–4.87
    pre-trial procedure, 4.88–4.92
    standard of proof, 4.104
    time limits, 4.12–4.33
  breach of abatement notice, against
    conviction for
      case stated, by way of, 5.122–5.125
      conviction, against, 5.117–5.121
      introduction, 5.116
  construction works noise
    generally, 9.114–9.115
    suspension of notices, 9.116–9.118
  fly tipping, 9.31–9.38
  housing repair notices, 9.26–9.29
  s 215 TCPA 1990 notice, against
    generally, 9.04
    grounds, 9.05
    suspension of notice, 9.06
Appeals against abatement notices
  amendment of grounds, 4.78–4.82
  appeals from
    introduction, 4.124–4.125

Appeals against abatement notices – *contd*
  appeals from – *contd*
    Human Rights Act 1998, and, 4.126–4.133
    preclusive provision, 4.134
  burden of proof, 4.105–4.107
  complaints
    applicants, 4.05
    form, 4.08–4.11
    grounds, 4.35–4.87
    nature, 4.07
    service, 4.34
    time limits, 4.12–4.33
  conduct of trial, 4.99–4.103
  costs
    Crown Court, in, 7.22–7.30
    magistrates' court, in, 7.03–7.21
  cost orders, 7.21
  costs in Crown Court
    abandonment of appeal, 7.27–7.28
    adjournments, 7.29
    interim hearings, 7.29
    introduction, 7.22
    proceedings in Crown Court, of, 7.23
    proceedings in magistrates' court, of,
      7.24–7.26
    withdrawal of notice, 7.29
  costs in magistrates' court
    abandonment of appeal, 7.18
    adjournments, 7.17
    discretion, 7.05
    interim hearings, 7.16–7.17
    introduction, 7.01–7.02
    outright success of party, 7.09
    partial success of party, 7.10–7.15
    withdrawal of notice, 7.19–7.20
  courts' powers
    generally, 4.110–4.117
    Human Rights Act 1998, and, 4.06
    third parties, against, 4.118–4.123
  date of facts, 4.108–4.109
  discretion
    extension of time, 4.13–4.16
  evidence
    burden of proof, 4.105–4.107
    disclosure, 4.88–4.89
    experts' reports, 4.92
    generally, 4.93–4.98
    hearsay, 4.93
    procedure at trial, 4.99–4.103
    relevant date, 4.108–4.109
    standard of proof, 4.104
  extension of time
    generally, 4.13–4.16
    Human Rights Act 1998, and, 4.17–4.22
  form of complaints
    oral complaint, 4.09
    written complaint, 4.08
  generally, 4.05–4.07
  grounds
    additional recipient to be served,
      4.72–4.77

Index

Appeals against abatement notices – *contd*
grounds – *contd*
  amendment, 4.78–4.82
  best practicable means used, 4.59–4.68
  defective notice, 4.37–4.41
  error in notice, 4.37–4.41
  introduction, 4.35
  refusal to accept alternative scheme, 4.42–4.49
  requirements are unreasonable, 4.50–4.52
  requirements more onerous than under statutory conditions, 4.69
  time for compliance is insufficient, 4.53–4.58
  unjustified issue of notice, 4.36
  wrong recipient, 4.70–4.77
Human Rights Act 1998, and
  appeals from magistrates' court, 4.126–4.133
  extension of time, 4.17–4.22
  introduction, 4.01
  listing of appeals, 4.126–4.133
issue of summons, 4.10–4.11
noise nuisances, and, 4.69
non-suspended notice, and, 4.83–4.87
order of speeches, 4.99–4.103
pre-trial procedure
  checklist, 4.90
  disclosure of evidence, 4.88–4.89
  evidence, 4.93–4.98
  experts' reports, 4.92
  particulars of appeal, 4.91
proof
  burden, 4.105–4.107
  standard, 4.104
service, 4.34
standard of proof, 4.104
third parties, orders against, 4.118–4.123
time limits
  calculation, 4.23–4.33
  excluded days, 4.30–4.33
  extension, 4.13–4.16
  Human Rights Act 1998, and, 4.17–4.22
  introduction, 4.12
  starting date, 4.23–4.24
  termination date, 4.25–4.29
trial procedure
  evidence, 4.93–4.98
  order of speeches, 4.99–4.103
Audible intruder alarms
generally, 9.140
Availability disclosure
breach of abatement notice, 5.48–5.64

BATNEEC
introduction, 10.03
Best practicable means
abatement notices, and, 3.51–3.58
accumulations, 1.49

Best practicable means – *contd*
animals, 1.57, 1.59
breach of abatement notice, and, 5.95–5.96
contaminated land exception, 1.95–1.104
deposits, 1.49
disused mines 1.75
ditches, 1.72
domestic water supply, 1.71
dust from business premises, 1.44
effluvia from business premises, 1.44
light pollution, 1.63
noise from premises, 1.67
noise from vehicles in street, 1.68
ponds, 1.72
quarries, 1.77
sheds, 1.75
smells from business premises, 1.44
smoke emissions, 1.44
state of premises, 1.35
steam from premises, 1.44
tents, 1.75
test
  compatibility with legal duty, 1.90–1.91
  compatibility with safety, 1.92–1.94
  introduction, 1.83–1.89
  local conditions and circumstances, 1.86–1.87
  means to be employed, 1.88–1.89
vans, 1.75
watercourses, 1.72
water supply, 1.71
BPEO
introduction, 10.03
Breach of abatement notice, proceedings for
appeals
  case stated, by way of, 5.122–5.125
  conviction, against, 5.117–5.121
  introduction, 5.116
availability disclosure, 5.48–5.67
best practicable means, 5.95–5.96
burden of proof
  defence case, 5.87–5.96
  prosecution case, 5.75–5.76
categories of offence, 5.19–5.25
conduct of trial
  defence case, 5.87–5.102
  introduction, 5.68
  no case to answer, submission of, 5.85–5.86
  prosecution case, 5.69–5.84
costs
  Crown Court, in, 7.37–7.46
  magistrates' court, in, 7.30–7.34
costs in Crown Court
  abandonment of appeal, 7.41
  failure of appeal, 7.38–7.40
  introduction, 7.37
  partially successful appeal, 7.46
  successful appeal, 7.42–7.44

Index

Breach of abatement notice, proceedings for – *contd*
  costs in magistrates' court
    abandonment of prosecution, 7.31–7.33
    outright success of defence, 7.31–7.33
    outright success of prosecution, 7.30
    partial success, 7.35
  defective service of abatement notice
    preconditions, 5.10–5.18
    requirement, 5.06–5.09
  defences
    best practicable means, 5.95–5.96
    invalidity of abatement notice, 5.98–5.102
    miscellaneous statutory defences, 5.97
    reasonable excuse, 5.78–5.84
    standard of proof, 5.90–5.94
  elements of offence
    failure to serve abatement notice, 5.06–5.18
    introduction, 5.03–5.04
  evidence
    advance information, 5.42–5.47
    caution, under, 5.58–5.59
    expert evidence, 5.52–5.53
    generally, 5.39–5.41
    information upon which prosecution not rely, 5.48–5.51
    PACE 1984, and, 5.55–5.59
    right against self-incrimination, 5.60–5.64
    unfair evidence, 5.65–5.67
  extension of time, 5.31
  failure to serve abatement notice
    preconditions, 5.10–5.18
    requirement, 5.06–5.09
  Human Rights Act 1998, and, 5.02
  information
    amendment, 5.34–5.35
    date of breach of notice, 5.38
    discretion to refuse to try, 5.36–5.37
    form, 5.26–5.30
    time limits, 5.31–5.33
  introduction, 5.01–5.02
  judicial review, 5.123–5.125, 5.130
  nature of offence
    discretion to prosecute, 5.23–5.25
    failure to serve abatement notice, 5.06–5.18
    identification of defendant, 5.22
    introduction, 5.05
  Newton procedure, 5.115
  proof of offence
    introduction, 5.75
    reasonable excuse, 5.78–5.84
    standard of proof, 5.76
  prosecution case
    generally, 5.69–5.86
    proof of offence, 5.75–5.77
  reasonable excuse, 5.78–5.84

Breach of abatement notice, proceedings for – *contd*
  sentencing
    corporate bodies, 5.114
    generally, 5.103–5.113
  standard of proof
    defence case, 5.87–5.89
    prosecution case, 5.77
  time limits
    date of breach of notice, 5.38
    extension, 5.31
    generally, 5.31–5.33
Breach of notices and orders
  abatement notices
    and see above
    appeals, 5.116–5.130
    availability disclosure, 5.48–5.67
    categories of offence, 5.19–5.25
    conduct of trial, 5.68–5.102
    elements of offence, 5.03–5.04
    evidence, 5.39–5.47
    information, 5.26–5.38
    introduction, 5.01–5.02
    nature of offence, 5.05–5.18
    Newton procedure, 5.115
    sentencing, 5.103–5.114
  housing repair notices, 9.30
  nuisance orders
    and see below
    costs in Crown Court, 7.38
    costs in magistrates' court, 7.24–7.26
    generally, 6.81–6.82
  s 215 TCPA 1990 notice, 9.02
Breach of nuisance order, proceedings for
  costs in Crown Court
    abandonment of appeal, 7.41
    failure of appeal, 7.38–7.40
    introduction, 7.37
    partially successful appeal, 7.45–7.46
    successful appeal, 7.42–7.44
  costs in magistrates' court
    abandonment of prosecution, 7.31–7.34
    outright success of defence, 7.31–7.34
    outright success of prosecution, 7.30
    partial success, 7.35
  generally, 6.81–6.82
British Standards (BS)
  industrial noises, 8.40–8.45
  quantification of sound levels, 8.15–8.16
Burden of proof
  appeals against abatement notices, 4.105–4.107
  breach of abatement notice
    defence case, 5.90–5.94
    prosecution case, 5.75
  complaints by individuals, 6.59–6.60
Burglar alarms
  generally, 9.140
Buses
  noise from, 1.68

Index

Business premises
definition, 1.80–1.82

Categories of statutory nuisance
accumulations, 1.46–1.50
animals, 1.51–1.58
deposits, 1.46–1.50
effluvia, 1.39–1.45
fumes, 1.36–1.38
gases, 1.36–1.38
introduction, 1.01
light pollution 1.61
noise, 1.56–1.57
relevant meanings, 1.78–1.81
smoke emissions, 1.34–1.35
state of premises, 1.26–1.32

Cesspools
local authorities' powers, 9.78–9.80

Challenging notices and orders
abatement notices
and see below
appeal, by, 4.05–4.151
complaint to Ombudsman, by, 4.145–4.151
introduction, 4.01–4.02
judicial review, by, 4.134–4.144
compensation orders, 7.105–7.106
costs orders
Crown Court, made in, 7.88
magistrates' court, made in, 7.87
s 215 TCPA 1990 notice, 9.14

Challenging an abatement notice
appeal, by
and see Appeals against abatement notices
appeals from, 4.124–4.133
burden of proof, 4.105–4.107
conduct of trial, 4.99–4.103
courts' powers, 4.110–4.123
date of facts, 4.108–4.109
evidence, 4.93–4.98
form, 4.08–4.11
generally, 4.05–4.07
grounds, 4.35–4.87
pre-trial procedure, 4.88–4.92
standard of proof, 4.104
time limits, 4.12–4.33
complaint to Ombudsman, by
injustice, 4.159–4.151
introduction, 4.145–4.147
maladministration, 4.149
introduction, 4.01–4.02
judicial review, by
recipient, by, 4.135–4.144
third parties, by, 4.144–4.145
recipients, by
appeal, by, 4.05–4.151
complaint to Ombudsman, by, 4.146–4.151
introduction, 4.01
judicial review, by, 4.135–4.145

Challenging an abatement notice – *contd*
third parties, by, 4.04

Clean air
introduction, 10.28–10.29
relationship with EPA, 10.30–10.33

Clearance of litter
control notices, 9.56–9.58
courts, yards and passages, 9.57
generally, 9.50–9.53

Closets, defective
local authorities' powers, 9.73–9.77

Coaches
noise from, 1.68

Codes of Practice
noise, 9.141–9.142

Compensation in criminal proceedings
amount, 7.94
beneficiaries, 7.90–7.91
challenging award, 7.105–7.106
deduction from civil claim, 7.107
discretion, 7.95–7.98
evidence, 7.99–7.103
introduction, 7.89
procedure, 7.101–7.103
relevant harm, 7.92–7.94
variation, 7.108

Complaints against abatement notices
applicants, 4.05
form
oral complaint, 4.09
written complaint, 4.08
grounds of appeal
additional recipient to be served, 4.72–4.77
amendment, 4.78–4.82
best practicable means used, 4.59–4.68
defective notice, 4.37–4.41
error in notice, 4.37–4.41
introduction, 4.35
refusal to accept alternative scheme, 4.42–4.49
requirements are unreasonable, 4.50–4.52
requirements more onerous than under statutory conditions, 4.69
time for compliance is insufficient, 4.53–4.58
unjustified issue of notice, 4.36
wrong recipient, 4.70–4.77
nature, 4.07
service, 4.34
time limits
calculation, 4.23–4.33
excluded days, 4.30–4.33
extension, 4.13–4.16
Human Rights Act 1998, and, 4.17–4.22
introduction, 4.12
starting date, 4.23–4.24
termination date, 4.25–4.29

555

Index

Complaints by individuals
aggrieved persons, 6.03–6.04
applying for summons
  introduction, 6.38
  laying of information, 6.38–6.53
burden of proof, 6.59–6.60
commencement of proceedings
  giving notice, 6.05–6.37
  introduction, 6.05
  laying of information, 6.38–6.53
conduct of hearing, 6.61–6.65
costs
  discretion, 7.54–7.55
  introduction, 6.81–6.82, 7.47
  liability of private prosecutor, 7.58
  local authority, order against, 7.56
  statutory right, 7.48–7.53
  successful defendants, 7.57
court's powers
  fines, 6.78
  introduction, 6.71–6.72
  local authority, order against, 6.79–6.80
  nuisance order, 6.73–6.77
defences, 6.66–6.70
elements to be proved
  existence of nuisance at hearing, 6.54
  existence of nuisance at laying of information, 6.55–6.58
  person aggrieved, 6.56–6.58
existence of nuisance, 6.14–6.19
fines
  amount, 6.72
  introduction, 6.71–6.72
giving notice of intention to start proceedings
  content of notice, 6.23–6.32
  introduction, 6.06
  local authority, to, 6.35–6.37
  period of notice, 6.20–6.22
  recipients of notice, 6.07–6.19
  service of notice, 6.33–6.34
  whereabouts of defendant unknown, when, 6.35–6.37
introduction, 6.01–6.02
laying of information
  defective information, 6.51–6.53
  form of information, 6.50–6.53
  introduction, 6.38–6.41
  supporting material, 6.44–6.49
  time limits, 6.42–6.43
local authority, order against, 6.79–6.80
nuisance order
  introduction, 6.70
  proceedings for breach, 6.83–6.84
  terms, 6.73–6.77
penalties
  fines, 6.78
  introduction, 6.71–6.72
  local authority, order against, 6.79–6.80
  nuisance order, 6.73–6.77

Complaints by individuals – *contd*
procedure at hearing
  burden of proof, 6.59–6.60
  elements to be proved, 6.54–6.58
  generally, 6.61–6.65
recipients of notice
  every possible defendant, 6.11–6.13
  existence of nuisance, 6.14–6.19
  general rule, 6.07–6.10
standard of proof, 6.59–6.60
Complaints to Ombudsman
injustice, 4.150–4.151
introduction, 4.146–4.148
maladministration, 4.149
Conduct of trial
appeals against abatement notices, 4.99–4.103
breach of abatement notice
  defence case, 5.87–5.102
  introduction, 5.68
  no case to answer, submission of, 5.85–5.86
  prosecution case, 5.69–5.84
complaints by individuals, 6.61–6.65
Construction works, noise from
appeals
  generally, 9.114–9.115
  suspension of notices, 9.116–9.118
criminal offences, 9.120
effect on other proceedings, 9.119
introduction, 9.109–9.113
prior consent
  effect on other proceedings, 9.124
  generally, 9.121
Consultation
local authorities' powers, and, 2.90–2.92
Contaminated land
background, 10.12
generally, 1.95–1.104
statutory provisions, 10.13–10.17
Control notices
litter, 9.55–9.56
Controlled waste
fly tipping, 9.33
Convention
considerations, and, 1.17
cost orders, 7.21
Costs
appeals against abatement notices
  Crown Court, in, 7.23–7.29
  magistrates' court, in, 7.03–7.21
application for
  evidence, 7.76–7.81
  procedure, 7.82–7.86
breach of abatement notices
  Crown Court, in, 7.37–7.42
  magistrates' court, in, 7.30–7.34
breach of nuisance order
  Crown Court, in, 7.37–7.46
  magistrates' court, in, 7.30–7.36

Index

Costs – *contd*
challenging costs order
Crown Court, made in, 7.88
magistrates' court, made in, 7.87
civil appeal to High Court, of, 7.71–7.73
complaints by individuals
discretion, 7.54–7.55
introduction, 6.81–6.82, 7.47
liability of private prosecutor, 7.58
local authority, order against, 7.56
statutory right, 7.48–7.53
successful defendants, 7.57
criminal appeal to Divisional Court, of, 7.74–7.75
Crown Court, in
appeals against abatement notices, 7.22–7.30
breach of abatement notices, 7.37–7.46
breach of nuisance order, 7.37–7.46
gathering evidence, of, 7.61–7.62
introduction, 7.01–7.02
investigation by salaried officers, of, 7.59
magistrates' court, in
appeals against abatement notices, 7.03–7.21
breach of abatement notices, 7.31–7.34
breach of nuisance order, 7.31–7.34
complaints by individuals, 7.47–7.58
relationship to level of fine, 7.63–7.67
service of abatement notice, of, 7.68–7.70

Courts' powers
appeals against abatement notices
generally, 4.110–4.117
Human Rights Act 1998, and, 4.06
third parties, against, 4.118–4.123
complaints by individuals
fines, 6.78
introduction, 6.71–6.72
local authority, order against, 6.79–6.80
nuisance order, 6.73–6.77

Courts, yards and passages
litter, 9.57

Criminal proceedings
breach of abatement notice, for
and see below
appeals, 5.116–5.130
availability disclosure, 5.48–5.67
categories of offence, 5.19–5.25
conduct of trial, 5.68–5.74
elements of offence, 5.03–5.04
evidence, 5.39–5.47
information, 5.26–5.38
introduction, 5.01–5.02
nature of offence, 5.05–5.18
Newton procedure, 5.115
sentencing, 5.103–5.113
breach of nuisance order, for, 6.83–6.85
local authorities' powers, and, 2.68–2.70

Criminal proceedings for breach of abatement notice
appeals
case stated, by way of, 5.122–5.125
conviction, against, 5.117–5.121
introduction, 5.116
availability disclosure, 5.48–5.67
best practicable means, 5.95–5.96
burden of proof
defence case, 5.87–5.96
prosecution case, 5.75–5.76
categories of offence, 5.19–5.25
conduct of trial
defence case, 5.87–5.102
introduction, 5.68
no case to answer, submission of, 5.85–5.86
prosecution case, 5.69–5.86
defective service of abatement notice
preconditions, 5.10–5.18
requirement, 5.06–5.09
defences
best practicable means, 5.95–5.96
invalidity of abatement notice, 5.98–5.102
miscellaneous statutory defences, 5.97
reasonable excuse, 5.78–5.84
standard of proof, 5.90–5.94
elements of offence
failure to serve abatement notice, 5.06–5.18
introduction, 5.03–5.04
evidence
advance information, 5.42–5.47
caution, under, 5.58–5.59
expert evidence, 5.52–5.54
generally, 5.39–5.41
information upon which prosecution not rely, 5.48–5.51
PACE 1984, and, 5.55–5.59
right against self-incrimination, 5.60–5.64
unfair evidence, 5.65–5.67
extension of time, 5.31
failure to serve abatement notice
preconditions, 5.10–5.18
requirement, 5.06–5.09
Human Rights Act 1998, and, 5.02
information
amendment, 5.34–5.35
date of breach of notice, 5.38
discretion to refuse to try, 5.36–5.37
form, 5.26–5.30
time limits, 5.31–5.33
introduction, 5.01–5.02
judicial review, 5.123–5.125, 5.130
nature of offence
discretion to prosecute, 5.23–5.24
failure to serve abatement notice, 5.06–5.18
identification of defendant, 5.22
introduction, 5.05

557

Index

Criminal proceedings for breach of abatement notice – *contd*
 Newton procedure, 5.115
 proof of offence
  introduction, 5.75
  reasonable excuse, 5.78–5.84
  standard of proof, 5.76
 prosecution case
  generally, 5.69–5.86
  proof of offence, 5.75–5.77
 reasonable excuse, 5.78–5.84
 sentencing
  corporate bodies, 5.114
  generally, 5.103–5.113
 standard of proof
  defence case, 5.87–5.89
  prosecution case, 5.77
 time limits
  date of breach of notice, 5.38
  extension, 5.31
  generally, 5.31–5.33
Crop reside premises, smoke from
 local authorities' powers, 9.100
Crown property
 introduction, 10.36–10.37

Damages for interference with human rights
 breach of convention rights, 7.113
 Crown Court proceedings, 7.112
 introduction, 7.109–1.111
 magistrates' court proceedings, 7.112
 principles in determining amount, 7.114–7.116
Dangerous premises
 local authorities' powers, 9.87–9.93
Defective closets
 local authorities' powers, 9.73–9.77
Defective premises
 local authorities' powers, 9.87–9.93
Defective service of abatement notice
 preconditions, 5.10–5.18
 requirement, 5.06–5.09
Defences
 appeals against abatement notice
  additional recipient to be served, 4.72–4.77
  amendment, 4.78–4.82
  best practicable means used, 4.59–4.68
  defective notice, 4.37–4.41
  error in notice, 4.37–4.41
  introduction, 4.35
  refusal to accept alternative scheme, 4.42–4.49
  requirements are unreasonable, 4.50–4.52
  requirements more onerous than under statutory conditions, 4.69
  time for compliance is insufficient, 4.53–4.58
  unjustified issue of notice, 4.36
  wrong recipient, 4.70–4.77

Defences – *contd*
 breach of abatement notice
  best practicable means, 5.95–5.97
  invalidity of abatement notice, 5.98–5.102
  miscellaneous statutory defences, 5.97
  reasonable excuse, 5.78–5.84
  standard of proof, 5.80–5.102
 complaints by individuals, 6.66–6.70
Delegation of powers
 local authorities' powers, and, 2.11
Demolition, waste on
 generally, 9.66–9.67
Deposits
 best practicable means
  introduction, 1.49
 meaning, 1.83–1.94
 prejudicial to health, 1.03–1.04
Development plans
 considerations, and, 1.21–1.25
Difficulty of avoidance of effects of activity to community
 considerations, and, 1.18–1.19
Directive waste
 fly tipping, 9.34
Disposal of litter
 generally, 9.60–9.62
Disused mines 1.77
Ditches
 meaning, 1.72–1.74
 local authorities' powers, 9.94
 meaning, 1.72–1.74
Dog fouling
 local authorities' powers, 9.98–9.99
Domestic water supply
 best practicable means
  introduction, 1.71
 meaning, 1.71
Drainage defects
 local authorities' powers, 9.81–9.82
Duration of activity
 considerations, and, 1.15
Dust from industrial, trade or business premises
 best practicable means
  introduction, 1.40
 meaning, 1.40, 1.83–1.94
 prejudicial to health, 1.03–1.05
 premises, 1.79–1.82

Ease of avoidance of effects of activity to community
 considerations, and, 1.19–1.20
Effluvia from industrial, trade or business premises
 best practicable means
  introduction, 1.43
 meaning, 1.38–1.45, 1.83–1.94
 prejudicial to health, 1.02
 premises, 1.80–1.81

Index

Engineering works, noise from
appeals
generally, 9.14–9.15
suspension of notices, 9.116–9.119
criminal offences, 9.120
effect on other proceedings, 9.122
introduction, 9.119–9.113
prior consent
effect on other proceedings, 9.121–9.123
generally, 9.121
Entry to premises
local authorities' powers, and, 2.56–2.66
Environmental Health criteria
quantification of sound levels, 8.13
Environmental information, availability of
local authorities' powers, and, 2.25–2.32
Environmental Protection Act 1990
abandoned shopping trolleys, 9.58–9.59
abatement notices, 3.02
categories of statutory nuisance, 1.02
challenging abatement notices, 4.03
complaints by individuals, 6.01
criminal proceedings, 5.01
definitions, 1.78
fly tipping, 9.31–9.38
litter, 9.47–9.48
local authorities' powers, 2.01
relationship with other controls, 10.01–10.06
smoke from crop reside burning, 9.100
Equipment in street, noise from
best practicable means
introduction, 1.68
meaning, 1.68–1.70, 1.83–1.94
prejudicial to health, 1.03–1.05
Evidence
appeals against abatement notices
burden of proof, 4.105–4.107
disclosure, 4.88–4.89
experts' reports, 4.92
generally, 4.94–4.98
hearsay, 4.93
procedure at trial, 4.99–4.103
relevant date, 4.108–4.109
standard of proof, 4.104
breach of abatement notice
advance information, 5.42–5.47
caution, under, 5.58–5.59
expert evidence, 5.52–5.54
generally, 5.39–5.41
information upon which prosecution not rely, 5.48–5.51
PACE 1984, and, 5.55–5.59
right against self-incrimination, 5.60–5.64
unfair evidence, 5.65–5.67
compensation orders, 7.95–7.98
costs application, 7.77–7.80

Extension of time
appeals against abatement notices
generally, 4.13–4.16
Human Rights Act 1998, and, 4.17–4.22
breach of abatement notice, 5.31

Failure to comply with abatement notice, proceedings for
appeals
case stated, by way of, 5.122–5.125
conviction, against, 5.117–5.121
introduction, 5.116
availability disclosure, 5.48–5.67
best practicable means, 5.95–5.96
burden of proof
defence case, 5.87–5.96
prosecution case, 5.75–5.76
categories of offence, 5.19–5.25
conduct of trial
defence case, 5.87–5.102
introduction, 5.68
no case to answer, submission of, 5.85–5.86
prosecution case, 5.69–5.86
costs
Crown Court, in, 7.37–7.46
magistrates' court, in, 7.31–7.34
costs in Crown Court
abandonment of appeal, 7.41
failure of appeal, 7.38–7.40
introduction, 7.37
partially successful appeal, 7.45–7.46
successful appeal, 7.42–7.44
costs in magistrates' court
abandonment of prosecution, 7.31–7.34
outright success of defence, 7.31–7.32
outright success of prosecution, 7.30
partial success, 7.35
defective service of abatement notice
preconditions, 5.10–5.18
requirement, 5.06–5.09
defences
best practicable means, 5.95–5.96
invalidity of abatement notice, 5.99–5.102
miscellaneous statutory defences, 5.97
reasonable excuse, 5.78–5.84
standard of proof, 5.90–5.94
elements of offence
failure to serve abatement notice, 5.06–5.18
introduction, 5.03–5.04
evidence
advance information, 5.42–5.47
caution, under, 5.58–5.59
expert evidence, 5.52–5.54
generally, 5.39–5.41
information upon which prosecution not rely, 5.48–5.51
PACE 1984, and, 5.55–5.59

559

Index

Failure to comply with abatement notice, proceedings for – *contd*
  expert evidence – *contd*
    right against self-incrimination, 5.60–5.64
    unfair evidence, 5.65–5.67
  extension of time, 5.31
  failure to serve abatement notice
    preconditions, 5.10–5.18
    requirement, 5.06–5.09
  Human Rights Act 1998, and, 5.02
  information
    amendment, 5.34–5.35
    date of breach of notice, 5.38
    discretion to refuse to try, 5.36–5.37
    form, 5.25–5.30
    time limits, 5.31–5.33
  introduction, 5.01–5.02
  judicial review, 5.123–5.125, 5.130
  nature of offence
    discretion to prosecute, 5.23–5.24
    failure to serve abatement notice, 5.06–5.18
    identification of defendant, 5.22
    introduction, 5.05
  Newton procedure, 5.115
  proof of offence
    introduction, 5.75
    reasonable excuse, 5.78–5.84
    standard of proof, 5.76
  prosecution case
    generally, 5.69–5.86
    proof of offence, 5.75–5.77
  reasonable excuse, 5.78–5.84
  sentencing
    corporate bodies, 5.114
    generally, 5.103–5.113
  standard of proof
    defence case, 5.87–5.89
    prosecution case, 5.77
  time limits
    date of breach of notice, 5.38
    extension, 5.31
    generally, 5.31–5.33

Failure to comply with notices and orders
  abatement notices
    and see above
    appeals, 5.116–5.130
    availability disclosure, 5.48–5.67
    categories of offence, 5.19–5.25
    conduct of trial, 5.68–5.102
    elements of offence, 5.03–5.04
    evidence, 5.39–5.47
    information, 5.26–5.38
    introduction, 5.01–5.02
    nature of offence, 5.05–5.18
    Newton procedure, 5.115
    sentencing, 5.103–5.114
  housing repair notices, 9.30
  nuisance orders
    and see below

Failure to comply with notices and orders – *contd*
  nuisance orders – *contd*
    costs in Crown Court, 7.37–7.38
    costs in magistrates' court, 7.39–7.41
    generally, 6.82–6.83
  s 215 TCPA 1990 notice, 9.02

Failure to comply with nuisance order, proceedings for
  costs in Crown Court
    abandonment of appeal, 7.41
    failure of appeal, 7.39–7.40
    introduction, 7.36
    partially successful appeal, 7.45–7.46
    successful appeal, 7.42–7.44
  costs in magistrates' court
    abandonment of prosecution, 7.31–7.34
    outright success of defence, 7.31–7.34
    outright success of prosecution, 7.30
    partial success, 7.35
  generally, 6.82–6.85

Failure to serve abatement notice
  preconditions, 5.10–5.18
  requirement, 5.06–5.09

Filthy premises
  local authorities' powers, 9.88–9.85

Fines
  complaints by individuals
    amount, 6.78
    introduction, 6.71

Fitness for habitation
  flats, 9.20
  flats in multiple occupation, 9.21
  houses, 9.18–9.24
  houses in multiple occupation, 9.19

Fly tipping
  appeals, 9.39–9.40
  criminal offences, 9.37–9.38
  definitions
    controlled waste, 9.38
    Directive waste, 9.34
    discard, 9.35
  enforcement, 9.41
  introduction, 9.31–9.32

Form of complaints
  oral complaint, 4.08
  written complaint, 4.09

Fouling by dogs
  local authorities' powers, 9.98–9.99

Frequency of activity
  considerations, and, 1.16

Fumes from dwellings
  best practicable means, 1.38
  meaning, 1.36–1.37
  prejudicial to health, 1.03–1.05

Gases from dwellings
  best practicable means, 1.38
  meaning, 1.36–1.37
  prejudicial to health, 1.03–1.05

Index

Gathering evidence
costs, and, 7.60–7.61
Grounds of appeal
abatement notice, against
and see below
generally, 4.35–4.77
s 215 TCPA 1990 notice, against
generally, 9.05
ordinary course of events, 9.15–9.17
Grounds of appeal against abatement notice
additional recipient to be served, 4.72–4.77
amendment, 4.78–4.82
best practicable means used, 4.59–4.68
defective notice, 4.37–4.41
error in notice, 4.37–4.41
introduction, 4.35
refusal to accept alternative scheme, 4.42–4.49
requirements are unreasonable, 4.50–4.52
requirements more onerous than under statutory conditions, 4.69
time for compliance is insufficient, 4.53–4.58
unjustified issue of notice, 4.36
wrong recipient, 4.70–4.77
Gutters
local authorities' powers, 9.94

Health, prejudicial to
meaning, 1.03–1.05
Highway, waste on
litter, 9.63–9.65
Housing repair notices
appeals, 9.25–9.27
contents, 9.23
failure to comply, 9.30
fitness for habitation
flats, 9.20
flats in multiple occupation, 9.21
houses, 9.18–9.24
houses in multiple occupation, 9.19
introduction, 9.18
local authority works, 9.28–9.29
recipients, 9.22–9.24
Human Rights Act 1998
abatement notices
generally, 3.38–3.43
practical advice, 3.43–3.44
appeals against abatement notices
appeals from magistrates' court, 4.124–4.133
extension of time, 4.17–4.22
introduction, 4.01
listing of appeals, 4.127–4.133
convention rights, 2.07
damages, 7.109
deference, 2.08–2.10
interpretation of legislation, 2.05
obligations of authorities, 2.03–2.04
breach of abatement notice, 5.02

Human Rights Act 1998 – *contd*
proportionality, 2.08–2.10
victims, 2.06

Importance of activity to community
considerations, and, 1.18
Individuals, complaints by
aggrieved persons, 6.03–6.04
applying for summons
introduction, 6.38
laying of information, 6.38–6.53
burden of proof, 6.59–6.60
commencement of proceedings
giving notice, 6.05–6.37
introduction, 6.05
laying of information, 6.38–6.53
conduct of hearing, 6.61–6.65
costs, 6.81–6.82
court's powers
fines, 6.78
introduction, 6.71–6.72
local authority, order against, 6.79–6.80
nuisance order, 6.73–6.77
defences, 6.66–6.70
elements to be proved
existence of nuisance at hearing, 6.54
existence of nuisance at laying of information, 6.55–6.58
person aggrieved, 6.55–6.58
existence of nuisance, 6.14–6.19
fines
amount, 6.78
introduction, 6.72
giving notice of intention to start proceedings
content of notice, 6.23–6.32
introduction, 6.06
local authority, to, 6.35–6.37
period of notice, 6.20–6.22
recipients of notice, 6.07–6.19
service of notice, 6.33–6.34
whereabouts of defendant unknown, when, 6.35–6.37
introduction, 6.01–6.02
laying of information
defective information, 6.51–6.53
form of information, 6.50–6.53
introduction, 6.38–6.41
supporting material, 6.44–6.49
time limits, 6.42–6.43
local authority, order against, 6.79–6.80
nuisance order
introduction, 6.71
proceedings for breach, 6.83–6.84
terms, 6.73–6.77
penalties
fines, 6.78
introduction, 6.71–6.72
local authority, order against, 6.79–6.80
nuisance order, 6.73–6.77

561

Index

Individuals, complaints by – *contd*
  procedure at hearing
    burden of proof, 6.59–6.60
    elements to be proved, 6.54–6.58
    generally, 6.61–6.65
  recipients of notice
    every possible defendant, 6.11–6.13
    existence of nuisance, 6.14–6.19
    general rule, 6.07–6.10
  standard of proof, 6.59–6.60
Industrial noises
  noise nuisance, 8.40–8.45
Industrial premises
  definition, 1.80–1.82
Information
  breach of abatement notice
    amendment, 5.34–5.35
    date of breach of notice, 5.38
    discretion to refuse to try, 5.36–5.37
    form, 5.26–5.30
    time limits, 5.31–5.33
  complaints by individuals
    defective information, 6.51–6.53
    form, 6.50–6.53
    introduction, 6.38–6.41
    supporting material, 6.44–6.49
    time limits, 6.42–6.43
Information, provision of
  local authorities' powers, and, 2.54–2.55
Injunctions
  local authorities' powers, and, 2.71–2.78
Inspection of area
  generally, 2.12–2.13
  remedies for non-compliance, 2.14–2.19
Integrated pollution control (IPC)
  enforcement, 10.05
  introduction, 10.03
Integrated pollution prevention and control (IPPC)
  background, 10.07–10.08
  introduction, 10.06
  regulations, 10.09–10.10
Interim hearings
  costs in Crown Court, 7.28
  costs in magistrates' court, 7.16
Interim injunctions
  local authorities' powers, and, 2.79
Intruder alarms
  generally, 9.140
Investigation by salaried officers
  costs, and, 7.59
Investigation of complaints
  local authorities' powers, and, 2.20–2.24

Judicial review
  challenging abatement notices
    recipient, by, 4.146–4.151
    third parties, by, 4.144–4.145
  breach of abatement notice, 5.123–5.125, 5.130

LAeq
  noise nuisance, 8.28–8.29
LAMax
  noise nuisance, 8.25
Land adversely affecting amenity of area
  affecting amenity of area, 9.08–9.09
  appeals
    generally, 9.04
    grounds, 9.05
    suspension of notice, 9.06
  challenging, 9.14
  discharge, 9.13
  failure to comply, 9.03
  grounds of appeal
    generally, 9.05
    ordinary course of events, 9.15–9.17
  introduction, 9.01
  legality, 9.14
  local authority works, 9.07
  personal nature, 9.10–9.12
LA90
  noise nuisance, 8.26
LA10
  noise nuisance, 8.27
Legislation
  duty to interpret in accordance with HRA 1998, 2.05
Letters before notice
  abatement notices, and, 3.53
Light pollution 1.61–1.63
Litter
  abandoned shopping trolleys, 9.58–9.59
  abatement actions, 9.53
  clearance duties
    control notices, 9.56–9.57
    courts, yards and passages, 9.57
    generally, 9.50–9.53
  control notices, 9.55–9.56
  criminal offences, 9.47–9.49
  definition, 9.45
  disposal duties, 9.60–9.62
  highway waste, 9.63–9.65
  introduction, 9.44–9.46
Local authorities, powers and duties of
  abatement notice, issue of
    effect of breach, 2.47–2.49
    generally, 2.33–2.43
    Ombudsman's decisions, 2.46
    power to restrict nuisance, 2.44–2.45
    suspension, 2.53
    variation, 2.82–2.85
    withdrawal, 2.82–2.85
  consultation, 2.90–2.92
  delegation of powers, 2.11
  enforcement
    acts outside area, of, 2.80
    criminal proceedings, 2.68–2.70
    injunctions, 2.71–2.78
    interim injunctions, 2.79
    permission from SoS, 2.81–2.82
  entry to premises, 2.56–2.66

Index

Local authorities, powers and duties of – *contd*
environmental information, availability of, 2.25–2.29
Human Rights Act 1998, and
  convention rights, 2.07, 2.93
  deference, 2.08–2.10
  interpretation of legislation, 2.05
  obligations of authorities, 2.03–2.04
  proportionality, 2.08–2.10
  victims, 2.06
information, provision of, 2.53–2.55
inspection of area
  generally, 2.12–2.13
  remedies for non-compliance, 2.14–2.19
introduction, 2.01–2.02
investigation of complaints, 2.20–2.24
'minded to act' notices, 2.86–2.89
opening vehicles, 2.56–2.66
restriction of nuisance, 2.44–2.45
seizure, 2.67
surveillance 2.67
Local authority, order against
costs, 7.56
generally, 6.79–6.80
Local authority, works by
housing repair notices, 9.28–9.29
s 215 TCPA 1990 notice, 9.07
Local Government Ombudsman, complaints to
injustice, 4.150–4.151
introduction, 4.146–4.148
maladministration, 4.149
Location of activity
considerations, and, 1.13
Loudspeakers
generally, 9.136–9.139

Maladministration
injustice, 4.150–4.151
introduction, 4.145–4.148
meaning, 4.149
Maximum levels
noise nuisance, 8.35–8.39
'Minded to act' notices
local authorities' powers, and, 2.86–2.89

Nature of statutory nuisance
introduction, 1.01–1.02
key considerations
  convention, 1.17
  development plans, 1.21–1.25
  ease of avoidance of effects, 1.19
  duration, 1.15
  frequency, 1.16
  importance of community activity, 1.18
  introduction, 1.12
  location, 1.13
  time, 1.14
  value of community activity, 1.18

Nature of statutory nuisance – *contd*
nuisance, 1.06–1.11
prejudicial to health, 1.03–1.05
breach of abatement notice, 5.31
***Newton* procedure**
failure to serve abatement notice, 5.115
Night time residential noise
local authorities' powers, 9.101–9.108
Noise abatement zones
designation, 9.125
excessive noise, 9.128–9.129
introduction, 9.124
noise level register, 9.126–9.127
reduction of noise, 9.130–9.133
relationship to statutory nuisance, 9.134–9.135
Noise from premises
best practicable means
  introduction, 1.67
  meaning, 1.64–1.69, 1.83–1.94
premises, 1.79–1.82
Noise from vehicles
generally, 9.143
Noise from vehicles in street
abatement notices, and, 3.74
best practicable means
  introduction, 1.69
  meaning, 1.68–1.69, 1.83–1.92
prejudicial to health, 1.03–1.05
Noise nuisances
appeals against abatement notices, 4.69
Codes of Practice, 9.141–9.142
indices
  introduction, 8.24
  L_{Aeq}, 8.28–8.29
  L_{AMax}, 8.25
  L_{A90}, 8.26
  L_{A10}, 8.27
industrial noises, 8.40–8.45
introduction, 8.01–8.05
maximum levels, 8.35–8.39
night time residential noise, 9.101–9.108
qualitative factor adjustments, 8.30–8.31
quantification of sound levels
  guidance, 8.11–8.17
  introduction, 8.06–8.10
  limitations, 8.18–8.19
  scientific summary, 8.21–8.23
times and seasons, 8.32–8.34
Non-suspended notice
appeals against abatement notices, 4.83–4.87
Notice of intention to start proceedings
content of notice, 6.23–6.32
introduction, 6.06
local authority, to, 6.35–6.37
period of notice, 6.20–6.22
recipients of notice, 6.07–6.19
service of notice, 6.33–6.34
whereabouts of defendant unknown, when, 6.35–6.37

Index

Notifiable diseases
local authorities' powers, 9.86
Nuisance
meaning, 1.06–1.109
Nuisance order
costs in Crown Court
abandonment of appeal, 7.41
failure of appeal, 7.38–7.40
introduction, 7.36
partially successful appeal, 7.45–7.46
successful appeal, 7.42–7.44
costs in magistrates' court
abandonment of prosecution, 7.31–7.34
outright success of defence, 7.31–7.34
outright success of prosecution, 7.30
partial success, 7.35
introduction, 6.71
proceedings for breach
costs in Crown Court, 7.37–7.46
costs in magistrates' court, 7.30–7.34
generally, 6.81–6.82
terms, 6.73–6.77
Nuisance prevention
local authorities' powers, 9.83

Offensive matter or liquid, removal of
local authorities' powers, 9.83
Ombudsman, complaints to
injustice, 4.150–4.151
introduction, 4.146–4.147
maladministration, 4.149
Opening vehicles
local authorities' powers, and, 2.56–2.66
Order of speeches
appeals against abatement notices, 4.99–4.103
Ordinary, decent people, test of
convention, 1.17
development plans, 1.21–1.25
ease of avoidance of effects, 1.19–1.20
duration, 1.15
frequency, 1.16
importance of community activity, 1.18
introduction, 1.11
location, 1.13
time, 1.14
value of community activity, 1.18

Permission from SoS
local authorities' powers, and, 2.81–2.82
Pests
local authorities' powers, 9.96–9.97
Planning Policy Guidance (PPG)
quantification of sound levels, 8.14
Pollution prevention and control (IPPC)
background, 10.07–10.08
introduction, 10.06
regulations, 10.09–10.10
Ponds
best practicable means
introduction, 1.60

Ponds – *contd*
best practicable means – *contd*
meaning, 1.83–1.92
local authorities' powers, 9.94
meaning, 1.72–1.74
Powers of local authorities
abatement notice, issue of
effect of breach, 2.47–2.53
generally, 2.33–2.43
Ombudsman's decisions, 2.46
power to restrict nuisance, 2.44–2.45
suspension, 2.53
variation, 2.83–2.85
withdrawal, 2.83–2.85
consultation, 2.90–2.92
delegation of powers, 2.11
enforcement
acts outside area, of, 2.80
criminal proceedings, 2.68–2.70
injunctions, 2.71–2.79
interim injunctions, 2.79
permission from SoS, 2.81–2.82
entry to premises, 2.56–2.66
environmental information, availability of, 2.25–2.32
Human Rights Act 1998, and
convention rights, 2.07
deference, 2.08–2.10
duties under RIPA 2000, 2.93–2.101
interpretation of legislation, 2.05
obligations of authorities, 2.03–2.04
proportionality, 2.08–2.10
victims, 2.06
information, provision of, 2.54–2.55
inspection of area
generally, 2.12–2.13
remedies for non-compliance, 2.14–2.19
introduction, 2.01–2.02
investigation of complaints, 2.20–2.25
'minded to act' notices, 2.86–2.89
opening vehicles, 2.56–2.66
restriction of nuisance, 2.44–2.45
seizure, 2.67
Prejudicial to health
meaning, 1.03–1.05
Premises, definition of
generally, 1.79
industrial, trade or business, 1.80–1.82

Qualitative factor adjustments
noise nuisance, 8.30–8.31
Quantification of sound levels
guidance
BS 4142, 8.15
BS 8233, 8.16
EH Criteria 12/1980, 8.13
introduction, 8.11–8.12
PPG 24, 8.14
introduction, 8.06–8.10
limitations, 8.18–8.19
scientific summary, 8.20–8.23

564

Index

Quarries 1.77

Radioactive substances
introduction, 10.11
Reasonable excuse
breach of abatement notice, 5.78–5.84
Remedies
introduction, 1.01
Repair notices
appeals, 9.25–9.27
contents, 9.23
failure to comply, 9.31
fitness for habitation
  flats, 9.21
  flats in multiple occupation, 9.22
  houses, 9.18–9.24
  houses in multiple occupation, 9.20
introduction, 9.18
local authority works, 9.28–9.30
recipients, 9.22–9.24
Restriction of nuisance
local authorities' powers, and, 2.44–2.45

Sanitary conveniences, defective
local authorities' powers, 9.73–9.77
s 59 EPA 1990 notice
appeals, 9.39–9.40
criminal offences, 9.41–9.43
definitions
  controlled waste, 9.33
  Directive waste, 9.34
  discard, 9.36
enforcement, 9.41
introduction, 9.31–9.32
s 60 COPA 1970 notice
appeals
  generally, 9.114–9.115
  suspension of notices, 9.116–9.118
criminal offences, 9.120
effect on other proceedings, 9.119
introduction, 9.109–9.113
s 61 COPA 1970 notice
effect on other proceedings, 9.122–9.123
generally, 9.121
s 215 TCPA 1990 notice
affecting amenity of area, 9.08–9.09
appeals
  generally, 9.04
  grounds, 9.05
  suspension of notice, 9.06
challenging, 9.14
discharge, 9.13
failure to comply, 9.03
grounds of appeal
  generally, 9.05
  ordinary course of events, 9.15–9.17
introduction, 9.01
legality, 9.14
local authority works, 9.07
personal nature, 9.10–9.12

Seizure
local authorities' powers, and, 2.67
Sentencing
breach of abatement notice
  corporate bodies, 5.114
  generally, 5.103–5.114
Service
abatement notices
  costs, 7.68
  generally, 3.77–3.80
appeals against abatement notices, 4.34
Sewers
local authorities' powers, 9.94
Sheds
best practicable means
  introduction, 1.59
  meaning, 1.75–1.76, 1.83–1.94
Shopping trolleys
litter, 9.58–9.59
Smells from industrial, trade or business premises
best practicable means
  introduction, 1.44
  meaning, 1.83–1.92
meaning, 1.42
prejudicial to health, 1.03–1.05
premises, 1.79–1.82
residential premises, from, 1.36–1.37
Smoke emissions
best practicable means
  introduction, 1.44
  meaning, 1.34–1.35, 1.83–1.92
crop reside burning, from, 9.100
prejudicial to health, 1.03–1.05
Standard of proof
appeals against abatement notices, 4.104
breach of abatement notice
  defence case, 5.90–5.94
  prosecution case, 5.70–5.71
complaints by individuals, 6.59–6.60
State of premises
best practicable means
  introduction, 1.35
  meaning, 1.26–1.33, 1.79–1.94
prejudicial to health, 1.03–1.05
premises, 1.79–1.82
Statutory nuisance
categories 1.26–1.104
  accumulations, 1.44–1.50
  animals, 1.51–1.59
  deposits, 1.46–1.50
  effluvia, 1.38–1.45
  fumes, 1.36–1.37
  gases, 1.36–1.37
  introduction, 1.02
  light pollution 1.61–1.63
  noise, 1.64–1.69
  other matters, 1.70–1.75
  relevant meanings, 1.78–1.85
  smoke emissions, 1.34–1.35
  state of premises, 1.26–1.33

Index

Statutory nuisance – *contd*
  contaminated land, 1.95–1.104
  nature
    introduction, 1.01–1.02
    key considerations, 1.12–1.20
    nuisance, 1.06–1.10
    prejudicial to health, 1.03–1.05
Steam from industrial, trade or business premises
  best practicable means
    introduction, 1.41
    meaning, 1.79–1.94
  meaning, 1.41
  prejudicial to health, 1.03–1.05
  premises, 1.79–1.81
Street noise
  abatement notices, and, 3.74
  loudspeakers, 9.136–9.139
Summary remedies
  introduction, 1.01
  surveillance 2.93–2.101
Suspension of abatement notice
  generally, 2.53

Tents
  best practicable means
    introduction, 1.69
    meaning, 1.75–1.76, 1.79–1.94
Third parties
  appeals against abatement notices
    complaints by third parties, 4.04
    orders against third parties, 4.118–4.123
  judicial review of abatement notices, 4.135–4.145
Time limits
  appeals against abatement notices
    calculation, 4.23–4.33
    excluded days, 4.30–4.33
    extension, 4.13–4.16
    Human Rights Act 1998, and, 4.17–4.22
    introduction, 4.12
    starting date, 4.23–4.24
    termination date, 4.25–4.29
  breach of abatement notice
    date of breach of notice, 5.38
    extension, 5.31
    generally, 5.31–5.33
Time of activity
  considerations, and, 1.14
Times and seasons
  noise nuisance, 8.32–8.34
Toilets, defective
  local authorities' powers, 9.73–9.77

Trade premises
  definition, 1.80–1.82
Traffic noise
  generally, 1.68

Value of activity to community
  considerations, and, 1.18
Vans
  best practicable means
    introduction, 1.59
    meaning, 1.75–1.76, 1.79–1.94
Vapours from dwellings
  meaning, 1.36–1.37
  prejudicial to health, 1.03–1.05
Variation of abatement notice
  generally, 2.83–2.85
Vehicles, abandonment of
  disposal, 9.68–9.70
Vehicles, noise from
  generally, 9.143
Vehicles in street, noise from
  best practicable means
    introduction, 1.69
    meaning, 1.68–1.69, 1.79–1.94
Vermin
  local authorities' powers, 9.96–9.97
Verminous premises
  local authorities' powers, 9.84–9.85

Waste management licensing
  introduction, 10.26
  overlap with statutory nuisance, 10.27
Water closets, defective
  local authorities' powers, 9.73–9.77
Water pollution
  introduction, 10.21–10.23
  overlap with statutory nuisance, 10.24–10.25
Water supply
  best practicable means
    introduction, 1.71
    meaning, 1.71, 1.79–1.84
Watercourses
  best practicable means
    introduction, 1.71
    meaning, 1.72–1.74, 1.79–1.94
Withdrawal of abatement notice
  costs
    Crown Court, in, 7.29
    magistrates' court in, 7.19–7.20
  generally, 2.83–2.85, 3.81
Works by local authority
  housing repair notices, 9.28–9.30
  s 215 TCPA 1990 notice, 9.07